Constitutional Rights
Sourcebook

Constitutional Rights Sourcebook

Peter G. Renstrom

ABC-CLIO

Santa Barbara, California
Denver, Colorado
Oxford, England

Library of Congress Cataloging-in-Publication Data

Renstrom, Peter G., 1943–
    Constitutional rights sourcebook / Peter G. Renstrom.
    p.   cm.
    Includes bibliographical references and index
    ISBN 1-57607-061-1
    1. Constitutional law–United States.   I. Title.
KF4550.Z9R463 1999   99-13197
342.73'02–dc21   CIP

ISBN 1-57607-061-1

04 03 02 01 00 99 9 8 7 6 5 4 3 2 1

ABC-CLIO, Inc.
130 Cremona Drive, P.O. Box 1911
Santa Barbara, California 93116-1911

This book is printed on acid-free paper ∞.

Typesetting by Straight Line Design

Manufactured in the United States of America

CONTENTS

To Bobbi, Dan, Joey, Ola, Michele, and Rowan—for the "good life" away from the computer screen.

NOTE ON HOW TO USE THIS BOOK

The *Constitutional Rights Sourcebook* is designed to introduce or reacquaint readers with the United States Constitution. The *Sourcebook* contains discussion of the concepts of constitutionalism, words and phrases common to American constitutional law, and leading United States Supreme Court decisions addressing contemporary constitutional rights questions. A number of techniques have been used to help readers easily locate the information they seek in the *Sourcebook*.

Before beginning any of the chapters, turn to Appendix A and read (at least skim) the text of the Constitution. Pay particular attention to the first nine amendments and the Fourteenth Amendment. Think about two things as you read: Imagine what was going on in the minds of the people who wrote these words, and think about the meanings you put on these words. Think about how these words might support different interpretations. This exercise will begin to sensitize you to the interpretative function of the Supreme Court. Choice of one interpretation over another has significant consequences. Much of our constitutional history involves the clash of interpretative arguments and the ultimate selection of one that will prevail over others.

The Supreme Court's business is conducted through cases. A case reflects a contest between two parties, both of whom have different views about a constitutional issue. It is valuable to imagine yourself first as one party to a case and then as the other. Try to envision what each side is claiming, and what it wants from the Supreme Court. In other words, try and get a sense of the stakes in a case. The Supreme Court not only determines which party will win, but it also explains why. It is the statement of rationale that addresses the underlying question of constitutional law contained in the case. The principle established in a decision defines what the Constitution means, at least at the time the case is decided.

The Court's ruling also becomes the basis or point of departure for future decisions throughout the court system. The ruling sets a precedent to guide future judgments and provide continuity and stability. Finding specific cases is possible by using citation numbers. Each Supreme Court decision has unique sets of numbers that refer to volumes of compiled cases. There are several series of volumes that contain Court decisions. The *Sourcebook* uses the citations from the *United States Reports*, the series produced by the U.S. government. A *U.S. Reports* citation number will be provided for each case included in this book. For example, the citation number for the case entitled *Roe v. Wade* is 410 U.S. 113 (1973). The number before the "U.S." abbreviation refers to the volume number in which *Roe v. Wade* is found. The number following the abbreviation indicates the page within the volume upon which the opinion for that case begins. You will find the year a case was decided in parentheses following the page number. So, *Roe v. Wade*, decided in 1973, can be found on page 113 of volume 410 of the *U.S. Reports*. Some of the most recent cases have citation numbers from another series of cases reports, the *Supreme Court Reporter*. This series is published by West Group of St. Paul, Minnesota. The *Supreme Court Reporter* citation numbers work the same way as the *U.S. Reports* citations with a volume number, abbreviation to identify the series (S. Ct.), and a page number. The *Supreme Court Reporter* citation for *Roe v. Wade* is 93 S. Ct. 705 (1973).

Chapter 1 provides some historical background on the development of the U.S. Constitution and examines the Supreme Court's role in interpreting its words. Chapters 2 through 7 are organized by constitutional amendment. More specific issues within the scope of the particular amendment are found within each chapter. The last chapter, Chapter 8, provides discussion of more than 140 terms and concepts that are important to the understanding of constitutional law. The terms and concepts entries are cross-referenced with the cases discussed in earlier chapters. The reader may locate a case or concept related to each covered constitutional amendment by scanning the summary of entries at the beginning of each chapter. A complete alphabetical listing of the cases that serve as the foundation entries for discussion is provided at the front of the book.

The reader can consider related information by using the cross-references provided in the *See also* section that follows the initial paragraphs on a case or concept. The references point to related materials included within the same chapter or in other chapters. Page numbers have been provided for all cross-references.

Finally, if readers are unsure about which chapter to consult for a particular case or concept, they may consult the comprehensive index at the end of the book. The index includes every case or concept contained in the volume, either as a major topic of discussion or as a reference topic within the discussion.

This volume has been designed to offer the student or general reader a variety of approaches to locating information. The *Sourcebook* may be used as: (1) a *dictionary* and *reference guide* to the language and major decisions of the United States Supreme Court in the field of constitutional rights; (2) a *study guide* for students enrolled in law school or in law-related courses in colleges or universities; (3) a *handbook* for use by lawyers, police officers, and others entrusted with enforcement of the law and/or protection of constitutional rights; (4) a *supplement* to textbooks in the field of constitutional law; (5) a source of *review materials* for the attorney, judge, professor, or student of constitutional law; and (6) a *social science aid* for use in cognate fields, such as business and commercial law, economics, history, political science, and sociology.

PREFACE

The objective throughout this project has been to assemble a volume that explicates the fundamental ideas of constitutionalism in general and American constitutional law in particular. The task involves the integration of many elements reflective of the multidimensional character of the subject. It is hoped that the *Sourcebook* reaches both general readers and specific audiences of academics and practitioners. A major objective is to introduce students who might be considering a career in law to some of the operational concepts in the field of constitutional rights. It is also intended that the volume reach the legal community, especially lawyers who may find themselves removed by circumstances of their specialized practices from easy access to the essentials of constitutional law.

The concepts, terms, and cases selected for this volume represent my best judgment about how to advance readers' understanding of constitutional rights. A large number of terms and cases could have been selected for discussion. I did not intend, however, that the volume be an exhaustive reference source. A number of such volumes already exist. My selections were guided by such questions as:

Does this term, concept, or case enhance the ability of the reader to communicate in the fundamental language of the field?
Will the discussion facilitate the reader's search for information and understanding?
Will the volume complement and supplement materials commonly used in courses in constitutional law?

By limiting this volume to fundamental concepts, I believe that a more thorough description and commentary has been made possible.

Two considerations were important in the selection of Supreme Court cases. One was that certain cases should be included because they are generally regarded as landmark cases. *Brown v. Board of Education* is such a case. No chapter on the Equal Protection Clause can be complete without it. The second consideration was that recent decisions should be used wherever possible. The idea is to present the current thinking of the Supreme Court and to provide some sense of how a particular line of decisions has evolved. The Rehnquist Court is therefore heavily represented. It should be this way because of the extensive activity of the Rehnquist Court in defining and redefining individual rights. As the Court making the most recent pronouncements, the Rehnquist Court's interpretative views currently govern. Citations for the most recent decisions are from the *Supreme Court Reporter* because, at the time of publication, the citations from the *United States Reports* were not available.

Inevitably, volumes on constitutional rights tend to resemble each other. However, the *Constitutional Rights Sourcebook* has some unique features. First, discussion is focused on the currently existing doctrine on constitutional rights. The volume has a subject matter chapter format within which key cases are grouped for study and review purposes. This allows the volume to be used in and out of class as a teaching and learning tool. The chapter organization attempts to closely parallel the content as found in the leading constitutional rights casebooks. A second unique feature is the *Significance* section. I have attempted to provide historical perspective and discuss current relevance in this portion of each entry. This section allows comments that underscore the importance of a concept, term, or case decision. A third feature is the inclusion of cross-references that function as suggestions about additional information found in the volume.

I wish to acknowledge the large number of scholars who have contributed to this volume by way of their own discussion of constitutional rights. I am greatly indebted to all of them. I also wish to acknowledge with deep gratitude the intellectual stimulation provided by my colleagues and students. Deserving of a special acknowledgment are Professor Ralph C. Chandler and U.S. District Judge Richard A. Enslen. For more than a decade, we collaborated on various projects. I learned very much from my association with them, and I greatly enjoyed the time we spent together—it was a great run. I undertook this project on my own, but not really. These colleagues and friends made this volume possible. I alone, however, accept full responsibility for any errors of commission or omission. Finally, a word about my family. Their encouragement and patience during all the hours I spent in front of my computer screen were immeasurably important. I also want to thank my wife, Bobbi, and my daughter, Joelle, for the many hours with a red pen.

Peter G. Renstrom
Professor of Political Science
Western Michigan University

ALPHABETICAL LIST OF CASE ENTRIES

Alphabetical List of Case Entries

Constitutional Rights Sourcebook

CHAPTER 1

The Constitution and the Supreme Court:
A Brief Introduction

There are several kinds of law in the American legal system. The source of the law distinguishes the categories. Elected legislative bodies enact law in the form of statutes and ordinances. Law is created by administrative agencies as they implement statutory law. Law may also be drawn from the customs and traditions of a society by courts. Law is also found in constitutions. Constitutional law is the "fundamental" or "highest" law. Statutes enacted by legislatures, common law established through judicial decisions, and rules created by executive agencies are all measured against the national Constitution. Provisions contained in the Constitution are the "supreme law of the land." Law of any other kind is always subordinate to the Constitution. Any law that conflicts with provisions of the Constitution is invalid.

The concept of constitutionalism has roots in the Greek and Roman legal systems. The notion that government must be guided by a rule of law was advanced by Plato. Aristotle further developed the fundamental character of constitutions and distinguished them from the more transitory and subordinate policies that a political system might adopt through the actions of governmental officials. The Romans contributed the idea of government with a written and codified foundation. Unlike the Greeks, the Romans recognized something similar to the natural law concept of equality. The second development, coupled with the elements of Judeo-Christian faith, substantially elevated the standing of human rights.

American constitutionalism is grounded in these ideas, but was also profoundly influenced by the British experience. Although the British do not have a written constitution as such, the Magna Carta of 1215 unmistakably served much the same function, as it sought to make sovereign power subject to a higher law. The desire to put a constitution in writing was distinctively American and reflected in such earlier documents as the Mayflower Compact of 1620. By the time of the American Revolution, the colonists believed strongly in having a written constitution. As for the document's content, the colonists were quite familiar with the work of such people as John Locke, who with other natural rights theorists focused the view that certain everlasting principles of human rights and justice transcend any law established by man—a point critically important to the thinking of those who fashioned the U.S. Constitution. Locke believed in democratic processes where popular consent served as the basis of government. Locke saw government as something to be controlled by legal means and advocated integrating protections of individual rights into the written charter of government. This view was given effect when the first Congress adopted a Bill of Rights and sent it to the states for ratification.

The Constitutions of the United States   One of the first collective actions of the American colonists was to convene the First Continental Congress in 1774. The delegates were called together to fashion a statement of complaints against the British. When the American Revolution began two years later, it became necessary for the colonists to form their own government. Up to this time, Britain had taken care of national defense and international relations on behalf of the colonists. When independence from Britain was declared, a governmental vacuum was created at the national level. The Second Continental Congress generally acted as the national or central government, but had no formal authority to do so. It was out of the need to establish a national government that the first U.S. constitution, the Articles of Confederation, was written in 1777.

The final version of the Articles of Confederation contained 13 articles and set forth a close confederation of sovereign states over which the central government had only limited powers. Because provisions were made only for a weak executive and no judiciary, what powers the central government had were essentially vested in the Congress. The structural arrangement under the Articles was fatally flawed from the outset, however. The states were so dominant that the central government was unable to protect the collective interests of the confederation against states acting in their own interests. The insufficient strength of the central government under the Articles also contributed to substantial economic and political instability and—ultimately—to the need to abandon the Articles altogether.

The defects of the Articles had been apparent to people such as Alexander Hamilton and George Washington since before the end of the Revolutionary War. In 1786 a serious attempt was made to convene delegates from all the states at a meeting in Annapolis, Maryland. The meeting was intended to address the shortcomings of the Articles, but was largely unsuccessful because only five states sent delegates. The delegates in attendance, however, urged Congress to initiate efforts to convene another constitutional convention. Support for such a convention grew as economic and political problems worsened. Congress eventually recognized the need to reconsider the Articles, and called for a constitutional convention to take place in Philadelphia in the spring of 1787.

The delegates at the Philadelphia Convention were divided into two groups: those who favored a substantially stronger central government and those who favored making the central government only marginally stronger. This was a serious difference, but a difference of degree. The delegates all agreed that the Articles were irreparably defective and that major changes were in order. The delegates also agreed that a basic function of government was to protect certain natural rights. Thomas Jefferson had labeled rights such as life, liberty, and the pursuit of happiness as "unalienable" in the Declaration of Independence. It was of paramount importance to Convention delegates that a government be able to effectively protect such rights. The delegates were trying to achieve a delicate balance by establishing a government powerful enough to be effective but not oppressive, and they seized upon several commonly shared principles to further their pursuit.

One was the principle of republicanism, which describes a form of government in which the people elect representatives to act on their behalf. Republicanism gives the people the capacity to hold public officials accountable because unresponsive or otherwise poorly performing officials can be removed at the next election. The delegates also turned to the Baron de Montesquieu's concept of separation of power. With separation of power, the authority of government is divided among several branches to prevent potentially troublesome concentration of control. The distribution of powers embodied in the Constitution distinguishes functionally between the people and the government and among legislative, executive, and judicial tasks. While the Constitution creates three separate branches, it also assigns them overlapping responsibilities that make them interdependent. The checks and balances system becomes operational through this interdependence. The Congress is assigned the responsibility for passing laws, for example, but those laws must be implemented by the executive. Interpretation of what the laws mean falls to the judiciary. Similarly, the president controls the executive branch, but the laws to be executed and the funding for implementation come from the Congress.

The system of checks and balances simultaneously softens and augments separation of powers. The softening is due to the fact that checks and balances require the concurrence of one branch in the functions primarily assigned to another branch. The presidential veto, for example, makes the president a participant in the legislative process. Separation of power is augmented because checks and balances specify the controls each part of government has over the other parts. Separation of power, in concert with checks and balances, is designed to limit improper exercise of governmental authority by dispersing control to several locations. As a result, governmental power is restricted and decentralized, and no branch can dominate the processes of government for a protracted period. A drawback is that separation of power may create fragmentation or disunity for government if sufficient interbranch conflict exists.

The Constitution presented to the states for ratification also embraced the concept of federalism. Federalism divides authority between a central government and constituent units, with each level governing the same people and the same territory. The U.S. system under the Articles of Confederation had been a federation, but what came out of the Philadelphia Convention had not been seen in previous federations. The central government was much stronger, and the document contained language such as the Supremacy Clause of Article VI that allowed the central government to become even stronger relative to the states as time passed. Federations historically have not survived for long periods but have tended to disintegrate or pull apart under stress. The federation established by the U.S. Constitution has mechanisms designed to pull in the opposite direction—inward.

The Bill of Rights   The Bill of Rights itemizes most of the individual rights protected by the U.S. Constitution. These rights are contained in the First through Ninth Amendments and the Fourteenth Amendment. The first nine amendments were ratified in 1791, while the Fourteenth Amendment was added to the Constitution in 1868, following the Civil War. One may wonder why the Bill of Rights came in the form of amendments to the Constitution and was not included in the text of the document that emerged from the Philadelphia Convention in 1787. There are several reasons.

First, one must keep in mind the principal reason the Philadelphia Convention took place. The central government under the Articles of Confederation was terribly ineffective. The highest priority of the Federalists, who had the majority of delegates at the Convention, was to structure an effective government at the national level. They did not want the issue of individual rights deflecting them from establishing a central government with enough authority to govern. Second, and more important, the Federalists believed that the federal government created under the Constitution was one of limited delegated powers. As such, the government could not exercise power beyond what was formally conveyed by the document. The government was not, for example, empowered to enact any law that abridged free speech or religious freedom. It seemed unnecessary and redundant to take up such issues as free speech or religious freedom by developing a list of recognized rights—those rights were already protected. The mechanism of separation of powers was utilized by the Framers to protect both the public good and individual rights from the arbitrary exercise of governmental power. Third, some Federalists, including Alexander Hamilton, believed that enumerating rights might suggest that any list of rights would, or later could, be considered fixed or final. Hamilton believed such an interpretation to be not only erroneous but also dangerous in that rights not specifically listed might be violated by government. Hamilton argued that social diversity and watchfulness were the ultimate guarantees of personal rights.

It was during the ratification process that absence of a bill of rights emerged as a major political problem. Indeed, ratification in several of the larger states was achieved only through assurance that a bill of rights would be immediately added to the Constitution. Upon becoming president, George Washington directed the first Congress to promptly attend to the issue. The Congress, however, was preoccupied with other governance questions. James Madison finally took the initiative and guided a set of proposals to adoption. Though Madison had originally shared Hamilton's view that a bill of rights was not necessary, he was moved by the tremendous expression of popular sentiment. He was also a very pragmatic politician who wanted to preserve the Constitution as it emerged from the Federalist-controlled Philadelphia Convention. Holding another convention to consider the bill of rights question was a strategy of the Anti-Federalists, and Madison feared such a convention would make more substantial revisions in the document.

Judicial Review   The Declaration of Independence first asserted the primacy of individual rights when it made reference to people's natural rights—those rights that are "unalienable." The use of a written constitution creating a federal government of limited power was heavily influenced by the concern for securing such rights. The Bill of Rights was added to the Constitution because most politicians of the time believed that explicit itemization in the document itself made these rights more secure. But rights may not be fully secured by enumeration alone. The protections are not self-executing, nor is their meaning always clear. A vigilant and independent judiciary is needed to authoritatively interpret the words and to act as guardian of the integrity of the Constitution. Judicial oversight or review varies depending on whose actions are under court scrutiny. One situation involves review of administrative actions, which is both common and has relatively little policy impact.

Two more significant types of review were cultivated by Chief Justice Marshall in the early 1800s. The first involves the Supreme Court's role as umpire of the federal-state relationship. This kind of review allows the courts of the national government to review actions of the constituent states and invalidate those that collide with national authority or interfere with the authority of other states. The power to perform this kind of review can be derived from the Supremacy Clause of Article VI of the U.S. Constitution and from language of the Judiciary Act of 1789. The second involves judicial capacity to review actions of the other branches and carries the potential of placing the courts in a position of policy dominance. The argument for this function is that the integrity of the Constitution must be safeguarded from actions that conflict with it. This kind of judicial review is not mentioned in the Constitution although it was debated at length by the Framers. Judicial review of this kind authorizes courts to examine governmental actions, including those of the legislative and executive branches, and declare those actions unconstitutional if necessary.

Appellate judges have divergent views on when and how to engage in judicial review of the actions of the other or "coordinate" branches of government. Two role orientations, judicial self-restraint and judicial activism, are useful in examining the behavior of Supreme Court justices. Judicial self-restraint is the self-imposed limitation used by judges who believe this approach is most compatible with democratic principles. Judges who subscribe to self-restraint will go to great lengths in deferring to the policy decisions of the elective branches. Such judges seek to limit their role to enforcing the norms established by those accountable to the electorate. Judicial self-restraint advocates that only when constitutional violations are flagrant should courts nullify actions of the elective branches. Self-restraint does not necessarily correspond to a conservative policy orientation, however. Deferring to legislative establishment of a minimum wage or to an aggressive pursuit of voting rights, for example, might yield a liberal policy result. According to judicial self-restraint, the exercise of judicial power should be limited because the legislative and executive branches are the appropriate sources of major policy initiatives as both branches can be held politically accountable by the voters. A more aggressive or active role is considered inappropriate by self-restraint advocates for several reasons. First, courts generally are not effectively accountable to the public. This is especially true of federal judges, who are appointed and enjoy life tenure. Second, courts seldom win confrontations with the other branches. Indeed, the courts tend to be vulnerable to reprisals aimed at limiting their power. Judicial independence therefore may be threatened by activist and provocative decisions. Finally, self-restraintists argue that the courts are not a well-suited forum for decision making on broad and complex social questions.

Judicial activists, on the other hand, see the appellate courts as playing a substantial and affirmative policy role. Judicial activism prompts judges to entertain new policies, even those that would depart from adherence to established legal rules and precedents. Judicial activism can manifest itself in a number of ways, but most important is a court's adoption of its own policy preferences over those of the legislative or executive branches, which is exactly what occurs when a court declares a governmental action unconstitutional. Judicial activism may also extend legal rules to establish specific requirements for governmental action. While both judicial activists and self-restraintists acknowledge that a certain degree of policy making is inevitable as a result of deciding legal questions, they differ on how aggressively and how extensively judges should pursue policy-making opportunities. Judicial activism is sometimes described as legislating by judges to achieve policy outcomes compatible with their own priorities. A judicial activist will find more issues appropriate for judicial response than a judge who subscribes to self-restraint. United States judges have engaged in judicial activism from the outset of U.S. history. The most obvious early example is Chief Justice John Marshall's establishment of the power of judicial review itself in *Marbury v. Madison*, 1 Cranch 137 (1803). Activism need not coincide with a liberal policy orientation. Classic examples of judicial activism can be found in the 1930s, when the Hughes Court struck down numerous pieces of New Deal legislation in the interest of preserving laissez-faire economic doctrine. The judicial activist sees the Court as appropriately and legitimately asserting itself in the policy-making process even if its policy objectives differ from those of the legislative and executive branches.

Constitutional Law and the Courts   United States courts process literally millions of cases each year, only a handful of which reach an appellate court, much less the U.S. Supreme Court. These cases begin in either federal or state trial courts, although very few of them result in actual trials. Only about 10 percent of the criminal cases in this country receive jury trials with the remainder concluded by plea agreements. The proportion of civil cases that are actually tried is about 2 percent. Virtually none of the settled cases, civil or criminal, ever go beyond the court where the case was filed. It is from the small minority of cases that are tried that almost all appeals are initiated, and only a small fraction of these cases contain an issue that may involve the Constitution. So it is important to recognize from the outset that a case that presents the Supreme Court with an opportunity to address a constitutional question is rare. But such cases do exist, and the following discussion tells how they progress through the judicial system.

Jurisdiction and Organizational Structure   One of the fundamental principles embedded in the U.S. Constitution is federalism, which divides political authority between national and state levels of government. Federalism was one of the methods used by the constitutional Framers to decentralize control. One structural manifestation of U.S. federalism is the dual court system, in which power is divided between federal and state courts. These judicial systems are quite separate—each has its own courts to discharge the trial and appellate functions. Once a case begins in either the state or the federal system, it virtually always stays in that system. More than 99 percent of cases are processed in state courts. Most criminal prosecutions, domestic relations matters, contractual and financial recovery disputes—to name a few categories—are governed by state law. Federal cases, on the other hand, are limited to matters of federal law or matters involving parties from different states.

A small area of overlap exists where state and federal courts have concurrent jurisdiction. This permits litigants to initiate a legal action in either a federal or a state court. The only other real point of linkage between the federal and state systems is the U.S. Supreme Court. Provided federal jurisdictional requirements are satisfied, decisions of state courts of last resort may be reviewed by the U.S. Supreme Court. Otherwise, the federal and state court systems are independent. The independence of federal and state court jurisdictions was designed to maintain the respective sovereignties of the two levels of government. The main consequence of this dual judicial system is that it promotes some policy and doctrinal diversity. Though states may have similar constitutional provisions, statutes, and common-law traditions, the state courts do not necessarily interpret them in exactly the same way. Different local attitudes as well as different social conditions account for some variations.

A court's authority to hear or decide a case is defined by its jurisdiction. It is through jurisdiction that the power of federal and state courts to "say the law" is distinguished. The overall jurisdiction of the federal courts is set forth in Article III of the Constitution. Federal judicial power was further defined by Congress as courts located beneath the Supreme Court in the organizational scheme were established. Any action by Congress, of course, must be compatible with the general directives of Article III. Federal judicial authority extends to particular categories of cases defined either by substance or party. Cases that stem directly from the federal Constitution, federal statutes, or treaties or cases that involve admiralty or maritime issues can be brought to federal courts. Federal judicial power also extends to cases involving specified parties. Regardless of substance, federal jurisdiction includes actions in which the federal government is itself a party, actions between two or more states, actions between a state and a citizen of another state, actions between citizens of different states, actions between a state and an alien, actions between a citizen of a state and an alien, and actions involving foreign ambassadors. In similar fashion, state constitutions and state statutes define the jurisdiction of the state courts.

The Supreme Court has extensive power to make constitutional doctrine. Through the exercise of its functions of judicial review and statutory interpretation, the Court can define the meaning of the Constitution. In doing so the Court can determine the boundaries of legislative, executive, and judicial authority. The Supreme Court receives its cases from two principal sources: the U.S. courts of appeals and state courts of last resort. The Supreme Court is headed by the chief justice of the United States, who presides over the eight associate justices. The size of the Court is set by Congress and has ranged from as few as five to as many as ten justices. As with all federal judges, Supreme Court justices are nominated by the president and must be confirmed by the Senate. If confirmed, the justices have life tenure.

How Cases Begin   A case that reaches the U.S. Supreme Court for consideration of a constitutional issue begins in a state or federal trial court. A case at the trial level involves a fact dispute that requires resolution. If a trial actually occurs, the parties present evidence to an impartial judge or jury under basic rules of evidence administered by the trial judge. Once the fact dispute is resolved, an appeal may be pursued by the losing party, at which time any constitutional questions that may be present can be developed. How cases are begun at the trial level depends in large part on whether the case is criminal or civil.

A criminal case begins with the government accusing a person of violating one or more provisions of the criminal code. The government initiates all criminal cases. A criminal case is an adversarial contest between the "State" or the "People" and the accused, who is called the defendant. The issue of fact in a criminal case is whether the state can prove beyond a reasonable doubt the guilt of the accused. No private party can take a criminal case directly into the courts. Once a criminal case is filed by a prosecutor, it is the responsibility of the trial court to conduct a series of proceedings up to and including a trial to determine as a matter of fact whether the accused is guilty. Most criminal cases are not concluded by trial, however. Rather, the government and the defendant resolve the case by means of a plea agreement, which typically involves the accused admitting guilt in exchange for some consideration by the prosecution. Cases settled in this way usually reflect the defendant's decision not to press any constitutional question(s) the case may have contained. Indeed, the objective of the settlement is to end the case rather than pursue any such questions on appeal. It is from the small proportion of cases that are tried that a constitutional question may emerge.

Constitutional issues in criminal cases may involve either process (procedure) or substance, although procedural questions are far more common. In these cases, it is virtually always the defendant who raises a question on appeal following a conviction. A wide range of procedural questions may be raised by convicted defendants. Most stem from alleged errors made by the police or as the case progressed through the criminal justice system. Procedural errors may originate at any of the many steps in the process beginning with the police investigation. The double jeopardy prohibition prevents the state from appealing an acquittal in a criminal case. An acquittal is a fact judgment that the prosecution did not establish the defendant's guilt beyond a reasonable doubt. The government does not have the right to keep bringing that question to trial. The government can appeal from an adverse ruling on a legal judgment, however, which is distinct from a fact judgment. An occasion for a government-initiated appeal is found in cases in which a convicted defendant is successful on appeal. If the ruling comes from other than the U.S. Supreme Court, the state is free to pursue further review of the underlying law issue.

Substantive appeals in criminal cases are quite rare because there is generally little doubt that the government can legitimately regulate or prohibit such conduct as burglary, assault, arson, or murder. A challenge of state law criminalizing arson or sexual assault as an unreasonable exercise of governmental power, for example, has no chance of succeeding. A prosecution for the crime of distributing obscene material, on the other hand, might raise substantive questions about whether the underlying obscenity law violates the First Amendment. The flag-burning cases of the late 1980s and early 1990s had similar First Amendment connections. The state case, *Texas v. Johnson*, 491 U.S. 397 (1989), serves as an example. The state of Texas made it a crime to desecrate the U.S. flag, and Gregory Johnson burned a flag as part of a protest against the policies of the Reagan administration. Johnson did not dispute that he had broken the law. He had done so deliberately, with the specific intention of putting himself in a position to challenge the law. The trial court's task was relatively easy in this case. But the trial was merely a step to an appeal. On appeal, Johnson claimed that his burning of a flag was an act of symbolic expression and was therefore protected by the First Amendment. The essential question Johnson put before the Court was whether a state could criminalize his action. The Supreme Court eventually ruled that it could not.

Civil challenges to government policies are a little different. Here the initiative rests exclusively with an individual or group who claim injury as a result of some governmental policy or practice. Obviously, the governmental action had to be taken prior to any legal action, but it is wholly up to an injured party to seek relief from the courts. A civil case contains an asserted claim by a litigant, who is called a plaintiff. The legal action is commenced to obtain court-ordered relief. Though a number of different remedies may be sought in civil cases, actions concerning constitutional questions usually involve a claim that the government has in some way violated a right protected by law. Through the lawsuit, a government policy or practice is challenged as unlawful. The remedy sought by the challenging party is most often the elimination or modification of the particular policy or practice, although compensation for any injury is often sought as well.

Several general propositions can be offered in summary. First, even landmark cases do not originate at the U.S. Supreme Court level. Rather, both civil and criminal cases enter the court system as disputes of fact in federal or state trial courts. Second, criminal cases are initiated by the government and tend not to contain constitutional or policy questions at the outset. If such a question develops, it is likely to involve an alleged procedural error that occurred as police investigated or the courts adjudicated. Seldom does a criminal case involve substantive challenges to criminal law. Finally, cases that contain a constitutional question from the outset are typically cases in which a lawsuit is brought for the specific purpose of challenging a particular government policy or practice.

The decisions that most authoritatively define constitutional rights come from the U.S. Supreme Court. The Supreme Court is at least two levels above the trial courts in which the cases enter the judicial system. The trial stage is as far as most cases go. Once the fact dispute is resolved, the case ends and the parties accept the outcome. For a relatively small number of cases, however, the trial process is merely a preliminary step. If an appeal is pursued, a case goes from the trial court having original jurisdiction to the appellate court structurally located just above that trial court. If the case was heard by a state trial court, an appeal would go to the first-level appellate court in the state system. Whether this would involve one or two levels depends on the state in which the trial was held. In larger states with a two-level appellate structure, appeal would occur in an intermediate-level court. In small states with only one appellate level, the court would be the court of last resort, usually called the supreme court of a state. A U.S. court of appeals would be the first step in the federal appellate process.

United States Supreme Court Review   Virtually all the cases that come before the U.S. Supreme Court are seeking review of a ruling by a U.S. court of appeals or a state supreme court. Cases get to the Supreme Court in essentially one of two ways. The first is by writ of appeal, a route established by federal statute. The Supreme Court was given substantial discretion over granting the writ of appeal in 1928, when the Congress gave the justices authority to determine whether the issues contained in any case otherwise satisfying writ of appeal conditions also raised a "substantial federal question." If the Court determined a "substantial" question was not present, it could then withhold the writ, which previously would have been granted automatically. Congress again modified the rules for the writ of appeal in 1988, confining it to certain cases coming from three-judge U.S. district courts. Prior to 1928 more than 80 percent of the Supreme Court's docket was writ of appeal cases. Once the Court obtained discretion to decide which of these cases were important enough to review, the number of cases coming to the Court on writ of appeal decreased substantially. Presently, less than 10 percent of the cases the Court decides come to it on writ of appeal.

The second route to the Supreme Court is through the writ of certiorari. This approach to the Court was established by Congress in the Everts Act of 1891, which established the certiorari power that gave the Court complete discretion over much of its caseload. Through certiorari the Court can decline to hear certain cases if a given number of justices feel that the cases are not sufficiently important. The writ is granted when at least four of the nine justices of the U.S. Supreme Court agree that a particular case should be reviewed. Since the late 1920s the proportion of certiorari petitions granted review by the Court has never exceeded 22 percent. More recently, the Court grants certiorari in fewer than 3 percent of the cases. Although the writ is granted in a small proportion of cases, in excess of 90 percent of the Court's cases presently come by certiorari.

The Decisional Process   The process by which the Supreme Court decides which cases to review is not complex. The chief justice prepares a list of cases to be discussed by the Court as a whole. This list is relatively short and represents the chief justice's best estimate of those cases worthy of consideration. A small number of cases are added by the other justices. Each justice, with the extensive assistance of his or her law clerks, has screened the cases petitioning for review. As a result, each justice has a good idea of which cases raise the most substantial questions. Unless a justice requests that a case be discussed by the Court as a whole, the petitions other than those on the chief justice's "discuss" list are summarily rejected. Generally, there is consensus on which cases should be selected for review.

The Constitution and the Supreme Court: A Brief Introduction

The conference is the place at which all important business of the Court is conducted. It is used at several stages in the decisional process. The conference is considered by many to be the core of the Court's decisional process. In conferences the justices engage in intensive discussions that yield decisions on which cases are to be reviewed and subsequently decided. The conference discussion shapes not only voting alignments but also the substance of the majority opinion in most cases. Conference sessions occupy the better part of two workdays per week during the period the Court hears oral arguments, and conferences are closed to everyone but the justices. The conferences held early in the Court's annual term are used to determine which cases are to be reviewed. At this point, preterm conferences have already disposed of many of the accumulated petitions. For a case to be selected, a minimum of four justices must agree the case warrants review.

It is difficult to know precisely why any particular case is selected or rejected because the justices seldom explain these judgments. Yet some discernible patterns do emerge. Certainly, some cases are chosen because they deal with particularly important questions that have significance beyond resolving the specific case out of which they arise. One characteristic of an important case may be that it contains an issue not previously addressed by the Court. Another factor that underscores the importance of a particular case might be that lower court rulings on the issue are unclear or in conflict. Clearly one of the Court's main functions is to resolve inconsistencies in constitutional interpretation coming from lower courts. Issues that have resulted in conflicting judgments from lower courts present situations in which the Court often feels compelled to establish a uniform principle of law.

The Court receives information about a case from several sources. The petitions that are filed are supported by documentation that provides some information about the case and the particular legal issue. This information is important, because the justices decide which cases to review based on the material provided with the petitions. Once the Court has agreed to review a case, written briefs on the merits of the issue are filed. A brief is a document submitted on behalf of each of the parties. The brief attempts to represent all the applicable legal materials, such as constitutional or statutory provisions and precedents. More important, the brief offers arguments in an effort to persuade the Court to rule in favor of one party over the other. The brief is a vehicle of advocacy. In addition to briefs submitted by the parties themselves, amicus curiae briefs are often submitted by third parties such as interest groups. There is some evidence to suggest that an indication of forthcoming amicus briefs from certain interest groups or from the federal government underscores the importance of a particular case and enhances the possibility that the case will be selected for review.

Once a case has been selected for review, it is scheduled for oral argument. Oral arguments occur after the written briefs have been filed. The oral argument is a very short presentation, usually 30 to 60 minutes, and is made before the full membership of the Court. Although limited in length, the oral argument represents each party's last chance to advance their position. The oral argument process is highly interactive because the justices are able to pose questions to the attorneys representing each party. The justices are already familiar with the issue and have probably heard most of the arguments before. Their questions are designed to clarify a particular point or to go beyond the arguments contained in the written briefs. For justices who are undecided on a case, the oral argument period can be the critical step in the decisional process.

The conference process is used again when the justices consider a case following the oral arguments. The chief justice speaks first, with each associate justice following in turn (in order of seniority). The Court can do one of three things with a particular case. First, it may determine that the case was mistakenly selected for review (review improvidently granted) and dismiss the case. The result here is as though the case had not been selected for review in the first place. Second, the Court may decide to resolve the case by summary judgment. This option means the decision will not have much policy significance; summary judgments typically are not accompanied by a lengthy opinion. Third, the Court may choose to decide the case on its merits and write a full accompanying opinion. Assignment of the opinion by the chief justice occurs after a nonbinding vote that provides a preliminary indication of how the Court will align itself on the issue. The justice assigned to draft the majority opinion must come from the winning side of any split vote. The chief justice may assign himself or herself this responsibility as long as he or she votes with the majority.

Each justice ultimately decides how to vote based on his or her response to the legal arguments advanced by the parties and to the arguments made by other justices in conference. Voting decisions are also affected by the views of each justice concerning the meaning of particular constitutional provisions. Each justice comes to the Court with well-developed opinions on these matters. Each justice will, for example, have a pretty clear idea of how far the First Amendment's free speech protection should extend. When a free speech case comes before the Court, these views come into play. Equally intelligent and well-trained lawyers often have differing views on constitutional provisions, so it is not uncommon for the Court to lack consensus in some cases, a split vote being the result. Each justice's vote on a case becomes final only when he or she actually agrees to or rejects the written opinion offered on behalf of the majority position. The discussion begun in conference continues after the opinion assignment has been made and a draft opinion has circulated; votes may be altered throughout this period. Ultimately a decision and accompanying majority and minority opinions emerge.

The Decision   The Supreme Court's decision does two things. It resolves the specific dispute between the two parties, and it also addresses any constitutional or policy question that underlies the case. In many ways, the latter function is more important, but first a word about the former.

Cases reaching the Supreme Court already have been before lower courts, so one party already is in the position of winner. The Supreme Court's options are to uphold the lower court ruling, to modify it, or to reverse it altogether. If the Supreme Court finds the previous decision to be correct on the merits, it affirms the lower court ruling. Remember that the court hearing the case immediately before the Supreme Court is typically an appeals court, so the ruling under review focuses on some procedural or substantive policy issue and not on the fact judgment. If the Court upholds the existing ruling, the losing party from the lower court—the party who sought review by the Supreme Court—remains the losing party. If this party is a criminal defendant, his or her conviction is upheld because the issue appealed was not considered valid. If, on the other hand, the Court decides the previous ruling is incorrect, it may reverse the lower court. Another term for setting aside a lower court ruling is *vacate*. The Court also has the intermediate option of modifying a lower court ruling, which is a partial or limited reversal.

When a decision is reversed or modified, the case is often remanded, or sent back, to the lower court for reconsideration consistent with the Supreme Court's decision. This is done because the effect of reversing or vacating is to set aside the outcome of the trial process on legal, rather than factual, grounds. The original factual question, such as a criminal defendant's guilt, is not addressed by the Supreme Court, thus, the case must be sent back for reconsideration of the factual issue. For example, assume a criminal defendant has been convicted of burglary. One of the pieces of evidence offered by the prosecution was an item stolen from someone's home. However, that item was found in the closet of the defendant's home during a search conducted without a warrant. The defense would have objected to the introduction of the evidence at the trial, but the trial judge allowed the jury to see the evidence. On appeal following conviction, the defense may have been able to convince the Supreme Court that the evidence had been discovered in an illegal search and that it should have been suppressed at the trial. It is impossible, however, for the Supreme Court to calculate what effect the evidence had on the original jury's decision to convict. As a result, the Court must remand the case for a new trial to determine whether the defendant is guilty. The prosecution is permitted in the new trial to do everything it did during the first trial except introduce the item that was ruled inadmissible on appeal.

More important than the decision declaring a winner in a case is the Supreme Court's accompanying opinion, which serves several purposes. First, the opinion may contain specific directions for any reconsideration undertaken by a lower court on remand. Such instructions might offer standards by which reconsideration is to take place. Any direction of this kind will provide guidance to lower courts as they handle similar cases in the future. Second, the opinion represents the Court's rationale for its decision. Finally, it is the opinion that speaks to the broader constitutional or policy questions and establishes clear principles that becomes controlling precedent in later cases.

There are several kinds of opinions. The most important is the majority opinion, or opinion of the court. The majority opinion includes the rationale for the court's conclusion on a question of law. It also defines the scope and reach of the decision. The legal basis for the opinion, called the *ratio decidendi*, is the central proposition that resolves a constitutional question—the irreducible core of the decision. The *ratio decidendi* is distinguished from *obiter dicta*, which are statements in a court opinion on matters that are not essential to the resolution of the law question before the court. It is the *ratio decidendi* that establishes the value of a decision as a legal precedent. Because *obiter dicta* generally go beyond what is necessary to resolve a point of law, they have no precedent value.

The majority opinion is written by a member of the court who votes with the majority side. Assignment of the majority opinion to an individual member of the court occurs at conference. On the U.S. Supreme Court, the chief justice assigns the opinion, provided he or she is also a member of the majority. If the chief justice is not among the majority, the opinion is assigned by the most senior associate justice on the majority side. The assigned justice drafts an initial version of the opinion, trying to integrate the views of all those among the majority. The opinion is then circulated, discussed, and probably redrafted several times. This rewriting is aimed at developing or holding a consensus on the reasons for a particular decision. While a decision can be made by a majority even if the members of the majority disagree on the reasons, the Court's decisions are much more authoritative if a consensus can be maintained on the reasons as well as the outcome. The Supreme Court may use a per curiam opinion instead of a full majority opinion. A per curiam opinion is an unsigned statement issued to briefly summarize a ruling without extensively developing the Court's reasoning. Per curiam opinions are generally used for cases that undergo abbreviated review, which means the case is reviewed on its merits but without oral argument. These are usually not the major decisions of the Supreme Court. Rather, they are cases in which the issues may be less complicated than those in cases receiving the "full treatment."

Individual justices may choose to depart from a majority opinion in one of two ways. One way is to issue a concurring opinion, which reflects agreement on the outcome but differs regarding rationale. Concurring opinions may vary widely in the extent to which they depart from the majority opinion. In some instances, the difference may be quite narrow. A justice may wish to mention an additional reason for arriving at the outcome or may want to place emphasis a little differently across several supporting points. On the other hand, a justice may disagree on virtually all the reasons underlying the majority position. In this instance, the justice may be among the majority "in result only" and his or her concurring opinion departs extensively from the majority opinion.

Justices often disagree not only with the language of the majority opinion but with the ruling itself. Justices on the losing side of a split decision usually issue a dissenting opinion, which is essentially a minority report. A dissenting opinion may represent the views of as few as one justice or as many as four. A dissenting opinion does not have precedent value in that it cannot authoritatively define a point of law. As a result, justices who write dissenting opinions have greater freedom regarding the arguments they advance. Because dissents need not attend to finely focused legal points as majority opinions must, they often are sweeping in scope and contain powerful language. It also is possible to dissent "in part." If the Court reviews a case containing multiple issues, a justice may agree with the majority position on some points but not all of them. In such a case, the justice's dissenting opinion would address only those one or two points of disagreement. In addition to representing a justice's disagreement with the majority, a dissenting opinion has two other purposes. First, a dissenter may try to limit the impact of a ruling. The dissenting opinion may invite Congress or a state legislature to modify the ruling if it is based on construction of a statute. A dissension may otherwise indicate ways to interpret the ruling narrowly, which can affect the way a lower court applies the ruling. Second, a dissenting opinion can encourage future appeals on the same question. Occasionally, a dissenting position in one case becomes the majority position when the issue is reviewed some time later.

Once all the opinions have been written and the alignment of the justices is finalized, the ruling is announced in open court. Though opinions may be read in their entirety in open court, they are usually summarized. The timing of an announcement rests with the Court, but most decisions are announced in May and June as the Court nears the conclusion of its term. There are a number of excellent titles in which the U.S. Supreme Court and its function of constitutional interpretation are discussed is detail. Several of the leading titles are:

Abraham, Henry J. *The Judiciary: The Supreme Court in the Governmental Process.* 9th ed. New York: New York University Press, 1996.

Baum, Lawrence. *The Supreme Court.* 6th ed. Washington DC: Congressional Quarterly Press, 1998.

Carp, Robert A., and Ronald Stidham. *Judicial Process in America.* 3d ed. Washington, DC: Congressional Quarterly Press, 1995.

Cooper, Phillip, and Howard Ball. *The United States Supreme Court: From the Inside Out.* Upper Saddle River, NJ: Prentice-Hall, 1996.

O'Brien, David M. *Storm Center: The Supreme Court in American Politics.* 4th ed. New York: W. W. Norton and Company, 1996.

Walker, Thomas G., and Lee Epstein. *The Supreme Court of the United States: An Introduction.* New York: St. Martin's Press, 1993.

CHAPTER 2

The First Amendment

Overview, 23

The First Amendment, 29

Freedom Speech, 79

Freedom of the Press, *100*

OVERVIEW

The First Amendment states:

> Congress shall make no law respecting an establishment of religion, or prohibiting the free exercise thereof; or abridging the freedom of speech, or of the press; or the right of the people peaceably to assemble, and to petition the Government for redress of grievances.

The several provisions of the First Amendment are designed to protect the sensitive area of personal belief and opinion. The Establishment Clause forbids creation of a state church or direct governmental subsidies to churches. The more troublesome question has been how much contact is permissible short of designation of a state church.

The first significant attempt to develop standards for religious establishment came in *Everson v. Board of Education*, 330 U.S. 1 (1947). In *Everson*, the Court upheld state legislation authorizing reimbursement of school transportation costs to parents of children attending either public or parochial schools. The Court indicated that the state ought to assume a position of "neutrality" with respect to religion, but concluded that the Establishment Clause should not prevent people from receiving general government services notwithstanding incidental benefit to institutionalized religion. So long as the student or individual citizen is the primary beneficiary of government service, the Establishment Clause is not violated. One criterion of establishment is whether an action of government has a secular purpose. The Court invalidated a state-sponsored prayer exercise for public schools in *Engel v. Vitale*, 370 U.S. 421 (1962), on secular purpose grounds. The Court modified the establishment standard in *Lemon v. Kurtzman*, 403 U.S. 602 (1971), as it struck down a state law authorizing public money to be used for nonpublic school expenses, including teacher salaries. The three-prong *Lemon* test held that, in addition to having a secular purpose, a government must not enact policies that advance or hinder religion as a primary effect or consequence. Furthermore, a government policy may not put church and state in an "excessively entangled" relationship. The teacher salary supplement program in *Lemon* failed the "entanglement" element. The *Lemon* test did not prohibit all forms of aid to nonpublic schools, however. Using the "child benefit" approach, the Court upheld a state income tax deduction for all costs of elementary and secondary level children in *Mueller v. Allen*, 463 U.S. 388 (1983). The deductions applied to expenses involved for both public and nonpublic schools. The Court ruled in *Agostini v. Felton*, 501 U.S. 203 (1997), that public school staff could provide remedial services to students on the premises of nonpublic schools. In *Agostini* the Court abandoned the previously held position that mere presence of public school employees on parochial school grounds created an impermissible "symbolic link between government and religion." Similarly, in *Rosenberger v. University of Virginia*, 515 U.S. 819 (1995), the Court concluded that providing financial support to a religious student group did not convey an endorsement or indicate a preference for the particular religion. The Court reasoned that if the university provided subsidies to nonreligious groups, it must provide the same kind of support to religious groups. The Court reached a similar conclusion in *Lamb's Chapel v. Center Moriches Union Free School District*, 508 U.S. 384 (1993), in which it ruled that public school districts could not deny access to religious groups to public school premises if other noncurriculum groups also had access to those facilities. Religious displays on public premises also presented highly sensitive establishment questions. In *Allegheny County v. American Civil Liberties Union*, 492 U.S. 573 (1989), the Court ruled that use of religious symbols in public displays may be permitted as long as no message of endorsement or preference is communicated. Finally, the Court struck down the use of clergy at public school graduation ceremonies in *Lee v. Weisman*, 505 U.S. 577 (1992), because school authorities had too great an influence on religious content.

The Free Exercise Clause of the First Amendment prohibits governmental interference with religious practices. Although the clause absolutely protects religious belief, conduct related to the pursuit of belief may be subject to limitation. As in establishment cases, the most contentious free exercise issue has been the standard to use when reviewing questions about religious exercise. Generally, a purely secular regulation must be obeyed even by those who find the regulation at odds with their religious belief system. The *Sunday Closing Law Cases*, 366 U.S. 421 (1961), permit secular regulation to encroach upon religious practice, but only in the absence of alternate means of achieving secular ends. The Warren Court added the "compelling interest" element to the free exercise standard in *Sherbert v. Verner*, 374 U.S. 398 (1963). This change elevated the free exercise standard to its most protective level. The Burger Court retained this standard in *Wisconsin v. Yoder*, 406 U.S. 205 (1972), but the Rehnquist Court returned to the secular purpose test in *Employment Division v. Smith*, 494 U.S. 872 (1990), which is where the standard presently remains. The Congress attempted to overturn the *Smith* decision and reinstate the more protective *Sherbert/Yoder* free exercise standard by statute. The Religious Freedom Restoration Act of 1993 was found unconstitutional by the Court, however, in *City of Boerne v. Flores*, 521 U.S. 507 (1997), on Fourteenth Amendment grounds. Two other decisions are included in the free exercise section of this chapter. In *Gillette v. United States*, 401 U.S. 437 (1971), the Court did not allow an exemption from the military draft process for persons asserting religion-based objection to particular wars as distinct from war generally. Finally, the Court upheld a state sales and use tax levied upon a religious organization's sale of religious materials in *Jimmy Swaggart Ministries v. Board of Equalization*, 493 U.S. 378 (1990).

The First Amendment prohibits impairment of free speech. The basic principles for free speech cases were first considered in *Schenck v. United States*, 249 U.S. 47 (1919), in which the Court held that expression may be regulated when the expression creates a "clear and present danger." *Gitlow v. New York*, 268 U.S. 652 (1925), modified the *Schenck* standard by permitting restriction of expression if it tended to lead to an injurious result. A sliding scale or balancing test for expression was developed in *Dennis v. United States*, 341 U.S. 494 (1951), in which speech that advocated illegal action was examined. Expression through an action substitute or symbolic gesture is generally protected speech as seen in *Tinker v. Des Moines Independent Community School District*, 393 U.S. 503 (1969), and the flag desecration case of *Texas v. Johnson*, 491 U.S. 397 (1989). The nature of speech as communication was examined in *Cohen v. California*, 403 U.S. 15 (1971), in which a state unsuccessfully sought to regulate "offensive" speech. A "hate speech" ordinance was struck down by the Court in *R.A.V. v. City of St. Paul*, 505 U.S. 377 (1992), because it was not content neutral. Statutory restrictions imposed on speech may not be too broad or vague. *Schaumburg v. Citizens for a Better Environment*, 444 U.S. 620 (1980), utilized the overbreadth doctrine to strike down a local ordinance. In *Lebron v. National Railroad Passenger Corp.*, 513 U.S. 374 (1995), the Court ruled that although Amtrak is legally a private entity, it is an agency of government and cannot ban advertising simply because of the political content of an advertisement. Similarly, the Court ruled in *United States v. National Treasury Employees Union*, 513 U.S. 454 (1995), that the federal government cannot prevent lower-level executive branch employees from receiving compensation for appearances, speeches, articles, or other expressive conduct.

The fundamental ingredient of a free press is the absence of prior restraint or government censorship. *Near v. Minnesota*, 283 U.S. 697 (1931), was the Court's first extensive discussion of prior restraint and its generally suspect character. The prior restraint doctrine provided, at least in part, the basis for the Court's review of the injunction preventing publication of the Pentagon Papers in *New York Times Co. v. United States*, 403 U.S. 713 (1971). The Court has permitted prior restraint under certain circumstances, however. In *Hazelwood School District v. Kuhlmeier*, 484 U.S. 260 (1988), for example, a school principal was permitted to remove articles from a high school paper before its publication. The free press protection extends beyond the prohibition on prior restraint. The extent to which libelous statements are protected was examined in *New York Times Co. v. Sullivan*, 376 U.S. 254 (1964). In *Hustler Magazine v. Falwell*, 485 U.S. 46 (1988), the Court refused to fashion new standards for public figures subjected to intentionally inflicted emotional distress. The press has claimed that the First Amendment provides special privileges to the press to give full effect to its news-gathering function. The Court gave this claim full consideration in *Branzburg v. Hayes*, 408 U.S. 665 (1972). The tension between the requirements of fair criminal trials and a free press has prompted numerous Supreme Court decisions. While the press may be kept from accessing pretrial proceedings, the Court ruled in *Richmond Newspapers, Inc. v. Virginia*, 448 U.S. 555 (1980), that trials must remain open to the press even over the contrary wishes of a criminal defendant. Commercial press now receives extensive protection from the First Amendment. The basic standards that apply in commercial speech or press cases were fashioned in *Central Hudson Gas & Electric Co. v. Public Service Commission*, 447 U.S. 557 (1980). The extent to which commercial press may be protected from government regulation is examined in *Glickman v. Wileman Bros.*, 521 U.S. 457 (1997). Although the broadcast medium falls within the scope of the Free Press Clause, it historically has been treated differently from the print medium. The most recent examination of the rationale for that distinction can be found in *Turner Broadcasting System, Inc. v. Federal Communications Commission*, 520 U.S. 180 (1997). The advent of Internet communication may provide the basis for a comprehensive reconsideration of broadcast and cable regulation. The first case involving regulation of content on the Internet was *Reno v. American Civil Liberties Union (ACLU)*, 521 U.S. 844 (1997), in which the Court struck down provisions of the Communications Decency Act of 1996.

The Supreme Court has consistently placed obscenity outside the protection of the First Amendment. Having done so, the central problem becomes fashioning definitional standards that allow protected speech to be distinguished from obscenity. The Court's first major effort to develop such standards came in *Roth v. United States*, 354 U.S. 476 (1957). After *Roth* consensus on standards eroded until there was little expression that remained unprotected. The Burger Court sought to reestablish clarity in the definition of obscenity in *Miller v. California*, 413 U.S. 15 (1973). In the wake of

Miller, many localities attempted to regulate obscenity and adult entertainment. The Court upheld one such attempt through the zoning process in *Young v. American Mini Theatres, Inc.,* 427 U.S. 50 (1976). The Court has allowed state regulations that prohibit production and distribution of child pornography and in *Osborne v. Ohio,* 495 U.S. 103 (1990), upheld criminal sanctions for the private possession of such material. Besides criminal sanctions, other techniques have been developed to control distribution of pornography. In *Kingsley Books, Inc. v. Brown,* 354 U.S. 436 (1957), for example, the Court considered the use of injunctions to prevent sales of materials found to be obscene.

Free expression occasionally involves conduct such as assembling, marching, picketing, or demonstrating. It is an area in which the speech itself is likely to be protected, but the associated conduct may be subject to regulation. The interests of expression must be balanced against the government's interest in maintaining public order. Government may impose restrictions on the time, place, and manner in which expression may occur. In *Adderley v. Florida,* 385 U.S. 39 (1966), the Court held that jail grounds may be off-limits for a demonstration. More recently the Court upheld the right of persons to access a privately owned shopping center to express political views in *PruneYard Shopping Center v. Robins,* 447 U.S. 74 (1980). Licensing or permit requirements have generally been viewed with suspicion by the Court, as have ex parte injunctive proceedings used to restrain assembly before it occurs. In *Carroll v. President and Commissioners of Princess Anne County,* 393 U.S. 175 (1968), the Court struck down an attempt to enjoin a rally of a militant white supremacist organization. The most troublesome assembly question before the Court in the last several years has been protests at abortion clinics. In *Schenck v. Pro Choice Network,* 519 U.S. 357 (1997), the Court reviewed judicial restraints placed on antiabortion protesters.

The First Amendment does not explicitly protect the right of association, but it is now understood that group organization is a legitimate means of expression. The freedom to associate is drawn from the several expressed protections of the First Amendment. The character of association as a means of expression is thoroughly developed in *National Association for the Advancement of Colored People (NAACP) v. Alabama,* 357 U.S. 449 (1958), a case involving an attempt by a state to compel disclosure of an organization's membership list. Although the Court decided the case on Fourteenth Amendment due process grounds, the principal thrust of the decision was to protect associational freedom. The Court also extended associational freedom in *Keyishian v. Board of Regents,* 385 U.S. 589 (1967), in which it held that mere membership in a particular organization cannot lead to dismissal from public employment. The Court acknowledged the expressive character of parades in *Hurley v. Irish-American Gay, Lesbian & Bisexual Group*, 515 U.S. 557 (1995), and held that private sponsors of parades could exclude groups from participating. Associational activity as it relates to the electoral process has been examined in several contexts. Portions of the Federal Election Campaign Act were stricken down in *Buckley v. Valeo*, 424 U.S. 1 (1976), because of impermissible interference with political campaign expenditures. Political parties are also protected associations. The Court held in *Tashjian v. Republican Party*, 479 U.S. 208 (1986), that parties can determine the rules by which their primary elections are conducted. At the same time, the Court has allowed states to regulate the electoral process as such. The Court upheld, for example, ballot access restrictions in *Munro v. Socialist Workers Party*, 479 U.S. 189 (1986), and allowed a state to prohibit a political party from nominating a candidate for political office who was already a candidate of one of the two major parties in the state. The Court, however, ruled that a state could not ban anonymous political campaign literature in *McIntyre v. Ohio Elections Commission*, 514 U.S. 334 (1995). Finally, the Court recently examined the issues of term limits and political patronage. In *U.S. Term Limits, Inc. v. Thornton*, 514 U.S. 779 (1995), the Court ruled that states could not establish term limits for either the United States Senate or House of Representatives, and in *Wabaunsee County v. Umbehr*, 518 U.S. 668 (1996), held that a government contract with a private service provider could not be terminated because the contractor expressed criticism of the contracting governmental unit.

The First Amendment protects personal belief and opinion, and action stemming from personal belief and opinion. The First Amendment to the Constitution of the United States was adopted in 1791. It addresses four basic freedoms that its authors deemed imperative to a free society functioning within a democratic political system. These include the freedom of religion, speech, the press, and the dual right to assemble peaceably and to petition the government. Freedom of religion is protected by two provisions: One prohibits the establishment of religion while the other ensures the free exercise of religion. The right of association has also been recognized as protected by the First Amendment. Some eminent jurists have argued that First Amendment protections are absolute, but this view has never been represented by a majority of Supreme Court justices. Instead, the Court has engaged in balancing First Amendment rights with the requirements of public order. The issues that come before the Court require drawing a line between constitutionally protected and unprotected activity. The Establishment Clause was included because those who wrote the Bill of Rights were mindful of the European experience of establishing state churches. The Establishment Clause certainly prohibits government from designating an "official" church, but also from showing preference for a particular church or sect. The Supreme Court, however, has construed the prohibitions more broadly. It has attempted to create standards by which it can distinguish those church and state interactions that are forbidden from those that are not. For government policy to withstand the limitations imposed by the Establishment Clause, a law must have a secular purpose, a primary effect that neither advances nor inhibits religion, and it must not excessively entangle church and state authorities. The neutral position to be occupied by the state applies both to spiritual practices such as devotional exercises and to the allocation of public funds for the benefit of religion.

The Free Exercise Clause prevents the government from interfering with religious practices. The Clause absolutely protects a person's right to believe. The line-drawing problem exists when some kind of conduct is required in addition to belief. As Justice Felix Frankfurter observed in the first flag salute case, "conscientious scruples" are insufficient to relieve an individual from "obedience to general law not aimed at the promotion or restriction of religious belief." Thus, a generally applicable law that has a legitimate secular purpose may impinge upon the ability of a person to act out religious beliefs. More recently the Court has held that regulations that interfere with religious practices may do so only in the absence of a less burdensome alternative to the accomplishment of the legitimate secular objective.

The Court did not have occasion to consider the free speech provision until shortly after World War I. The first important free speech case, *Schenck v. United States*, 249 U.S. 47 (1919), held that the First Amendment does not provide absolute freedom of expression, but rather conditional protection. Justice Holmes emphasized this point by making use of the often quoted example that the First Amendment would not protect a person who falsely shouted "fire" in a crowded theater and thus caused a panic. The authors of the First Amendment, however, were not as concerned with an utterance such as "fire" as they were with political and social expression. The problems of interpretation for the Court have come largely because the right of expression requires that there must be both a sender and a receiver of messages for communication to occur. Even if the participants in a communicative exchange are of limited numbers, there may be circumstances in which governmental intervention is appropriate. The key is determining *when* that intervention might be justified. The interests of those wishing to express themselves must be weighed against the public interest. That balancing process is complex and has given rise to a typology of expression that distinguishes among speech that requires no additional conduct, called pure speech; speech that does require additional conduct, sometimes referred to as speech "plus"; and speech that occurs through symbolic surrogates. The Court has fashioned various standards by which it can separate protected from unprotected communication within each of these categories.

The fundamental freedom of the press is also included within the First Amendment. The Framers of the Constitution believed that liberty could not be maintained without a free press. A free press must serve as the public's "watchdog" of the government. If the press is truly free, it can criticize all branches of the government, public employees, and—particularly—public policy. The reality of a free press means the press must be free from government control, printing what it desires without fear of censorship or prior restraint. There are many related issues the Framers did not anticipate, however. Since radio and television were unknown in the late eighteenth century, the Framers did not anticipate the power of electronic news media. Interference with the rights of those accused of crimes and the fairness of their trials could not be jeopardized in 1791 by prejudicial publicity broadcast over the airwaves. Neither were certain questions of obscenity and commercial speech perceived at the beginning of the American constitutional era. The Supreme Court has had to address each of these issues as they have developed in American history, all the while trying to balance the freedoms mandated in the First Amendment with other individual rights.

The enunciated right of peaceful assembly contains elements of expression found both in the right of free speech and in the right of association. In recent years assembly rights have been associated with the civil-rights movements of the 1960s, with anti–Vietnam War demonstrations in the late 1960s and early 1970s, and with other political assemblies. Once again the Court has had to balance peaceful assembly against the protection of other rights, including private property rights and state property rights. Assembly cases usually involve marching, picketing, demonstrating, petition gathering, and similar activities. While free speech may be protected, associated conduct may be subject to regulation by the state. Not only is government interested in protecting property rights, it is also interested in maintaining public order. The essential rule is that government may impose restrictions on the time, place, and the manner in which an expression may occur through assembly. The First Amendment does not expressly protect the right of association. That right is inferred from the free speech, peaceful assembly, and right to petition clauses of the First Amendment. While free speech focuses on one's right to express his or her views, the association right focuses on one's right to join a group, and be present at group meetings, but not necessarily to express oneself directly. It is the right to be a member of a group while the group expresses itself without regard to whether an individual member agrees with the group or not. *See also* BILL OF RIGHTS, p. 621; INCORPORATION, p. 665; NATURAL LAW AND NATURAL RIGHTS, p. 679.

Significance   The First Amendment was conceived as a constraint on the power of central government. With the exception of the Alien and Sedition Acts of 1798, Congress enacted little legislation that found its way to the Supreme Court on First Amendment free speech grounds until *Schenck v. United States*, 249 U.S. 47 (1919). Soon thereafter the Court was involved in a series of decisions that extended the various components of the First Amendment to the states through the Fourteenth Amendment. Early evidence of this intention was found in *Meyer v. Nebraska*, 262 U.S. 390 (1923), in which the Court struck down a state statute prohibiting the teaching of German to any student below the ninth-grade level in either public or private school. The Court said in *Meyer* that the term "liberty" included, among other things, the right to "acquire useful knowledge" and engage in "common occupations of life," such as teaching. The Court said the Nebraska statute arbitrarily and unreasonably interfered with that liberty to the degree that the due process protections of the Fourteenth Amendment had been violated. The free speech protection of the First Amendment was formally linked to the states two years later in *Gitlow v. New York*, 268 U.S. 652 (1925), in which the

31

Court concluded that freedom of speech was "among the fundamental personal rights and 'liberties' protected by the Fourteenth
Amendment from impairment by the states." Nationalization of the
press and assembly components of the First Amendment followed
soon thereafter in *Near v. Minnesota*, 283 U.S. 697 (1931), and *De
Jonge v. Oregon*, 299 U.S. 353 (1937), respectively. The Court said in
Near that it is "no longer open to doubt that the liberty of the press is
within the liberty safeguarded by the Due Process Clause of the
Fourteenth Amendment from invasion by state action." The right of
assembly was incorporated because the Court saw the right of "peace-
able assembly" as a right "cognate" and "equally fundamental" to
those of free speech and press. The two religious freedom provisions
were incorporated in the 1940s. The Free Exercise Clause was
absorbed in *Cantwell v. Connecticut*, 310 U.S. 296 (1940), and the
Establishment Clause was made applicable to the states in *Everson v.
Board of Education*, 330 U.S. 1 (1947). The result of these decisions is
that the safeguards residing within the First Amendment stand
against unreasonable actions by both national and state governments
in circumscribing personal belief and opinion.

ESTABLISHMENT OF RELIGION
Child Benefit Doctrine

Everson v. Board of Education, **330 U.S. 1 (1947),** upheld reimbursement of costs of transporting nonpublic school students. At issue in
Everson was a New Jersey statute that authorized local school districts
to make "rules and contracts for the transportation of children to
and from schools." The Ewing Township Board of Education authorized reimbursements to parents covering costs of transporting their
children to private schools, including local church-affiliated schools.
These church schools gave their students regular religious instruction conforming to the religious tenets of their faith in addition to
secular education. The Court upheld the reimbursement program.
Justice Hugo Black considered the nature of the establishment
prohibition and concluded, as did Thomas Jefferson, that the
Clause "intended to erect 'a wall of separation between Church and
State.'" But the wall need not be so high as to require the state to
"make it far more difficult" for church schools. The Establishment
Clause, Black said, "requires the state to be neutral in its relations
with groups of religious believers and non-believers; it does not
require the state to be their adversary." The Court found the reimbursements were not an aid to religion, but rather an attempt to
promote the safe travel of schoolchildren. Providing safe transportation is like other governmental services such as police and fire
protection, and sewer and water service. Prohibiting access to these

kinds of services, services "separable and indisputably marked off from the religious function," would handicap religion unnecessarily. Crucial to the Court's holding was the proposition that institutional religion was not the recipient of aid. Rather, services (reimbursement in this case) were extended directly to students and their parents. The transportation program "does no more than provide a general program to help parents get their children, regardless of their religion, safely and expeditiously to and from accredited schools." This view has become known as the "child benefit" theory, and has been invoked frequently to place certain aid programs outside the coverage of the Establishment Clause. Justices Jackson, Rutledge, Frankfurter, and Burton dissented. Justice Jackson responded to the child benefit concept by saying the "prohibition against establishment of religion cannot be circumvented by a subsidy, bonus, or reimbursement of expense to individuals receiving religious instruction and indoctrination." Justice Rutledge observed that religious content is the reason parents send their children to religious schools. He viewed transportation as an essential component in delivering that religious content, and would have prohibited government from facilitating religious indoctrination in any way. *See also Agostini v. Felton*, p. 45; CHILD BENEFIT DOCTRINE, p. 624; ESTABLISHMENT CLAUSE, p. 644; FIRST AMENDMENT, p. 29; *Lemon v. Kurtzman*, p. 35.

Significance   *Everson* placed state policies within reach of the Establishment Clause. At the same time, the Court took an "accommodationist" position in *Everson*. While urging that the wall between church and state be kept "high and impregnable," the Court pursued neutrality through the child benefit concept, an approach that allowed religious institutions to benefit indirectly from government programs that are themselves "neutral" with regard to religion, provided that the institutional church is not the primary or principal beneficiary of government aid. The child benefit approach has been used extensively in school aid cases since. In *Board of Education v. Allen*, 392 U.S. 236 (1968), for example, a New York program to loan textbooks to nonpublic school students was upheld. The Court concluded that the program's purpose was the "furtherance of the educational opportunities available to the young," and that the law "merely makes available to all children the benefits of a general program to lend school books free of charge." The only books available for loan were books found to be suitable for use in public schools and books that were confined to secular substance.

With comparable limitations, textbook lending practices have consistently been upheld in such cases as *Wolman v. Walter*, 433 U.S. 229 (1977). *Wolman*, however, examined several other kinds of aid programs for nonpublic elementary and secondary schools including standardized testing services, diagnostic and therapeutic services, instructional materials and equipment, and field trip services. All disbursements authorized under the law had equivalent expenditure categories for public schools. The amount of aid for each program was limited by the amount of per pupil expenditure for public school students. The Court upheld four programs and invalidated two. The two invalidated were those providing instructional materials and equipment and field trip services. *Wolman* provides a useful example of the way the Court has used the three-pronged establishment test from *Lemon v. Kurtzman*, 403 U.S. 602 (1971). Most of the assistance in question was sufficiently circumscribed to satisfy establishment concerns. The textbooks, for example, were lent upon pupil request and their choices were confined to texts approved for use in public schools. The Court upheld the testing, diagnostic (speech, hearing, and psychological), and therapeutic services because no nonpublic school personnel delivered the services, the services were obtained in "neutral" locations off public school grounds, none of the services advanced ideology, and the activities required no monitoring. These components of the aid package passed the purpose, primary effect, and entanglement tests. The instructional materials and field trip services did not pass Establishment Clause muster. The Court found that because of the sectarian mission of the nonpublic school, "aid to the educational function of such schools necessarily results in aid to the sectarian school enterprise as a whole." Despite limiting materials to those "incapable of diversion to religious use," these materials "inescapably had the primary effect of providing direct and substantial advancement of the sectarian enterprise." The Court also concluded that the child benefit doctrine could not avoid the primary effect problem; loaning the materials to the pupil rather than the nonpublic school directly only "exalts form over substance." The field trips were found defective because the nonpublic schools controlled the timing and, within a certain range, the "frequency and destinations" of the trips. The trips are an "integral part of the educational experience, and where the teacher works within and for a sectarian institution, an unacceptable risk of fostering religion is an inevitable byproduct." The result of the *Wolman* ruling was that services that can be identified as going directly to the nonpublic school student are permitted. Thus, transportation, textbooks, and most off-premises auxiliary services do not violate the Establishment Clause. Other forms of aid relate too closely to the religious purpose of the nonpublic school or run afoul of the entanglement prohibition when monitoring is used to check against impermissible advancement of religion. Failing one or both of these tests are tuition reimbursements, facility maintenance, instructional materials and equipment, and teacher salary supplements.

In 1980 the Court narrowly upheld a reimbursement program for mandated testing in *Committee for Public Education & Religious Liberty v. Regan*, 444 U.S. 646 (1980). The reimbursement program was similar to one struck down in *Levitt v. Committee for Public Education & Religious Liberty*, 413 U.S. 472 (1973), but in *Regan*, nonpublic schools had no control over test content and cost-reporting procedures had been tightened. At the conclusion of the majority opinion, Justice White commented on the Court's difficulty in handling the school aid issue. "Our decisions have tended to avoid categorical imperatives and absolutist approaches at either end of the range of possible outcomes. This course sacrifices clarity and predictability for flexibility."

Establishment Standards

***Lemon v. Kurtzman*, 403 U.S. 602 (1971),** prohibited salary supplements for nonpublic school teachers. *Lemon* involved a Pennsylvania statute that authorized reimbursement to nonpublic schools for expenditures "for teachers, textbooks, and instructional materials." The reimbursement was limited to "courses presented in the curricula of the public schools." A school seeking reimbursement needed to identify the separate costs of the eligible "secular educational service." The contested statute specifically prohibited reimbursement for "any course that contains any subject matter expressing religious teaching, or the morals or forms of worship of any sect." A unanimous Supreme Court struck down the statute on the ground that the statute fostered an "excessive entanglement" of government and religion. In assessing the entanglement question, the Court indicated it must "examine the character and purposes of the institutions which are benefitted, the nature of aid that the state provides, and the resulting relationship between the government and the religious authority." The main problem was the "ideological character" of teachers. The Court could not "ignore the dangers that a teacher under religious control and discipline poses to the separation of the religious from the purely secular aspects of pre-college education." Although parochial teachers may not intentionally violate First Amendment proscriptions, "a dedicated religious person, teaching in a school affiliated with his or her faith and operated to inculcate its tenets, will inevitably experience great difficulty in remaining religiously neutral." If a state is to make reimbursements available, it must be certain that subsidized teachers do not inculcate religion. The comprehensive and continuing surveillance required to maintain that limit itself becomes an establishment defect because the "prophylactic contacts will involve excessive and enduring entanglement between state and church." Ongoing inspection of school records is a "relationship pregnant with dangers of excessive government direction in church schools." Finally, the Court found entanglement of a different character created by the "divisive political potential of state programs." Continuation of such state assistance will "entail considerable political activity." While political debate is normally a "healthy manifestation of our democratic system," political division along religious lines was one of the principal evils against which the First Amendment was intended to protect." *See also Agostini v. Felton*, p. 45; ESTABLISHMENT CLAUSE, p. 644; FIRST AMENDMENT, p. 29; *Lee v. Weisman*, p. 60; *Mueller v. Allen*, p. 38.

Significance   The Court articulated a three-prong establishment test in *Lemon v. Kurtzman*. The Court's ruling reflected the decisive role of the entanglement criterion in school aid establishment cases. The Court again noted the difference between precollege levels of education and higher education as it had in *Tilton v. Richardson*, 403 U.S. 672 (1971). Religious indoctrination is only an incidental purpose of education at the college level, while educational objectives at the lower levels have a "substantial religious character." In addition, the college-level student is more discriminating than the younger student, thus less susceptible to religious indoctrination. *Lemon* emphasizes that the Court sees programs at the elementary and secondary levels as inherently susceptible to religious indoctrination. *Lemon* cast serious doubt on purchase-of-service programs. Monitoring personnel, especially teachers, would be an ongoing obligation that would excessively entangle government and the church school. Transportation and books, on the other hand, have no content to be evaluated or they are subject only to a onetime review. Service items are much more difficult to fit into child benefit coverage than are books and transportation. *Lemon* involved an irresolvable establishment problem. Religion would obviously be advanced in violation of the purpose and effects criteria without the surveillance of teachers. At the same time, the maintenance of a monitoring system produces entanglement defects.

A year prior to *Lemon*, the Court upheld tax exemptions on church-owned property in *Walz v. Tax Commission [of the City of New York]*, 397 U.S. 664 (1970). *Walz* addressed the question of whether tax exemptions for religious property are compatible with the Establishment Clause. The exemption authorized by state law included "real or personal property used exclusively for religious, educational, or charitable purposes as defined by law and owned by any corporation or association organized or conducted exclusively for one or more such purposes and not operating for profit." Walz, a property owner and taxpayer, contended that the exemption indirectly compelled him to financially support religious organizations owning exempted properties. The Supreme Court upheld the exemption. Chief Justice Burger said that the First Amendment "will not tolerate either governmentally established religion or governmental interference with religion." As long as those proscribed acts are avoided, "there is room for play in a benevolent neutrality which will permit religious exercise to exist without sponsorship and without interference." Evaluation of policies using the religion clauses rests on "whether particular acts in question are intended to establish or interfere with religious beliefs and practices or have the effect of doing so." The legislative purpose served here is legitimate, Burger said. Historically common exemptions recognize the "beneficial and stabilizing influences" of the nonprofit groups exempted from taxation. The policy also responds to the "latent danger inherent in the imposition of property taxes." What New York is doing is "simply sparing the exercise of religion from the burden of property taxation levied on private profit institutions." On considering primary effect, the Court introduced the entanglement criterion that would become a decisive factor in many subsequent establishment cases. The chief justice argued that government involvement with religion existed with or without the exemption. Indeed, "elimination of the exemption would tend to expand the involvement of government by giving rise to tax valuation of church property, tax liens, tax foreclosures, and the direct confrontations and conflicts that follow in the train of those legal processes." Although some indirect economic benefits and some involvements result from granting the exemption, they are lesser involvements than collecting the property tax. Finally, the Court concluded there was no "nexus between tax exemption and establishment of religion." The tax exemption is clearly not "sponsorship since the government does not transfer part of its revenue to churches but simply abstains from demanding that the church support the state." *Walz* provided the Supreme Court a comparatively easy way to handle the establishment issue. Unlike direct aid programs, tax exemption had a long history. The history created a presumption for the practice. Although benefits may be conveyed at least indirectly to religion, such tax exemptions were quite distinct from grant programs. The exemptions were also different politically in that they did not generate the divisive debate often associated with direct grant programs.

The tax exemption issue reappeared in *Texas Monthly, Inc. v. Bullock*, 489 U.S. 1 (1989), in which the Rehnquist Court considered a state sales and use tax exemption for religious publications. The law exempted periodicals published or distributed by a "religious faith" that consisted entirely of writings either "promulgating the teachings of the faith" or "sacred to a religious faith." The exemption was challenged by the publisher of a "general interest" periodical not entitled to the exemption. The Court struck down the exemption because it had no secular purpose. When exemptions are granted, they must fall to a "wide array of nonsectarian groups as well as religious organizations." That did not occur here. Rather, the exemption was confined exclusively to religious publications, which gave it insufficient "breadth" to serve a secular objective. The Court noted a second establishment problem. Under the exemption, public officials were to determine whether a message or activity is "consistent with the teachings of the faith." Such a requirement produces a level of entanglement between government and religion greater than would occur through enforcement of the tax laws without the exemption.

The issue before the Court in *Hernandez v. Commissioner of Internal Revenue*, 490 U.S. 680 (1989), was whether fees collected by the Church of Scientology for "auditing" and "training" were deductible charitable contributions or nondeductible payments for services. The IRS disallowed the deductions, and the Supreme Court affirmed. The Court held that Congress had tried to distinguish charitable, "unrequited payments" from payments made with "some expectation of a quid pro quo in terms of goods or services." The former are deductible, while the latter are not. The Court found the payments to the church had been quid pro quo in character.

Primary Effects

Mueller v. Allen, **463 U.S. 388 (1983),** upheld a state income tax deduction for certain costs associated with the education of elementary and secondary-level students. Deductions applied to expenses incurred by students attending either public or private schools. Justice Rehnquist said that the Establishment Clause does not necessarily prohibit a program that "in some manner aids an institution with a religious affiliation." With that perspective, Rehnquist proceeded to the establishment test set forth in *Lemon v. Kurtzman*, 403 U.S. 602 (1971). The tax deduction clearly served a secular purpose. The Court, said Rehnquist, is reluctant to "attribute unconstitutional motives to the states, particularly when a plausible secular purpose ... may be discerned from the face of the statute." The Court found a state's decision to defray educational costs regardless of the type of school to evidence a purpose that is both "secular and understandable." A state may endeavor to assist parents of schoolchildren meet the rising costs of education. Such a policy "plainly serves" the secular purpose of ensuring that the state's population is well educated. Rehnquist also noted the state's interest in "assuring the continued financial health of private schools" because nonpublic schools relieve public schools from a substantial number of students. A "more difficult" question for the Court was whether the Minnesota law had the "primary effect" of advancing religion. Several features of the tax deduction led the Court to conclude the policy met the effects test. First, the educational deduction was but one of many available under Minnesota tax laws. State legislatures ought to have "especially broad latitude" in developing deductions as a means of both equalizing the tax burden of its citizens and encouraging educational expenditures. Second, the educational deduction was available to *all* parents; it did not target only parents of students attending nonpublic schools. Third, any assistance to nonpublic schools was not transmitted directly to the nonpublic schools. Rather, assistance was "channeled" through individual parents and only got to parochial schools as a consequence of "numerous private choices of individual parents of school-age children." Justices Marshall, Brennan, Blackmun, and Stevens dissented. They saw the tax deduction as a form of tuition reimbursement that provided an "incentive" to parents to send their children to sectarian schools. Although all parents may benefit, the benefits did not fall evenly. Those parents who paid tuition to send their children to private schools received greater tax deductions. The approach, said Justice Marshall, was "little more than a subsidy of tuition masquerading as a subsidy of general educational expenses." *See also Agostini v. Felton,* p. 45; ESTABLISHMENT CLAUSE, p. 644; FIRST AMENDMENT, p. 29; *Lemon v. Kurtzman,* p. 35.

Significance The decision in *Mueller v. Allen* was a departure from the Burger Court's response a decade earlier to similar issues raised in *Committee for Public Education & Religious Liberty v. Nyquist,* 413 U.S. 756 (1973). *Nyquist* invalidated three financial aid programs for nonpublic elementary and secondary schools established by the New York legislature. One program provided direct money grants to qualified schools in low-income urban areas for maintenance and repair of school facilities and equipment. A second program created a tuition reimbursement plan for parents with annual taxable income of less than $5,000. The third program provided tax deductions to parents failing to qualify for direct reimbursement. The Court found a secular legislative purpose for all three programs, but noted the "propriety of a legislature's purposes may not immunize from further scrutiny a law which either has a primary effect that advantages religion or which fosters excessive entanglement between church and state." The maintenance and repair grants failed the primary effect criterion because there was no restriction on the grant usage. This program advanced religion "in that it subsidized directly the religious activities of sectarian elementary and secondary schools." The key issue in the reimbursement and tax relief programs was whether use of parents as conduits removed the primary effect and entanglement obstacles. The Court concluded that reimbursement and tax relief were incentives. It was therefore irrelevant "whether or not the actual dollars given eventually find their way into sectarian institutions." The establishment problem was that the program provided incentive or encouragement to send a child to a nonpublic school. The Court explicitly refused to accept the argument that reimbursements to low-income parents protected their free exercise options. In the Court's view, the reimbursements and tax relief constituted "encouragement and reward" for sending students to nonpublic schools, a prohibited primary effect. The Court said in *Mueller* that Minnesota's tax deduction was "vitally different" from the programs struck down in *Nyquist*. The Court pointed specifically to the broader class of recipients—parents of all schoolchildren—and the channeling of assistance directly to the parents as the decisive differences.

The Court allowed use of federal construction monies for projects at church-affiliated institutions of higher education in *Tilton v. Richardson*, 403 U.S. 672 (1971), however. *Tilton* upheld Title I of the Higher Education Facilities Act of 1963, which provided construction grants to church-related colleges and universities for buildings and facilities "used exclusively for secular educational purposes." It also prohibited use of funds for any project that may be used for "sectarian instruction, religious worship, or the programs of a divinity school." Applicants for funds were required to "provide assurances that these restrictions will be respected," and enforcement was to be accomplished by government on-site inspections. Key to upholding the Act was the Court's opinion that "excessive entanglement did not characterize the relationship between government and church under the Act." The Court cited three factors that diminished the extent and the potential danger of the entanglement. First, institutions of higher learning are significantly different from elementary and secondary schools. Because "religious indoctrination was not a substantial purpose or activity of these church-related colleges and universities, there was less likelihood than in primary and secondary schools that religion will permeate the area of secular education." Second, the aid provided through the building grants was of a "non-ideological character." The need to monitor buildings was less than monitoring teachers, for example. Third, entanglement was lessened because the aid came in the form of a "one-time, single purpose construction grant." There were "no continuing financial relationships or dependencies." The inspections that occurred to monitor use of funds created only minimal contact. These factors also substantially lessened the potential for divisive religious fragmentation in the political arena. Justices Douglas, Black, Marshall, and Brennan dissented. They argued excessive entanglement and the insufficiency of the restrictions contained in the Act. The dissenters pointed out that even if the specific buildings funded under the grant were used only for secular purposes, religious institutions were aided by being able to use for religious purposes funds freed by the receipt of the federal grant.

Tilton had substantial impact on First Amendment standards in two ways. First, the entanglement criterion introduced the year before in *Walz v. Tax Commission*, 397 U.S. 664 (1970), was decisive in *Tilton*. It marked the first application of the standard in a school aid case. Second, Chief Justice Burger developed the distinction between higher education and the elementary-secondary levels of education as a key element in determining the degree to which entanglement existed. Combined with the nature of the bricks and mortar character of the aid, excessive entanglement was not found in *Tilton*. The Court expanded this view in *Hunt v. McNair*, 413 U.S. 734 (1973), as it upheld a state financing arrangement that involved making proceeds from the sale of revenue bonds available to finance building projects at institutions of higher education, including nonpublic colleges and universities. The monitoring required during the payback period of the program was more extensive than in *Tilton*, but not yet excessive. Similarly, the Court upheld a broad, noncategorical grant program for private colleges, including religiously affiliated institutions, in *Roemer v. Board of Public Works*, 426 U.S. 736 (1976). The Court said the Establishment Clause requires "scrupulous neutrality by the State" but not a "hermetic separation." Although the grants were made annually, the need for close surveillance of secular activities was limited enough that it did not constitute excessive entanglement.

Title VII of the Civil Rights Act of 1964 prohibits employment discrimination, but contains an exemption for religious organizations. This exemption was challenged on establishment grounds if applied to secular activities in *Church of Jesus Christ of Latter-Day Saints v. Amos*, 483 U.S. 327 (1987). Amos had been discharged from his job at a church-owned facility that was open to the public and that served no religious purpose. He argued that the church should not be able to discriminate on religious grounds in employment practices for nonreligious jobs. The Court unanimously ruled, however, that the exemption did not violate the Establishment Clause. The Court said that the secular purpose test does not mean the law's purpose "must be unrelated to religion." The purpose requirement is aimed at preventing government from abandoning neutrality and acting to promote a particular point of view on religious matters. It is a permissible legislative purpose to "alleviate significant government interference with the ability of religious organizations to define and carry out their religious missions." Neither did the Court find that the exemption advanced religion. A law is not unconstitutional "simply because it allows churches to advance religion." For a law to have forbidden effects, it is necessary for the government itself to "advance religion through its own activities and influence." Here the advancement was attributable to the church and not the government.

Public Displays

County of Allegheny v. American Civil Liberties Union (ACLU), **492 U.S. 573 (1989),** examined the question of religious displays on public property. The decision actually considered two displays. The first was a display of a creche depicting the Christian nativity scene on the main inside staircase of the Allegheny County Courthouse. With the creche was a banner saying "Glory to God in the Highest." The creche was donated by a Roman Catholic group, a fact indicated on a sign attached to the display. The second display was an 18-foot Hanukkah menorah placed next to a Christmas tree and sign saluting liberty on the steps of the Pittsburgh City Hall. The menorah was owned by a Jewish group, but was stored and placed on display by the city. The ACLU and several local residents sought to permanently enjoin both displays on Establishment Clause grounds. In a five-to-four decision, the Court ruled that the creche display impermissibly advanced religion, but by a six-to-three vote allowed display of the menorah. On the creche display, Justice Blackmun said that the "essential principle" of the Establishment prohibition is that government does not "take a position on questions of religious belief." Government's use of symbolism becomes unconstitutional if it "has the effect of endorsing religious beliefs." The effect of the government's use of symbolism, Blackmun continued, "depends upon its context." In ruling on the creche and menorah displays, the task of the Court is to determine whether, in their "particular physical settings," either has the effect of "endorsing or disapproving religious beliefs." The creche used "words as well as the picture of the nativity scene, to make its religious meaning unmistakably clear." Unlike the nativity scene in *Lynch v. Donnelly*, 465 U.S. 668 (1984), there is nothing in the context of the courthouse display that "detracts from the creche's religious message." Allegheny County, said Blackmun, sent an "unmistakable message that it supports and promotes the Christian praise to God that is the creche's religious message." While government may celebrate Christmas "in some manner," it may not do so in a way that "endorses Christian doctrine." Justice Kennedy, joined by Chief Justice Rehnquist, Justice White, and Justice Scalia, dissented on the creche display. Kennedy said that the striking down of the creche display reflected "unjustified hostility toward religion." He saw displays of the creche and the menorah as comparable and equally permissible, and he charged the majority with creating an orthodoxy of secularism. Kennedy objected to government being limited to acknowledging only a Christmas "in which references to religion have been held to a minimum."

The menorah display brought a different result and a different alignment of justices. Here the creche dissenters joined Blackmun and O'Connor and found no Establishment defect. Although the menorah is a "religious symbol," its "message is not exclusively religious." Setting was again the key. At city hall, the menorah stood "next to a Christmas tree and a sign saluting liberty." This display was not an endorsement of religion, but "simply a recognition of cultural diversity." Thus, for Establishment Clause purposes, the city's "overall display" must be seen as conveying a "secular recognition of different traditions for celebrating the winter holiday season." Justices Brennan, Marshall, and Stevens dissented from the part of the decision allowing display of the menorah. They saw no difference in the religious messages sent by either display. *See also Engle v. Vitale*, p. 54; ESTABLISHMENT CLAUSE, p. 644; FIRST AMENDMENT, p. 29; *Lamb's Chapel v. Center Moriches Union Free School District*, p. 57.

Significance   Allegheny County was not the Court's first encounter with nativity scenes. The first came five years earlier in *Lynch v. Donnelly*, 465 U.S. 668 (1984). There a municipality had included a creche in its Christmas celebration display. When the creche was challenged as a violation of the Establishment Clause, the Court allowed the display. The Court said that it had consistently rejected a "rigid, absolutist view" of the Establishment Clause. In addition, the Court said the "wall of separation" metaphor inaccurately represented the relationship of church and state. "Our society cannot have segments or institutions which exist in a vacuum or in total isolation from all other parts, much less from government." The Court maintained that history shows unbroken acknowledgment of the role of religion in American life, and the creche scene merely depicted the historical origins of Christmas. The Court concluded that the city's motives for including the creche were secular, that religion was not impermissibly advanced, and that excessive entanglement of religion was not created.

The related question of whether a state violates the Establishment Clause when a private party is permitted to display an unattended religious symbol in a public forum was examined in *Capitol Square Review & Advisory Board v. Pinette*, 515 U.S. 753 (1995). Vincent Pinette, on behalf of the Ku Klux Klan, sought a permit from the Capitol Square Review and Advisory Board to place a cross in Capitol Square in Columbus, Ohio. The state capitol building is located on the Square, and the Square qualifies as a "public forum" for First Amendment purposes. Already located on the site was a Christmas tree displayed by the state, and a Hanukkah menorah displayed by a private group. Although Pinette proposed to display a disclaimer with the cross indicating that the government neither sponsored nor endorsed its presence on the site, the Board denied his application. The Supreme Court ruled in favor of Pinette, but the seven-justice majority was unable to agree on the establishment standard to be used in this case. Justice Scalia spoke for the plurality of himself, Chief Justice Rehnquist, and Justices Kennedy and Thomas, and concluded that the Klan's religious display in Capitol Square was private expression. Private religious speech, said Scalia, "far from being a First Amendment orphan," is as fully protected by the Free Speech Clause as secular speech. The Board had rejected the display because it recognized the state's interest in avoiding any official endorsement of Christianity. The plurality saw no endorsement in permitting the display. Scalia drew heavily on *Lamb's Chapel v. Center Moriches Union Free School District*, 508 U.S. 384 (1993), in which the Court had held that public school facilities, already open to a wide variety of uses, must be open to religious groups as well. The equal access factors that the Court found in *Lamb's Chapel* were also present here—the state did not sponsor the Klan's expression, the expression took place on public property already open to the public for expressive activity, and permission was requested on the same terms as applied to other groups. The Court saw no promotion of religion in this situation. Scalia found it "peculiar" to say that the government "promotes" or "favors" a religious display by giving it the "same access to a public forum that all other displays enjoy." The Board had contended that any distinction between private speech and government speech disappears when the private speech is conducted too closely to the "symbols of government"; when private speech can be mistaken for government speech. The Court disagreed, at least when the "government has not fostered or encouraged the mistake." In fact, the four-justice plurality chose not to use the "perception of endorsement" standard here. In Scalia's view, private religious expression cannot be "subject to veto by those who see favoritism where there is none." The contrary view "exiles private religious speech to a realm of less-protected expressions heretofore inhabited only by sexually explicit displays and commercial speech." Ohio may require all private displays in Capitol Square to be identified as such. Such a regulation would be a content-neutral "manner" restriction, which is "assuredly constitutional." The state may not, however, based on a misperception of official endorsement, ban all private religious speech or "discriminate against it requiring religious speech alone to disclaim public sponsorship." Justices O'Connor, Souter, and Breyer chose to retain the endorsement test here and concluded that no reasonable observer would "interpret the State's tolerance of the

Klan's private religious display in Capitol Square as an endorsement of religion." Justice Stevens dissented saying that the Establishment Clause should be read to create a "strong presumption against the installation of unattended religious symbols on public property." The fact that a sign is placed on public property "implies official recognition and reinforcement of its message." That implication, said Stevens, is "especially strong" when the display is located in front of the seat of government itself.

Aid to Nonpublic Education

Agostini v. Felton, **501 U.S. 203, 138 L. Ed. 2d 391, 117 S. Ct. 1997 (1997)** Title I of the Elementary and Secondary Act of 1965 was intended to provide remedial instruction to educationally deprived students. The remedial instruction supported by Title I funding could not cover religious content and was typically confined to such subjects as mathematics and reading. The Supreme Court held in *Aguilar v. Felton*, 473 U.S. 402 (1985), that services funded under Title I could not be provided to students on religious school premises. It was the Court's conclusion in *Aguilar* that offering such services in religious school facilities excessively entangled church and state in a way that violates the establishment of religion prohibition of the First Amendment. As a result of *Aguilar*, services to students at religious schools were provided on public school premises. The School Board of New York City and parents of religious school students eligible for Title I were of the view that implementation of the program under the conditions set forth in *Aguilar* created problems relating to both quality and cost. The Supreme Court agreed. Justice O'Connor indicated that the Court's rulings following *Aguilar* "modified in two significant respects the approach we use to assess indoctrination." First, the Court has "abandoned the presumption" that the placement of public school employees on parochial school grounds "invariably results in the impermissible effect of state-sponsored indoctrination or constitutes a symbolic union between government and religion." Second, O'Connor said that the Court had departed from the rule relied on in *Aguilar* that "all government aid that directly aids the educational function of religious schools is invalid." O'Connor concluded that it was evident from the Court's current position that New York City's Title I program first reviewed in *Aguilar* would "not be deemed to have the effect of advancing religion through indoctrination." The dissenters contended that *Aguilar* must be maintained. It was their view that no line could be drawn between "instruction paid for at taxpayers' expense and the instruction in any subject that is not identified as formally religious." *See also* ESTABLISHMENT CLAUSE, p. 644; FIRST AMENDMENT, p. 29; *Lemon v. Kurtzman*, p. 35.

Significance   The Court reaffirmed the establishment standards from *Lemon v. Kurtzman*, 403 U.S. 602 (1971), in two shared-time cases in 1985. In *Grand Rapids School District v. Ball*, 473 U.S. 373 (1985), and *Aguilar v. Felton*, 473 U.S. 402 (1985), it struck down programs in public school systems that sent teachers into nonpublic schools to provide remedial instruction. These programs were seen as advancing religion and fostering an excessively entangled relationship between government and religion. The Court said that state-paid teachers, "influenced by the pervasively sectarian nature of the religious schools in which they work," may subtly or overtly indoctrinate students with particular religious views at public expense. The symbolic union of church and state inherent in the provision of secular, state-provided instruction in religious school buildings "threatens to convey a message of state support for religion." The "conveying a message" criterion was coupled with the "student benefit" doctrine in *Witters v. Washington Department of Services for the Blind*, 474 U.S. 481 (1986). Witters suffered from a condition that made him eligible for state vocational rehabilitation assistance for blind persons. He sought the assistance to cover the costs of his studies at a Christian college where he was engaged in a program leading to a religious vocation. The aid was denied on the ground that public money could not be used to obtain religious instruction. The Court ruled that such aid did not advance religion because the aid was given directly to Witters. Any money that eventually got to religious institutions came as a result of the "genuinely independent and private choices of the aid recipients." That Witters chose to use the aid in this way did not confer any message of state endorsement of religion.

The Court reiterated the *Witters* rationale in *Zobrest v. Catalina Foothills School District*, 509 U.S. 1 (1993), ruling that a public school district could place a sign-language interpreter for a deaf child in a parochial school without violating the Establishment Clause. Chief Justice Rehnquist said that the First Amendment has never "disabled" religious institutions from participating in publicly sponsored social welfare programs. To the contrary, the Court has "consistently held that government programs that neutrally provide benefits to a broad class of citizens defined without reference to religion are not readily subject to an Establishment Clause challenge just because sectarian institutions also receive an attenuated financial benefit." Rehnquist observed that if religious groups were precluded from receiving general governmental benefits, a church could not, for example, be protected by police or fire departments. The Court saw the service at issue in this case as a general government program that distributes benefits neutrally to any student qualifying as handicapped under terms of the Individuals with Disabilities Education Act (IDEA).

Because the IDEA "creates no financial incentive for parents to choose a sectarian school," said Rehnquist, "an interpreter's presence there cannot be attributed to state decision-making." Instead, the question posed in this case was relatively "eas[y]" because under the IDEA, "no funds traceable to the government ever find their way into the sectarian schools' coffers." Finally, the Court held that the Establishment Clause does not categorically prohibit the placement of a public school employee in a sectarian school. The Court saw nothing in the record to suggest that a sign-language interpreter "would do more than accurately interpret whatever material is presented to the class as a whole." In other words, the interpreter was seen as an entirely content-neutral medium who neither added to nor subtracted from the substantive discussions taking place at school. Justices Blackmun, Souter, Stevens, and O'Connor dissented. They saw the effect of the Court's ruling as authorizing a public employee "to participate directly in religious indoctrination." The "distinguishing purpose" of Zobrest's school is the "inculcation ... of the faith and morals of the Roman Catholic Church." The sign-language interpreter was not seen by the dissenters as a neutral party. Instead, the communication of religious content to Zobrest required the participation of the state-employed sign-language interpreter. In an environment "so pervaded by discussions of the divine, the interpreter's every gesture would be infused with religious significance."

The Village of Joel is a community in southeast New York populated exclusively by Satmar Hasidic Jews. The village was incorporated in 1977 out of what was formerly a portion of the town of Monroe. The Satmars are an extremely conservative Jewish sect, and wish to prevent interactions with nonresidents of the village as much as possible. Virtually all of the school-age children of the village attend private religious schools. There are a number of village children, however, who are handicapped or disabled in some way and require special attention. At the time the village was incorporated, these students received state and federally funded special services at the religious schools from teachers and other staff of the Monroe-Woodbury School District at the religious schools. Several years later, the Supreme Court ruled in *Aguilar v. Felton* that public school staff could not deliver services at religious school sites. The arrangement between the Monroe-Woodbury School District and the Satmar village fell within the reach of the ruling and subsequently was terminated. Hasidic parents then had to choose whether to send their children to public schools in order to receive the special services or have their children go without those services. Most chose the latter, fearing that their children would be ridiculed because of their language (the students spoke only Yiddish), dress, and manner. In 1989 New York enacted a law establishing a separate public school district, Kiryas Joel Village School District (KJVSD), for the village. The sole function of the new district was to provide special education services to the special-needs children of the village and other Hasidic communities located nearby. The law was challenged on establishment grounds by Louis Grumet and Albert Hawk as individual taxpayers and on behalf of the New York State School Boards Association. The Supreme Court held the law unconstitutional in *Board of Education v. Grumet* , 512 U.S. 687 (1994). Justice Souter said that the Constitution "allows the state to accommodate religious needs by alleviating special burdens." Accommodation, however, is not a "principle without limits." What New York attempted here was an "adjustment to the Satmars' religiously grounded preferences that our cases do not countenance." Souter suggested a number of alternatives for providing bilingual and bicultural education to the Satmar children. The problem with the New York statute was that it was "tantamount to an allocation of political power on a religious criterion." Accommodation is possible as long as it is "implemented through generally applicable legislation," but the line chosen for drawing the Kiryas Joel Village School District was one "purposely drawn to separate Satmars from non-Satmars." Justice Scalia offered a dissent, which was joined by Chief Justice Rehnquist and Justice Thomas. He said the Founding Fathers would be "astonished" to find that the Establishment Clause could be employed to "prohibit characteristically and admirably American accommodation of the religious practices (or more precisely, cultural peculiarities) of a tiny minority sect." The Court invalidated the statute, said the dissenters, because it "does not trust New York to be as accommodating toward other religions in the future."

The Rehnquist Court reviewed a different kind of initiative in *Bowen v. Kendrick*, 487 U.S. 589 (1987). Congress passed the Adolescent Family Life Act in 1981 in response to the "severe adverse health, social and economic consequences" that frequently come after pregnancy and childbirth among unwed adolescents. The Act authorized federal grants to public or nonprofit private organizations for "services and research in the area of premarital adolescent sexual relations and pregnancy." Recipients of a grant were required to provide certain services, such as counseling and education relating to family life. Various individuals and organizations challenged the program on Establishment Clause grounds because funding under the Act had gone to religious institutions whose counsel emphasized abstention and rejection of abortion as a pregnancy option. The Court ruled that the Act was not facially defective. The Act was aimed at the legitimate and secular objective of "eliminating or reducing social and economic problems caused by teenage sexuality, pregnancy and parenthood." The increased role for religious agencies was viewed as part of a more general attempt to enlist various private-sector organizations and reflected the "entirely appropriate aim of increasing broad-based community involvement" to deal with the problem. The Act did not require that grantees have religious affiliation, and the services provided were "not religious in character." While the approach chosen to deal with adolescent sexuality and pregnancy may "coincide" with those of religious denominations, the approach was not "inherently religious." Once Congress determined that development of close family ties would help prevent adolescent sexual activity, it was "sensible" for Congress to recognize that religious organizations could "influence family life."

Endorsement

Rosenberger v. University of Virginia, **515 U.S. 819 (1995)** The University of Virginia collected fees from all its students for a Student Activities Fund (SAF) that was used to support student activities and organizations on campus. Policy governing distribution of the funds did not permit subsidizing religious activities. The line separating "religious activities" from nonreligious activities, however, was not altogether clear. Some organizations that were "religious" could be subsidized if they were engaged in "cultural" rather than "religious" activities. There were also categories of nonreligious groups that could not be subsidized under the allocation policy. Ronald Rosenberger and several other students began publishing a magazine entitled *Wide Awake*. The magazine was intended to provide a "Christian perspective on both personal and community issues" and was distributed without charge on the campus. Rosenberger's organization, which was able to access University facilities, applied for funding to underwrite the publication costs for *Wide Awake*. Production of the magazine was seen as a religious activity, however, and the application was rejected. Rosenberger, the editor in chief of *Wide Awake*, and two other students brought suit in federal court. They agreed with the University that publication of the magazine was a religious activity, but contended that denial of funding for *Wide Awake* discriminated against a particular religious view. The Supreme Court ruled for Rosenberger in a five-to-four decision. Justice Kennedy said that it is "axiomatic" that the government may not regulate speech based on the message it conveys. Once the state opens a limited forum, however, it may not exclude speech "where its distinction is not reasonable in light of the purpose served by the forum, nor may it discriminate against speech on the basis of its viewpoint." The Court determined that the University's objection to *Wide Awake* constituted viewpoint discrimination. The SAF guidelines did not categorically exclude religious groups from support, but rather selected for "disfavored treatment those student journalistic efforts with religious editorial viewpoints." That the SAF guidelines excluded an "entire class" of viewpoints, said Kennedy, reflected an "insupportable assumption that all debate is bipolar and that anti-religious speech is the only response to religious speech." The "neutrality" required by the First Amendment "was compromised by the University's course of action." The funds used to support organizations came from student fees rather than the state treasury, and *Wide Awake* did not receive the SAF funds directly. Rather, the payments went to the non-University printers who produced the publication. According to Kennedy, "This is a far cry from a general public assessment designed and effected to provide financial support for a church."

Justice O'Connor provided the decisive fifth vote in *Rosenberger*, but offered a different rationale. She sought to confine herself to the specific circumstances of this case. The student organizations receiving support were "strictly independent" from the University. Assistance provided to religious publications made "improbable any perception of government endorsement of the religious message." Justice Souter, joined by Justices Stevens, Ginsburg, and Breyer, dissented. The majority decision approves "direct funding of core religious activities by an arm of the state," said Souter. He suggested that the Court's reasoning would commit the Court to approving "direct religious aid beyond anything justifiable for the sake of access to speaking forums." The Establishment Clause "absolutely" prohibits government-financed "indoctrination into the beliefs of a particular religious belief." Souter also took issue with the "novel assumption" that only direct aid financed by tax revenue is prohibited. He rejected any distinction between a tax and the student fee; the University "exercises the power of the State to compel a student to pay it." The "corrupting effect" of government support does not turn on how the government raises the money. Finally, Souter suggested that there was no viewpoint discrimination in the University's application of the SAF guidelines. The guidelines applied to religious advocacy generally; it applied to "agnostics and atheists as well as it does to deists and theists." As a consequence, the guidelines did not "skew debate by funding one position but not its competitors." *See also* ESTABLISHMENT CLAUSE, p. 644; *Everson v. Board of Education*, p. 32; FIRST AMENDMENT, p. 29; *Lamb's Chapel v. Center Moriches Union Free School District*, p. 57; *Lemon v. Kurtzman*, p. 35.

Significance   Issues involving religious content and its place in public educational institutions had been to the Court many times prior to the *Rosenberger* case. In *Zorach v. Clauson*, 343 U.S. 306 (1952), for example, the Court upheld off-campus "released time" for religious education. *Zorach* explored the extent to which the Establishment Clause requires strict separation of church and state with regard to such religious instruction. The case dispelled some of the criticism generated by the invalidation of a slightly different program four years earlier in *Illinois ex rel. McCollum v. Board of Education*, 333 U.S. 203 (1948). In the New York program reviewed in *Zorach*, students were released from regular classes to receive religious instruction. The religion classes were taught by nonschool personnel and were conducted off the school grounds, a point of difference from *McCollum*. Release from school in *Zorach* was voluntary and was initiated by a written request from the student's parents. Students not attending religious instruction remained in their regular classrooms. Verification of attendance at religion classes had to be submitted to public school authorities. The Court in *Zorach* found this released-time approach to be satisfactory in that the program involved "neither religious instruction in public school classrooms nor the expenditure of public funds." Justice Douglas observed in his majority opinion that "[w]e are a religious people whose institutions presume a Supreme Being." As a result, when government "cooperates with religious activities by adjusting the schedule of public events to sectarian needs, it follows the best of our traditions." Although government may not aid or favor religion or any religious sect, there is "no constitutional requirement which makes it necessary for government to be hostile to religion." Justices Black, Jackson, and Frankfurter dissented. Given the presence of the compulsory education law in both *McCollum* and *Zorach*, the dissenters viewed the two situations as comparable. Justice Black observed that the state "makes religious sects the beneficiaries of its power to compel children to attend secular schools." *Zorach* softened the separationist position taken in *McCollum*. In doing so, *Zorach* provided a key underpinning for subsequent decisions, especially the decisions of the Burger Court, which speak of government taking a position of "benevolent neutrality" toward religion. By contrast, *McCollum* had found an on-premises released-time program to be a governmentally assisted religious activity, and had come closer to the strict separationist language of *Everson* than the *Everson* decision itself. *McCollum* was an unambiguous decision using the Establishment Clause to invalidate a state enactment. Over the sole dissent of Justice Reed, *McCollum* held the program to be promotion of religious education through use of tax-supported property and close cooperation between school and religious authorities. *McCollum* advanced the view that the Establishment Clause rested "upon the premise that both religion and government can best work to achieve their lofty aims if each is left free from the other within its respective sphere." The reaction to *McCollum* was fierce because many communities throughout the nation had some form of released-time religious instruction program in place.

A somewhat different question was raised in *Edwards v. Aguillard,* 482 U.S. 578 (1987), in which the Court struck down Louisiana's creation science law. The state's Balanced Treatment for Creation-Science and Evolution-Science in Public School Instruction Act reviewed in *Aquillard* prohibited the teaching of the theory of evolution in public schools unless accompanied by instruction in the theory of creation science. No school was required to teach evolution or creation science, but if either theory was taught, the other must be taught as well. The stated purpose of the law was protection of academic freedom. The Court found the law constitutionally defective. Determination of whether challenged legislation comports with the Establishment Clause is based on the three-pronged test first defined in *Lemon v. Kurtzman,* 403 U.S. 602 (1971). Under that standard, the legislature must have adopted the law for a secular purpose, the law's principal or primary effect may neither advance nor inhibit religion, and the law must not produce an excessive entanglement of church and state. A law failing any of these three elements violates the Establishment Clause. Justice Brennan noted that the Court has been particularly vigilant in monitoring the Establishment Clause in elementary and secondary schools. "Families entrust public schools with the education of their children, but condition their trust on the understanding that the classroom will not purposely be used to advance religious views." This vigilance is necessary because students at these levels are "impressionable," and because their attendance is involuntary. The Court concluded that the Louisiana law failed the secular purpose test. While noting that the stated purpose of the law was the protection of academic freedom, the Court said it was clear from the law's legislative history and sponsor comments that the Act was not designed to further that goal. Under the Act, teachers "once free to teach any and all facets of this subject are now unable to do so." In addition, the Act failed to ensure instruction in creation science. Rather than protecting academic freedom, the Court concluded that the Act had the "distinctly different purpose of discrediting evolution by counter-balancing its teaching at every turn with the teaching of creation science." Brennan said the Court "need not be blind to the legislature's preeminent religious purpose," which was "to advance the religious viewpoint that a supernatural being created humankind." The Act's legislative history documented the fact that the proposed change in the science curriculum was done in order "to provide persuasive advantage to a particular religious doctrine that rejects the factual basis of evolution in its entirety." As a result, the Court concluded that the primary purpose of the Act was to endorse particular religious doctrine through use of the symbolic and financial support of government and therefore violated the Establishment Clause. Justice Scalia, joined by Chief Justice Rehnquist, disagreed, concluding that the Act pursued a secular purpose. Scalia saw "abundant evidence" of the sincerity of the stated secular purpose and was highly critical of the Court, saying that the constitutionality of a law "cannot rightly be disposed of on the gallop, by impugning the motives of its supporters."

The Court's ruling in *Aquillard* closely paralleled *Epperson v. Arkansas*, 393 U.S. 97 (1968), a case decided two decades earlier. *Epperson* invalidated a state law that prohibited a teacher in a state-supported school from teaching "the theory or doctrine that mankind ascended or descended from a lower order of animals." Epperson's school district adopted a biology text that contained a chapter on evolution. Epperson was faced with the "literal dilemma" of using the adopted text and simultaneously committing an offense that could subject her to dismissal. The Court said that the First Amendment does not "permit the State to require that teaching and learning must be tailored to the principles or prohibitions of any religious sect or dogma." The Arkansas statute did not satisfy that condition. To the contrary, the Arkansas law "selects from the body of knowledge a particular segment which it proscribes for the sole reason that it is deemed to conflict with a particular religious doctrine." *Epperson* reflected a strict separation position much like that found in *Engel v. Vitale*, 370 U.S. 421 (1962), and *Abington v. Schempp*, 374 U.S. 203 (1963). The problem in *Epperson*, however, involved embracing a particular religious perspective or doctrine rather than the broader issue of religion versus nonreligion. *Epperson* required that government refuse to favor any particular religious doctrine or any attempt to disadvantage religious belief that may be distasteful to other religious views. In maintaining its neutral posture, a state may not avoid establishment problems by simply stating a secular purpose or disclaiming religious preference. A Kentucky statute, for example, required the posting of a copy of the Ten Commandments in every public school classroom in the state. Each posted copy had a small disclaimer saying that "secular application of the ten commandments is clearly seen in its adoption as the fundamental legal code of western civilization and the common law of the United States." A notation was also made that all posted copies were purchased with funds other than public funds. The Supreme Court nonetheless struck down the statute in *Stone v. Graham*, 449 U.S. 39 (1980), calling the declaration of secular purpose "self-serving." The Ten Commandments is "undeniably a sacred text" and "no legislative recitation of a supposed secular purpose can blind us to that fact," said the Court. While the state may integrate the Commandments into the school curriculum used in the study of history or comparative religions, the "posting of religious texts on the wall serves no such educational purpose." Thus the enactment failed the secular purpose test, and, despite private funding, the Establishment Clause was violated by the "mere posting of the copies under auspices of the legislature."

School Prayer

***Engel v. Vitale*, 370 U.S. 421 (1962),** decided that the Establishment Clause prohibited daily recitation of the New York Regents' Prayer. *Engel* generated a great deal of controversy because the spiritual exercise at issue was a prayer composed by a public body. The New York State Board of Regents, an agency with broad supervisory authority over the public schools in New York, recommended to school districts that the school day begin with a prayer they specified, although no pupil was to be compelled to join in the recitation of it. The prayer was as follows:

> "Almighty God, we acknowledge our dependence on Thee, and we beg Thy blessings upon us, our parents, our teachers and our Country."

The Supreme Court held that by "using its public school system to encourage recitation of the prayer, the State of New York has adopted a practice wholly inconsistent with the Establishment Clause." Justice Black wrote that the Establishment Clause must "at least mean that in this country it is no part of the business of government to compose official prayers for any group of the American people to recite as part of a religious program carried on by government." The exercise "officially establishes the religious beliefs embodied in the Regents' prayer." That the prayer was not overtly denominational or that participation was voluntary could not save the prayer from a fatal establishment defect, argued Black. The establishment prohibitions go beyond just keeping governmental power and influence from coercing religious minorities to conform to the prevailing officially approved religion. The Establishment Clause rests on the belief that "a union of government and religion tends to destroy government and to degrade religion." The Court said its decision did not indicate a hostility toward religion or prayer. Rather, the problem was the state's role in a spiritual exercise. The Court concluded by saying that it is "neither sacrilegious nor anti-religious to say that each separate government in this country should stay out of the business of writing or sanctioning prayers and leave that purely religious function to the people themselves." Justice Stewart disagreed that the "simple prayer" involved in this case created "an official religion." On the contrary, he maintained that "to deny the wish of these school children to join in reciting this prayer is to deny them the opportunity of sharing in the spiritual heritage of our Nation." *See also* ESTABLISHMENT CLAUSE, p. 644; *Everson v. Board of Education*, p. 32; FIRST AMENDMENT, p. 29; *Lee v. Weisman*, p. 60; *Lemon v. Kurtzman*, p. 35.

Significance   *Engel v. Vitale* took a decidedly different direction from previous establishment decisions such as *Everson v. Board of Education*, 330 U.S. 1 (1947), and *Zorach v. Clauson*, 343 U.S. 306 (1952). These cases suggested that the Establishment Clause allowed a limited interaction between church and state. Under such a view, religious practitioners could benefit from general secular purpose enactments. *Engel*, however, held that strict separation is required when governmental interaction involves actual spiritual practices. The *Engel* case prompted a wave of criticism. The Court held firm, however, and in the following year struck down other school practices in *School District v. Schempp*, 374 U.S. 203 (1963), and *Murray v. Curlett*, 374 U.S. 203 (1963). At issue in these cases were legislative enactments that designated recitation of the Lord's Prayer and the reading of Bible passages as spiritual activities to begin each public school day. As in *Engel*, the Court found the states' involvement with such practices to be incompatible with the establishment prohibition. The Court said in *Abington* that separation of church and state was based on a recognition of the teachings of history that powerful sects or groups might bring about a fusion of governmental and religious institutions. The other prohibited possibility would be to "convert a dependence of one upon the other to the end that official support of the State or Federal Government would be placed behind the tenets of one or of all orthodoxies." The Court further noted that such establishment limitations do not interfere with free exercise protections. Although a state may not use its power to prevent someone from religious exercise, the Free Exercise Clause "has never meant that a majority could use the machinery of the State to practice its beliefs." The reactions to the school prayer and Bible-reading decisions led to various attempts formally to amend the Constitution to permit voluntary prayer. Given the politically volatile nature of the issue, the Court has generally steered clear of further establishment cases involving school prayer. Instead it has concentrated in recent years on cases related to financial assistance programs.

Closely elated to school prayer is the so-called moment of silence. The Court struck down a state statute authorizing a moment of silence to be used for meditation or voluntary prayer in public schools in *Wallace v. Jaffree*, 472 U.S. 38 (1985). The case began as a challenge to three statutes in Alabama. The first was enacted in 1978 and authorized a one-minute period of silence in all public schools "for meditation." The second was passed in 1981 and provided for a period of silence "for meditation or voluntary prayer." In 1982 Alabama adopted yet another statute allowing teachers to lead "willing students" in prayer at the beginning of class. The 1982 statute prescribed that the prayer be to "Almighty God the Creator and Supreme Judge of the World." A U.S. district court found no defect in the 1978 law, but ruled the other two statutes to be an attempt by the state to encourage religious activity. The Supreme Court held the 1981 statute to be unconstitutional. Justice Stevens said the right to speech and the right to refrain from speaking are "complementary components of a broader concept of individual freedom of mind." The right to "choose his own creed" is the counterpart of one's right to "refrain from accepting the creed established by the majority." Stevens said the Court historically had unambiguously conceded that the freedom of conscience protected by the First Amendment "embraces the right to select any religious faith or none at all." This conclusion derives support not only from protection of the interest of freedom of conscience but also from the view that "religious beliefs worthy of respect are the product of free and voluntary choice by the faithful." The establishment standards require that any law must have a secular purpose. This criterion is "most plainly implicated" by *Jaffree.* In applying the secular purpose standard, the Court asked whether government's actual purpose was to endorse or disapprove of religion. The legislative record provided an "unambiguous" affirmative answer at this point. It showed the bill's sponsor to say that the law was "an effort to return voluntary school prayer" to the public schools of Alabama. The Court also based its conclusion on a comparison of the Alabama statutes. The only significant difference between the 1978 and 1981 laws was the addition of the words "or voluntary prayer." This was done, said Stevens, to convey a message of state endorsement and promotion of prayer. Addition of the words "or voluntary prayer" indicated that the state "intended to characterize prayer as a favored practice." Such an endorsement was not consistent with the principle that government must pursue a course of complete neutrality toward religion. Justice O'Connor offered a concurring opinion that distinguished the defective Alabama law from those laws that simply call for a moment of silence. The latter do not deal with an exercise that is "inherently religious," she said, and the participating student "need not compromise his or her beliefs." O'Connor argued that when a state mandates a moment of silence, it does not necessarily "endorse any activity that might occur during the period." The dissenters in *Wallace* were Chief Justice Burger and Justices White and Rehnquist. Burger said the law did not establish a religion, but only endorsed the view that religious observance "should be tolerated, and, where possible, accommodated." Burger said the Court's decision "manifests not neutrality but hostility toward religion." Rehnquist attacked the "wall of separation" metaphor frequently used in establishment cases, saying it was based on bad history and had proven useless as a guide. He saw the Establishment Clause as prohibiting only the designation of a national church or giving preference to one sect or denomination over another. Accordingly, the Free Exercise Clause did not preclude government from giving nondiscriminatory encouragement to religion. Neither did it require governmental neutrality between religion and irreligion. The Court refused to allow a moment of silence law in *Jaffree* because it concluded the statute conveyed a message of endorsement and promotion of religion. The *Jaffree* decision was a strong reiteration of the Court's position in *Engel v. Vitale.* At the conclusion of the 1982 term, the Court upheld the practice of opening legislative sessions with a prayer offered by a state-paid chaplain in *Marsh v. Chambers,* 463 U.S. 783 (1983). The Court distinguished legislative prayer from school prayer by citing the unique history of the former. The Court noted the practice was first begun with the writing of the Bill of Rights, a clear indication, it said, that the Framers of the Constitution did not view legislative prayer as prohibited activity.

Public Access

Lamb's Chapel v. Center Moriches Union Free School District, **508 U.S. 384 (1993)** New York law allows local public school districts to establish policies permitting use of school property after school hours. The statute sets forth 10 specific purposes for which school property may be used, but does not include the use of property for religious purposes. Under terms of this law the Center Moriches School District fashioned rules allowing, among other things, use of its school facilities for social, civic, and recreational purposes, but categorically prohibited use by any group for religious purposes. A local church unsuccessfully sought access to school property to show a film series on family values and child rearing. A unanimous Supreme Court ruled in *Lamb's Chapel* that denying the church group access to the school facilities was unconstitutional on free speech grounds. The First Amendment forbids the government from regulating speech in ways that "favor some viewpoints or ideas at the expense of others." The District's categorical denial of access to all religious groups did not make the policy viewpoint neutral. Justice White said the film the religious group wished to exhibit dealt with otherwise permissible subject matter and that denial of access for its presentation was "solely because the film dealt with the subject from a religious standpoint." The denial of access was thus discrimination on the basis of viewpoint. White linked the free speech rationale to the establishment standards from *Lemon v. Kurtzman*, 403 U.S. 602 (1971). The District had asserted that the refusal of access to all religious groups was necessary to avoid establishment of religion problems. The Court disagreed. When school property was widely used by a variety of private organizations, there was "no realistic danger than the community would think that the District was endorsing religion or any particular creed." Further, any benefit to religion or to the church would be, said White, "no more than incidental." Justices Kennedy, Scalia, and Thomas concurred in the Court's judgment, but were unwilling to ground their conclusions on the *Lemon* standards. Justice Kennedy called the use of *Lemon* in this case as "unsettling and unnecessary." Justice Scalia was more outspoken. He reiterated his criticisms that the test permitted the Court to rationalize virtually any outcome. He compared *Lemon* to a "ghoul in a late-night horror movie" that "stalks" our Establishment Clause jurisprudence. In his view, *Lemon* allows the Court to strike down governmental initiatives that might endorse religion, at least religion in general. *See also* ESTABLISHMENT CLAUSE, p. 644; *Everson v. Board of Education*, p. 32; FIRST AMENDMENT, p. 29; *Lemon v. Kurtzman*, p. 35; *Rosenberger v. University of Virginia*, p. 49.

Significance The access issue raised in *Lamb's Chapel* was not new to the Court. In *Board of Education v. Mergens*, 496 U.S. 226 (1990), the Court reviewed provisions of the Equal Access Act of 1984, a federal law that requires public secondary schools receiving federal educational funds to allow political or religious student groups to meet on school premises, provided other noncurriculum-related groups are allowed to do so. Under the Act, a school need not permit any student group to use facilities beyond those related to the curriculum. If at least one group unrelated to the school curriculum has access, however, the school becomes a "limited open forum," and religious or political groups must be able to access the same facilities as well. The Court upheld the Act against an Establishment Clause challenge in *Mergens*. The school district had a formal policy recognizing that student clubs are a "vital part of the education program," and about 30 noncurriculum student clubs met on school premises at the time Mergens sought access for a Christian Bible club, which triggered the Act's equal access requirements. The question then was whether the Act violated the Establishment Clause. It was argued by the school district that if it permitted religious groups to use school facilities, that action would constitute an official recognition or endorsement of religion. The Court disagreed. The Court had previously ruled that an equal access policy was constitutional at the university level in *Widmar v. Vincent*, 454 U.S. 263 (1981). In *Widmar* a state university denied use of its facilities to a group wishing to use those facilities for religious worship and religious discussion. The Court held that the denial of access was unjustified. The Court found the university had "discriminated against student groups and speakers based on their desire to use a generally open forum to engage in religious worship and discussion." Although religious groups may benefit from use of the university facilities, "enjoyment of merely 'incidental' benefits does not violate the prohibition against the 'primary advancement' of religion." That the benefits would be incidental was based on the Court's view that "an open forum does not confer any imprimatur of state approval on religious sects or practices." Furthermore, the facilities were available to a "broad class of non-religious as well as religious speakers." The provision of benefits to "so broad a spectrum of groups is an important index of secular effect."

The Court applied the three-pronged test articulated in *Lemon v. Kurtzman* and concluded that the "logic of *Widmar* applies with equal force to the Equal Access Act." Congress's reason for enacting the law was to "prevent discrimination against religious and other types of speech." Such a purpose, said Justice O'Connor, "is undeniably secular." Access to facilities did not advance religion either. There is a "crucial difference between *government* speech endorsing religion, ... and *private* speech endorsing religion." The Court concluded that high school students were "mature enough" to understand that a school does not endorse religion or support student speech that it merely permits on a nondiscriminatory basis." The proposition, O'Connor continued, that "schools do not endorse everything they fail to censor is not complicated." Indeed, Congress specifically rejected the contention that high school students are "likely to confuse an equal access policy with state sponsorship of religion." Furthermore, the Act limits participation of school officials at meetings of student religious organizations and requires that meetings occur during noninstructional time. As a result, the Act "avoids the problems of the students' emulation of teachers as role models' and 'mandatory attendance requirements.'" The Court acknowledged that the possibility of student peer pressure remained, but concluded that a school can make it clear that permitting a religious club to use facilities is not an endorsement of the club members' views. In addition, the district recognized a "broad spectrum" of organizations and invited the organization of more clubs. This "counteract[s] any possible message of official endorsement of or a preference for religion or a particular belief." Justice Stevens dissented. He would have interpreted the Act in a way that some access could be restricted. In his view, the Court's ruling required an open-door policy for any group "no matter how controversial or distasteful its views may be." *Mergens* once again gave the Court the opportunity to examine that zone of ambiguity between First Amendment expression and establishment of religion interests. As in *Widmar* before it, the Court chose in favor of the expression interests.

Content-based limitations on expression are particularly suspect. As the Court held in *Carey v. Brown*, 445 U.S. 914 (1980), a case involving selective regulation of labor picketing, "government may not grant the use of a forum to people whose views it finds acceptable, but deny use to those wishing to express less favored or more controversial views." The Court concluded that "selective exclusions from a public forum may not be based on content alone, and may not be justified by reference to content alone." Nevertheless, a state may be able to justify time, place, and manner restrictions on expression so long as they are not selective. In *Heffron v. International Society for Krishna Consciousness, Inc.*, 449 U.S. 1109 (1981), the Court upheld a state fair regulation that required the sale, exhibition, or distribution of printed material only from assigned locations. The Court found the regulation reasonable and applicable to all groups, not merely religious organizations.

Public Ceremonies

Lee v. Weisman, **505 U.S. 577 (1992),** struck down prayers at public school graduation ceremonies. Justice Kennedy wrote for a five-justice majority comprised of Blackmun, Stevens, O'Connor, and Souter. The Court saw the state's involvement with religious content as "pervasive" in this case. Kennedy focused the choices attributable to the state in this case. First, the school principal had authority to decide whether to have clergy-led prayers. Second, the principal had the choice of which community clergy would participate. Finally, the principal provided the clergy with guidance as to the content of the prayers. It was the Court's conclusion that such state involvement with these prayers violated "central principles" of the Establishment Clause. Kennedy said, "One timeless lesson [of the First Amendment] is that if citizens are subjected to state-sponsored religious exercises, the State disavows its duty to guard and respect that sphere of inviolable conscience and belief which is the mark of a free people." If the prayers are allowed at these ceremonies, objectors would face the dilemma of "participating, with all that implies, or protesting." Primary and secondary-level students ought not be forced to make such a choice. Voluntary attendance at these ceremonies was seen as insufficient to save them. High school graduation is "one of life's most important occasions." It is for this reason that the school district argued that prayer ought to be included, but the Court saw this as a fatal establishment defect. The state is not allowed "to exact religious conformity from a student as the price of attending her own high school graduation." Justice Scalia issued a dissent joined by Rehnquist, White, and Thomas. He said the Court's decision to prohibit invocations and benedictions "lays waste a tradition that is as old as public school graduation ceremonies themselves," and eliminates a component of an "even more long-standing American tradition of nonsectarian prayer to God at public celebrations generally." The "deeper flaw" in the Court's ruling, according to Scalia, was that no one was "legally coerced" into reciting or subscribing to the content of the officially sponsored nondenominational invocation and benediction read by the clergyman at these ceremonies. *See also* ESTABLISHMENT CLAUSE, p. 644; *Lemon v. Kurtzman*, p. 35.

Significance   It was anticipated that *Lee v. Weisman* could provide the Court with an opportunity to reconsider the three-pronged test fashioned more than two decades earlier in *Lemon v. Kurtzman*, 403 U.S. 602 (1971). The school district argued that the proper establishment test should hinge on whether the government coerces people toward some "official" view of religion. This coercion of the religious belief test was seen as providing the appropriate balance between keeping government away from matters of conscience, but at the same time protecting a right of public expression of religious beliefs. Because the state's involvement with religious content was so "pervasive" in this case, the Court found it possible to make a decision "without reconsidering the general constitutional framework" by which establishment issues are examined.

FREE EXERCISE OF RELIGION
Compelling Interest Test

Sherbert v. Verner, **374 U.S. 398 (1963),** held that a state may not disqualify a person from unemployment compensation because she refused to work on Saturdays for religious reasons. *Sherbert* said the protection of free exercise interests may produce a religion-based exemption from secular regulation. Sherbert was a Seventh-Day Adventist who was discharged from her job because she would not work on Saturday. Failing to find other employment because of her "conscientious scruples not to take Saturday work," Sherbert filed for unemployment compensation benefits under provisions of South Carolina law. The law required that any claimant is ineligible for benefits if he or she has failed, without good cause, to accept suitable work when offered. Through appropriate administrative proceedings, Sherbert's unwillingness to work on Saturdays was determined to disqualify her from benefits. The Supreme Court held for Sherbert in a seven-to-two decision. The Court saw the burdens imposed on her in this case as too great. She was forced to choose between "following the precepts of her religion and forfeiting benefits" or "abandoning one of the precepts of her religion in order to accept work." Facing such a choice "puts the same kind of burden upon the free exercise of religion as would a fine imposed against appellant for her Saturday worship." The Court failed to find that protection of the unemployment compensation fund from fraudulent claims by unscrupulous claimants feigning religious objections to Saturday work was a sufficiently compelling state interest. Even if the fund were threatened by spurious claims, South Carolina would need to demonstrate that no alternative forms of regulation would combat such abuses. In requiring the religion-based exemption for Sherbert, the Court imposed a requirement of possible differential treatment for those seeking unemployment benefits for refusal to work on Saturdays. The Court suggested, however, that such classification was not the establishment of religion. The decision "reflects nothing more than the governmental obligation of neutrality in the face of religious differences." The holding requires only that "South Carolina may not constitutionally apply the eligibility provisions so as to constrain a worker to abandon his religious convictions." Justices Harlan and White dissented on the ground that the decision required an exemption based upon religion. The decision required South Carolina to "single out for financial assistance those whose behavior is religiously motivated, even though it denies such assistance to others whose identical behavior (in this case, inability to work on Saturdays) is not religiously motivated." *See also Employment Division v. Smith*, p. 68; FIRST AMENDMENT, p. 29; FREE EXERCISE CLAUSE, p. 652; *The Sunday Closing Law Cases*, p. 67; *Wisconsin v. Yoder*, p. 64.

Significance   *Sherbert v. Verner*, was something of a replay of the free exercise issues seen in two of the *Sunday Closing Law Cases, Braunfeld v. Brown*, 366 U.S. 599 (1961), and *Gallagher v. Crown Kosher Super Market, Inc.*, 366 U.S. 617 (1961). Sherbert was subjected to economic hardship, like the merchants in *Braunfeld* and *Gallagher*, but the burden in the *Sunday Closing Law Cases* was less extensive and less direct. The merchants claiming a religious freedom violation had to close their businesses on Sunday under the law, but also had to be closed on Saturday to adhere to the tenets of their faith. While this resulted in some economic hardship, they could be open for business on the five weekdays. The choice of these merchants thus was not between practicing their religion and having to close their businesses altogether, but choosing between their religious obligations or a sixth day of commercial activity. Sherbert's choice was more categorical—if she chose her religion, she had neither job nor unemployment benefits. It was the Court's judgment that government could not require of someone the kind of choice Sherbert faced, but could require the kind of choice the merchants had to make under the Sunday commercial restrictions. The compelling interest criterion is far more demanding than merely showing secular purpose. Coupled with the alternate means requirement carried over from the *Sunday Closing Law Cases, Sherbert* substantially expanded the protection afforded by the Free Exercise Clause. At the same time, the broadened protection for free exercise raised serious establishment questions. They can be seen clearly in *Thomas v. Review Board of Indiana Employment Security Division*, 450 U.S. 707 (1981). Thomas was denied unemployment compensation after voluntarily quitting his job for religious reasons. The Court held the denial of benefits a violation of Thomas's free exercise rights. Only Justice Rehnquist dissented. The Court was even more emphatic than in *Sherbert*, saying: "Where the state conditions receipt of an important benefit upon conduct proscribed by religious faith, or where it denies such a benefit because of conduct mandated by religious belief," a believer's free exercise rights are burdened. Although the compulsion may be indirect, the infringement upon free exercise is nonetheless substantial. Justice Rehnquist was wholly dissatisfied with the Court's preferential treatment of Thomas. In his view, the Court applied the Free Exercise Clause too broadly and in a manner that conflicted with the Court's establishment doctrine. The Court took a step back from *Thomas* and *Sherbert* in *Estate of Thornton v. Caldor, Inc.*, 472 U.S. 703 (1985), invalidating a state law that gave any employee the absolute right to refuse to work on his or her Sabbath. The Court said the statute failed the primary effect test of *Lemon v. Kurtzman*, 403 U.S. 602 (1971), in that it required religious concerns automatically to control all secular interests in the workplace.

The *Sherbert* and *Thomas* decisions had essentially said that a state imposes an unacceptable burden on religion when it denies an important benefit because of conduct mandated by religious belief. *Hobbie v. Unemployment Appeals Commission*, 480 U.S. 136 (1987), extended that reasoning. *Hobbie* differed from *Sherbert* and *Thomas* in that Hobbie had been employed some two and one-half years before undergoing the religious conversion that produced the employment conflict. Indeed, Florida attempted to distinguish Hobbie's situation from the other two cases by arguing that she was the agent of change herself and was responsible for the consequences of the conflict between her job and her religious beliefs because her conversion came subsequent to her employment. The Court rejected this position by saying that Florida had asked the Court "to single out the religious convert for different, less favorable treatment than that given an individual whose adherence to his or her faith precedes employment." The timing of Hobbie's conversion was characterized as immaterial to the issue of a free exercise burden. Justice Brennan said that the First Amendment protects the free exercise rights of those who "adopt religious beliefs or convert from one faith to another after they are hired." The Court concluded that *Sherbert, Thomas,* and *Hobbie* presented a situation in which the employee was forced to choose between fidelity to religious belief and continued employment. The forfeiture of benefits for choosing fidelity brings "unlawful coercion to bear on the employee's choice." The sole dissent in *Hobbie* came from Chief Justice Rehnquist. He repeated the concerns expressed in his *Thomas* dissent about requiring special accommodation for employees in Hobbie's position. In each of the unemployment compensation cases through *Hobbie,* all the claimants had been members of a particular religious sect. In *Frazee v. Illinois Department of Employment Security,* 489 U.S. 829 (1989), the Court considered the case of a claimant who called himself a Christian but was not a member of an established religious sect. He did not contend that his refusal to work rested on a tenet or teaching of an established religious body, but rather that as a Christian, he could not work on "the Lord's day." The Court ruled for Frazee saying that none of the previous decisions "turned" on the matter of sect membership. Neither did they require that a tenet of an established sect prohibited the kind of work the claimant refused to perform. Rather, the prior cases "rested on the fact that each of the claimants had a sincere belief that religion required him or her to refrain from the work in question." Membership in an organized religion, especially one with a specific tenet forbidding Sunday work, "undoubtedly" would "simplify the problem of identifying sincerely held religious beliefs," but the Court rejected the notion that to claim free exercise protection, "one must be responding to the commands of a particularly religious organization." Finally, the Court responded to the state court's reference to America's "weekend way of life," one which requires many to work. If all Americans were to abstain from Sunday work, said the Illinois Appellate Court, "chaos would result." The Supreme Court, however, was "unpersuaded that there will be a mass movement away from Sunday employ if William Frazee succeeds in his claim."

Compulsory Education

Wisconsin v. Yoder, **406 U.S. 205 (1972),** created a free exercise exemption to a state compulsory school attendance law. Jonas Yoder did not contest the attendance law as discriminatory against religion, nor was the legitimacy of the state's interest in advancing education challenged per se. The respondents were members of the Old Order Amish and the Conservative Amish Mennonite Church. They had sent their children to public schools through the eighth grade, but they refused to keep their children in public schools until age 16 as required by law. The respondents argued that attendance of Amish children in high school was contrary to their religious beliefs and way of life, might endanger their salvation, and possibly threaten the ongoing existence of the sect by drawing teenagers away from their beliefs. The Court unanimously found for the Amish. The Court acknowledged the state's paramount responsibility for education, but held that even a fundamental function such as education was not "totally free from the balancing process when it impinges on other fundamental rights and interests." In this instance, the "impact of the compulsory attendance law on respondents' practice of the Amish religion is not only severe, but inescapable." The impact is not confined to "grave interference with important Amish religious tenets," but also the "very real threat of undermining the Amish community and religious practice as it exists today." The effective choice left the Amish was to "abandon belief and be assimilated into society or be forced to migrate to some other and more tolerant region." The Court attempted to confine the holding by emphasizing that the Amish were disputing only one or possibly two years of high school–level education. It was training that would be of little value in the agrarian Amish community. Further, the Court noted the character of the Amish, specifically mentioning such characteristics as their self-reliance, their peaceful and law-abiding lifestyle, and their unique history. The Amish history and tradition were crucial in connecting their religious beliefs to their unusual way of life, which in turn created a unique free exercise injury when the compulsory attendance law was enforced against them. *See also* FIRST AMENDMENT, p. 29; FREE EXERCISE CLAUSE, p. 652; *Sherbert v. Verner*, p. 61.

Significance   *Wisconsin v. Yoder* illustrates the extent to which secular regulation has been modified by the Supreme Court. Wisconsin's compulsory education law was clearly a statute of general application with nothing to suggest ill intent with respect to religion or any religious group. The state's substantial interest in educating its young was not questioned, but when the state's interest in requiring Amish children to attend a year or two of high school was weighed against the Amish religious freedom interest, the state's interest was found to be subordinate. The main consequences of *Yoder* are seen in the expansion of free exercise protection at the expense of establishment protection. *Yoder* expanded *Sherbert v. Verner*, 374 U.S. 398 (1963), by requiring a religion-based exemption from an enactment established pursuant to a substantial state interest. As a result, *Yoder* reflected the inevitability of free exercise and establishment conflict when exemptions are created for certain religious groups.

Despite the Court's use of the compelling interest standard into the 1980s, it became evident in the cases of *United States v. Lee*, 435 U.S. 252 (1982), and *Goldman v. Weinberger*, 475 U.S. 503 (1986), that the Court was considering a change in this standard. In *Lee* the Court examined a challenge brought by a member of the Old Order Amish who refused to withhold social security taxes from his employees or pay the employer's portion of these taxes. Lee argued that payment of these taxes as well as the receipt of any benefits under the program would violate tenets of the Amish religion. The Court acknowledged the conflict between the Amish faith and the obligation of employers under the social security system, but concluded that not all "burdens on religion are unconstitutional." Chief Justice Burger indicated that the government may limit religious liberty if it can show that its action is "essential to accomplish an overriding governmental interest." Burger went on to say that to maintain a society that protects widely diverse religious faiths requires that "some religious practices yield to the common good." The Court's seeming revision of the compelling interest standard in *Lee* became more apparent in *Goldman*. Goldman, an Orthodox Jew and ordained rabbi, was serving in the air force as a psychologist at a military hospital. Throughout his service, Goldman complied with the requirement of his religion to keep his head covered by wearing a yarmulke at all times. He was told that wearing the yarmulke violated a regulation contained in the air force dress code. Goldman challenged the dress regulation arguing that his conduct interfered with no one and could be readily accommodated, and that there was no governmental interest that justified interference with his religious practice. The Court concluded that different standards apply when military regulations are involved. Justice Rehnquist suggested that the military "by necessity" is a "specialized society separate from civilian society." The "essence" of military service, Rehnquist continued, is the "subordination of the desires and interests of the individual to the needs of the service." Accordingly, the courts must "give great deference" to the judgment of military authorities. Indeed, that deference is "at its apogee when legislative action under the congressional authority to raise and support armies and make rules and regulations for their governance is challenged." Soon after the *Goldman* ruling, Congress enacted legislation to overturn the decision. The law allowed members of the armed forces to wear items of religious apparel, even while in uniform, as long as the religious item is "neat and conservative" and does not interfere with the performance of assigned military duties. Notwithstanding the congressional override of *Goldman*, the Court's decisions in *Lee* and *Goldman* suggested that the Court was withdrawing from the compelling interest standard of *Sherbert* and *Yoder*. This doctrinal change was confirmed in *Employment Division v. Smith*, 494 U.S. 872 (1990).

Alternative and Least Restrictive Means

The *Sunday Closing Law Cases*, 366 U.S. 421 (1961), upheld Sunday restrictions on commercial activity. Four cases (called the *Sunday Closing Law Cases* in aggregate) challenging state and local prohibitions on Sunday business activities came to the Supreme Court in 1961. Two of the four cases were decided essentially on establishment and equal protection grounds. *McGowan v. Maryland*, 366 U.S. 420 (1961), and *Two Guys from Harrison—Allentown, Inc. v. McGinley*, 366 U.S. 582 (1961), upheld the retail restrictions. In the other two cases, *Gallagher v. Crown Kosher Super Market, Inc.*, 366 U.S. 617 (1961), and *Braunfeld v. Brown*, 366 U.S. 599 (1961), the petitioners, both Orthodox Jews, added free exercise allegations to their establishment and equal protection claims. This tactic weakened their constitutional position, because only Justices Douglas, Brennan, and Stewart found the Sunday closing laws defective by free exercise standards. The Court said the commercial restrictions in *Gallagher* and *Braunfeld* were legitimate secular regulations, the purpose of which was the designation of a uniform day of rest. The Court held that while the regulation may impose some free exercise burden on the litigants, they were not denied the opportunity for free exercise. They merely had to forego a day's work. Free exercise only made the practice of their religious beliefs more expensive. The Free Exercise Clause cannot, except in rare circumstances, be used to strike down legislation "which imposes only an indirect burden on the exercise of religion." The Court said the Free Exercise Clause does not require that "legislators enact no law regulating conduct that may in some way result in an economic disadvantage of some religious sects and not to others because of the special practices of the various religions." The Court did offer one important qualification, however. A state may enact a general law the purpose of which is to advance the state's secular goals and that may impose an indirect burden on religious observance. But it may do so only if the state may not "accomplish its purpose by means which do not impose such a burden." Thus the Court fashioned an alternative means factor for evaluating general secular regulations against free exercise challenges. *See also* ESTABLISHMENT CLAUSE, p. 644; FIRST AMENDMENT, p. 29; FREE EXERCISE CLAUSE, p. 652; *Sherbert v. Verner*, p. 61.

Significance   The *Sunday Closing Law Cases* modified the secular regulation rule, although the Court rejected free exercise arguments in each of the four cases. The secular regulation doctrine was an attractive approach for the Court because of its simplicity. As applied, however, the doctrine proved undesirably "rigid," and produced results deemed "harsh" by many. The Warren Court began modification in the doctrine in the *Sunday Closing Law Cases.* The Court resolved the free exercise issue in the four Sunday closing cases by weighing the burdens on religious practice flowing from the secular rule. After assessing the competing interests, the Court concluded the burden borne by the sabbatarians was indirect. If the state had required Saturday work, the burden would have been direct and prohibited. What the state did, instead, was deny a person closing a business on Saturday the opportunity to be open on Sunday. The Court's use of the direct-indirect burden approach clearly suggested that at least certain kinds of secular regulations would require exemptions if they survived First Amendment scrutiny at all. The secular regulation rule was altered further by the addition of the alternate means provision. This placed an affirmative obligation on the state to show the lack of alternatives that could accomplish the secular end without imposing a burden on religious exercise. The real impact of this change became apparent in *Sherbert v. Verner,* 374 U.S. 398 (1963).

General Secular Regulation Test

Employment Division v. Smith, **494 U.S. 872 (1990),** ruled that a state could withhold benefits from employees terminated from their jobs for ceremonial use of peyote. Oregon had refused to pay benefits because use of a controlled hallucinogen was a crime in the state, and was "misconduct" for which an employee could be dismissed and rendered ineligible for unemployment benefits. The employees in this case had used the peyote in the sacramental rituals of the Native American Church and sought exemption on free exercise grounds. The Court ruled that although the state legislature could have established such an exemption, the Free Exercise Clause did not require it. "We have never held," said Justice Scalia, that an "individual's beliefs excuse him from compliance with an otherwise valid law prohibiting conduct that the State is free to regulate." As long as religion is not itself the object of the regulation, and any burden is "merely the incidental effect of a generally applicable and otherwise valid provision, the First Amendment has not been offended." To permit individuals to exempt themselves from such regulations would make "professed doctrines of religious belief superior to the law of the land," and in effect "permit every citizen to become a law unto himself." The *Sherbert* test, said the Court, was "developed in a context that lent itself to individualized governmental assessment of the reasons for the relevant conduct," and was seen as inappropriate for a challenge of an "across-the-board criminal prohibition on a particular form of conduct." The government's ability to enact and enforce generally applicable regulations of "socially harmful conduct cannot depend on measuring the effects of a governmental action on a religious objector's spiritual development." To make an individual's obligation to comply with a law "contingent on the law's coincidence with his religious beliefs, except where the State's interest is 'compelling,' contradicts both constitutional tradition and common sense." Justices Blackmun, Brennan, and Marshall applied the *Sherbert* test and concluded that the failure of Oregon to make an exception for religious uses of peyote did not outweigh Smith's free exercise interests. *See also City of Boerne v. Flores*, p. 76; FIRST AMENDMENT, p. 29; FREE EXERCISE CLAUSE, p. 652; *Sherbert v. Verner*, p. 61.

Significance The secular regulation rule to which the Court returned in *Employment Division v. Smith* was first applied in *Reynolds v. United States*, 98 U.S. 145 (1878). Congress had made the practice of polygamy illegal. The Mormons challenged the law, arguing that polygamy was required by their religion and that enforcement of the law would violate their right to free exercise. The Court disagreed in *Reynolds*, upholding the law as a generally applicable secular regulation, and as such, a constitutional exercise of congressional power to regulate the territories of the United States. Similarly, the Court upheld compulsory smallpox vaccinations over religious objections in *Jacobson v. Massachusetts*, 197 U.S. 11 (1905). In doing so, the Court indicated the presence of a strong presumption that attaches to legislation enacted for public health purposes.

The Court struck down compulsory flag salute requirements for public school students in *West Virginia State Board of Education v. Barnette*, 319 U.S. 624 (1943). *Barnette* invalidated a compulsory flag salute, but it did not exempt religion from secular laws. Three years prior to *Barnette*, in *Minersville School District v. Gobitis*, 310 U.S. 586 (1940), the Court had upheld a flag salute requirement, with only Justice Stone dissenting. Both cases raised the question of whether public school pupils could be compelled, under threat of expulsion and fine, to salute the flag. The Barnette and Gobitis children, members of the Jehovah's Witnesses sect, refused to participate because to do so would have put them in conflict with their religious beliefs, which forbade oaths to "images" such as flags. Through Justice Jackson, the six-justice majority in *Barnette* sought to resolve the case on free expression grounds. As an expression issue, the Jehovah's Witnesses' behavior could be evaluated by using the "clear and present danger" test, a criterion established in *Schenck v. United States*, 249 U.S. 47 (1919). Justice Jackson concluded that the children's silence was a form of expression that did not create a clear and present danger. Neither did their refusal to salute the flag "interfere with or deny rights of others to do so." Clear and present danger could justify restriction of expression, but "it would seem that involuntary affirmation could be commanded on even more immediate and urgent grounds than silence." The Court judged that the First Amendment permitted no authority to impose participation in a ceremony "so touching matters of opinion and political attitude." To the contrary, "if there be any fixed star in our constitutional constellation, it is that no official, high or petty, can prescribe what shall be orthodox in politics, nationalism, religion, or other matters of opinion." *Barnette* reversed the heavily criticized *Gobitis* decision, but it did so without dismantling the secular regulation rule or encouraging religious preference. The Court opted instead to view free exercise interests as largely contained within expression protections. The compulsory flag salute was offensive because it dealt with matters of belief and opinion, a transgression the First Amendment cannot tolerate regardless of religion. Because the state could not require any child to salute the flag, the Court avoided carving out an exception for Jehovah's Witnesses. The implications of the broader basis for the decision can readily be seen by comparing the *Barnette* outcome to the outcome of the earlier flag salute case. *Gobitis* was an example of the secular regulation approach in its purest form. Justice Frankfurter's majority opinion argued that protection of religion does not preclude legislation of a general scope as long as the legislation is not directed against the doctrinal loyalties of particular sects. Even "conscientious scruples" cannot relieve the individual from obedience to general law not aimed at the promotion or restriction of religious beliefs. The secular interest being promoted by flag ceremonies is a preeminent interest. What it seeks is cohesion and national unity, an interest "inferior to none." National unity is the basis of national security. The secular regulation doctrine, decisive in *Gobitis*, emerged from *Murdock* and *Barnette* just three years later as a much less generally applicable justification for state enactments overriding religious expression.

The case of *Church of the Lukumi Babalu Aye, Inc. v. City of Hialeah*, 508 U.S. 520 (1993), involved the practices of the Santeria religion. The faith originated in the nineteenth century as many Yorubas from Africa were brought to Cuba as slaves. Santeria was the result of a combination of traditional Yoruba religion with elements of Roman Catholicism. A basic tenet of the religion is the development of personal relationships with spirits (orishas). These spirits, while possessing substantial power, are not immortal. Rather, they are sustained by periodic ritual sacrifice of animals. In April 1987 the Church of the Lukumi Babalu Aye leased land in Hialeah, Florida, and announced its intention to establish a Santeria church in the community. The prospect of a Santeria church in the area was "distressing" to many members of the Hialeah community. In September 1987 the City of Hialeah adopted ordinances that increased the penalty for animal cruelty, prohibited "possession, sacrifice or slaughter" of certain animals within the city (licensed slaughterhouses were excepted), and enlarged the authority of local officials to prosecute those involved in the sacrifice of animals. Sacrifice was defined as to "unnecessarily kill, torment, torture, or mutilate an animal in a public or private ritual or ceremony not for the primary purpose of food consumption." The ordinances were challenged by the Church on free exercise grounds. A unanimous Supreme Court ruled for the Church. Justice Kennedy delivered the opinion of the Court, which was joined by Chief Justice Rehnquist, and Justices White, Stevens, Scalia, and Thomas. Their review of the ordinances "confirm[ed] that the laws in question were enacted by officials who did not understand, failed to perceive, or chose to ignore the fact that their official actions violated the nation's essential commitment to religious freedom." There was no doubt that Santeria is a "religion" entitled to First Amendment protection. Although animal sacrifice may be unacceptable or abhorrent to some, religious beliefs need not be "acceptable, logical, consistent, or comprehensible to others" to qualify for First Amendment protection. If the purpose of a law is to "infringe upon or restrict practices because of their religious motivation, the law is not neutral," and it is invalid unless the government can demonstrate that the law serves a compelling interest and is narrowly tailored in doing so. Kennedy said that in this case, the record "compels the conclusion that suppression of the central element of the Santeria worship service was the object of the ordinances." Kennedy acknowledged that legitimate concerns such as public health and animal protection are represented in the ordinances. Nonetheless, when the ordinances are considered together, they "disclose an object remote from ... legitimate concerns." Instead, the design of the ordinances impermissibly targets the religious practices of the Church—something Kennedy referred to as a "religious gerrymander." The inquiry into the neutrality of the ordinances led the Court to conclude that they "had as their object the suppression of religion." Essential to the protection of free exercise rights is the principle that government cannot "in a selective manner impose burdens only to conduct motivated by religious belief." Without precisely defining a general applicability standard, it was the Court's judgment that Hialeah's ordinances "fall well below the minimum standard" necessary to protect First Amendment rights. The ordinances pursued the city's interests "only against conduct motivated by religious belief." Kennedy said the ordinances "had every appearance" of restrictions that society was willing to impose on the Santeria worshippers, "but not upon itself." In his view, this is the "precise evil" the general applicability requirement is intended to avoid. Kennedy concluded by saying that legislators "may not devise mechanisms, overt or disguised, designed to persecute or oppress a religion or its practices." Justices Blackmun and Souter wrote separate concurring opinions. Souter was concerned that the general applicability standard be more than merely formally neutral. He urged a "substantive neutrality." If the Free Exercise Clause secures only protection against "deliberate discrimination, a formal requirement will exhaust the Clause's neutrality command." If, on the other hand, the Clause "safeguards a right to engage in religious activity free from the unnecessary governmental interference, the Clause requires substantive as well as formal neutrality."

Religion and Taxation

Jimmy Swaggart Ministries v. Board of Equalization, **493 U.S. 378 (1990),** upheld a state sales and use tax imposed on a religious organization's sale of religious materials. The California law required retail sellers to register with the state. In addition, the law levied a 6 percent tax on in-state sales and a 6 percent use tax on materials purchased outside the state. The Swaggart Ministries, incorporated in Louisiana, offered materials for sale in California over a period of years. In 1981 the Board of Equalization conducted an audit and advised the Ministries that it needed to pay accumulated taxes on articles sold at its "evangelical crusades" dating back to 1974. The tax was challenged by the Ministries as a violation of both religion clauses. A unanimous Supreme Court rejected the challenge. The Swaggart Ministries based its Free Exercise Clause challenge on cases such as the license tax ruling in *Murdock v. Pennsylvania*, 319 U.S. 105 (1943). The Court, however, distinguished the flat license taxes that operated as a "prior restraint on the exercise of religious liberty" in *Murdock* from the sales tax in this case. In *Murdock*, the license tax acted as a precondition to free exercise. That defect was "simply not present where a tax applies to all sales and uses of tangible personal property in a State." The California tax was not a tax on the right to "disseminate religious information, ideas, or beliefs per se." Rather, the tax was on the "privilege of making retail sales of tangible personal property," and was owed regardless of the motivation of the sale. The sale of a Bible by a religious organization is treated like the sale of a Bible by a bookstore. Consequently, the Court saw "no danger" that religious activity was being "singled out for special and burdensome treatment." The Ministries also contended that an impermissible burden was produced by diminishing their income and thereby decreasing the resources it could devote to religious pursuits. The Court recognized that the Ministries incurred some economic cost, but the tax was no different from other generally applicable laws and regulations such as health and safety regulations to which the Ministries must adhere. Justice O'Connor indicated that a "more onerous tax rate, even if generally applicable, might effectively choke off an adherent's religious practices," but concluded that "we face no such situation in this case." The Establishment Clause challenge focused on whether administration of the tax produced an unacceptable degree of entanglement between government and religion. The Court ruled that the administration and record-keeping burdens involved in collection and payment of the California tax did not "rise to a constitutionally significant level." The contact required only "routine regulatory interaction," a level that was not seen as violating the nonentanglement command. Imposition of the tax, said O'Connor, did not "require the State to inquire into the religious content of the items sold or the religious motivation for selling or purchasing the items, because the materials are subject to the tax regardless of content or motive." *See also* FIRST AMENDMENT, p. 29; FREE EXERCISE CLAUSE, p. 652; *Sherbert v. Verner,* p. 61.

Significance   The Jimmy Swaggart Ministries attempted to base its challenge of the California sales and use tax on *Murdock. Murdock* involved a municipal license tax that was imposed on all persons selling or canvassing door-to-door. The tax was challenged by Jehovah's Witnesses as an infringement of their ability freely to exercise their religious beliefs. Justice Douglas observed that the distribution of religious tracts is "an age old form of missionary evangelism." Such distribution is "as evangelical as the revival meeting," and is a form of religious activity as protected as "worship in the churches and preaching from the pulpit." That monies are obtained through distribution of literature does not transform evangelism into a commercial enterprise. Besides the evangelical character of the Witnesses' solicitation, the Court noted the financial realities of survival and exempted missionary evangelism from taxation on those grounds. Although an income tax might be collected from a member of the clergy, it is "quite another thing to exact a tax from him for the privilege of delivering a sermon." If taxes could be collected on religious exercises, the state could make such exercises "so costly as to deprive religion of the resources necessary for its maintenance." Finally, the Court did not find the nondiscriminatory character of the tax sufficient to save it. The tax "does not acquire constitutional validity because it classifies the privileges protected by the First Amendment along with the wares and merchandise of hucksters and peddlers and treats them all alike." Free exercise holdings had established previous to *Murdock* that freedom of religious exercise was not absolute and that religious beliefs would not free an individual from the demands of general secular regulation. Just a year prior to *Murdock*, for example, the Court upheld a similar license tax in *Jones v. Opelika*, 316 U.S. 584 (1942). It said the tax imposed only an incidental burden upon free exercise while allowing a state to "insure orderly living." *Murdock*, however, suggests that injury created by a secular regulation may be too great. In this case, the license tax was imposed on the religious exercise of evangelism, a protected religious practice. Certain regulations, despite their secular purpose and nondiscriminatory administration, simply cannot be applied in some situations. This is especially true when a particular secular regulation has the potential of interfering with the ability of a sect to perpetuate itself.

Conscientious Objection: Selective Service

Gillette v. United States, **401 U.S. 437 (1971),** held that religion-based objections to a particular war, as distinct from wars generally, does not entitle a person to exemption from the military draft. *Gillette* examined the language of the Selective Service Act, which exempts registrants who are "conscientiously opposed to participation in war in any form." Gillette had attempted to limit his objection to participation in the Vietnam War, but the Supreme Court, with only Justice Douglas dissenting, held he was not entitled to such a free exercise exemption. The Court also determined that Congress could provide exemptions to the draft for those having religion-based objections to wars generally without violating establishment prohibitions. While conscription of those with "conscientious scruples" against all wars would violate the free exercise proscription, there are governmental interests of "sufficient kind and weight" to justify drafting people who object to particular wars. The Court determined that the draft laws were not "designed to interfere with any religious ritual or practice, and do not work a penalty against any theological position." In addition, the burdens imposed are incidental when compared to the substantial government interest in creating and administering an equitable exemption policy. The Court also noted the interest of the government in "procuring the manpower necessary for military purposes," an interest of sufficient weight to permit burdening Gillette's free exercise rights. The establishment claim was based on the argument that allowing exemption only to those with objection to all wars discriminated against faiths which "distinguish between personal participation in 'just' and 'unjust' wars." The Court held that congressional objectives in requiring objection to all wars were neutral, secular, and did not reflect a religious preference. The Court focused on the need for the exemption to have a neutral basis. Because a virtually "limitless variety of beliefs are subsumable under the rubric objection to a particular war, the difficulties of operating a fair and uniform conscription system would be substantial." Sorting through the various claims creates a great "potential for state involvement in determining the character of persons' beliefs and affiliations, thus entangling government in difficult classifications of what is or is not religious, or what is or is not conscientious." Acknowledging that some discretion exists under any process that takes individual differences into account, establishment problems would be even greater if conscientious objection of indeterminate scope were involved. *See also* FIRST AMENDMENT, p. 29; FREE EXERCISE CLAUSE, p. 652; *Sherbert v. Verner*, p. 61.

Significance   *Gillette* was unique in singling out a particular war for religion-based conscientious objection to an American draft law. The Selective Service and Training Act of 1940 provided that conscientious objector status did not require affiliation with a religious sect. The claim of exemption required only "theistic religious beliefs" and training, and not a "merely personal moral code." The Court addressed this language in *United States v. Seeger*, 380 U.S. 163 (1965), holding that a conscientious objector claimant need not declare a belief in a Supreme Being as long as the claimant had beliefs that served in the place of an orthodox belief in God. The term "Supreme Being" was said to mean a broader view of something to which everything else is subordinate. In *Welsh v. United States*, 398 U.S. 333 (1970), the Court required exemption for a claimant without the basis of his objections resting on religious training or belief as long as the claimant genuinely believed in pacifism. A selective conscientious objector such as Gillette, on the other hand, created problems of implementation "so wrought with establishment defects" as to outweigh the free exercise interest served by the exemption. More recent considerations were offered on this issue in *Rostker v. Goldberg*, 453 U.S. 57 (1981), *Selective Service System v. Minnesota Public Interest Research Group*, 468 U.S. 841 (1984), and *Wayte v. United States*, 470 U.S. 598 (1985). *Rostker* upheld a 1980 presidential proclamation issued pursuant to the Military Selective Service Act requiring every male citizen and resident alien to register for potential conscription. In the *Minnesota Public Interest Research Group* case, the Court permitted denial of federal student aid to persons failing to register for the draft, saying the policy had been aimed at securing compliance rather than seeking punishment of nonregistrants. The policy had been challenged on bill of attainder, self-incrimination, and equal protection grounds.

In *Wayte*, the Court allowed the temporary use of a passive enforcement of the draft registration law whereby initial prosecutions were undertaken only against those nonregistrants who publicized their own resistance to the policy or were reported by others to be in violation. The Court said such an approach would be impermissible only if discriminating motive and effect could be shown.

Religious Freedom Restoration Act

City of Boerne v. Flores, **521 U.S. 507 (1997)** In response to the Court's free exercise ruling in *Employment Division v. Smith*, 494 U.S. 872 (1990), Congress enacted the Religious Freedom Restoration Act (RFRA), which provided that government at any level may not "substantially burden" religious exercise without demonstrating a compelling governmental interest pursued in the least restrictive way. Congressional authority to adopt such a law was based on Section 5 of the Fourteenth Amendment. The RFRA was intended to replace the free exercise standards articulated by the Court in *Smith* with the more protective standards that had been in place prior to *Smith*. The Court had an opportunity to determine whether the Fourteenth Amendment enabled Congress to take such action in *City of Boerne v. Flores*. The membership of St. Peter's Catholic Church, located in Boerne, Texas, had outgrown the capacity of its church building. The Church unsuccessfully sought permission from the city to raze the building and then construct a larger structure on the same spot. The city denied the building permit because the area in which St. Peter's was located had been zoned for historic preservation. The Church brought suit in federal court claiming a violation of the RFRA, but the case was dismissed on the grounds that the RFRA was unconstitutional. The Supreme Court agreed. The case was resolved on federalism rather than religious freedom grounds. The central question was whether Section 5 of the Fourteenth Amendment, which empowers Congress to "enforce" constitutional guarantees by "appropriate legislation," was an acceptable constitutional basis for the RFRA. P. F. Flores, Archbishop of San Antonio, and the United States as amicus curiae argued that RFRA was permissible enforcement legislation in that Congress was attempting to protect the right to free exercise of religion—a right guaranteed by the First and Fourteenth Amendments. Legislation that "deters or remedies constitutional violations," said Justice Kennedy, "can fall within the sweep of Congress's enforcement power even if in the process it prohibits conduct which is not itself unconstitutional and intrudes into legislative spheres of autonomy previously reserved to the states." Kennedy pointed to the upholding of federal laws suspending literacy tests and other voting requirements as examples of a recognized and broad enforcement power under the Fourteenth and Fifteenth Amendments "despite the burdens those measures placed on the states." As broad as congressional enforcement power is, however, "it is not unlimited." Congressional power under Section 5 extends only to enforcing the provisions of the Fourteenth Amendment. The design of the Amendment and the provisions of Section 5 are "inconsistent with the suggestion that Congress has the power to decree the substance of the Fourteenth Amendment's restrictions on the states." Legislation which "alters the meaning of the Free Exercise Clause," said Kennedy, "cannot be said to be enforcing the Clause." Congress does not "enforce a constitutional right by changing what the right is." Congress has the power to "enforce," not the power to "determine what constitutes a constitutional violation." The line between congressional measures that "remedy or prevent" unconstitutional actions and laws that make a "substantive change in the governing law is not easy to discern." While Congress must have "wide latitude" in determining where the distinction lies, the distinction "exists and must be observed." Although preventive rules are "sometimes appropriate remedial measures," there must be a "congruence" between the objectives being sought and the means chosen to achieve them. The appropriateness of remedial measures must be considered, said Kennedy, "in light of the evil presented." Strong measures appropriate to address one harm "may be an unwarranted response to another, lesser one." Evidence was presented to document the "subsisting and pervasive discrimination," and therefore unlawful uses of such devices as the literacy test. The "unprecedented remedies" of the Voting Rights Act were justified given the "ineffectiveness" of existing voting rights law, and the close and costly character of litigation. The legislative record that accompanied the RFRA lacked evidence of "modern instances of generally applicable laws passed because of religious bigotry." The Court was unconvinced that the examples of burdensome regulations offered in support of the RFRA were enacted or enforced "due to animus or hostility to the burdened religious practices or that they indicate some widespread pattern of religious discrimination in this country." In the Court's view, the RFRA could not be considered "remedial, preventive legislation, if those terms are to have any meaning." The Court found the law "so out of proportion to a supposed remedial or preventive objective that it cannot be understood as responsive to, or designed to prevent unconstitutional behavior." Rather, the Court saw the RFRA as an attempt to effect "substantive change in constitutional protections." Furthermore, its "sweeping coverage ensures its intrusion at every level of government, displacing laws prohibiting official actions of almost every description and regardless of subject matter." Justices O'Connor, Souter, and Breyer dissented. O'Connor indicated her preference that this case be used to reexamine the Court's position in *Smith*. The Free Exercise Clause is not an "anti-discrimination principle that protects only against those laws that single out religious practice for unfavorable treatment." Instead, the Clause is an "affirmative guarantee of the right to participate in religious practices and conduct without impermissible governmental interference, even when such conduct conflicts with a neutral, generally applicable law." *See also Employment Division v. Smith*, p. 68; FIRST AMENDMENT, p. 29; FOURTEENTH AMENDMENT, p. 651; FREE EXERCISE CLAUSE, p. 652; VOTING RIGHTS ACT OF 1965, p. 709.

Significance   *City of Boerne v. Flores* was not decided on free exercise grounds even though the Religious Freedom Restoration Act was enacted by Congress in an attempt to overturn the Court's decision in *Employment Division v. Smith*. Congressional attempts to reverse Supreme Court decisions by statute is not novel, but reflective of normal legislative-judicial interaction. Two recent examples serve to illustrate. The Court ruled in *Goldman v. Weinberger*, 475 U.S. 503 (1986), that a military dress regulation could be used to prevent an Orthodox Jew from wearing a yarmulke while in military uniform and performing his duties as a clinical psychologist at a military hospital. The ruling generated extensive debate in Congress, which eventually produced legislation enabling armed forces members to wear religious apparel while in uniform as long as the apparel was "neat and conservative" and did not "interfere with the performance" of any military duties. Three years after *Goldman*, the Court decided several cases involving federal civil-rights laws. Among them were *Wards Cove Packing Co. v. Atonio*, 490 U.S. 642 (1989), *Martin v. Wilks*, 490 U.S. 755 (1989), and *Lorance v. AT&T Technologies, Inc.*, 490 U.S. 900 (1989). These decisions made it more difficult for plaintiffs in employment discrimination cases to access federal courts, and elevated evidentiary standards for claims that did access federal courts, thus making it harder to actually demonstrate illegal conduct by employers. The Civil Rights Act of 1991 was enacted by Congress to reverse the effect of these Court decisions. These two examples reflect the conflict that often occurs when the Court makes statutory interpretations. In such instances, if the Congress disagrees with the Court's interpretation of a statute, it may respond to the ruling by statute. The *Boerne* case involved congressional response to the Court's interpretation of the Constitution, not federal statute. Here, the Court ruled that Congress may not use the Fourteenth Amendment to "correct" or change a substantive judicial interpretation of the Constitution. Rather, federal remedial power must be limited to actual enforcement of constitutional protections.

FREEDOM OF SPEECH
Clear and Present Danger Standard

Schenck v. United States, **249 U.S. 47 (1919),** established the clear and present danger test for evaluating restrictions of expression. *Schenck* was the first significant free speech case to come before the Supreme Court. At issue was the constraint on speech imposed by the Espionage Act of 1917. The Act made it a crime to interfere with recruitment of persons into the armed services. Schenck was convicted of obstructing the draft by printing and distributing materials that urged draft-eligible men to resist conscription. The Court unanimously upheld the conviction with Justice Holmes speaking for the Court. He said the right of expression is not absolute, but rather is conditional and has boundaries set by the circumstances in which it is undertaken. Even the most "stringent protection of free speech would not protect a man in falsely shouting fire in a theater and causing a panic." Having established a situational context for evaluating expression, Justice Holmes then described a "clear and present danger" standard by which expression can be assessed. The issue in every case involving expression is "whether the words used are used in such circumstances and are of such a nature as to create a clear and present danger that they will bring about the substantive evil that Congress has a right to prevent." If speech is linked closely enough to illegal action, it is speech that can be restricted. As Justice Holmes put it, "it is a question of proximity and degree." Schenck's expression was intended to have an effect on persons subject to the draft, a point conceded by Schenck. Under certain circumstances such as peacetime, Schenck's expression would not have been dangerous enough to warrant prosecution. But his words were disseminated while the nation was at war, and the war context gave quite a different effect to his expression. The clear and present danger test allowed certain speech to be regulated through prosecution as long as the government could show that the expression endangered legitimate governmental functions and societal interests. The test required that the danger be both recognizable and immediate. *See also* CLEAR AND PRESENT DANGER TEST, p. 629; *Dennis v. United States,* p. 82; FIRST AMENDMENT, p. 29; FREE SPEECH CLAUSE, p. 654; *Gitlow v. New York,* p. 80.

Significance   *Schenck v. United States* provided a basic rubric by which expression issues might be examined. Several cases immediately following *Schenck* provided the Court an opportunity to refine further the clear and present danger criterion. In *Frohwerk v. United States,*

249 U.S. 204 (1919), a unanimous Court upheld the conviction of an author of several newspaper articles that were highly critical of American involvement in World War I. The Court felt the language of the articles was effectively comparable to Schenck's leaflets. The Court also upheld the conspiracy conviction of Eugene Debs for a speech critical of the war effort in *Debs v. United States*, 249 U.S. 211 (1919). The speech focused on socialism, "its growth and a prophecy of its success." The Court had no objection to the content of the speech, but made it clear that if the "manifest intent" of a speech encourages those hearing it to obstruct the recruiting service, the "immunity of the general theme may not be enough to protect the speech." In cases involving the Sedition Act of 1918, however, Justices Holmes and Brandeis parted company from the rest of the Court. In *Abrams v. United States*, 250 U.S. 616 (1919), the Court upheld Abrams's conviction for distribution of materials critical of the government's commitment of forces to Russia in the wake of the Russian Revolution. Holmes and Brandeis argued that neither sufficient danger nor proximity had been demonstrated in the case. Only "present danger of immediate evil" warrants limitation of expression, they said, not the "surreptitious publishing of a silly leaflet by an unknown man."

Bad Tendency Standard

Gitlow v. New York, **268 U.S. 652 (1925),** created the "bad tendency" standard for evaluating freedom of expression issues. *Gitlow* modified the clear and present danger test to allow suppression of speech that might tend to produce "substantive evil." *Gitlow* also formally linked the provisions of the Free Speech Clause of the First Amendment to state enactments through the Due Process Clause of the Fourteenth Amendment. Gitlow, a member of the Left Wing Section of the Socialist Party, was convicted under provisions of New York's criminal anarchy statutes for his advocacy of the "overthrow of the government by force, violence, and unlawful means." The criminal advocacy was demonstrated in two published tracts entitled "The Left Wing Manifesto" and "The Revolutionary Age." The Court held the statute did not deprive Gitlow of his "liberty of expression," nor did it "penalize the utterance or publication of abstract 'doctrine' or academic discussion having no quality of incitement to any concrete action." Rather, the statute aimed at "language advocating, advising, or teaching the overthrow of organized government by unlawful means." The Court felt the statute was properly focused on advocacy of action directed toward the accomplishment of an illegal purpose, i.e., overthrowing the government. The Court said the police power of the state is appropriately used to "punish those who abuse freedom of expression by utterances inimical to the public welfare." Judgment as to what utterances might be so inimical to the general welfare and "involve such danger of substantive evil" essentially rests with the state's legislative body, and "every presumption is to be indulged in favoring the validity of the statute." Utterances that incite to overthrow the government were found to be "within the range of legislative discretion." As for the point at which the state may intervene, the Court said the "State cannot reasonably be required to measure the danger from every such utterance in the nice balance of a jeweler's scale." A state cannot be said to have acted arbitrarily or unreasonably when it "seeks to extinguish the spark without waiting until it has enkindled the flame or blazed into the conflagration." A state may, in the exercise of its judgment, "suppress the threatened danger in its incipiency." Justices Holmes and Brandeis dissented. Neither felt sufficient danger had been demonstrated. Gitlow's "redundant discourse" simply "had no chance of starting a present conflagration." As in prior speech cases, Holmes invoked the marketplace of ideas argument, asserting that free speech must permit ideas to "compete for acceptance within society." *See also* BAD TENDENCY TEST, p. 619; *Dennis v. United States*, p. 82; FIRST AMENDMENT, p. 29; FREE SPEECH CLAUSE, p. 654; *Schenck v. United States*, p. 79.

Significance   *Gitlow v. New York* had the practical effect of permitting legislatures to restrict expression that might lead to unlawful ends. The unlawful consequences need not be immediate. *Gitlow* permitted the government to take preventive action to keep expression from jeopardizing public safety. The ruling was characterized as allowing the government to "kill the serpent while it is still in the egg." *Gitlow* reflected the Court's generally deferential position toward legislative judgments. It explicitly noted a presumption of constitutionality to be indulged in reviewing legislative enactments. In the years following *Gitlow*, however, the Court began to suggest it would be more demanding in cases involving the First Amendment. As distinct from enactments involving economic regulation, legislation touching First Amendment protections would be viewed with suspicion because the Constitution elevates First Amendment freedoms to a "preferred position." The preferred position doctrine had its origin in Justice Stone's celebrated Footnote 4 in *United States v. Carolene Products Co.*, 304 U.S. 144 (1938). The burden of demonstrating the need for impairment of First Amendment freedoms falls directly on the government in "preferred position" cases. The footnote was frequently cited in the 1940s, especially in labor picketing and free exercise of religion situations. An intermediate position between the preferred position and the *Gitlow* bad tendency doctrine began to evolve after World War II with the balancing test articulated in *Dennis v. United States*, 341 U.S. 494 (1951).

Political Association

***Dennis v. United States*, 341 U.S. 494 (1951),** upheld Sections 2 and 3 of the Alien Registration Act of 1940, the first federal attempt to restrict political expression and association since the Alien and Sedition Acts of 1798. *Dennis* examined the constitutionality of the Act, particularly the sections that prohibited advocacy of over-throwing the government by force and organizing groups with that objective. Dennis was a leader of the Communist Party of the United States. The criminal charges brought against him and others were confined to illegal advocacy and conspiracy. The Court upheld the Alien Registration Act, which was also known as the Smith Act. The Vinson Court could have developed a rationale along the lines of *Gitlow v. New York*, 268 U.S. 652 (1925), which permitted the govern-ment to declare that even advocacy of governmental overthrow is unprotected expression. Instead, it utilized the clear and present danger test to determine if the Communist Party members posed a sufficient threat to warrant restriction. The Court opted for the latter approach although Chief Justice Vinson reshaped the clear and present danger standard in doing so. Vinson said the severity of the threat involved was heavier than the immediacy or probability of the danger. Regarding immediacy he reasoned, "obviously, the words of the test cannot mean that before the Government may act, it must wait until the putsch is about to be executed, the plans have been laid, and the signal is awaited." Not only is governmental response allowed in such a situation, it is required if the government is "aware that a group aiming at its overthrow is attempting to indoctrinate its members and to commit them to a course whereby they will strike when the leaders feel the circumstances permit." The likelihood of the threat actually materializing is not required either. An attempt to overthrow the government by force, even though "doomed from the outset, is a sufficient evil for Congress to prevent it." The Court adopted the sliding scale concept of clear and probable danger as articulated by Judge Learned Hand in the Court of Appeals review of the case. Judge Hand's formulation required that courts "ask whether the gravity of the evil, discounted by its improbability, justi-fies such invasion of free speech as is necessary to avoid the danger." Applying Judge Hand's standard, the Court found the conspiracy to advocate sufficient to bring sanctions against Dennis. Justices Black and Douglas dissented. Justice Black charged the decision "watered down the First Amendment so that it amounts to little more than an admonition to Congress. The Amendment as so construed is not likely to protect any but those safe or orthodox views which rarely need its protection." *See also* CLEAR AND PRESENT DANGER TEST, p. 629; FIRST AMENDMENT, p. 29; FREE SPEECH CLAUSE, p. 654; *Gitlow v. New York*, p. 80; *Schenck v. United States*, p. 79.

Significance   The first test of associational rights came in *Whitney v. California*, 274 U.S. 357 (1927), in which the Court upheld a state criminal syndicalism statute that prohibited organizing and being a member of a group advocating unlawful force as a political weapon. Whitney had participated in a convention of the Communist Labor Party of California, which had passed resolutions advocating various revolutionary acts. Whitney claimed she had neither supported the resolutions nor wished the party to urge violation of California's laws. She was convicted nonetheless because she had remained at the convention and had not disassociated herself from the party and its adopted resolutions. The Supreme Court upheld her conviction. The Court refused to reexamine the jury's fact determination that Whitney had not sufficiently detached herself from the party's objectives. The Court concluded that remaining in attendance until the close of the convention and maintaining membership "manifested her acquiescence." The justices said that California's law did not impermissibly restrain free speech or assembly. The "essence of the offense denounced by the Act is the combining with others in an association for the accomplishment of the desired ends through the advocacy and use of criminal and unlawful methods." Because such united and joint action constituted an even greater threat to public peace and security, a state may reasonably exercise its police power to prevent groups from "menacing the peace and welfare of the State." The *Whitney* ruling seemed to provide license for convicting political radicals because of their association alone, but the Court began to disengage from *Whitney* almost immediately. In *DeJonge v. Oregon*, 299 U.S. 353 (1937), and *Herndon v. Lowry*, 301 U.S. 242 (1937), the Court reversed convictions of admitted members of the Communist Party because, as individuals, neither defendant had violated a criminal law. While an organization may have criminal objectives, simply attending a peaceful meeting called by such an organization cannot transfer criminal liability to individual members. The formal end to *Whitney* came in *Brandenburg v. Ohio*, 395 U.S. 444 (1969), in which the Court unanimously struck down a state syndicalism statute. The defendant in *Brandenburg* was the leader of a Ku Klux Klan group who had spoken at a Klan rally. The Court said "the mere abstract teaching of the moral propriety or even moral necessity for a resort to force and violence is not the same as preparing a group for violent action and steeling it for such action." Accordingly, a statute that fails to draw this distinction impermissibly intrudes on First Amendment freedoms.

The Smith Act imposed significant restraints on political speech and association. *Dennis v. United States* cleared the way for numerous conspiracy convictions under the Smith Act between 1951 and 1957. In *Yates v. United States*, 354 U.S. 298 (1957), however, the Court set evidentiary requirements that substantially diminished the likelihood of securing convictions under the Smith Act. The Court said the *Dennis* distinction between advocacy of illegal acts and abstract doctrinal advocacy had been ignored by trial courts subsequent to *Dennis*. Whether *Dennis* had really made this distinction is debatable, but the key result of *Yates* was that the government was now required to demonstrate specific illegal acts by party members in order to convict under the Smith Act. Abstract advocacy and mere membership were insufficient bases for a Smith Act conviction. This clarification limited the impact of *Dennis*, but four years later the Court upheld the section of the Smith Act making it a crime to be a member of a group advocating forcible overthrow in *Scales v. United States*, 367 U.S. 203 (1961). In *Scales* the Court did require evidence comparable to that required in *Yates*, saying, for example, that in order to gain a conviction under the membership provision, a person's membership had to be both knowing and active, and that the person had to have shown "specific intent to bring about violent overthrow" of the government. Prosecutions under the Smith Act were essentially abandoned soon thereafter. The Internal Security Act of 1950 traveled a parallel course. The Act required Communist organizations to register with the federal government, and created a Subversive Activities Control Board to determine which organizations needed to register. The government had little success in implementing provisions of the Act, and in *Albertson v. Subversive Activities Control Board*, 383 U.S. 70 (1965), the Court unanimously held that individual members of the Communist Party could not be compelled to register on self-incrimination grounds.

Symbolic Speech

***Tinker v. Des Moines Independent Community School District*, 393 U.S. 503 (1969),** upheld the wearing of armbands as a protected substitute for speech. *Tinker* involved three public school students in Des Moines, Iowa, who were suspended from school for their symbolic protest of the government's policy in Vietnam, which involved the wearing of black armbands. They brought suit to enjoin the school district from enforcing its regulation against the wearing of armbands. The Supreme Court ruled in favor of the students. The Court found the "silent, passive expression of opinion, unaccompanied by any disorder or disturbance" to be "closely akin" to pure speech. Although the wearing of the armbands used a symbolic action instead of speech as such, the action warranted First Amendment protection. The state may not prohibit expression of opinion without evidence that the rule is necessary to avoid interference with school discipline or the rights of others. Anticipation of a disturbance cannot provide the basis for regulating speech. The Court also found the ban defective in that it selectively singled out the symbol representing opposition to the Vietnam War while ignoring other political symbols. Justices Black and Harlan dissented in separate opinions. Both thought school officials must be given the "widest authority in maintaining discipline and good order." Justice Black said a person cannot engage in demonstrations "where he pleases and when he pleases." The armbands in the school setting distracted from the educational process and could, in Justice Black's view, be regulated. Black also lamented the revolutionary era of permissiveness that allowed the public schools to be subjected to the "whims and caprices of the loudest-mouthed." *See also Cohen v. California*, p. 89; FIRST AMENDMENT, p. 29; FREE SPEECH CLAUSE, p. 654; SYMBOLIC SPEECH, p. 706; *Texas v. Johnson*, p. 85.

Significance   *Tinker* affirmed the principle that symbolic expression may be protected by the Free Speech Clause of the First Amendment. *Tinker* was decided at a time when the United States was undergoing a painful public dialogue about the rights of a minority of its citizens to protest political actions. The nation was reassessing institutional values that had long gone uncontested. Justice Black's reference to "permissiveness" may be understood as reference to a code word of the era for opposition to certain policy choices such as the American involvement in Southeast Asia. A year later, the Court upheld a conviction for the burning of a draft card in protest of the Vietnam War in *United States v. O'Brien*, 391 U.S. 367 (1968). The Court agreed that O'Brien's gesture was communicative, but it also found the act of destroying the draft card impaired a legitimate function of the government. Although certain symbolic acts may be protected, Chief Justice Warren said that the Court "cannot accept the view that an apparently limitless variety of conduct can be labelled 'speech' whenever the person engaging in the conduct intends thereby to express an idea." In *California v. La Rue*, 409 U.S. 109 (1972), the Court upheld a liquor control regulation forbidding establishments with liquor licenses from having nude entertainment. The Court did not find performances with sexual overtones protected as symbolic speech.

***Texas v. Johnson,* 491 U.S. 397 (1989),** upheld the right of persons to express their political views by burning the American flag. Johnson was part of a group that gathered in Dallas to demonstrate at the 1984 Republican National Convention. The group marched through downtown Dallas to city hall where Johnson set fire to the flag. He was arrested and subsequently convicted for violation of the Texas law prohibiting flag desecration. The Supreme Court overturned the conviction and struck down the law. Texas' principal interest advanced in support of its conviction of Johnson was preservation of the flag as a "symbol of national unity." Justice Brennan pointed to prior decisions "recognizing the communicative nature of conduct relating to flags." He said that while government generally has a "freer hand in restricting expressive conduct" than the written or spoken word, it may not "proscribe particular conduct because it has expressive elements." Preservation of the flag as a symbol, on the other hand, relates to "suppression of expression." If there is a "bedrock principle underlying the First Amendment," said Brennan, it is that government may not "prohibit expression of an idea simply because society finds the idea itself offensive or disagreeable." Prior cases have not recognized an exception where the flag is involved nor have they allowed government to "insure that a symbol be used to express only one view of that symbol." To allow government to "designate symbols to be used to communicate only a limited set of messages would be to enter territory having no discernible or defensible boundaries." The question, said Brennan, is how should the Court determine where symbols are "sufficiently special" to qualify for this "unique status." Judges would be forced to consult their own "political preferences, and impose them on the citizenry, in the very way the First Amendment forbids us to do." The First Amendment does not so protect other "sacred concepts" from "going unquestioned in the market place of ideas," and Brennan said the Court declines "to create for the flag an exception to the joust of principles protected by the First Amendment." Brennan concluded by saying that the decision strengthens the flag's "deservedly cherished place in our community." The decision reflects the conviction that "our toleration of criticisms such as Johnson's is a sign and source of our strength." The way to "preserve the flag's special role" is not, he said, to punish those who "feel differently about these matters." Rather, it is to "persuade them that they are wrong." We do not "consecrate the flag by punishing its desecration, for in doing so we dilute the freedom that this cherished emblem represents." Chief Justice Rehnquist, one of the dissenters, argued the unique position of the flag "as the symbol of our nation" that warrants a "governmental prohibition against flag burning." Justice Stevens referred to the "intangible dimension" of this case that makes use of established symbolic expression rules "inapplicable." The flag, he said, is a symbol of more than "nationhood and national unity." In addition, it signifies "ideas that characterize the society ... as well as the special history that has animated the growth and power of those ideas." The symbolic value of the flag, therefore, "cannot be measured." Nonetheless, Stevens continued, the government has a significant and legitimate interest in "preserving that value." Occasionally, restrictions must prevail over expression interests. Creating a right to post "bulletin boards and graffiti" on the Washington Monument might "enlarge the market for free expression, but at a cost I would not pay." Similarly, Stevens concluded, "sanctioning the public desecration of the flag will tarnish its value." That tarnish is not justified by the "trivial burden on free expression occasioned by requiring an available, alternative mode of expression—including words critical of the flag—be employed." *See also* FIRST AMENDMENT, p. 29; FREE SPEECH CLAUSE, p. 654; SYMBOLIC SPEECH, p. 706; *Tinker v. Des Moines Independent Community School District*, p. 84.

Significance   The flag desecration case of *Texas v. Johnson* was among the more controversial decisions in recent years, but was not the first case involving flags. The Court has recognized since the 1930s that flags have symbolic value as expression. In 1931 the Court struck down a state law in *Stromberg v. California*, 283 U.S. 359 (1931), that outlawed the display of a red flag because it symbolized "opposition to organized government." The Court felt that if such symbolic expression as this could be restricted, more general political debate would be seriously jeopardized. Although it has recognized the government's authority to punish certain improper conduct regarding the flag, the Court has generally permitted its symbolic use. *Street v. New York*, 394 U.S. 576 (1969), for example, struck down a state law prohibiting flag mutilation. This case involved flag burning, but the Court focused on the overbroad character of the restriction. In *Smith v. Goguen*, 415 U.S. 566 (1974), the Court reversed a conviction for the "contemptuous" conduct of a person who had sewn a small flag to the seat of his pants. That same year, the Court ruled in *Spence v. Washington*, 418 U.S. 405 (1974), that superimposing a peace symbol on the flag and flying it upside down was protected. These decisions notwithstanding, symbolic expression may be subject to regulation. The line is drawn by examining the action or conduct through which the message is conveyed.

Following the Court's decision in *Texas v. Johnson*, Congress enacted the Flag Protection Act of 1989. The Act made it a crime to "knowingly mutilate, deface, physically defile, burn, maintain on the floor or ground, or trample upon any flag of the United States." Upon passage of the federal law, flags were burned in a number of political demonstrations. *United States v. Eichman* and *United States v. Haggerty*, 496 U.S. 310 (1990), arose out of prosecutions for flag-burning incidents in Seattle and Washington, D.C., respectively. The cases were combined for review by the Supreme Court. The Court held that the federal law, like the state law in *Johnson,* violated the free speech protection of the First Amendment. Justice Brennan spoke for the same five-justice majority from *Johnson,* and his opinion substantially reiterated the rationale from that case. While conceding that flag burning is "expressive conduct," the government sought to have the Court declare flag burning a kind of expression that falls outside the full protection of the First Amendment. In drafting the federal law, an effort had been made to avoid the defect identified in *Johnson*—that is, regulating conduct on the basis of content. Although the Flag Protection Act contained no explicit content-based limitation on prohibited conduct, Justice Brennan said it was "nevertheless clear that the Government's asserted interest is related to the suppression of free expression, and is concerned with the content of such expression." The government's interest in "protecting the physical integrity of a privately owned flag" is based on the "perceived need to preserve the flag's status as a symbol of our nation and certain national ideals." The destruction of a flag, by itself, however, "does not diminish or otherwise affect the symbol." The government's desire to "preserve the flag as a symbol for certain national ideals is implicated only when a person's treatment of the flag communicates a message to others that is inconsistent with those ideals." The language of the Act "confirms" congressional intent to prevent the "communicative impact of flag destruction." Each of the terms chosen to define the criminal conduct "unmistakably connotes disrespectful treatment of the flag and suggests a focus on those acts likely to damage the flag's symbolic value." Allowing the government to prohibit flag burning when it endangers the flag's symbolic role would permit the state to "prescribe what shall be orthodoxy by saying that one may burn the flag to convey one's attitude toward it ... only if one does not endanger the flag's representation of nation-hood and national unity." Notwithstanding congressional effort to approach flag desecration differently from Texas, the Court still found the same fundamental flaw—"it suppresses expression out of concern for its likely communicative impact." Finally, the Court refused to reassess the *Johnson* ruling in light of Congress's asserted recognition of a "national consensus" favoring a prohibition on flag burning. Even presuming such a consensus exists, "any suggestion that the Government's interest in suppressing speech becomes more weighty as popular opposition to that speech grows is foreign to the First Amendment." Justice Stevens said for the dissenters that the government should be able to "protect the symbolic value of the flag without regard to the specific content of the flag burners' speech." Following the Court's ruling in *Haggerty* and *Eichman,* the Congress considered a constitutional amendment that would have permitted prosecution of flag burning notwithstanding First Amendment protection of symbolic expression. The proposed amendment was defeated in the House of Representatives on 21 June 1990.

Offensive Speech

Cohen v. California, **403 U.S. 15 (1971),** held that even "offensive" expression is entitled to First Amendment protection. Cohen was arrested in the Los Angeles County Courthouse for wearing a jacket upon which were the words "Fuck the Draft." At his trial Cohen testified that the jacket was his means of stating his intensely held feelings about the draft and American involvement in Vietnam. Cohen was convicted of violating a statute prohibiting "malicious and willful disturbing of the peace" by conduct that is "offensive." The Supreme Court set aside Cohen's conviction. The Court ruled that the words were the issue rather than Cohen's conduct; it was his "speech" that was prohibited by enforcement of the law. The Court also held that the words on Cohen's jacket were not directed at anyone. Furthermore, a state cannot excise arguably offensive epithets by functioning as a guardian of public morality. Justice Harlan said the First Amendment is "designed and intended to remove governmental restraints from the arena of public discussion." A consequence of free speech "may often appear to be only verbal tumult, discord, and even offensive utterance," but that is the "price of the freedom." The Court cannot lose sight of the fact, said Harlan, that, "in what otherwise might seem a trifling and annoying instance of individual distasteful abuse of a privilege, fundamental societal values are truly implicated." The majority also was troubled by the "inherently boundless" nature of what California was attempting through this law. "Surely the State has no right to cleanse public debate to the point where it is grammatically palatable to the most squeamish among us." Finally, Harlan pointed out that language serves a dual communicative function. Language conveys not only ideas capable of relatively precise and detailed explication, but it conveys otherwise inexpressible emotions as well. Words are often chosen as much for their "emotive as their cognitive force." He concluded: "We cannot sanction the view that the Constitution, while solicitous of the cognitive content of individual speech, has little or no regard for that emotive function which, practically speaking, may often be the more important element of the overall message sought to be communicated." Chief Justice Burger and Justices Blackmun, Black, and White dissented. They said Cohen's "absurd and immature antic" was primarily conduct and could be regulated. *See also* FIRST AMENDMENT, p. 29; FREE SPEECH CLAUSE, p. 654; *R.A.V. v. City of St. Paul,* p. 90; SYMBOLIC SPEECH, p. 706; *Tinker v. Des Moines Independent Community School District,* p. 84.

Significance   Cohen v. California involved an attempt to regulate offensive speech through criminal prosecution for breach of the peace. The Court has ruled that obscene or libelous utterances are not protected by the First Amendment because they are of such minimal communicative value that any possible benefit is clearly outweighed by the social interest in order and morality. The Court included so-called fighting words in the category of unprotected speech in *Chaplinsky v. New Hampshire*, 315 U.S. 568 (1942). In *Terminiello v. Chicago*, 337 U.S. 1 (1949), however, the Court reversed the breach of the peace conviction of a highly provocative speaker, holding that a municipal ordinance was inappropriately applied to limit speech that "invites dispute." Two years later, however, the Court upheld the disorderly conduct conviction of a street-corner speaker in *Feiner v. New York*, 340 U.S. 315 (1951). The Court said that when "clear and present danger of riot, disorder, interference with traffic upon the public street, or other immediate threat to public safety, peace, or order appears, the power of the State to prevent or punish is obvious." The dissenters in *Feiner* argued that the speaker ought to have been protected from the hostile crowd and allowed to speak rather than placed under arrest. The case of *Rankin v. McPherson*, 483 U.S. 378 (1987), involved the right of a public employee to engage in "offensive" speech. McPherson, an employee of a county constable, was fired from her job for saying to a coworker following the assassination attempt on President Reagan that "if they go for him again, I hope they get him." The Court ruled that McPherson's remarks should not have caused her to be fired because her remarks were made in the course of discussion of a matter of public concern. While a threat to kill the president would not be protected expression, McPherson's statement was not itself a threat and could not be criminalized. The inappropriate or controversial character of a remark is irrelevant to the question of whether it deals with a matter of public concern. Debate on such matters must be given "breathing space" to allow discussion to remain "uninhibited, robust, and wide-open." A different kind of offensive expression problem was examined in *Federal Communications Commission (FCC) v. Pacifica Foundation*, 438 U.S. 726 (1978). Upon receipt of a listener's complaint, the FCC found that a radio station had aired an indecent program. The FCC issued an order to the station threatening subsequent sanction if such broadcasting reoccurred. The Supreme Court upheld the FCC's authority to issue such an order.

Hate Speech

***R.A.V. v. City of St. Paul*, 505 U.S. 377 (1992)** The City of St. Paul, Minnesota, made it a crime to engage in "hate speech." An ordinance made it a misdemeanor to engage in speech or conduct likely to "arouse anger, alarm, or resentment in others on the basis of race, color, creed, religion or gender." The ordinance was challenged by a juvenile charged with violating the law by burning a cross on a black family's lawn. All nine members of the Court agreed in *R.A.V. v. City of St. Paul* that the ordinance violated the First Amendment, but the Court was deeply split on its reasons for that conclusion. Justice Scalia's opinion, joined by Rehnquist, Kennedy, Souter, and Thomas, regarded the regulation as facially unconstitutional because it prohibited speech solely on the basis of its content. Under the ordinance, expression containing "abusive invective" is permissible unless it "addressed one of the specified disfavored topics." The First Amendment, said Scalia, does not permit St. Paul to "impose special prohibitions" on speakers who express views on subjects public officials place out-of-bounds. The St. Pail ordinance had not focused on threatening expression, but rather proscribed "fighting words of whatever manner" that communicated intolerant messages about race, gender, or religion. "Selectivity of this sort creates the possibility that the city is seeking to handicap the expression of particular ideas." The question for those five justices joining Scalia's opinion was whether "content discrimination is reasonably necessary" to achieve a compelling interest. Their answer was "plainly not." The only interest served by the content limitations was the city council's "special hostility towards the particular biases thus singled out." Justice White felt the ordinance was fatally overbroad, but was critical of Scalia's "simplistic, all or nothing-at-all approach" to dealing with fighting words. White said Scalia's opinion signaled that "expressions of violence ... are of sufficient value to outweigh the social interest in order and morality that has traditionally placed such fighting words outside the First Amendment." White felt regulation of all or some fighting words to restrict the "social evil of hate speech" could be crafted "without creating the danger of driving viewpoints from the market place." Like White, Justice Blackmun saw no First Amendment values "compromised by a law that prohibits hoodlums from driving minorities out of their homes." To the contrary, he saw "great harm in preventing the people of St. Paul from specifically punishing the race-based fighting words that so prejudice their community." *See also Cohen v. California*, p. 89; FIRST AMENDMENT, p. 29; FREE SPEECH CLAUSE, p. 654; HATE SPEECH, p. 660; OFFENSIVE SPEECH, p. 684.

Significance The Supreme Court returned to the hate crimes issue a year after *R.A.V.* in *Wisconsin v. Mitchell*, 509 U.S. 476 (1993). The Wisconsin approach to hate speech was to authorize longer sentences for those criminal offenders who select their victims on the basis of "race, religion, color, disability, sexual orientation, national origin or ancestry." Todd Mitchell was convicted of aggravated battery, an offense that typically carries a two year maximum sentence in Wisconsin. Mitchell was sentenced to four years, however, because the jury determined that he intentionally had chosen his victim on the basis of race. The Wisconsin Supreme Court, citing *R.A.V.*, ruled for Mitchell. According to the state court, the Wisconsin legislature criminalized "bigoted thought with which it disagree[d]." A unanimous U.S. Supreme Court upheld the Wisconsin law, however, finding the argument that the enhanced sentence punishes only conduct to be persuasive. A physical assault "is not by any stretch of the imagination expressive conduct protected by the First Amendment." At the same time, the threshold condition for triggering the enhanced sentence is discriminatory motive in the selection of a particular victim. In other words, the Wisconsin law punishes someone more severely for conduct "motivated by a discriminatory point of view" than for the same conduct "engaged in for some other reason or for no reason at all." The Court resolved the problem in the state's favor in two ways. State legislatures possess "primary responsibility for fixing criminal penalties." As a result, state legislatures may reasonably decide that bias-motivated offenses warrant more substantial penalties. Motive plays the "same role" in Wisconsin's statute as it plays in federal and state antidiscrimination laws. Furthermore, judges who are about to sentence criminal offenders have traditionally been able to consider a "wide variety of factors" beyond the evidence directly bearing on guilt in determining an appropriate sentence. One such important factor is the defendant's motive for committing the crime. The Court saw the definition of aggravating circumstances for capital crimes as analogous. The Court also distinguished the Wisconsin law from the ordinance struck down in *R.A.V. v. City of St. Paul.* In *R.A.V.*, the ordinance had selectively targeted speech deemed offensive and, thus, violated the prohibition against "content-based discrimination." The Wisconsin law, on the other hand, aimed at "conduct unprotected by the First Amendment." In addition, the Wisconsin statute selected bias-motivated crimes for enhanced penalty because this kind of conduct is "thought to inflict greater individual and societal harm." The Court concluded that a state's "desire to redress these perceived harms provides an adequate explanation for its penalty-enhancement provisions over and above mere disagreement with offenders' beliefs or biases."

Overbreadth Doctrine

Schaumburg v. Citizens for a Better Environment, **444 U.S. 620 (1980)**, struck down a local ordinance on the basis of the overbreadth doctrine. The Supreme Court examined a local ordinance that prohibited door-to-door solicitations for contributions by organizations not using at least 75 percent of their receipts for charitable purposes. A charitable purpose excluded such items as salaries, overhead, solicitation costs, and other administrative expenses. An environmental group was denied permission to solicit because it could not demonstrate compliance with the 75 percent requirement. The organization challenged the ordinance on First Amendment grounds, and the Court struck it down over the single dissent of Justice Rehnquist. The Court's primary objection was that the ordinance covered too much. The Court noted that a class of organizations existed to which the 75 percent rule could not constitutionally be applied. These were organizations "whose primary purpose is not to provide money or services to the poor, the needy, or other worthy objects of charity, but to gather and disseminate information about and advocate positions on matters of public concern." The costs of research, advocacy, or public education is typically in excess of 25 percent of funds raised. The Court felt that to lump all organizations failing to meet the 75 percent standard together imposed a direct and substantial limitation on protected activity. Although the village interest in preventing fraud may generally be legitimate, the means to accomplish that end must use more precise measures to separate one kind of solicitation from another. *See also* FIRST AMENDMENT, p. 29; FREE SPEECH CLAUSE, p. 654; OVERBREADTH DOCTRINE, p. 686.

Significance   Schaumburg v. Citizens for a Better Environment is important because it produced a requirement that statutes distinguish sufficiently between lawful and unlawful expression or behavior. In *Coates v. Cincinnati*, 402 U.S. 611 (1971), the Court struck down a city ordinance that prohibited three or more persons from assembling on public sidewalks and conducting themselves in such a way as to "annoy any police officer or other persons who should happen to pass by." The Court found the ordinance "makes a crime out of what under the Constitution cannot be a crime." It was also impermissibly vague. It conveyed no standard of conduct and "men of common intelligence must necessarily guess at its meaning." Although the overbreadth and vagueness doctrines have often been invoked to invalidate enactments as in *Schaumburg* and *Coates*, some ordinances survive such challenges.

In *Grayned v. Rockford*, 408 U.S. 104 (1972), the Court allowed an antinoise ordinance prohibiting disturbances in the proximity of schools in session. The specific school context separated the restriction from the typically vague and general breach of the peace ordinance. The enactment was seen as a reasonable time, place, and manner restriction. It was narrowly tailored to further Rockford's compelling interest in having undisrupted school sessions and was not an impermissibly broad prophylactic.

In *Hoffman Estates v. Flipside, Inc.*, 456 U.S. 950 (1982), the Court upheld an ordinance requiring a license to sell items designed or marketed for use with illegal drugs against claims that the ordinance was both vague and overbroad. The Court ruled that the ordinance merely sought to regulate the commercial marketing of illegal drug paraphernalia and did not reach other than commercial speech. The only potential limit on Flipside's conveying of information was confined to the commercial activity related to illegal drug use. The Court also found the vagueness claim unpersuasive. The "designed for use" provision of the ordinance covered at least some of the items sold at Flipside. The "marketed for use" language provided ample warning to the retailer about licensure and the display practices that could result in violation of the ordinance.

The *Schaumburg* reasoning was later applied to a state limitation on charity fund-raising expenses in *Secretary of State v. Joseph H. Munson Company*, 467 U.S. 947 (1984). Maryland had enacted a statute designed to prevent abusive and fraudulent fund raising by prohibiting a charity from spending more than 25 percent of its gross income for expenses. The Court invalidated the law, saying fund raising for charities was so intertwined with speech that it required First Amendment protection. The Maryland statute was based on the "fundamentally mistaken premise" that fund-raising costs that exceed 25 percent are fraudulent. In another case closely resembling *Munson*, the Court struck down a North Carolina "charitable solicitation" law that regulated the practices of professional fund raisers. The law divided fees charged by fund raisers into three categories. A fee up to 20 percent of receipts was deemed "reasonable." A fee between 20 and 35 percent was "unreasonable" if it could be shown that the solicitation did not involve certain activities, such as advocacy on a public issue as directed by the recipient of the solicitation proceeds. A fee of greater than 35 percent was presumed "unreasonable" but was rebuttable by the fund raiser. The law also required fund raisers to disclose the amounts of money actually turned over to charities during the past 12 months. This information was to be made available to potential donors before the solicitation campaign began. In addition, licensure of all fund raisers was mandated. A coalition of fund raisers and charitable organizations successfully challenged the provisions on free speech grounds. The Supreme Court found the provisions unconstitutional in *Riley v. National Federation for the Blind*, 487 U.S. 781 (1988). The Court first dealt with the three-tiered fee schedule. Noting that solicitation of contributions for charities is protected speech, the Court found that the formula for characterizing fees was "not narrowly tailored to the State's interest in preventing fraud." Neither did the Court see maximizing funds to charities or guarantees of reasonable fees charged as sufficiently "motivating interests" to warrant regulation of this kind. The Court characterized as "unsound" the asserted justification that charities' speech must be regulated "for their own benefit." The First Amendment "mandates the presumption that speakers, not the government, know best what they want to say and how to say it." The Court found the disclosure requirement defective as a content-based regulation mandating speech a speaker would not otherwise make. Even if the speech is regarded as commercial in an "abstract sense," it "does not retain its commercial character" when it is "inextricably intertwined" with the "fully protected speech involved in charitable solicitations." Finally, the Court struck down the licensing requirement. A speaker's rights "are not lost merely because compensation is received." Further, the asserted power to license brings with it, in the Court's view, the "power directly and substantially to affect the speech they may utter."

The Court also used the overbreadth doctrine to invalidate a local ordinance in *Board of Airport Commissioners v. Jews for Jesus*, 482 U.S. 589 (1987). This case involved an ordinance banning "all First Amendment activities within the Central Terminal area of Los Angeles International Airport." The defect in the regulation was the policy went further than regulating expressive activity that might create problems, such as congestion or disruption in the airport. Such a regulation might be a permissible time, place, and manner restriction. Instead, this ordinance banned all expression in an effort to create a "virtual First Amendment Free Zone." Not only were groups such as Jews for Jesus reached by the regulation, but the ban extended "even to talking and reading, or the wearing of campaign buttons or symbolic clothing." Under such a sweeping ban virtually everyone entering the airport could be found in violation of the ordinance.

Regulation of Political Advertising

Lebron v. National Railroad Passenger Corp., **513 U.S. 374 (1995)**
Michael Lebron sought to display a political advertisement on a large electronic billboard, known as the Spectacular, located in Penn Station, a facility owned by the National Railway Passenger Corporation (Amtrak). At the time Lebron signed a contract to lease space on the Spectacular, he indicated his ad would be political. He subsequently submitted a photograph of his ad and was informed that Amtrak did not allow political advertising on the Spectacular. Lebron filed suit in federal court claiming that refusal to display his advertisement was content-based censorship by a government agency. The district court ruled for Lebron, but the Court of Appeals for the Second Circuit reversed, concluding that Amtrak is not a government agency but a private entity. As a result,

the Second Circuit ruled that Amtrak and its advertising policies were outside the reach of the First Amendment. The Supreme Court disagreed. Justice Scalia traced the "long history" of corporations created by the United States for the "achievement of governmental objectives," and found that Amtrak is not "unusual" in this respect. Although its authorizing statute declares that Amtrak is not an agency of the federal government, its board of directors is "controlled by Government appointees." Amtrak contended, however, that the disclaimer of government agency status "prevents it from being considered a Government entity." Scalia suggested that Amtrak's reliance on the disclaimer was "misplaced." Charter provisions can define Amtrak's status for those matters that are within congressional control, but Congress may not make final determination of Amtrak's status for purposes of "determining the constitutional rights of citizens affected by its actions." If by its nature Amtrak is a governmental entity under the Constitution, congressional pronouncement to the contrary "can no more relieve it of its First Amendment restrictions than a similar pronouncement could exempt the Federal Bureau of Investigation from the Fourth Amendment." The Constitution limits governmental action, Scalia continued, "by whatever instruments or in whatever modes that action may be taken," and "under whatever congressional label." Scalia noted the strong basis in both past practice and reason for corporations created and controlled by government to be regarded as part of the government itself. Neither state nor federal government is "able to evade the most solemn obligations imposed in the Constitution by simply resorting to the corporate form." If such a thesis were true, *Plessy v. Ferguson*, 163 U.S. 537 (1896), which allowed railroads to segregate passengers by race, could be "resurrected by the simple device of having the State of Louisiana operate segregated trains through a state-owned Amtrak." Scalia concluded that when the government creates a corporation "by special law, for the furtherance of governmental objectives, and retains for itself permanent authority to appoint a majority of the directors of the corporation, the corporation is part of the Government for purposes of the First Amendment." Justice O'Connor was the only dissenter. In her view, there was no evidence to suggest that the government "controlled, coerced, or even influenced" Amtrak's decision to disallow Lebron's advertisement. *See also* FIRST AMENDMENT, p. 29; FREE SPEECH CLAUSE, p. 654; STATE ACTION, p. 703; *United States v. National Treasury Employees Union*, p. 97.

Significance   The Bill of Rights is intended to protect individuals from unlawful actions of government. A plaintiff like Michael Lebron must demonstrate, among other things, that a rights violation was committed by an agency (or agent) of government. State action has been a centrally important issue in equal protection cases, but in *Lebron* the Second Circuit held that First Amendment claims require meeting a more stringent state action standard. The *Lebron* case provided the Supreme Court with an opportunity to clarify the standard by which state action is defined in First Amendment cases. Lebron argued that Amtrak was a governmental entity because, among other things, it was established by federal law, wholly owned by the federal government, subsidized by federal funds, and managed by a board of directors appointed by the federal government. Amtrak's contention that it was a private entity was based on the proposition that its function was commercial rather than governmental. It was further contended that language in the federal law creating Amtrak expressly declared that it was not a federal agency or instrumentality. The Court concluded that where the government creates a corporation by special law for the "furtherance of governmental objectives" and retains permanent authority to appoint the corporation's board of directors, the corporation is "part of the Government for purposes of the First Amendment." The Court also concluded that it was not for Congress to determine by statute the status of an entity such as Amtrak for the purposes of determining the applicability of constitutional rights. The government cannot evade its constitutional obligations by insulating its agencies from constitutional reach by merely configuring them as corporate entities or designating them as private.

Government Employee Expression

***United States v. National Treasury Employees Union*, 513 U.S. 454 (1995)**
The Federal Ethics in Government Act of 1978 was amended in 1989 to prohibit federal officials and employees from receiving compensation for any appearance or expressive activity, even if the subject matter was unrelated to their work responsibilities. The honorarium ban included members of Congress, federal judges, certain executive branch employees above the salary grade of GS-15, and virtually all remaining federal employees up through the GS-15 grade level. The Act did not prohibit appearances or expressive activity on the part of covered officials and employees, but prohibited compensation for that activity. Violators were subject to civil penalty of up to $10,000 or the amount of compensation received. Several individual employees and unions representing them filed suit in federal court asserting that the ban on compensation violated the First Amendment. The Supreme Court found the ban to be unconstitutional and enjoined enforcement of the Act. Previous rulings such as *Pickering v. Board of*

Education, 391 U.S. 563 (1968), had recognized, Justice Stevens suggested, that Congress may impose restraints on job-related speech of public employees that would be "plainly unconstitutional if applied to the public at large." Here, however, the government asked the Court to apply *Pickering* as a "wholesale deterrent to a broad category of expression by a massive number of potential speakers." The honoraria ban as applied to these employees "burdens speech" because the ban "deters an enormous quantity of speech before it is uttered, based only on speculation that the speech might threaten the Government's interests." Stevens pointed to the "significant contributions to the marketplace of ideas" made by federal employees such as Nathaniel Hawthorne, Walt Whitman, and Herman Melville. While the employees involved in this case had yet to make "comparable contributions to American culture," they share "important characteristics" with those artists. Even though these employees work for the government, said Stevens, they have not relinquished the First Amendment rights "they would otherwise enjoy as citizens to comment on matters of public interest." With few exceptions, the content of the employees' messages has "nothing to do with their jobs and does not even arguably have any adverse effect on their efficiency of the offices in which they work." The government's concern in enacting the honoraria ban was that federal employees not misuse or appear to misuse power by accepting compensation for their unofficial and nonpolitical expressive activities. The Court judged this interest "undeniably powerful," but noted the absence of any evidence of misconduct related to honoraria. Instead of a concern about the "cumulative effect of a widespread practice" that Congress deemed to "menace the integrity and the competency of service," the government relied on "limited evidence of actual or apparent impropriety." The Court concluded that the "speculative benefits the honoraria ban may provide the Government are not sufficient to justify this crudely crafted burden on [the employee's] freedom to engage in expressive activities." The Court found the lower courts' injunction "overinclusive," however, to the extent it reached senior executives not party to this case and to those situations in which an "obvious nexus" existed between the employee's job and either the subject matter of his or her expression or the interest of the person paying an honorarium. Chief Justice Rehnquist, joined by Justices Scalia and Thomas, dissented. He contended that the Court "understate[d]" the weight that should have been given the government's justifications for the ban on honoraria and "overstate[d]" the volume of expression that will actually be deterred by the ban. Rehnquist also suggested that the Court "largely ignore[d] the Government's foremost interest—prevention of impropriety and the appearance of impropriety." In the dissenters' view, the honoraria ban neither prohibited nor penalized expression. Rather, the only "stricture affected by the statute is a denial of compensation." *See also* FIRST AMENDMENT, p. 29; FREE SPEECH CLAUSE, p. 654; *Lebron v. National Railroad Passenger Corp.*, p. 95.

Significance Federal employees are subject to regulations that affect their free expression rights. The Hatch Act, for example, prohibits federal employees from participating in various political activities. The Hatch Act was upheld in *United Public Workers v. Mitchell*, 330 U.S. 75 (1947), in which the Court concluded that such regulation does not violate the First Amendment if Congress reasonably believes it will interfere with the efficient performance of public service. The restriction at issue in *National Treasury Employees Union* was prompted by ethics concerns. Notwithstanding the importance of setting high ethical standards for those in government, most strong ethics reform proposals have the potential to impinge on free speech rights. The government argued in this case that expression was not prohibited under the regulation, only compensation for that expression. It also was asserted that the purpose of the ban on honoraria was to preserve the integrity of the federal workforce. The government contended that the controlling precedent in this case was *Pickering*. In that case, a public school teacher was dismissed because of his extensive criticism of both the school board and the school superintendent. The dismissal was based on the school board's determination that the teacher's views were "detrimental to the efficient operation and administration of the schools in the district." The Court ruled that Pickering's dismissal was not justified in this instance, but also recognized that government may restrict expression of its employees under some circumstances. *Pickering* requires courts to weigh an employee's interest in commenting on matters of "public concern" against the government's interest in having its employees perform effectively. Using the *Pickering* standard, the government argued in *National Treasury Employees Union* that the ban on compensation imposed only a minimal burden on expressive activity, a burden that was outweighed by the governmental interest in preserving the integrity of the federal workforce. The lower courts ruled that the regulation was too broad—that a more narrowly focused ban on honoraria could be created that applied only when there was a close enough relationship between the compensated expressive activity and the recipient's government responsibilities. The Supreme Court agreed.

FREEDOM OF THE PRESS
Prior Restraint

Near v. Minnesota, **283 U.S. 697 (1931),** struck down a state law that imposed an unconstitutional prior restraint. Prior restraint is governmental censorship, and typically takes one of two forms. Prior restraint occurs when government must approve all content, or categorically bans particular content before publication.

The Court emphasized that the core of the free press protection is freedom from governmental censorship. The doctrine of prior restraint is built on the proposition that restraint of expression *before* it can occur constitutes a grave threat to free speech. Near published a weekly newspaper that engaged in vicious attacks on various public officials in Minneapolis. He was subsequently enjoined from publication under provisions of a Minnesota statute authorizing the abatement of any "malicious, scandalous and defamatory newspaper, magazine or periodical" as a "public nuisance." The Court found the statute unconstitutional. Before addressing the prior restraint question, the Court first determined that the free press provision fell within the liberty safeguarded by the Due Process Clause of the Fourteenth Amendment and applies to the states. The Court found the Minnesota statute defective because it was "not aimed at the redress of individual or private wrongs." Rather, it was aimed at distribution of material "for the protection of the public welfare." Although prosecution might occur against such publications after the fact, the state had insufficient interest to warrant a prior restraint. Chief Justice Hughes argued that the "object of the statute is not punishment, in the ordinary sense, but suppression." The suppression is "accomplished by enjoining publication, and that restraint is the object and effect of the statute." In short, the objectives and means embodied in the statute were the essence of censorship. The Court also pointed out that the statute too seriously limited what might be said about public officials. References to public corruption, malfeasance, or neglect of duty create a public scandal by their very nature. Under the statute, such content is scandalous and defamatory by definition. The Court said, "the recognition of authority to impose previous restraint upon publication in order to protect the community against the circulation of charges of misconduct, and especially of official misconduct necessarily would carry with it the admission of the authority of the censor against which the constitutional barrier was erected." While "charges of reprehensible conduct, and in particular official malfeasance, unquestionably create a public scandal, the theory of the constitutional guaranty is that even a more serious public evil would be caused by authority to prevent publication." Justices Van DeVanter, McReynolds, and Sutherland joined in a dissent written by Justice Butler. The dissenters argued that the injunction was not a prior restraint in that it could be issued only after a publication had been found to be a nuisance. The dissenters also felt that libel laws were insufficient to deter such publications or redress injury caused by libelous publication. *See also* FIRST AMENDMENT, p. 29; FREE PRESS CLAUSE, p. 653; *Hazelwood School District v. Kuhlmeier*, p. 104; *New York Times Co. v. United States*, p. 101; PRIOR RESTRAINT, p. 690.

Significance Near v. Minnesota was the Court's first significant censorship decision and provided the baseline standard in the critical matter of defining prior restraint. *Near* holds such restraint to be heavily suspect, but possibly justifiable in the instance of threats to national security, obscenity, incitements to governmental overthrow or other violence, or interference with private interests. The prior restraint exceptions set forth in *Near* have remained largely undisturbed. The Court struck down a "gag order" intended to safeguard jury selection in a criminal trial in *Nebraska Press Association v. Stuart*, 427 U.S. 539 (1976), and freed the publication of the so-called Pentagon Papers in *New York Times Co. v. United States*, 403 U.S. 713 (1971). The "papers" were classified Defense Department documents that were illegally taken from the Pentagon and given to the *New York Times* and *Washington Post*. The documents contained a detailed and somewhat embarrassing historical account of American involvement in Vietnam. The Court also held that a group wishing to criticize the way a businessman conducted his business could circulate leaflets near the businessman's home and church in *Organization for Better Austin v. Keefe*, 402 U.S. 415 (1971). Prior restraints have been allowed, however, within the exceptions stated in *Near*. In *Snepp v. United States*, 444 U.S. 507 (1980), the Court required an ex–Central Intelligence Agency agent to obtain clearance from the agency prior to publication of any material relating to his former employment with the CIA, a regulation in place because agents have "frequent access to classified information, including information regarding intelligence sources and methods." The authority of school officials to exclude certain content from student publications was upheld in *Hazelwood School District v. Kuhlmeier*, 484 U.S. 260 (1988).

New York Times Co. v. United States (The Pentagon Papers Cases), 403 U.S. 713 (1971), dissolved an injunction against the *New York Times* restraining publication of the Pentagon Papers. The *Pentagon Papers Cases* examined the question of whether a prior restraint upon publication may be warranted if national security is threatened. The *New York Times* and the *Washington Post* came into possession of copies of Defense Department documents detailing the history of American involvement in the Vietnam War. After failing to prevent publication by direct request to the newspapers, injunctions were sought in federal court by the Nixon administration against the two papers to stop publication of the documents on national security grounds. An injunction was obtained against the *Times*, but not against the *Post*. The Supreme Court determined that injunctive restraints against either paper were unwarranted. In a brief per curiam opinion, the Court said there is a "heavy presumption" against prior restraint and that the "heavy burden" had not been carried in these cases. Each member of the Court entered an individual opinion. Justices Black and Douglas both categorically rejected prior restraint. Justice Black said that "every moment's continuance of the injunction against these newspapers amounts to a flagrant, indefensible, and continuing violation of the First Amendment." Justice Black recited the history of the amendment and noted the essential function assigned to the press. The press he said, "was to serve the governed, not the governors. The Government's power to censor the press was abolished so that the press would remain forever free to censure the Government." Of all the press functions, "paramount among the responsibilities of the free press is the duty to prevent any part of the government from deceiving the people and sending them off to distant lands to die of foreign fevers and foreign shot and shell." Justice Brennan allowed that prior restraint might be possible in the most extreme circumstance, but found no such circumstances present in these cases. The other members of the majority, Justices Stewart, White, and Marshall, focused on the absence of statutory authority for federal courts to issue injunctions such as those sought by the government. Indeed, it was pointed out that Congress had directly rejected such an option in the debate leading to the passage of the Espionage Act of 1917. Justices White and Stewart, however, expressed concern that national security had been compromised, and suggested that the criminal process could be utilized against the newspapers in this instance. The three dissenters, Chief Justice Burger and Justices Harlan and Blackmun, rejected the majority's First Amendment position, but they were also concerned with the "irresponsibly feverish" and "frenzied" manner in which the cases were handled. Describing the way the cases reached the Court as "frenetic," the chief justice said, "the consequence of all this melancholy series of events is that we literally do not know what we are acting upon." *See also* FIRST AMENDMENT, p. 29; FREE PRESS CLAUSE, p. 653; *Hazelwood School District v. Kuhlmeier*, p. 104; *Near v. Minnesota*, p. 100; PRIOR RESTRAINT, p. 690.

Significance   The *Pentagon Papers Cases* represented an important free press challenge. The Supreme Court decision was expected to provide a definitive statement on when prior restraint might constitutionally be imposed, but the decision did not produce such a ruling. The Court's judgment actually hinged on the fairly narrow issue of whether the government had sufficiently demonstrated that immediate and irreparable harm would result from publication of the documents. Although the *Times* prevailed, the various opinions did not constitute a strong ruling for press freedom. The criminal prosecution of Daniel Ellsberg, who had furnished copies of the documents to the *Times* and the *Post* in the first place, was ultimately dismissed. Thus the Court was precluded from another opportunity to consider the free press issues contained in the Pentagon Papers imbroglio. Similarly, an attempt to prevent publication of an article in *The Progressive* about the manufacture of a hydrogen bomb was resolved prior to the matter reaching the Supreme Court.

Almost all the states have laws designed to prevent criminals from profiting from their crimes by selling their stories to book publishers or filmmakers. The Court's ruling in *Simon & Schuster, Inc. v. Members of the New York State Crime Victims Board*, 502 U.S. 105 (1991), declared such laws unconstitutional. New York enacted such a law in 1977 soon after the arrest of David Berkowitz, an alleged serial killer. Berkowitz was popularly known as "Son of Sam," and New York's law became known as the "Son of Sam" law. Under terms of the law, any money earned by persons who admit to criminal conduct through their expressive works is placed in escrow and held for distribution to eligible victims for a five-year period. Initially, the New York law applied only to those convicted of a crime. Ironically, because Berkowitz was found incompetent to stand trial, the law was never applied to him. This case arose out of a contractual agreement between Simon & Schuster and an organized crime figure, Henry Hill. Hill and an author had produced a book, entitled *Wiseguy*, about his criminal life. The book was a commercial success, selling more than a million copies. The book was subsequently made into a film entitled, "Goodfellas," which enjoyed both critical and commercial success. The Crime Victims Board determined the book to be covered by the Son of Sam law. The Board ordered Hill to turn over payments already received, and ordered Simon & Schuster to turn over all future money payable to Hill. Simon & Schuster brought suit seeking declaration that the law was incompatible with the First Amendment. A unanimous Supreme Court agreed. Justice O'Connor said that a statute is "presumptively inconsistent" with the First Amendment if it "imposes a financial burden on speakers because of the content of their speech." The Court found the Son of Sam law to be such a content-based statute. The law "singles out income derived from expressive activity for a burden the State places on no other income, and it is directed only at works with a specified content." The financial disincentive of the law, said O'Connor, was placed "only on speech of a particular content." Furthermore, the Court concluded that the law was fatally "overinclusive," because it applied to works on "any subject, provided that they express the author's thoughts or recollections about his crime, however tangentially or incidentally." The law also covered crimes that the author wrote about committing, but for which he was never charged. The Court concluded that such a law reached too "wide a range of literature" to pass First Amendment scrutiny.

Hazelwood School District v. Kuhlmeier, **484 U.S. 260 (1988),** upheld the broad authority of school officials to monitor and censor content thought to be objectionable for student publications. Former staff members of a high school newspaper brought suit claiming Hazelwood School District violated their First Amendment rights by deleting articles from a particular issue of the newspaper. The articles described student pregnancy experiences and the effect on students of parental divorce. The newspaper was produced by a journalism class as a part of the high school curriculum. The procedure established by the school district was that the principal reviewed all page proofs prior to publication. In this case, the principal objected to the article on pregnancy as inappropriate for some of the school's younger students. The article on divorce was found objectionable because it actually identified a parent by name and included accusations of abusive conduct. With publication imminent, the principal ordered the pages on which the two articles appeared to be withheld from the paper even though these pages contained other, unobjectionable material. The Supreme Court ruled that there was no First Amendment violation. While acknowledging that students do not "shed their constitutional rights to freedom of speech or expression at the schoolhouse gate," the Court said that the rights of students in public schools are not "automatically coextensive with the rights of adults in other settings." Rather, they must be applied in light of the "special characteristics of the school environment." A school "need not tolerate" student speech that is "inconsistent" with its "basic educational mission, even though the government could not censor similar speech outside the school." The Court rejected the assertion that the paper was a forum for public expression. School facilities are public forums only if they are open for "indiscriminate use" by the "general public" or a portion of the general public. On the other hand, if facilities have been "reserved for other intended purposes," no public forum exists and school authorities may impose "reasonable restrictions." In this case, the school district merely adhered to its policy that publication of the newspaper was part of the educational process and an activity subject to the control of the school staff. Because there was no intent to open the paper to "indiscriminate use" by the student body or even the newspaper's student staff, the Court ruled that the school officials were entitled to reasonably regulate the content of the paper. Educators may exercise greater control over certain expression to assure that participants "learn whatever lessons the activity is designed to teach," that readers or listeners are not exposed to material that may be "inappropriate for their level of maturity," and that the positions taken are not "erroneously attributed to the school." Educators, said the Court, do not violate the First Amendment by "exercising editorial control over the style and content of student speech in school-sponsored expressive activities" so long as their actions are "reasonably related to legitimate pedagogical concerns." Justices Brennan, Marshall, and Blackmun disagreed, seeing the principal's action as unconstitutional prior restraint. In their view, the expression did not interfere with the educational process and should have been protected. They also objected to the breadth of discretion permitted the school authorities. *See also* FIRST AMENDMENT, p. 29; FREE PRESS CLAUSE, p. 653; *Near v. Minnesota*, p. 100; *New York Times Co. v. United States*, p. 101; PRIOR RESTRAINT, p. 690.

Significance   *Hazelwood School District v. Kuhlmeier* contained the central free press issue of censorship. Some distinctions can be drawn within the general prohibition against government censorship. Florida law, for example, prohibited publication of identifying information about the victim of a sex crime. The newspaper had been ordered to pay damages for publishing a victim's name although lawfully obtained from police records. The information had been included in a police report left in a law enforcement agency press room. Access to the room or documents located there was not restricted. The police report in which an individual was identified had been discovered by a reporter-trainee who copied the entire report. The information was subsequently published in a story appearing in the *Florida Star*. B. J. F., the identified victim, filed suit against the newspaper claiming negligent violation of the statute and was awarded both compensatory and punitive damages. The Supreme Court reversed in *Florida Star v. B.J.F.*, 491 U.S. 524 (1989). The Court chose not to establish the "broad" principle that damages for encroachment on privacy rights could never prevail over truthful publication. Instead, the Court resolved the issue on "limited principles" that "sweep no more broadly" than the "appropriate context" of this particular case. The Court drew heavily on *Smith v. Daily Mail Publishing Co.*, 443 U.S. 61 (1979), that held that if a newspaper "lawfully obtains truthful information," it may not be punished for publication of that information "absent a need to further a state interest of the highest order." In this case the newspaper had accurately reported information lawfully obtained from a government agency. The Court saw "ample" and "less drastic means" open to the state to safeguard information than limiting publication. While acknowledging that protecting the privacy of sexual assault victims was "highly significant," imposing liability under these circumstances is "too precipitous a means" of protecting those interests.

Another state law permanently prohibited a grand jury witness from disclosing his or her testimony. To the extent the prohibition applied to a person's own testimony after the grand jury term ended, a unanimous Supreme Court struck down the regulation in *Butterworth v. Smith*, 494 U.S. 624 (1990). The Court recognized the "tradition of secrecy" that has evolved as one of the ways to ensure grand jury impartiality and protect against "overreaching" by the state. At the same time, mere "invocation of grand jury interests is not 'some talisman that dissolves all constitutional protections.'" In this case the state sought to prevent Smith, a reporter, from "publication of information relating to alleged government misconduct—speech which has traditionally been recognized as lying at the core of the First Amendment."

***New York Times Co. v. Sullivan*, 376 U.S. 254 (1964),** held that publications may not be subjected to libel damages for criticism of public officials and their official conduct unless deliberate malice could be shown. *Sullivan* attached stringent conditions to certain kinds of libel actions involving speech attacking public officials. A state libel action was brought by a police commissioner in an Alabama court against the *New York Times* for its publication of a paid advertisement that charged police mistreatment of black students protesting racial segregation. It was stipulated that the advertisement contained errors of fact. The trial judge found the statements in the advertisement to be libelous and instructed the jury that injury occurred through publication, and that both compensatory and punitive damages could be presumed. Substantial damages were awarded by the jury, which also found malice on the part of the *Times*. The Supreme Court reversed the judgments in a unanimous decision. The Court's position was that libel law must provide free speech safeguards. To allow unrestricted libel actions "would discourage newspapers from carrying 'editorial advertisements' of this type, and so might shut off an important outlet for the promulgation of information and ideas." Such laws would shackle the First Amendment in its attempt to secure the widest possible dissemination of information from diverse and antagonistic sources. Even the factual errors did not jeopardize the advertisement's protected status. The protection of the advertisement, clearly "an expression of grievance and protest on one of the major public issues of our time," is not contingent on the truth, popularity, or social utility of the ideas and beliefs that are offered. Mistakes or errors of fact are inevitable in free debate and must be protected if freedom of expression is to have the "breathing space" it needs. Neither does injury to the reputation of a public official itself justify limiting expression. "Criticism of their official conduct does not lose its constitutional protection merely because it is effective criticism and hence diminishes their official reputations." Any rule "compelling the critic of official conduct to guarantee the truth of all his factual assertions—and to do so on pain of libel judgments virtually unlimited in amount—leads to a comparable self-censorship." Such a rule severely dampens the vigor and limits the variety of public debate. The Court did allow for recovery of damages when it can be proved that statements were made with actual malice, that is, with knowledge that statements were false, or with reckless disregard of whether they were false or not. In concurring opinions, Justices Black and Goldberg argued for the unconditional insulation of the press from libel suits, at least with regard to public officials. *See also* FIRST AMENDMENT, p. 29; FREE PRESS CLAUSE, p. 653; *Hustler Magazine v. Falwell*, p. 110; LIBEL, p. 675.

Significance   *New York Times Co. v. Sullivan* expanded the Court's experience with seditious libel, a special category of libel that involves defamation of government and its officials. The Alien and Sedition Acts of 1798 would have provided a basic test of seditious libel, but they never reached the Court. The Court has generally included libel in the category of unprotected speech. *Sullivan* provided the Court an opportunity to refine that classification. Libel laws cannot inhibit debate on public issues even if the debate includes strong and unpleasant attacks on the government and its officials. *Sullivan* held that public officials could protect themselves through libel actions in situations in which false statements were made with "actual malice" or with "reckless disregard of their falsity." The *Sullivan* decision approached an almost unconditional free press position relative to public officials. The Court soon extended *Sullivan* to criminal libel prosecutions in *Garrison v. Louisiana*, 379 U.S. 64 (1964). In *Garrison* the Court said that regardless of limitations in other contexts, "where the criticism is of public officials and their conduct of public business, the interest in private reputation is overborne by the larger public interest, secured by the Constitution in the dissemination of the truth." Yet in *McDonald v. Smith*, 472 U.S. 479 (1985), the Court held that communications to governmental officials influencing reputation are not immune from libel suits. McDonald had written to President Reagan urging the president not to nominate Smith to the position of United States attorney. Smith did not receive the nomination and subsequently filed a libel action against McDonald, claiming his letters to be malicious and knowingly false. McDonald argued that he was immune from such suit under his First Amendment right to petition the government. In a unanimous decision, the Court said that while the right to petition is guaranteed, "the right to commit libel with impunity is not."

The question of whether groups may be protected from defamatory statements was addressed in *Beauharnais v. Illinois*, 343 U.S. 250 (1952). The Court upheld an Illinois statute prohibiting derogatory comment about any racial or religious group. The Court said that "we are precluded from saying that speech concededly punishable when directed at individuals cannot be outlawed if directed at groups with whose position and esteem in society the affiliated individual may be inextricably involved." The dissenters in *Beauharnais* vigorously argued that such a law would greatly inhibit public debate. This view eventually prevailed in *Sullivan* and diminished the current applicability of *Beauharnais*.

The Court reinforced the "deliberate malice" standard in *Bose Corp. v. Consumers Union of United States, Inc.*, 466 U.S. 485 (1984). The Court held that determination of malice in defamation suits is subject to full and thorough review on appeal. *Bose* called for appellate courts to exercise independent judgment and to make their own determination as to whether actual malice had been established with "convincing clarity." This is a more rigorous standard than is normally utilized at appellate levels, and it offers greater protection to publishers defending libel actions by creating a two-tiered system for finding actual malice. *Sullivan* protected publications from libel suits when critical comment had been made about governmental officials. Soon thereafter the category of government official was expanded to include public figures, private citizens who are in the midst of public events, or persons who attract wide public attention. In *Rosenbloom v. Metromedia, Inc.*, 403 U.S. 29 (1971), the Court went so far as to require reckless falsity in all actions, whether the plaintiff was a public official, a public figure, or a private individual. Rosenbloom, a distributor of nudist magazines, had been charged with possession of obscene materials. The Court ruled that Rosenbloom could not collect damages for radio broadcasts that referred to him as a "smut peddler" even after he was acquitted on the obscenity charges. *Gertz v. Robert Welsh, Inc.*, 418 U.S. 323 (1974), held that an individual did not become a public figure simply because the public was interested in a particular event with which he was associated. After a police officer had been convicted of murder, the attorney who represented the victim's family in a civil action against the officer was characterized in a magazine article as the "architect of a frame-up" of the officer, as having a criminal record, and as a Communist. The Court concluded the attorney was not a public figure, and thus did not need to show reckless falsity as a public figure must. Similarly, a federally funded researcher's media response to receipt of a senator's award for wasting public funds was held insufficient to establish public figure status in *Hutchinson v. Proxmire*, 443 U.S. 111 (1979). U.S. Senator William Proxmire regularly conferred "Golden Fleece" awards to federal agencies he believed had engaged in "egregiously wasteful spending." The agency funding Hutchinson's research on various behavior patterns of animals received an award, and Hutchinson sought damages for defamation.

Yet another aspect of libel was addressed in 1984. In *Keeton v. Hustler Magazine, Inc.*, 465 U.S. 770 (1984), and *Calder v. Jones*, 465 U.S. 783 (1984), the Court found that courts have jurisdiction over out-of-state magazines and newspapers if the publications are regularly circulated in the state in which the court is located. Thus plaintiffs are afforded greater discretion in choosing which court will hear their libel actions. The Court maintained that the First Amendment had no direct bearing on the matter of jurisdiction and that the potential for danger to activities protected by the First Amendment is well integrated into the substantive law governing libel actions.

In 1985 the Court added a content criterion for private libel cases in *Dun & Bradstreet, Inc. v. Greenmoss Builders, Inc.*, 472 U.S. 749 (1985). It ruled that no finding of actual malice need occur unless the case involves a matter of public concern. Greenmoss had sued Dun & Bradstreet for damages based on the circulation of an erroneous credit report. Dun & Bradstreet claimed that Greenmoss must show the erroneous report was published with actual malice. The Court responded that purely private matters are of less First Amendment concern than public matters, thus underscoring the difference between private cases and cases involving public figures. *Greenmoss* increased the likelihood that private parties will collect damages in libel actions by eliminating the focus on actual malice. In *Philadelphia Newspapers, Inc. v. Hepps*, 475 U.S. 767 (1985), however, the Court opined that a private figure suing a newspaper for defamation carries the burden of proving that defamatory statements of public concern are false. This is the converse of traditional libel law in which the defense must prove the statements true in order to prevail and that this switch in the burden of proof makes it more difficult for plaintiffs to win, especially because proving a negative is already very difficult. Soon after *Hepps*, the Court added the detail in *Anderson v. Liberty Lobby, Inc.*, 477 U.S. 242 (1986), that trial judges should summarily dismiss, before a trial begins, public figure libel suits unless there is clear and convincing evidence of actual malice. This is the standard of proof any public figure plaintiff must demonstrate in order to succeed in a libel trial. The *Anderson* ruling enhances the probability that defendants will win pretrial dismissals in libel actions brought by public figures.

Libel: Parodies and Misquotes

Hustler Magazine v. Falwell, **485 U.S. 46 (1988),** held that a public figure cannot be awarded damages for the "intentional infliction of emotional distress" caused by the publication of a parody. Campari Liqueur conducted an advertising campaign in which celebrities discussed their first experiences with the liqueur—their "first times." *Hustler* published an advertisement parody, so labeled in small print at the bottom of the page, in which Falwell, a prominent religious and political personality, was represented as recalling his "first time" as a drunken and incestuous affair with his mother in an outhouse. Falwell brought suit against *Hustler*, claiming that publication of the parody entitled him to damages for libel and intentional infliction of emotional distress. The jury found that the parody could not reasonably be understood as representing actual facts, and it ruled for the magazine on the libel claim. The jury awarded Falwell damages on the emotional distress claim, however. The U.S. Court of Appeals for the Fourth Circuit affirmed, saying that in an emotional stress action brought by public figures, actual malice need not be shown. The Fourth Circuit further held that even if the ad parody was constitutionally protected opinion, the only relevant factor was whether the publication was sufficiently outrageous to constitute the intentional infliction of emotional distress. The Supreme Court unanimously reversed the lower courts and ruled for *Hustler*. The case presented the Court with a "novel" First Amendment question: whether a public figure may recover damages for "emotional harm" caused by publication of material "offensive to him, and doubtless gross and repugnant in the eyes of most." Falwell asked the Court to find that a state's interest in protecting public figures from emotional distress is "sufficient to deny First Amendment protection to speech that is patently offensive and is intended to inflict emotional injury," even when that speech could not "reasonably have been interpreted as stating actual facts about the public figure involved." This, said Rehnquist, "we decline to do." The sort of "robust" political debate encouraged by the First Amendment will necessarily produce expression that is "critical" of public figures who are "intimately involved in the resolution of important public issues." Such criticism will not always be "reasoned or moderate," and public figures will be subjected to "vehement, caustic, and sometimes unpleasantly sharp attacks." Only defamatory falsehoods uttered with knowledge that they are false or with "reckless disregard" for the truth provide a public figure with an opportunity to hold a speaker liable for damage to reputation. Falwell argued that as long as the utterance was "intended to inflict emotional distress, was outrageous, and did in fact inflict serious emotional distress," it did not matter whether the statement was fact or opinion or whether it was true or false. The Court rejected this contention. Rehnquist said that while the law does not regard the intent to inflict emotional distress as one that should "receive much solicitude," many things done with motives that are "less than admirable are protected by the First Amendment." Although bad motives may be "deemed controlling for purposes of tort liability" in other areas of the law, the First Amendment prohibits such a result in the "area of public debate about public figures." Were the Court to hold otherwise, said Rehnquist, there can be "little doubt" that political cartoonists and satirists "would be subject to damages awards without any showing that their work falsely defamed its subject." Rehnquist examined the history of political cartoons and caricatures. He concluded that despite their "sometimes caustic nature, ... graphic depictions and satirical cartoons have played a prominent role in public and political debate." From a historical perspective, it is "clear that our political discourse would have been considerably poorer without them." He then rejected Falwell's contention that the *Hustler* parody was "so outrageous as to distinguish it from more traditional political cartoons." Rehnquist acknowledged that the *Hustler* caricature of Falwell was "at best a distant cousin" of the traditional political cartoon. If it were possible, he said, to lay down a "principled standard" to separate them, "public discourse would probably suffer little or no harm." Rehnquist doubted, however, that such a standard existed and "was certain" that the "pejorative description 'outrageous' does not supply one. "Outrageousness" in the field of political and social discourse has "an inherent subjectiveness" that would allow a jury to "impose liability on the basis of the jurors' tastes or views, or perhaps on the basis of their dislike of a particular expression." An "outrageousness" standard thus "runs afoul" of the "long-standing refusal" to permit damages to be awarded because expression may have an "adverse emotional impact on the audience." *See also* FIRST AMENDMENT, p. 29; FREE PRESS CLAUSE, p. 653; LIBEL, p. 675; *New York Times Co. v. Sullivan*, p. 106.

Significance   The Court's decision in *Hustler Magazine v. Falwell* was important for two reasons. First, the decision indicated that the Court was not interested in making it easier for public figures to collect damages when subjected to criticism and satire. On the contrary, the decision discouraged plaintiffs who felt offended by media treatment from resorting to litigation as a means of recovery. Second, the decision dispelled speculation that the Court was on the verge of abandoning the "actual malice" rule established in *New York*

Times Co. v. Sullivan, 376 U.S. 254 (1964). The so-called *Sullivan* rule has served as the basis for publications defending themselves in libel actions. During the past decade, the Court seemed to be in doubt as to whether the *Sullivan* rule provided public figures with enough room to protect themselves. The Court's decision in the *Hustler* case was squarely founded on *Sullivan*, and it was apparent that the Court was satisfied with the *Sullivan* rule as the basis for evaluating "public figure" libel actions. Since *Sullivan*, statements of opinion about public figures, as opposed to statements of "fact," have enjoyed virtual protection from libel actions. In addition to *Sullivan*, further support for a privilege for "comment" can be found in *Gertz v. Robert Welch, Inc.*, 418 U.S. 323 (1974), in which the Court said that under the First Amendment, "there is no such thing as a false idea. However pernicious an opinion may seem, we depend for its correction not on the conscience of judges and juries, but on the competition of other ideas." In *Milkovich v. Lorain Journal*, 497 U.S. 1 (1990), the Court clarified this point and ruled that opinions are not categorically insulated from being found defamatory. Chief Justice Rehnquist said that the Court did not think that "this passage from *Gertz* was intended to create a wholesale defamation exception for anything that might be labeled opinion." Such an interpretation is not only contradictory to the "tenor and context" of the *Gertz* opinion, but would "ignore the fact that expressions of opinion may often imply an assertion of objective fact." The Court was satisfied that the "breathing space" needed for free expression was "adequately secured without the creation of an artificial dichotomy between 'opinion' and 'fact.'" A statement as a matter of public concern "must be provable as false before there can be liability under state defamation law." The key in these cases is separating "pure" opinion from opinion that "contains actionable assertions of fact."

The question in *Masson v. New Yorker Magazine, Inc.*, 501 U.S. 493 (1991), was whether fabricated quotations attributed to a public figure constituted sufficient cause to go to trial in a libel action. Masson, a psychoanalyst, was the subject of an unfavorable article by Janet Malcolm that appeared in *The New Yorker*. Before writing the article, Malcolm interviewed Masson extensively. Most of the interview sessions were taped. There were, however, several statements attributed to Masson for which there was no recording. Masson filed a libel action claiming that several statements enclosed in quotation marks were fabricated or deliberately misquoted. A U.S. district court granted summary judgment for *The New Yorker*, concluding that while Malcolm had deliberately altered the quotations, the inaccuracies did not raise a question of actual malice to put to a jury. The Supreme Court disagreed. According to Justice Kennedy, the constitutional question was whether the evidence was sufficient to show that a publisher "acted with the requisite knowledge of falsity or reckless disregard as to truth or falsity." Key to the Court's inquiry was the concept of falsity—whether the "requisite falsity inheres in the attribution of words to the petitioner [Masson] which he did not speak." Kennedy acknowledged that any "alteration of a verbatim quotation is false," but this falsity is only technical. Some alterations may make only minor changes to correct grammar or syntax. This kind of alteration clearly does not show actual malice. If an author, said Kennedy, changes a speaker's words, but "effects no material change in meaning, including any meaning conveyed by the manner or fact of expression, the speaker suffers no injury to reputation that is compensable as defamation." The Court refused to make determination of the falsity of quotations as a special kind of libel inquiry. Rather, the Court applied its longstanding definition of actual malice. A deliberate alteration of a speaker's words does not constitute knowledge of falsity, Kennedy concluded, "unless the alteration results in a material change in the meaning of the statement." Using quotation marks to attribute words not in fact spoken "bears in a most important way on the inquiry, but it is not dispositive in every case." Justices White and Scalia dissented, finding sufficient proof of malice in the knowing publication of false attribution.

Newsperson's Privilege

Branzburg v. Hayes, **408 U.S. 665 (1972),** held that newspersons must disclose sources of information to a grand jury. After having published reports about drug use and manufacture, Hayes was subpoenaed to appear before a state grand jury and identify those persons he had seen using and making illegal narcotics. Hayes refused to testify and was cited for contempt. Through Justice White, the Supreme Court found that the First Amendment "does not invalidate every incidental burdening of the press that may result from the enforcement of civil or criminal statutes of general applicability." In balancing the interests of protecting the criminal process and the news-gathering function of the press, the former must prevail. The burden on the press was seen as too uncertain to justify treating newspersons differently from ordinary citizens. Journalists must respond to relevant questions put to them in the course of a valid grand jury investigation or criminal trial. The press burden in *Branzburg* was not prior restraint, a tax, a penalty on content, or a compulsion to publish. The Court suggested, however, that the impact of its holding would be limited. "Only where news sources themselves are implicated in crime or possess information relevant to the grand jury's task need they or the reporter be concerned about grand jury subpoenas. Nothing before us indicates that a large number or percentage of all confidential news sources fall into either category." Finally, the Court argued that abuse or harassment of the press would be subject to judicial scrutiny and possible intervention. Justice Stewart issued a dissent joined by Justices Brennan and Marshall. He said the Court had undermined the historic independence of the press by attempting to annex the journalistic profession as an investigative arm of the government. Justice Stewart argued that freedom of the press requires the ability to gather news that, in turn, is often contingent on a confidential relationship of reporter and source. The dissenters would have required the state to show that probable cause exists to believe a newsperson has relevant information, that the information cannot be obtained from any other source, and that the state has a compelling interest in the information. Justice Douglas also dissented. He said that forcing a reporter before a grand jury has "two retarding effects upon the ear and pen of the press." One is that fear of exposure will cause dissidents to communicate less openly to reporters. The other is that concerns about accountability will cause editors and critics to write with more restrained pens. Douglas suggested more generally that the press has a "preferred position in our constitutional scheme." The position of the press is not designed to enhance profit or set newspersons apart as a favored class. It is intended to "bring fulfillment to the public's right to know." *See also* EDITORIAL PRIVILEGE, p. 642; FIRST AMENDMENT, p. 29; FREE PRESS CLAUSE, p. 653; NEWSPERSON'S PRIVILEGE, p. 681.

Significance   *Branzburg* rejected the argument of newspersons that they possess a privileged relationship with their sources, and had the effect of leaving information gathering largely unprotected. *Branzburg* said that even an unconditional freedom to publish would be of limited value if information gathering was unprotected. To protect the news-gathering function, several states have adopted shield laws designed to protect the confidentiality of sources. No such legislation exists at the federal level, although *Branzburg* did prompt introduction of such proposals.

The Burger Court rejected other claims of the press regarding its rights in the gathering of information. In *Saxbe v. Washington Post Co.*, 417 U.S. 843 (1974), the Court upheld federal prison regulations that prohibited press interviews with particular inmates. The Court said that the Constitution does not impose upon government the "affirmative duty to make available to journalists sources of information not available to members of the public generally." Four years later, in *Houchins v. KQED, Inc.*, 438 U.S. 1 (1978), the Court upheld a refusal to allow media access to a county jail that had been the site of a prisoner's suicide and other alleged violent incidents, as well as charges of inhumane conditions. The majority saw the case as one involving a "special privilege of access" such as that denied in *Saxbe.* This is "a right which is not essential to guarantee the freedom to communicate or publish."

The Court refused to defer to editorial privilege in the libel case of *Herbert v. Lando,* 441 U.S. 153 (1979). Herbert was a retired army officer with extended service in Vietnam. He received widespread media attention when he accused his superior officers of covering up reports of atrocities and other war crimes. Some three years after Herbert's disclosures, the Columbia Broadcasting System broadcast a report on Herbert and his charges on the television program *60 Minutes.* Lando produced and edited the program. He also published an article on Herbert in the *Atlantic Monthly.* Herbert's suit alleged that the "program and article falsely and maliciously portrayed him as a liar and a person who had made war crime charges to explain his relief from command." In attempting to develop proofs for his case, Herbert tried to obtain the testimony of Lando before trial, but Lando refused, claiming that the First Amendment protected against "inquiry into the state of mind of those who edit, produce, or publish, and into the editorial process." The Supreme Court found against Lando, holding that the First Amendment does not restrict the sources from which a plaintiff can obtain evidence. Indeed, "it is essential to proving liability that plaintiffs focus on the conduct and state of mind of the defendants." If demonstration of liability is potentially possible, "the thoughts and editorial processes of the alleged defamer would be open to examination." Such examination includes being able to inquire directly from the defendants whether they knew or had reason to suspect that their damaging publication was in error. The editorial privilege sought by Lando would constitute substantial interference with the ability of a defamation plaintiff to establish the ingredients of malice.

The Court ruled in *Cohen v. Cowles Media Co.,* 501 U.S. 663 (1991), that the news media is not protected from damage suits if the promise of confidentiality is breached. Cohen was closely associated with a gubernatorial campaign. He offered to render certain information about the opposing candidate for lieutenant governor, but only if the media promised not to disclose him as the source. The promise was given, and the information was exchanged. Over the objection of the reporters who had promised confidentiality, the editorial staff of two newspapers decided to reveal Cohen's name. It was their editorial judgment that readers were entitled to know the source and his interest in the outcome of the gubernatorial election. Cohen subsequently lost his job. He brought suit in state court alleging, among other things, breach of contract. The Minnesota Supreme Court ruled that the First Amendment prevented enforcement of such civil claims against the newspapers. The U.S. Supreme

Court disagreed. The newspapers relied on previous decisions holding that states could not "punish" publication of lawfully obtained information. The Court, however, did not see that line of cases as governing here. Rather, the Court drew upon decisions rejecting special privilege for the press. Justice White said for the majority that it is "beyond dispute" that a newspaper has "no special immunity from the application of general laws." Generally applicable laws such as Minnesota's do not offend the First Amendment "simply because their enforcement against the press has incidental effects on its ability to gather and report the news." Further, the Court rejected the argument that the law punished publication of truthful information. The Minnesota law that provided for compensatory damages did not inflict a form of punishment. Rather, it was intended to "simply require those making promises to keep them." Justices Souter, Marshall, Blackmun, and O'Connor dissented. Justice Souter argued that publication of Cohen's identity significantly "expanded the universe of information" relevant to Minnesota voters, and that the First Amendment should be interpreted in a way to protect the public's right to that information.

Coverage of Criminal Trials

Richmond Newspapers, Inc. v. Virginia, **448 U.S. 555 (1980),** determined that the press has a constitutional right of access to criminal trials. In *Richmond Newspapers* the defendant's counsel requested that a murder trial be closed to the public. The prosecutor expressed no objection, and the trial judge ordered the courtroom cleared. Under Virginia law, a trial judge has the discretion to exclude from a trial any person whose "presence would impair the conduct of a fair trial." The Supreme Court held the closure order was a violation of the right of access, a press right protected by the First Amendment. Chief Justice Burger traced the history of open trials and concluded "that a presumption of openness inheres in the very nature of a criminal trial under our system of justice." The Court said the open trial serves a therapeutic purpose for the community, especially in the instance of shocking crimes. Open trials offer protection against abusive or arbitrary behavior, and allow criminal processes "to satisfy the appearance of justice." Although access to trials is not specifically provided in the First Amendment, it is implicit. Without the freedom to attend trials, important aspects of free speech and a free press could be diminished. The closure order was defective because the trial judge made no finding of fact that an order was required. Alternatives to closure were not explored, there was no recognition of any constitutional right for the press or the public to attend the proceeding, and there was no indication that witness problems could not have been handled otherwise. In a concurring opinion Justice Brennan said that "open trials play a fundamental role in furthering the efforts of any judicial system to assure the criminal defendant a fair and accurate adjudication of guilt or innocence." Justice Rehnquist dissented and recast the issue. For him the issue was "whether any provision in the Constitution may fairly be read to prohibit what the trial judge in the Virginia state court system did in this case." Rehnquist would have permitted the trial judge's order to stand. *See also Branzburg v. Hayes,* p. 113; FIRST AMENDMENT, p. 29; FREE PRESS CLAUSE, p. 653.

Significance   Richmond Newspapers, Inc. v. Virginia rested on a distinction between the trial itself and pretrial proceedings, and elevated the press interest to prevailing weight in the former. In most instances, the Supreme Court has found that a criminal defendant needed to be shielded from media coverage in pretrial hearings as a basic requirement of due process.

Consistent with the objective of minimizing adverse pretrial publicity, the Court allowed closure of pretrial proceedings in *Gannett Co. v. De Pasquale,* 443 U.S. 368 (1979). The Court held in *Nebraska Press Association v. Stuart,* 427 U.S. 539 (1976), that material from a public proceeding or record could not be kept from the public through a court gag order. *Nebraska Press Association* also said the press cannot be restrained from reporting what it observes.

A balance of press and criminal defendant interests was struck in *Chandler v. Florida,* 449 U.S. 560 (1980), in which the Court upheld a policy whereby trials might be broadcast as long as broadcast coverage was not disruptive, intrusive, or prejudicial to the outcome of the trial.

In *Press-Enterprise Co. v. Superior Court* (I), 464 U.S. 501 (1984), the Court added the detail that the voir dire examination must also be open to the public and the press. The presumption of openness can only be overcome by an "overriding interest" that needs protection through narrowly tailored closure. Two years later the Court softened the distinction between trials and pretrial criminal proceedings in *Press-Enterprise Co. v. Superior Court* (II), 478 U.S. 1 (1986). It narrowed the scope of *Gannett* by saying that closure of pretrial proceedings can only occur when such action is "essential to preserve higher values and is narrowly tailored to serve the interest," a standard that will likely make the closure of pretrial proceedings more difficult.

Commercial Press

Central Hudson Gas & Electric Co. v. Public Service Commission, 447 U.S. 557 (1980), established standards by which commercial content in speech may be evaluated. The United States experienced fuel shortages in the early 1970s, and New York's Public Service Commission ordered all electric utilities in the state to stop promoting the use of electricity. Even after the fuel shortage eased, however, the Commission sought to continue the ban on promotional advertising. Central Hudson Gas & Electric Co. unsuccessfully challenged the advertising ban in the state courts on First Amendment grounds. The Supreme Court found the categorical elimination of promotional advertising by electric utilities to violate the First Amendment. Commercial speech is expression exclusively related to the "economic interests of the speaker and its audience." What First Amendment protection is afforded commercial speech is "based on the informational function of advertising." Although government may regulate commercial messages that inaccurately inform the public about lawful activity, the government's power is "more circumscribed" if the communication is neither "misleading nor related to unlawful activity." A review of previous cases suggested a "four-part analysis" to be applied in cases involving the regulation of commercial messages. First, the Court must determine whether the expression is protected by the First Amendment; the commercial message must concern lawful activity and not be misleading. Second, the Court must determine whether the regulatory interest asserted by the government is "substantial." If both these conditions are met, the Court then must determine whether the regulation "directly advances the governmental interest asserted," and whether the regulation is "more extensive than necessary to serve that interest." The ban on promotional advertising in *Central Hudson* related neither to an inaccurate communication nor to an unlawful activity. New York argued, however, that because Central Hudson had a monopoly on the sale of electricity, any information provided by the advertising could not "improve the decisionmaking of consumers." The Court rejected this contention by suggesting that Central Hudson's monopoly over its supply of a product provides "no protection from competition with substitutes for that product." Even in a monopoly market, suppression of advertising "reduces the information available for consumers' decisions and thereby defeats the purpose of the First Amendment." New York offered two interests as justification for the ban on promotional advertising—energy conservation and concern that promotional advertising would "aggravate inequities caused by the failure to base the utility's rates on marginal cost." The Court agreed that conserving energy and "fair and efficient" energy rates are substantial governmental interests. The Court then examined the relationship between the state's interests and the advertising ban—the "fit" of means and ends. The fit between the advertising ban and rate structure was seen as "tenuous" and "highly speculative." The state's interest in energy conservation was, in contrast, "directly advanced" by the advertising ban. The final consideration was whether the Commission's "complete suppression of speech ordinarily protected by the First Amendment is no more extensive than necessary to further the State's interest in energy conservation." The order applied to all advertising "regardless of the impact of the touted service on overall energy use." The Court concluded that as important as the energy conservation rationale was, it could not justify suppression of information about, for example, "electric devices or services that would cause no net increase in total energy use." In the absence of a showing that more limited speech regulation would be ineffective, the Court could not "approve the complete suppression of Central Hudson's advertising." Justice Rehnquist dissented, arguing that the monopoly status the state conferred on Central Hudson justified a state's "wide-ranging supervision and control," including regulation of the monopoly's commercial speech. *See also* COMMERCIAL PRESS, p. 630; FIRST AMENDMENT, p. 29; FREE PRESS CLAUSE, p. 653; *Glickman v. Wileman Bros.*, p. 120.

Significance   The Burger Court was responsible for expanding the protections afforded commercial content. *Central Hudson* established the currently used criteria for reviewing commercial expression. *Pittsburgh Press Co. v. Pittsburgh Commission on Human Relations*, 413 U.S. 376 (1973), demonstrated several years earlier that particular kinds of commercial speech may be regulated. Restrictions such as that in *Pittsburgh Press* were not altered by *Central Hudson*. The Pittsburgh Press Company was found to be in violation of a Human Relations Commission ordinance because it placed help-wanted advertisements in sex-designated columns. The Commission ordered the newspaper to end the gender-referenced layout of the advertisements, and the Supreme Court ruled that the order was not prior restraint. The Court first determined that the advertisements were commercial speech, not merely because they were advertisements but because of their commercial content. They were, in fact, "classic examples of commercial speech" because of the proposal of possible employment. They were therefore unlike the political advertisement in *New York Times Co. v. Sullivan*, 376 U.S. 254 (1964). The Pittsburgh Press Company argued that editorial judgment about where to place an advertisement should control, rather than its commercial content. The Court answered that "a newspaper's editorial judgments in connection with an advertisement take on the character of the advertisement and, in those cases, the scope of the newspaper's First Amendment protection may be affected by the content of the advertisement." The kind of editorial judgment involved in this case did not strip commercial advertising of its commercial character. Even more crucial was the fact that the commercial activity involved was illegal employment discrimination. In the Court's view, advertisements could be forbidden in this instance just as advertisements "proposing a sale of narcotics or soliciting prostitution" could be forbidden. The justices concluded that any First Amendment interest that applies to an ordinary commercial proposal is "altogether absent when the commercial activity itself is illegal and the restriction on advertising is incidental to a valid limitation on economic activity." Dissents were entered by Chief Justice Burger and Justices Douglas, Stewart, and Blackmun. The chief justice wrote that the First Amendment "includes the right of a newspaper to arrange the content of its paper, whether it be news items, editorials, or advertising, as it sees fit." Justice Douglas argued that no ordinance justifies censorship, and that employment discrimination can be otherwise handled. Justice Stewart felt that, given the Court's holding, there is "no reason why Government cannot force a newspaper publisher to conform in the same way in order to achieve other goals thought socially desirable." If government can "dictate the layout of a newspaper's classified advertising pages today, what is there to prevent it from dictating the layout of the news pages tomorrow?"

The commercial speech holding in *Central Hudson* had its origin in *Valentine v. Chrestensen*, 316 U.S. 52 (1942). The latter decision clearly put commercial speech outside First Amendment coverage. *New York Times Co. v. Sullivan*, 376 U.S. 254 (1964), substantially narrowed the *Chrestensen* concept of commercial speech, and following *Pittsburgh Press*, the Burger Court narrowed the definition even further. In *Bigelow v. Virginia*, 421 U.S. 809 (1975), the Court protected the publication of an advertisement by an organization offering services related to legal abortions in another state. The Court held the advertisement "conveyed information of potential interest and value to a diverse audience," not merely a commercial promotion of services. The next year, in *Virginia State Board of Pharmacy v. Virginia Citizens Consumer Council, Inc.*, 425 U.S. 748 (1976), the Court struck down a statute that made advertising of prescription drugs a form of conduct possibly leading to a suspension of license. The Court argued that even if the advertiser's interest is a purely economic one, such speech is not necessarily disqualified from protection. The consumer and society in general have a "strong interest in the free flow of commercial information." Such a free flow is indispensable in a predominantly free enterprise economy that requires many private economic decisions.

***Glickman v. Wileman Bros.*, 521 U.S. 457 (1997)**   Under terms of the Agricultural Marketing Agreement Act, the secretary of agriculture may assess a fee from those engaged in the "handling" of agricultural commodities to help underwrite the costs of advertising initiatives designed to promote particular products. A number of California handlers of peaches, plums, and nectarines including Wileman Brothers and Elliott, Inc. challenged on First Amendment grounds the secretary's authority to issue such "marketing orders." The Supreme Court rejected the free speech challenge in *Glickman*. Instead, Justice Stevens set a context from which the Court approached this case. The claimed disagreement with the content of the generic advertising and the effectiveness of the advertising had "no bearing on the validity of the entire program." Furthermore, the businesses required to pay for the generic advertising "do so as part of a broader collective enterprise in which their freedom to act independently is already constrained by the regulatory scheme." Justice Stevens suggested that three characteristics of this regulatory scheme distinguish it from laws the Court has struck down in the past. The marketing orders "impose no restraint on the freedom of any producer to communicate any message to any audience," do not compel anyone to "engage in any actual or symbolic speech," and do not compel the producers to "endorse or to finance any political or ideological view." Because Wileman Brothers engaged in the business of marketing California nectarines, plums, and peaches, "it is fair to presume that they agree with the central message" of the generic advertising. Accordingly, the Court saw no reason to subject the regulations to closer scrutiny than that applicable to the other anticompetitiveness features of the marketing orders. The First Amendment has never been construed, said Justice Stevens, "to require heightened scrutiny of any financial burden that has the incidental effect of constraining the size of a firm's advertising budget." The "compelled speech" case law was seen as inapplicable here because the use of assessments to pay for the generic advertising did not require Wileman Brothers to "repeat an objectionable message" or "engender any crisis of conscience." Wileman Brothers' preference to foster an independent message that might better promote its own products did not, in the Court's view, make this case "comparable to those in which objection rested on political or ideological disagreement with the content of the message." Similarly, Wileman Brothers' criticisms of generic advertising "provide no basis for concluding that factually accurate advertising constitutes an abridgment of anybody's right to speak freely." Although Wileman Brothers might question the wisdom of the generic advertising program, "its debatable features are insufficient to warrant special First Amendment scrutiny." Whether the advertising program is cost effective is a question that involves the "exercise of policy judgments that are better made by producers and administrators than judges," said Stevens. In the Court's view, the advertising program is a "species of economic regulation that should enjoy the same strong presumption of validity that we accord to other policy judgments made by Congress." Justice Souter, joined in dissent by Chief Justice Rehnquist and Justices Scalia and Thomas, suggested that the reasons for recognizing commercial speech as worthy of First Amendment protection "likewise justifies the protection of those who object to subsidizing it against their will." Justice Thomas observed that if the Court is "taken at face value," we are left with "two disturbing consequences": Either paying for advertising is "not speech at all," while such activities as draft card and flag burning, the wearing of arm bands, and nude dancing are, or compelling payment for third-party communication "does not implicate speech," and thus the government would be free to force payment for a "whole variety of expressive conduct that it could not restrict." In either case, he concluded, "surely we have lost our way." *See also Central Hudson Gas & Electric Co. v. Public Service Commission*, p. 117; COMMERCIAL PRESS, p. 630; FIRST AMENDMENT, p. 29; FREE PRESS CLAUSE, p. 653.

Significance   Regulation of commercial content by professional associations was at issue in *Shapero v. Kentucky Bar Association*, 486 U.S. 466 (1988). Lawyers are able to advertise, but are not permitted by rules of the profession to directly solicit legal business. Shapero wished to send a letter to potential clients threatened with foreclosure, but approval was withheld by the state bar association on the ground that the letter violated a state court rule barring targeted advertising. The court rule was grounded on the American Bar Association's Model Rules of Professional Conduct, which prohibit such solicitation. The Supreme Court held that the comprehensive ban on targeted, direct-mail solicitation violated the First Amendment. The Court saw the sending of "truthful and nondeceptive" letters to potential clients as protected commercial speech. Such speech, said the Court, can only be restricted in order to pursue "substantial governmental interests" and only in ways that "directly advance" such interests. The "possibility of improper conduct and the improbability of effective regulation" are diminished in the direct-mail situation. The direct-mail approach, said the Court, is less "coercive" than in-person solicitation and can be scrutinized as are other forms of advertising.

The Florida Bar Association sought to change a number of its regulations for attorney advertising. Among the proposed changes was a categorical prohibition on direct-mail advertising by lawyers or lawyer-referral services to accident victims who had potential wrongful death or personal injury claims. The Florida Supreme Court did not approve a total ban on direct-mail advertising, but fashioned a rule that prohibited direct-mail contact to accident victims for 30 days from the date of an accident. The Supreme Court ruled that the modified rule did not violate the First Amendment in *Florida Bar v. Went For It, Inc.*, 515 U.S. 618 (1995). Attorney advertising is commercial speech, a category of communication entitled to limited First Amendment protection. The analytic framework for commercial speech cases comes from *Central Hudson Gas & Electric Co. v. Public Service Commission*, 447 U.S. 557 (1980). Provided that the advertising is not misleading nor involves illegal activity, *Central Hudson* allows regulation of commercial speech if the government can demonstrate that a narrowly drawn regulation materially advances a substantial governmental interest. The Florida Bar Association contended that the regulation protected the privacy of personal injury victims and their families from "intrusive" unsolicited contact by attorneys, and protected the reputation of the legal profession by keeping its members from engaging in inappropriate conduct. Justice O'Connor said the Court had "little trouble" finding the interest of protecting potential clients' privacy to be substantial. Indeed, the state's interest in protecting the "well-being, tranquility, and privacy of the home is certainly of the highest order." The Court also found the regulation to advance the state's interest in a "direct and material" way. The regulation attempted to forestall irritation with the state-licensed legal profession that direct solicitation engenders, and throwing the letter away does not abate the irritation that comes from simply receiving such a targeted solicitation. Those challenging the direct-mail regulation argued that the rule prohibited targeted mailing even to those with relatively minor injuries. The Court was not convinced that a regulation distinguishing potential recipients of direct mail by degree of pain or grief could be developed. It certainly did not see "numerous and obvious less-burdensome alternatives" open to the bar association. Prospective litigants, however, had "ample alternative channels" to learn about the availability of legal representation during the 30-day ban on direct-mail solicitations. Justice Kennedy dissented on behalf of Justices Stevens, Souter, and Ginsburg. It was their view that the communications sent by lawyers to potential clients were protected speech. They also felt the harm caused by direct mail was minimal—a letter can be "put in a drawer to be considered later, ignored, or discarded." In other words, recipients of the mailings were not a "captive audience." Further, the dissenters thought that more speech was regulated than was necessary to achieve the state interest. Indeed, Kennedy referred to the "wild disproportion" between the supposed harm and a ban on speech that applies to all accidental injuries "whatever their gravity." Most important, the regulation kept accident victims from information that "may be critical to their right to make a claim for compensation for injuries." Kennedy concluded by calling the regulation "censorship pure and simple."

Ladue, Missouri, had an ordinance banning all residential signs except those falling within 10 specified exemptions. Among the exemptions were "residence identification" signs, "for sale" signs, and signs warning of safety hazards. Commercial establishments, churches, and nonprofit organizations were allowed to place certain signs that were not allowed at residential sites. Margaret Gilleo placed a two-foot by three-foot sign in her yard expressing her opposition to the Persian Gulf War. She was informed that she was in violation of the sign ordinance. She first sought a variance from the ordinance from the city council. When she failed to obtain the variance, she obtained a temporary injunction against enforcement of the ordinance. The city council amended the ordinance by eliminating the language allowing for variances and grandfathering signs already exempted under the original ordinance. Gilleo then amended her complaint and pursued a permanent injunction against the modified ordinance. In late 1991 a federal district court granted a permanent injunction against enforcement of the more recent version of the ordinance, and the Supreme Court unanimously agreed in *City of Ladue v. Gilleo*, 512 U.S. 43 (1994). Justice Stevens acknowledged that signs are a "form of expression" protected by the Free Speech Clause. Unlike oral speech, however, signs pose a variety of problems that "legitimately call for regulation." Stevens suggested that there are two "analytically distinct" grounds for challenging municipal regulation of signs. One is that the regulation "restricts too little" because its exemptions discriminate on the basis of the signs' content. An impermissibly underinclusive regulation may either attempt to give one side of a "debatable public question an advantage" or place government in a position to "select the permissible subjects for public debate." The second ground on which sign regulations might be attacked is that they "simply prohibit too much protected speech." The Ladue ordinance covered "even such absolutely pivotal speech as a sign protesting an imminent government decision to go to war." The ordinance left residents of Ladue with virtually no way to display any sign on their property. Indeed, Ladue had "almost completely foreclosed a venerable means of communication that is unique and important." Signs that "react to a local happening or express a view on a controversial issue both reflect and animate change in the life of a community." The Court also was unpersuaded that Ladue's ordinance was nothing more than a "time, place or manner" regulation that left residents with sufficient alternate means to express themselves. Displaying a sign from one's own residence, said Stevens, "often carries a message quite distinct from placing the same sign somewhere else, or conveying the same text or picture by other means." The location of signs provides information about the identity of the speaker, an "important component of many attempts to persuade." Although government may need to "mediate among various competing uses, including expressive ones," for public streets and facilities, its "need to regulate temperate speech from the home is surely much less pressing." In conclusion, Stevens observed homeowners have strong incentives for preventing "visual clutter" in their own yards. Such self-interest "diminishes the danger of unlimited proliferation of residential signs." The Court was convinced that "more temperate measures" could satisfy Ladue's stated regulatory needs without harm to the First Amendment interests of its residents.

The Federal Alcohol Administration Act was passed in 1935 and imposed various regulations on the marketing of alcoholic beverages. The Act prohibits, among other things, statements about the alcohol content of beer and other malt beverages on container labels or in product advertising. Coors Brewing Company sought approval of proposed labels and advertising that included alcohol content statements for its beer. The applications were denied by the Bureau of Alcohol, Tobacco, and Firearms, the federal agency that administers the Act. The regulation covering advertising was upheld, and Coors did not appeal. The labeling regulation, however, was struck down by a federal district court, a decision affirmed by the Supreme Court in *Rubin v. Coors Brewing Co.*, 514 U.S. 476 (1995). Both the government and Coors agreed that the labels bore only "truthful, verifiable, and nonmisleading factual information," thus the Court's inquiry focused on the two asserted governmental interests for the beer label regulation. The government claimed that the label restriction "facilitated" efforts to effectively regulate alcohol, but the Court was unpersuaded that the government's interest in facilitating state regulatory initiatives was substantial enough. The second interest advanced by the government was to curb "strength wars"—that is, to deter competition for customers on the basis of the alcohol content of beer. The Court agreed that deterring strength wars was a substantial interest. Justice Thomas turned to the closeness of "fit" between the government's objective in deterring strength wars and the means chosen to achieve that end. The government, he said, carries the burden of showing that the label ban advances the government's interest in a "direct and material way," and that burden is not met by "mere speculation and conjecture." The Court concluded that the label regulation could not directly and materially advance the government's asserted interest because of the "overall irrationality of [its] regulatory scheme." Although the federal label restriction prohibited disclosure of alcohol content on labels unless required by state law, federal law applied a contrary policy to advertising. The federal restriction on statements about alcohol content in advertising applied only in states that prohibited such statements. Because only

18 states had such advertising limitations, brewers remained "free to disclose alcohol content in advertisements, but not on labels, in much of the country." Thomas suggested that advertising seemed to be a "more influential weapon" in strength wars than labels, thus the failure to prohibit disclosure of alcohol content in advertising made "no rational sense" if the true governmental objective was suppression of strength wars. Thomas also noted that brewers were able to "signal" higher alcohol content through use of terms such as "malt liquor." One would think, he continued, that if the government sought to suppress strength wars by prohibiting use of numbers reflecting alcohol content, it would also preclude brewers from "indicating higher alcohol beverages by using descriptive terms." Although the government's interest in combating strengths wars "remains a valid goal," Thomas continued, the "irrationality of this unique and puzzling regulatory framework ensures that the labeling ban will fail to achieve that end."

The state of Rhode Island prohibited the advertising of liquor prices as part of a more comprehensive set of regulations applying to alcoholic beverages. All media within the state were prohibited from carrying any such advertising, and all retail liquor outlets were prohibited from posting advertising visible from outside their premises. These restrictions applied to all such price advertising, including ads that were truthful and did not mislead. Two retail liquor outlets successfully sought to enjoin enforcement of the price advertising regulation. The Supreme Court struck down the ban in *44 Liquormart, Inc. v. Rhode Island*, 517 U.S. 484 (1996). Although several opinions were issued, there was consensus on that part of the ruling stemming from the Twenty-First Amendment, which repealed Prohibition, and delegated to the states the authority to regulate alcohol, including its transport. Justice Stevens said that the amendment "does not qualify" the prohibition against laws abridging free speech; it does not "license the States to ignore their obligations under other constitutional provisions." There was less consensus on the commercial speech aspects of the case. Stevens attempted to differentiate between commercial messages. Regulation of commercial messages undertaken to protect consumers from misleading or untruthful sales practices "justifies less than strict review." On the other hand, when a state imposes a categorical ban on truthful, nonmisleading commercial messages for purposes unrelated to the preservation of a fair bargaining process, there is "far less reason to depart from the rigorous review that the First Amendment generally demands." There are, Stevens noted, "special dangers that attend complete bans on truthful, nonmisleading commercial speech" that cannot be explained away by reference to "commonsense" differences between commercial and noncommercial speech. Bans that target truthful and nonmisleading commercial messages rarely protect consumers from "commercial harms." Rather, they often serve only to "obscure an 'underlying governmental policy' that could be implemented without regulating speech." Indeed, bans against truthful, nonmisleading commercial speech usually are based on the "offensive assumption that the public will respond irrationally to the truth." The First Amendment, Stevens concluded, requires the Court to be especially skeptical of restrictions that seek to "keep people in the dark for what government perceives to be their own good." That skepticism "applies equally" to attempts to "deprive consumers of accurate information about their chosen products." This decision suggests that proposed regulation of cigarette advertising will face stringent examination by the Court. Justice Thomas categorically rejected that the government can keep "legal users of a product or service ignorant in order to manipulate their choices in the marketplace." Because the proposed restrictions on cigarette advertising are aimed at advertising to minors—that is, to nonlegal users of cigarettes—it might be possible for the Court to uphold the restrictions notwithstanding the ruling in *44 Liquormart.*

The Discovery Network is a private company that broadcasts educational and social programs. In addition, it publishes a magazine promoting its programming, but also containing information about current events. The magazines were distributed from freestanding newsracks, 62 of which were located by permit on public property in Cincinnati, Ohio. In March 1990 the city revoked the Discovery Network's permit to place newsracks on public property. The revocation notice said the magazines were "commercial handbills" within the meaning of a city ordinance that prohibited the distribution of that class of material on public property. The Supreme Court ruled against the prohibition in *Cincinnati v. Discovery Network, Inc.,* 507 U.S. 410 (1993). The Court concluded that Cincinnati had not "carefully calculated the costs and benefits associated with the burden on speech associated with the prohibition." Justice Stevens focused on the city's contention that the restriction could be justified because commercial speech, as distinct from noncommercial speech such as the reporting of news, "has only a low value." In his view, the argument "seriously underestimates the value of commercial speech," and provides insufficient justification for the "selective and categorical ban on news racks dispensing commercial handbills." Even though the city had not acted with animus toward the content of the Discovery Network's publication, whether a newsrack was subject to the regulation was determined by the "commercial" content of the magazines in any newsrack. Cincinnati did not regulate newsracks generally. Rather, it sought only to eliminate newsracks containing commercial publications. The Court found no

justification for such a prohibition other than the city's "naked assertion that commercial speech has low value." The absence of a neutral
justification for the "selective ban" on newsracks precluded
Cincinnati from "defending its newsrack policy as content-neutral."

Broadcast and Cable Regulation

***Turner Broadcasting System, Inc. v. Federal Communications Commission
(FCC) (Turner II), 520 U.S. 180 (1997)*** The Cable Television
Consumer Protection Act of 1992 included "must carry" provisions
that required cable television operators to carry programming of
certain local and public broadcast stations. This requirement was
immediately challenged. The Court ruled in *Turner Broadcasting
System, Inc v. FCC,* 512 U.S. 622 (1994) *(Turner I),* that review of the
FCC's "must carry" regulations should be conducted at the intermediate scrutiny level. Applying that standard, the Court placed the
burden on the FCC of demonstrating that the requirement advanced
important governmental interests in the least restrictive way. The
Court then remanded the case for further consideration of whether
the "must carry" requirement actually met this test. On remand, a
three-judge district court upheld the provisions by a two-to-one vote.
The cable industry pursued direct appeal to the Supreme Court in
Turner II, but was unsuccessful in persuading the High Court that the
regulation was unconstitutional. Three interrelated interests were
identified in *Turner I* as being served by the "must carry" requirements: (1) preservation of local broadcast television carried over the
air; (2) promotion of multiple-source information dissemination;
and (3) promotion of fair market competition for television
programming. The Court reaffirmed in *Turner II* that each constituted an important government interest. Congress was reasonably
concerned that without the "must carry" regulations, significant
numbers of broadcast stations would be refused carriage on cable
systems, and that those stations not carried on cable would "deterio-
rate to a substantial degree or fail altogether." Further, Congress was
concerned that without regulatory action, there would be a reduced
number of "media voices available to consumers." Employing an
approach that extended deference to legislative judgments, the
Court concluded that Congress had a substantial basis for believing
that a "real threat" to the broadcast industry justified enactment of
the "must carry" provisions. Among the evidence supporting the
congressional conclusions were: (1) the "considerable and growing
market power" that cable operators had over local programming
markets; (2) the local "monopoly" that cable operators possess over
cable households; (3) the increasing capacity and inclination of
cable operators to reposition local broadcast stations to less-viewed

channels or drop those stations from their systems altogether; and (4) the growing number of stations that had lost operating revenue as a result of "adverse carriage decisions" of the cable systems. Taken together, the Court was satisfied that Congress had sufficient basis to conclude that local broadcast stations were "endangered" in the absence of regulation, and that the "must carry" approach served the government's interests in a "direct and effective way." Finally, the Court examined the "fit" between the asserted interests and the means chosen to advance them. The "must carry" regulations potentially interfered with protected speech in two ways: restraint of editorial discretion of those operating cable systems, and the greater difficulty cable operators might have in competing for programming on the channels remaining available to them after meeting the "must carry" requirements. The Court concluded that the "must-carry" requirement was "narrowly tailored to preserve a multiplicity of broadcast stations for the 40 percent of American households without cable." Justice O'Connor dissented on behalf of Justices Scalia, Thomas, and Ginsburg. They disputed the strength of the evidence used to support the "must carry" regulation. Specifically, they disputed that the broadcast industry was "at risk" without government intervention of this kind. They concluded instead that only the most "marginal" of stations would not be carried by cable systems without the "must carry" requirement. They also saw the growth of such technology as direct-broadcast satellite television as diminishing the argument that cable operators possess something approaching monopolistic strength. *See also* FIRST AMENDMENT, p. 29; FREE SPEECH CLAUSE, p. 654.

Significance   Regulation of the cable industry was preceded by extensive regulation of the broadcast medium. In *Red Lion Broadcasting Co. v. FCC*, 395 U.S. 367 (1969), for example, the Court upheld a Federal Communications Commission regulation known as the fairness doctrine. Red Lion broadcast a particular program during which the honesty and character of a third party were impugned. The third party demanded free time for a response, but was refused. The FCC then held that Red Lion had failed to satisfy a requirement of equity and equal access. The Supreme Court unanimously upheld the constitutionality of the FCC position. The Court acknowledged that broadcasting is clearly a medium affected by First Amendment interests, but it emphasized some critical differences from the print medium. Among these are the limited number of channels available and the incomparably greater reach of the radio signal. Scarcity of access means Congress "unquestionably has the power to grant and deny licenses," a power vested by Congress in the Federal Communications Commission. The license permits broadcasting, but the licensee "has no constitutional right to be the one who holds the license or to monopolize a radio frequency to the exclusion of his fellow citizens." The Court said the First Amendment does not prevent the government from requiring a licensee to share a frequency with others and to "conduct himself as a proxy" with obligations to present views that are representative of his or her community and that would otherwise be barred from the airwaves. Government has an obligation to preserve access for divergent views because of the unique character of the broadcast medium. Justice White said the people retain their interest in free speech through broadcast and have a collective right to the medium functioning consistently with the ends and purposes of the First Amendment. It is the "right of the viewers and listeners, not the right of broadcasters, which is paramount." Without regulations such as the fairness doctrine, station owners and a few networks would have "unfettered power to make time available only to the highest bidders, to communicate only their own views on public issues, people and candidates, and to permit on the air only those with whom they agreed." The Court concluded that there is no sanctuary in the First Amendment for unlimited private censorship operating in a medium not open to all. The thrust of *Red Lion* is that a balance must be struck between the First Amendment interests of the broadcast medium and the need to regulate governmentally granted channel monopolies. The fairness doctrine at issue in *Red Lion* had not kept the station from expressing its own views. It had only required that reply time be provided when a station carries a broadcast that attacks an individual personally.

The print media may not be required to do the same thing, however. In *Miami Herald Publishing Co. v. Tornillo*, 418 U.S. 241 (1974), the Court struck down a Florida right-to-reply statute that required reply space in a newspaper for any political candidate who was attacked. Such required space was found to be a constitutionally impermissible prior restraint. Such a law authorizes governmental "intrusion into the function of editors in choosing what material goes into a newspaper."

Similarly, the Court typically has held that the airwaves need not become a common carrier with access guaranteed to any private citizen or group. *Columbia Broadcasting System, Inc. v. Democratic National Committee*, 412 U.S. 94 (1973), determined that a broadcaster policy of refusing to sell editorial advertisements was an acceptable practice and not incompatible with the fairness doctrine, but upheld a right of reasonable access for candidates for federal office in *Columbia Broadcasting System, Inc. v. Federal Communications Commission*, 449 U.S. 950 (1980).

The power of Congress to prohibit editorials on stations receiving funds from the Corporation for Public Broadcasting was disallowed in *FCC v. League of Women Voters,* 468 U.S. 364 (1984). Congressionally imposed editorial restrictions affect "precisely that form of speech the Framers were most anxious to protect." Content-defined discussion of public issues is the purest example of discourse that must be allowed to proceed unfettered.

A 1988 amendment to the Federal Communications Act made it a crime to use a telephone to send an "indecent" as well as an "obscene" message for commercial purposes. Although the objective of earlier regulations had been to protect minors from such communications, the 1988 amendment banned "obscene and indecent" communications to any recipient. Challenge to the amendment was considered by the Supreme Court in *Sable Communications of California, Inc. v. FCC,* 492 U.S. 115 (1989). The Court ruled for Sable Communications with respect to the regulation of "indecent" messages, but upheld the authority of Congress to impose a total ban on "obscene" messages. It had been argued by Sable Communications that the law created a "national standard of obscenity" in a manner incompatible with *Miller v. California,* 413 U.S. 15 (1973). Although *Miller* allowed localities to enforce their own "communities' standards," it did not preclude Congress from prohibiting "communications that are obscene in some communities under local standards even though they are not obscene in others." The sender, while obligated to comply with the ban, said the Court, is free to "tailor its messages, on a selective basis, to the communities it chooses to serve." The Court was unanimous in striking down the regulation of "indecent" content as an overly broad restriction. The amendment was designed to protect minors from the messages, an interest the Court acknowledged to be "compelling." The ban, however, denied adult access to messages that are "indecent but not obscene," a policy that "far exceeds that which is necessary to limit the access of minors to such messages." The Court distinguished regulation of "indecent" radio broadcasts from the "dial-it medium" because the latter requires the listener to take "affirmative steps to receive the communications." The government's contention that only a total ban could protect against access by minors was, accordingly, seen as "unpersuasive" by the Court.

Among other things, the Cable Television Consumer Protection and Competition Act of 1992 required (in Sections 4 and 5) that most cable systems use a third of their cable capacity to retransmit local broadcast channels. These provisions are referred to as the "must carry" rules. The cable industry argued that the Act prevented it from carrying the content it wished, and thus violated the First Amendment. Broadcasters, on the other hand, contended that cable systems are essentially local monopolies, and as such, are subject to regulations designed to protect broadcasters from unfair competition. Passage of the Act brought immediate challenge from Turner Broadcasting System and a number of cable programmers. The Supreme Court held in *Turner Broadcasting System, Inc. v. FCC,* 512 U.S 622 (1994), that the First Amendment does not broadly insulate the cable industry from federal regulations, and that the "must carry" provisions are content neutral. Justice Kennedy said that the "must carry" provisions must be evaluated using a heightened or intermediate level of First Amendment scrutiny. Cable technology has virtually none of the characteristics of broadcast, such as a finite number of frequencies, that provide the rationale for extensive regulation of broadcasters. At the same time, the Court found the "must carry" provisions justified by the "special characteristics of the cable medium: the bottleneck monopoly power" exercised by cable operators and the "danger this power poses to the viability of broadcast television." Cable's position as a "bottleneck" was controlling in the Court's thinking. By virtue of its "ownership of the essential pathway for cable speech," said Kennedy, a cable operator can "prevent its subscribers from obtaining programming it chooses to exclude." The "potential for abuse," he continued, of this private power "over a central avenue of communication cannot be overlooked." The First Amendment prohibits governmental interference with free speech, but it does not "disable the Government from taking steps to insure that private interests not restrict, through physical control of a critical pathway of communication, the free flow of information and ideas." The Court also rejected the contention of the cable industry that the "must carry" regulations were not content neutral, and as a result, required compelling justification by the government. The "overriding objective" of Congress in enacting the "must carry" requirement was "not to favor programming of a particular subject matter, viewpoint or format," but rather, said Kennedy, to "preserve access to free television programming" for those Americans without cable service. The case was remanded to the three-judge court to enable further fact finding on the government's contention that without the "must carry" requirements, cable systems would bring about the failure of broadcast stations. The Court reviewed the findings of the three-judge court in *Turner II.* Justice O'Connor offered a dissent that was joined by Justices Scalia, Thomas, and Ginsburg. It was their view that the "must carry" provisions were an unconstitutional restraint on the cable operators' "editorial discretion as well as on the cable programmers' speech." The dissenters also concluded the regulation was based on content. No matter how praiseworthy the objective of maintaining access and diverse sources of information, said O'Connor, the regulation here is "directly tied to the content of what speakers are likely to say." In their view, no governmental interest could justify that kind of interference with free speech.

Internet Regulation

Reno v. American Civil Liberties Union (ACLU), **521 U.S. 844 (1997)**
The Congress sought to protect minors from objectionable content available on the Internet by enacting the Communications Decency Act of 1996 (CDA). Among other provisions, the Act prohibited the knowing transmission of "indecent communications" to minors. More generally, the Act prohibited the transmission or display of obscene material. This case presented two questions for the Supreme Court. The first focused on the manner in which the government might protect minors from indecent communications—that is, how were adults and minors to be effectively separated? The Act suggested that Internet users who made a "good faith" effort to prevent access by minors would not violate the Act. Access is most commonly restricted through such devices as access codes or identification numbers. The issue was whether the Act was narrowly tailored enough to pass First Amendment scrutiny. The second issue was whether such terms as "indecency" and "patently offensive" were defined clearly enough in the Act. Upon passage of the Act, actions were filed in federal district court to prevent implementation of the law. One suit was commenced by a wide range of groups including the American Civil Liberties Union, groups of online users, service providers, and nonprofit organizations. A second suit was filed by such groups as the American Library Association, American Booksellers Association, and a number of major Internet access providers such as America Online and Microsoft. These two cases were consolidated as *Reno v. ACLU*. A three-judge district court found the Act unconstitutional on its face because the language of the statute was vague, and because age verification is too expensive and technologically unfeasible. The Supreme Court agreed. The Court's focus was on the terms "indecent" and "patently offensive." Notwithstanding the "legitimacy and importance" of protecting minors from harmful materials, the Court concluded that the terms were sufficiently vague and ambiguous to render the CDA "problematic" for First Amendment purposes. Justice Stevens suggested that the vagueness of the CDA was of "special concern" for two reasons. First, the Act is "content-based regulation of speech." The vagueness of such a regulation has an "obvious chilling effect on free speech." Secondly, the CDA is a criminal statute. The "severity of criminal sanctions may well cause speakers to remain silent rather than communicate even arguably unlawful words, ideas, and images." The objective of denying access of minors to potentially harmful material "effectively suppresses a large amount of speech that adults have a constitutional right to receive and address to one another." This burden on adult expression is unacceptable if "less restrictive alternatives would be at least as effective in achieving the legitimate

purpose the statute was enacted to serve." The government had argued that adult communication was not diminished, but the Court found the claim to be based on the "incorrect factual premise" that prohibiting transmissions when one of the recipients is a minor would not interfere with communication among adults. Justice O'Connor wrote a separate concurring opinion and suggested that the attempt to create "adult zones" on the Internet was different from those created for sexual content found in the "physical world." She saw the physical world as having two characteristics that make it possible to create "adult zones"—geography and identity. A minor needs to actually enter establishments to obtain adult material, and if such an attempt is made, the minor will be unable to "conceal completely his identity (or, consequently, his age)." The electronic world, by contrast, is "fundamentally different." It allows both speakers and listeners to conceal their identities. Until effective "gateway technology" is available, the only way for a speaker to avoid liability under the CDA is to "refrain completely from using indecent speech." When a minor enters an Internet chat room otherwise occupied by adults, the CDA "effectively requires the adults in the room to stop using indecent speech." *See also* FIRST AMENDMENT, p. 29; FREE SPEECH CLAUSE, p. 654; *Turner Broadcasting v. FCC II*, p. 128.

Significance   The Cable Communications Policy Act of 1984 prohibited cable television operators from interfering with programming on channels leased to commercial programmers or channels designated for public, educational, or governmental programming. Congress became concerned with the levels of sexually explicit programming permitted under the 1984 Act and sought to enable cable operators to restrict access to such programming. Section 10 of the Cable Television Consumer Protection and Competition Act of 1992 required certain cable operators either to ban "indecent programming" or to block access except to adult subscribers who requested that channels be unblocked. The Federal Communications Commission (FCC) was charged with implementing Section 10 of the Act and issued regulations that enabled a cable system operator to ban any programming the operator determined to be indecent. Cable programmers, including the Denver Area Educational Telecommunications Consortium, challenged the FCC regulations on free speech grounds. In a fragmented ruling, the Supreme Court upheld parts of the Act, but struck down others in *Denver Area Educational Telecommunications Consortium, Inc. v. FCC*, 518 U.S. 727 (1996). The Court upheld the provision permitting cable operators to ban "patently offensive" material from leased channels, but struck down the provision enabling cable operators to impose similar bans on the public access channels. The Court also struck down the requirement that cable operators segregate and block offensive content. The permission to ban offensive material from leased channels was upheld for two reasons—a "compelling" need to protect children from sexual material, and a "balance[d] flexibility" of implementation. Broadcasting is "uniquely accessible" to children, said Justice Breyer, and he called the child protection justification for the regulation "extremely important." In addition, the provision is permissive in character, which creates a flexibility that gives cable operators options short of banning programs altogether, such as rescheduling broadcast times to minimize the risk of reaching a young audience. The existence of this "complex balance of interests" persuaded the Court that the permissive nature of the provision, "coupled with its viewpoint neutral application," is a constitutional way to "protect children from the kind of sexual material that concerned Congress while also accommodating First Amendment interests." The Court struck down the language permitting cable operators to restrict programming on public access channels, concluding that there was a history of neither indecent programming on these channels nor a record of cable operator interference with public access channel programming. Allowing cable operators the same authority with respect to public access channels would "greatly increase the risk that certain categories of programming will not appear." Finally, the separation and blocking provisions were found unconstitutional. Although protecting children remained a "compelling interest," the Court did not find that speech restrictions "properly accommodate[d] ... the legitimate objective they seek to attain." The delays encountered by a subscriber in unscrambling segregated channels would be substantial (up to 30 days) and would prevent viewers who select programs on a day-by-day basis from viewing programming on those channels. Given the availability of less-intrusive alternatives, it was the Court's conclusion that this provision was not "narrowly or reasonably tailored ... to protect children."

Obscenity Regulation

Roth v. United States, **354 U.S. 476 (1957),** established definitional standards for obscenity. *Roth* and its companion case, *Alberts v. California*, addressed the issue of whether "obscenity is utterance within the area of protected speech and press." Roth had been convicted of violating the federal obscenity statute by using the mail to distribute "obscene, lewd, lascivious, filthy, or indecent" material. The Supreme Court upheld both convictions. The Court indicated that the First Amendment was not intended to protect every utterance. Obscenity is not protected because it is "utterly without redeeming social importance." If obscenity falls outside the reach of the First Amendment, it is imperative to develop a precise definition of obscenity that permits distinguishing between protected and unprotected speech. Key to the identification of obscenity is its appeal to prurient interests. Treatment of sex per se "is not itself sufficient reason to deny material the constitutional protection of speech and press." Justice Brennan sought to establish a standard sufficiently proscribed as not to encroach on material legitimately treating sex. The standard chosen was "whether to the average person, applying contemporary community standards, the dominant theme of the material taken as a whole appeals to prurient interest." Prurient interest is referred to in *Roth* and subsequent cases as a "shameful, excessive, obsessive," or "unnatural" interest in nudity or sex. Using this standard, the Court concluded that the two statutes under consideration did not offend the First Amendment. Justices Douglas and Black dissented in both cases saying "any test which turns on what is offensive to the community's standards is too loose, too capricious, too destructive of freedom of expression to be squared with the First Amendment." Justice Harlan concurred in *Alberts*, but dissented in *Roth*, saying the "federal interest in dealing with pornography is attenuated," and ought to be left to the states. *See also* FIRST AMENDMENT, p. 29; FREE PRESS CLAUSE, p. 653; *Miller v. California*, p. 137; OBSCENITY, p. 682.

Significance   *Roth* clearly established that obscenity is not protected speech and upheld a federal attempt to regulate obscenity. The more troublesome issue was differentiating protected speech from unprotected obscenity. The leading definition prior to *Roth* had come from an English case, *Queen v. Hicklin*, 3 Q.B. 360 (1868). The *Hicklin* test allowed "material to be judged merely by the effect of an isolated excerpt upon particularly susceptible persons." Although *Roth* represented progress from the highly restrictive *Hicklin* standard, many questions remained. As the Warren Court struggled with these questions, it lost consensus on standards, and its definition became even less restrictive. In *Jacobellis v. Ohio*, 378 U.S. 184 (1964), for example, the Court essentially held that material need be pornographic in order to be restricted, but no more than two justices could agree on a rationale for the policy. *A Book Named "John Cleland's Memoirs of a Woman of Pleasure" v. Attorney General of Massachusetts*, 383 U.S. 413 (1966), was the most permissive of the Warren Court pronouncements on obscenity. It held that the three previously established obscenity criteria—prurient interest, social value, and patent offensiveness—were separate and independent. This was especially important for the social value criterion. If any redeeming social value could be detected, material could not be adjudged obscene, despite its appeal to prurient interest and its patently offensive character. Although the

Court was badly divided in *Memoirs*, it could be inferred from the case that only hard-core pornography remained as an unprotected class of material. *Memoirs* also marked the Warren Court's last real effort to grapple with definitional standards for obscenity.

In *Redrup v. New York*, 386 U.S. 767 (1967), the Court declared it would uphold obscenity statutes only to prohibit distribution of obscene materials to juveniles or in cases in which such materials were obtrusively thrust upon an unwilling audience. *Redrup* allowed the Court to by-pass its stalemate on standards and handle the obscenity matter pragmatically. Earlier the Court had upheld a state prohibition on sale of indecent material to minors in *Ginsberg v. New York*, 390 U.S. 629 (1968), and later it upheld federal prosecution of firms sending a second mailing to persons in *Rowan v. Post Office*, 397 U.S. 728 (1970). The only case producing a more restrictive outcome was *Ginzburg v. United States*, 383 U.S. 463 (1966). The Court upheld Ginzburg's conviction because he commercially exploited the sexual content of the materials he offered for sale. He engaged in pandering, purviewing material that appeals to the prurient interest of prospective customers. Ginzburg's materials were viewed "against a background of commercial exploitation of erotica solely for the sake of their prurient appeal." In situations in which the "purveyor's sole emphasis is on the sexually provocative aspects of his publications, that fact may be decisive in the determination of obscenity." *Ginzburg* modified *Roth* in that materials may pass the initial *Roth* test and yet still be found obscene. Although the materials themselves may not be obscene, they can become illicit merchandise through the "sordid business of pandering."

Miller v. California, 413 U.S. 15 (1973), tightened definitional standards for obscenity. In *Miller* the Burger Court redesigned Warren Court obscenity criteria. Miller had been convicted of distributing obscene material through the mail. A five-justice majority upheld Miller's conviction and offered a modification of the test developed in *Roth v. United States*, 354 U.S. 476 (1957). The Burger Court found no fault with *Roth* as such, but subsequent Warren Court decisions had "veered sharply away from the *Roth* concept." The Burger Court felt a need to return to *Roth*. Although many Warren Court rulings prompted this view, the most distressing decision to the Burger Court's view was *A Book Named "John Cleland's Memoirs of a Woman of Pleasure" v. Attorney General of Massachusetts*, 383 U.S. 413 (1966), which was also known as the *Fanny Hill* case. This decision had "drastically altered" the *Roth* standards. Under *Fanny Hill*, the prosecution had to prove that material was "utterly without redeeming social value—a burden virtually impossible to discharge." In establishing a revised standard, the Burger Court drew heavily from *Roth*. An obscenity statute must be limited to works that, taken as a whole, appeal to a prurient interest in sex or that portray sexual conduct in a patently offensive way. The material, when taken as a whole, must lack "serious literary, artistic, political, or scientific value." The Court specifically rejected the social value test of *Memoirs*. It also proposed some flexibility in applying its guidelines to specific cases. The nation is "simply too big and too diverse" for a uniform standard of prurient interest or patently offensive sexual conduct. The Court viewed it as unrealistic to base proceedings around an abstract formulation. To require a state to try a case around evidence of a national community standard would be an exercise in futility. The Court asserted that people in different states vary in their tastes and attitudes, and "this diversity is not to be strangled by the absolutism of imposed uniformity." State obscenity trials can therefore base evaluation of materials on the contemporary community standards of the particular state. Justices Brennan, Douglas, Marshall, and Stewart dissented. They argued that obscenity regulations ought to be confined to the distribution of obscene materials to juveniles and unwilling audiences. In his dissent in *Paris Adult Theater I v. Slaton*, 413 U.S. 49 (1973), a companion case to *Miller*, Justice Brennan also warned of another expression problem. He said, "The State's interest in regulating morality by suppressing obscenity, while often asserted, remains essentially unfocused and ill-defined." When attempts are made to curtail unprotected speech, protected speech is necessarily involved as well. Thus the effort to serve this speculative interest through regulation of obscene matter "must tread heavily on the rights protected by the First Amendment." *See also* FIRST AMENDMENT, p. 29; FREE PRESS CLAUSE, p. 653; *Roth v. United States*, p. 135.

Significance   *Miller* represented the first consensus statement on obscenity standards since *Roth* in 1957. *Miller* is significant because the Court's rejection of national community standards prompted highly diverse outcomes relative to obscenity regulations. It also removed the social value criterion as an insurmountable obstacle to prosecution. *Miller* provided examples of the kinds of materials that may be offensive enough to be regulated, but a lack of doctrinal clarity remained. Just a year after *Miller*, the Court unanimously reversed an obscenity conviction in *Jenkins v. Georgia*, 418 U.S. 153 (1974), overturning a local judgment that the film *Carnal Knowledge* was obscene. The Court cautioned that local juries and their application of community standards are not free from First Amendment limitations. *Miller* prompted more stringent regulatory initiatives, and these regulations have generally been supported by the Court. In *New York v. Ferber*, 458 U.S. 747 (1982), for example, the Court unanimously upheld a statute prohibiting "persons from knowingly promoting a sexual performance by a child under the age of 16." Speaking for a unanimous Court, Justice White offered several reasons that states are "entitled to greater leeway in the regulation of pornographic depictions of children." First, it was evident to the Court "beyond the need for elaboration" that a state's interest in safeguarding the "physical and psychological well-being" of children is compelling. Second, the distribution of photographs and films depicting sexual activities by minors is "intrinsically related to the sexual abuse of children" because they are a "permanent record" of the child's participation and the distribution network for child pornography must be closed if the production of such material, "which requires the sexual exploitation of children is to be effectively controlled." Third, advertising and selling of child pornography provide an "economic motive for and are thus an integral part of the production of such materials." Finally, the artistic value of photographic reproductions of children engaged in "lewd sexual conduct is exceedingly modest, if not *de minimis.*"

The most noteworthy modification of *Stanley* came in *Paris Adult Theater I v. Staton*, 413 U.S. 49 (1973), a companion to *Miller. Paris* held that obscene films do not "acquire constitutional immunity from state regulation simply because they are exhibited for consenting adults only." The Court recognized the "legitimate state interests at stake in stemming the tide of commercialized obscenity." It is an interest that includes protecting "the quality of life and the total community environment."

In *Brockett v. Spokane Arcades, Inc.*, 472 U.S. 491 (1985), however, the Court held that a state obscenity law could not ban "lustful" material. Just because sexual response is aroused, expression may not therefore be automatically regulated. The Court said that material that does no more than "arouse 'good, old fashioned, healthy' interest in sex" is constitutionally protected.

The Protection of Children Against Sexual Exploitation Act of 1977 prohibits "knowingly" transporting, receiving, distributing, or reproducing any materials that depict minors engaged in sexually explicit acts. The issue in *United States v. X-Citement Video, Inc.*, 513 U.S. 64 (1994), was whether the knowledge requirement meant that prosecutors must demonstrate that the defendant was aware that performers were actually minors. A number of the videotapes sold by Rubin Gottesman, the owner of X-Citement Video, Inc., featured a performer who was not yet 18 at the time the videos were produced. The U.S. Court of Appeals for the Ninth Circuit ruled that the Act was unconstitutional because it did not clearly require proof that the defendant had knowledge that any of the performers was a minor. The Supreme Court concluded that the Act was properly read as containing a knowledge requirement on the element of performer age. Chief Justice Rehnquist suggested that a statute should be interpreted "where fairly possible" so as to avoid substantial constitutional questions, and that some form of *scienter* (knowledge) is to be implied in a criminal statute even if not expressed. The prosecution is required to demonstrate that the accused had knowledge of each of the essential components of any other crime. From this perspective, the Court concluded that knowledge of the age of performers was implicit in the federal child pornography law. The critical element in separating wrongful conduct from lawful or protected conduct is the age of the performers. Knowledge that at least one performer in sexually explicit material is under age thus must be seen as an essential component for the offenses of transporting and distributing child pornography because neither transporting nor distributing sexually explicit material involving only adult performers is criminal. Justices Scalia and Thomas strongly objected to the Court writing in a knowledge requirement that Congress had failed to provide.

The federal government, through the National Endowment for the Arts (NEA), supports "individuals of exceptional talent engaged in or concerned with the arts" with grants-in-aid. The chairperson of the NEA, in consultation with the National Council on the Arts (NCA) and other advisory panels, approves and disapproves grant applications. The controversial character of artists awarded NEA grants prompted Congress to pass legislation in 1990 barring the funding of art that does not meet the legal standards for obscenity. Congress also directed the NEA chairperson to consider "general standards of decency and respect for the diverse beliefs and values of the American public" in reviewing grant applications. A number of grant applicants, including Karen Finley, applied for NEA grants. The applications were supported by both the NCA and an advisory panel, but in June 1990 the NEA chair John Frohnmeyer decided not to fund these applicants. Although many of these applicants submitted successful proposals subsequently, they filed suit in federal courts challenging the rejection of the earlier proposals and the decency provision. A federal district court struck down the "decency and respect" provisions on vagueness grounds. A settlement was then reached between the new Clinton administration and the applicants. At the same time, however, the Department of Justice unsuccessfully appealed. The U.S. Supreme Court upheld the "decency and respect for diverse values" provisions in *National Endowment for the Arts v. Finley*, 118 S.Ct. 2168 (1998). Justice O'Connor indicated that Finley had to demonstrate a "substantial risk" that application of the "decency and respect" provisions will "lead to the suppression of speech." Finley argued that the provision is a "paradigmatic example of viewpoint discrimination" because it rejects artistic speech that either "fails to respect mainstream values or offends standards of decency." The NEA disputed the contention and characterized the provisions as "merely hortatory." The NEA argued that it did not implement the provision in a way that discriminated against particular viewpoints—that the provision "stops well short of an absolute restriction." The Court found it "clear" that the language of the decency provision "imposes no categorical requirement." The advisory language of the statute "stands in sharp contrast to congressional efforts to prohibit the funding of certain classes of speech." In addition, the Court found the political context existing at the time the "decency and respect" language was adopted was "inconsistent with [Finley's] assertion that the provision compels the NEA to deny funding on the basis of viewpoint discriminatory criteria." The language of the law merely admonished the NEA to "take 'decency and respect' into consideration." This "undercut" the argument that the provision "inevitably will be utilized as a tool for invidious viewpoint discrimination." The Court did not perceive a "realistic danger" that the provision would compromise First Amendment values. In other words, the Court concluded that the "decency and respect" criteria would not, in practice, "effectively preclude or punish" the expression of particular views. O'Connor suggested that any "content-based considerations" that may be evaluated in the grant-making process "are a consequence of the nature of arts funding." It would be impossible, she said, "to have a highly selective grant program without denying money to a large amount of constitutionally protected expression." O'Connor suggested that although the First Amendment applies in the subsidy context, the government may "allocate competitive funding according to criteria that would be impermissible were direct regulation of speech or a criminal penalty at stake." As long as legislation does not infringe on any other protected rights, Congress has "wide latitude to set spending priorities." Finally, the Court rejected the contention that the "decency and respect" language was unconstitutionally vague. Although the language was "undeniably opaque," and could raise vagueness concerns if it appeared in a criminal statute or regulatory scheme, the Court found it unlikely that speakers "will be compelled to steer too far clearly of any forbidden area in the context of grants of this nature." When government is acting as "patron rather than as sovereign, the consequences of imprecision are not constitutionally severe." Justices Scalia and Thomas said the "decency and respect" language "unquestionably constitutes viewpoint discrimination," but viewed such discrimination as permissible in the selective funding of arts projects. Justice Souter was the lone dissenter finding the provision the "very model of viewpoint discrimination." Unlike Scalia and Thomas, however, Souter found this to be a violation of the First Amendment.

Obscenity and Zoning

Young v. American Mini Theatres, Inc., **427 U.S. 50 (1976)**, upheld zoning ordinances regulating locations of adult theaters. *Young* approved amendments to Detroit zoning ordinances providing that adult theaters be licensed. They could not be located within 1,000 feet of any two other "regulated uses" or within 500 feet of any residential area. The other "regulated uses" included some 10 categories of adult entertainment enterprises. An adult theater was defined as one that presented material characterized by emphasis on "specified sexual activities" or "specified anatomical areas." The Court rejected several lines of challenge in *Young*. First, the Court rejected assertions of vagueness in the ordinance because "any element of vagueness in these ordinances has not affected the respondents." The application of the ordinances to the American Mini Theatres "is plain." As for the licensure requirement, the Court noted that the general zoning laws in Detroit imposed requirements on all motion picture theaters. The Court said: "We have no doubt that the municipality may control the location of theaters as well as the location of other commercial establishments." Establishment of such restrictions in themselves is not prohibited as prior restraint. The "mere fact that the commercial exploitation of material protected by the First Amendment is subject to zoning and other licensing requirements is not sufficient reason for invalidating these ordinances." The Court also considered whether the 1,000-foot restriction constituted an improper content-based classification. The Court said that "even within the area of protected speech, a difference in content may require a different governmental response." Citing the public figure category in libel law and prohibitions on exhibition of obscenity to juveniles and unconsenting adults, the Court held that the First Amendment did not foreclose content distinctions. They "rest squarely on an appraisal of the content of the material otherwise within a constitutionally protected area." Even though the First Amendment does not allow total suppression, the Court held that a state may legitimately use the content of minitheater materials as the basis for placing them in a different classification from other motion pictures. Finally, the Court upheld the regulated-use classification on the basis of the city's interest in preserving the character of its neighborhoods. Detroit has a legitimate interest in attempting to preserve the quality of urban life. It is an interest that "must be accorded high respect," and the city must be allowed "a reasonable opportunity to experiment with solutions to an admittedly serious problem." Justices Brennan, Stewart, Marshall, and Blackmun dissented, basing their opinion on the vagueness and content orientation of the ordinance. *See also* FIRST AMENDMENT, p. 29; FREE PRESS CLAUSE, p. 653; *Miller v. California*, p. 137; OBSCENITY, p. 682.

Significance *Young v. American Mini Theatres, Inc.* represents a new wave of cases raising issues about the local regulation of "adult entertainment." The Court has generally supported local regulation as long as expression is not completely prohibited and as long as a compelling interest can be demonstrated. Meeting these conditions is not always easy, however. In *Erznoznik v. Jacksonville*, 422 U.S. 205 (1975), the Court struck down an ordinance that prohibited the exhibition of films containing nudity, if the screen could be seen from a public street. The Court cited the limited privacy interest of persons on the streets, but it also stressed the overly broad sweep of the ordinance. In *Schad v. Borough of Mt. Ephraim*, 452 U.S. 61 (1981), the Court invalidated a zoning ordinance that banned live entertainment in a borough establishment. Convictions under the ordinance had been secured against an adult bookstore operator for having live nude dancers performing in the establishment. The borough argued that permitting such entertainment would conflict with its plan to create a commercial area catering only to the "immediate needs of residents." The Court considered such justification "patently insufficient." The ordinance prohibited a "wide range of expression that has long been held to be within the protection of the First and Fourteenth Amendments."

Ten years after *Young*, the Court once again reviewed a local attempt to regulate the location of adult theaters in *City of Renton v. Playtime Theatres, Inc.*, 475 U.S. 41 (1986). Using the rationale from *Young*, the Court upheld a municipality's authority to require dispersal of such establishments. Because the municipal ordinance did not bar adult theaters entirely, it was reviewed as a time, place, and manner regulation. Such regulations are acceptable as long as they serve a substantial interest and do not unreasonably limit avenues of communication. Justice Rehnquist said that the First Amendment requires only that a local unit refrain from denying individuals a "reasonable opportunity to open and operate an adult theater within the city." He said the City of Renton easily met that requirement in the ordinance under review.

FW/PBS, Inc. v. City of Dallas, 493 U.S. 215 (1990), reviewed a comprehensive city ordinance regulating "sexually oriented" businesses, including bookstores. Dallas sought to regulate such businesses through a variety of licensing and zoning requirements. All owners of sexually oriented businesses were required to obtain a license from the city as well as pay an annual fee. The ordinance contained civil disability provisions that prohibited people convicted of certain crimes from obtaining a license. Licenses could also be revoked, or not renewed, if the owner (or his or her spouse) was convicted of certain specified offenses. The ordinance defined "adult motels" as establishments renting rooms for periods under 10 hours.

"Adult" motels were a "sexually oriented" business subject to the licensure provisions of the ordinance, and had to be more than 1,000 feet from parks, churches, and residential or business structures. The Court struck down the licensing provision as a prior restraint. Any system of prior restraint, said the Court, carries a "heavy presumption against its constitutional validity" for two reasons. First, such schemes give government "unbridled discretion" that may result in censorship. Second, prior restraint systems seldom impose stringent time limits on the decision maker. The Dallas ordinance not only created the possibility that protected speech could be censored through the licensing requirements, but that the city had "unlimited time within which to issue a license" as well. This created the "risk of indefinitely suppressing permissible speech." The Court found the legislative judgment that short rental periods are likely to "foster prostitution" to be reasonable and unanimously upheld the 10-hour restriction. It was contended that this ordinance provision violated privacy rights by impinging on the right to intimate association. The Court rejected this contention by saying that limiting motel room rentals will not have any "discernable effect on the sorts of traditional personal bonds" referred to in previous right of association cases. Such "personal bonds" that are formed through the use of a motel room for less than 10 hours are not those that have "played a critical role in the culture and traditions of the Nation by cultivating and transmitting shared ideals and beliefs."

The Court rejected in *Barnes v. Glen Theater*, 501 U.S. 560 (1991), the argument that the First Amendment precludes a state from enforcing a public decency law to prohibit nude dancing. The parties had agreed that the nude performances were not obscene. As a result, the five-justice majority used symbolic expression standards to resolve the constitutional question. A regulation can withstand First Amendment scrutiny only if it furthers a substantial governmental interest. That interest must be unrelated to the suppression of expression, may only incidentally affect expression, and is to be only as extensive as is required to further the substantial interest. Chief Justice Rehnquist noted the state's "traditional interest in protecting societal order and morality." This interest was seen as both substantial and not directed at expression. Indecency statutes, said Rehnquist, "reflect moral disapproval of people appearing in the nude among strangers in public places." Although nude dancing is expressive conduct within the "outer perimeters" of the First Amendment, it is only "marginally so." In Rehnquist's view, the state was not attempting to regulate nudity because of any erotic message, but because the nudity was public. It is the public nudity that is the targeted "evil the state seeks to prevent, whether or not it is combined with expressive activity." Justices O'Connor and Kennedy joined Rehnquist's plurality opinion, while Justices Scalia and Souter issued concurring opinions. Scalia saw the indecency law as a general law not specifically directed at expression. As a result, the law was "not subject to First Amendment scrutiny at all." Souter deferred to the state's substantial interest in "combatting the secondary effects of adult entertainment establishments." Justice White issued a dissent joined by Justices Blackmun, Marshall, and Stevens. He saw the regulation as aimed at the message communicated by nude dancing. It is only because such performances "may generate emotions and feelings of eroticism and sensuality among the spectators that the State seeks to regulate such expressive activity." Generating thoughts and emotions is the "essence of communication." The nudity component of nude dancing cannot, said White, "be neatly pigeonholed as conduct independent of any expression component of the dance."

Private Obscenity

Osborne v. Ohio, **495 U.S. 103 (1990),** held that states can outlaw the private possession of pornographic materials featuring minors. Crucial to the decision was the choice of *New York v. Ferber*, 458 U.S. 747 (1982), rather than *Stanley v. Georgia*, 394 U.S. 557 (1969), as the controlling precedent. The law struck down in *Stanley* was intended to prevent "poison[ing] the minds" of those who observed such material. In this case, however, the state did not "rely on a paternalistic interest in Osborne's mind." Rather, Ohio enacted the law in an attempt to "protect the victims of child pornography; it hopes to destroy a market for the exploitive use of children." The Ohio legislature made the judgment that using children as subjects in pornographic materials is "harmful to the physiological, emotional, and mental health of the child." That judgment, said the Court, "easily passes muster" under the First Amendment. Furthermore, it is "surely reasonable" for Ohio to conclude that it will "decrease the production of child pornography if it penalizes those who possess and view the product, thereby decreasing demand." Given the importance of Ohio's interest in protecting the child victims, "we cannot fault Ohio for attempting to stamp out this vice at all levels in the distribution chain." The Court also rejected Osborne's overbreadth contention finding that the state supreme court had interpreted the law in such a way as to sufficiently focus or confine the materials that could be reached under the regulation. Justices Brennan, Marshall, and Stevens felt the Ohio law was overbroad. Brennan said he shared the Court's concerns on the issue, but was dissatisfied with the way the interests were balanced. In his view, the Court was "so disquieted by the possible exploitation of children" in the production of pornographic materials that it was "willing to tolerate the imposition of criminal penalties for simple possession." *See also* FIRST AMENDMENT, p. 29; FREE PRESS CLAUSE, p. 653; OBSCENITY, p. 682; OVERBREADTH DOCTRINE, p. 686.

Significance   *Stanley v. Georgia* held that a state could not prohibit private possession of obscene materials. Stanley was convicted of possessing obscene films. The films were discovered while federal and state agents searched Stanley's home under authority of a warrant issued in connection with an investigation of Stanley's alleged involvement in bookmaking. The Supreme Court unanimously reversed Stanley's conviction. Stanley's First Amendment claim was based on his "right to read or observe what he pleases— the right to satisfy his intellectual and emotional needs in the privacy of his own home and the right to be free from state inquiry into the contents of his library." Georgia's statute was based on the view that there are "certain types of materials that the individual may not read or even possess." The Court was unpersuaded, however, saying that "mere categorization of these films as 'obscene' is insufficient justification for such drastic invasion of personal liberties." Although privacy was a key consideration, the Court stressed the First Amendment aspects of *Stanley*. Justifications for regulation of obscenity "do not reach into the privacy of one's own home." If the First Amendment means anything, it means that a state "has no business telling a man, sitting alone in his own house, what books he may read or what films he may watch." Our whole constitutional heritage "rebels at the thought of giving government the power to control men's minds." Neither may the state justify the prohibition of privately held obscene materials as a means of forestalling antisocial conduct. The state "may no more prohibit mere possession of obscenity on the ground that it may lead to anti-social conduct than it may prohibit possession of chemistry books on the ground they may lead to the manufacture of homemade spirits."

The Burger Court followed *Stanley* by closing off the means of delivering obscene matter. *United States v. Reidel*, 402 U.S. 351 (1971), held that obscene material was unprotected expression and could constitutionally be excluded from the mail. On the same day, in *United States v. Thirty-Seven Photographs*, 402 U.S. 363 (1971), the Court allowed a prohibition on the importation of obscenity from abroad even if it were intended for private use. The following year, in *United States v. Twelve 200-Ft. Reels of Super 8 mm. Film*, 413 U.S. 123 (1973), the Court allowed seizure of materials coming into the country from Mexico. The justices declared that the right privately to possess obscene materials did not afford "a correlative right to acquire, sell, or import such material even for private use only."

Censorship

Kingsley Books, Inc. v. Brown, **354 U.S. 436 (1957),** upheld restrictions on the sale of obscene materials through court order. A section of the New York Code of Criminal Procedure authorized enforcement officials in municipalities to invoke injunctive remedies against the "sale and distribution of written and printed matter found after due trial to be obscene," and to obtain an order for "the seizure, in default of surrender, of the condemned publications." The section entitled the person subject to the injunction to have a trial within one day and a decision within two days of the trial. Certain items found in the Kingsley Books establishment were determined obscene, their further distribution enjoined, and their destruction ordered. Kingsley Books did not challenge New York's authority to prohibit the distribution of obscenity. The appeal focused on the remedial technique that included the power to enjoin during the course of the litigation. Kingsley Books asserted that such use of the injunctive remedy amounted to an unconstitutional prior restraint, but the Supreme Court upheld the method. In approving the approach, the Court compared it to imposing criminal sanctions on booksellers. Rather than requiring the seller "to dread that the offer for sale of a book may without prior warning subject him to criminal prosecution with the hazard of imprisonment," the section of the Code at issue "assures him that such consequences cannot follow unless he ignores a court order specifically directed to him for a prompt and carefully circumscribed determination of the issue of obscenity." The Court concluded that the Code "moves after publication" by enjoining from display or sale "particular booklets theretofore published and adjudged to be obscene." When compared with criminal penalties, the "restraint upon appellants as merchants in obscenity was narrower." The restriction imposed under the Code was altogether different from the injunctive restraint disallowed in *Near v. Minnesota,* 283 U.S. 697 (1931). Unlike *Near,* the New York Code provision "is concerned solely with obscenity," and it "studiously withholds restraints upon matters not already published and not yet found to be offensive." Chief Justice Warren dissented on the ground that the statute "places the book on trial" with no criteria for "judging the book in context." The matter of use should determine obscenity rather than the quality of the art or literature. Justices Douglas and Black found the provision for injunction during litigation excessive in that it gave the state "the paralyzing power of a censor." Justice Brennan's dissent cited the absence of a jury as a fatal defect. *See also* FIRST AMENDMENT, p. 29; FREE PRESS CLAUSE, p. 653; *Near v. Minnesota,* p. 100; OBSCENITY, p. 682; PRIOR RESTRAINT, p. 690.

Significance   *Kingsley Books* held that techniques of censoring written materials, especially books, must contain extensive procedural safeguards. In *Smith v. California*, 361 U.S. 147 (1959), the Court required in addition that a defendant in an obscenity proceeding must be shown to have knowledge of the material's contents. Without such knowledge, the bookseller will "restrict the books he sells to those he inspected," and this will constitute a state-imposed "restriction upon the distribution of constitutionally protected as well as obscene literature." Neither can material be prohibited from distribution until it has been subjected to a formal hearing as in *Kingsley Books*. In *Bantam Books, Inc. v. Sullivan*, 372 U.S. 58 (1963), the Court struck down a statute that established a commission to convey to booksellers the potential for prosecution if objectionable material was sold. The Court felt these informal sanctions were effective censorship wholly lacking in necessary safeguards.

Censorship of films occurred from the time films were first produced, and Supreme Court decisions extended virtually no free press protections for them. As motion pictures evolved, however, their unprotected status changed and censorship techniques such as those in *Freedman v. Maryland*, 380 U.S. 51 (1965), demanded Court attention. A key case in elevating films to partial coverage by the First Amendment was *Joseph Burstyn, Inc. v. Wilson*, 343 U.S. 495 (1952). The Court found that it "cannot be doubted that motion pictures are a significant medium for the communication of ideas." Although films may possess a "greater capacity for evil," such potential "does not authorize substantially unbridled censorship." The Court was asked in *Freedman* to prohibit film censorship altogether. Although it refused to do so, the Court established procedures for the licensing of films that closely parallel the procedures outlined in *Kingsley Books*. Freedman had refused to submit a film to the State Board of Censors prior to showing it. Maryland stipulated that the film would have been licensed had it been submitted. The Court said a prior restraint mechanism bears a "heavy presumption against its constitutional validity." Specifically, the "administration of a censorship proceeding puts the initial burden on the exhibitor or distributor." The justices went on to outline procedural safeguards "designed to obviate the dangers of the censorship system." First, the "burden of proving that the film is unprotected expression must rest with the censor." Second, although advance submissions may be required, no film may be banned through means "which would lend an effect of finality to the censor's determination." Third, a film cannot be banned unless the process permits judicial determination of the restraint. Fourth, various steps in the process must not take too long. "The exhibitor must be assured that the censor will within a specified brief period, either issue a license or go to court to restrain the showing of the film." Any restraints imposed prior to final judicial determination must be "limited to preservation of the status quo for the shortest fixed period." In *Roaden v. Kentucky*, 413 U.S. 496 (1973), the Court unanimously determined that a warrantless seizure by a county sheriff of a film during its showing was a prior restraint. Similarly, in *Southeastern Promotions, Ltd. v. Conrad*, 419 U.S. 892 (1974), the Court held that a city's refusal to rent a city facility for a performance of *Hair* was a prior restraint. The Court said city officials may deny a forum to an obscene production, but such a decision must be made through a properly safeguarded process. In *Heller v. New York*, 413 U.S. 483 (1973), the Court upheld the seizure of a film under authority of a warrant from a judge who had viewed it prior to signing the warrant. Finally, in *New York v. P.J. Video, Inc.*, 475 U.S. 868 (1986), the Court reviewed a lower court ruling that established a higher probable cause standard for issuing warrants to seize suspect books or films as opposed to other contraband, such as weapons. The Burger Court ruled that the First Amendment required no higher standard. Such warrant applications should be reviewed with the same standards used for warrant applications generally: that there is a fair probability evidence of a crime will be found in the location to be searched.

FREEDOM OF ASSEMBLY AND PROTEST
Public Premises

Adderley v. Florida, **385 U.S. 39 (1966),** held that demonstrators may be barred from assembling on the grounds of a county jail. *Adderley* considered whether certain public locations might be put off-limits to demonstrations or assemblies. Adderley and a number of others were convicted of trespass for gathering at a county jail to protest the arrest of several students the day before, as well as local policies of racial segregation at the jail itself. When the demonstrators would not leave the jail grounds when asked, they were warned of possible arrest for trespass. Adderley and others remained on the premises, were arrested, subsequently tried, and convicted. The Court upheld the convictions. The Court concluded that "nothing in the Constitution of the United States prevented Florida from even-handed enforcement of its general trespass statute against those refusing to obey the sheriff's order to remove themselves from what amounted to the curtilage of the jailhouse." The fact that the jail was a public building did not automatically entitle the protesters to unconditional assembly. The state, no less than a private owner of property, has power to preserve the property under its control for the use to which it is lawfully dedicated. The security purpose for which the jail was dedicated outweighed the expression interests of the protesters. Justice Black said that to find for Adderley would be to endorse "the assumption that people who want to propagandize protests or views have a constitutional right to do so whenever and wherever they please." The Court categorically rejected that premise and concluded by saying the Constitution does not forbid a state to "control the use of its own property for its own lawful nondiscriminatory purposes." Justice Douglas dissented, joined by Chief Justice Warren and Justices Brennan and Fortas. Justice Douglas considered the jailhouse "one of the seats of government" and was an "obvious center for protest." *See also* ASSEMBLY, RIGHT TO, p. 616; ASSOCIATION, RIGHT TO, p. 617; FIRST AMENDMENT, p. 29; *PruneYard Shopping Center v. Robins*, p. 152; SPEECH PLUS, p. 700.

Significance   *Adderley* illustrates the "speech plus" concept. In certain situations speech involves accompanying conduct beyond verbal utterances. The conduct may be regulated even if the regulation impairs expression. In *Cox v. Louisiana*, 379 U.S. 536 (1965), the Court upheld a state statute that prohibited picketing near a courthouse. It said that a state could legitimately insulate its judicial proceedings from demonstrations.

While restrictions were said to be warranted in *Adderley* and *Cox*, breach of the peace convictions of persons demonstrating on the grounds of a state capitol were reversed in *Edwards v. South Carolina*, 372 U.S. 229 (1963). Similarly, a peaceful sit-in at a public library was protected in *Brown v. Louisiana*, 383 U.S. 13 (1966). More recently, the Court struck down an ordinance that prohibited picketing in the proximity of school buildings when classes were in session in *Chicago Police Department v. Mosley*, 408 U.S. 92 (1972). The ordinance was invalidated largely because it excepted labor picketing from the ban. The Court noted the city had a legitimate interest in preventing school disruption, however. Time, place, and manner restrictions have generally been recognized by the Court, provided that significant governmental interests can be demonstrated. Trespass on private property was subject to punishment for many years, although civil-rights sit-ins forced a legislative reevaluation of that policy. A Washington, D.C., regulation prohibiting display of signs conveying criticism of foreign governments within 500 feet of embassies was struck down in *Boos v. Barry*, 485 U.S. 312 (1988). While recognizing the need to shield foreign governments from criticism, the Court found the display prohibition to be content-based regulation of particular expression. Parallel language banning assembly within 500 feet of embassies was upheld, however, because its application had been confined to security-threatening situations.

The question in *United States v. Kokinda*, 497 U.S. 720 (1990), was whether a Postal Service regulation banning solicitation on sidewalks located entirely on Postal Service property violated the First Amendment. The Court upheld the regulation. Sidewalks have generally been regarded as a forum traditionally open to the public for expressive activity. Regulation of speech on government property that has been traditionally open to the public for expressive activity, such as public streets or parks, is examined under strict scrutiny. On the other hand, expressive activity where the government has not dedicated its property to First Amendment activity is examined only for reasonableness. The Court rejected the argument that all sidewalks be regarded as a traditional public forum. The "mere physical characteristics of the property cannot dictate forum analysis." The "location and purpose" of a public sidewalk "is critical to determining whether such a sidewalk constitutes a public forum." The sidewalk subject to regulation in this case did not have the "characteristics of public sidewalks traditionally open to expressive activity." Rather, this postal sidewalk was constructed "solely to provide for the passage of individuals engaged in postal business," thus it was not a traditional public forum sidewalk.

The public forum concept was also the critical consideration in *International Society for Krishna Consciousness, Inc. v. Lee*, 505 U.S. 672 (1992). Members of Krishna Consciousness are required by their faith to go to public places and engage in activities that include literature distribution and solicitation of donations. The Port Authority of New York and New Jersey operates the three major airports in and near New York City. The Port Authority permitted the Krishnas to engage in various activities in the common areas of the airport grounds, but prohibited the same conduct in those airport locations that had been leased to private airlines. Much of the terminal space fell into the latter category. The Krishnas sought to extend their access to all airport locations and challenged the restrictions on First Amendment grounds. The Supreme Court agreed that the Krishnas were engaged in activities generally protected by the First Amendment, but upheld the ban on solicitations for money. At the same time, the restriction on distribution of literature was held to be unconstitutional. The Court's rulings hinged on whether the air terminals were historically dedicated to expressive activities. The "tradition of airport activity," said Chief Justice Rehnquist, "does not demonstrate that airports have historically been available for speech activity." Rather, the Court saw airline terminals as designed to serve airline passengers and personnel and not the public at large. The ban on direct solicitation was found to be a reasonable way to avoid excessive congestion and disruption to passengers as they moved through the terminals. The members of the Court who would have overturned the regulation of solicitation, Justices Souter, Blackmun, and Stevens, saw the airport as a public forum where solicitation should be protected conduct. Justices O'Connor and Kennedy joined the dissenters on the solicitation question to strike down the restriction on literature distribution. They felt the regulation could not satisfy even the reasonableness standard applied to a nonpublic forum.

151

A city's authority to regulate concerts held in a municipal park was before the Court in *Ward v. Rock Against Racism*, 491 U.S. 781 (1989). The city issued a set of use guidelines governing all band shell concerts that, among other things, specified that the city would furnish the amplification equipment and employ an experienced sound technician to operate it. The Supreme Court ruled the guidelines to be a valid place and manner regulation. The city had two objectives in instituting the guidelines: controlling noise and ensuring sound quality. Neither of these purposes, concluded the Court, had anything to do with content.

Private Property

PruneYard Shopping Center v. Robins, 447 U.S. 74 (1980), declared that demonstrators may access privately owned shopping malls to circulate petitions and distribute political pamphlets. *PruneYard* involved a group of high school students who sought to express their opposition to a United Nations Resolution against Zionism. They set up a table near the central courtyard of the shopping center, began distributing pamphlets, and asked patrons of the shopping center to sign a petition. The students were orderly and no objection to their presence was registered by any shopping center customer. The students were informed by a shopping center security guard that their activity was in violation of a center policy that prohibited all such conduct. The group subsequently filed suit, seeking access to the center through a court order. The trial court refused to issue such an order, but the California Supreme Court held that the state constitution entitled the students access to the mall. The United States Supreme Court unanimously upheld the California Supreme Court. The crucial issue for the Court was whether state-protected rights of expression infringed upon the property rights of PruneYard's owners. Citing the state court opinion, Justice Rehnquist said that "a handful of additional orderly persons soliciting signatures and distributing handbills do not interfere with normal business operations." They "would not markedly dilute defendant's property rights." Three other arguments were developed to support the judgment of the California Supreme Court. First, PruneYard "by the choice of its owner is not limited to the personal use of the appellants." PruneYard is rather a "business establishment that is open to the public." Any views expressed by center patrons "thus will not likely be identified with those of the owner." Second, the state's insistence that PruneYard's private property be made available was content neutral in that there was "no danger of governmental discrimination for or against a particular message." Finally, PruneYard and its constituent shop owners could easily disclaim any connection to the expression of the demonstrators. They could explain that the "persons are communicating their own messages by virtue of state law." *See also Adderley v. Florida*, p. 149; ASSEMBLY, RIGHT TO, p. 616; FIRST AMENDMENT, p. 29.

Significance   PruneYard Shopping Center v. Robins treated the troublesome issue of demonstrator access to private property. The Burger Court position in *PruneYard* represents a compromise between several of its own previous decisions and those of the Warren Court. The Warren Court view is best illustrated by *Amalgamated Food Employees Union v. Logan Valley Plaza, Inc.*, 391 U.S. 308 (1968). In *Logan Valley* the Court upheld the picketing of a business located in a privately owned shopping center. The Burger Court reconsidered *Logan Valley* in *Lloyd Corp. v. Tanner*, 407 U.S. 551 (1972), and upheld a restriction on handbilling. Although the shopping center invites patrons, the Burger Court said, it is not an invitation of unlimited scope. The invitation is to do business with the tenants of the center. There is "no open-ended invitation to the public to use the center for any and all purposes, however incompatible with the interests of both the stores and the shoppers whom they serve." In addition, the restriction did not deprive the persons from distributing their handbills on the public sidewalks surrounding the center.

The Burger Court abandoned *Logan Valley* altogether in *Hudgens v. National Labor Relations Board (NLRB)*, 424 U.S. 507 (1976). In *Hudgens*, union members attempted to picket the retail store of their employer, which was located in a privately owned mall. Citing *Lloyd Corp.*, the Court held that the First Amendment "has no part to play in such a case as this." Thus, the Burger Court divorced privately owned shopping centers from First Amendment reach. Through the *PruneYard* decision, however, it did allow protection of expression to flow from state constitutional provisions.

Enjoining Assembly

Carroll v. President and Commissioners of Princess Anne County, **393 U.S. 175 (1968),** struck down an ex parte injunction prohibiting a rally of a militant white supremacist organization. An ex parte proceeding is one in which only one party participates or appears. Injunctions are frequently, but not always, used in situations in which permits or licenses to march or demonstrate have been denied. Carroll, a member of a white supremacist organization known as the National States Rights Party, participated in a rally at which aggressively and militantly racist and anti-Semitic speeches were made. At the conclusion of the speeches, it was announced that the rally would be resumed the next night. Local government officials obtained a restraining order in the meantime in an ex parte proceeding. The injunction restrained Carroll and others from holding public meetings for 10 days. The Supreme Court unanimously struck down the order. The Court's primary objection was to the ex parte procedure. The order was issued "without notice to petitioners and without any effort, however informal, to invite or permit their participation in the proceedings." The Court recognized that ex parte orders may be appropriate in some situations, "but there is no place within the area of basic freedoms guaranteed by the First Amendment for such orders." The absence of an adversary proceeding deprives a trial court of the facts necessary to make a judgment. There is "insufficient assurance of the balanced analysis and careful conclusions which are essential in the area of First Amendment adjudication." The same absence of information makes it more difficult to construct an order in the narrowest and least stifling terms. *See also Adderley v. Florida*, p. 149; ASSEMBLY, RIGHT TO, p. 616; FIRST AMENDMENT, p. 29.

Significance   *Carroll v. President of Princess Anne* established procedural guidelines through which court orders might be obtained against demonstrators. The permit-injunction approach had often been used against civil-rights demonstrators. In *Walker v. Birmingham*, 388 U.S. 307 (1967), the Court upheld an injunction issued following denial of a parade permit. Walker, Martin Luther King Jr., and others involved in the proposed parade disobeyed the injunction without seeking appellate review of either the injunction or the permit denial that precipitated the court order. The Court found the potentially persuasive objections to the Birmingham permit system to be subordinate to the failure of the demonstrators to obey the court order. The dissenters in *Walker* would have voided the injunction on the grounds that the permit system was unconstitutionally discriminatory. Permits are satisfactory as long as they are confined to reasonable time, place, and manner limitations. Permit or license requirements that are not content neutral or that allow too much discretion to permit-granting officials are unacceptable to the Court.

A more recent injunction episode involved attempts by the Village of Skokie, Illinois, to prevent an assembly of the National Socialist Party of America, a self-proclaimed Nazi organization. More than half of Skokie's residents are Jewish and a sizeable number were survivors of German concentration camps. Prior to the assembly, an injunction was secured from a state court enjoining the National Socialist Party from a uniformed march, display of swastikas, and distribution of materials that might "promote hatred against persons of the Jewish faith or ancestry." The Illinois Supreme Court refused to stay the injunction. The United States Supreme Court, in *National*

Socialist Party v. Skokie, 432 U.S. 43 (1977), reversed because the denial of the stay at the state level deprived the party of its right to demonstrate for the period until an appellate review could occur, a period estimated to be a year or more. The Court said that if a state seeks to impose a restraint of this kind, "it must provide strict procedural safeguards including appellate review." Absent such review, the state must instead allow the stay." The party never assembled in Skokie, choosing instead to hold a rally in a Chicago park.

The Court dealt with a different kind of permit requirement in *Forsyth County v. Nationalist Movement*, 505 U.S. 123 (1992). In 1987 Forsyth County, Georgia, was the site of a number of civil-rights demonstrations and counterdemonstrations. In response Forsyth County adopted a permit ordinance that imposed a fee as a condition for obtaining permission to use public property for expressive activity. The county administrator had authority to set the amount of the fee up to a maximum of $1,000 for each day the public properties were used. The Supreme Court found the ordinance unconstitutional. The central objection was that the ordinance gave the local government, in the person of the county administrator, "unbridled discretion," and "created the possibility that assessments might be influenced by the content of the expression." Justice Blackmun said, "Speech cannot be financially burdened, any more than it can be punished or banned, simply because it might offend a hostile mob."

Abortion Clinic Protest

Schenck v. Pro-Choice Network, **519 U.S. 357 (1997),** reviewed a federal district court restraining order that prohibited antiabortion protesters from coming within 15 feet of entrances and driveways to an abortion clinic. The order also created "floating" zones of 15 feet around all persons entering the clinic. Two protesters were permitted to engage in "sidewalk counseling" within the zones, but were required to approach patients or staff in a nonconfrontational manner and "cease and desist" from any interaction if the person receiving the "counseling" objected to it. Sidewalk counseling typically involves talking with and distributing literature to people entering abortion clinics. The Pro-Choice Network filed motions with a federal court alleging violations of the restraining order by protesters led by Reverend Paul Schenck. The U.S. Supreme Court upheld parts of the injunction, but struck down the "floating buffer zone" component. The Court concluded that the governmental interests of ensuring public safety and order, maintaining free traffic flow, property protection, and protecting a woman's "freedom to seek pregnancy-related services" were present. Those interests, considered "in combination, are certainly significant enough to justify an appropriately tailored injunction to secure unimpeded physical access to the clinics." The fixed buffer zone was upheld because the issuing court could have reasonably concluded that the only way to ensure access was to move the demonstrators away from the driveways and parking lot entrances. The protesters argued that a 15-foot fixed zone constituted a ban on "peaceful, nonobstructive demonstrations." Chief Justice Rehnquist suggested that such an argument ignored the history of this case. The court that had issued the restraining order initially was "entitled to conclude" that some of the protesters "aggressively follow and crowd individuals" seeking entry to the clinics "right up to the clinic door" and then "refuse to move … in an effort to impede or block" clinic staff and patients. In addition, protester harassment of police limited the capability of law enforcement to function effectively, making a "prophylactic measure even more appropriate." The protesters also argued that the "cease and desist" provision of the injunction was too restrictive. The Court disagreed, saying that the exception for the two sidewalk counselors was a good faith effort of the trial court to "enhance" the speech rights of the protesters, and the limitation "must be assessed in that light." The "floating zones," however, were found defective because they "burden more speech than is necessary to serve the relevant governmental interests." The floating zones largely prevented the communication of any message from a "normal conversational distance or handing leaflets to people entering or leaving the clinics." Leafletting and commenting on matters of public concern are "classic forms of speech that lie at the heart of the First Amendment," and speech in public areas is "at its most protected on public sidewalks, a prototypical example of a traditional public forum." Rehnquist noted that it would be difficult for a protester who wishes to engage in lawful expression to "know how to remain in compliance with the injunction." This "lack of certainty" leads to a substantial risk that "much more speech will be burdened than the injunction by its terms prohibits." Justices Scalia, Kennedy, and Thomas concluded that there is no right to be "free of unwelcome speech on the public streets" while seeking to enter or exit from abortion clinics. The First Amendment obligates courts to "bend over backwards to accommodate speech rights." *See also Adderley v. Florida,* p. 149; ASSEMBLY, RIGHT TO, p. 616; FIRST AMENDMENT, p. 29.

Significance   One of the tactics used by abortion opponents is to demonstrate near abortion clinics. The clinics have responded by seeking judicial intervention. Two cases decided by the Rehnquist Court prior to *Schenck* examined the statutory bases for possible intervention. The first was *Bray v. Alexandria Women's Health Clinic,* 506 U.S.

263 (1993). The issue in *Bray* was whether federal judges have authority under an 1871 statute to enjoin antiabortion protesters from obstructing entry to abortion clinics. The law bans conspiracies to deprive persons, or classes of persons, of equal protection under the law. In order to prove a conspiracy in violation of the law, plaintiffs need to show that the conspirators were motivated, at least in part, by a "class-based invidiously discriminatory animus." A plaintiff would further need to show that the conspiracy was designed to interfere with rights protected against encroachment by private parties. It was asserted by the clinics that because only women can have abortions, the demonstrators discriminated against women as a class by interfering with access to legal abortions. The Supreme Court ruled that the plaintiffs did not prove a private conspiracy in violation of the statute. Absent such a finding, the federal courts are without power to restrict demonstrations such as the one involved here. The Court did not see in the record any indications that the abortion protesters were motivated by a purpose directed at women as a class. Opposition to voluntary abortion, said Justice Scalia, "cannot possibly be considered an irrational surrogate for opposition to (or paternalism toward) women." Regardless of one's position on abortion, it "cannot be denied that there are common and respectable reasons for opposing it, other than hatred of or condescension toward (or indeed any view at all concerning) women as a class."

The Racketeer Influenced and Corrupt Organizations Act (RICO) makes it a federal crime to conduct the "affairs" of an "enterprise" through "patterned" racketeering activity. The National Organization for Women (NOW) attempted to use RICO in an action against the Pro-Life Action Network (PLAN), an antiabortion coalition including such groups as Operation Rescue. NOW claimed that PLAN had engaged in a criminal conspiracy to close down abortion clinics through patterned use of intimidation and extortion. The lower courts dismissed the suit, finding the actions of PLAN to be political rather than economic as required under RICO. The Supreme Court disagreed. It was the Court's view that there need not be a property interest or economic motive for engaging in illegal activity; it need only be an association in fact that engages in a pattern of racketeering activity. In ruling that an economic motive was required, the lower courts had overlooked that fact that predicate acts, such as an alleged extortion, "may not benefit the protesters financially but still may drain money from the economy by harming businesses such as clinics." The Court found the requirement of economic motive to be neither expressed nor fairly implied in RICO. Although the Act may have been passed to combat organized crime, Congress enacted a more general statute; it "was not limited in application to organized crime."

The Rehnquist Court reviewed a restraining order in *Madsen v. Women's Health Center*, 512 U.S. 753 (1994), which closely paralleled the injunction at issue in *Schenck*. A number of abortion clinics in Florida secured an injunction from a state court restraining such activities as trespassing on clinic property, blocking access to clinic entrances, and harassing persons associated with the clinics as staff or patients. The following year, a more extensive injunction created "buffer zones" of 36 and 300 feet from the clinics. The abortion protesters were forbidden from approaching persons seeking clinic services inside the 300-foot zone. An exception was allowed for potential clinic patients who consented to talk with protesters. Nonthreatening communication and the distribution of literature could occur within the 300-foot zone until the 36-foot perimeter was reached, at which point all interaction between the prospective patients and protesters was prohibited. The amended injunction also prohibited making sounds that could be heard inside the clinics, and prohibited the exhibiting of "images" observable to patients of the clinic. The Supreme Court upheld the 36-foot buffer zone, but struck down the restrictions within the 300-foot zone. The Court rejected the protesters' contention that because the injunction prohibits only the speech of the protesters, it is necessarily viewpoint or content based. To accept their claim, said Chief Justice Rehnquist, would be to classify "virtually every" injunction as content based because, by its nature, it applies only to particular individuals and perhaps their speech. Content neutrality hinges on the purpose of the regulation—a purpose chosen without interference to the content of the regulated speech. The injunction was issued here because the protesters "repeatedly violated" the original restraining order. That protesters all shared the same view on abortion did not in itself demonstrate a viewpoint-based purpose. Rather, the order reflected that the persons "whose *conduct* violated the court's order happen to share the same opinion regarding abortions being performed at the clinic." The Court concluded that the state had "few other options to protect access given the narrow confines around the clinic." The Court also noted that an "even narrower order was issued originally, and that it had failed to protect clinic access." The Court also upheld the noise restriction. The First Amendment, said Rehnquist, "does not demand that patients at a medical facility undertake Herculean efforts to escape the cacophony of political protests." If overamplified loudspeakers "assault the citizenry, government may turn them down." Here the Court distinguished the sound restrictions from the restrictions on observable "images." The latter restriction was too broad—it was more burdensome than necessary to achieve the purpose of limiting threats to clinic patients or their families. Similarly, the Court concluded that there was insufficient justification for creating the 300-

foot buffer zone—the desired result could have been accomplished with less burdensome restrictions. Justices Scalia, Kennedy, and Thomas dissented. In their view, the restraining order was unconstitutional because it was content based; it targeted a particular group that had broken no laws and imposed restrictions on only that group. The danger with such restrictions, said Scalia, is that they "may be designed and used precisely to suppress the ideas in question rather than to achieve any other proper governmental aim."

FREEDOM OF ASSOCIATION
Origin

National Association for the Advancement of Colored People (NAACP) v. Alabama, **357 U.S. 449 (1958),** established a constitutional protection for the freedom of association. This case involved an attempt by the state of Alabama to compel disclosure of the NAACP's membership list as a means of inhibiting the operation of the organization. Alabama sought to enjoin NAACP activities within the state because the NAACP had failed to comply with a statutory requirement that all out-of-state corporations file certain information. Among the documents the NAACP was ordered to produce was a list of all names and addresses of members and agents in Alabama. The Association refused to disclose such a list and was cited for contempt and fined. The Supreme Court unanimously reversed the contempt judgment and determined that the First Amendment included a right of association. The Court first had to resolve the matter of standing. Alabama argued that the NAACP could not "assert constitutional rights pertaining to the members," but the Court found the Association's "nexus with them is sufficient to permit that it act as their representative." Indeed, the Court concluded that the NAACP was the "appropriate party to assert these rights, because it and its members are in every practical sense identical." The Court turned to the associational rights threatened by the compulsory disclosure of NAACP members. Justice Harlan suggested that "effective advocacy of both public and private points of view, particularly controversial ones, is undeniably enhanced by group association." The compelled disclosure was viewed as affecting "adversely the ability of the petitioner and its members to pursue their collective effort to foster beliefs which they admittedly have a right to advocate." The Court saw disclosure as impairing the NAACP in two ways. First, the Association would likely suffer diminished financial support and fewer membership applications. Second, disclosure of the identity of members might prompt "economic reprisal, loss of employment, threat of physical coercion, and other manifestations of public hostility." The Court found that Alabama had not shown a "controlling justification for the deterrent effect on the free enjoyment of the right to associate which disclosure of membership lists is likely to have." *See also* ASSOCIATION, RIGHT TO, p. 617; FIRST AMENDMENT, p. 29; *Keyishian v. Board of Regents*, p. 160.

Significance   A number of associational rights questions reached the Court soon after. *NAACP v. Alabama* marked the beginning of a new era for associational rights. In *Shelton v. Tucker*, 364 U.S. 479 (1960), the Court struck down a state statute requiring every public school teacher to disclose annually every organization supported by his or her membership or contribution. The Court determined that even a legitimate inquiry into a teacher's fitness and competence "cannot be pursued by means that broadly stifle fundamental personal liberties when the end can be more narrowly achieved." Associational ties have also been an issue with respect to admission to the bar. In *Baird v. State Bar of Arizona*, 401 U.S. 1 (1971), the Court held that applicants to the bar may not be compelled to disclose organizational memberships. "Views and beliefs are immune from bar association inquisitions designed to lay a foundation for barring an applicant from the practice of law." In *Law Students Civil Rights Research Council, Inc. v. Wadmond*, 401 U.S. 154 (1971), however, the Court upheld bar admission inquiries into character and fitness, including questions probing membership in associations advocating unlawful overthrow of the government.

The NAACP was able to affirm another dimension of associational freedom in *NAACP v. Button*, 371 U.S. 415 (1963). *Button* upheld the NAACP's strategy of representing membership interests through litigation. Many states had enacted antisolicitation laws prohibiting the "stirring up" of lawsuits. The Court recognized such activity as a means for achieving lawful objectives and a form of political expression for organizations like the NAACP. Indeed, "for such a group, association for litigation may be the most effective form of political association." The Court distinguished litigation seeking vindication of constitutional rights from "avaricious use" of the legal process purely for personal gain.

Political Association

***Keyishian v. Board of Regents*, 385 U.S. 589 (1967),** required that more than "mere membership" in organizations be demonstrated before the imposition of restrictions on associational rights. *Keyishian* examined provisions of New York's Feinberg Law, which authorized the State Board of Regents to monitor organizational memberships of state employees. The Board was required to generate a list of subversive organizations. Membership in any one of them was prima facie evidence of disqualification from public employment, including appointments to academic positions. Although the person being terminated could have a hearing, the hearing could not address the matter of the state's classification of an organization as "subversive." Keyishian and several other faculty members in the state university system were dismissed because of their membership in the Communist Party. The Supreme Court struck down the Feinberg Law. The Court rejected the premise that "public employment, including academic employment, may be conditioned upon the surrender of constitutional rights which could not be abridged by direct government action." The Court found "mere membership" to be an insufficient basis for exclusion. "Legislation which sanctions membership unaccompanied by specific intent to further the unlawful goals of the organization or which is not active membership violates constitutional limitations." The Court also said the statute "sweeps overbroadly in association which may not be proscribed." The regulations "seek to bar employment both for association which legitimately may be proscribed and for association which may not be sanctioned." The flaw of overbreadth was as constitutionally defective as the flaw of vagueness. The dissenters, Justices Clark, Harlan, Stewart, and White, reacted strongly by saying the Court "has by its broadside swept away one of our most precious rights, namely the right of self-preservation." *See also* ASSOCIATION, RIGHT TO, p. 617; *Dennis v. United States* , p. 82; *NAACP v. Alabama,* p. 159.

Significance   The right of association is not explicitly provided in the First Amendment, yet there is a recognized relationship between voluntary association with groups and the protected freedoms of expression and assembly. Decisions such as *Keyishian* reaffirm the notion that the First Amendment extends to associational activity. That was not always the view, however. The first serious test of associational rights came in *Whitney v. California,* 274 U.S. 357 (1927), in which the Court upheld California's Criminal Syndicalism Act, which prohibited organizing and being a member of a group advocating unlawful force as a political weapon. Whitney had participated in a convention of the Communist Labor Party of California, which had passed resolutions advocating various revolutionary acts. Whitney asserted that she had not supported the resolutions nor had she wished the party to urge violation of California's laws. She was convicted nonetheless because she had remained at the convention and had not disassociated herself from the party after the resolutions were adopted. The Supreme Court upheld her conviction. The Court refused to reexamine the jury's finding that Whitney had not sufficiently detached herself from the party. The Court noted that remaining in attendance until the close of the convention and maintaining her membership "manifested her acquiescence." The justices said that California's approach did not restrain free speech or assembly. The "essence of the offense denounced by the Act is the combining with others in an association for the accomplishment of the desired ends through the advocacy and use of criminal and unlawful methods." Because such united and joint action constituted an even greater threat to public peace and security, a state may reasonably exercise its police power to prevent groups from "menacing the peace and welfare of the State."

Whitney seemed to provide license for convicting political radicals because of their association alone, but the Court began to disengage from *Whitney* almost immediately. In *DeJonge v. Oregon*, 299 U.S. 353 (1937), and *Herndon v. Lowry*, 301 U.S. 242 (1937), the Court reversed convictions of admitted members of the Communist Party, because as individuals neither defendant had violated a criminal law. While an organization may have criminal objectives, simply attending a peaceful meeting called by such an organization cannot transfer criminal liability to an individual. The formal end to *Whitney* came in *Brandenburg v. Ohio*, 395 U.S. 444 (1969), in which the Court unanimously struck down a state syndicalism statute. The defendant in this case was the leader of a Ku Klux Klan group who had spoken at a Klan rally. The Court said "the mere abstract teaching of the moral propriety or even moral necessity for a resort to force and violence is not the same as preparing a group for violent action and steeling it for such action." Accordingly, a statute that fails to draw this distinction impermissibly intrudes on First Amendment freedoms. *Keyishian* specifically overturned *Adler v. Board of Education*, 342 U.S. 485 (1952), decided 15 years earlier. *Adler* had found the Feinberg Law constitutional, deciding that teachers "have no right to work for the State in the school system on their own terms." The state may inquire into the fitness and suitability of a person for public service, and past conduct may well relate to present fitness. In addition, one's associates, past and present, may properly be considered in determining fitness and loyalty. "From time immemorial, one's reputation has been determined in part by the company he keeps."

Shortly after *Keyishian*, in *United States v. Robel*, 389 U.S. 258 (1967), the Court voided a McCarron Act provision that prohibited any member of a Communist-action organization from working in a defense facility. As in *Keyishian*, the Court found the statute "casts its net across a broad range of associational activities, indiscriminately trapping membership which can be constitutionally punished and membership which cannot be so proscribed."

In a decision predating *Keyishian* and *Robel* by a year, but using a similar rationale, the Court struck down a loyalty oath provision that imposed penalties upon anyone taking the oath who might later become a member of a subversive organization. The case was *Elfbrandt v. Russell*, 384 U.S. 11 (1966). The Burger Court upheld a loyalty oath in *Cole v. Richardson*, 405 U.S. 676 (1972). The oath required public employees to uphold and defend the federal and state constitutions and to oppose the overthrow of federal or state governments by illegal means. *Cole* found the oath permissible in that it did not impose specific action obligations on persons taking it. It required only a general commitment to abide by constitutional processes.

Associational Privacy

***Hurley v. Irish-American Gay, Lesbian & Bisexual Group*, 515 U.S. 557 (1995)** Each year, the city of Boston simultaneously celebrates St. Patrick's Day and Evacuation Day (the day the British troops evacuated Boston during the War of Independence) with a parade. The South Boston Allied War Veterans Council has organized the annual parade since 1947. The parade typically includes thousands of participants and historically has been open for the participation of local groups. An organization known as the Irish-American Gay, Lesbian, and Bisexual Group of Boston was formed in 1992. One of its objectives was to march in the parade. The Group's applications to participate were denied by the Council in 1992 and 1993, and the Group obtained a court order enabling its members to march in the parade. The state court ruled for the Group because historically the Council had allowed virtually all other groups to participate in the parade, thus the parade was not seen as an expressive associational activity falling within the reach of the First Amendment, and exclusion of the Group violated the state public accommodations law that prohibits, among other things, discrimination on the basis of sexual preference. Rather than permit Group members from marching in the 1994 parade under court order, the Council canceled the parade and then fashioned written criteria for selecting parade participants. The standards declared that the purpose of the parade was to commemorate "traditional values" and the role of "traditional families." The Council contended that as sponsors of a private parade, it could not be required to include any messages with which it disagreed. The Group contended that state antidiscrimination laws continued to protect their participation, but argued that carrying a banner identifying marchers as gay Irish Americans did not convey a message that could justify their exclusion from participation in the parade. The Court unanimously ruled that private sponsors could exclude the Group from marching in the parade. The ruling rested on three conclusions: The parade was a private event, a parade is an expressive activity, and the Group's self-identifying presence in the parade was viewed by the Court as "equally expressive." The expression that "inheres" in a parade need not be precisely defined; a "narrow, succinctly articulable message is not a condition of constitutional protection." So even though the Council let many community groups participate in the parade, it did not forfeit constitutional protection "simply by combining multifarious voices, or by failing to edit their themes to isolate an exact message as the exclusive subject matter of the speech." The Court rejected the notion that the state, even for the "enlightened purpose" of discouraging discrimination, could interfere with the expressive rights of a private organization. The state court order compelling participation of the Group required the Council to "alter the expressive content" of their parade. Such use of state power violates the "fundamental rule" of First Amendment protection that a speaker has the "autonomy to choose the content of his own message." All speech, Souter continued, "inherently involves choices of what to say and what to leave unsaid"; one important manifestation of free speech is that "one who chooses to speak may also decide 'what not to say.'" The free speech tradition requires that a speaker should be free from state interference based on the content of his or her expression. Souter concluded by saying that while law can be used to promote "all sorts of conduct in place of harmful behavior," law cannot be used to "interfere with speech for no better reason than promoting an approved message or discouraging a disfavored one." *See also* ASSOCIATION, RIGHT TO, p. 617; FIRST AMENDMENT, p. 29.

Significance   Several associational rights cases have involved the use of fees collected from members for political purposes. Two rulings illustrate the point. In *Communications Workers v. Beck*, 487 U.S. 735 (1988), the Court ruled that unions cannot compel nonmembers to pay "agency fees" if these fees are used for political or other purposes that are not directly related to collective bargaining. Prior to this decision, unions were free to use agency fees for noncollective-bargaining activities. A number of nonmember employees challenged the Communication Workers of America's (CWA's) use of agency fees to support endorsed political candidates, organize employees at other companies, and to conduct various lobbying activities. They contended that use of fees for such purposes violated the CWA's "duty of fair representation." The issue in this case was whether the collection of agency fees allows a union to financially support "union activities beyond those germane to collective bargaining, contract administration, and grievance adjustment." The Court ruled that it did not.

A similar decision was rendered in a case involving a state bar association. The state bar association of California is "integrated," which means those who wish to practice law in California are statutorily required to become dues-paying members. Virtually all state bar activities are financed by the membership dues, including those that could be characterized as political or ideological. An action was brought by Keller and other state bar association members who wished to prevent use of the mandatory dues for those political activities with which they disagreed. A unanimous Court ruled in *Keller v. State Bar of California*, 496 U.S. 1 (1990), that the state bar's use of compulsory dues for political purposes violated the free speech rights of members who might disagree. The decision effectively limited bar association expenditures to those activities required for the effective regulation of the profession and the improvement of the quality of legal services.

Electoral Process: Campaign Finance

Buckley v. Valeo, **424 U.S. 1 (1976),** examined the constitutionality of the Federal Election Campaign Act of 1974. *Buckley* considered the Act against First Amendment challenge that regulation of the electoral process impinges upon individual and group expression. The Federal Election Campaign Act was passed in the wake of Watergate. It sought to protect the electoral process by limiting political campaign contributions, establishing ceilings on several categories of campaign expenditures, requiring extensive and regular disclosure of campaign contributors and expenditures, providing public financing for presidential campaigns, and creating a Federal Election Commission (FEC) to administer the Act. Suit was filed by a diverse collection of individuals and groups including United States Senator James Buckley, the Eugene McCarthy presidential campaign, the Libertarian Party, the American Conservative Union, and the New York Civil Liberties Union. By differing majorities, the Court upheld those portions of the Act that provided for campaign contribution limits, disclosure, public financing, and the creation of the FEC. The section imposing limits on expenditures was invalidated. In a per curiam opinion, the Court said the Act's contribution and expenditure ceiling "reduces the quantity of expression because virtually every means of communicating ideas in today's society requires the expenditure of money." The Court distinguished, however, between limits on contributions and limits on expenditures—in other words, on those things for which the contributions might be spent. While the latter represents substantial restraint on the quantity and diversity of political speech, limits on contributions involve "little direct restraint." Indeed, the contributor's freedom to discuss candidates and issues is not infringed in any way. Even though contributions may underwrite some costs of conveying a campaign's views, the contributions must be transformed into political expression by persons other than the contributor. The Court acknowledged a legitimate governmental interest in protecting the "integrity of our system of representative democracy" from quid pro quo arrangements that might arise from financial contributions. Expenditure limits, on the other hand, severely burden one's ability to speak one's mind and engage in vigorous advocacy. Neither is the First Amendment to be used to equalize political influence. "The concept that government may restrict the speech of some elements of our society in order to enhance the relative voice of others is wholly foreign to the First Amendment." By striking the expenditure limits, the Court allowed unlimited use of personal wealth or expenditures made on behalf of campaigns separate from the actual campaign organization of a candidate. On the matter of disclosure, the Court agreed that the requirement might deter some contributions, but viewed it as a "least restrictive means of curbing the evils of campaign ignorance and corruption." The Court also upheld the Act's public financing provisions by rejecting a claim that a differential funding formula for major and minor parties was unconstitutional. *See also* ASSOCIATION, RIGHT TO, p. 617; FIRST AMENDMENT, p. 29; *Keyishian v. Board of Regents*, p. 160; *NAACP v. Alabama*, p. 159.

Significance   *Buckley* generated important follow-up questions regarding regulation of the electoral process. In *First National Bank v. Bellotti*, 435 U.S. 765 (1978), the Court struck down a state statute prohibiting the use of corporate funds for the purpose of influencing a referendum question. Without a showing that the corporation's advocacy "threatened imminently to undermine democratic processes," the state has no interest sufficient to limit a corporation's expression of views on a public issue. *In Citizens Against Rent Control v. Berkeley*, 450 U.S. 908 (1981), the Court struck down a municipal ordinance limiting contributions to organizations formed to support or oppose ballot issues. With only Justice White dissenting, the Court drew heavily on *Buckley* and concluded that the ordinance went too far in restraining individual and associational rights of expression. The Court extended the *Buckley* reasoning in *Federal Election Commission v. National Conservative Political Action Committee*, 470 U.S. 480 (1985), saying the Federal Election Campaign Act could not limit political action committees to an expenditure of $1,000 for promoting the candidacies of publicly funded presidential aspirants. Such an expenditure limit impermissibly infringed on First Amendment speech and association rights.

The Federal Election Campaign Act came under further review in *Federal Election Commission v. Massachusetts Citizens for Life*, 479 U.S. 238 (1986). Under challenge was the section prohibiting corporations from using general funds to make expenditures related to an election to any public office. Massachusetts Citizens for Life (MCFL), a nonprofit, nonstock corporation, was formed to promote pro-life causes. MCFL used its general treasury to prepare and distribute a special election edition of its newsletter. This publication categorized all candidates for state and federal offices in terms of their support or opposition to MCFL's views. The Supreme Court unanimously ruled that the special edition of the newsletter fell within the scope of the prohibition of the law, but that the provision created unacceptable First Amendment violations for corporations such as MCFL. Most of the rationale supporting regulations of this kind stems from the special characteristics of the corporate structure. The "integrity of the marketplace of political ideas" must be protected from the "corrosive influence of corporate wealth." The availability of resources may make a corporation a "formidable political presence, even though the power of the corporation may be no reflection of the power of its ideas." The Court held that such groups as MCFL simply do not pose that danger of corruption. MCFL was formed for the expressed purpose of promoting political ideas, and its activities cannot be considered as business activities.

The Court upheld, however, the power of the federal and state governments to regulate the campaign expenditures of business corporations in *Austin v. Michigan Chamber of Commerce*, 494 U.S. 652 (1990). The Michigan Campaign Finance Act prohibited corporations from using general treasury funds for independent expenditures for state political candidates. Rather, corporations were required to use funds specifically segregated for political purposes. The state regulation did allow business corporations to establish political action committees to make such independent expenditures. The Michigan Chamber of Commerce wished to use general treasury funds on behalf of a specific candidate for state office, and it sought to enjoin enforcement of the restriction. The Chamber claimed that, like Massachusetts Citizens for Life, it, too, was a nonprofit ideological corporation. The Court disagreed, citing the organizational characteristics developed in the MCFL decision. MCFL was formed for the "express purpose of promoting political ideas, and cannot engage in business activities." Its "narrow political focus" ensured that its political funding "reflects its political support." The Chamber, on the other hand, had "more varied purposes." Second, MCFL was "independen[t] from the influence of business corporations." Indeed, it was on this basis that the Court found the Chamber to differ "most greatly from the Massachusetts organization." MCFL did not accept contributions from business corporations. Thus, it could not serve as a "conduit for the type of direct spending that creates a threat to the political marketplace." In "striking contrast," the Chamber's members are largely business corporations, whose "political contributions and expenditures can be constitutionally regulated by the State." Business corporations therefore could "circumvent the Act's restrictions by funneling money through the Chamber's general treasury."

The Colorado Republican Party spent in excess of $15,000 for some radio spots and printed material challenging claims made by an incumbent Democratic member of Congress. The question in *Colorado Republican Federal Campaign Committee v. Federal Election Commission*, 518 U.S. 604 (1996), was whether this ad campaign was an independent or a coordinated expenditure. An independent expenditure is beyond the reach of federal limits, while a coordinated expenditure—an expenditure made "in connection" with a candidate's campaign—is subject to federal spending limits. The Colorado Democrats filed a complaint with the FEC contending that the ads constituted a coordinated expenditure and that the cost of the ads exceeded the limit for such spending. The FEC agreed and proposed to settle the matter with a minimal civil penalty. The Colorado Republicans declined, and the FEC brought suit. The Supreme Court ruled that party expenditures may not be restricted unless there is direct evidence that the spending was coordinated with an individual candidate's campaign. Justice Breyer reviewed prior decisions involving federal regulation of campaign financing and identified two relevant propositions: that restrictions on independent expenditures neither impair political advocacy nor relate directly to preventing political corruption. It was Breyer's view that limits on a party's independent expenditures cannot "escape the controlling effect" of these prior rulings. Indeed, the independent expression of a party's views is "core First Amendment activity no less than is the independent expression of individuals, candidates, or other political committees." The Court, said Breyer, was not aware of any "special dangers of corruption associated with a political party's independent expenditures to tip the constitutional balance in another direction." The absence of "prearrangement" and "coordination" do not eliminate but help diminish any danger that a candidate will understand the spending as an "effort to obtain a *quid pro quo.*" The diminished risk of corruption, in other words, could not justify the "burden on basic freedoms" produced by the party expenditure restriction. Indeed, Breyer continued, an expenditure made possible by a donation, but "controlled and directed" by a party rather than the donor, would seem "less likely to corrupt than ... [an] independent expenditure made directly by that donor." This prevents the Court from "assuming, absent convincing evidence to the contrary, that the limitation on political parties' independent expenditures is necessary to combat a substantial danger of corruption of the electoral system." Finally, Justice Breyer rejected the "conclusive presumption" of the FEC that all party expenditures are "coordinated"—that is, that the party and its candidates are "identical." While noting that a party's coordinated expenditures share some "constitutionally relevant features" with its independent expenditures, the Court remanded the question for further examination. The Court also chose not to respond to the contentions of the two major parties that any regulation of party expenditures, independent or otherwise, is barred by the First Amendment. That position, however, was embraced by Chief Justice Rehnquist and Justices Scalia, Kennedy, and Thomas. Justice Thomas would have gone even further. He called for the overturning of *Buckley v. Valeo*, 424 U.S. 1 (1976), and said the regulation of contributions is as burdensome on political speech and association as expenditure restrictions. Justices Stevens and Ginsburg dissented on this point. Stevens said government had an important interest in "leveling the electoral playing field," and urged the strengthening of regulations on party finances, both income and spending.

The question in *Federal Election Commission v. Akins*, 118 S.Ct. 1777 (1998), was whether lobbying organizations that engage in only minimal electioneering activity must comply with the disclosure requirements of the Federal Election Campaign Act (FECA). The American Israel Public Affairs Committee (AIPAC) is a tax-exempt organization that attempts to improve the relationship between the United States and Israel. AIPAC has an annual budget of about $10 million, the bulk of which is used to lobby Congress and the executive branch. The Federal Election Commission (FEC) has taken the position that unless campaign spending is the principal objective of an organization, the campaign finance law disclosure requirements do not apply. The plaintiffs in this case, including James Akins, former Ambassador to Saudi Arabia, were critical of American support for Israel. The plaintiffs filed a complaint with the FEC in 1989 contending that the AIPAC was sufficiently engaged in electoral activity to qualify as a political committee under the terms of the FECA. Specifically, the plaintiffs alleged that AIPAC was violating provisions of federal campaign finance law by making unreported contributions and direct expenditures on behalf of candidates for federal office, and expending funds that were not from a designated and separated political expenditure fund. The FEC dismissed the complaint, concluding that the campaign involvement of AIPAC was not its major objective and involved only a fraction of its overall expenditures. Akins then challenged the FEC dismissal of the complaint in the U.S. District Court for the District of Columbia. The district court eventually upheld the FEC decision to dismiss, but the U.S. Court of Appeals for the District of Columbia Circuit, sitting en banc, reversed, concluding that AIPAC was a political committee subject to all provisions of the FECA. The FEC, on the other hand, argued that the plaintiffs did not have standing to bring the suit. The U.S. Supreme Court ruled that Akins and the others had standing to bring suit against the FEC for its failure to enforce disclosure requirements against AIPAC. At the same time, the Court remanded the case back to the FEC for it to apply its new definition of a political committee. The new definition would expand the scope of a "membership organization," which, in turn, would categorize expenditures like those of AIPAC as "membership communications" rather than political expenditures. The latter would be subject to disclosure, but the former would not. The Court chose not to address the disputed definition of a "political committee" because the new FEC definition would probably make the question moot, at least with respect to AIPAC. On the standing issue, Justice Breyer said that the plaintiffs had suffered "informational injury...directly related to voting." The Court concluded that Congress had intended to protect voters from the kind of injury at issue in this case. Furthermore, this injury was both "concrete and specific," and even though the injury may be "widely shared," Congress has the constitutional power to "authorize its vindication in the Federal courts." Justices Scalia, O'Connor, and Thomas dissented, concluding that the Court had taken the standing concept "beyond what the Constitution permits."

Electoral Process: Political Parties

Tashjian v. Republican Party, **479 U.S. 208 (1986),** ruled that states may not require political parties to hold primary elections open only to registered party members. Connecticut law required that voters in a party primary must be registered members of that party. In an effort to broaden its own electoral base, the Republican Party of Connecticut changed its rules of participation in primaries for federal and state offices to allow registered voters not affiliated with any political party to vote in Republican primaries. The Supreme Court ruled for the Party on associational grounds. Justice Marshall said courts must first consider the character and magnitude of the asserted injury to protected rights, and then evaluate the precise interests offered by the state as justification for any burden. The Party's First Amendment interest was clearly evident to the Court; the freedom to engage in association is an inseparable aspect of the liberty embraced by freedom of speech. Associational freedom extends to partisan political organizations, and the right to associate with the party of one's choice was viewed as an integral part of this basic constitutional freedom. Accordingly, the Party's attempt to broaden its base is conduct "undeniably central to the exercise of the right to association." The statute in this case limited whom the Party could invite to participate in the basic function of selecting the

Party's candidates. The law thus limited the Party's "associational opportunities at the crucial juncture at which the appeal to common principle may be translated into concerted actions, and hence to political power in the community." Connecticut attempted to defend the regulation on several grounds, but the Court found each unpersuasive. First, the state claimed the administration of primaries under the Party's rule would cost too much. Even if the state were accurate in its projections, the Court said that the possibility of future cost increases in administering the election policy is not a sufficient basis in this case for interfering with the Party's associational rights. Second, Connecticut contended that the law prevented raiding, a practice whereby voters sympathetic to one party participate in another party's primary in hope of influencing the result. While acknowledging a legitimate state interest in preventing raiding and thereby protecting the integrity of the electoral process, the Court felt a raid on the Republican primary by independents was seen as substantially different from a raid by members of opposing parties. The Court also rejected Connecticut's contention that the law prevented voter confusion. The state argued that the public might not understand what a candidate stands for when he or she is nominated by an "unknown, amorphous body outside the party, while nevertheless using the party name." The Court deferred, however, to the ability of voters to remain sufficiently informed without the state's assistance. Finally, Connecticut contended that its law protected the integrity of the two-party system and the responsibility of party government. Here the Court refused to consider the wisdom of open versus closed primaries and was unwilling to let the state substitute its own judgment for that of the Party, even if the latter's course of conduct was destructive of its own interests. Speaking for himself and Chief Justice Rehnquist and Justice O'Connor, Justice Scalia said in dissent that the Court's view exaggerated the importance of the associational issue involved. He said the Party's only complaint was that it could not leave selection of its candidates to persons unwilling to become Party members. He thought it "fanciful" to see an associational linkage between the Republican Party and putative independent voters, where there was no meaningful connection. *See also* ASSOCIATION, RIGHT TO, p. 617; *Munro v. Socialist Workers Party*, p. 178.

Significance   The Court's ruling in *Tashjian* permitted a political party to determine the rules by which it conducted its own state primaries. A similar ruling was made in *Eu v. San Francisco County Democratic Central Committee*, 489 U.S. 214 (1989). California election law contained a provision forbidding governing bodies of political parties from endorsing or opposing candidates in primary elections. Another provision made it a misdemeanor for a primary candidate to claim official party endorsement. The Court invalidated these provisions on associational grounds. The ban on primary endorsements keeps a party from "stating whether a candidate adheres to the tenets of the party or whether party officials believe that the candidate is qualified" for office. The law "directly burdens" the party's capacity to "spread its message," said the Court, and it "hamstrings" voters as they attempt to inform themselves about issues and candidates. The party's associational rights allow it to "identify the people who constitute the association," and select candidates who best represent the party's "ideologies and preferences." Interfering with the party's power to endorse "suffocates this right."

The Court has generally steered clear of intervention in partisan political processes. In *O'Brien v. Brown*, 409 U.S. 1 (1972), for example, the Court invoked the "political question" doctrine when it held that federal courts did not possess the authority to interject themselves into the deliberative processes of a presidential nominating convention. A decade later the Court ruled in *Democratic Party v. LaFollette*, 450 U.S. 107 (1981), that a state could not require national party convention delegates to support the candidacy of the winner of the state's presidential primary.

Notwithstanding this generally noninterventionist tendency, the Court has found state interest in some restrictions on the electoral process to be compelling. In *Rosario v. Rockefeller*, 410 U.S. 752 (1973), it upheld a requirement that voters register in a party at least 30 days prior to a general election in order to participate in the next primary. In *Burson v. Freeman*, 504 U.S. 191 (1992), the Court permitted a state to ban political activities, including the distribution of political campaign materials, within 100 feet of a polling place on election day. Upon examination of the history of election regulation, the Court found a "wide-spread and time-tested consensus that some restricted zone is necessary to serve the States' compelling interest in preventing voter intimidation and election fraud." The law was challenged on the grounds that it was content based—it only regulated political expression around polling places. Justice Blackmun said that failure to regulate all speech does not "render the statute fatally under-inclusive." Blackmun also focused on the secret ballot as an integral effort to curb electoral abuses. The only way to preserve the secrecy of the ballot, he argued, "is to limit access to the area around the voter." Justice Stevens, joined by Justices O'Connor and Souter, dissented. They saw the law as a restriction of speech based on its content. Creation of campaign-free zones may protect orderly access to the polls, but at the same time prevent last-minute campaigning. It was the dissenters' view that this regulation unnecessarily "hindered" the latter.

In *Burdick v. Takushi*, 504 U.S. 245 (1992), the Court ruled that a state ban on write-in voting imposed only a "very limited burden" on the right to vote. Noting several different ways party or independent candidates may appear on Hawaii's primary ballot, the Court concluded that the restriction on write-in voting did not unreasonably "interfere with the right of voters to associate and have candidates of their choice placed on the ballot." The Court also rejected the contention that a voter is entitled both to cast and have counted a "protest vote." The function of the election process, said Justice White, is to "'winnow out and finally reject all but the chosen,' not to provide means of giving vent to 'short-range political goals, pique, or personal quarrels.'" Justices Kennedy, Blackmun, and Stevens saw the ban on write-in voting as preventing voters dissatisfied with choices available "from participating in Hawaiian elections in a meaningful manner."

Timmons v. Twin Cities Area New Party, **520 U.S. 351 (1997)** Most states prohibit candidates for public office from appearing on the ballot as the nominee of more than one political party. Minnesota has such an "antifusion" candidacy law, and it prevented the Twin Cities Area New Party from nominating a state legislative candidate who was already the candidate of one of the two major parties in the state. The fusion or cross-nomination strategy is often important to the viability of minor parties that would otherwise have no chance of electing candidates on their own. The Twin Cities Area New Party brought suit asserting that the law violated New Party members' First Amendment right to associational expression. The Supreme Court disagreed in *Timmons*. Chief Justice Rehnquist said that the First Amendment protects the right of citizens to "associate and to form political parties for the advancement of common political goals and ideas." At the same time, "it is also clear that States may, and inevitably must, enact reasonable regulations of parties, elections, and ballots to reduce election and campaign related disorder." The states have been granted "broad power" to prescribe the time, place, and manner of elections for federal offices, a power "matched by state control over the election process for state offices." When deciding whether a state election law violates associational rights, the Court must "weigh the 'character and magnitude' of the burden the State's rule imposes on those rights against the interests the State contends justify that burden." Regulations that impose "severe burdens" must advance a compelling interest and be narrowly tailored. Lesser burdens "trigger less exacting review," however, and a state's "important regulatory interests" are typically sufficient to justify "reasonable, nondiscriminatory restrictions." Rehnquist called the New Party's right to select its own candidates "uncontroversial," but that a party was not "absolutely entitled to have its nominee appear on the ballot as that party's candidate." The Minnesota law did not regulate the party's "internal affairs or core associational activities." Rather, it simply kept one party's candidate from appearing on the ballot "as that party's candidate, if already nominated by another party." The Minnesota law, in the Court's view, neither directly precluded minor political parties from "developing and organizing" nor "excluded a particular group of citizens, or a political party from participation in the election process." Thus, the New Party remained free to "endorse whom it likes, to ally itself with others, to nominate candidates for office, and to spread its message to all who will listen." The Court agreed that the ban on fusion candidacies did prevent the New Party from using the ballot to "communicate" its support of a particular candidate who is already another party's nominee. The Court was unpersuaded, however, by the Party's claim that it had a right to use the ballot itself to "send a particularized message" to its candidates or voters. Ballots serve "primarily to elect candidates, not as fora for political expression." Even with the ban, the Party retained "great latitude" to communicate ideas to voters through its participation in the campaign. In short, the Court concluded that the Minnesota ban did not restrict the ability of the Party and its members to "endorse support, and vote for anyone they like." The law was silent on the Party's "internal structure, governance, and policy-making," and the fusion ban did not directly limit ballot access by the Party. The burdens imposed on the Party's associational rights, "though not trivial, are not severe." The Constitution, said Rehnquist, does not require that Minnesota "compromise the policy choices embodied in its ballot-access requirements to accommodate the New Party's fusion strategy." Minnesota possesses a valid interest in making sure that minor parties that are granted ballot access are "bona fide and actually supported, on their own merits, by those who have provided the statutorily required petition or ballot support." The states also possess a strong interest in the "stability of their political systems." These interests enable the states to "enact reasonable election regulations that may, in practice, favor the traditional two-party system." As a result, states "need not remove all the many hurdles third parties face in the American political arena today." Justice Stevens, in dissent, characterized the premises upon which the Court's conclusions were based as "dubious." It was Stevens's view that while the ballot is not primarily a forum for individual expression of political sentiment through the act of voting, the ballot still serves an expressive function. Stevens saw a legitimate state interest in preventing political factionalism, but he suggested that the activity banned by the Minnesota policy was coalition formation, not the "division and dissension of 'splintered parties and unrestrained factionalism.'" *See also* ASSOCIATION, RIGHT TO, p. 617; FIRST AMENDMENT, p. 29; *Munro v. Socialist Workers Party*, p. 178.

Significance States typically have been permitted to condition ballot access on some level of support from the electorate. The access requirements may impinge on third parties and independents, however. The Court upheld a California law that denied ballot access to independents who had been registered party members within 17 months prior to an election in *Storer v. Brown*, 415 U.S. 724 (1974). This case was explicitly distinguished from the Connecticut law in *Tashjian v. Republican Party*, 479 U.S. 208 (1986). Justice Marshall said the regulations upheld in *Storer* were designed to protect parties from the "disorganizing effect of independent candidacies launched by unsuccessful putative nominees." This action was undertaken to protect the disruption of the political parties from without, and not to prevent parties from taking internal steps affecting their own process for the selection of candidates. Marshall was careful to point out, however, that *Tashjian* should not be read as blanket support for open primaries, or that no state regulation of primary voting qualifications could be sustained.

The Court addressed the issue of ballot access by a third party in *Norman v. Reed*, 502 U.S. 279 (1992). Illinois law required that new political parties wishing to run candidates for offices within a political subdivision must obtain signatures of 5 percent of the voters from the last election in the subdivision, or 25,000 voters, whichever was less. Another provision of the statute required the same minimum number of signatures to qualify a candidate running for statewide office. If the political unit was divided into separate districts, the signature requirement had to be met in each of the districts. Yet another statute prohibited new parties from using the same name as an established party. The Harold Washington Party (HWP), named after the former mayor of Chicago, was established in 1989. Its candidate in the 1989 mayoral election in the City of Chicago received more than 40 percent of the vote. The 40 percent support level established the party for ballot access purposes in the city. The following year, a group of people sought to expand the party throughout Cook County. The Cook County Board elects members from two districts, a city district and a suburban district. As an established party within the city, the HWP was able to run candidates in Chicago for countywide office and the city district seats. The party was not permitted, however, to run candidates for the suburban district seats because it had not met the 25,000-signature requirement in the district outside the city. The Supreme Court ruled that the signature requirement for the suburban district was not unduly burdensome under the specific facts of the case. Justice Souter said that citizens have a constitutional right to "create and develop" new political parties. As a result, a state must demonstrate a "sufficiently weighty" interest in order to justify an access limitation for new parties. The state has an interest in preventing misrepresentation caused by unaffiliated groups using the name of an established party, but the Court saw the categorical bar preventing candidates from one political subdivision from using the name of a party established only in another as broader than necessary to protect against misrepresentation. The 25,000-signature-per-district requirement was viewed as excessive because the same number of signatures would qualify a candidate to run statewide; organizers of a new party could access the statewide ballot with 25,000 signatures from the City of Chicago, but fail to qualify for the Cook County ballot in the suburban district. Souter concluded that if the state "deems it unimportant" to require new statewide parties to demonstrate any distribution of support, it requires "elusive logic" to demonstrate a serious state interest in demanding such a distribution for new local parties.

The Arkansas Educational Television Commission, a public agency of the state of Arkansas, operates a five-station noncommercial network (AETN). Although the Commission's members were political appointees and AETN received state funding, AETN exercised editorial judgment about the content broadcast over its stations. The AETN broadcast a number of debates involving congressional candidates in 1992. Two months after the Democratic and Republican Party candidates for Arkansas' Third Congressional District were invited to participate in a debate, Ralph Forbes, an independent candidate for the congressional seat, asked to be included in the debate. AETN concluded that Forbes was not a viable candidate for the office and declined his request. Forbes sought an injunction directing that AETN allow him to participate in the debate. He asserted that AETN's refusal to allow him to participate violated his First Amendment right of free speech. He was unable to obtain the injunction, however, and the debate took place without his participation. Forbes also was unsuccessful in his suit for damages. A jury was instructed that Forbes was required to show that AETN had excluded him because it either disagreed with his viewpoint or had been subjected to political pressure to exclude him. The jury concluded that Forbes had not demonstrated either circumstance and ruled in favor of AETN. The Court of Appeals for the Eighth Circuit reversed the judgment, however. The Supreme Court ruled in *Arkansas Education Television Commission v. Forbes*, 118 S.Ct. 1633 (1998), that stations have sufficient editorial discretion to exclude nonviable candidates from debates as long as the decision is not based on the candidate's issue positions. The Court first rejected the contention that "public forum" principles applied to this case. The public forum doctrine, said Justice Kennedy, should not be "extended in a mechanical way to the very different context of public television broadcasting." Broad rights of access for outside speakers would be "antithetical ... to the discretion that stations and their editorial staff must exercise to fulfill their journalistic purpose and statutory obligations." Public and private broadcasters both are required to exercise "substantial editorial discretion in the selection and presentation of their programming." If the courts were to define and require "pre-established criteria for access, it would risk implicating the courts in judgments that should be left to the exercise of journalistic discretion." Candidate debates, Kennedy acknowledged, present a "narrow exception" to the rule that public broadcasting does not lend itself to forum analysis. A candidate debate is different from other programming in that it is designed to be a forum for political speech, and debates have "exceptional significance" in the electoral process. Government does not create a "designated public forum," however, when it "does no more than reserve eligibility for access to the forum to a particular class of speakers, whose members must then, as individuals, obtain permission to use it." The AETN debate did not have an "open-microphone" format. Rather, the AETN made candidate-by-candidate determinations of which candidates would participate. Kennedy said that the Eighth Circuit's ruling that the debate was a public forum open to all candidates would place a "severe burden" on public broadcasters who air candidates' views. A public television editor might decide that the inclusion of all ballot-qualified candidates would "actually undermine the educational value and quality of debates." Were it faced with the prospect of "cacophony," on the one hand, and "First Amendment liability," on the other, a public television broadcaster might "choose not to air candidates' views at all." A broadcaster might decide instead that the "safe course" is to avoid controversy, and by doing so, "diminish the free flow of information and ideas." The debate's status as a "nonpublic forum," however, did not give AETN "unfettered power to exclude any candidate it wished." Exclusion must not be based on the speaker's viewpoint and must be "otherwise reasonable in light of the purpose of the property." In this case, it was "beyond dispute" that Forbes was excluded not because of his views but because he had "generated no appreciable public interest." His own "objective lack of support, not his platform," was the basis of his exclusion. Thus, AETN's decision to exclude Forbes was a "reasonable, viewpoint-neutral exercise of journalistic discretion consistent with the First Amendment." Justice Stevens, joined by Justices Souter and Ginsburg, dissented. They saw the publicly owned status of AETN as decisive because it made the central issue the right of a state-owned network to "regulate speech" in the electoral process. Because AETN was publicly owned, deference to its editorial discretion in making decisions about the "political content of its programs necessarily increases the risk of government censorship and propaganda in a way that protection of privately owned broadcasters does not."

Electoral Process: Ballot Access

Munro v. Socialist Workers Party, **479 U.S. 189 (1986),** upheld a state law limiting general election ballot access to those candidates receiving at least 1 percent of the primary vote total. The state of Washington established a two-step process for minor party candidates seeking to get on the general election ballot. Each candidate had first to secure the convention nomination of his or her party. As the nominee, the candidate would appear on the primary election ballot. In order to access the general election ballot, the candidate needed to receive at least 1 percent of all votes cast for that office in the primary election. Candidate Dean Peoples was placed on the primary election ballot as the nominee of the Socialist Workers Party. Peoples received only 596 of the 681,690 votes cast in the primary, or .09 percent. Accordingly his name was not placed on the general election ballot. An action was brought in federal court by Peoples, the Party, and two registered voters claiming abridgment of rights secured by the First Amendment. The Supreme Court upheld the restrictions on ballot access. The Court noted that restrictions on ballot access for political parties impinges both on the rights of individuals to associate for political purposes and the rights of qualified voters to cast their votes efficaciously. Such rights are not absolute, however, and are necessarily subject to qualification if elections are to be run fairly and effectively. In reviewing the restrictions of this type, Justice White said it is clear that states may condition access to the general election ballot by minor party or independent candidates upon a showing of a modicum of support among the potential voters for the office. When states attempt to justify access restrictions, there is no requirement of a "particularized showing of the existence of voter confusion, ballot overcrowding, or the presence of frivolous candidates prior to the imposition of reasonable restrictions." Such a requirement would necessitate that a state's electoral processes sustain some level of damage before the legislature could act. The Court preferred that legislatures be able to respond to potential deficiencies proactively as long as the response is reasonable and does not significantly impinge on protected rights. In this case, the Court concluded that Washington had created no impediment to voting in primary elections. Candidates and members of any organization, regardless of size or duration of existence, were viewed as wholly free to associate, to proselytize, to speak, to write, and to organize campaigns for any school of thought they wished. States do not have a constitutional imperative to reduce voter apathy or assist unpopular candidates to enhance their chances of gaining access to the general election ballot. All Washington did here was to require a candidate to demonstrate a significant modicum of voter support, a condition it was entitled to impose. Justices Marshall and Brennan dissented, and spoke to the role of minor parties in the American political system and argued that their contributions cannot be realized if they are unable to participate meaningfully in the phase of the electoral process in which policy choices are most seriously considered. In their view, the state had impermissibly preempted participation by minor parties and allowed them to be "excised from the electoral process before they have fulfilled their central role in a democratic political tradition: to channel dissent into that process in a constructive fashion." *See also* ASSOCIATION, RIGHT TO, p. 617; FIRST AMENDMENT, p. 29.

Significance   The ballot access issue examined in *Munro v. Socialist Workers Party* is not new. For years the Court refrained from engaging in direct supervision of state electoral processes. That policy began to change with the Warren Court's decision to address the issue of legislative apportionment. Regulations that made it difficult for new or minor parties to get on the ballot began to be scrutinized more carefully. In *Williams v. Rhodes*, 393 U.S. 23 (1968), for example, the Court voided an Ohio statute that required new parties to file a substantial number of petition signatures to access the ballot. Established parties were exempt from the requirement, and the Court ruled that the policy unfairly burdened new parties.

Similarly, the Court struck down an early filing date for candidates other than those nominated by the two major parties in *Anderson v. Celebrezze*, 460 U.S. 780 (1983). But as Justice White said in *Munro*, there were cases decided during this same period that established with unmistakable clarity that states may, as a manifestation of their interest in preserving the integrity of the election process, require candidates to make a preliminary showing of support to qualify for ballot access. In *Jenness v. Fortsen*, 403 U.S. 431 (1971), the Court sustained a Georgia requirement that independent and minor party candidates submit petitions signed by at least 5 percent of those eligible to vote in the election for the office involved. Likewise, the Court upheld a state requirement in *American Party of Texas v. White*, 415 U.S. 767 (1974), that minor party candidates demonstrate support through signatures of voters numbering at least 1 percent of the total votes cast in the most recent gubernatorial election. What is clearly reflected in such cases as *Jenness*, *White*, and *Munro* is that the Court will permit states significant latitude in restricting ballot access as long as access conditions are not excessive.

Campaign Regulations

McIntyre v. Ohio Elections Commission, **514 U.S. 334 (1995)**   An Ohio statute required the name and address of the person(s) or organization(s) that distributes literature designed to influence the outcome of an election. The Ohio Elections Commission (OEC) found that Margaret McIntyre had violated the law by distributing unsigned campaign literature opposing a local tax initiative and fined her $100. The U.S. Supreme Court declared the Ohio law unconstitutional, concluding that an author's decision to remain anonymous, like other decisions concerning publication content, is "an aspect of the freedom of speech protected by the First Amendment." Ohio sought to justify the regulation as a means of preventing dissemination of fraudulent, false, or libelous statements. The Court was unpersuaded, however, noting that the Ohio statute contained no language so limiting its application to such statements. Instead, the category of speech regulated by Ohio, said Stevens, "occupies the core of the protection afforded by the First Amendment." Discussion of political issues must be afforded the broadest constitutional protection in order to ensure the fullest possible debate. Stevens continued that "[n]o form of speech is entitled to greater constitutional protection." Although deterrence of misleading or false statements was regarded as a legitimate state interest, the Court was satisfied that Ohio had other means of protecting that interest without the "extremely broad" prohibition on anonymous expression. The state's interest in informing the public was also seen as insufficient to justify the ban on anonymous speech. The identity of a speaker is "no different from other components of [a] document's content that the author is free to include or exclude." The simple interest in providing voters with additional relevant information "does not justify a state requirement that a writer make statements or disclosures she would otherwise omit." Anonymous pamphleteering is "not a pernicious, fraudulent practice, but an honorable tradition of advocacy and of dissent," and anonymity is a "shield from the tyranny of the majority." The right to remain anonymous "may be abused when it shields fraudulent conduct," but political speech will inherently have "unpalatable consequences." While Ohio can attempt to regulate fraud directly, it cannot seek to punish fraud indirectly by "indiscriminately outlawing a category of speech, based on its content, with no necessary relationship to the danger sought to be prevented." Justice Thomas preferred an approach that examined whether the free speech protection, as "originally understood," protected anonymous leafletting. He concluded that it did, and voted to strike down the Ohio law. Chief Justice Rehnquist and Justice Scalia were of the view that protection of the election process is a most compelling interest, one that "justifies limitations upon speech that cannot constitutionally be imposed generally." Further, Scalia and Rehnquist were convinced that the ban on anonymous campaigning was effective in protecting democratic elections. A person who is required to put his or her name on a document is "much less likely to lie than one who can lie anonymously." The Ohio law, Scalia suggested, not only deters campaign falsehoods but also promotes a "civil and dignified level of campaign debate—which the State has no power to command, but ample power to encourage by such undemanding measures as a signature requirement." *See also* FIRST AMENDMENT, p. 29.

Significance Anonymous pamphleteering and leafletting have been recognized as legitimate forms of expression since the beginning of our constitutional history. Indeed, the *Federalist* was authored by James Madison, Alexander Hamilton, and John Jay under the pseudonym of "Publius." The Court has typically found regulations such as found in *McIntyre* to be suspect.

The Burger Court, however, upheld a ban on the posting of political campaign signs on utility poles in *Members of City Council v. Taxpayers for Vincent*, 466 U.S. 789 (1984). The ban was seen to be content neutral and directed toward a legitimate aesthetic interest. The purpose of the regulation was "unrelated to the suppression of ideas," and interfered with expression only to the extent necessary to eliminate visual clutter. The Court noted that the ban on posting signs did not impinge on any alternative modes of communication.

The Rehnquist Court recognized the value of speaker identity in *Ladue v. Gilleo*, 512 U.S. 43 (1994). Ladue, Missouri, banned residential signs except for a number of exempted categories of signs; for example, signs that identified property, indicated property was for sale, or conveyed safety warnings, among others. Margaret Gilleo placed a sign in her yard indicating her opposition to the Persian Gulf War and was cited for violating the sign ordinance. The Supreme Court unanimously struck down the sign ban as affording residents of Ladue insufficient alternative means to express themselves. Displaying a sign from one's own residence, said Justice Stevens, "often carries a message quite distinct from placing the same sign somewhere else, or conveying the same text or picture by other means." Unlike in *McIntyre*, the Court assigned value to the identity of the speaker in *Ladue*. The location of signs provides important information about the identity of the speaker, often an "important component of many attempts to persuade."

Term Limits

***U.S. Term Limits, Inc. v. Thornton*, 514 U.S. 779 (1995)**   Twenty-three states have adopted some form of term limits on members of

Congress. The voters of Arkansas adopted a constitutional amendment (Amendment 73) in 1992 effectively limiting membership in the U.S. House of Representatives to three terms (6 years), and U.S. Senate membership to two terms (12 years). Specifically, Amendment 73 prohibited placing on the ballot the name of an otherwise qualified candidate for Congress if that candidate had already served three terms in the U.S. House or two terms in the U.S. Senate. The amendment permitted incumbents who reached the term limits to run and be reelected by write-in campaigns. Suits were filed in an Arkansas court challenging the constitutionality of Amendment 73. There were a number of plaintiffs, including Congressman Ray Thornton. Various organizations supporting term limits, including U.S. Term Limits, Inc., intervened as defendants. The U.S. Supreme Court ruled against Amendment 73. Constitutionality of Amendment 73 "depends critically" on the resolution of two issues, said Justice Stevens. The first is whether the Constitution prohibits states from adding to or altering the qualifications "specifically enumerated" in Article I. Second, if the Constitution does forbid such change, the issue of whether Amendment 73 is a ballot access restriction rather than an "outright disqualification" of otherwise qualified incumbents must be resolved. The majority was guided by the Court's ruling in *Powell v. McCormack*, 395 U.S. 486 (1969). The issue in *Powell* was whether Congress's power to judge the qualifications of its own members included the power to impose qualifications other than those enumerated in Article I. The Court concluded that it did not. The Court recognized in *Powell* that the ratification debates "confirmed that the framers understood the qualifications in the Constitution to be fixed and unalterable by Congress." The Court also noted in *Powell* that allowing Congress to impose additional qualifications "would violate that 'fundamental principle of our representative democracy … that the people should choose whom they please to govern them.'" He also rejected the argument that, because *Powell* dealt with House power to exclude a member, it did not control the more general question of whether Congress has the power to add qualifications. *Powell*, said Stevens, is "not susceptible to such a narrow reading."

Powell, however, did not reach the question of whether the Constitution prohibits additional qualifications imposed by states. The supporters of term limits argued that in the absence of an explicit constitutional prohibition, the reserved powers in the Tenth Amendment should allow states to add such qualifications. The Court was unpersuaded for two reasons. First, historical materials showed that the Framers drew a basic distinction between the powers of the newly created national government and the powers retained by the preexisting sovereign states. Contrary to the assertions of those supporting Amendment 73, the power to add qualifications is not part of the sovereignty the Tenth Amendment reserved to the states. Petitioners' Tenth Amendment argument, said Stevens, "misconceives the nature of the right at issue because that amendment could only 'reserve' that which existed before." Second, even if states had some original power on this subject, the Court concluded that the Framers intended the Constitution to be "the exclusive source of qualifications for members of Congress," and that the Framers thereby "divested" states of any power to add qualifications. When the Framers decided to create an entirely new national government at the Constitutional Convention, they "envisioned a uniform national system, rejecting the notion that the nation was a collection of states, and instead creating a direct link between the national Government and the people of the United States." Rather, any power the state might have to set congressional membership qualifications must derive from the delegated powers of national sovereignty. In the absence of explicit delegation of such power to the states, state power to add qualifications does not exist. Further, permitting states to fashion diverse qualifications for members of Congress, said Stevens, would result in a "patchwork of state qualifications, undermining the uniformity and the national character that the framers envisioned and sought to ensure." The Court was convinced that allowing states to adopt term limits for Congress would "effect a fundamental change in the constitutional framework." A change of that kind cannot come from legislation adopted by either Congress or the states, but must come through the amendment procedures set out by the Constitution in Article V.

Justice Thomas issued a lengthy dissent that was joined by Chief Justice Rehnquist and Justices O'Connor and Scalia. He pointed to the irony of the Court's recognition of the people's right to freely choose their representatives, but not allowing elected legislatures or the people themselves through ballot initiatives to "prescribe any qualifications for those representatives." It was the dissenters' view that nothing in the Constitution bars the people of each state the power to establish eligibility requirements for candidates. When the Constitution is "silent" on an issue, it "raises no bar to action by the states or the people." Thomas also suggested that the Court had made more of the Qualifications Clauses than was appropriate. They restrict state power only in that they keep states from ignoring or abolishing "all eligibility requirements for membership in Congress." Historical evidence is "simply insufficient" to warrant the Court's conclusion that the Article I provisions on qualifications "mean any more than they say." The Qualifications Clauses give the people of other states no basis to complain if the people of Arkansas elect a new representative in preference to a long-term incumbent. Similarly, it is "hard to see why the rights of the people of other states have been violated when the people of Arkansas decide to enact a more general disqualification of long-term incumbents." As long as the candidate sent to Congress meets the age, citizenship, and inhabitancy requirements of Article I, the "people of Arkansas have not violated the Qualifications Clauses." *See also* FEDERALISM, p. 649.

Significance   States typically have wide-ranging authority to regulate elections. Occasionally, the Court invalidates provisions of state election law because they conflict with specific provisions of the U.S. Constitution. The term limit ruling is an example of such a conflict. A similar ruling came in the Louisiana primary case. Since 1978 Louisiana has conducted an "open" primary for congressional offices in October of federal election years. All candidates, regardless of party affiliation, are listed on the same ballot, and all voters are entitled to vote. If a candidate for a particular office receives a majority at the primary, the person is elected to the office without any voting necessary on the federal election day in November. Since this system went into effect, over 80 percent of the state's contested congressional elections have ended with the October open primary. G. Scott Love and other Louisiana voters challenged the primary on the grounds that it violated a federal law that establishes a uniform date in November for congressional elections. A federal district court upheld the Louisiana process, but the U.S. Court of Appeals for the Fifth Circuit reversed that ruling. The Supreme Court ruled in *Foster v. Love*, 118 S.Ct. 464 (1998) that the process conflicts with federal law in that it allows potentially final election of U.S. senators and representatives before the designated federal election day. The Elections Clause of Article I permits states to determine the "times, places, and manner" of congressional elections, but also permits Congress to "alter such regulations" at any time. The Clause, said Justice Souter, is a "default provision; it invests the States with responsibility for the mechanics of congressional elections, but only so far as Congress declines to pre-empt state legislative choices." The Elections Clause thus gives Congress the power to "override state regulations" by establishing uniform rules for federal elections that are binding on the states. Without "paring the term 'election' in [the federal law] down to the constitutional bone," it is sufficient to resolve this case that a "contested selection of candidates for a congressional office that is concluded as a matter of law before the federal election day, with no act in law or in fact to take place on the date chosen by Congress, clearly violates [the federal law]." Louisiana sought to save the election process by suggesting that there was provision for a "general" election on the federal election day, and that the Louisiana open primary concerns only the manner for electing federal representatives and not the time of the election. Justice Souter characterized this argument as "mere wordplay." After a candidate receives a majority of votes in the open primary, Louisiana law requires no further act by anyone to "seal the election; the election has already occurred." When Congress established the uniform election day, it was concerned with the "distortion" of the voting process threatened when the results of an early federal election in one state can "influence later voting in other States, with the burden on citizens forced to turn out on two different election days to make final selections of federal officers in presidential election years." The Louisiana open primary process has tended to "foster both evils," said Souter. It has had the effect of "conclusively electing more than 80% of the state's Senators and Representatives before the election day elsewhere," and, in presidential election years, having "forced voters to turn out for two potentially conclusive federal elections."

Government Contractors and Patronage

***Wabaunsee County v. Umbehr*, 518 U.S. 668 (1996),** examined the political speech rights of an independent government contractor. Umbehr was under contract to provide trash collection for Wabaunsee County, Kansas. He was also openly critical of the performance of the Wabaunsee County Commission. Umbehr filed suit in federal court when his contract was terminated by the Commission, contending that the action was prompted by his expressed criticism of county government. The Supreme Court ruled that a private contractor was entitled to the same free speech protections as a government employee. Justice O'Connor acknowledged that the Court had never examined whether the First Amendment limits the capacity of the government to terminate relationships with independent contractors because of the contractors' speech. She noted, however, the "obvious" similarities between government employees and government contractors, and the government employment precedents were seen as controlling this case. Although government needs to be able to terminate both employees and independent contractors for various legitimate reasons, the threat of the loss of a "valuable financial benefit" on the basis of speech "may chill speech on matters of public concern."

In choosing the government employee precedents, especially the balancing test from *Pickering v. Board of Education*, 391 U.S. 563 (1968), the Court rejected a "bright line" distinction between government employees and independent contractors. The "bright line" approach advocated by the Board would give the government "carte blanche to terminate independent contractors for exercising First Amendment

185

rights." Furthermore, such an approach would leave First Amendment rights, said O'Connor, "unduly dependent" on whether state law defines a contract for provision of government services as a contract of employment or a contract for services, a "distinction which is at best a very poor proxy for the interests at stake." Finally, the Court was unconvinced by Justice Scalia's dissenting view on three points—fear of excessive litigation, compatibility with longstanding practice, and serving the best interests of the government. O'Connor said fear of excessive litigation cannot justify government practices that "deprive independent government contractors of protection." Equally insufficient as a justification for allocating government contracts on the "basis of political bias" is the claimed "long and unbroken tradition of our people." The Court does not believe "that tradition legitimizes patronage contracting." Finally, O'Connor said the Court did not believe that a "deferentially administered requirement" that the government not "unreasonably terminate its commercial relationships on the basis of speech or political affiliation poses a greater threat to legitimate government interests than the complex and detailed array of modern statutory and regulatory government contracting laws." The case was remanded for further proceedings, and O'Connor described how the proper balancing approach would apply in this case. On remand, Umbehr would have to demonstrate that the termination of his contract was "motivated by his speech on a public concern," a showing that would require him to prove "more than the mere fact he criticized the Board members before they terminated him." If Umbehr could make such a showing, the Board would have a "valid defense" if it could show that "in light of their knowledge, perceptions, and policies at the time of termination, the Board members would have terminated the contract regardless of his speech." Justice Scalia, joined by Justice Thomas, dissented. Among other things, he argued for perspective. This case involves "petty-tyrant politicians" acting with unacceptable arrogance. Further, Wabaunsee County won a summary judgment with only the plaintiffs "tale" before the trial court. Even if the plaintiff's allegations were true, the behavior present in this was "highly unusual." For every "extreme" case of the kind seen here, there are "thousands of contracts awarded on a 'favoritism' basis that no one would get excited about." Scalia criticized the Court for "living in another world," and throwing out "vast numbers of practices that are routine in American political life in order to get rid of a few bad apples." *See also* ASSOCIATION, RIGHT TO, p. 617; FIRST AMENDMENT, p. 29; FREE SPEECH CLAUSE, p. 654; *United States v. National Treasury Employees Union*, p. 97.

Significance   The Burger Court extensively dealt with political appointments. In *Elrod v. Burns*, 427 U.S. 347 (1976), the Court held that an incoming county official could not fire department employees because they belonged to the wrong party. *Branti v. Finkel*, 445 U.S. 507 (1980), involved assistant public defenders also terminated on the basis of partisanship. The rationale shared by these two cases was that firings based on party affiliation penalized political thought.

This principle was broadened by the Rehnquist Court in *Rutan v. Republican Party*, 497 U.S. 62 (1990). In *Rutan*, the Court ruled that hiring decisions for public positions could not be based on party affiliation. Justice Brennan said that political victors are entitled to "only those spoils that may be constitutionally obtained." Unless party affiliation is an "appropriate requirement" for a position, the First Amendment precludes use of party affiliation in hiring, promotion, recall, and transfer decisions. Employees who do "not compromise their beliefs" stand to lose in a variety of ways if party affiliation may be used in making job decisions. For example, an employee may lose "increases in pay or job satisfaction attendant to promotion." These are "significant penalties … imposed for the exercise of rights guaranteed by the First Amendment." Unless use of patronage is "narrowly tailored" to further a "vital" governmental interest, it encroaches on the First Amendment. Illinois asserted that patronage both produced a more effective workforce and protected political parties. The Court disagreed. Justice Brennan said that government can secure "effective" employees by sanctioning workers whose work is "deficient." Party affiliation is not a proxy for deficient performance as such. Neither is the democratic process furthered by patronage. Parties are "nurtured by other, less intrusive and equally effective methods." To the contrary, patronage "decidedly impairs the elective process by discouraging free political expression by public employees." Justice Scalia said in dissent that a legislature could determine that patronage "stabilizes political parties and prevents excessive political fragmentation—both of which are results in which states have a strong governmental interest."

The Rehnquist Court decided another case with *Umbehr* in 1995 that focused even more tightly on the question of whether patronage-based awarding of government contracts violates the First Amendment. A towing company was among those included on a police dispatch list in Northlake, Illinois. Each company was called "in rotation" with other companies whenever police needed vehicles moved. The company owner openly supported the incumbent mayor's opponent in an election. The incumbent mayor was reelected, and the towing company was removed from the dispatch list. The company's owner claimed that the city's action was in retaliation for his support of the mayor's opponent. The case of *O'Hare Trucking Services, Inc. v. Northlake*, 518 U.S. 712 (1996), differed from

Umbehr in that it focused more extensively on the patronage issue, and the Court's reasoning drew more extensively from patronage precedents such as *Elrod, Branti,* and *Rutan.* These cases had established that public employees may not be discharged for failure to support a political party or its candidates unless political affiliation is a reasonably appropriate requirement for the job. The question in *O'Hare* was whether the same protection extends to an independent contractor. The Supreme Court ruled that it did. There is "no doubt," said Justice Kennedy, that the towing company's owner could not have been removed from the list for refusing to contribute to the mayor's campaign if he had been a public employee. Northlake contended that the protective rulings of *Elrod, Branti,* and *Rutan* did not apply here—that unlike a public employee, an independent contractor's First Amendment rights "must yield to the government's asserted countervailing interest in sustaining a patronage system." Kennedy said, however, that the Court could not accept the contention that those who "perform the government's work outside the formal employment relationship" are subject to the "direct and specific" abridgment of First Amendment rights. Government officials are accorded a "large measure of freedom" as they make decisions about contracting for goods and services. As long as government terminates its affiliation with a service provided "for reasons unrelated to political association," there will be no First Amendment violation. The "absolute right to enforce a patronage scheme" as a means of maintaining control over independent contractors, Kennedy concluded, has not been shown to be a "necessary part of a legitimate political system in all instances." As in *Umbehr,* Justice Scalia, joined by Justice Thomas, dissented. When a practice not expressly prohibited by the Constitution "bears the endorsement of a long tradition of open, widespread, and unchallenged use that dates back to the beginning of the Republic, we have no proper basis for striking it down."

CHAPTER 3

The Fourth Amendment

Overview, 191

The Fourth Amendment, 193

OVERVIEW

The Fourth Amendment states:

> The right of the people to be secure in their persons, houses, papers, and effects, against unreasonable searches and seizures, shall not be violated, and no Warrants shall issue, but upon probable cause, supported by Oath or affirmation, and particularly describing the place to be searched, and the persons or things to be seized.

The Fourth Amendment requires that invasions of privacy occur only under authority of a warrant. A warrant is to be issued by a neutral party based upon probable cause and must particularly describe what is to be searched for or seized. The basic definition of probable cause is provided in *Draper v. United States*, 358 U.S. 307 (1959), while the neutral party and particularity requirements are discussed in *Coolidge v. New Hampshire*, 403 U.S. 443 (1971), and *Ybarra v. Illinois*, 444 U.S. 85 (1979), respectively.

Contemporary application of the Fourth Amendment involves other warrant issues as well. *Illinois v. Gates*, 462 U.S. 213 (1983), weighed the use of information from informants to establish probable cause. *Zurcher v. Stanford Daily*, 436 U.S. 547 (1978), decided whether a state is prevented from issuing a search warrant simply because the possessor of the place to be searched is not suspected of criminal conduct. *Katz v. United States*, 389 U.S. 347 (1967), extended Fourth Amendment provisions to electronic surveillance. The exclusionary rule is a rule of evidence that disallows use of evidence secured by means of an unreasonable search and seizure. *Mapp v. Ohio*, 367 U.S. 643 (1961), held that the rule must be used in state as well as federal criminal trials. *United States v. Leon*, 468 U.S. 897 (1984), examined a "good faith" exception to the exclusionary rule.

Failure to secure a warrant does not necessarily make an arrest or a search unreasonable, but *Minnesota v. Olson*, 495 U.S. 95 (1990), established that a warrantless arrest must be accompanied by both probable cause and an exigent circumstance. *Riverside County v. McLaughlin*, 500 U.S. 44 (1991), held that when an individual is arrested without a warrant, a judicial officer must determine within 48 hours whether the arrest was justified. Several warrant exceptions have been recognized for searches, most of which stem from some kind of exigent circumstance. *Chimel v. California*, 395 U.S. 752

(1969), explored warrantless searches conducted incident to lawful arrests. The duration of an exigent circumstance exception is examined in *Michigan v. Tyler*, 436 U.S. 499 (1978). The plain view exception is described in *Washington v. Chrisman*, 455 U.S. 1 (1982). Searches of automobiles have generally been viewed as exigent situations as reflected in *Chambers v. Maroney*, 399 U.S. 42 (1970). *California v. Acevedo*, 500 U.S. 565 (1991), revisited the troublesome issue of searching closed containers seized from automobiles. The case of *Terry v. Ohio*, 392 U.S. 1 (1968), provided the Court an opportunity to consider the "stop and frisk" search technique even in the absence of probable cause. Investigative stops and "protective sweeps" are discussed in *Maryland v. Buie*, 494 U.S. 325 (1990). Waiver of Fourth Amendment protection through consent is the featured issue in *Ohio v. Robinette*, 519 U.S. 33 (1996). The very sensitive matter of drug testing was considered by the Court in *Vernonia School District 47J v. Acton*, 515 U.S. 646 (1995). The question of whether the common-law rule of "knock and announce" is part of the Fourth Amendment reasonable search protection was considered in *Richards v. Wisconsin*, 520 U.S. 385 (1997).

Helling v. McKinney, 509 U.S. 25 (1993), examines the nature of Fourth Amendment protections afforded persons housed in detention facilities. The fairness aspects of early release from incarceration were taken up in *Lynce v. Mathis*, 519 U.S. 433 (1997). Finally, the Court reviewed the asset forfeiture process in *Bennis v. Michigan*, 517 U.S. 1163 (1996).

The Fourth Amendment   The Fourth Amendment safeguards American citizens from unreasonable searches and seizures. The Fourth Amendment was included in the Bill of Rights as the direct result of the British imposition in the American colonies of writs of assistance. These general warrants allowed for arbitrary searches and seizures of persons and property. They proliferated in the years immediately preceding the American Revolution when they were issued to seize contraband smuggled into the colonies in violation of acts of Parliament imposing duties and tariffs on imports. In *Lopez v. United States*, 373 U.S. 427 (1963), Justice William J. Brennan said, "The evil of the general warrant is often regarded as the single immediate cause of the American Revolution." As early as 1761 James Otis, a prominent Boston lawyer and merchant, was railing against the use of writs of assistance. John Adams considered such condemnations the foundation of the Revolution. Of Otis's denunciations Adams wrote, "Then and there was the first scene of the first act of opposition to the arbitrary claims of Great Britain. Then and there the child Independence was born." When the child was more mature, it insisted on specific language to ensure that probable cause existed to issue a warrant. It said that name, place, and things sought must be identified. Further, the warrant must issue from a neutral magistrate who would be a disinterested third party between the individual citizen and the law enforcement officer seeking the warrant. Yet the Fourth Amendment only extended to the federal government in early American history. Passage of the Fourteenth Amendment in 1868 enabled eventual extension of the Fourth Amendment to the states. Nationalization of the Fourth Amendment was dramatically interpreted by the Supreme Court in such cases as *Mapp v. Ohio*, 367 U.S. 643 (1961), *Ker v. California*, 374 U.S. 23 (1963), *Aguilar v. Texas*, 378 U.S. 108 (1964), and *Chimel v. California*, 395 U.S. 752 (1969).

The wind changed, however, with Richard M. Nixon's "law and order mandate" in 1968, and with his appointment of Warren E. Burger as chief justice of the United States. With more conservative appointments, decisions of the Court have gradually moved from limiting the scope of permissible searches and seizures to limiting the scope of the rights of criminal defendants, including the boundaries of permissibility. In 1973, for example, the Burger Court upheld full searches of individuals lawfully arrested for traffic violations without evidence of probable cause in *United States v. Robinson*, 414 U.S. 218 (1973), and *Gustafson v. Florida*, 414 U.S. 260 (1973). Thus specific abuses under the Fourth Amendment are reinterpreted over time. *See also* EXCLUSIONARY RULE, p. 646; NEUTRAL MAGISTRATE, p. 680; PROBABLE CAUSE, p. 691; WARRANT, p. 710.

Significance   The Fourth Amendment established an absolute right against threat of unreasonable intrusion by agents and officials of the newly formed American government. The clamor for the Fourth Amendment, as well as the other amendments in the Bill of Rights, came out of the state constitutional ratifying conventions. The delegates to the Maryland convention said, for example, that the adoption of the Fourth Amendment was necessary because "a free people" must be provided a constitutional check effective to "safeguard our citizens" against the issuance of general warrants. In making their arguments, many of the states relied heavily on the language of Sir William Blackstone's *Commentaries on the Laws of England*, Volume IV, in which general warrants were declared to be illegal. Elements of Blackstone's language found their way into both the Constitution and the Bill of Rights. The English constitution did forbid the issuance of general writs. In 1766 Parliament expressly declared all general warrants for search and seizure illegal, but abuses of both common and statutory law were prevalent in Great Britain and in the American colonies in the late eighteenth century. Just prior to the American Revolution, members of Parliament were in fact debating the abuses of the general warrant process. Among the discussants were Sir Edward Coke, Sir Matthew Hale, and especially Lord Camden, who found the general warrant wholly outside the spirit of the English constitution. Lord Camden was quoted by a justice of the United States Supreme Court as late as 1886 when Joseph P. Bradley wrote in *Boyd v. United States*, 116 U.S. 616 (1886), that Camden's exposition expressed "the true doctrine on the subject of searches and seizures." It furnished "the true criteria of the reasonable and unreasonable character of such searches." The true doctrine and the true criteria are settled in American jurisprudence as the sanctity of a citizen's home and person. Hopefully the fundamental values safeguarded by the Framers' prohibition against unreasonable searches and seizures will far outlast changing historical circumstances.

Probable Cause

***Draper v. United States*, 358 U.S. 307 (1959),** clarified the basic definition of probable cause. Draper was arrested in Chicago by a federal agent who neither knew Draper nor had seen him commit any criminal offense. The experienced agent had been told by a "previously reliable" informant that Draper was engaged in narcotics distribution and that Draper would be arriving in Chicago by train. The arrest of Draper occurred at the railroad station where the officer recognized Draper from the physical description provided by the informant. A search conducted incident to the arrest yielded heroin. Draper was subsequently convicted on narcotics charges, and the heroin was admitted into evidence. With only Justice Douglas dissenting, the Supreme Court upheld the search. The critical question for the Court was whether the arresting officer had probable cause to take Draper into custody. The Court emphasized that the evidence needed to satisfy the probable cause standard is quite different from that needed to prove guilt. The Court said: "We deal with probabilities. These are not technical; they are the factual and practical considerations of everyday life on which reasonable and prudent men, not legal technicians, act." The arresting officer had found the informant reliable in the past, and "would have been derelict in his duties" had he not pursued the information. As a standard of probable cause, the Court suggested it exists when reasonably trustworthy information known to authorities is sufficient "to warrant a man of reasonable caution in the belief that an offense has been or is being committed." Thus the arresting officer had probable cause, his arrest of Draper was valid, and the search of Draper incident to the arrest produced admissible evidence. *See also* FOURTH AMENDMENT, p. 193; PROBABLE CAUSE, p. 691.

Significance   Arrest and search incident to an arrest without a warrant depend upon whether the arresting officer has probable cause. Even when acting on hearsay information, an arresting officer is entitled to consider such information in determining whether probable cause exists within the meaning of the Fourth Amendment. *Draper* provided the perspective that although an arrest or search is a governmental intrusion and a warrant can authorize the intrusion, a warrantless arrest and search are legally permitted if probable cause exists. Probable cause is defined as the level of evidence or knowledge required to convince a neutral third party, typically a judge or magistrate, to issue a warrant. The test applied is essentially the same test an officer must use in searching without a warrant. *Draper* establishes that probable cause relates to reasonable inferences rather than technical judgments drawn from rigid legal requirements. It is clear that probable cause does not require support conclusive of guilt. Instead, it deals with probabilities. The probabilities must be sufficiently high in the judgment of the magistrate to focus closely enough on a person or a place to justify an invasion of privacy by government. The probable cause standard can be met by evidence such as direct observation of criminal acts by a law enforcement officer, indirect observation by citizens or informants, physical evidence, or accounts of crimes by witnesses. The *Draper* test requires a nonneutral police officer to exercise the same judgment as a judicial officer, at least to a large degree. When an officer makes a warrantless search, the question is whether the officer had probable cause to make an arrest and a search pursuant to that arrest. The related deadly force issue is discussed in *Tennessee v. Garner,* 471 U.S. 1 (1985), in which the Court said that the use of deadly force is a seizure subject to the reasonableness requirement of the Fourth Amendment. Deadly force may be used only when it is necessary to prevent an escape. Even then an officer must have probable cause to believe the suspect "poses a significant threat of death or serious physical injury to the officer or to others." The use of deadly force to prevent any and all escapes, whatever the circumstances, is constitutionally unreasonable.

Neutral Magistrate

Coolidge v. New Hampshire, **403 U.S. 443 (1971),** examined the indispensable role of a neutral judicial officer in making the determination of probable cause. During an investigation of Coolidge, some evidence was obtained from his home without a search warrant. After his arrest, following warrantless seizure of guns and other evidence, a warrant to search Coolidge's automobile was obtained by the state. The arrest and search warrants, however, had been authorized by the state attorney general acting as a justice of the peace, a practice permitted under New Hampshire law. Prior to issuing the warrants, the attorney general had supervised the police investigation of the case, and subsequently served as chief prosecutor at Coolidge's trial. An incidental issue was that during the investigation, Coolidge's automobile, parked in his driveway, was towed to the police station where it was searched three times over the course of more than a year. Several search exemption questions stemmed from this fact. The Supreme Court concluded that the warrants issued by the attorney general were irreparably flawed. The Court said the Fourth Amendment offers protection by requiring that inferences made from evidence "are drawn by neutral and detached magistrates instead of being judged by the officer engaged in the often competitive enterprise of ferreting out crime." The Court felt that "there could hardly be a more appropriate setting than this for a *per se* rule of disqualification" because "prosecutors and police simply cannot be asked to maintain the requisite neutrality with regard to their own investigations." Because the attorney general could not be regarded as the "neutral and detached magistrate required by the Constitution, the search stands on no firmer ground than if there had been no warrant at all." *See also* FOURTH AMENDMENT, p. 193; NEUTRAL MAGISTRATE, p. 680; WARRANT, p. 710.

Significance The holding in *Coolidge* was that the search warrant issued by the state attorney general was invalid inasmuch as he was not a "neutral and detached magistrate." The appropriate authorizing party must have no direct interest in the search. Officials within the judicial branch are typically viewed as the neutral party most appropriately vested with the power to approve warrants. The basic constitutional rule is that searches conducted outside the judicial process, without prior approval by a judge or magistrate, are per se unreasonable under the Fourth Amendment.

In *Johnson v. United States*, 333 U.S. 10 (1948), the Court said the Fourth Amendment would become a "nullity" and would leave privacy to "police discretion" if judgments relative to the sufficiency of cause to conduct a search were left to other than "neutral and detached" magistrates. The required neutrality can also disappear if the magistrate issuing the warrant stands to gain financially. In *Connally v. Georgia*, 429 U.S. 245 (1977), the Court found a Georgia statute allowing warrants to be issued by unsalaried justices of the peace who collected a fee only when a warrant was issued to be in violation of the neutrality requirement. A judge may compromise neutrality by participating in the execution of the warrant as well. In *Lo-Ji Sales, Inc. v. New York*, 442 U.S. 319 (1979), a judge issued an open-ended warrant for seizure of allegedly obscene materials. He accompanied the police in the execution of the warrant and listed on the warrant additional seized items that he determined to be obscene. The Court unanimously condemned the practice because the judge "undertook to telescope the processes of the application for warrants, the issuance of the warrant, and its execution," and because it was "difficult to discern when he was acting as a 'neutral and detached' judicial officer and when he was one with the police and prosecutors in the executive seizure." The clear effect of *Coolidge* is that judicial officers typically possess the requisite neutrality to issue warrants, but a warrant issued by a nonneutral official makes the search essentially warrantless.

Warrant Particularity

Ybarra v. Illinois, **444 U.S. 85 (1979),** considered the degree of particularity that must be included in search warrants. Ybarra was a customer at a tavern that underwent a warrant-authorized search. The warrant specified the tavern and the bartender as the subjects of the search. In executing their duties, officers performed a "cursory weapons search" on all the tavern patrons under provisions of Illinois law. The officer patting down Ybarra "felt a cigarette pack with objects in it," but did not remove the packet from Ybarra's pocket. The officer eventually returned to Ybarra, removed the packet, and found heroin. Ybarra's motion to suppress this evidence was denied, and he was convicted of possession of a controlled substance. The Supreme Court reversed the conviction. Illinois attempted to justify the search on two bases. First, Illinois contended that the initial weapons search was reasonable and that the follow-up search was sufficient as an outgrowth of a reasonable frisk. The Court rejected this argument, saying the state was "unable to articulate any specific fact that would have justified a police officer at the scene in even suspecting that Ybarra was armed and dangerous." Illinois' second argument was to justify the search as included in the warrant issued for the search of the bar and bartender. That argument was rejected as well. The Court said, "a person's mere propinquity to others inde- pendently suspected of criminal activity does not, without more, give rise to probable cause to search that person." It is necessary to focus on an individual in order to effect a search. The Court concluded that "a search or seizure of a person must be supported by probable cause particularized with respect to that person." The expectations of privacy require the protection of particularity, and this "requirement cannot be undercut or avoided by simply pointing to the fact that coincidentally there exists probable cause to search or seize another or to search the premises where the person may happen to be." The dissenters in *Ybarra*, Chief Justice Burger and Justices Blackmun and Rehnquist, argued that the search was reasonable as incident to the execution of the warrant. They would also have upheld the seizure on stop and frisk grounds. *See also* FOURTH AMENDMENT, p. 193; PROB- ABLE CAUSE, p. 691; WARRANT, p. 710.

Significance   *Ybarra* invalidated an Illinois statute that authorized officers in the execution of a valid search warrant to search any person encountered on the warrant-covered premises. The problem with the statute was its failure to meet the Fourth Amendment's "particularity" requirement for warrants. The particularity provision in the amendment reflects the strongly held feelings of the Constitution's Framers against invasions of privacy committed under authority of the "general warrant" common in eighteenth-century England. The general warrant was a broad license under which virtu- ally unrestricted searches could occur. Warrants obtained in compli- ance with the Fourth Amendment must make some reference to the person who is to be searched. That reference may be other than an actual name as long as it allows a reasonably reliable identification of the person to be searched. In the absence of any warrant reference, an officer must have a reasonable suspicion that a person encoun- tered in a search is armed and dangerous. Such suspicion would permit a frisk as described in *Terry v. Ohio*, 392 U.S. 1 (1968). In the *Ybarra* case no reasonable inference of danger existed. The Court noted that the warrant "did not allege that the bar was frequented by persons illegally purchasing drugs." This reference suggests that had it been established at the time the warrant was obtained that patrons were often engaged in related criminal conduct in the tavern, this fact would have had a bearing on determining the sufficiency of the search of Ybarra, even though it occurred incidental to the execution of a warrant search of the tavern itself. Nonetheless, the clear message of *Ybarra* is the necessity for particularity in warrants.

Informants and Probable Cause

***Illinois v. Gates*, 462 U.S. 213 (1983),** established new standards for obtaining warrants on the basis of informant tips. Bloomingdale, Illinois, police received an anonymous letter indicating that Lance and Susan Gates were engaged in illegal drug trafficking. The letter contained a detailed description of an upcoming trip the Gateses were planning to Florida to obtain the drugs and the manner in which the drugs would be transported back to Illinois. The police corroborated the information contained in the letter. On the basis of the letter and the subsequent corroboration, the police obtained a warrant and searched the Gateses' automobile upon its return from Florida. They found 350 pounds of marijuana. The Gateses sought to suppress the evidence, asserting that under the then-existing standard, probable cause had not been shown. The state courts excluded the marijuana at trial, but the Supreme Court concluded the evidence was admissible. The standard applicable at the time required satisfying two independent conditions: the basis of the informant's knowledge and the reliability of the informant. The Court agreed that basis of knowledge and informant reliability were "highly relevant" in determining the value of the informant's tip, but ruled that these elements should not be understood as "entirely separate and independent requirements to be rigidly exacted in every case." Rather, they should be understood as "closely intertwined issues that may usefully illuminate the commonsense, practical question whether there is probable cause to believe that contraband or evidence is located at a particular place." A "totality-of-the-circumstances" approach was seen as "far more consistent" with prior standards than a "rigid demand that specific tests be satisfied by every informant's tip." Justice Rehnquist said probable cause is a "fluid concept" driven by an assessment of probabilities in particular contexts. Probable cause is not, he continued, "readily, or even usefully, reduced to a neat set of legal rules." The Court found "persuasive" the argument against according basis of knowledge and informant reliability independent status. Those factors are better understood as considerations in a totality of circumstances analysis in which a "deficiency in one may be compensated for, in determining the overall reliability of a tip, by a strong showing as to the other, or by some other indicia of reliability." The Court saw the "strictures that inevitably accompany the 'two-pronged test' cannot avoid seriously impeding the task of law enforcement." The Court concluded it was "wiser to abandon the two-pronged test" in favor of the "totality-of-the-circumstances" analysis because the "flexible, easily applied standard will better achieve the accommodation of public and private interests that the Fourth Amendment requires." In this case, the anonymous letter contained a "range of details" relating to future actions not easily predicted. The informant's accurate information was "of a character likely obtained only from the Gateses themselves, or from someone familiar with" their plans. It was "apparent" to the Court that the judge issuing the warrant had "substantial basis" for concluding that probable cause to search the Gateses' home and car existed. Justices Brennan, Marshall, and Stevens would have retained the "two-pronged" test for evaluating the validity of the warrant. *See also Draper v. United States*, p. 194; INFORMANT, p. 666; PROBABLE CAUSE, p. 691.

Significance   *Aguilar v. Texas*, 378 U.S. 108 (1964), had established two key criteria for determining probable cause based on information provided by an informant. First, supporting information must be provided that speaks to the reliability and trustworthiness of the informant, a special problem when the informant is unnamed or anonymous. Second, the substance of the informant's information must be supported by other evidence. In *Spinelli v. United States*, 393 U.S. 410 (1969), the Court reversed a conviction because insufficient support had been provided for a tip from an anonymous informant. The Court said the identity of an informant was clearly a factor in assessing his or her credibility. If the identity is either withheld or unknown, *Spinelli* required additional support to compensate for the informant's anonymity. *Spinelli* also demanded the full development of the basis upon which the informant concluded that criminal conduct had occurred. In *United States v. Harris*, 403 U.S. 573 (1971), the Court said that hearsay may be used when seeking a warrant, thus modifying *Spinelli* by holding that information about the reputation of the person to be searched could be used to support the warrant request. Further, *Harris* held that the previous receipt of reliable information was not required to demonstrate an informant's reliability. *Harris* reinterpreted both *Aguilar* and *Spinelli* by assigning weight to a suspect's reputation and by deferring to the experience and knowledge of police officers in assessing the credibility of information from informants.

Massachusetts v. Upton*, 466 U.S. 727 (1984), reaffirmed the Burger Court's reformulation of policy relative to the use of informant information in the warrant process begun in *Gates*. The affidavit submitted in *Upton* did not establish probable cause based on the two-pronged test established in *Aguilar*, according to the state supreme court. The U.S. Supreme Court disagreed, ruling that the probable cause requirement could be adequately maintained through a "totality of circumstances" approach. The two-pronged test required that affidavits submitted in support of warrants establish the means by which the informant came to know the information given to authorities, the so-called "basis of knowledge" prong. The other requirement was that the affidavit must establish either the general veracity of the informant or the specific reliability of his or her information in the specific case. The Court chose to move away from both requirements in *Upton*, with the language of the Court's opinion making its new position unmistakably clear. The Court said it now rejected the two-pronged test as "hypertechnical" and "divorced from the 'factual and practical considerations of everyday life on which reasonable and prudent men, not legal technicians, act.'" The Court said it is "wiser" to abandon the two-pronged test and replace it with a totality-of-circumstances approach that is more in keeping with the practical, common sense decisions demanded of magistrates granting warrants. The totality analysis permits necessary flexibility rather than encouraging "an excessively technical dissection" of informant tips. The previous standard allowed undue attention to isolated issues. The new approach is a "more deferential standard of review," which permits the magistrate to put together pieces of evidence in a more general way to support his or her decision to issue a warrant.

Third-Party Searches

Zurcher v. Stanford Daily, **436 U.S. 547 (1978),** examined whether a state is able to issue a search warrant if the owner of the place to be searched is not suspected of criminal conduct. A demonstration occurred on the hospital premises of Stanford University. During the demonstration a number of persons, including police officers sent to contain the demonstration, were injured. The *Stanford Daily*, a student newspaper, published several articles and photographs of the incident. It was thought the *Daily* had photographs that could lead to the identification of the demonstrators who had assaulted the officers. A warrant was issued and the police searched the *Daily* offices. The *Daily* unsuccessfully sought a declaratory judgment against those connected with the warrant authorizing the search. First, probable cause relates to evidence sought. When the state can show probable cause in regard to evidence that may be found by a search, a warrant is issued and an invasion of privacy is justified. Second, warrants may be issued to search any property. "Nothing on the face of the Amendment suggests that a third-party search warrant should not normally issue." Third, the Court rejected the argument that only the property of those suspected of an offense may be subject to a search. Justice White said it is "untenable to conclude that property may not be searched unless its occupant is reasonably suspected of crime and is subject to arrest." Finally, the Court felt that the press interests were handled within the warrant process. The "preconditions for a warrant ... should afford sufficient protection against the harms that are assertedly threatened by warrants for searching newspaper offices." The three dissenters, Justices Stewart, Stevens, and Marshall, argued that the newspaper should not be subjected to a warrant search. They would have issued a subpoena, which would allow the "newspaper itself an opportunity to locate whatever material might be requested and produce it." *See also* FOURTH AMENDMENT, p. 193; PROBABLE CAUSE, p. 691; WARRANT, p. 710.

Significance   *Zurcher v. Stanford Daily* held that no special protection of privacy interests flows from the First Amendment. Further, the conditions necessary for the issuance of a search warrant provide adequate safeguards to First Amendment rights—that is, if applied with exactitude, the conditions of issuance of such a warrant do not endanger the press's ability to gather, analyze, and disseminate news. *Zurcher* permits warrant searches of places neither owned nor occupied by persons actually suspected of criminal conduct. The sole protection is the process through which warrants are obtained. That process requires demonstration that there is a reasonable expectation that evidence relating to a criminal investigation is located in the place to be searched. Relevant evidence can often be found with third parties. Evidence for investigations of white-collar crime might be located in bank, medical, and insurance records, for example. As computer-dependent record keeping develops, probabilities increase dramatically that potentially valuable evidence is stored in anonymous third-party locations. The Court was asked in *Zurcher* to preclude such searches, but the Court found the safeguards afforded by the warrant process to be adequate. Another policy option rejected by the Burger Court in *Zurcher* was the subpoena approach to obtaining evidence from third parties. Because subpoenas do not require a showing of probable cause, they possess the liability of possible indiscriminate use. At the same time, the subpoena technique does allow the third party to control the search and maintain the privacy of other materials on the premises. Justice Stewart, in dissent, joined by Justice Marshall, was very concerned that freedom of the press was endangered by this discussion. Not only would the newsroom be "disrupted" by a lengthy search, but the possibility of disclosure of information received from confidential sources would tend to prevent the press from fulfilling "its constitutionally designated function of informing the public."

Electronic Surveillance

Katz v. United States, 389 U.S. 347 (1967), extended the Fourth Amendment provisions to electronic surveillance. Katz was convicted on federal gambling charges. The key evidence against him were recordings of telephone conversations obtained by the FBI through a microphone installed in a public telephone booth. With only Justice Black dissenting, the Supreme Court held that the incriminating recordings could not be used against Katz. The Court said the protection of the Fourth Amendment "protects people, not places." The phone booth itself is not a protected area as such. Rather, as Katz entered the phone booth, he brought with him expectations of privacy. What Katz "seeks to preserve as private, even in an area accessible to the public, may be constitutionally protected." Even if he could be seen from outside, he deserved protection from the "uninvited ear," and he should be able to "assume that the words he utters into the mouthpiece will not be broadcast to the world." A person's expectations of privacy are critical to application of the Fourth Amendment. The Court qualified its decision, however, by adding that the protections of the Fourth Amendment are not absolute. Electronic surveillance is not foreclosed altogether. The government's surveillance of Katz was flawed because it failed to secure prior authorization. Even though the government had probable cause to believe Katz was using the phone for criminal purposes, and despite the limited scope and duration of the surveillance, the Court insisted on advance authorization. If probable cause, appropriate limitations on scope and duration, and prior review are all present, invasions of privacy through electronic surveillance techniques are permissible. *See also* ELECTRONIC SURVEILLANCE, p. 643; FOURTH AMENDMENT, p. 193.

Significance   Technology has allowed invasions of privacy in ways unimagined at the time the Fourth Amendment was written. *Katz v. United States* established that wiretaps and electronic surveillances are searches of a kind covered by the Fourth Amendment. The decision brought to an end a longstanding policy to the contrary. The first critical decision on wiretapping came in *Olmstead v. United States*, 277 U.S. 438 (1928). Olmstead and a number of others were convicted on conspiracy to violate the Prohibition Act. The convictions were gained largely through evidence obtained by tapping telephone lines. The Court held that the Fourth Amendment only protected an individual from the seizure of tangible things, and the conversations were not tangible. Further, the amendment only protected against physical entry onto Olmstead's property. The conversations presented in evidence were obtained without trespass. While not going so far as to declare that wiretaps and electronic surveillance violated the Fourth Amendment, *Katz* and *Berger v. New York*, 388 U.S. 41 (1967), reversed *Olmstead* and tightly proscribed this kind of evidence gathering. Such surveillance could only be undertaken with prior judicial authorization, and such approval was contingent on a demonstration of probable cause that the intercepted conversations will yield evidence of criminal conduct. Further, *Katz* and *Berger* applied more stringent standards relative to the scope and duration of authorized surveillance. These standards were subsequently embodied in the Omnibus Crime Control and Safe Streets Act of 1968. This act moved wiretap and electronic surveillance into a different era by prohibiting interception of communications except under particular conditions. The exceptions were structured around controls such as prior judicial approval and the other limitations required in *Katz*. In addition, the statute permitted emergency surveillance without judicial authorization for up to 48 hours in cases involving national security.

The Burger Court, however, unanimously found that surveillance of domestic political activists under the emergency provisions violates the Fourth Amendment. In *United States v. District Court*, 407 U.S. 297 (1972), the Burger Court upheld remaining provisions of the Act and demonstrated a very literal approach to construction of the Act's language. For example, in *United States v. Giordano*, 416 U.S. 505 (1974), the Court had occasion to examine the procedures by which applications for approved interceptions are made. The Act required that applications be signed by the attorney general or a specially designated assistant attorney general. In this case, however, the applications were signed by an executive assistant, and the Court reversed Giordano's conviction because of the process deviation.

In *Dalia v. United States*, 441 U.S. 238 (1979), the Court upheld covert entry as a means of implementing an approved surveillance. Dalia tried to have certain evidence suppressed on the ground that the surveillance equipment used to intercept various conversations was illegally installed. The *Dalia* decision said, among other things, that covert entry to install surveillance equipment need not be explicitly and separately authorized by the judicial authority approving the surveillance request. The Court rejected the argument that the Fourth Amendment proscribes all covert entries, noting that it is "well established that law officers may constitutionally break and enter to execute a search warrant where such entry is the only means by which the warrant effectively may be executed." Second, the Court rejected the argument that Title III of the Omnibus Crime Control and Safe Streets Act of 1968 itself limited use of covert entry. Need for the surveillance must be demonstrated in accordance with the statute's requirements, but "nowhere in Title III is there any indication that the authority of courts ... is to be limited to approving those methods of interception that do not require covert entry for installation of intercepting equipment." Finally, the Court rejected the assertion that even if Title III allows covert entry, explicit authorization is required prior to implementation. Justice Powell said such explicit authorization would "promote empty formalism." The Fourth Amendment does not "require that a Title III surveillance order include a specific authorization to enter covertly the premises described in the order." At the same time, *Dalia* reflects the Court's unwillingness to demand more than the statute explicitly requires. The case suggests that the key element in providing protections from abuse in this sensitive area is the prior judicial authorization for the surveillance. Once the surveillance is approved, the means of executing the surveillance do not require judicial approval.

Exclusionary Rule

Mapp v. Ohio, **367 U.S. 643 (1961),** held that evidence obtained by unreasonable searches or seizures must be excluded from state criminal proceedings. The police who conducted a warrantless search of Mapp's residence were looking for evidence of a bombing and for materials associated with gambling. Instead they found "obscene" materials. The materials were confiscated and Mapp was subsequently convicted for their possession. The Supreme Court held that state trial courts were required to exclude illegally obtained evidence. In applying the exclusionary rule to the states, the Court concluded that the right of privacy was of sufficient priority to require the most effective method of implementing the Fourth Amendment. The means of protecting privacy other than the exclusionary rule were seen as "worthless and futile." The Court felt compelled to "close the only courtroom door remaining open to evidence secured by official lawlessness in flagrant abuse of that basic right." The Court had refused to extend the rule to state proceedings in earlier cases, but in *Mapp* the Warren Court determined that the Fourth Amendment remains "an empty promise" unless secured through the exclusionary rule. Justices Harlan, Frankfurter, and Whittaker dissented and focused on three areas of concern: First, they were unsatisfied that *Mapp* was the proper case through which to reconsider prior decisions on the exclusionary rule because *Mapp* was brought and argued primarily on obscenity grounds. Second, the dissenters asserted that prior cases had sufficiently addressed general due process dimensions of privacy. Third, they concluded that states ought to be free to adopt or reject the exclusionary rule at their discretion. The key concern was state power versus federal power. The proper position of the Supreme Court should be to "forbear from fettering the States with an adamant rule which may embarrass them in coping with their own peculiar problems in criminal law enforcement." *See also* EXCLUSIONARY RULE, p. 646; FOURTH AMEND-MENT, p. 193.

Significance   *Mapp v. Ohio* extended the exclusionary rule to state criminal proceedings. The exclusionary rule is aimed at deterring police misconduct in the conduct of searches. It also preserved the integrity of trial courts by insulating them from tainted evidence. The exclusionary rule is a highly controversial means of pursuing these objectives because its utilization has substantial crime control costs. Further, imposition of the rule by the United States Supreme Court preempts a policy decision previously retained by the states. Clearly *Mapp* was a decision that had fundamental policy impact. The decision had evolved over many years. Initially, admissibility of search evidence was governed by common law. In *Weeks v. United States*, 232 U.S. 383 (1914), the Supreme Court adopted the rule in federal cases, at least for evidence illegally obtained by federal agents. The Court chose not to extend the rule to the states, however. As late as 1949 the Court held in *Wolf v. Colorado*, 338 U.S. 25 (1949), that the rule was not required at the state level despite the linkage of the Fourth Amendment to the states via the Fourteenth Amendment. Although the *Wolf* decision was maintained through the next decade, there were signs that the Court was moving closer to extending the exclusionary rule to the states. In *Elkins v. United States*, 364 U.S. 206 (1960), the Court ended the "silver platter" practice. *Elkins* closed a loophole left from *Weeks* that allowed evidence illegally seized by state authorities to be handed on a "silver platter" to federal authorities for use in federal proceedings.

Extension of the exclusionary rule to all state proceedings in *Mapp* was extremely significant. It was an attempt by the Warren Court to deter police misconduct while conducting searches. Since the early 1970s, however, the Court has shown a growing disaffection with the exclusionary rule in two ways: First, when presented with situations in which the rule might have been extended, the Burger Court consistently chose not to do so. In *United States v. Calandra*, 414 U.S. 338 (1974), for example, the Court held that the rule did not apply to grand jury proceedings. It said the rule had "never been interpreted to proscribe the use of illegally seized evidence in all proceedings," and that "extension of the exclusionary rule would seriously impede the grand jury." Second, the Court has been receptive to a narrowing application of the rule. *Stone v. Powell*, 428 U.S. 465 (1976), is illustrative. The Burger Court used *Powell* to limit federal habeas corpus jurisdiction through which state prisoners could receive collateral review on search issues. The case diminished the possibility of federal judges intervening in state cases featuring search issues when those issues have had a "full and fair" review within the state courts. *Powell* conveyed greater conclusiveness to state determinations about the applicability of the exclusionary rule.

An alternative to the exclusionary rule is to bring a civil action against offending officers. In *Bivens v. Six Unknown Named Agents of the Federal Bureau of Narcotics*, 403 U.S. 388 (1971), the Court ruled that individuals could recover damages under federal law for Fourth Amendment violations by federal agents.

"Good Faith" Exception

United States v. Leon, **468 U.S. 897 (1984),** recognized a "good faith" exception to the exclusionary rule. *United States v. Leon* involved an attempt to suppress evidence obtained through a search conducted under warrant. It was determined that the affidavit supporting the application for the warrant did not actually establish probable cause. The lower courts ruled that, despite the fact that police officers acted in "good faith" pursuant to what they believed was a legally sufficient warrant, the evidence had to be suppressed. The Supreme Court reversed. The issue in *Leon* was whether the exclusionary rule should be modified to allow admission of evidence seized "in reasonable, good faith reliance" on a search warrant that is subsequently held to be defective. Justice White said there is no provision in the Fourth Amendment "expressly precluding the use of evidence in violation of its commands." Instead, the exclusionary rule operates as a judicially created remedy designed to protect Fourth Amendment rights generally rather than as a "personal constitutional right of the person aggrieved." White pointed to the "substantial social cost" exacted by the rule and argued that unbending application of it "impedes the truth-finding functions of judge and jury." A collateral consequence is that some guilty defendants go free or receive reduced sentences through plea bargaining as a result of the exclusionary rule. Indiscriminate application of the rule also "generates disrespect for the law and the administration of justice." For these reasons, decisions of the Burger and Rehnquist Courts have narrowed the scope of the rule. Justice White said that the rule must be used when a Fourth Amendment violation is substantial and deliberate, but the rule should not disallow use of evidence obtained by officers reasonably relying on a warrant. Appellate courts must be sure that affidavits supporting warrants are not knowingly false, or issued by judicial officers who may not be neutral and detached. Extending the rule further serves no deterrent function. The rule was designed to limit police misconduct rather than punish errors of judges and magistrates, and is contrary to the rule's purpose to apply it to diminish objectively reasonable police conduct. Once the warrant has been issued, there is "literally nothing more the policeman can do in seeking to comply with the law." Penalizing the officer for a magistrate's error rather than his or her own "cannot logically contribute to the deterrence of Fourth Amendment violations." In the case of *Leon*, because the officers' reliance on the judge's determination was objectively reasonable, the exclusion of evidence based on their activity was not necessary. Justices Brennan, Marshall, and Stevens dissented. Brennan called the decision one of a series aimed at the "gradual but determined strangulation of the exclusionary rule." Brennan felt the Court ignored the fundamental constitutional importance of what was at stake in *Leon*. He said fighting crime will always be a sufficiently critical and pressing concern to present "temptations of expediency" leading to "forsaking our commitment to the protection of individual liberty and privacy." *See also* EXCLUSIONARY RULE, p. 646; FOURTH AMENDMENT, p. 193; *Mapp v. Ohio*, p. 205.

Significance   The Court said in *United States v. Leon* that the exclusionary rule need not be applied to evidence seized by police officers when executing a warrant, even though that warrant may subsequently be found to be defective. *Leon* represented a potentially substantial alteration of the exclusionary rule, but the Court was careful to point out that the "good faith" exception does not apply widely. The police may not mislead a magistrate or knowingly offer false information in support of an affidavit, for example. Reasonable reliance on a warrant cannot exist when it lacks specificity or is otherwise facially defective.

Maryland v. Garrison, 480 U.S. 79 (1987), ruled that search evidence obtained by police through an "honest mistake" also could be used in a criminal prosecution. The Baltimore police obtained and executed a search warrant for a third-floor apartment believing there was only one apartment on the floor when in reality there were two. One was occupied by the party named in the warrant, the other by Garrison. Before it was apparent to the police that they were in Garrison's apartment, they discovered and seized drugs that subsequently were introduced as evidence in the successful prosecution of Garrison. The constitutionality of police conduct must be judged in light of the information available to them at the time they acted. Information that emerges after the warrant is issued has no bearing on the validity of the warrant—just as finding illegal items cannot validate a warrant that was invalid when issued. It is equally clear that a later determination that a valid warrant was too broad does not retroactively invalidate the warrant. Had the officers been aware that there were two apartments and that the warrant was in error, however, they would have been obligated not to search Garrison's apartment. Although the purposes justifying a search limit the scope of the search, the Court recognized the need "to allow some latitude for honest mistakes that are made by officers in the dangerous and difficult process of making arrests and executing search warrants." The validity of a search such as this depends on whether the officers' failure to realize the overbreadth of the warrant was objectively understandable and reasonable. The Court concluded that it was in this instance. Justices Brennan, Marshall, and Blackmun rejected the view that reasonable error prevents a Fourth Amendment violation.

Several other decisions have provided police with greater latitude when conducting searches. In *Immigration & Naturalization Service v. Delgado*, 466 U.S. 210 (1984), the Court upheld use of factory sweeps as a means of apprehending illegal aliens. The practice involved entry into a workplace without advanced notice to question employees about the status of their citizenship. The Court did not see this practice as a seizure and ruled that no warrant was required.

The Supreme Court expanded the "good faith" exception in *Arizona v. Evans*, 514 U.S. 1 (1995). Isaac Evans was stopped by police for driving the wrong way on a one-way street. The officer ran Evans's name through the computer in his car and found an outstanding misdemeanor arrest warrant on Evans. While taking Evans into custody, the officer found marijuana. Evans sought to suppress admission of the marijuana on the grounds that the warrant on which he had been arrested had been quashed 17 days earlier. It was established at the suppression hearing that Evans would not have been arrested or searched for the traffic infraction alone. There was evidence to suggest that failure to remove the warrant from the computer record was probably a clerical error by court personnel, but there remained, however, the possibility that police had been notified of the decision to quash the warrant and that the police had failed to update the record. The trial court suppressed the marijuana evidence without resolving who was responsible for the error. The Supreme Court ruled that the evidence could be used as long the computer error was not the fault of the police. Chief Justice Rehnquist based his reasoning on *Leon*. He indicated that the exclusionary rule was historically designed to deter police misconduct, not mistakes made by court employees. The Court saw no evidence that court employees were "inclined to ignore or subvert" the Fourth Amendment or that "lawlessness" among court employees required use of the "extreme sanction of exclusion." If the court clerk was responsible for the erroneous computer entry, use of the exclusionary rule could not reasonably be expected to "alter the behavior of the arresting officer." Justices Stevens and Ginsburg criticized the Court for "overlook[ing] the reality that computer technology has changed the nature of threats to citizens' privacy." The "offense to the dignity of the citizen who is arrested, handcuffed, and searched on a public street simply because some bureaucrat has failed to maintain an accurate computer database" struck Stevens as "outrageous." Ginsburg was critical of the artificial distinction between court personnel and police officers. In the electronic age, particularly as it involves record keeping, court employees and police are not "neatly compartmentalized actors." Rather, they serve together to carry out the state's "information gathering objectives." As a result, whether records are maintained by the police or courts "should not be dispositive where a single computer database can answer all calls."

Warrantless Arrest

Minnesota v Olson, **495 U.S. 95 (1990),** held that a warrantless arrest of a guest in another's residence violates the Fourth Amendment. An armed robbery of a gas station occurred during which the station manager was killed. The gunman was caught, but the getaway car driver avoided arrest. Police later concluded that the driver was in the apartment of two others. Police surrounded the building and telephoned the apartment ordering the suspect to come out. A voice was heard saying "Tell them I left." Police then entered the residence without seeking consent and found Olson hiding in a closet. A short time later, Olson made incriminating statements during interrogation at police headquarters. The Supreme Court ruled that his statements should have been suppressed, concluding that the guest had an expectation of privacy sufficient to protect him from warrantless arrest. To find that a guest has such an expectation of privacy "merely recognizes the everyday expectations of privacy we all share." Staying overnight in another's home "is a longstanding social custom that serves functions recognized as valuable by society." That the host possesses ultimate control is not incompatible with a guest having a legitimate expectation of privacy. The houseguest is there "with the permission of the host, who is willing to share his house and his privacy with his guest." Guests share the expectation of privacy "despite the fact that they have no legal interest in the premises and do not have the legal authority to determine who may or may not enter the household." It is unlikely that the guest will be "confined to a restricted area of the house; and when the host is away or asleep, the guest will have a measure of control over the premises." Hosts will likely "respect the privacy interests of their guests," who are entitled, said Justice White, to a "legitimate expectation of privacy despite the fact that they have no legal interest in the premises and do not have the legal authority to determine who may or may not enter the household." As a result, warrantless entry can only occur under exigent circumstances. In other words, there must be probable cause to believe, among other things, that destruction of evidence is imminent, the suspect will escape, or danger to the officer(s) or others is likely. *See also* EXIGENT CIRCUMSTANCE, p. 647; FOURTH AMENDMENT, p. 193; PROBABLE CAUSE, p. 691; WARRANT, p. 710.

Significance   The Court has insisted on an exigency as a precondition for a warrantless arrest. The Court ruled in *Welsh v. Wisconsin*, 466 U.S. 740 (1984), for example, that police officers may not enter a person's home at night without a warrant to make an arrest for a nonjailable traffic violation unless there are exigent circumstances. *Welsh* involved an erratic driving incident reported to authorities by a witness. The driver abandoned the car, but officers learned his address by checking the registration. Without a warrant, they went to Welsh's residence, entered it, and found him in bed. He was arrested and taken to police headquarters, where he refused to take a breath test. The Supreme Court invalidated the arrest.

In 1980 the Court held in *Payton v. New York*, 445 U.S. 573 (1980), that a warrantless arrest in a person's home was prohibited unless both probable cause and exigent circumstances existed. *Welsh* focused on the characteristics of exigent circumstances. Justice Brennan said it is axiomatic that "the physical entry of the home is the chief evil against which the wording of the Fourth Amendment is directed." Accordingly, warrantless searches and arrests that occur inside a home are presumptively unreasonable, and exceptions are few and carefully delineated. The police bear a heavy burden when attempting to demonstrate an urgent need that might justify a warrantless search or arrest, a burden that is heavier when the offense is relatively minor. The warrant exception for exigent circumstances is narrowly drawn to cover real and not contrived emergencies, thus the exception is typically limited to the investigation of serious crime.

In *Steagald v. United States*, 451 U.S. 204 (1981), the Court held that an arrest warrant for one individual cannot cover the search of the home of another individual. Federal agents, possessing an arrest warrant for Ricky Lyons, went to the home of Gary Steagald in search of Lyons. The officers did not find Lyons, but found evidence leading to the arrest of Steagald. The search of Steagald's home that produced the evidence was conducted with only the arrest warrant for Lyons. The Court disallowed the search. The Court distinguished between arrest and search warrants and ruled that the arrest warrant for Lyons had no bearing on "petitioner's privacy interest in being free from an unreasonable invasion and search of his home." Given that no exigent circumstances could be shown, Steagald was entitled to independent judicial determination of probable cause before a search of his residence could legally occur. To hold otherwise "would create a significant potential for abuse." Police, using only an arrest warrant for a particular person, "could search all the homes of that individual's friends and acquaintances." An arrest warrant might thus "serve as the pretext for entering a home in which police have a suspicion, but not probable cause to believe that illegal activity is taking place." The *Payton* case, upon which *Olson* and *Welsh* rest, did not attempt to define what constituted a sufficiently exigent circumstance to support a warrantless arrest, however. The pursuit of a fleeing suspect into a private residence was permissible, but beyond that the contours of a sufficiently compelling exigency remained vague. The Court attempted to clarify the nature of an emergency in *Welsh* insisting that the state show an urgent need for a warrantless arrest. Demonstration of an actual exigency may be virtually impossible if the underlying offense is minor, and if a state has classified an offense as minor, not even the preservation of evidence produces a sufficiently compelling need for a warrantless arrest.

Incriminating statements made following a warrantless in-house arrest present different problems. The question in *New York v. Harris*, 495 U.S. 14 (1990), was whether the existence of probable cause and administration of the *Miranda* warnings might overcome the taint of an unlawful arrest. Police had probable cause to believe that Harris had committed murder. They entered his house without a warrant, placed him under arrest, and advised him of his rights. Harris then confessed to the crime. He was taken to the police station where he was again given the *Miranda* warnings. Harris signed a written confession at the station. The Supreme Court permitted use of the confession made outside the house despite the defective arrest. The *Payton* ruling, said the Court, was intended to "protect the physical integrity of the home." It was not intended to grant suspects "protection from statements made outside their premises where the police have probable cause to arrest the suspect for committing a crime." Statements Harris made at the police station were not an "exploitation of the illegal entry into his home." Suppressing the station house statement would, in the Court's view, not serve the purpose of *Payton* because evidence stemming from the defective arrest was already inadmissible under *Payton*.

The Court ruled in *California v. Hodari D.*, 499 U.S. 621 (1991), that a fleeing suspect had not been "seized" and was not yet subject to Fourth Amendment protections. As a result, evidence discarded prior to actual seizure was admissible at trial regardless of the degree of suspicion the police had for instigating the chase. A group of youths including Hodari D. were standing on a street corner. They fled upon sighting a police car approaching. One of the officers gave chase on foot, but did not chase Hodari directly. Rather, he circled around the block, which eventually placed him in front of Hodari as he ran up an adjacent street. Hodari had been watching behind him as he ran and was almost face-to-face with the officer before seeing him. On seeing the officer, Hodari turned and set off in the opposite direction. As he fled, he discarded a small rock. The officer gave chase and subsequently tackled Hodari. The discarded article was recovered and turned out to be crack cocaine. The cocaine was introduced as evidence in the juvenile proceeding against Hodari. A California appellate court ruled the evidence should have been suppressed under terms of the Fourth Amendment because Hodari had been "seized" from the time of his face-to-face confrontation with the officer. In the appellate court's view, the officer did not have cause to seize Hodari. The cocaine was thus the fruit of an illegal seizure. The Supreme Court reversed the California court by using the common-law concept of arrest. An arrest occurs when a person is restrained by application of physical force, or when a person submits to the "assertion of authority" by an officer. Hodari was not "seized" until he was physically restrained. Because the cocaine was discarded before the arrest, its recovery was not unlawful. Justice Stevens and Marshall dissented. Stevens felt the decision was not focused on the reasonableness of police conduct, but rather the response of the suspect. The "character of a citizen's response," he said, "should not govern the constitutionality of the officer's conduct."

Review of Warrantless Arrests

County of Riverside v. McLaughlin, **500 U.S. 44 (1991)**   *Gerstein v. Pugh,* 420 U.S. 103 (1975), required that persons arrested without warrants have "prompt" judicial determinations of whether probable cause existed. In *McLaughlin,* the Court more fully defined promptness. Riverside County incorporated probable cause determinations into its arraignment procedure. Under county policy, arraignments were to take place within two days of arrest exclusive of weekends and holidays. The Court, speaking through Justice O'Connor, said *Gerstein* had established a "practical compromise" between the interests of arrested persons and the "realities" of law enforcement. *Gerstein* allowed local jurisdiction some latitude in procedures used to make probable cause determinations. Riverside County was free under *Gerstein* to combine probable cause determinations with arraignments. The Court recognized that some delays are "inevitable." For that reason, it is reasonable to postpone probable cause hearings in some situations as police "cope with the everyday problems of processing suspects through an overly burdened criminal justice system." At the same time, said O'Connor, "flexibility has its limits; *Gerstein* is not a blank check." The Court concluded that probable cause hearings held within 48 hours of arrest will, "as a general matter, comply with the promptness requirement of *Gerstein.*" *Gerstein* violations may still occur within the first 48 hours, but the burden of demonstrating unreasonable delay rests with the arrested party. After 48 hours, the "calculus changes." The burden then shifts to the government to demonstrate the existence of a "bona fide emergency or other extraordinary circumstance." Delay in a case beyond 48 hours in order to consolidate pretrial proceedings, said O'Connor, will not qualify as an extraordinary circumstance. Nor will intervening weekends or holidays provide the basis for permissible delay. Using this standard, the Riverside County policy did not comply with the *Gerstein* promptness requirement. Justices Scalia, Marshall, Blackmun, and Stevens felt that the Fourth Amendment requires that a probable cause hearing occur "immediately upon completion of the administrative steps incident to arrest." Justice Scalia said that 24 hours should define the outer limit of reasonable delay. *See also* FOURTH AMENDMENT, p. 193; WARRANT, p. 710.

Significance   All individuals who are arrested are entitled to appear before a judicial officer. This is especially important when the arrest has taken place without a warrant. Unlike the arrest pursuant to an arrest warrant, the cause for the warrantless arrest has yet to be considered by a judicial officer. *Gerstein* required that this appearance occur "without unnecessary delay." The *Gerstein* ruling, however, did not establish a specific standard for delay in this review. The Rehnquist Court recognized the vagueness of the *Gerstein* rule in *McLaughlin*. While *McLaughlin* indicated that judicial review of warrantless arrests should occur within 48 hours, the time limit was not rigidly set. Rather, the Court spoke of shifting burdens of proof at the 48-hour point. Thus, it may be possible under *McLaughlin* for the government to show the existence of an exigent circumstance and delay beyond the 48 hours, but delay beyond the time limit is presumptively unreasonable.

Warrantless Search: Incident to Lawful Arrest

***Chimel v. California*, 395 U.S. 752 (1969),** examined limitations on warrantless searches when conducted incident to a legal arrest. Chimel was arrested at his home. The police proceeded to conduct a warrantless search of Chimel's home, including the garage and attic. Certain items were found and admitted into evidence over his objection at his trial. The Supreme Court reversed his conviction. The Court said that officers have two primary interests when making an arrest: The first is to "remove any weapons that [the arrestee] might seek to use in order to resist or effect his escape." Second, the Court concluded that it is "entirely reasonable for the arresting officer to search for and seize any evidence on the arrestee's person in order to prevent its concealment or destruction." The question in *Chimel* was the extent to which an actual search may be conducted toward either or both these ends. *Chimel* concluded that the area to be searched incident to an arrest is narrowly confined. The Court defined this area as one "within his [the arrestee's] immediate control"; an area "from within which he might gain possession of a weapon or destructible evidence." Such an area clearly cannot extend to an entire residence. The Court argued that there is "no comparable justification ... for routinely searching through all the desk drawers or other closed or concealed areas in that room itself." The latter kind of search may only proceed under authority of a search warrant. *Chimel* significantly closed the scope of a permissible search stemming from a valid arrest. Justices Black and White dissented on the ground that, although authorities failed to obtain the warrant, probable cause existed. The dissenters felt that reliable evidence would be needlessly jeopardized by requiring a warrant under these circumstances. Black and White also argued that the arrest "supplies an exigent circumstance justifying police action." *See also* FOURTH AMENDMENT, p. 193; WARRANT, p. 710; WARRANTLESS SEARCH, p. 711.

Significance   *Chimel v. California* reaffirmed the warrant exception that applies when searches are conducted while making a lawful arrest. Such searches are justified as a means of protecting the safety of arresting officers and others, as well as preventing the destruction of evidence. *Chimel* addressed the extensiveness of a search attending an arrest. In cases prior to *Chimel*, the Court had held in such cases as *Harris v. United States*, 331 U.S. 145 (1947), and *United States v. Rabinowitz*, 339 U.S. 56 (1950), that full premises searches could occur. *Chimel*, however, imposed more stringent limits on the area that could reasonably be searched. While prior cases had given consideration to the "control" an arrestee might have over weapons or evidence on the premises, *Chimel* both restricted and supplanted such precedents as *Harris* and *Rabinowitz* by inserting the qualifier "immediate" on the term "control." Officers may search only that area from which an arrestee might be able to access a weapon or evidence. If a fuller search of the premises becomes necessary, *Chimel* requires that officers obtain a warrant.

United States v. Edwards, 415 U.S. 800 (1974), examined whether the warrant exception permitting a search incident to a lawful arrest allows a search to occur the next day. Edwards was arrested around 11 P.M. for attempting to break into a post office. From paint chips found at the scene, investigators had reason to believe Edwards's clothing contained material evidence of the crime. Edwards's clothing was taken from him without a warrant the following morning, some 10 hours after his arrest. The clothing yielded paint chips similar to those on the windowsill of the post office, and over Edwards's objection, the clothing was admitted into evidence at his trial. Edwards appealed his conviction on the ground that the seizure had occurred so much later that it could not have been incident to his arrest. The Supreme Court disagreed. The Court emphasized that seizure of Edwards's clothing would have been permitted at the time Edwards was taken into custody. The delay in this instance occurred because it "was late at night," and no substitute clothing was then available at that time for Edwards to wear. It would certainly have been unreasonable for the police to have "stripped respondent of his clothing and left him exposed in his cell throughout the night." Delaying the seizure "does not change the fact that Edwards was no more imposed upon than he could have been at the time and place of the arrest or immediately upon arrival at the place of detention." If too much time elapses, or the arrestee is fully secured, however, the necessity for the warrant exception diminishes. The greater the delay, the greater the burden of demonstrating continuing necessity.

Distinct from a search conducted incident to an arrest is an inventory search of an arrested person and any article in his or her possession. In *Illinois v. Lafayette*, 462 U.S. 640 (1983), the Court upheld the search of an arrestee's shoulder bag saying, "justification for such searches does not rest on probable cause." A warrant is not required in this case because "every consideration of orderly police administration benefiting both police and the public points toward the appropriateness of the examination of the shoulder bag prior to [the defendant's] incarceration." The Court concluded that "even if less intrusive means existed of protecting some particular types of property, it would be unreasonable to expect police officers to make fine and subtle distinctions in deciding which containers or items may be searched."

Duration of Incident to Arrest Exception

Michigan v. Tyler, **436 U.S. 499 (1978),** considered how long an exigent circumstance might justify an exception to the search warrant requirement. A fire began about midnight in a store co-owned by Tyler. Before the fire was fully extinguished, the fire chief made a cursory inspection of the fire scene. Among the things noted at the time were containers of flammable liquid. The police were immediately informed and a fuller investigation commenced. After leaving the scene for several hours, both police and fire officials returned to the unsecured location around 8 A.M., more systematically examined the scene, and seized evidence. In the days that followed, additional visits to the scene were made and additional evidence, largely in the form of photographs, was obtained. None of the inspections—neither those taking place during the fire itself nor those occurring up to 30 days after the fire—were conducted with a warrant or Tyler's consent. The Supreme Court unanimously ruled that the searches occurring during and immediately after the fire had satisfied the conditions of the exigent circumstance exception, but those occurring more than nine hours after the fire did not. The Court rejected the argument that no privacy interests remained in the badly burned premises, and that searches by officials other than police are not encompassed by the Fourth Amendment. Warrants are generally required, and an official must show more than "the bare fact that a fire has occurred." Even though there is a "vital social objective in ascertaining the cause of the fire, the magistrate can perform the important function of preventing harassment by keeping that invasion to a minimum." However, the initial search was clearly subject to the exigent circumstance exception; "a burning building clearly presents an exigency of sufficient proportions to render a warrantless entry 'reasonable.'" The authorities were properly on the premises, and could thus seize evidence in plain view. Justice Stewart argued that "it would defy reason to suppose that a fireman must secure a warrant or consent before entering a burning structure to put out the blaze. And once in the building for this purpose, firefighters may seize evidence of arson that is in plain view." Justices Marshall and White would have prohibited the warrantless search after the fire was extinguished. Justice Rehnquist considered the search of a "routine, regulatory" nature and would have placed it outside the conventional Fourth Amendment coverage. *See also* EXIGENT CIRCUMSTANCE, p. 647; FOURTH AMENDMENT, p. 193; WARRANT, p. 710; WARRANTLESS SEARCH, p. 711.

Significance   Warrantless searches are permitted if emergency circumstances exist. *Michigan v. Tyler* examined the exigent circumstance exception associated with entry onto burning property. The exigent circumstance exception is based upon the recognition that prior authorization through a warrant may simply be impossible under compelling conditions. To expect an officer to interrupt the "hot pursuit" of a suspect to obtain a warrant to continue the chase onto private property is generally regarded as unreasonable. Key to proceeding without a warrant is the presence of an emergency. In *Tyler* the presence of fire fighters at a fire scene was clearly justified, and once legally on the property, the fire fighters could reasonably investigate the origin of the fire. The investigation was permitted because it could be related not only to the preservation of potential evidence of crime, but also because it was necessary to reduce the likelihood of the fire recurring. The legal presence also allowed warrantless investigation for a reasonable time following the onset of the fire. Those searches that occurred in days following the fire were not seen as contemporaneous with the exigency that permitted the initial legal entry onto the property. Once property can be secured, the exigency ends and no necessity for proceeding without a warrant remains.

In a more recent arson search case, *Michigan v. Clifford*, 464 U.S. 287 (1984), the Court held that when "expectations of privacy" remain for fire-damaged premises, administrative warrants are required for searches intended to determine the cause and place of origin of the fire. Privacy expectations are "especially strong" for a private home, and a delay between the fire and the search brings with it warrant requirements. Once the cause and place of the fire's origin have been determined, the scope of the search is limited, and the search for additional evidence of criminal conduct can proceed only under a search warrant obtained on a showing of probable cause.

In *Thompson v. Louisiana*, 469 U.S. 17 (1984), the Court held that a search does not qualify for a warrant exception simply because it occurred at a murder scene. Lillian Thompson fatally shot her husband and ingested some pills in a suicide attempt. Apparently changing her mind, she called her daughter for help. The daughter, in turn, called the police and admitted them on their arrival at the Thompson residence. The police transported Thompson to the hospital for treatment and secured the premises. A full search followed, which produced, among other things, the murder weapon and a suicide note. The Court ruled that the warrantless seizure of the evidence was reasonable and need not be suppressed. Thompson's phone call for emergency medical services would have allowed seizure of evidence in plain view. Her call could not be regarded as an "invitation to the general public that would have converted her home into the sort of public place for which no warrant to search would be necessary." The Court suggested that a blanket "murder scene" exception was inconsistent with the Fourth Amendment.

Arizona v. Hicks, 480 U.S. 321 (1987), decided the limited character of the plain view warrant exception. A shot was fired through the floor of Hicks's apartment, injuring a man on the floor below. Police entered Hicks's apartment without a warrant to search for the shooter and to determine if there were other victims. While there, an officer noticed two sets of stereo equipment. Suspecting they were stolen, the officer recorded their serial numbers and telephoned them to headquarters. In order to read some of the numbers, however, it was necessary to move the equipment. The numbers revealed that the stereos had indeed been stolen in an armed robbery. The equipment was seized and used as evidence in the successful prosecution of Hicks. The Supreme Court, however, ruled the evidence to be inadmissible. The Court said that merely recording the numbers did not constitute a seizure, but moving the equipment was a search separate and apart from the search for the shooter, victims, and weapons that was the lawful objective of the entry. By moving the stereo sets, an independent invasion of Hicks's privacy occurred. The second search was not covered by the exigent circumstance that justified the initial entry. It was irrelevant that the search produced only the serial numbers, something possessing no inherent value in itself. A search is a search, even if it happens to disclose nothing but the bottom of a turntable. The Court went on to consider whether the plain view doctrine might allow the search to stand as reasonable and concluded that without probable cause it could not. To rule otherwise would be to draw the plain view doctrine too far from its theoretical and practical moorings. The doctrine was used to avoid some of the inconvenience and risk that may be associated with obtaining a warrant under certain circumstances. The "search of a dwelling no less than a dwelling place seizure, requires probable cause, and there is no reason why application of the plain view doctrine would supplant that requirement." Although the interests protected by the Fourth Amendment relative to unreasonable searches and seizures are quite different, "neither is of inferior worth or necessarily requires only lesser protection."

"Plain View" Exception

Washington v. Chrisman, **455 U.S. 1 (1982),** involved a plain view seizure of evidence located in a residence some distance from the place of a legitimate arrest. Chrisman was stopped by a campus police officer for illegally possessing liquor. The officer asked Chrisman for identification. Chrisman had no identification on him and requested that he be permitted to return to his dormitory room to obtain it. The officer agreed and accompanied him to the residence hall. The officer stood at the open door of Chrisman's room and watched him look for identification. While waiting, the officer noticed what he believed to be marijuana lying "in plain view" on a desk in the room. The officer entered the room, confirmed that the substance was marijuana, and advised Chrisman and his roommate of their rights. The students consented to a broader search of the room, which yielded more marijuana and LSD. The students subsequently sought to have the evidence suppressed on the ground that the officer was not entitled to enter the room and seize the marijuana and LSD without a warrant. The Supreme Court allowed the seizure on plain view grounds. The plain view doctrine "permits a law enforcement officer to seize what clearly is incriminating evidence or contraband when it is discovered in a place where the officer has a right to be." The Court concluded that the officer had properly accompanied Chrisman to his room, and that remaining at the doorway was irrelevant to sustaining the warrantless search. The officer had "an unimpeded view of and access to the area's contents and its occupants." The officer's "right to custodial control did not evaporate with his choice to hesitate briefly in the doorway." He had a "right to act" as soon as he observed the seeds and the pipe. This was a "classic instance" of incriminating evidence found in plain view when a police officer "obtains lawful access to an individual's area of privacy." Justices Brennan, Marshall, and White dissented, saying the plain view doctrine "does not authorize an officer to enter a dwelling without a warrant to seize contraband merely because the contraband is visible from outside the dwelling." For them, the failure of the officer to enter the room with Chrisman was a fatal defect. *See also Coolidge v. New hampshire*, p. 196; FOURTH AMENDMENT, p. 193; WARRANTLESS SEARCH, p. 711.

Significance   *Washington v. Chrisman* rested upon the plain view exception to the warrant requirement. *Chrisman* drew heavily on the Warren Court's ruling in *Harris v. United States*, 390 U.S. 234 (1968), and *Coolidge v. New Hampshire*, 403 U.S. 443 (1971). *Harris* involved discovery of evidence while the police were securing an impounded car as required by department regulations. *Harris* held that evidence may be seized when it is "in the plain view of an officer who has the right to be in a position to have that view." Controlling in *Harris* was the recognition that the officer had legally opened the door to Harris's car before finding the seized evidence. The *Harris* decision did not permit warrantless entry of a residence, however, simply because an officer notes contraband through a window. *Coolidge* sharpened *Harris* by saying that "plain view alone is never enough to justify the warrantless seizure of evidence."

Coolidge also required that plain view discoveries "must be inadvertent," but the Court reconsidered the inadvertence issue in *Horton v. California*, 496 U.S. 128 (1990). A warrant was obtained to search Horton's home for evidence related to an armed robbery. Although the supporting affidavit referred to weapons used in commission of the crime, the warrant authorized a search only for the crime's proceeds. The officer who executed the search did not find stolen property, but seized weapons discovered in plain view during the search. The officer subsequently testified that while he was searching for the stolen property covered by the warrant, he was also "interested in finding other evidence" linking Horton to the offense. His seizure of the weapons was, thus, not inadvertent, but the Court found the

Coolidge rationale on inadvertence flawed in two ways: First, law enforcement standards ought not to "depend upon the subjective state of mind" of an officer. That an officer "is interested" in particular evidence and "expects to find it" during the search "should not invalidate its seizure if the search is confined in area and duration by terms of the warrant." If an officer has a valid warrant to search for one item, and merely a suspicion concerning a second item, "we fail to see why that suspicion should immunize the second item from seizure if it is found during a lawful search for the first." Second, the Court was not persuaded that the inadvertence requirement prevented general searches or the conversion of specific warrants into general warrants. That interest, said Justice Stevens, "is already served by the requirement that no warrant issue unless it 'particularly describes the place to be searched and the person or things to be seized.'" "Scrupulous adherence to these requirements," Stevens continued, "serves the interests in limiting the area and duration of the search that the inadvertence requirement inadequately protects." Once those requirements have been met and lawful access has been established, no other Fourth Amendment interest is "furthered by requiring that the discovery of evidence be inadvertent." Thus, while inadvertence is a characteristic of most legitimate plain view seizures, inadvertence is not a necessary condition of them.

A variation on the plain view theme was developed in *United States v. Jacobsen*, 466 U.S. 109 (1984). Several bags of a white powder were found concealed in a tube by freight company employees as they examined a damaged package. The employees notified authorities, who subjected the powder to tests without a warrant. The substance was confirmed to be cocaine. A warrant was subsequently obtained to search the location where the package was addressed. The Court held that a warrant was not necessary for the chemical test. The original discovery had been made by private persons who are not subject to Fourth Amendment limitations. The subsequent inspection by law enforcement agents did not materially expand the scope of the search conducted by the freight company personnel. The law enforcement search "impinged no legitimate expectation of privacy." The Court saw the seizure of the bags as appropriate because it was apparent the bags contained contraband. Given what the agents came to know about the package, the Court found the contents to be virtually in plain view and thus seizable.

The issue in *California v. Greenwood*, 486 U.S. 35 (1988), was whether the Fourth Amendment prohibits warrantless searches and seizures of trash left for collection outside a residence. Believing Greenwood to be engaged in drug trafficking, the police obtained from his regular trash collector garbage bags left by him in front of his house. Largely on the basis of material found in the bags, warrants were obtained to search the house. The search yielded narcotics, and Greenwood was arrested. The trial court concluded that probable cause to search did not exist without the evidence from the garbage bags and dismissed charges under a state court ruling that warrantless trash searches violate the Fourth Amendment and the California Constitution. The Supreme Court disagreed, saying that Greenwood had "voluntarily" left the trash for collection in an area "particularly suited for public inspection." Having done so, his claimed "expectation of privacy" in the discarded items was not "objectively reasonable." Garbage bags left along a public street are "readily accessible to animals, children, scavengers, snoops, and other members of the public." When Greenwood left the garbage at the curb for the collector, he was conveying it to a "third party" who might then sort through it or permit others, including the police, to do so. The police cannot "reasonably be expected to avert their eyes from the evidence of criminal activity that could have been observed by any member of the public." In *Oliver v. United States* and *Maine v. Thornton*, 466 U.S. 170 (1984), the Court said that police officers do not need a warrant to search for drugs in open fields. An "open field" was not found to be a person, house, or effect entitled to Fourth Amendment protection because it possessed no expectation of privacy. Similarly, the Court upheld warrantless aerial observation in *California v. Ciraolo*, 476 U.S. 207 (1986). The police suspected that marijuana was being grown on the property and obtained a warrant based on aerial inspection of Ciraolo's property. Applying reasoning similar to the "open fields" cases, the Court concluded that the Fourth Amendment does not require that police officers flying in public airspace must obtain a warrant to observe what is visible to the naked eye.

The question in *Florida v. Riley*, 488 U.S. 445 (1989), was whether observing a private greenhouse from a helicopter in search of marijuana required a search warrant. The Court extended its holding in *Ciraolo* by ruling that helicopter observations were not a search and did not require a warrant. *Ciraolo* had involved surveillance from a higher altitude (1,000 feet) from a fixed-wing aircraft. Key to extending *Ciraolo* to *Riley* was the conclusion that police do not need a warrant when they make "naked eye" observations from public airspace. The Court also considered the extent of Riley's expectations of privacy for his greenhouse. He had taken precautions against ground-level observations, but because the sides and top of the greenhouse were at least partially open, the greenhouse was subject to view from above. Using *Ciraolo*, the Court concluded that Riley "could not reasonably have expected" the contents of the greenhouse to be "immune" from inspection from the air. Riley also argued that the helicopter had been too low, at least 100 feet below the minimum for fixed-wing aircraft. The Court pointed out that different regulations apply to helicopters, and that the helicopter used by the police had not been in violation of existing altitude restrictions applicable to helicopters.

In *Dow Chemical Co. v. United States*, 476 U.S. 227 (1986), the Court permitted the Environmental Protection Agency to use aerial photographic equipment for measuring emissions at Dow's production facilities to determine whether Dow was in compliance with Clean Air Act standards. The Court said that open areas of an industrial complex are comparable to open fields for which persons cannot demand privacy.

United States v. Dunn, 480 U.S. 294 (1987), examined yet another variation on the open fields theme. Through the use of electronic tracking devices and aerial surveillance, drug enforcement agents traced supplies used in drug manufacture to a barn on Dunn's ranch. The ranch was encircled by a perimeter fence and several barbed wire fences. Around the front of the barn was a wooden fence. Without a warrant, but prompted by the smell of chemicals and the sound of a motor coming from the barn, the officers traversed the fences and moved to a point outside the barn. They did not enter the barn, but they shone a flashlight into it from outside and observed what they believed to be a drug laboratory. The agents then left the ranch but entered it twice the following day to confirm their judgment that it was a place of drug preparation. A warrant was subsequently obtained and executed. Evidence was seized at that time and Dunn was arrested. The Supreme Court ruled there was no Fourth Amendment violation. In this case, the barn was 50 yards from the fence surrounding the house and 60 yards from the house itself and did not lie within the area surrounded by the fence. Another consideration was the nature of the uses to which the area was put. Here law enforcement officers had objective data indicating the barn was not being used for intimate activities of the home. Furthermore, Dunn had taken no action to protect the barn from observation by those standing in the open fields.

Warrantless Search: Vehicles

Chambers v. Maroney, **399 U.S. 42 (1970),** applied the automobile exception to Fourth Amendment warrant requirements. Following an armed robbery, a description of the robbers and their car was broadcast. Police stopped a car meeting the description and arrested the occupants. The car was taken to the police station and subsequently searched without a warrant. The search produced both weapons used and property taken in the robbery. Following his conviction, Chambers sought review on illegal search grounds, but the Supreme Court unanimously rejected Chambers's claim. The Court cited prior cases that recognized "a necessary difference between a search of a store, dwelling house or other structure ... and a search of a ship, motor boat, wagon or automobile." The Court said that "the circumstances that furnish probable cause to search a particular auto for particular articles are most often unforeseeable; moreover, the opportunity to search is fleeting, since a car is readily movable." Given this situation an "immediate search is constitutionally permissible." The Court could have chosen to require immobilization of the car until a warrant could be obtained, but it rejected this course as only a "lesser" intrusion. In the Court's view there was no difference between "seizing and holding a car before presenting the probable cause issue to a magistrate and ... carrying out an immediate search without a warrant." As long as probable cause exists, either course is permitted. Because Chambers's car was properly under the control of the police, there was "little to choose in terms of practical consequences between an immediate search without a warrant and the car's immobilization until a warrant is obtained." *See also* FOURTH AMENDMENT, p. 193; HABEAS CORPUS, p. 658.

Significance   *Chambers v. Maroney* provided a reiteration of the "moving vehicle" exception to the warrant requirement first introduced in 1925 in *Carroll v. United States*, 267 U.S. 132 (1925). The moving vehicle doctrine allows a warrantless vehicle search because the mobility of vehicles creates a particular exigency—that is, the possibility that the vehicle could be moved out of the jurisdiction. The same standards of probable cause exist, however, as would apply if a warrant could be sought. The searching officer must be able to support a belief that the vehicle contains seizable materials. *Carroll* distinguished between vehicles and places of residence. Mobility of the former creates a generally applicable warrant exception. *Chambers* expanded upon *Carroll* by allowing the mobility exigency to continue even if the vehicle was first taken to the police station. *Chambers* rejected the need to obtain a warrant once the vehicle had been secured, which broadened the scope of the exception.

California v. Carney, 471 U.S. 386 (1985), examined the vehicle exception in the special case of mobile homes. It is clear from cases such as *Chambers* that the exigency created by mobility applies to other movable conveyances such as trucks, ships, and planes. Carney argued that his mobile home was more like a dwelling than a vehicle and thus should not fall within the vehicle warrant exception. The Court disagreed. Although recognizing that the vehicle possessed many of the attributes of a home, it was also readily mobile, a characteristic that made the mobile home comparable to an automobile.

In addition, because the mobile home was a vehicle, there were diminished expectations of privacy. Because it was licensed to operate on public streets and highways, it was more subject than a residence to extensive regulation and inspection. Carney also contended that mobile homes should be distinguished from other vehicles because they are capable of functioning as a residence, but the Court refused to do so. Rather, the Court chose to retain the established basis for application of the exception—ready mobility and the presence of the vehicle in a setting that objectively indicates the vehicle is being used for transportation.

United States v. Robinson, 414 U.S. 218 (1973), considered whether a traffic violation may trigger an arrest that then provides the basis for a full search. Robinson was stopped by a police officer who had reason to believe Robinson was driving with a revoked license. Probable cause was satisfied in that the same officer had stopped Robinson only four days earlier and had found Robinson's license to have been revoked. The officer put Robinson under a full-custody arrest and conducted a thorough search. The search yielded a packet containing heroin capsules, and Robinson sought to have the evidence suppressed. The Supreme Court upheld the search. The question faced by the Court was whether the full search was justified because it could not yield any evidence pertaining to the traffic offense. The Court argued that a custodial arrest allowed a full search and that such a situation was not bound by the limits placed on investigative searches. Further, custodial arrests subject officers to "extended exposure" to danger, more so than the "fleeting contact" of stop and frisks, thus a fuller search than a cursory weapons frisk could be justified. The Court concluded that if the arrest is lawful, authority to search is established, and the full search is "not only an exception to the warrant requirement of the Fourth Amendment, but is also a 'reasonable' search under that Amendment." The dissenters, Justices Douglas, Brennan, and Marshall, disagreed with the Court on two crucial points: First, they felt it was necessary to establish probable cause relative to the seized evidence. Without having to justify such searches, the full arrest might simply be "a pretext for searching the arrestee." Second, the dissenters rejected the argument that a search of personal effects was appropriate even if it could be justified that Robinson was required to empty his pockets. The dissenters could not agree that "simply because some interference with an individual's privacy and freedom of movement has lawfully taken place, further intrusions should automatically be allowed despite the absence of a warrant that the Fourth Amendment would otherwise require." The primary impact of *Robinson* is found in the breadth of the warrant exception permitted. *Robinson* allowed a full search, not a search confined to discovery of weapons. The Court explicitly distinguished the situation from *Terry v. Ohio*, 392 U.S. 1 (1968), and the stricter stop and frisk guidelines. The *Robinson* search was not connected to finding evidence related to the offense for which Robinson was under arrest. The search in *Robinson* also differed from such incident-to-arrest searches as in *Chimel v. California*, 395 U.S. 752 (1969), in that no arrest warrant authorized Robinson's detention. The Court took *Robinson* one step further in *Gustafson v. Florida*, 414 U.S. 260 (1973). *Gustafson* permitted a search incident to a custodial arrest from a traffic violation even though state law and department regulations permitted the officer merely to issue a traffic citation.

Robinson and *Gustafson* are among the more permissive decisions relative to Fourth Amendment limits upon unreasonable search conduct. *Robinson* is limited, however, to the "traffic stop" for a full custodial arrest. In *Robinson*, the officer had probable cause to believe the driver was driving on a revoked license, a serious offense in the traffic codes of all states. More generally, the traffic stop can provide sufficient cause for a variety of actions. In *New York v. Class*, 475 U.S. 106 (1986), for example, the Court ruled that the Fourth Amendment was not violated by an officer's confiscation of a gun found when he was reaching into the car to move papers obscuring the vehicle's registration number. The Court offered three reasons: (1) the number played an important role in the government's scheme of automobile regulation, a clearly legitimate governmental activity; (2) because the number was to be placed in plain view, the motorist had a diminished expectation of privacy; and (3) the officer had directly observed the driver commit two traffic violations. The search was limited and sufficiently unintrusive to be permissible given the diminished expectations of privacy.

South Dakota v. Opperman, 428 U.S. 364 (1976), involved a warrant-less inventory search of an impounded automobile. Opperman's car was impounded for numerous parking violations. A police officer noted some personal property in the car, and, following established inventory practices, inventoried the contents of Opperman's car. During the inventory marijuana was discovered in the unlocked glove compartment. Opperman was subsequently prosecuted for possession of marijuana. He sought to have the evidence suppressed, but his motion was denied, and he was convicted. The Supreme Court affirmed the conviction. The Court stressed that there is a diminished "expectation of privacy with respect to one's automobile" as distinct from "one's home or office." The primary function of automobiles is transportation, and a car "seldom serves as one's residence or as the repository of personal effects." In the course of its "community caretaking functions," police often take automobiles into custody. Impounded cars are routinely secured and inventoried in order to protect the owner's property, minimize claims against the police over lost or stolen property, and to protect police from potential danger. The Court found these "caretaking procedures" to be an established practice within state law. The search was not unreasonable because the inventory was "prompted by the presence in plain view of a number of valuables inside the car." *Opperman* never suggested that this "standard procedure, essentially like that followed throughout the country, was a pretext concealing an investigatory police motive." A dissent authored by Justice Marshall was joined by Justices Brennan, Stewart, and White and emphasized there was "no reason to believe that the glove compartment of the impounded car contained any particular property of any substantial value." In addition, the dissenters suggested that Opperman's locking of the car was adequate protection of his property. The dissenters also objected to the result of the holding that "elevates the conservation of property interests—indeed mere possibilities of property interests—above the privacy and security interest protected by the Fourth Amendment."

Since *Opperman*, the Court has broadened the scope of permissible impoundment searches without warrant. In *Michigan v. Thomas*, 458 U.S. 259 (1982), the Court upheld the warrantless search of an impounded automobile made subsequent to a routine inventory. The *Thomas* decision was reiterated in *Florida v. Myers*, 466 U.S. 380 (1984). At the time of Myers's arrest, his car was searched by authorities and taken to an impound lot. Some eight hours later, a second search was conducted without a warrant. The Court upheld the second search because police officers had cause to believe evidence was still located in the car. The Court said the impounded search was justified on the same grounds as the initial search incident to the arrest.

The Court ruled in *Florida v. Wells*, 495 U.S. 1 (1990), that law enforcement officials do not have unlimited discretion to search closed containers found while conducting a vehicle inventory. Wells had been arrested for driving under the influence of alcohol. He gave his permission to open the trunk of his impounded car. A locked suitcase was found in the trunk. The suitcase was opened and found to contain marijuana. The Court ruled that the opening of the suitcase violated the Fourth Amendment. The Court held that the key defect was the absence of a specific policy on closed containers that could govern the officers in conducting inventory searches. Individual officers must not have so much discretion in those situations that inventory searches can become a "purposeful and general means of discovering evidence of crime." The Court did not say, however, that all officer discretion must be removed. In prohibiting "uncanalized discretion" in the inventory situation, there is "no reason to insist that they be conducted in a totally mechanical 'all or nothing' fashion." Police policies that mandate the opening of all containers or no containers are "unquestionably permissible." The Court said it would be "equally permissible to permit officers sufficient latitude" to determine whether a particular container may be opened "in light of the nature of the search and the characteristics of the container itself." The allowance of the exercise of judgment based on concerns related to the purpose of an inventory search does not violate the Fourth Amendment.

Container Searches

California v. Acevedo, **500 U.S. 565 (1991),** modified doctrine on closed-container searches. Acevedo was seen leaving an apartment carrying a paper bag the size of marijuana packages the police knew to be in the apartment. Acevedo placed the bag in the trunk of his car and was stopped by police as he began to drive away. A search of the trunk revealed a bag containing marijuana. Under terms of *Arkansas v. Sanders*, 442 U.S. 753 (1979), a warrant was required for such a search. *Sanders* distinguished between a vehicle and container found inside a vehicle. Under *Sanders*, officers could open any container, even one that was not suspicious, if there was probable cause to conduct a search of the car. At the same time, suspicious containers could not be opened without a warrant if there was no probable cause to search the car as a whole. Justice Blackmun said that *Sanders* did not set out a "clear and unequivocal guideline." To the contrary, *Sanders* not only "failed to protect privacy interests effectively," but it also "confused courts and police officers and impeded effective law enforcement." Cases such as *Sanders* had established, Blackmun continued, a "curious line between the search of an automobile that coincidentally turns up a container and the search of a container that coincidentally turns up in an automobile." The protections of the Fourth Amendment "must not turn on such coincidences." The Court concluded it was better to adopt a clear rule for automobile searches generally and eliminate the warrant requirement established for closed containers in *Sanders*. *Acevedo* interpreted the vehicle exception as providing "one rule to govern all automobile searches." The new ruling allowed police to search an automobile and containers within it "where they have probable cause to believe contraband or evidence is contained." Justice Stevens issued a dissenting opinion joined by Justices Marshall and White, and noted that the police are required to have a warrant to open containers like luggage that people may carry on the street. He felt it "anomalous" that the requirement does not apply when a person puts the same container into an automobile. *See also* FOURTH AMENDMENT, p. 193; WARRANTLESS SEARCH, p. 711.

Significance   The transition from *Sanders* began in *United States v. Ross*, 456 U.S. 798 (1982), in which the Court permitted the warrantless search of a container found in a lawfully stopped automobile. *Ross* held that as long as probable cause exists, police authority to perform a warrantless search is coextensive with a magistrate's authority to issue a warrant. It was the Court's view that the vehicle warrant exception did not diminish the probable cause requirement. The only warrantless automobile search permissible is one "supported by probable cause." Once the probable cause requirement has been met, the practical consequences of the automobile warrant exception would be largely nullified if the scope of the search did not include containers and packages found inside the vehicle. A warranted search of any premises extends to the entire area in which the object of the search may be found. This rule applies equally to all containers and carries over to warrantless vehicle searches. Justice Stevens noted that the protection of the Fourth Amendment "varies in different settings." A container that is in a person's possession at the time of arrest may be searched "even without any specific suspicion concerning its contents." The privacy interests of an individual must give way to the finding of probable cause. Stevens concluded by saying that the scope of a warrantless automobile search is not defined by the nature of the container. It is defined by "the object of the search and the places in which there is probable cause to believe that it may be found." Justices White, Brennan, and Marshall dissented. Marshall said the decision repeals the Fourth Amendment warrant requirement. The value of a probable cause determination by a neutral and detached magistrate is lost by permitting police officers to make the same judgment.

The *Ross* case constituted a significant change in Court policy in this sensitive area. Prior to *Ross*, the Court had held that containers found in cars were protected unless their contents were in plain view, a rule derived from several cases having to do with the expectations of privacy attaching to luggage. In *United States v. Chadwick*, 433 U.S. 1 (1977), for example, the Court refused to permit the warrantless search of a secured footlocker taken from an automobile trunk. It said the locked container conveyed a privacy expectation that required warrant protection. *Sanders* rejected the automobile exception as the basis for a warrantless search of anything, including a suitcase, found in the course of the examination of an automobile.

In *Robbins v. California*, 453 U.S. 420 (1981), which followed *Ross* by two years, the Court held that a closed container found during a lawful automobile search was constitutionally protected to the same extent as closed items of luggage found anywhere else. *Ross* distinguished *Chadwick* and overruled *Robbins*. The Court maintained that the *Chadwick* decision did not rest on the automobile exception

229

because the footlocker itself "was the suspected locus of the contra-band." But not all movable containers are subject to warrantless search after seizure even if they come in contact with an automobile. Thus, *Ross* retained *Chadwick*. *Robbins*, on the other hand, involved cause to search a whole automobile, not just a footlocker. The *Robbins* prohibition on the search of a closed container found in the execution of the lawful search of an automobile was rejected by *Ross*. So long as probable cause exists to search an automobile, the expectation of privacy does not extend to closed containers that might be capable of concealing the object of the search.

In *United States v. Johns*, 469 U.S. 478 (1985), the Court extended *Ross* to warrantless searches of packages occurring three days after the packages were seized. Given the fact that authorities could have opened the containers at the time of the seizure under the *Ross* rule, the Court found no requirement that the containers be examined immediately.

Florida v. Jimeno, 500 U.S. 248 (1991), involved the added element of consent. Police followed Jimeno after overhearing him arrange what seemed to be a narcotics transaction. His car was stopped by police for failure to stop at a traffic light. The officer who stopped the car told Jimeno that he had reason to believe there were drugs in the car. The officer asked Jimeno for permission to search the vehicle and Jimeno consented. Cocaine was discovered in a closed paper bag found on the floor of the vehicle. The cocaine was suppressed at trial because Jimeno's consent to have his car searched was ruled not to include consent to search the paper bag. The Supreme Court ruled, however, that Jimeno's consent to search his car implicitly extended to closed containers found in the course of the vehicle search, provided the container might reasonably hold the object of the search. Chief Justice Rehnquist said that the "touchstone" of the Fourth Amendment is reasonableness. The basis for assessing the scope of a suspect's consent is "objective reasonableness—what would the typical reasonable person have understood by the exchange between the officer and the suspect." Rehnquist said the terms of the search authorization in this case were "simple." The officer conveyed the belief that drugs were in the car. Jimeno was aware of that suspicion, but did not place any explicit limitation on the scope of the search. Under these circumstances, the Court thought it was "objectively reasonable for the police to conclude that the general consent to search the respondent's [Jimeno's] car included consent to search containers within that car which might bear drugs." The Court acknowledged that Jimeno could have limited the scope of the search. If, however, his consent would "reasonably be understood to extend to a particular container, the Fourth Amendment provides no grounds for requiring a more explicit authorization." Justices Marshall and Stevens dissented, saying that they were not persuaded that consent to search the interior of a car and closed containers inside a car are "one and the same from the consenting individual's standpoint." A person's expectation of privacy in a container is "distinct from, and far greater than, his expectation of privacy in the interior of his car."

Stop and Frisk

Terry v. Ohio, **392 U.S. 1 (1968),** examined the practice of "stop and frisk" and established basic guidelines for a limited warrantless search conducted on persons behaving in a suspicious manner. A police officer of 39 years' service observed two men, later joined by a third, acting "suspiciously." The officer approached the men, identified himself as a police officer, and requested identification. Upon receiving an unsatisfactory response to his request, the officer frisked the men. Terry was found to have a gun in his possession, and was subsequently charged and convicted for carrying a concealed weapon. The Supreme Court upheld the validity of the stop and frisk practice, with only Justice Douglas dissenting. It was admitted in *Terry* that the officer did not have "probable cause" to search Terry. The Court concluded, nonetheless, that the officer was entitled to conduct a cursory search for weapons. Such a search is "protective," and while it constitutes an "intrusion upon the sanctity of the person," it is briefer and more limited than a full search. The frisk was justified by the need to discover weapons that may be used to harm the officer or others. Thus, when an officer "observes unusual conduct which leads him [or her] reasonably to conclude in light of his [or her] experience that criminal activity may be afoot," when the officer identifies himself or herself as a police officer, and when "nothing in the initial stages of the encounter serves to dispel his [or her] reasonable fear for his [or her] own or others' safety," the officer is entitled to conduct a cursory search. Justice Douglas argued in dissent that the officer had no basis to believe Terry was carrying a weapon, thus, the search was invalid. *See also* FOURTH AMENDMENT, p. 193; STOP AND FRISK, p. 704.

Significance   *Terry v. Ohio* provided law enforcement authorities with the capability to take preventive action. Not only did *Terry* allow police to stop a person in situations deemed to be "suspicious," but also authorized a limited weapons patdown. Critical in *Terry* was reasonable suspicion based on observed behavior that could justify the stop. If reasonable suspicion to stop is present, the officer is entitled to make an investigative stop, including a cursory weapons patdown. *Terry* does not allow a full search unless the cursory search yields a weapon that leads to custodial arrest.

In *Sibron v. New York*, 392 U.S. 40 (1968), a case decided with *Terry*, the Court disallowed a stop and frisk that netted a package of narcotics because the searching officer could not demonstrate cause for the stop. There was no reason to infer that Sibron was armed at the time of the stop or presented a danger to the officer. The Court felt the search of Sibron was a search for evidence, not for weapons. A similar absence of suspicion led the Court to strike down the "stop and identify" practice in *Brown v. Texas*, 443 U.S. 47 (1979).

In *United States v. Brignoni-Ponce*, 422 U.S. 873 (1975), the Court held that vehicle stops to search for illegal aliens were impermissible unless specific cause could be shown. Random stops of vehicles simply on the basis of observed substantial trafficking in aliens was inadequate.

More recently the Court held in *Delaware v. Prouse*, 40 U.S. 648 (1979), that police could not randomly stop automobiles to check license and registration without some suspicion of a violation. To stop a driver, an officer must have cause comparable to the cause required to stop a person on foot. However, the Supreme Court upheld the use of so-called sobriety check lanes against Fourth Amendment challenge in *Michigan Dept. of State Police v. Sitz*, 496 U.S. 444 (1990). Law enforcement officers had briefly stopped all drivers at checkpoints in an attempt to detect signs of intoxication. The question in *Sitz* was "whether such seizures are reasonable." The question was resolved by weighing the state's interest in preventing drunk driving against the intrusion on drivers as individuals. Chief Justice Rehnquist began by characterizing the scope of the problem. "No one can seriously dispute the magnitude of the drunk driving problem or the state's interest in eradicating it." Rehnquist referred to both media accounts of "alcohol-related death and mutilation," and the statistical data, which show an annual death toll in excess of 25,000. At the same time, the "intrusion on motorists stopped briefly at sobriety checkpoints is slight." The Court found these stops similar to highway stops to detect illegal aliens. Such stops do not involve "standardless and unconstrained discretion" on the part of law enforcement officers. Empirical data showed that operation of the checkpoints produces arrests for alcohol impairment. Although the check lanes may not be the best means available for enforcement of drunk driving laws, the approach "can reasonably be said to advance" the state interest in preventing alcohol-impaired driving. Justices Brennan, Marshall, and Stevens dissented, saying the Fourth Amendment precluded any stop without "some level of individualized suspicion." Justice Stevens also doubted the utility of the checkpoints. The check lanes create the "disquieting" possibility that "anyone, no matter how innocent, may be stopped for police inspection." He referred to the check lanes as "publicity stunts" designed for their "attention-getting ... shock value."

The Burger Court expanded upon *Terry* in *Adams v. Williams*, 407 U.S. 143 (1972), when it permitted a frisk based upon an informant's tip as opposed to an officer's own observations. In *Pennsylvania v. Mimms*, 434 U.S. 106 (1977), the Court held that an officer could order a lawfully detained driver out of his or her automobile. The Court concluded that an officer's safety justified having a driver leave a car, and if cause exists to proceed with a frisk, a patdown is permissible. *Terry* and the cases that build upon it authorize substantial latitude for a cursory weapons search if observed or reported behavior can focus sufficient suspicion.

In *United States v. Place*, 462 U.S. 696 (1983), the Court held that suspicious luggage may be seized at an airport and subjected to a sniff test by a narcotics detection dog. In this case the permissible limits of a *Terry* stop were exceeded, however, when the luggage was kept for 90 minutes, the suspect was not informed of where the luggage would be taken, and detention officers failed to specify how the luggage might be returned.

Terry was extended in *Michigan v. Long*, 463 U.S. 1032 (1983), in which the Court allowed a protective search of the passenger compartment of a stopped car. The Court ruled that "*Terry* need not be read as restricting the preventative search to the person of the detained suspect." Search of the passenger compartment of a car is permissible as long as the police "possess an articulable and objectively reasonable belief that the suspect is potentially dangerous." Contraband discovered in the course of such a protective search is admissible evidence.

The Court used the reasonable suspicion standard of *Terry* to uphold searches by school officials in *New Jersey v. T.L.O.*, 469 U.S. 325 (1985). In that case the Court held that searching a student is justified if there are "reasonable grounds for suspecting" the search will yield evidence that laws or school rules are being violated. Such searches are permissible if they are related to the objectives of the school rules and are not excessively intrusive, given the age of the student and the nature of the infraction. The Court recognized that searches are a "severe violation" of the student's privacy. It therefore urged school officials to limit their conduct "according to the dictates of reason." But the Court said society must recognize that drug use and crime are "major social problems," and that searches are justified as a means of maintaining an appropriate school environment. Although it noted that constitutional protections apply to students, the Court permitted the search based on the existence of reasonable suspicion.

Further evolution of *Terry* occurred in *United States v. Sharpe*, 470 U.S. 675 (1985), in which the Court upheld "short-term" (e.g., 20-minute) investigative detention when reasonable suspicion exists. In

Hayes v. Florida, 470 U.S. 811 (1985), however, the Court said that police officers may not take a suspect to police headquarters for fingerprinting in the absence of probable cause, a warrant, or the person's consent. The Court left the door open for a brief detention for field administration of fingerprinting when reasonable suspicion exists. It said such detention "is not necessarily impermissible." A vagueness criterion has been incorporated into this analysis as well. In *Kolender v. Lawson*, 461 U.S. 352 (1983), the Court struck down a California law requiring persons who "loiter or wander on the streets" to provide "credible and reliable" identification, and to "account for their presence" when requested. The Court ruled that the statute was vague and that it vested virtually absolute discretion in police officers to determine if the law's requirements had been satisfied. While stop and frisk remains a valuable law enforcement practice, *Brown* firmly reiterated that reasonable suspicion must exist for such a stop to occur.

The question in *Minnesota v. Dickerson*, 508 U.S. 366 (1993), was whether police may seize articles other than weapons detected during a weapons frisk. A unanimous Court ruled that such seizures are constitutional so long as officers stay within the limits established by *Terry*, but found the search in this instance to go beyond the bounds of *Terry*. Timothy Dickerson was observed leaving a building known to be used for drug trafficking. In addition, his behavior was felt to be "suspicious" to officers who observed him. He was subsequently stopped and subjected to a weapons frisk. No weapons were found, but the officer touched a small lump in Dickerson's pocket. Believing the lump to be crack cocaine, the officer reached into the pocket and seized a small bag of cocaine. Dickerson unsuccessfully sought to suppress the cocaine and was convicted of possession. The Court saw discoveries of contraband by touch as analogous to plain view discoveries. Justice White said that if a police officer lawfully pats down a suspect and "feels an object whose contour or mass makes its identity immediately apparent, there has been no invasion of the suspect's privacy beyond that already authorized by the officer's search for weapons." If the object discovered by touch is indeed contraband, its warrantless seizure is "justified by the same practical considerations that inhere in the plain view context." The Court also rejected the argument that touch intrudes more extensively into privacy than does sight. The intrusion "has already been authorized by the lawful search for weapons." The seizure of an item, the identity of which is already known, "occasions no further invasion of privacy." The Court then turned to the specifics of the cocaine seizure from Dickerson. The seizure from Dickerson did not meet *Terry* standards because the "lump" in Dickerson's pocket was not "immediately" recognized as crack cocaine. Instead, the officer did not determine the lump to be contraband until it was squeezed and otherwise manipulated in Dickerson's pocket. The officer's "continued exploration" of Dickerson's pocket after having concluded there was no weapon was unrelated to the "sole justification" of a search based on *Terry*. The inspection of Dickerson's pocket thus "amounted to the sort of evidentiary search that *Terry* expressly refused to authorize."

Investigative Searches

Maryland v. Buie, **494 U.S. 325 (1990),** extended the reasoning from *Terry v. Ohio*, 392 U.S. 1 (1968), to an action known as a protective sweep. A protective sweep is a "quick and limited search of a premises incident to an arrest." Such a sweep is conducted to "protect the safety of police officers or others." The sweep is "narrowly confined to a cursory visual inspection of those places in which a person might be hiding." The Court emphasized that the sweep is not to be a full search of the premises. Rather, it may extend only to those spaces where a person may be found, and it may last no longer than necessary to "dispel the reasonable suspicion of danger." The Court acknowledged that an arrestee has an expectation of privacy in the remaining areas of his residence, but this did not mean, however, that such rooms were immune from entry. Determinations of reasonableness of a search require a balancing of the intrusion on individual Fourth Amendment interests against the "protection of legitimate governmental interests." The "ingredients to apply the balance struck in *Terry*," said the Court, "are present in this case." In *Terry*, the Court was concerned with the interest of the officers in "taking steps to assure themselves that the persons with whom they were dealing were not armed with or able to gain immediate control of weapons that could unexpectedly and fatally be used against them." The Court saw an "analogous interest" in law enforcement officers taking steps to assure themselves that "the house in which a suspect is being or has just been arrested is not harboring other persons who are dangerous and who could unexpectedly launch an attack." Furthermore, the Court said that neither a warrant nor probable cause was required for such a protective sweep. Rather, the sweep can commence with a "reasonable, articulable suspicion that the house is harboring a person posing a danger to those on the arrest scene." Justices Brennan and Marshall dissented. They argued that because of the "special sanctity" of a house, and the "highly intrusive nature of a protective sweep," officers must have "probable cause to fear that their personal safety is threatened by a hidden confederate of an arrestee before they may sweep through the entire house." *See also* FOURTH AMENDMENT, p. 193; STOP AND FRISK, p. 704; *Terry v. Ohio*, p. 231.

Significance   *Buie* is representative of a number of recent Fourth Amendment decisions in which the Court supported actions taken on the basis of reasonable suspicion. The key issue in most situations of stop and frisk or protective sweeps is how much information is needed to establish reasonable suspicion. The question in *Alabama v. White*, 496 U.S. 325 (1990), was whether an anonymous tip could provide the basis for an investigative stop and frisk. The tip provided very specific information. The unknown informant indicated that White would leave a particular apartment at a particular time, drive away in a particular car, go to a particular destination, and have drugs in a brown attaché case. Officers observed White leave in the described vehicle and go to the described destination. White was stopped by the officers as she approached her destination and consented to a search for drugs. Drugs were found in the attaché case, and White was arrested. The Court ruled that such a tip, if sufficiently supported by independent evidence, could provide reasonable suspicion. Like probable cause, said Justice White, reasonable suspicion is "dependent upon both the content of information possessed by the police and its degree of reliability." If a tip has a "relatively low degree of reliability," more corroborative information is necessary to "establish the requisite quantum of suspicion that would be required if the tip were more reliable." A tip's reliability is determined by consideration of the totality of circumstances. In this case, police were able to corroborate significant aspects of the informer's tip that, in turn, imparted some degree of reliability to the allegations. In addition, the tip contained a "range of details" related to "future actions of third parties ordinarily not easily predicted." This information of future conduct "demonstrated inside information," and a "special familiarity" with the suspect's activities. This familiarity, said the Court, made it reasonable for police to believe that a person "with access to such information is likely to also have access to reliable information about the individual's illegal activities." Although Justice White characterized the judgment as "close," the majority concluded that the tip, as corroborated, "exhibited sufficient indicia of reliability to justify the investigatory stop" of White. The dissenters, Justices Stevens, Brennan, and Marshall, felt the anonymous tip provided "anything but a reliable basis" of criminal conduct. Under the ruling, said Stevens, "every citizen is subject to being seized and questioned by any officer prepared to testify that the warrantless stop was based on an anonymous tip predicting whatever conduct the officer just observed."

Police officers are permitted to order the driver of a vehicle stopped for a traffic violation to step out of the car. The Fourth Amendment question in *Maryland v. Wilson*, 519 U.S. 408 (1997), was whether that authority extended to anyone else riding in the car.

Jerry Wilson was a passenger in a car lawfully stopped for speeding. While the driver was searching for registration and other information, the officer ordered Wilson, who had been acting "nervously," to exit the vehicle. As Wilson stepped out, he dropped what seemed to the officer to be crack cocaine. Wilson and the driver were arrested and indicted on several drug charges. Wilson sought to suppress admission at trial of the drugs seized during the traffic stop, arguing that the officer did not have authority to order him to leave the car. The trial judge ruled that the officer did not have reasonable suspicion to order Wilson from the car, and that the officer could not automatically order a passenger from a car based on the traffic stop alone. As a result of these findings, the trial court ordered suppression of the drugs, a decision upheld by two appellate courts in Maryland. The state petitioned the Supreme Court for review of whether the officer could order a passenger from a stopped vehicle even in the absence of cause. The Supreme Court ruled that officers could order passengers out of stopped vehicles. Chief Justice Rehnquist referred to *Pennsylvania v. Mimms*, 434 U.S. 106 (1977), in which the Court held that an officer "as a matter of course" may order the driver of a lawfully stopped car to exit the vehicle. The question in *Wilson* was whether the *Mimms* rule extends to passengers. On the "public interest" side of the balance, the same "weighty interest in officer safety is present regardless of whether the occupant of the stopped car is a driver or a passenger." On the "personal liberty" side of the balance, the case for the passengers is "in one sense" stronger than that for the driver. There is probable cause to believe that the driver has committed a driving offense, but there is no such cause for the passenger. But, said Rehnquist, "as a practical matter, the passengers are already stopped by virtue of the stop of the vehicle." The only "change in their circumstance" is that they will be outside rather than inside the stopped vehicle. While outside, the passenger will be denied access to any weapon that might be hidden inside the car. In the Court's view, the possibility of a "violent encounter" does not occur from the "ordinary reaction" of a motorist stopped for a driving violation, but from a concern that evidence of a more serious crime might be revealed by the stop. The "motivation of a passenger to employ violence to prevent apprehension of such a crime is every bit as great as that of the driver." The danger to an officer from a traffic stop, Rehnquist concluded, is "likely to be greater when there are passengers in addition to the driver in the stopped car." Although the basis for ordering passengers from the car is not the same as for ordering drivers to exit the vehicle, the "additional intrusion on the passenger is minimal." Justices Stevens and Kennedy objected to the authorization of seizures "unsupported by any individual suspicion whatsoever." Kennedy feared that the ruling would put "tens of millions of passengers at risk of arbitrary control by the police."

Two Washington, D.C., police officers stopped Michael Whren and James Brown for traffic violations. As one of the officers approached the vehicle, he observed plastic bags that appeared to contain cocaine in the car. Whren and Brown were arrested and the bags were seized. At the suppression hearing, the defendants showed that a police department regulation prohibited plainclothes officers driving unmarked cars from making stops for the driving infractions involved in this case. Notwithstanding the department regulation, a federal district court found that the officers had cause to make the stop and denied the motion to suppress the drugs. The case of *Whren v. United States*, 517 U.S. 806 (1996), thus raised the question of whether a traffic stop prohibited by department regulations is a pretextual stop barred by the Fourth Amendment. It was the Supreme Court's unanimous judgment that it is not. The determining consideration is whether the police have probable cause to believe a traffic violation has occurred. The mere fact that an officer does not have the "state of mind which is hypothecated by the reasons which provide the legal justification for the officer's actions," said Justice Scalia, "does not invalidate the action taken as long as the circumstances, viewed objectively, justify that action." The defendants had contended that because automobiles are so "heavily and minutely regulated," officers could almost invariably catch a motorist in violation of some regulation or another, thus creating the temptation to use traffic stops as a way of stopping cars for impermissible reasons—such as racial bias. The Court refused, however, to make the reasonableness of traffic stops a function of the "actual motivations" of the officers. The Constitution, Scalia acknowledged, prohibits race-based police actions, but the constitutional framework for objecting to intentionally discriminatory law enforcement is the Equal Protection Clause, not the Fourth Amendment. "Subjective intentions," Scalia concluded, "play no role in ordinary, probable-cause Fourth Amendment analysis." Accordingly, it was the Court's conclusion for cases such as this, there is "no realistic alternative to the traditional common-law rule that probable cause justifies a search and seizure."

The question in *United States v. Sokolow*, 490 U.S. 1 (1989), was whether reasonable suspicion exists when an individual fits the characteristics of a drug courier "profile," a composite of factors based on law enforcement experience that correlate with involvement in drug trafficking. Sokolow was stopped as he entered a taxi at the Honolulu airport. When Sokolow was stopped, Drug Enforcement Administration (DEA) agents knew, among other things, that he had paid over $2,000 for two round-trip airline tickets from a large roll of

$20 bills. He was also traveling under a name that did not match the name under which his telephone number was listed. His original destination had been Miami, a "source" city for illicit drugs. He had stayed in Miami only a short time despite a 20-hour one-way flight. Further, he had appeared nervous throughout the flight and had checked none of his luggage. Warrants were subsequently obtained after a drug-detection dog alerted officers to a shoulder bag Sokolow was carrying. A search of the shoulder bag yielded an amount of cocaine in excess of 1,000 grams. The court of appeals had reversed Sokolow's conviction, saying that the stop was impermissible because there was no objective evidence of "ongoing criminal behavior" prior to the stop. The Supreme Court reversed the court of appeals. The Court characterized the lower court's standard as creating "unnecessary difficulty" by drawing an "unnecessarily sharp line between types of evidence." Rather, the Court recognized the probative significance of the "probabalistic" factors from the profile. Although none of these factors was itself proof of illegal conduct, and may even be "quite consistent with innocent travel," when the factors here are "taken together, they amount to reasonable suspicion." The factors observed here have evidentiary value by themselves, and the fact that these factors were listed in the profile does not "detract from their evidentiary significance as seen by a trained agent." Finally, Sokolow contended that the agents were obligated to use the "least intrusive means to verify or dispel their suspicions." Sokolow argued that the agents should have "approached and spoken with him" rather than detaining him. The Court disagreed. The reasonableness of a stop "does not turn on the availability of less intrusive investigatory techniques." Such a rule would "unduly hamper the police's ability to make swift on-the-spot decisions, ... and it would require courts to indulge in unrealistic second-guessing."

Consent Searches

Ohio v. Robinette, **519 U.S. 33 (1996)** An officer stopped Robert Robinette for speeding. After returning Robinette's driver's license and administering a verbal warning, the officer asked him if he was carrying anything illegal in the car. Robinette said he was not, but consented to a search of the car. The search revealed a small amount of marijuana and a pill. Robinette was arrested and charged with possession of a controlled substance. Robinette unsuccessfully sought to suppress the evidence and was found guilty. The Ohio Supreme Court, however, ruled that an officer must inform a motorist detained in this way that he or she is "legally free to go" as a precondition for any consensual interrogation. The Supreme Court disagreed and ruled that an officer may ask permission to search a car without an indication that the motorist is free to leave. Chief Justice Rehnquist indicated a strong reluctance to resolve the question on the basis of any "bright-line" rule. Rather, the reasonableness of police searches must be "measured in objective terms" by examining the totality of circumstances. Rehnquist based much of his brief opinion on *Schneckloth v. Bustamonte*, 412 U.S. 218 (1973), in which the Court had said that it would be "thoroughly impractical to impose on the normal consent search the detailed requirements of an effective warning." So, too, said Rehnquist, it would be "unrealistic to require police officers to always inform detainees that they are free to go before a consent search may be deemed voluntary." Justice Stevens was the only dissenter. It was his view that a motorist "in [Robinette's] shoes" would have believed that he was obligated to answer the question about contraband and that he was not free to "get back in his car and drive away." It "inexorably follows" that when an officer either arrests or reprimands the driver of a speeding car, any "continued detention of that person constitute[s] an illegal seizure." *See also* CONSENT SEARCH, p. 633; EXIGENT CIRCUMSTANCE, p. 647; FOURTH AMENDMENT, p. 193; WARRANTLESS SEARCH, p. 711.

Significance   The central issue in cases like *Robinette* and *Schneckloth* is whether the consent to search is voluntary. In *Schneckloth*, a police officer stopped an automobile occupied by six persons including Robert Bustamonte. After requesting identification and establishing that the car was owned by the brother of one of the occupants, the officer asked if he could search the interior of the car. The owner's brother agreed. When the officer asked whether the trunk opened, the owner's brother took the car keys and opened the trunk. Several stolen checks were found in the trunk and were subsequently entered into evidence at Bustamonte's intent to defraud trial. The Supreme Court upheld the use of the evidence. The Court said "two competing concerns must be accommodated in determining the meaning of a 'voluntary' consent—the legitimate need for such searches and the equally important requirement of assuring the absence of coercion." Such problems cannot be "resolved by any infallible touchstone." The Court stressed the "totality of circumstances" in making judgments in these kinds of cases and concluded that consent had been voluntarily given in this case. The Court rejected the argument that consent must be evaluated in the same way as a waiver of rights pertaining to a fair trial. The Court opted not to require that individuals know of their right to refuse consent in order to establish a voluntary consent. The dissenters, Justices Douglas, Brennan, and Marshall, on the other hand, argued that before consent could be obtained, a person must be informed of his or her right to refuse consent. The *Schneckloth* ruling distinguished between search and custodial interrogation situations, holding that an individual need be apprised of legal options only in the instance of the latter. *Schneckloth* did not require knowledge of the right to withhold consent as an element of showing voluntary consent. Beyond the issue of voluntariness, there remains the question of how much the consent allows authorities to search. Consent may be limited to specific places to be searched or specific items to be searched for. If it cannot be shown that a person has voluntarily consented to an unlimited search, authorities tend to carefully limit searches based on consent. A person may also withdraw consent, and searches continued after consent is withdrawn must be otherwise defensible. Even a suspect's consent may be insufficient to uphold a search. The Court held in *Florida v. Royer*, 460 U.S. 491 (1983), a case quite similar to *Robinette*, that if a suspect is detained beyond the permissible bounds of an investigative stop, his or her consent to a search of his or her suitcases becomes "tainted by the illegal detention."

A Rehnquist Court decision further illustrates the direction of recent consent doctrine. Law enforcement officers board buses laid over at a stop and seek the consent of passengers to submit to searches of their luggage. The action is known as "working the buses," and it is a fairly common drug interdiction tactic on interstate buses. The Court upheld the practice in *Florida v. Bostick*, 501 U.S. 429 (1991). Permission was sought to search Bostick's luggage, even though there was no reason to suspect Bostick was carrying drugs. Bostick consented to a search, which yielded cocaine. The Florida Supreme Court ruled that "working the buses" was categorically unconstitutional because a reasonable person would not have felt free to leave the bus to avoid the request for permission to search. The U.S. Supreme Court, however, did not see the practice as unlawful in every situation. A "consensual encounter," said Justice O'Connor, does not "trigger Fourth Amendment scrutiny," and merely asking a passenger to consent does not constitute a "seizure." Even without particularized suspicion, police may ask questions of individual passengers and request consent to search. The request becomes improper if it conveys that compliance is not optional. Consent that is the product of any kind of intimidation is "not consent at all." The appropriate test is whether, considering all the circumstances, a passenger would feel free to refuse the request to search. The Court rejected Bostick's argument that, because the encounter occurred on a bus, he was less "free to leave." It was this "free to leave" test that governed the thinking of the Florida Supreme Court. O'Connor said the focus on freedom to leave was misplaced. The fact that Bostick did not feel free to leave was largely because of his decision to take the bus in the first place. When someone is seated on a bus and has no wish to leave, inquiry into whether he or she should leave is "not an accurate measure of the coercive effect of the encounter." Rather, said O'Connor, the crucial test is whether, on the basis of all the circumstances surrounding the encounter, the police conduct "would have communicated to a reasonable person that he was not at liberty to ignore the police presence and go about his business." Justices Marshall, Blackmun, and Stevens dissented. Marshall regarded these "dragnet-style sweeps" as highly coercive. Consent is obtained, he observed, because few passengers are willing to leave the bus and risk being "stranded in unfamiliar locations."

United States v. Matlock, 415 U.S. 164 (1974), considered whether a third party may consent to a search. Matlock was convicted of bank robbery. Part of the evidence used against him was stolen money that was found during a warrantless search of a bedroom that Matlock shared with someone else. Consent for the search yielding the stolen money was obtained from the other person, not Matlock. The Supreme Court upheld the search. The decisive element in determining the adequacy of a third-party consent was joint occupancy or control. The Court found such joint control present in this case because Matlock had often represented the other person as his wife, the consenting person "harbored no hostility" toward Matlock, and the person admitted cohabitation out of wedlock with Matlock, a criminal offense in the state of the search. The Court concluded she was in a position to give valid consent to the search. The dissent was similar to that in *Schneckloth v. Bustamonte*, 412 U.S. 218 (1973). Justices Douglas, Brennan, and Marshall argued that consent cannot be obtained unless the consenting party is informed of the right to refuse consent. Their central thrust was that a waiver of the right to privacy cannot be effectively made if "he is totally ignorant of the fact that, in the absence of his consent, such invasions of privacy would be constitutionally prohibited." Justice Douglas also pointed out that no exigent circumstance prevailed here, thus authorities had every opportunity to secure a warrant prior to the conduct of the search. *Matlock* provided guidance in the matter of third-party consent searches. If the suspect does not offer consent, the question becomes whether anyone may legally consent to a search of the suspect's premises. In *Matlock*, the Court focused on the "common authority" criterion. If a third party shares common authority over a place or items within a place, that person may properly consent to the search. Generally, common authority would cover consent by a spouse or persons otherwise living together such as in *Matlock*. Consent in these situations, however, may be limited if there are places or items within the shared premises that are "exclusively used" by the nonconsenting other party. Parents may generally consent to searches of rooms that are occupied by minor children within the parents' premises.

Minors, on the other hand, may not provide consent to search shared premises. The ability to consent is independent from possessing title to the premises to be searched. Accordingly, a landlord may not legally consent to the search of a leased room or rooms, nor may the employee or agent of any landlord consent to a search on behalf of a tenant. This applies even to short-term renters in hotels or motels.

The question before the Court in *Illinois v. Rodriguez*, 497 U.S. 177 (1990), was whether a warrantless entry is lawful if based on the consent of a third party whom the police reasonably believe to have common authority over the premises, but who does not in fact possess such authority. The Court upheld the entry nonetheless. The Court, through Justice Scalia, said there are various elements that can make the search of a person's home reasonable, one of which is "consent of the person or his cotenant." The general rule, said Scalia, is that factual determinations made by agents of government be reasonable, but not necessarily correct. The Constitution is no more violated in this case than it is when police "enter without a warrant because they reasonably (though erroneously) believe they are in pursuit of a violent felon who is about to escape." The Court said its decision "does not suggest that law enforcement officials may always accept a person's invitation to enter premises." As with other factual judgments bearing on searches and seizures, consent entries must be judged against the objective standard: "[W]ould the facts available to the officer at the moment ... warrant a man of reasonable caution in the belief that the consenting party had authority over the premises?" If not, a warrantless entry "without further inquiry is unlawful unless authority actually exists. But if so, the search is valid."

Knock and Announce Requirement

Richards v. Wisconsin, **520 U.S. 385 (1997),** Police officers typically announce themselves prior to executing a search warrant on private property. The Court held in *Wilson v. Arkansas,* 514 U.S. 927 (1995), that announcement prior to entry is a general expectation for a reasonable search. Wisconsin had a policy that categorically excepted searches in drug cases from the knock and announcement requirement prior to the *Wilson* ruling. *Richards* provided the Court with the opportunity to determine whether a blanket or automatic exception to the knock and announcement rule is permissible within *Wilson.* Police sought to enter Richards's motel room to perform a warrant-authorized search for cocaine. There was no dispute concerning the warrant or the evidence used to obtain it. An officer first attempted to gain entry to the room by posing as a maintenance person, but Richards closed the door. The first officer, joined by another, then forced his way into the room without announcing his intent to execute the warranted search. Richards sought to suppress the evidence seized from the room, citing the officers' failure to knock and announce their intention to search. The trial judge ruled against Richards, who then pled no contest on several charges and was sentenced. He appealed to Wisconsin's intermediate appellate court, but the U.S. Supreme Court decided *Wilson* before the Wisconsin Supreme Court could rule on his case. The Wisconsin Supreme Court then ruled that the state drug search exception to the knock and announce rule was not affected by the *Wilson* decision. The Supreme Court unanimously reversed the Wisconsin court's decision, but concluded that the forcible, no-knock entry was justified in this case. Justice Stevens reiterated the view expressed in *Wilson* that the "knock and announce" requirement could "give way" in situations that presented a threat of physical violence or when officers had reason to believe that evidence would be destroyed. He termed "indisputable" that felony drug investigations "may frequently involve both these circumstances." The question in this case, however, was whether felony drug investigations could justify exception from the knock and announce requirement in every case. Wisconsin had cited the needs attaching to the "special circumstances of today's drug culture" as justification for the categorical exception. Stevens suggested that creating exceptions to the knock and announce rule based on the "culture" surrounding a category of criminal behavior presented at least two "serious concerns." First, the bright line exception contained "considerable overgeneralization." Although drug investigations "frequently pose special risks to officer safety and the preservation of evidence, not every drug investigation will pose these risks to a substantial degree." In some situations, the government interest in preserving evidence and maintaining safety "may not outweigh the individual privacy interests intruded upon by a no-knock entry." Wisconsin's blanket rule impermissibly "insulates these cases from judicial review." Second, a criminal category exception to the no-knock requirement is too easily transferable to other criminal categories. If a "per se exception" were allowed for each category of criminal investigation that includes "considerable—albeit hypothetical—risk" of danger to officers or destruction of evidence, the knock and announce element of the Fourth Amendment's reasonableness requirement "would be meaningless." The Court concluded that the fact that felony drug investigations may frequently present circumstances warranting no-knock entry "cannot remove from the neutral scrutiny of a reviewing court the reasonableness of the police decision not to knock and announce in a particular case." In order to justify a "no-knock" entry, police must have a reasonable suspicion that knocking and announcing their presence, "under the particular circumstances," would be "dangerous or futile," or that it would "inhibit the effective investigation of the crime" by allowing the destruction of evidence. Although the Court rejected Wisconsin's blanket exception to the knock and announce requirement, it concluded that in this case officers had a "reasonable suspicion that Richards might destroy evidence if given the further opportunity to do so." *See also* FOURTH AMENDMENT, p. 193; KNOCK AND ANNOUNCE, p. 674; WARRANTLESS SEARCH, p. 711.

Significance   The "knock and announce" question was before the Rehnquist Court on several occasions, beginning with *Wilson v. Arkansas*, 514 U.S. 927 (1995). Indeed, *Richards* evolved directly from *Wilson v. Arkansas*. In *Wilson* authorities obtained warrants to arrest Wilson (and her boyfriend) and search her residence based on Wilson's sale of drugs to a police informer. Police entered Wilson's residence through an unlocked front door and found both narcotics and a weapon. Wilson unsuccessfully sought to suppress the evidence seized during the search on the grounds that the officers had failed to comply with the "knock and announce" requirement found in common law. The issue in *Wilson* was whether this common-law rule is required by the Fourth Amendment. The U.S. Supreme Court said it was, but not categorically. Justice Thomas spoke for a unanimous Court. He used historical evidence to determine the original meaning of the reasonable search requirements of the Fourth Amendment. At the time the amendment was written, common law recognized that officers had authority to "break open the doors of a dwelling, but generally indicated that he first ought to announce his presence and authority." As a result, the Court concluded that the common-law "knock and announce" principle "forms a part of the reasonableness inquiry under the Fourth Amendment." The principle was "quickly woven into the fabric of early American law." Most of the states that ratified the Fourth Amendment, said Thomas, enacted constitutional provisions or statutes generally incorporating English common law. The announcement principle need not apply in every case, however. The Fourth Amendment's "flexible requirement of reasonableness should not be read to mandate a rigid rule of announcement that ignores countervailing law enforcement interests." Arkansas sought to preserve Wilson's conviction by claiming that unannounced entry was justified because prior announcement would have endangered the officers executing the warrants, and produced an "unreasonable risk" that Wilson would destroy "easily disposable narcotics evidence." Thomas suggested that these considerations "may well provide the necessary justification" for unannounced entry, but refused to fashion an inflexible rule.

Bureau of Alcohol, Tobacco, and Firearms (ATF) agents were

attempting to find and arrest Alan Shelby. They received information from a reliable informant that he had been seen near the home of Hernan Ramirez and subsequently obtained a no-knock warrant to enter and search Ramirez's residence. A number of agents converged around the Ramirez home to execute the warrant. The agents announced their presence over a loudspeaker and indicated they intended to serve the warrant. At the same time, an agent broke a garage window and directed his gun inside. Ramirez, who had been sleeping inside the house, awoke and used his own gun to fire a shot into the ceiling of the garage. He explained that he had believed someone was breaking into his home. Ramirez was subsequently taken into custody where he admitted firing the shot. Based on this incident, officers obtained another search warrant to search Ramirez's home for the guns. Ramirez was a convicted felon and was charged with the federal offense of being a felon in possession of a firearm. He sought to suppress the admission of the weapons at trial, arguing that insufficient exigency existed to justify destruction of his property while making the no-knock search for Shelby. The U.S. Supreme Court unanimously rejected this argument in *United States v. Ramirez*, 118 S.Ct. 992 (1998). Police may make no-knock entry when there is reasonable suspicion that knocking and announcing their presence before entering would be "dangerous or futile, or … inhibit the effective investigation of the crime." The issue presented in Ramirez was whether the Fourth Amendment imposes a higher standard when no-knock entry results in the destruction of property. The Court concluded that it does not. Whether reasonable suspicion exists for a no-knock entry "depends in no way on whether police must destroy property in order to enter." In this case, police had ample reason to believe that Shelby presented a danger to themselves and others. The garage window was broken in an effort to discourage Shelby or anyone else from "rushing to the weapons that the informant had told them [Ramirez] might have kept there." The Court concluded that police conduct was "clearly reasonable" in this case and that no Fourth Amendment violation occurred.

Drug Testing

***Vernonia School District 47J v. Acton*, 515 U.S. 646 (1995)** The Vernonia School District 47J required students wishing to participate in athletics to submit to urine testing for drug and alcohol use. A drug test was performed on all student athletes wishing to participate in a particular sport prior to the beginning of the season, with random testing occurring on at least 10 percent of the athletes every week thereafter. The Actons challenged the drug-testing policy on behalf of their son James, who was kept from participating in the District's football program because he refused to submit to the testing. The Supreme Court upheld the policy in *Vernonia School District 47J v. Acton.* Justice Scalia indicated that when the Court attempts to determine the reasonableness of a search, it first must look to practices at the time the constitutional provision was adopted. There was no clear practice, either "approving or disapproving," the kind of search involved in this case, however. As a result, whether a search meets the reasonableness standard is determined by "balancing its intrusion on the individual's Fourth Amendment interests against its promotion of legitimate governmental interests." The critical question in this case was the absence of individualized suspicion as a precondition for testing student athletes—the testing of students was unsupported by probable cause of any drug use by students subjected to the test. A search of this kind may still be constitutional, said Scalia, when "special needs, beyond the normal need for law enforcement, make the warrant and probable cause requirement impracticable." The Court found "special needs" in the "sharp increase" in drug use in the District's schools. Central to the Court's conclusion about "special needs" was that the testing policy targeted children who had been "committed to the temporary custody of the State as schoolmaster." Unemancipated minors generally "lack some of the most fundamental rights of self-determination," and Fourth Amendment rights are "different" in the public school context than elsewhere. The consideration of "reasonableness" cannot ignore the schools' "custodial and tutelary responsibility for children." The nature of student rights depends on "what is appropriate" for children in the school setting, even if privacy expectations are compromised. Scalia used mandatory physical examination and vaccination programs as examples of governmental requirements students must undergo "for their own good and that of their classmates." Scalia focused on the population subset of students participating in athletics. Privacy interests are particularly diminished for the student athlete. Athletes routinely change clothes and shower in public school locker rooms. Such sites are "not notable for the privacy they afford." Indeed, in Scalia's view, participation in school sports is "not for the bashful." Furthermore, students who choose to participate "voluntarily subject themselves to a greater degree of regulation than that imposed on students generally." The Court noted that the testing program was a narrowly tailored initiative as it was limited to student athletes only. The Court also concluded that the District's concern was important, if not compelling. School years are the time when the "physical, psychological, and addictive effects of drugs are most severe." In addition, the effects of a "drug-infested" school are not limited to the users, but affect the entire student body and faculty because of the disruptions they have on the education process. The need for the state to act under these circumstances is "magnified" by the fact that the "evil is being visited not just upon individuals at large but upon children for whom it has undertaken a special responsibility of care and direction." Finally, the Court was persuaded that the testing program was efficacious. Scalia suggested that it was "self-evident" that a drug problem "fueled" by the "role model effect of athletes' drug use," and of particular danger to athletes, is "effectively addressed by making sure athletes do not use drugs." Justice O'Connor, joined by Justices Stevens and Souter, dissented. They were most troubled by the absence of individualized suspicion. It was their view that the Court's ruling made millions of students partici- pating in interscholastic sports, an "overwhelming" majority of whom have given school officials "no reason whatsoever to suspect they use drugs at school, ... open to an intrusive body search." They felt the Court had "sidestep[ped]" powerful privacy considerations. Blanket searches can involve large numbers of searches that pose a "greater threat to liberty than do suspicion-based ones, which affect one person at a time." *See also* FOURTH AMENDMENT, p. 193; PROBABLE CAUSE, p. 691; WARRANTLESS SEARCH, p. 711.

Significance   Several drug testing cases preceded the *Vernonia* case to the Supreme Court. *Skinner v. Railway Labor Executives Association*, 489 U.S. 602 (1989), upheld drug testing as a condition of employ- ment. The Court rested its decision on the nature of the job respon- sibilities. At issue in *Skinner* were regulations issued by the Federal Railroad Administration (FRA) under authority given the secretary of transportation (Skinner) to adopt industry safety standards. Two particular regulations were challenged. The first required blood and urine tests of covered employees following major train accidents or incidents. The second authorized administration of breath and urine tests to employees who violate certain safety rules. The court of appeals ruled that the Fourth Amendment requires "particularized suspicion" prior to testing. The Supreme Court disagreed. The Court ruled the regulations reasonable under the Fourth Amendment despite the absence of warrant or reasonable suspicion require- ments. The Court saw the government interest in regulating conduct of railroad employees as critical. Such employees have "safety-sensi- tive" responsibilities that bear directly on the traveling public. This creates a "special needs" interest that "plainly justifies" prohibiting covered employees from drug or alcohol use while on duty. In addi- tion, these "special needs" create an interest that "goes beyond normal law enforcement" that may justify "departures from" usual probable cause and warrant requirements. The Court held that neither the requirements for warrant nor individualized suspicion were "essential to render the intrusions reasonable." After reviewing the purposes of warrants, the Court concluded that in this context the use of warrants would "do little to further those aims." The intrusions are "narrowly and specifically defined" and "well known to the covered employees." Furthermore, the warrant requirement would "significantly hinder" and otherwise "frustrate" the purposes of testing in the time needed to obtain a warrant and would result in "destruction of valuable evidence." As for individualized suspicion, the Court saw the testing as posing only "limited threats" to employee privacy expectations, especially in an industry already subject to "pervasive" safety regulation at both the federal and state levels. Justices Brennan and Marshall dissented, arguing that testing should not occur without individualized suspicion that an employee was using drugs or alcohol. Justice Marshall also refused to defer to the public safety rationale. "History teaches," he said, "that grave threats to liberty come in times of urgency, when constitutional rights seem too extravagant to endure."

The Court's decision in *National Treasury Employees Union v. von Raab*, 489 U.S. 656 (1989), was similar to *Skinner*, but varied somewhat because of the difference in job responsibilities. The Customs Service required urinalysis of employees seeking transfer or promotion to positions having direct involvement with drug interdiction, requiring the carrying of firearms, or requiring the handling of "classified" information. The Court ruled that requiring mandatory urine samples as a condition of promotion or transfer must meet Fourth Amendment standards of reasonableness, but held the drug-screening requirement was reasonable even without a warrant or individualized suspicion provisions. The warrant requirement would "divert valuable agency resources" and provide "little or no protection of personal privacy" because the testing purpose was "narrowly and specifically" defined. The procedures were specifically set forth and were not subject to discretion. As a result, there was no determination to be made by a judicial officer because "implementation of the process becomes automatic" upon the employee's pursuit of one of the defined Service positions. Moreover, the Court reasoned that affected employees are aware of the testing requirement and the procedures used. In assessing the reasonableness of the process, the Court had to balance the public interest in the program against the individual privacy concerns of the employees. The Court referred to the Customs Service as our nation's "first line of defense against one of the greatest problems affecting the health and welfare of our population." Many of the Service's employees are "often exposed" to both the criminal element involved with drug smuggling and the controlled substances they attempt to bring into the country. Because of this exposure, the government has a "compelling interest in ensuring that front-line interdiction personnel are physically fit, and have unimpeachable integrity and judgment." Unlike private citizens or other government personnel, Service employees engaged in interdiction "reasonably should expect effective inquiry into their fitness." The same is true of those carrying firearms. Successful performance of their job responsibilities depends "uniquely on their judgment and dexterity," and these employees cannot reasonably expect to "keep from the Service information that bears directly on their fitness." Although screening designed to elicit this information "doubtless infringes on some privacy expectations," the Court concluded "we do not believe these expectations outweigh the Government's interest in safety and the integrity of our borders." Justices Brennan and Marshall were joined in dissent in the Customs case by Justices Stevens and Scalia. The dissenters focused on the same individual suspicion issue discussed in the railroad case. Justice Scalia said that without evidence of Service personnel abusing drugs or alcohol, the screening was "particularly destructive of privacy and offensive to personal dignity."

The "war on drugs" has provided the basis for a number of intriguing Fourth Amendment decisions. The Supreme Court authorized warrantless seizure of nonresident alien property located outside the United States in *United States v. Verdugo-Urquidez*, 494 U.S. 259 (1990). This decision removed one potentially effective line of defense for foreign nationals prosecuted in the United States for drug trafficking. Verdugo-Urquidez, a Mexican resident, was taken into custody by Mexican officials in Mexico for various drug-related violations of American law. He was transported to a border station and turned over to American officers, who placed him under arrest. Several days later, U.S. Drug Enforcement Agency (DEA) officers, working with Mexican authorities, searched two of Verdugo-Urquidez's residences in Mexico and seized a variety of documents. The Court ruled that the Fourth Amendment did not apply in this situation. Chief Justice Rehnquist said that the Fourth Amendment "functions differently" from other rights of the accused protections. The Framers of the amendment chose to use the term "people" in the amendment as opposed to any "person" or an "accused." This was meant to refer to a "class of persons who are part of a national community or who have otherwise developed sufficient connection with this county to be considered part of that community." The purpose of the Fourth Amendment was to "protect the people of the United States against arbitrary action by their own Government." It was not intended to restrain the federal government's "actions against aliens outside United States territory." Clearly, warrants are required to search overseas property of American citizens. Further, Rehnquist indicated that aliens with "substantial connections" to the United States are reached by the protections of the Fourth

Amendment. Verdugo-Urquidez's involuntary presence on American soil, however, does not establish such a connection. He had no "previous significant voluntary connection" with the United States that "might place him among 'the people'" of the national community. Justices Brennan, Marshall, and Blackmun dissented. In Brennan's view, Verdugo-Urquidez had "sufficient connection" to the United States by virtue of the government's own action; he is a member of "our community" and is entitled to Fourth Amendment protection because the government is "attempting to hold him accountable under United States criminal laws." Verdugo-Urquidez, said Brennan, "has become, quite literally, one of the governed."

In *United States v. Alvarez-Machain*, 511 U.S. 350 (1994), the Court ruled that agents of the United States may ignore the terms of extradition agreements and forcibly bring a criminal suspect from a foreign country to the United States to stand trial. Alvarez-Machain, a Mexican citizen and a physician, was sought by the United States for his alleged involvement in the kidnapping and murder of a Drug Enforcement Administration (DEA) agent. Under terms of a 1980 agreement with Mexico, the United States could have requested extradition. Because Alvarez-Machain was a Mexican citizen, Mexico could have chosen either to extradite him or undertake its own prosecution of him. No extradition request was made, however. Instead, Alvarez-Machain was seized in Mexico by Mexican bounty hunters, taken to El Paso, Texas, and delivered to DEA authorities. Alvarez-Machain contended that having an extradition agreement would make no sense "if either nation were free to resort to forcible kidnapping to gain the presence of an individual for prosecution in a manner not contemplated by the treaty." Chief Justice Rehnquist said, "We do not read the treaty in such a fashion." Rather, the treaty "does not purport to specify the only way in which one country may gain custody of a national of the other country for the purposes of prosecution." Viewing the terms of the treaty literally, Rehnquist said the agreement "says nothing about the obligations of the United States and Mexico to refrain from forcible abductions" and should not be read as though such limitations are contained implicitly. Justice Stevens, in a dissent joined by Blackmun and O'Connor, argued that failure to specifically prohibit forcible abductions should not be interpreted to create an "optional method of obtaining jurisdiction over alleged offenders." Indeed, he concluded that it is "shocking that a party to an extradition treaty might believe that it has secretly reserved the right to make seizures of citizens in the other party's territory."

A Georgia law required that candidates for state office submit to a drug test within 30 days of the filing deadline and file a certificate stating that the test results were negative. Several candidates of the

Libertarian Party, including Walker Chandler, unsuccessfully attempted to bar implementation of the testing requirement prior to the 1994 election. The Libertarian candidates complied with the law, but renewed their challenge after the election. The Supreme Court struck down the law in *Chandler v. Miller*, 520 U.S. 305 (1997). Both Georgia and the challengers agreed that the drug-testing requirement was a search within the meaning of the Fourth Amendment. The case essentially turned on whether Georgia could demonstrate "special needs" beyond the normal need for law enforcement on which to base an exception from the individualized suspicion condition normally associated with a reasonable search. Such "special needs" had been found in *Acton, Skinner,* and *von Raab.* Georgia argued that the "special needs" review in this case was grounded in the state's sovereign power reserved by the Tenth Amendment. While acknowledging that states enjoy "wide latitude" to establish conditions of candidacy for state offices, the Court expressed the view that states may not "disregard basic constitutional protections" in doing so. Neither a state's power to establish qualifications for state office nor its sovereign power to prosecute crimes "diminishes the constraints on state action imposed by the Fourth Amendment." Because Georgia's testing requirement had "effectively limited the invasiveness" of such a procedure, the "core issue" in this case was whether the certification requirement was "warranted by a special need." Georgia sought to establish a substantial interest on the "incompatibility of unlawful drug use with holding high state office." Use of illegal drugs draws into question the "judgment and integrity" of an elected official, "jeopardizes" the discharge of public functions, and "undermines public confidence and trust" in public officials. Georgia claimed that certification of an individual's drug-free status would deter users of illegal drugs from seeking elective office. The Court failed to see, however, "any indication of a concrete danger demanding departure from the Fourth Amendment's main rule." It was the Court's view that Georgia's certification requirement was neither "well designed to identify candidates who violate anti-drug laws" nor was the scheme a "credible means to deter illicit drug users from seeking election to state office." Indeed, the Court found no reason why ordinary law enforcement methods would not suffice in this circumstance. The only purpose the Court saw as served by the Georgia law was projection of an antidrug image. However well intended, the drug testing law, "diminishes personal privacy for a symbol's sake." Only Chief Justice Rehnquist dissented. Rehnquist saw preventing persons who use illegal drugs from concealing that fact from the public as a legitimate government interest, an interest sufficient to justify the use of drug testing.

Prisoners' Rights: Searches

Block v. Rutherford, **468 U.S. 576 (1984)** held that persons detained in a pretrial circumstance do not have the right to contact visits and can have their cells searched in their absence. *Block v. Rutherford* involved a policy of the Los Angeles County jail, which denied any contact visits with relatives or friends of pretrial detainees. Also under review in *Block* was the practice of jail authorities to conduct irregularly scheduled searches of individual jail cells when the occupants were not present. A number of pretrial detainees brought a class action challenging the policy and practice, but the Supreme Court ruled against them. Chief Justice Burger described the security concerns that attended the case. The Los Angeles County jail annually houses some 200,000 persons awaiting trial. Those who must be detained before trial constitute a serious security problem "given the ease with which one can obtain release on bail or personal recognizance." Holding a person before trial thus becomes "a significant factor bearing on the security measures that are imperative to proper administration of a detention facility." The Court defined the inquiry as whether the challenged condition or policy is imposed for the purpose of punishment or is incidental to some other legitimate government purpose. Without proof of intent to punish, the issue hinges on whether there is an alternative purpose for the restriction and whether the restriction is excessive. Before applying these guidelines to *Block,* the Court expressed its belief prison administrators should be accorded wide-ranging deference in the adoption and execution of policies and practices that are needed to preserve internal order and maintain institutional security. In considering the ban on contact visits, the Court focused on the question of legitimate government objective since it was conceded the prohibition was not intended as punishment. The Court found a "rational connection" between the ban and internal security at the facility. Contact visits "invite a host of security problems" by opening the institution to the introduction of drugs, weapons, and other contraband. The visits also pose the danger of exposing visitors to risk from detainees awaiting trial for serious, violent offenses. In this respect, pretrial detainees are as much a security risk as convicted prisoners. The Court did not find a total ban on contact visits excessive. Burger reinterated the Court's unwillingness "to substitute our judgment on these difficult and sensitive matters" for that of persons charged with and trained in the running of such facilities. The Court concluded that the prohibition was "an entirely reasonable, nonpunitive response to legitimate security concerns." The Court similarly deferred to the "informed discretion of prison authorities" by upholding the shakedown searches of cells conducted in the absence of detainees. Justices Brennan, Marshall, and Stevens dissented.

Brennan said the Court appeared willing to sanction any prison condition for which it could imagine a "colorable rationale," no matter how oppressive or ill justified that condition is in fact. *See also* FOURTH AMENDMENT, p. 193.

Significance   Security interests provided the Court with the basis to hold that detention facility officials may prohibit all contact visits in *Block v. Rutherford.* For similar reasons the Court also upheld searches of detention facility cells in the absence of the detainee. While prisoners are constitutionally protected, recent decisions such as *Block* clearly indicate that the scope of their protection is more significantly restricted than that of the general public.

In *Hudson v. Palmer* 468 U.S. 517 (1984), the Court said prisoners could be subjected to random searches. If a prisoner's lawfully possessed property is destroyed during such a search, a constitutional violation occurs only if the state provides no mechanism to obtain remedy for the property lost. Chief Justice Burger said in *Hudson* that "the recognition of privacy rights for prisoners in their individual cells simply cannot be reconciled with the need for incarceration and the needs of penal institutions." These words are reflective of the Court's recent response to prisoner challenges to detention facility practices.

Asset Forfeiture

***Bennis v. Michigan,* 517 U.S. 1163 (1996)** Asset forfeiture has become quite common in dealing with drug offenders, and a number of forfeiture issues have been before the Supreme Court during the last several years. *Bennis* gave the Court an opportunity to consider the "innocent owner" aspect of property forfeiture. Michigan allows the seizure of property that creates a public nuisance. John Bennis was arrested and charged with gross indecency; he engaged in sexual acts with a prostitute in his car. As part of an effort to crack down on prostitution, the nuisance abatement law was used to seize the Bennis's automobile. Tina Bennis, John's wife, appealed the forfeiture order on the grounds that she was an innocent co-owner of the automobile and that her interest in the car could not be forfeited unless it could be shown that she had prior knowledge of her husband's use of the car. The Michigan Supreme Court concluded that an innocent owner's property can be seized if that owner consented to the other owner's use of the property, regardless of the propriety of the use, and the Supreme Court agreed. Chief Justice Rehnquist referred to a "long and unbroken line" of cases establishing that an owner's interest in property may be forfeited because of the way the property is used "even though the owner did not know that it was to be put to such use." In addition, it has "long been settled" that forfeiture of property "entrusted by the innocent owner" to another who uses the property unlawfully does not violate due process protections. Rehnquist characterized the deterrent objectives of the forfeiture law—that Michigan sought to deter illegal activity that "contributes to neighborhood deterioration and unsafe streets." The Bennis car was used in criminal activity, and Michigan simply followed "long-standing practice" to seize it. Justices Thomas and Ginsburg both registered some concerns about asset forfeiture, but supported the seizure of the Bennis vehicle. Thomas suggested that the case provided a reminder that the Constitution does not "prohibit every-thing that is intensely undesirable." Ginsburg did not see Michigan's forfeiture statute as an "experiment to punish innocent third parties." Rather, Michigan has decided to "deter Johns from using cars they own (or co-own) to contribute to neighborhood blight, and that abatement endeavor hardly warrants this Court's disapproba-tion." The dissenters, Justices Stevens, Kennedy, Souter, and Breyer, were of the view that the wife's interest in the vehicle was not subject to forfeiture because fundamental fairness "prohibits the punish-ment of innocent people." *See also* ASSET FORFEITURE, p. 617; *Austin v. United States*, p. 404; DUE PROCESS CLAUSES, p. 641.

Significance The Comprehensive Drug Abuse Prevention and Control Act of 1970 (Act) authorizes the federal government, among other things, to confiscate property acquired with the proceeds of drug crimes. The issue in *United States v. A Parcel of Land*, 507 U.S. 111 (1993), concerned forfeiture of property belonging to someone other than the person involved in criminal conduct. One provision of the Act says that title to a property vests with the government at the time any crime connected to the property is committed. The Act also contains an "innocent owner" provision, however, that allows a person to establish that any criminal act(s) was committed "without the knowledge or consent of the owner." Beth Ann Goodwin lived with Joseph Brenca for a period of six years. Brenca gave Goodwin money she used to purchase a house in which she lived with Brenca. Two years after Goodwin ended the relationship, the government seized the property on the grounds that the money Brenca had given Goodwin to buy the house came from his illicit sales of marijuana. A lower court had ruled that the innocent owner defense was available only to persons who owned the property prior to the criminal act(s) that prompted the forfeiture action. The Supreme Court disagreed. Justice Stevens pointed to language in the Act establishing the inno-cent owner exception and noted that the term "owner" was used several times without qualification of the term. Such language, said Stevens, "is sufficiently unambiguous to foreclose any contention that it applies only to bona fide purchasers." It was the Court's view that Goodwin ought not be disqualified from claiming that she had no knowledge that the funds she had used to purchase the property were "proceeds traceable" to illegal drug transactions. Stevens said Congress would not create a "meaningless" defense for innocent owners. The government cannot profit from the statutory language adopting the doctrine until the owner has an opportunity to "invoke and offer evidence to support the innocent owner defense." Justice Kennedy, joined by Chief Justice Rehnquist and Justice White, dissented. It was their view that Goodwin was not a bona fide owner. Rather, forfeiture is determined by the "title and ownership of the asset in the hands of the donor, not the donee."

The Court considered the procedural protections associated with forfeiture in *United States v. Good Real Property*, 510 U.S. 43 (1993). James Good pleaded guilty to a drug charge in 1985 and was sentenced to a year of imprisonment and five years of probation. In 1989 the federal government began a civil forfeiture action against Good's property. A federal magistrate determined that there was probable cause to believe that the property was connected to Good's drug offense and issued a seizure warrant against it. Good, who was living in Nicaragua at the time, was not notified that the forfeiture action had been commenced. Furthermore, there was no hearing on the issue of whether the property was forfeitable. The United States argued that because the civil forfeiture served a law enforcement purpose in this case, that it need only comply with the Fourth Amendment when seizing property. The Court disagreed. The seizure of property "implicates two explicit textual sources of constitutional protection," the Fourth Amendment and the Due Process Clause of the Fifth. The proper question in this case, said Justice Kennedy, is not "which Amendment controls but whether either Amendment is violated." The Court agreed that the Fourth Amendment applies to civil seizures, but held that the "purpose and effect" of the government's action in this case went beyond the traditional meaning of search and seizure. The government did not seize the property to preserve evidence of criminal conduct, but rather to "assert ownership and control over the property itself." Legal action that can result in loss of property must comply with the Due Process Clause of the Fifth and Fourteenth Amendments. The Court said that the right to prior notice and a hearing is "central to the Constitution's command of due process." The purpose of this requirement is to protect an individual's use and possession of property from "arbitrary encroachment—to minimize substantively unfair or mistaken deprivations of property." The Court found Good's right to maintain control over his home without governmental interference of both "historic and continuing importance." Governmental seizure gives the government the right to prohibit sale, evict occupants, modify the property—generally to "supersede the owner in all rights pertaining to the use, possession, and enjoyment of the property." These interests are substantial. The Court also concluded that the practice of ex parte seizure created an "unacceptable risk of error." Although the intent of the drug forfeiture statute was not to deprive innocent owners of property, the ex parte approach "affords little or no protection to the innocent owner." Finally, the Court found no sufficiently important governmental interest to require asserting control over the property without first affording notice and hearing. To the contrary, postponement of seizure until after an adversary hearing, said Kennedy, "creates no significant administrative burden." Any harm resulting from the delay, he continued, "is minimal in comparison to the injury occasioned by erroneous seizure." Chief Justice Rehnquist, joined by Justices O'Connor and Scalia, were of the view that the ex parte warrant process required by the Fourth Amendment was sufficient for property forfeitures and arrests alike.

A federal grand jury in Nevada indicted Brian Degen on several charges stemming from his involvement with marijuana trafficking. Degen, a dual citizen of the United States and Switzerland, moved to Switzerland prior to his indictment. Under terms of an extradition treaty, Switzerland is not required to surrender a citizen for criminal prosecution. At no time after his indictment had Degen returned to the United States. Immediately following his indictment, the federal government sought to take possession of Degen's extensive property holdings in the United States on the grounds that the properties were either used in the furtherance of his criminal activities or obtained with proceeds from criminal activity. Degen had counsel contest the forfeiture action, but did not submit to the jurisdiction of the court on the criminal charges. The district court ruled that as a fugitive, Degen was not entitled to contest the attempt to seize his property. The Court of Appeals for the Ninth Circuit affirmed, concluding that the district court had reasonably dismissed Degen's property claims under the principle of fugitive disentitlement. The Supreme Court unanimously found disentitlement because of fugitive status unjustified in *Degen v. United States*, 517 U.S. 820 (1996). The Court saw no risk of "delay or frustration" in resolving the forfeiture claims or in enforcing any resulting judgment. Further, it was the Court's view that the lower court had sufficient alternative means to ensure that the criminal prosecution was not compromised by participation in the civil forfeiture proceeding. The Court recognized the need to "redress the indignity" caused the trial court by Degen's absence from the criminal proceeding, and the need to deter flight from prosecutions by Degen and others. Justice Kennedy characterized both interests as "substantial," but called disentitle-ment "too blunt an instrument for advancing them."

Austin v. United States, 509 U.S. 602 (1993), raised a substantially different forfeiture issue. Richard Austin sold two grams of cocaine to an individual working with local police. The buyer approached Austin at his place of business. Austin left his shop, went to his nearby trailer home, returned, and delivered the drugs to the buyer. Austin eventually pleaded guilty to one state count of possession of drugs with intent to distribute. Following his sentencing, a federal civil forfeiture proceeding was initiated. Austin's trailer home and place of business were both confiscated without trial on the grounds that these properties had been used in the drug transaction. Austin argued that the Excessive Fines Clause of the Eighth Amendment applied to civil forfeitures, and a unanimous Supreme Court agreed. Justice Blackmun said the general purpose of the Eighth Amendment was to "limit the government's power to punish." The Excessive Fines Clause more specifically limits the government's power to "extract payments, whether in cash or in kind, 'as *punishment* for some offense.'" The United States had argued that the civil forfeiture process is not limited by the Eighth Amendment. The issue according to Justice Blackmun, however, was not "whether forfeiture was civil or criminal, but rather whether it is punishment." Sanctions frequently serve more than one purpose. It is not necessary to "exclude the possibility that a forfeiture serves remedial purposes to conclude that it is subject to the limitations of the Excessive Fines Clause." All that must be shown is that the forfeiture "serv[es] in part to punish." The Court found the objective of punishment reflected several ways: in the legislative history of the federal forfeiture law; in the Congress's choice of linking forfeiture directly to drug offenses; and in the inclusion of an "innocent owner defense." Despite arguments by the United States that the statutory provision was remedial, the Court ruled that the government failed to show that the civil forfeiture process was exclusively remedial. A civil sanction that "cannot fairly be said *solely* to serve a remedial purpose, but rather can only be explained as also serving either retributive or deterrent purposes, is punishment, as we have come to understand the term."

Production and/or distribution of obscenity is one of the offenses falling under the forfeiture provisions of the Racketeer Influenced and Corrupt Organizations Act (RICO). RICO provides that persons convicted of two or more obscenity offenses can have all property directly or indirectly traceable to the convictions confiscated. Ferris Alexander was convicted of 18 counts of obscenity offenses and three RICO violations stemming from them. In addition to prison terms, fines, and assessed costs, the trial court ordered Alexander to forfeit his entire business. Under the RICO forfeiture, Alexander lost almost $9 million in cash plus the property and inventory connected to his business activities. Alexander challenged the RICO forfeiture as an unconstitutional prior restraint on expression and as an excessive or disproportionate punishment prohibited by the Eighth Amendment. The Supreme Court rejected his prior restraint argument, but unanimously concluded that the forfeiture was a form of punishment for Eighth Amendment purposes in *Alexander v. United States*, 509 U.S. 544 (1993). Alexander contended that the practical effect of the RICO forfeiture order imposed a "complete *ban* on his future expression because of previous unprotected speech." The Court did not see the RICO forfeiture as forbidding Alexander from future expressive conduct, nor was he required to obtain prior approval for any expressive activities. Rather, the order only deprived him of particular assets determined to be connected to his RICO violations. The Court saw no legal ingredient to his future expressive activity. Indeed, he was "perfectly free to open an adult bookstore or otherwise engage in the production and distribution of erotic materials." The order simply prevented Alexander from financing any such enterprise with assets derived from prior RICO offenses. Alexander also contended that the RICO forfeiture provisions may have an unlawful "chilling effect" on expression. The Court acknowledged that "cautious" booksellers may practice "self-censorship," but said that deterrence of the sale of obscenity is "a legitimate end of state antiobscenity laws." Justice Kennedy, joined by Justices Blackmun, Stevens, and Souter, dissented on the First Amendment question. The Court's decision allowed the "destruction" of a book or film business and its entire inventory of legitimate expression for "a single past speech offense." This "ominous, onerous threat undermines free speech and press principles essential to our personal freedom." Kennedy concluded that the Court had not recognized forfeiture of this kind as a "new kind of government control with unmistaken dangers of official censorship." Simply because forfeiture follows a lawful obscenity conviction is insufficient. Nonetheless, forfeiture of assets remains a significant component of the current efforts to combat drug trafficking.

CHAPTER 4

The Fifth Amendment

Overview, 263

The Fifth Amendment, 265

OVERVIEW

The Fifth Amendment states:

No person shall be held to answer for a capital, or otherwise infamous crime, unless on a presentment or indictment of a Grand Jury, except in cases arising in the land or naval forces, or in the Militia, when in actual service in time of War or public danger; nor shall any person be subject for the same offence to be twice put in jeopardy of life or limb; nor shall be compelled in any criminal case to be a witness against himself, nor be deprived of life, liberty, or property, without due process of law; nor shall private property be taken for public use, without just compensation.

The Fifth Amendment provides protection for the individual at both ends of the criminal process. It requires a charge by means of a grand jury indictment, and when the process is concluded, it prohibits a person from being "twice put in jeopardy" for the same offense. The protections of the Fifth Amendment were not applied to the states until well into the twentieth century, however. Chief Justice John Marshall said in *Barron v. Baltimore*, 32 U.S. 243 (1833), that the Bill of Rights applied only in federal cases. Although *Barron* has never been formally overturned, ratification of the Fourteenth Amendment created new possibilities for applying all or part of the Bill of Rights to the states. In *Palko v. Connecticut*, 302 U.S. 319 (1937), the Court rejected the view that the Fourteenth Amendment made safeguards of the Bill of Rights against double jeopardy effective against the states. But the *Palko* decision established a doctrine of "selective incorporation," which by 1983 had left only the grand jury clause of the Fifth Amendment and the excessive fines and bail clause of the Eighth Amendment outside the corpus of criminal procedures that had been incorporated into the states' laws.

The evolution of Fifth Amendment standards includes a number of benchmark cases. *Costello v. United States*, 350 U.S. 359 (1956), allowed relative informality in grand jury inquiries and established wide operating room for them. Several themes have emerged from double jeopardy cases. *Waller v. Florida*, 397 U.S. 387 (1970), found that "sameness" is constituted when multiple sovereignties, in this case a state and a municipality, simultaneously prosecute for the same offense. *Schiro v. Farley*, 510 U.S. 222 (1994), considered retrial situations in which the concept of "implicit acquittal" applies. The Court decided that the "same evidence" test rather than the "same conduct" test is more appropriate for determining whether two offenses are the same in *United States v. Foster*, 509 U.S. 688 (1993). The issue of whether the Double Jeopardy Clause prohibits multiple punishments is examined in *Department of Revenue v. Kurth Ranch*, 511 U.S. 767 (1994).

The Fifth Amendment also protects persons from having to provide testimony against themselves. *Carter v. Kentucky*, 450 U.S. 288 (1981), dealt with inferences that can be drawn from a defendant's failure to testify and jury instructions regarding that silence. The landmark decision of *Miranda v. Arizona*, 384 U.S. 436 (1966), required that any person undergoing custodial interrogation be apprised of his or her right to say nothing. Statements made without prior warning are inadmissible, although the Court has allowed use of such statements to impeach the defendant's own testimony at trial. *James v. Illinois*, 493 U.S. 307 (1990), held, however, that inadmissible statements cannot be used to impeach other defense witnesses. *North Carolina v. Butler*, 441 U.S. 369 (1979), examined waiver of the *Miranda* protections and the status of statements made following partial *Miranda* warnings. A recent decision of potentially great significance is *Arizona v. Fulminante*, 499 U.S. 279 (1991), in which the Court extended harmless error analysis to coerced confessions. *Nix v. Williams*, 467 U.S. 431 (1984), decided that improperly obtained evidence may be used in a trial if it would have been ultimately or "inevitably" discovered by lawful means.

Self-incrimination questions have also arisen relative to evidence other than testimony that may be derived from a defendant. *Schmerber v. California*, 384 U.S. 757 (1966), and *Neil v. Biggers*, 409 U.S. 188 (1972), took into account identification techniques and defendant-derived evidence such as line-ups, show-ups, photographic identification, and blood samples in relation to the privilege against self-incrimination. *Kastigar v. United States*, 406 U.S. 441 (1972), looked at immunity as an approach to satisfying the self-incrimination protection.

The Fifth Amendment provides protections for persons in the criminal process, particularly that no one shall be deprived of life, liberty, or property, without due process of law. The Fifth Amendment was an American adaptation of elements of the English common-law tradition. In contrast to the language of the Fourth Amendment, which was derived from specific colonial experiences with the General Warrant, the language of the Fifth Amendment was based on what Blackstone referred to as "universal maxims." The Fifth Amendment contains five separate clauses. The first provides that: "No person shall be held to answer for a capital, or otherwise infamous crime, unless on a presentment or indictment of a Grand Jury, except in cases arising in the land or naval forces, or in the Militia, when in actual service in time of War or public danger." The language is James Madison's, which he adapted from several state constitutions. The Supreme Court has held that the Grand Jury Clause of the Fifth Amendment does not extend to the states under the construction of the Due Process Clause of the Fourteenth Amendment. Hence, the right to indictment by grand jury is held absolute only in federal criminal proceedings.

The second component of the Fifth Amendment directs: "[N]or shall any person be subject for the same offence to be twice put in jeopardy of life or limb." Blackstone said that it was "a universal maxim of the common law of England that no man is to be brought into jeopardy of his life more than once for the same offence." This principle was based initially on a holding in twelfth-century English courts that if a person were tried for violation of an ecclesiastical canon, he could not then be tried for the same infraction in the civil courts. John Locke added in his draft of the North Carolina Fundamental Constitutions of 1669 that "no cause shall be twice tried in any one court, upon any reason or pretense whatsoever." In modern American criminal proceedings, jeopardy attaches when a defendant is formally charged with an offense and the trial has commenced before a competent court. The word "commence" applies in a jury trial to the time the jury is impaneled and sworn. In a court trial it applies to the time the first witness is sworn. The protection against double jeopardy was extended to state actions by the Due Process Clause of the Fourteenth Amendment in *Benton v. Maryland*, 395 U.S. 784 (1969).

The third clause of the Fifth Amendment provides that no person "shall be compelled in any criminal case to be a witness against himself." The origins of this clause were in the practices of the English Star Chamber Court, where persons even suspected of some offense were interrogated before any formal accusation had been made. The questions were leading and were intended to elicit a confession. It was not uncommon to gain confessions in Star Chamber with the help of threats or torture. As late as the seventeenth century it was common practice in England for a defendant to be questioned at trial only by the prosecutor or the judge. Thus the English system of justice at the time was redolent with forced confessions. The early American knowledge of and determination to reform this system was reflected in the Virginia Bill of Rights. It stated flatly that no one can be "compelled to give evidence against himself." A number of state constitutional ratifying conventions later insisted that the Virginia model be followed. By 1886 Justice Joseph P. Bradley could affirm what had become the American tradition in *Boyd v. United States*, 116 U.S. 616 (1886): "Any compulsory discovery made by extorting the oath is contrary to the principles of free government." Ten years later the tradition was summarized by Justice Henry B. Brown in *Brown v. Walker*, 161 U.S. 591 (1896):

> The change [from abject coercion to more humane influences] in the English criminal procedure in that particular seems to be founded upon no statute and no judicial opinion, but upon a general and silent acquiescence of the court in a popular demand. But, however adopted, it has become firmly imbedded in English, as well as in American jurisprudence. So deeply did the inequities of the ancient system impress themselves upon the minds of the American colonists that the states, with one accord, made a denial of the right to question an accused person a part of their fundamental law, so that a maxim, which in England was a mere rule of evidence, became clothed in this country with the impregnability of a constitutional enactment.(161 U.S. at 597)

Malloy v. Hogan, 378 U.S. 1 (1964), mandated applicability of the Self-Incrimination clause to the states under the Fourteenth Amendment.

The fourth clause of the Fifth Amendment provides that no person shall "be deprived of life, liberty, or property, without due process of law." The words "due process of law" came from Article XIII of the Constitution of New York. The drafter of the Bill of Rights, James Madison, was greatly influenced in his word choice by fellow *Federalist* author Alexander Hamilton. Hamilton argued persuasively that insertion of the phrase "due process" would remove any doubt that it was "the process and proceedings of the courts of justice" being addressed. Thus the *courts* would interpret the legitimate rights of citizens, not legislative bodies, which could presumably enact legislation to "disfranchise or deprive" citizens of *any* right. Because of the clause's general thrust and applicability, the Supreme Court historically has been reluctant to give it precise definition. The Court prefers to rely on "the gradual process of judicial inclusion and exclusion," as in *Davidson v. New Orleans*, 96 U.S. 97 (1878).

The central meaning of procedural due process is that parties whose rights are to be affected are entitled to be heard and, in order that they may enjoy that right, they must be notified. *Parham v. Cortese*, 407 U.S. 67 (1972). Reasonable notice and opportunity to be heard and present any claim or defense are embodied in the term "procedural due process."

Substantive due process requires that the Supreme Court be convinced not only that the procedure for enforcing the law, but that *the law itself* is fair, reasonable, and just. Thus the Court has struck down laws regulating hours of labor and forbidding employers to discharge workers for union membership and activity, as in *West Coast Hotel Co. v. Parrish*, 300 U.S. 379 (1937). The perils of such power under substantive due process review were articulated by Justice Lewis F. Powell Jr. in *Moore v. East Cleveland*, 431 U.S. 494 (1977):

[S]ubstantive due process has at times been a treacherous field for this Court. There are risks when the judicial branch gives enhanced protection to certain substantive liberties without the guidance of the more specific provisions of the Bill of Rights. As the history of the *Lochner* era demonstrates, there is reason for concern lest the only limits to such judicial intervention become the predilections of those who happen at the time to be members of this Court. That history counsels caution and restraint. But it does not counsel abandonment.... (431 U.S. at 502)

Finally, the Fifth Amendment provides: "[N]or shall private property be taken for public use, without just compensation." The Founding Fathers considered property rights to be absolute and inherent. Again, this holding is based in English common law dating from the Magna Carta. The citizens' power of eminent domain is described in *Black's Law Dictionary* as "the highest and most exact idea of property remaining in the government, or in the aggregate body of the people in their sovereign capacity." The precise perimeters for the legitimate taking of private property for public use remain elusive. The Supreme Court has followed a case-by-case approach to definition of them. In *Penn Central Transportation Company v. New York City*, 438 U.S. 104 (1978), the Court recognized the guarantee contemplated by the Eminent Domain Clause of the Fifth Amendment. It was designed to bar government from forcing certain few people to bear public burdens that, in all fairness and justice, should be borne by the public as a whole. This Court quite simply has been unable to develop any set formula for determining when justice and fairness require that economic injuries caused by public action be compensated by the government, rather than disproportionately afflict a few persons. *See also* BILL OF RIGHTS, p. 621; COMMON LAW, p. 631; DOUBLE JEOPARDY, p. 640; MAGNA CARTA, p. 677; SELF-INCRIMINATION CLAUSE, p. 695.

Significance The Fifth Amendment protects citizens from government authority in several ways. Property rights are secured by the Due Process and Just Compensation Clauses. The Due Process Clause has been significant in that it requires the government to act with fundamental fairness, particularly procedural fairness. It is the view of many that the Due Process Clause also places substantive restrictions on the unreasonable exercise of federal governmental power. The Fourteenth Amendment similarly restricts governmental action at the state level. The Just Compensation Clause, also called the Takings Clause, protects private property owners by limiting the power of the government to seize property through the process of eminent domain. The scope of the Takings Clause has been expanded by the Rehnquist Court as it restricted governmental actions that diminish the value of private property.

The Fifth Amendment clauses that deal with criminal procedure are probably better known by most people. The Double Jeopardy Clause, made applicable to the states in *Benton v. Maryland*, 395 U.S. 784 (1969), limits the capacity of the federal and state governments to subject citizens to successive prosecutions. The Burger and Rehnquist Courts have rendered upwards of 60 double jeopardy rulings that take up such critical double questions as "sameness" of offense, dual sovereignty, implicit acquittal, and multiple punishment.

The most common understanding of the Fifth Amendment involves its protection against self-incrimination. Indeed, "taking the Fifth" is a familiar phrase to most citizens. The Warren Court decision in *Malloy v. Hogan*, 378 U.S. 1 (1964), made the privilege applicable at the state level. This decision became the basis for the Warren Court's landmark ruling in *Miranda v. Arizona*, 384 U.S. 436 (1966). *Miranda*, in turn, established procedural protections for custodial interrogations, often the most vulnerable step in the criminal process. In addition to protecting individuals from unknowingly and involuntarily contributing to their own conviction, the privilege against self-incrimination is designed to protect the integrity of the criminal process. The privilege ensures that disclosures made by criminal suspects are reliable as evidence; that statements have not been coerced in some way that might compromise their truthfulness.

Incorporation of the Bill of Rights

***Palko v. Connecticut*, 302 U.S. 319 (1937),** established "selective incorporation" as the preferred approach for determining whether Bill of Rights protections should be applied to the states. *Palko* came to the

Supreme Court as a double jeopardy case. Under provisions of state law, the prosecution successfully appealed a trial in which Palko had been convicted of second-degree murder and sentenced to life imprisonment. At the retrial Palko was convicted of first-degree murder and sentenced to death. Palko said he had been "twice put in jeopardy," a violation of the Fifth Amendment. He maintained that the double jeopardy prohibition reached Connecticut through the Due Process Clause of the Fourteenth Amendment. The Court disagreed with Palko and upheld the conviction from the retrial.

Justice Benjamin N. Cardozo accepted the task of distinguishing between those Bill of Rights guarantees such as freedom of speech and freedom of the press that had already been extended to the states by 1937, and protections such as double jeopardy that the Court said in *Palko* did not apply. The "rationalizing principle" of Justice Cardozo was based on the judgment of whether a particular right is "of the very essence of a scheme of ordered liberty." Certain processes such as a jury trial or grand jury indictment "may have value and importance," but to abolish or by-pass them would not violate "a principle of justice so rooted in the tradition and conscience of our people as to be ranked as fundamental." The rights that the states must protect are of a "different plane of social and moral values." The absorption process must consider "the belief that neither liberty nor justice would exist if they were sacrificed." In determining on which side of the incorporation line a challenged practice falls, Justice Cardozo said the Court must ask if the defendant has been subjected to a "hardship so acute and shocking that our polity would not endure it." In the instance of double jeopardy, the Court said the answer must surely be no. Connecticut was not "attempting to wear the accused out" through endless trials, but only to have a trial "free from the corrosion of substantial legal error." No fundamental principle had been violated. Palko was executed. *See also* BILL OF RIGHTS, p. 621; INCORPORATION, p. 665.

Significance　Incorporation focuses on whether federal Bill of Rights guarantees apply to the states. The question assumed great significance soon after ratification of the Fourteenth Amendment. The *Palko* Court rejected the view that the Fourteenth Amendment automatically made provisions of the Bill of Rights effective against the states, adopting instead Cardozo's selective incorporation reasoning.

Palko was decided well into the incorporation controversy. More than five decades earlier, in *Hurtado v. California*, 110 U.S. 516 (1884), for example, the Court rejected the argument that states are required to indict on presentment of a grand jury. The *Hurtado* view of incorporation prevailed until the 1920s and *Hurtado* remains the governing case on the grand jury provision of the Fifth Amendment;

states are still not required to use grand juries. Although the Court refused to apply the self-incrimination protection to the states in *Twining v. New Jersey*, 211 U.S. 78 (1908), it did consider the possibility that certain national citizenship rights might be protected from state violations. It said "fundamental" rights might qualify. The decisive break on the incorporation question came in *Gitlow v. New York*, 268 U.S. 652 (1925), in which the Court held that the free speech protection of the First Amendment applied to the states. Ten years after *Palko* the Court retained the selective approach and refused to apply the privilege against self-incrimination to the states in *Adamson v. California*, 332 U.S. 46 (1947). Justice Black's dissent in *Adamson* is regarded as the classic presentation of the "total incorporation" position. The Court's unwillingness to extend the Bill of Rights provisions to the states was based, said Black, on a "natural law" theory of the Constitution that "degrades the constitutional safeguards of the Bill of Rights." Black argued that the people of no nation "can lose their liberty so long as a Bill of Rights like ours survives and its basic purposes are conscientiously interpreted, enforced, and respected so as to afford continuous protection against old, as well as new, devices and practices which might thwart those purposes." When the search and seizure provision of the Fourth Amendment was incorporated in *Wolf v. Colorado*, 338 U.S. 25 (1949), it was applied within the "ordered liberty" approach of *Palko*.

The Warren Court made extensive changes in criminal justice policy by drawing the incorporation line of *Palko* to include most of the rights of the accused in the Bill of Rights. The Warren Court's reliance on *Palko* is illustrated in *Malloy v. Hogan*, 378 U.S. 1 (1964), and *Duncan v. Louisiana*, 391 U.S. 145 (1968), which incorporated into the states' laws the right against self-incrimination from the Fifth Amendment and the right to a trial by jury from the Sixth Amendment, respectively. Only the Grand Jury Clause of the Fifth Amendment and the Excessive Fines and Bail Clause of the Eighth Amendment currently stand outside the corpus of incorporated criminal procedures.

Grand Jury

***Costello v. United States*, 350 U.S. 359 (1956),** examined whether grand juries must utilize the same procedural and evidentiary rules as are required for jury trials. Costello, an organized crime figure, was indicted by a grand jury for tax evasion. He claimed that the grand jury indictments had been based on hearsay evidence and should be dismissed. Costello was subsequently convicted. A unanimous Court upheld the conviction based on the challenged indictments. The Court held that no constitutional provision "prescribes the kind of evidence upon which grand juries must act." The work of grand juries was intended not to be "hampered by rigid procedural or evidentiary rules." Citing the history out of which the English grand jury system evolved, the Court noted that grand jurors could "act on their own knowledge and were free to make their presentments or indictments on such information as they deemed satisfactory." The Court noted the excessive delays that would be produced by challenges to indictments on grounds of evidentiary inadequacy. It would mean that a defendant could "insist on a kind of preliminary trial to determine competency and adequacy of the evidence before the grand jury." Such is not required by the Fifth Amendment. The Court concluded its opinion by reiterating that a preliminary trial "would run counter to the whole history of the grand jury institution, in which laymen conduct their inquiries unfettered by technical rules." *See also Branzburg v. Hayes*, p. 113; GRAND JURY, p. 657.

Significance   *Costello v. United States* graphically demonstrated the broad operating latitude the Supreme Court has typically extended to grand juries. *Costello* is grounded in the categorical distinction between the charging process and processes designed to adjudicate guilt. Grand juries can operate more informally. Procedural and evidentiary rules are typically seen as "impediments" to the charging role of grand juries. Although decided in 1953, the position of *Costello* remains virtually unaltered, and the consequences of the case are apparent in at least three ways: First, *Costello* underscored the investigative function of grand juries, and the Court's view that grand juries must be exposed to the widest range of information in performing the accusatorial function. All other interests are generally subordinate to this end. Second, because of the primacy of the investigatory role, *Costello* enhances the influence of the prosecutor in guiding the operations of a grand jury. The greater the level of informality allowed in grand jury proceedings, the greater the discretion that can be utilized by the prosecutor in selecting witnesses and other evidence for grand jury consideration. Third, *Costello*'s emphasis on informality raises certain questions regarding protection of witnesses' rights, specifically the right against self-incrimination and the right of assistance of counsel. Other problems have been noted related to the use of immunity and the threat of the contempt power. The latter can be seen in *Branzburg v. Hayes*, 408 U.S. 665 (1972), in which a reporter was compelled to disclose information to a grand jury or be subjected to penalties for contempt.

In *United States v. Washington*, 431 U.S. 181 (1977), the Court considered the question of whether a grand jury witness must be specifically warned that he or she may be indicted by that grand jury. Further, must he or she be explicitly informed that if he or she is indicted, his or her testimony may be used against him or her at the actual trial? Washington was not warned of either possibility, but the Supreme Court held that his grand jury statements were admissible at his trial nonetheless. The Court concluded that the Fifth Amendment does not "preclude a witness from testifying voluntarily in matters which may incriminate him." Unless compulsion can be shown, the Fifth Amendment does not automatically apply because testimony has an incriminating effect. Once Washington had been warned generally that he could remain silent and that statements he made could be used against him, that advice "eliminated any possible compulsion to self-incrimination which may otherwise exist."

The Burger Court rendered several additional decisions involving grand jury practices. In *United States v. Mandujano*, 425 U.S. 564 (1976), a person was indicted by a grand jury for making false statements to the grand jury. The defendant attempted to have the grand jury testimony suppressed on the ground that he had not received complete *Miranda* warnings prior to his appearance. A unanimous Court stressed two themes in *Mandujano* in concluding that the testimony need not be suppressed. First, the *Miranda* decision "did not perceive judicial inquiries and custodial interrogation as equivalents." The grand jury setting is so "wholly different from custodial police interrogation" that to apply *Miranda* to grand juries is an "extravagant expansion never remotely contemplated by the Court in *Miranda*." Second, the Court deferred to the broadest view of the grand jury's investigative function. The Court spoke of witnesses being "legally bound to give testimony" and having an "absolute duty to answer all questions." While the privilege against self-incrimination can be asserted, the Court clearly did not wish to interfere with the grand jury's capacity to conduct a complete inquiry.

In *United States v. Calandra*, 414 U.S. 338 (1974), the Court refused to extend the exclusionary rule to grand jury proceedings. Once again the Court spoke of the need to maintain broad investigative powers for grand juries. Extending the exclusionary rule would "seriously impede" grand jury inquiries and "unduly interfere with the effective and expeditious discharge of the grand jury's duties." The policy preferences reflected in *Washington* prevailed because the grand jury function is clearly distinct from guilt adjudication at the trial stage. Because the grand jury is designed to investigate and accuse, the Court decided it can best perform that function by using the widest range of evidence available. That evidence may properly come before a grand jury through procedures that are substantially less formal and protective than those found at the trial stage.

This same view was recently reflected in the Rehnquist Court's ruling in *United States v. Williams*, 504 U.S. 36 (1992). In *Williams*, the Court held that federal district courts do not have the authority to dismiss indictments in cases in which prosecutors withhold evidence favorable to the accused. Such authority, said Justice Scalia, would "neither preserve nor enhance the traditional functioning of the institution that the Fifth Amendment demands." Rather, to require prosecutors to present exculpatory as well as inculpatory evidence would alter the grand jury's historical role, transforming it from an accusatory to an adjudicatory body. Further, given the grand jury's "operational separateness" from the court constituting it, the Supreme Court's view was that district courts could not invoke the "judicial supervisory power as a basis for prescribing modes of grand jury procedure."

Double Jeopardy: Dual Sovereignty

Waller v. Florida, 397 U.S. 387 (1970), examined the question of whether a state and a municipality may each prosecute criminal offenses based on the same act. Waller was convicted in municipal court for destruction of city property, an ordinance violation. The property was damaged while it was being stolen, and the state later tried Waller for grand larceny. Waller appealed his state conviction on double jeopardy grounds, and the Supreme Court unanimously set aside the grand larceny conviction. The Court rejected the argument that a state and a municipality each possess sovereignty. The Court said that political subdivisions of states have never been "considered as sovereign entities." Instead, they have been viewed as "subordinate governmental instrumentalities created by the State to assist in carrying out state governmental functions." Although the Constitution permits dual prosecution of an individual for federal and state offenses stemming from the same act, Waller could not be so prosecuted by a state and a municipal government. As applied in that context, the Court said the "dual sovereignty theory is an anachronism, and the second trial constituted double jeopardy." *See also Department of Revenue v. Kurth Ranch*, p. 283; DOUBLE JEOPARDY, p. 640; FIFTH AMENDMENT, p. 265; *Schiro v. Farley*, p. 279; *United States v. Foster*, p. 274.

Significance   The issue of successive federal-state prosecutions was first treated in *United States v. Lanza*, 260 U.S. 377 (1922). *Lanza* held that successive federal-state prosecutions were permissible on dual sovereignty grounds. The two sovereignties derive "power from different sources," and are "capable of dealing with the same subject-matter within the same territory." When each level defines certain behaviors as crimes and undertakes prosecution of violators, each "is exercising its own sovereignty, not that of the other." Federal and state authorities typically coordinate their activities, and, as a general practice, the federal government does not commence prosecution of cases for which state prosecutions have been initiated. For the same reasons of dual sovereignty, the double jeopardy prohibition does not preclude simultaneous prosecutions in two or more states if the criminal act occurred in more than one state. An example is *Heath v. Alabama*, 474 U.S. 82 (1985). Heath had contracted for the murder of his wife. She was kidnapped from his Alabama home, killed, and her body abandoned in Georgia. After pleading guilty to a murder charge in Georgia, Heath sought to prohibit his indictment on a similar charge in Alabama on double jeopardy grounds. The Court permitted successive prosecutions by the two states for the same crime, concluding that each state possesses its own "inherent sovereignty" preserved by the Tenth Amendment. Given their distinct sources of power to prosecute, the states are "no less sovereign with respect to each other than they are with respect to the Federal Government." The Court came to the far-reaching conclusion that to deny a state its power to enforce its criminal laws because another state "won the race to the courthouse" would be "a shocking and untoward deprivation" of states' rights and obligations to maintain peace and order within their confines. Considering that sovereignty flows from the source of authority, the dual sovereignty concept cannot apply in the *Waller* instance because local units of government are creations of state power. Conclusion of a criminal proceeding in a municipal jurisdiction or a state court constitutionally precludes a subsequent prosecution for the same criminal act in the other.

Double Jeopardy: Sameness

***United States v. Foster*, 509 U.S. 688 (1993)** The determining issue in double jeopardy cases is often what constitutes the "same offense." Since 1932 the "sameness" test established in *Blockburger v. United States*, 284 U.S. 299 (1932), has controlled this inquiry. *Blockburger* focuses on elements of the offenses and says offenses are not the same if one offense "contains an element not contained in the other." In other words, offenses are not the same if conviction for one requires factual proof not required for the other.

In 1989 the Court ruled in *Grady v. Corbin*, 495 U.S. 508 (1989), that in addition to meeting the *Blockburger* test, a subsequent prosecution must also satisfy a "same conduct" test. The *Grady* rule says that a second prosecution is not permitted if the conduct needed to prove the second charge is conduct for which the person has already been prosecuted. *Grady* was a controversial double jeopardy decision, and the consolidated cases of *United States v. Foster* and *United States v. Dixon*, 509 U.S. 688 (1993), gave the Supreme Court the opportunity to overrule the "same conduct" test from *Grady*. Both Dixon and Foster were convicted of criminal contempt. The double jeopardy question in both was whether the contempt convictions barred subsequent prosecutions on the offenses upon which the contempt was based. Michael Foster's ex-wife obtained a protective order from a District of Columbia court requiring that he not molest, assault, or threaten physical abuse to his former wife or her mother. Foster violated the order a number of times, and he was found in contempt of the protective order. He was subsequently indicted on charges of simple assault (one count), assault with intent to kill (one count), and threatening to injure (three counts). The court of appeals dismissed the indictment on all five counts based on *Grady*. The Supreme Court agreed that prosecution for simple assault was barred under *Blockburger*, but prosecution of Foster could occur on the remaining four counts even though these prosecutions would have been barred under the "same conduct" test of *Grady*. Justice Scalia, an outspoken dissenter in *Grady*, said that unlike *Blockburger*, *Grady* lacked constitutional roots. The "same conduct" rule announced in *Grady* is "wholly inconsistent" with earlier Supreme Court decisions and with the "clear common-law understanding of double jeopardy." In Scalia's view, there is simply "no authority except *Grady*" for the proposition that the Double Jeopardy Clause has different meanings in the successive prosecution and successive punishment contexts. That is because, Scalia continued, it is "embarrassing to assert that the single term 'same offence' (the words of the Fifth Amendment at issue here) has two different meanings—that what *is* the same offense is yet *not* the same offense." He criticized Justice Souter's dissent for "totally ignor[ing]" the many early cases interpreting the Double Jeopardy Clause to support "only an 'elements' test." Not only was *Grady* "wrong in principle," Scalia suggested that *Grady* "has already proved unstable in application." *Foster* was "yet another situation" in which a pre-*Grady* understanding would have allowed a second trial only to be barred by the "same conduct" test. Scalia thought it time to acknowledge what is "compellingly clear," the *Grady* decision "was a mistake." The Court does not "lightly reconsider" a precedent, Scalia concluded, "but because *Grady* contradicted an 'unbroken line of decisions,' contained 'less than accurate' historical analysis, and has produced 'confusion,' we do so here." Chief Justice Rehnquist and Justices O'Connor and Thomas were of the view that "as a general matter, double jeopardy does not bar a subsequent prosecution based on conduct for which a defendant has been held in criminal contempt." Because the crime of contempt has different elements from any substantive criminal charge, they would have permitted the prosecution of Foster on the simple assault indictment because they are separate offenses under the *Blockburger* test. A crime such as possession with intent to distribute cocaine, for example, is a "serious felony," said Rehnquist, "that cannot easily be conceived of as a lesser included offense of criminal contempt." To the contrary, to say that criminal contempt is an aggravated form of the drug offense "defies common sense." Justices White, Souter, Blackmun, and Stevens dissented. They believed that all of Foster's counts were barred from prosecution without relying on *Grady*. They found it both "unwarranted and unwise" to reconsider *Grady* in these cases. Since *Grady* was on the table, however, the dissenters expressed their view that *Grady* had been correctly decided and should not be overruled. *See also* DOUBLE JEOPARDY, p. 640; FIFTH AMENDMENT, p. 265; *Schiro v. Farley*, p. 279; *Waller v. Florida*, p. 273.

Significance   The most troublesome double jeopardy issue is "sameness"—that is, whether the two offenses are the same or not. If two offenses can be distinguished, both may be prosecuted without double jeopardy problems. *Ashe v. Swenson*, 397 U.S. 436 (1970), considered whether the principle of collateral estoppel is contained within the double jeopardy protection in state criminal proceedings. Collateral estoppel is a legal principle that prohibits relitigation of an issue once a valid judgment has been made on that issue. Six persons were robbed while they were playing poker. Ashe was charged with armed robbery of each of the six players, but tried on only one of the charges in his first trial. The jury found the evidence "insufficient" to convict. Several weeks later Ashe was tried for the robbery of another of the victims and was convicted. The Supreme Court reversed Ashe's conviction. The Court felt the only issue in dispute in the first trial was the identification of Ashe as one of several suspects. The jury resolved that question in the negative. Substituting one victim for another "had no bearing whatever upon the issue of whether the petitioner was one of the robbers." The Court found the fact issue of the two trials to be identical and suggested the "situation is constitutionally no different" than had the state attempted to reprosecute Ashe for the robbery of the first victim.

The double jeopardy protection prevents a second prosecution only if charges are brought for the same offense. Thus determination of sameness is fundamental. With a large number of acts defined as crimes, it is likely that multiple prosecutions can arise out of overlapping offenses and single transactions. Prior to *Ashe*, one of two criteria was typically used in handling this problem. The first related to evidence required to convict on particular charges. If the "same evidence" was required for both, the offenses were deemed the same for purposes of double jeopardy. If, however, at least one element of each offense could not be proved with common evidence, the offenses were said to be different. The "same evidence" approach created limits to the protection afforded against reprosecution because of the overlapping character of contemporary criminal codes. The same evidence criterion does, however, preclude prosecution for included offenses, that is, offenses that are generally less serious than a connected greater offense, but are so tightly related that one cannot convict on the greater charge without convicting on the lesser charge as well.

Grady v. Corbin, 495 U.S. 508 (1989), produced a new but short-lived test for sameness. Corbin was responsible for an automobile accident in which a person died. Corbin was ticketed at the scene for drunk driving and driving on the wrong side of the road. Shortly thereafter, Corbin pleaded guilty to those charges. The prosecution failed to inform the trial court that the accident had resulted in a fatality before the court accepted Corbin's plea on the traffic offenses and imposed sentence. Two months later, Corbin was indicted on several charges stemming from the accident, including negligent homicide and third-degree reckless assault. Under the test established in *Blockburger v. United States*, the indictments covered charges that were not the same as those to which Corbin had earlier pleaded. The Supreme Court said that a subsequent prosecution must do more than "merely survive" *Blockburger* standards, however. The state had admitted in this case that it would attempt to establish the essential elements of the homicide and assault charges on the basis of Corbin's conduct that had led to the earlier convictions. The Court ruled that the state is precluded from establishing an essential element of a crime on the basis of the same conduct for which a defendant has been convicted. The Court made it clear this was not a "same evidence" test. Rather, the "critical inquiry is what conduct the State will prove, not the evidence the State will use to prove that conduct." Subsequent prosecutions for homicide and assault could have been pursued in this case if they did not rely on proving the conduct for which Corbin had already been convicted. The "same conduct" standard from *Grady* was overturned only three years later in *Foster*.

Two cases decided between *Grady* and *Foster* focus on different double jeopardy issues. The Court ruled in *Dowling v. United States*, 493 U.S. 342 (1990), that the double jeopardy prohibition did not prevent the admission of evidence relating to another alleged crime for which a defendant had been acquitted. Dowling was prosecuted in federal court for bank robbery. The prosecution sought to introduce evidence that Dowling had been involved in other crimes. Specifically, the prosecution attempted to introduce testimony from a woman into whose home Dowling had allegedly broken. In both the break-in and the robbery, the perpetrator had worn a ski mask and carried a small hand gun. The woman had unmasked Dowling during the break-in and was able to identify him. Notwithstanding that identification, Dowling had been acquitted on charges associated with that break-in. The prosecution for the bank robbery wished to have the woman describe Dowling to strengthen identification of him as the bank robber. The woman could also identify a second man from the break-in. This same man had been seen outside the bank in what was believed to be the intended getaway car, and the prosecution wished to reinforce the link between Dowling and the second man. As the woman concluded her testimony, the jury was informed that Dowling had been acquitted on the charge involving the witness. The jury was also instructed of the limited purpose for which the testimony was introduced. The Supreme Court ruled that neither the doctrine of collateral estoppel nor considerations of due process precluded her testimony. In this case, the prior acquittal did not "determine the ultimate fact issue" in the bank robbery because the prosecution was not required to prove that Dowling had entered the witness's home. The Court was also of the view that the judge's limiting jury instruction kept the testimony from being "fundamentally unfair" because the jury could assess the truthfulness and significance of the witness's testimony. The Court ruled in *United States v. Felix*, 503 U.S. 378 (1992), that *Grady* did not preclude prosecution for substantive offenses even if some of the evidence used by the government was based on offenses for which the defendant was previously convicted. "Mere overlap" in proof between two prosecutions, said Chief Justice Rehnquist, "does not establish a double jeopardy violation."

The double jeopardy protection requires determining when jeopardy actually begins. The Court addressed the question in *Breed v. Jones*, 421 U.S. 519 (1975), which decided when jeopardy actually begins or "attaches." The case involved a 17-year-old boy who was adjudicated in a juvenile court proceeding, but was later transferred to adult court for prosecution because he was "unfit for treatment as a juvenile." Jones appealed his adult court conviction, claiming he had been "in jeopardy" in his juvenile proceeding and that initiation of charges against him in the adult court was foreclosed by the double jeopardy prohibition. The Supreme Court agreed. The Court's holding rested primarily on its perception of jeopardy. The Court said it was "simply too late in the day" to think that a juvenile is "not put in jeopardy at a proceeding whose object is to determine whether he has committed acts that violate criminal law," a proceeding "whose potential consequences include both the stigma inherent in such a determination and the deprivation of liberty for many years." So, despite attempts to make juvenile proceedings different from trials of adults, the juvenile process resembles the adult process closely enough to create jeopardy. The Court also rejected the contention that the prosecution of Jones as an adult was merely a continuation of the prosecution begun at the juvenile level. Although the Court agreed that the case "had not yet reached its conclusion" in the juvenile proceeding in that no sentence had been imposed, it determined that the failure to sentence Jones had not in any way limited Jones's risk or jeopardy. Putting Jones "at risk" was viewed as the decisive aspect of jeopardy. The juvenile court, "as the trier of facts, began to hear evidence," and at that point Jones's jeopardy began. If the juvenile authorities wished to preserve flexibility in terms of treatment or sentence options, those matters should have been considered prior to initiating proceedings in the juvenile court. For double jeopardy purposes, the risk begins at the time a jury is chosen or when a court begins to take evidence. A judgment on that evidence by a jury or a court need not occur.

Immunity from future prosecution on the original charges does not extend to cases in which the defendant initiated a cessation to trial proceedings. Nor does it extend to those cases in which the defendant successfully appeals following a conviction and has the conviction vacated on grounds other than evidentiary insufficiency. A case that does not reach the evidence stage, stopping at some preliminary point, affords no protection from further prosecution on the same charges. Neither dismissal of charges at a preliminary hearing nor dismissal of an indictment before a trial actually commences precludes those same charges from being brought again.

Double Jeopardy: Implicit Acquittal

Schiro v. Farley, **510 U.S. 222 (1994)**   Thomas Schiro was charged with "knowing murder," murder while committing a rape, and murder during the commission of a criminally deviant act, following his confession of killing a young woman. The trial jury found him guilty of only the murder while committing rape charge, and did not return a verdict on the other two counts. Following Schiro's sentencing hearing, the jury recommended life imprisonment. The trial judge concluded that Schiro had intentionally killed the woman notwithstanding the jury's failure to convict of knowing murder, and sentenced Schiro to death. Schiro pressed two double jeopardy claims. The first was that he could not be sentenced to death based on the aggravating circumstance of intentional murder because the sentencing stage amounted to successive prosecution for intentional murder. In other words, Schiro urged the Court to treat the sentencing phase as a separate and successive prosecution. Schiro's second claim was that the jury's failure to return a verdict on the knowing murder charge reflected a finding by the jury that Schiro did not intend to kill. As a result, the state was precluded from pursuing the issue of intent as an aggravating circumstance for death penalty purposes. The Supreme Court rejected both claims in *Schiro v. Farley*.

Justice O'Connor rejected the assertion that the sentencing phase of a single prosecution is a successive or multiple prosecution. She cited cases upholding resentencing after retrial and suggested that if a second sentencing proceeding typically does not violate the double jeopardy protection, "we fail to see how an initial sentencing proceeding could do so." O'Connor also pointed to recidivist laws that provide for sentence enhancement on the basis of prior convictions. The Court has generally allowed such enhanced sentences even though it requires a defendant to, in a sense, "relitigate in a sentencing proceeding conduct for which he was previously tried." The state is entitled to one fair opportunity to prosecute, concluded O'Connor, "and that opportunity extends not only to prosecution at the guilt phase, but also to present evidence at an ensuing sentencing proceeding." The Court also rejected Schiro's second claim based on the jury's unwillingness to convict him of intentional killing. The central question in this inquiry was whether the jury could have based its verdict on something other than Schiro's intent to kill. The Court concluded that there were "any number of possible explanations for the jury's acquittal verdict." As a result, the verdict could not be viewed as having definitively resolved the intentional killing question; the Court did not "draw any particular conclusion from its failure to return a verdict" on the intentional killing count. Justices Stevens and Blackmun dissented. They saw the failure of the jury to return a verdict on the intentional killing count as constituting an acquittal. Once the jury so resolved the issue of intent, said Stevens, "it was constitutionally impermissible for the trial judge to reexamine the issue." In their view, an "egregious violation of the collateral estoppel principle" occurs if the judge can base a capital sentence on a factual predicate that the jury has rejected." *See also* DOUBLE JEOPARDY, p. 640; FIFTH AMENDMENT, p. 265; IMPLICIT ACQUITTAL, p. 663.

Significance The Court considered the concept of implicit acquittal more than 20 years prior to *Schiro* in *Price v. Georgia*, 398 U.S. 323 (1970). Price was convicted of manslaughter although the state had charged him with murder. Price appealed his conviction on jury instruction grounds and had his conviction set aside by a Georgia appellate court. Price was then retried with the indictment again charging him with murder. The jury again convicted Price of manslaughter, and Price appealed on double jeopardy grounds, claiming impermissible jeopardy on the murder charge in the second trial. The Supreme Court agreed with Price in a unanimous decision. Chief Justice Burger said that "the first verdict, limited as it was to the lesser included offense, required that the retrial be limited to that lesser offense." The chief justice emphasized that the double jeopardy protection "flows inescapably" from a concern about "risk of conviction," and Price was twice put in jeopardy. Price's jeopardy on the murder charge "ended when the first jury 'was given a full opportunity to return a verdict' on that charge and instead reached a verdict on a lesser charge." Burger concluded that there was no effective difference between direct or explicit acquittal and one "implied by a conviction on a lesser included offense when the jury was given a full opportunity to return a verdict on the greater charge."

Price raised and settled the question of implicit acquittal, but it also addressed the more general question of the extent to which the double jeopardy protection applies to a case in which a defendant successfully appeals a conviction. When an appellate court sets aside a conviction, the case is typically sent back to the jurisdiction of the trial. The prosecution has the discretion to reprosecute or not. The Court advanced a waiver rationale in *Green v. United States*, 355 U.S. 184 (1957), saying that an appealing defendant waives double jeopardy protection by pursuing appellate review. The "implicit acquittal" principle of *Price* applies at the point of retrial—it limits the charge on reprosecution to no greater than the equivalent of the original conviction. *Price* set the limit on the charge(s) in any retrial that may follow a successful appeal. The Court held in *North Carolina v. Pearce*, 395 U.S. 711 (1969), however, that the double jeopardy protection did not prohibit a more severe sentence following retrial. As a safeguard against vindictive sentence increases, however, *Pearce* required that the more severe sentence be based on new information not available at the initial sentencing.

On a related matter, the Court ruled in *Ohio v. Johnson*, 467 U.S. 493 (1984), that the Double Jeopardy Clause did not preclude prosecution for offenses not included in a guilty plea to other charges stemming from the same indictment. Johnson was indicted for four offenses. Over the prosecution's objection, he pled guilty to two of the charges at his arraignment. The trial judge dismissed the two remaining charges on the ground that further prosecution would constitute double jeopardy. The Supreme Court reversed the trial judge, ruling that dismissal of the remaining and more serious charges did more than prevent cumulative punishment; it precluded a verdict on the charges. Johnson had not been "exposed to conviction" on the charges to which he did not plea, and the state is entitled to have an opportunity to marshal its evidence on these charges.

The question examined in *Lockhart v. Nelson*, 488 U.S. 33 (1988), was whether a state could seek resentencing following an appellate court decision that crucial evidence in the initial sentencing was inadmissible. Arkansas secured a supplemented sentence for Nelson as a habitual offender by demonstrating to a jury that he had four prior felony convictions. Nelson subsequently filed a habeas corpus petition, claiming that one of the convictions used to support the recidivist sentencing had been pardoned. The district court found that the conviction in question had indeed been pardoned, and set aside the supplemental sentence. It also ruled that the state was prohibited on double jeopardy grounds from attempting to resentence Nelson as a habitual offender because the initial sentence had been based on insufficient evidence. The Supreme Court disagreed. Rather, the Court held that retrial is not barred when the evidence submitted by the state, erroneously or not, would have been "sufficient to sustain a guilty verdict." The trial court's judgment was founded on the proposition that appellate reversal for evidence insufficiency is the "functional equivalent" of an acquittal. The trial court erred here by admitting the conviction for which Nelson had been pardoned. Using that evidence, however, there clearly had been enough evidence to support the supplemental sentence. The decision not to bar resentencing "merely recreates" the situation that would have existed had the trial judge excluded the conviction in the first place.

California law provides that a "second-strike" felony conviction will result in a term of imprisonment twice that imposed for the second offense. Prior convictions qualify as "first strikes" if they were violent or serious felony offenses. The state failed to establish a "second-strike" prior felony to double Angel Monge's drug-dealing sentence, but the California Supreme Court allowed the state opportunity to attempt to demonstrate the "second-strike" offense at his second sentencing hearing. The U.S. Supreme Court ruled in *Monge v. California*, 118 S.Ct. 2246 (1998), that the double jeopardy prohibition does not generally apply to criminal sentences, thus clearing the way for reconsideration of Monge's sentence. Justice O'Connor said that sentencing determinations do not place a defendant in jeopardy for an "offense" as such. Similarly, sentencing judgments are not analogous to acquittals.

Monge grounded his double jeopardy claim on the Court's ruling in *Bullington v. Missouri*, 451 U.S. 430 (1981), which held that a jury decision on sentence in a capital case "bore the hallmarks" of a trial on the guilt or innocence issue. The Court found that the *Bullington* rationale does not extend to noncapital proceedings, however. Even if sentencing determinations have the "hallmarks" of a trial, a "critical component" of the *Bullington* reasoning was the capital sentencing context. In many ways, O'Connor said, "a capital trial's penalty phase is a continuation of the trial on guilt or innocence of capital murder." The "qualitative difference" between a capital sentence and other penalties "calls for a greater degree of reliability when it is imposed." Monge attempted to minimize the relevance of the capital context by contending that the application of double jeopardy standards turns on the "nature rather than the consequences" of the proceeding. The Court saw *Bullington* as hinging on the "trial-like proceedings," but also the severity of the penalty. Justices Scalia, Souter, Ginsburg, and Stevens were of the view that the Double Jeopardy Clause precluded the state's attempt to reestablish a second-strike prior felony. The prosecution was attempting to prove that Monge had previously been convicted of a qualifying felony. Had the prosecution proved the qualifying felony, Monge would have been sentenced to an additional five years in prison. The prosecution failed, however, to prove the qualifying felony, and Stevens said the Double Jeopardy Clause prohibits a "second bite at the apple." Scalia suggested that the California Code is "full of sentencing enhancements that look exactly like separate crimes, and that expose the defendant to additional maximum punishment."

Double Jeopardy: Multiple Punishment

Department of Revenue v. Kurth Ranch, **511 U.S. 767 (1994)** The Supreme Court ruled in *Kurth Ranch* that states could not levy a drug tax on persons who have been subjected to criminal penalties for the same conduct. The Montana Dangerous Drug Tax Act provided that if a person stored or possessed marijuana (or other specified controlled substances), he or she could be taxed at 10 percent of the drug's market value or $100 per ounce of marijuana, whichever is greater. The Act further provided that the tax could be "collected only after any state or federal fines or forfeitures have been satisfied." Six members of the Richard Kurth family were charged with various drug offenses following a raid on the family farm during which federal officers seized a variety of contraband including 2,155 live marijuana plants. The local prosecutor also filed a civil action seeking forfeiture of cash and equipment confiscated from the Kurth ranch. An officer participating in the raid completed a tax assessment form totaling $865,000 (at $100 an ounce of seized marijuana). The Kurths filed for bankruptcy and challenged the constitutionality of the tax on double jeopardy grounds. The Supreme Court ruled for the Kurths. As a general proposition, said Justice Stevens, the "unlawfulness of an activity does not prevent its taxation." The Court had no doubt that Montana could collect its marijuana possession tax had it not previously punished the taxpayer for the same offense. The issue in this case was whether the tax had punitive characteristics that brought it under the constraints of the Double Jeopardy Clause. Previous decisions, Stevens said, suggest that a tax should not be invalidated simply because "its enforcement might be oppressive or because the legislature's motive is suspect." Nonetheless, the penalizing features of a tax can cause it to lose its character as a tax and become a "mere penalty with the characteristics of regulation and punishment." Legislative labeling does not control whether a tax is immune from double jeopardy scrutiny. At some point, an exaction labeled as a tax approaches punishment, and the Court's task was to determine whether the tax under review crossed that line. Neither a high rate of taxation nor an obvious deterrent purpose automatically makes a tax a form of punishment. Here, however, these factors are "consistent with a punitive character." There were several other features that "set the Montana statute apart from most taxes." First, the tax was conditioned on the commission of a crime. This is indicative of "penal and prohibitory intent" rather than the raising of revenue. Second, the tax was exacted only after the taxpayer had been arrested for the "precise conduct that gives rise to tax obligation in the first place." People arrested for possession of marijuana in Montana "constitute the entire class of taxpayers subject to the Montana tax." Stevens distinguished taxes imposed on illegal activities from "mixed motive" taxes such as those imposed on cigarettes. The justifications for so-called mixed motive taxes do not apply when the taxed activity is completely prohibited, however. In such instances, the need to raise revenue would be "equally well served" by simply increasing the fine imposed on conviction. Third, the Montana tax was purportedly a form of property tax—a tax on the possession and storage of controlled substances. At the time the tax was imposed, the property was likely to have been confiscated by the state and destroyed. A tax on possession of goods that no longer exist or that could not have been lawfully possessed also reflects the punitive character of the Montana tax. Taken as a whole, Stevens concluded, the Montana drug tax was a concoction of anomalies, too far removed in crucial respects from a standard tax assessment to escape characterization as punishment for the purpose of double jeopardy analysis. Chief Justice Rehnquist, joined by Justices O'Connor and Scalia, dissented. They were of the view that the Montana tax had a nonpenal purpose of raising revenue as well as a legitimate deterrence purpose. Because the tax did not have a punitive purpose, it could not be regarded as a second punishment. Justice Scalia, joined by Justice Thomas, said the Double Jeopardy Clause prohibits, "not multiple punishments, but only multiple prosecutions." *See also* DOUBLE JEOPARDY, p. 640; FIFTH AMENDMENT, p. 265; *Waller v. Florida*, p. 273.

Significance   Although it is a point not shared by all justices, the Supreme Court has ruled that included in the double jeopardy protection is a prohibition on multiple punishment for the same crime. *Rutledge v. United States*, 517 U.S. 292 (1996), examined whether a defendant can have concurrent sentences imposed following conviction in a single trial for offenses based on the same conduct. Rutledge was part of a large drug distribution network in Chicago. He was convicted on a variety of federal charges, including conspiracy to distribute cocaine, distribution of cocaine, and operating a continuing criminal enterprise (CCE). A provision of federal law makes it a crime to participate in a conspiracy to distribute controlled substances, while a CCE conviction involves actions taken "in concert" with others to engage in the unlawful distribution of cocaine. The "in concert" element of Rutledge's CCE offense was based on the same criminal plan as the conspiracy. He was sentenced to separate life terms of imprisonment without the possibility of parole for the conspiracy and CCE offenses. The life sentences for continuing criminal enterprise and conspiracy to distribute were concurrent. The Supreme Court unanimously ruled that the life sentences were cumulative and violated the double jeopardy prohibition. Justice Stevens began with the common- law presumption that when statutory language proscribes the "same offense," a legislature "does not intend to impose two punishments for that offense." He then cited the "same evidence" test from *Blockburger v. United States,* 284 U.S. 299 (1932), that is, whether each provision requires proof "of a fact which the other does not." Applications of this test have often led the Court, Stevens continued, to conclude that two different statutes defined the "same offense," typically because "one is a lesser included offense of the other."

The Court considered whether criminal prosecution and a separate property forfeiture based on the same offense was double jeopardy in the consolidated cases of *United States v. Ursery* and *United States v. $405,089.23,* 518 U.S. 267 (1996). The government sought to seize Ursery's property, claiming that it was used to further unlawful possession and distribution of marijuana. Ursery eventually paid an agreed sum of money instead. Ursery sought to overturn his criminal conviction on double jeopardy grounds because it occurred after the property forfeiture action. In *$405,089.23,* Charles Arlt and James Wren were convicted on several federal drug-trafficking and money-laundering charges. A civil forfeiture complaint was filed following the indictment of Arlt and Wren, but by mutual consent deferred until the conclusion of the criminal proceedings. Following the defendants' conviction, the government successfully sought summary judgment on the forfeiture complaint. The Supreme Court ruled that the government can both seek criminal penalties and use civil forfeiture to seize property without violating the prohibition against double jeopardy. Chief Justice Rehnquist found that prior double jeopardy cases revealed a "remarkably consistent theme"; civil forfeiture is a "remedial civil sanction," distinct from civil penalties, and "does not constitute a punishment." Further, civil forfeiture as it is typically used is not primarily punitive.

Kurt Witte was indicted on federal drug charges for attempting to buy marijuana from a federal agent. He pled guilty to the marijuana charge and was sentenced under the Federal Sentencing Guidelines. The marijuana offense considered alone would have produced a Guideline sentence range of 63 to 78 months of incarceration. Witte had also been involved in a cocaine buy from the same federal agent. At the time of his marijuana sentencing, Witte had not been charged on the cocaine incident. The sentencing court, however, included the uncharged cocaine transaction in calculating Witte's sentence. With the cocaine transaction included, Witte's sentencing range was 292 to 365 months. Witte was subsequently indicted for the cocaine offense. Witte sought to dismiss the indictment on double jeopardy grounds. He argued that prosecution and possible punishment on the cocaine charge after it had been factored into his marijuana sentence constituted multiple punishment. The Supreme Court concluded in *Witte v. United States*, 515 U.S. 389 (1995), that the trial court had not punished Witte for the cocaine transaction, but only enhanced his marijuana sentence. Sentencing courts have traditionally been allowed to "conduct an inquiry broad in scope," generally unlimited either as to the content of information to be considered or its source. This inquiry includes consideration of a defendant's prior criminal behavior, "even if no conviction resulted from that behavior." Justice O'Connor acknowledged that Witte's sentence was substantially higher than it would have been without consideration of the cocaine offense. At the same time, the uncharged conduct used to enhance Witte's sentence was within the "range authorized by statute"; it still fell within the "scope of the legislatively authorized penalty."

John Hudson and two other former officers of federally chartered banks were subjected to civil sanctions by the Office of the Comptroller of the Currency (OCC) for violations of federal banking law. All three were assessed civil money penalties and were barred from participating in any banking business without OCC authorization. Three years after the civil sanctions were imposed, Hudson and the others were indicted on federal criminal charges stemming from the same acts as those upon which the civil penalties had been based. Each defendant sought to have the indictments dismissed on double jeopardy grounds. The Supreme Court ruled in *Hudson v. United States*, 522 U.S. 93 (1998), that the civil sanctions were not punishments. Chief Justice Rehnquist said for the Court that whether a particular penalty is criminal or civil is "at least initially, a matter of statutory construction." The Court must then determine whether the statutory scheme was so "punitive either in purpose or effect" so as to "transform" what was intended as a civil remedy into a criminal penalty. Applying "traditional" double jeopardy principles to this case, the Court concluded that it was "evident that Congress intended the OCC money penalties and debarment sanctions ... to be civil in nature."

Self-Incrimination

Carter v. Kentucky, **450 U.S. 288 (1980)** Lonnie Joe Carter was charged with burglary and tried before a jury in a Kentucky court. He chose not to take the witness stand and testify in his own defense. Carter requested a specific jury instruction indicating he was not obligated to testify and that his failure to testify should not prejudice him in any way. The trial judge refused the request, and Carter was convicted. The Supreme Court reversed the conviction, concluding that the Fifth Amendment does more than simply preclude adverse comment on the defendant's silence. The "defendant must pay no court-imposed price for the exercise of his constitutional privilege not to testify." That penalty "may be just as severe when there is no adverse comment" and the jury "is left to roam at large with only its untutored instincts to guide it." A defendant is entitled to request special mention of his choice not to testify so as to "remove from the jury's deliberations any influence of unspoken adverse inferences." The Court noted the impact of the jury instruction and concluded that a trial judge "has an affirmative constitutional obligation to use that tool when a defendant seeks its employment." Although those instructions may not prevent jurors from speculating about a defendant's silence, the "unique power of the jury instruction ... [can] reduce that speculation to a minimum." Justice Rehnquist argued in dissent that the instruction requested by Carter was a matter to be determined at the state level rather than by construction of the Fifth Amendment. Rehnquist felt Carter was not constitutionally entitled to such special instruction. *See also* FIFTH AMENDMENT, p. 265; *Miranda v. Arizona,* p. 290; SELF-INCRIMINATION CLAUSE, p. 695.

Significance *Carter v. Kentucky* represents the end of a lengthy consideration of the no-comment issue. The opposite position was first seen in *Twining v. New Jersey,* 211 U.S. 78 (1908), in which the Court refused to examine a New Jersey law permitting a jury instruction that an unfavorable inference could be drawn from the defendant's unwillingness to take the stand in his or her own defense. The Court held in *Twining* that the Fifth Amendment privilege against self-incrimination did not extend to the states, thus no specific practice allegedly abridging it could be considered. Essentially the same position was taken 40 years later in *Adamson v. California,* 332 U.S. 46 (1947), in which prosecutorial comment on a defendant's failure to testify was permitted. When the Supreme Court extended the self-incrimination protection to the states in *Malloy v. Hogan*, 378 U.S. 1 (1964), the practice of commenting on defendants' failure to testify became an immediate target, and it was declared unconstitutional a year later in *Griffin v. California*, 380 U.S. 609 (1965). *Carter* extends the no-comment rule one last step—to protective jury instructions even in the absence of comment.

Baltimore City Department of Social Services v. Bouknight, 493 U.S. 549 (1990), considered whether the privilege against self-incrimination applied to a woman who was ordered to produce her child to juvenile authorities. The Baltimore City Department of Social Services sought to remove the child from Bouknight's custody. The child had been removed once before on grounds of child abuse and was only returned to her custody subject to extensive conditions contained in a protective order. Bouknight was ordered to produce the child, and when she refused, she was held in civil contempt. The Maryland Court of Appeals ruled that the order was unconstitutional on self-incrimination grounds. It held that the production order compelled Bouknight to acknowledge control over the child in a situation in which she could have "reasonable apprehension that she would be prosecuted." The Supreme Court reversed the Maryland court, however. Justice O'Connor suggested the privilege against self-incrimination is generally reserved for testimonial communication, but she acknowledged that compliance with the production order might constitute a "limited testimonial assertion" for purposes of the privilege. The mere possibility of testimonial assertions, however, "does not, in all contexts, justify involving the privilege to resist production." O'Connor indicated that if the production order was complied with, parents such as Bouknight could assert self-incrimination protection if the government sought to prosecute on the basis of information derived from production. The Court concluded that Bouknight could not invoke the privilege in this case for two reasons: First, her prior abusive conduct had required that she submit herself to assistance and supervision by juvenile authorities as a condition of custody. As a result, she cannot invoke the privilege to prevent enforcement of those conditions. Second, the production of the child was not ordered in furtherance of the state's prosecutorial function. Rather, production of the child was required as part of a "noncriminal regulatory regime." The state has a legitimate interest in the well-being of children. When a person has control over things, like children, that are the object of government's noncriminal regulatory control, "the ability to invoke the privilege is reduced." Justices Marshall and Brennan found the regulatory approach used here closely connected to the enforcement of criminal child abuse laws, which creates a substantial need for protection against self-incrimination.

Aloyzaz Balsys was born in Lithuania and immigrated to the United States in 1961. He declared on his application for an immigrant visa that he had served in the Lithuanian army until the beginning of the Second World War, at which time he went into hiding for several years. The Office of Special Investigations (OSI), an agency of the Department of Justice, began to investigate Balsys on the belief that he had collaborated with the German Nazis to persecute Lithuanian Jews and civilians during the period he claimed he was in hiding. Balsys was subpoenaed by the OSI to answer questions about his possible collaboration with the Nazis. While he appeared at the hearing convened to examine his wartime activities, he refused on Fifth Amendment grounds to answer questions about this period or about his immigration to the United States. The U.S. Supreme Court ruled in *United States v. Balsys*, 118 S.Ct. 2218 (1998), that fear of prosecution in another country falls outside the Fifth Amendment protection from self-incrimination. Both Balsys and the government agreed that testimony that might subject him to deportation was an insufficient ground for asserting the privilege against self-incrimination because of the civil character of a deportation proceeding. If Balsys could show that any testimony he might give in a deportation hearing could be used in a federal or state criminal prosecution, he would be entitled to invoke the privilege. Balsys asserted his right to invoke the privilege because of "real and substantial fear" that his testimony could be used against him in a foreign criminal prosecution. Balsys made a textual argument that the Fifth Amendment provides that a person cannot be compelled "in any criminal case" to be a witness against himself or herself. Justice Souter responded by saying that the "cardinal rule" is to construe provisions in context. None of the other provisions of the Fifth Amendment "is implicated except by action of the government that it binds." Further, there is "no known clear common-law precedent or practice ... for looking to the possibility of foreign prosecution as a premise for claiming the privilege." The judiciary could not recognize the fear of foreign prosecution, suggested Souter, while at the same time preserving the government's "existing rights to seek testimony in exchange for immunity," because extending the privilege would "change the balance of private and governmental interests that has been accepted for as long as there has been Fifth Amendment doctrine." Cooperative conduct between the United States and foreign nations may evolve to a point at which fear of foreign prosecution might be recognized under the Self-Incrimination Clause, Souter concluded, but Balsys had neither presented an "interest rising to such a level of cooperative prosecution" nor shown that the "likely costs and benefits justify expanding the privilege's scope." Justices Breyer and Ginsburg dissented. It was their view that the "basic values" that underlie the Fifth Amendment's protections are "each diminished if the privilege may not be claimed here."

Self-Incrimination: Custodial Interrogation

***Miranda v. Arizona*, 384 U.S. 436 (1966),** established fundamental protections for arrested persons during custodial interrogation. The *Miranda* decision was based on the linkage of the Fifth Amendment's privilege against self-incrimination and the Sixth Amendment's right to counsel in the pretrial period. The groundwork for *Miranda* began two years earlier in *Escobedo v. Illinois,* 378 U.S. 478 (1964). In a controversial decision, the Court overturned the conviction of Escobedo, holding that when a police investigation begins to focus on a particular individual, and when interrogation turns from mere information gathering to eliciting incriminating statements, the suspect must be allowed to consult with legal counsel. *Miranda* and three companion cases allowed the Warren Court to broaden this principle. The Court was particularly concerned with the interrogation environment, believing it to be a "closed process and inherently coercive." Chief Justice Warren said that "[e]ven without employing brutality ... custodial interrogation exacts a heavy toll on individual liberty and trades on the weaknesses of individuals." He added: "It is obvious that such an interrogation environment is created for no other purpose than to subjugate the individual to the will of the examiner. This atmosphere carries its own badge of intimidation." The Court specified four warnings that must be administered prior to beginning any interrogation following arrest. The *Miranda* rules require that an arrested person be told of his or her right to remain silent, that anything he or she says can be used against the accused in court, that he or she has a right to consult with an attorney prior to questioning and that failure to request counsel does not constitute waiver of the right, and that counsel will be provided to the accused in the event that he or she cannot afford counsel. *See also Edwards v. Arizona,* p. 295; FIFTH AMENDMENT, p. 265; *North Carolina v. Butler,* p. 300; SELF-INCRIMINATION CLAUSE, p. 695.

Significance *Miranda* instituted extensive changes in constitutional policy involving rights of the accused. No single decision of the Warren Court has had more impact, except perhaps *Mapp v. Ohio,* 367 U.S. 643 (1961). The Warren Court clearly assigned high priority to confronting inappropriate police practices. It recognized the utility of defense counsel as a means of discouraging misconduct. Protection against self-incrimination, for example, could be achieved by extending the right to counsel to critical pretrial stages, thus the linkage of the two constitutional provisions in *Miranda.* The decision intensified criticism of the Warren Court's approach to defining rights of the accused. The Court's detractors felt that *Miranda* made confessions virtually impossible to secure, thus handcuffing law enforcement authorities.

The direction change in *Miranda* prompted many follow-up issues. *Michigan v. Tucker*, 417 U.S. 433 (1974), examined questions about the administration of *Miranda* rules. Tucker was arrested and questioned before the *Miranda* ruling was made, but his trial occurred afterward. Tucker was advised that statements he made could be used against him, but was not thoroughly advised about his right to access an attorney. In particular he was not told that counsel could be furnished him because of his indigent status. In fact, it was undisputed that he was not told he could have a lawyer without cost. During the ensuing interrogation, Tucker named an alibi witness. The statements of this witness turned out to discredit Tucker's alibi, however, and Tucker was convicted. Thus, without assistance of counsel, Tucker provided the damaging evidence against himself. With only Justice Douglas dissenting, the Court upheld Tucker's conviction. The Court said *Miranda* indeed precluded admission at trial of the statements made by Tucker during his interrogation. But this did not cover the naming of a third party, which was done voluntarily. The Court found that *Miranda* was "disregarded" to the extent that the full warnings were not executed, but the disregard was "inadvertent." So long as "the police conduct did not abridge respondent's constitutional privilege against self-incrimination, but departed only from the prophylactic standards set by this Court in *Miranda*," testimony from the witness named by the defendant need not be excluded. The Court felt that use of the exclusionary rule in cases in which police actions were "pursued in complete good faith" served no purpose relative to deterring police misconduct. The Court emphasized the flexible character of *Miranda*. Failure to give full *Miranda* warnings "does not entitle the suspect to insist that statements made by him be excluded in every conceivable context." *Miranda* protections must be evaluated from a broader perspective. Justice Rehnquist remarked: "Just as the law does not require that a defendant receive a perfect trial, just a fair one, it cannot realistically require that police investigating serious crimes make no errors whatsoever." Furthermore, the information provided by the witness was reliable and subject to the "testing process" of an adversary trial. There was no reason to believe that the witness's testimony was "untrustworthy simply because [Tucker] was not advised of his right to appointed counsel." Evidence derived from statements or confessions that are improperly obtained generally is inadmissible—the derived evidence is contaminated by the tainted confession. *Tucker* reflected the Burger Court's strong predisposition for exposing the trial process to the fullest range of reliable evidence, even if the evidence was derived from a flawed and inadmissible confession. Because Tucker disclosed the witness voluntarily and the witness's subsequent testimony was viewed as trustworthy, failure fully to advise Tucker of his *Miranda* protections was a subordinate interest.

Several Rehnquist Court decisions have narrowed the scope of *Miranda*. The Court defined the term "interrogation" in *Arizona v. Mauro*, 481 U.S. 520 (1987). Mauro was taken into custody for allegedly killing his son. He was advised of his *Miranda* rights, and he indicated he did not wish to make a statement in the absence of his lawyer. At that point, all questioning stopped and Mauro was placed in a police captain's office because no other detention area was available. Mauro's wife, who had herself been questioned in another room, insisted on seeing her husband. A meeting was allowed in the captain's office on the condition that an officer remain in the room. The police used a plainly visible recording device to tape Mauro's entire conversation with his wife. During the conversation, Mauro instructed his wife to answer no further questions in the absence of counsel. At the trial, the prosecutor used the recording to challenge Mauro's insanity claim. The question in this case was whether the police decision to permit and monitor the meeting between Mauro and his wife was the functional equivalent of an interrogation. The Court concluded it was not. Interrogation includes any practice "reasonably likely to elicit an incriminating response." The purpose of *Miranda* warnings is not to prevent the government from capitalizing on the coercive nature of confinement to extract incriminating statements. Mauro was not subjected to compelling influences, psychological ploys, direct questioning, or any other practice of interrogation, and the police had not initiated the meeting. Given various safety and security considerations, the Court considered the officer's presence at the meeting between Mauro and his wife to be permissible. The Court also examined the situation from Mauro's perspective and concluded that it was unlikely he felt coerced to incriminate himself simply because he was allowed to speak with his wife. Although the police might have been aware of the possibility that Mauro would say something incriminating during the meeting, an interrogation does not occur simply because the police may hope that a suspect will confess.

The Burger Court rejected opportunities to overrule *Miranda*, preferring instead to reexamine the *Miranda* standards on a case-by-case basis, and the Rehnquist Court has essentially followed the same course. The Court considered the requirements for adequately conveying *Miranda* warnings in *Duckworth v. Eagan*, 492 U.S. 195 (1989). Among other things, persons are to be advised of their right to counsel, and that counsel will be appointed if the suspect is indigent. Eagan was "Mirandized" at the time he was first questioned about a sexual assault and stabbing, although he was not placed under arrest. The warnings he received contained additional language on appointment of counsel for indigent persons. After being told that a lawyer could be provided to persons who could not afford to hire one, Eagan was told that appointment would occur "if and when you go to court." He was further advised that he need not answer any questions in the absence of counsel. Eagan signed a waiver form and answered questions about the crime. Eagan was formally placed in custody 29 hours later at which point he was again advised. He signed a second waiver form that contained a statement of rights without the "if and when you go to court" language. Eagan then confessed to the crimes. At his trial, Eagan sought to suppress statements made after both warnings. The question before the Court in this case was whether the additional language interfered with Eagan's securing "clear and unequivocal" warning of his rights prior to interrogation. The Supreme Court ruled that Eagan's warnings were adequate notwithstanding the additional phrase. The Court said it has "never insisted that *Miranda* warnings be given in the exact form described in that decision." Indeed, *Miranda* itself refers to the adequacy of a "fully effective equivalent" in meeting the requirements of the ruling. The "prophylactic" *Miranda* warnings are not themselves constitutional rights, but instead are "measures to insure that the right against compulsory self-incrimination is protected." Eagan's initial warning "touched all of the bases required by *Miranda*."

The Burger Court held in *Berkemer v. McCarty*, 468 U.S. 420 (1984), that *Miranda* warnings are not required for ordinary traffic stops. The Rehnquist Court affirmed that rule in *Pennsylvania v. Bruder*, 488 U.S. 9 (1988). Bruder was stopped for erratic driving and was given field sobriety tests. While awaiting the results of the tests, Bruder was asked to recite the alphabet and respond to some questions. When it was determined that he failed the sobriety tests, Bruder was arrested and properly advised of his rights. He sought to suppress all prearrest statements. The issue was whether Bruder's prearrest statements were elicited through custodial interrogation. The Supreme Court ruled that Bruder had not been subjected to improper custodial interrogation. Persons "temporarily detained" by traffic stops are not "in custody for the purposes of *Miranda*." Such stops "typically are brief, unlike a prolonged station house interrogation." Furthermore, traffic stops occur in "public view," and in an atmosphere less "dominated" by police than the kind of interrogation involved in *Miranda*.

Stansbury v. California, 511 U.S. 293 (1994), considered the question of when the custodial interrogation threshold for *Miranda* warnings has been crossed. Robert Stansbury was asked to accompany police to a police facility for questioning as a possible witness in the investigation of the death of a 10-year-old girl. Because Stansbury was not considered a suspect initially, he was not given *Miranda* warnings. Suspicion of Stansbury's involvement in the murder was triggered by some of his disclosures during the interview. At the point police began to consider Stansbury a suspect, the interview was stopped and Stansbury was advised of his rights. The state trial court did not suppress the statements made by Stansbury prior to his being advised, on the ground that he was not in custody until the point at which suspicion, absent at the outset of the interview, was actually aroused. The U.S. Supreme Court unanimously reversed, however, ruling that an officer's "subjective and undisclosed view" concerning whether the person under interrogation is a suspect is "irrelevant" to the assessment of whether the person is in custody. The Court said it was well established that the initial determination of custody depends on the "objective circumstances of the interrogation," and not on the "subjective views harbored by either the interrogating officers or the person being questioned." The officer's undisclosed view that a person being questioned is a suspect "does not bear upon the question whether the individual is in custody for purposes of *Miranda.*" Unless communicated or otherwise manifested to the person being questioned, an officer's "evolving but unarticulated suspicions do not affect the objective circumstances of an interrogation or interview, and thus cannot affect the *Miranda* custody inquiry." An officer's beliefs are relevant only to the extent that they "would affect how a reasonable person in the position of the individual being questioned would gauge the breadth or his or her 'freedom of action.'" Even a clear statement from an officer that a person is a suspect is not, in itself, dispositive of the custody issue, as some suspects remain free to leave prior to the police decision to arrest. In other words, the impact of an officer's degree of suspicion is bound to the facts and circumstances of the particular case. In short, an officer's views concerning the nature of an interrogation, or beliefs concerning the potential culpability of an individual being questioned, may be "one among many factors" that bear upon the assessment of whether that individual is in custody, but only if the officer's views or beliefs are "somehow manifested to the individual under interrogation and would have affected how a reasonable person in that position would perceive his or her freedom to leave."

Finally, in *McNeil v. Wisconsin,* 501 U.S. 171 (1991), the Court distinguished between the right to counsel based on the Sixth Amendment and the Fifth Amendment right to counsel attached to custodial interrogation. McNeil was arrested on an armed robbery warrant. He was "Mirandized" and declined to respond to police attempts to question him. He did not request an attorney immediately, but was represented by appointed counsel at his arraignment. While he was detained on the armed robbery charge, McNeil was questioned about other crimes. He was given his *Miranda* warnings on the second set of crimes, and he signed the appropriate waiver forms prior to making incriminating statements. McNeil unsuccessfully sought to have the statements suppressed by the trial court. The Supreme Court ruled that McNeil's request for representation at his arraignment on the armed robbery charge did not invoke the Fifth Amendment right to counsel as derived through *Miranda*. The Court's position was that McNeil had invoked only his Sixth Amendment right to counsel. The Sixth Amendment right, said Justice Scalia, is "offense-specific," and cannot be invoked for "all future prosecutions." As distinct from the Fifth Amendment right, the right to counsel based on the Sixth Amendment "does not attach until a prosecution is commenced." This occurs when adversary judicial criminal proceedings are begun—whether by way of "formal charge, preliminary hearing, indictment, information, or arraignment." The Court rejected McNeil's argument to combine coverage of the two rights because they protect distinct interests. The purpose of the Sixth Amendment guarantee is to protect the "unaided layman at critical confrontations with his 'expert adversary,' the government." This protection is designed to come after the adverse positions of the government and the defendants have "solidified with respect to a particular alleged crime." The Fifth Amendment right as guaranteed by *Miranda* is designed to protect "quite a different interest: the suspect's desire to deal with the police only through counsel." The Fifth Amendment right is both narrower and broader than the Sixth Amendment right. It is narrower in that it relates only to custodial interrogation. It is also broader because it relates to interrogation regarding any suspected crime and "attaches whether or not the adversarial relationship produced by a pending prosecution has yet arisen." Justices Marshall and Blackmun joined the dissent of Justice Stevens, who saw the offense-specific limitation on the attorney-client relationship as one that "could only generate confusion."

***Edwards v. Arizona*, 451 U.S. 477 (1981),** held that police cannot continue or reinitiate questioning once a defendant wishes to see an attorney. Edwards was lawfully arrested for several offenses, including murder, and advised of his rights. He indicated he would submit to questioning, but later said he wished to speak to an attorney before proceeding further. The following day, two officers returned to the jail and sought to speak to Edwards. He said he did not wish to talk with them, but was told "he had to." The officers again administered the *Miranda* warnings. The officers played a tape of an alleged accomplice, and Edwards implicated himself in the crimes. The Arizona courts found Edwards's disclosures to be voluntary, but the U.S. Supreme Court reversed. Waiver of *Miranda* protections needs to be "knowing and intelligent" in addition to voluntary. The Court concluded that a valid waiver cannot be established by "showing only that he responded to further police-initiated custodial interrogation even if he has been advised of his rights." This is particularly true when the accused asks for counsel. Indeed, when an accused expresses a desire to deal with police only through counsel, no further interrogation by authorities can occur "until counsel has been made available to him, unless the accused himself initiates further communication, exchanges, or conversations with the police." The Fifth Amendment, said Justice White, "identified in *Miranda* is the right to have counsel present at any custodial interrogation." Absent such interrogation, there would have been "no infringement of the right that Edwards invoked and there would be no occasion to determine whether there had been a valid waiver." *See also* FIFTH AMENDMENT, p. 265; *Miranda v. Arizona*, p. 290; SELF-INCRIMINATION CLAUSE, p. 695.

Significance   Police-initiated conversations that produce incriminating statements have been a particularly problematic aspect of *Miranda*. In *Edwards*, the Court refused to allow use of a confession obtained the day following a defendant's request for counsel. Even the rereading of the *Miranda* warnings was insufficient to overcome the failure to have counsel present. Once the right to assistance of counsel is invoked, no subsequent conversation may occur except on the defendant's initiative. The reasoning in *Edwards* was applied in *Michigan v. Jackson*, 475 U.S. 625 (1986). Following his arraignment on a murder charge, Jackson requested that counsel be appointed. Before he could meet with his lawyer, officers administered *Miranda* warnings to Jackson and interrogated him. The interrogation yielded a confession. The Court said that when the officers initiated the interview after the defendant requested counsel "at arraignment or similar proceeding," any subsequent waiver of the right to counsel for that police-initiated interrogation is invalid.

   Arizona v. Roberson, 486 U.S. 675 (1988), raised the issue of whether the *Edwards* rule reaches separate investigations of wholly independent offenses. Roberson was arrested for burglary and advised of his rights. He indicated that he wished to consult counsel before responding to any questions. Three days later, while Roberson was still detained and awaiting contact with a lawyer, a different officer who was unaware that Roberson had requested counsel again advised Roberson of his rights and began questioning him about another burglary. The interrogation on the second offense produced an incriminating statement. The Supreme Court held that *Edwards* extended to such situations. The *Edwards* rule, said the Court, "benefits the accused and the State alike." It protects the suspect against "inherently compelling pressures of custodial interrogation" by "creating a presumption" that a waiver of counsel is defective. At the same time, the rule provides "clear and unequivocal" guidelines for conducting custodial interrogations. Given these benefits, the Court saw no reason to create an exception to *Edwards* for the interrogation relating to a separate offense. The "eagerness" of officers to question a suspect is comparable for the officers engaged in separate investigations and those involved in a single inquiry. If the suspect is unable to "cope with" custodial interrogation, additional questioning without counsel will "exacerbate whatever compulsion to speak" the suspect may feel. Simply giving "fresh sets" of warnings will "not necessarily reassure" a suspect who is yet to receive requested counsel. Neither did the Court regard the second officer's ignorance of the earlier request for counsel to be relevant. The *Edwards* rule "focuses on the state of mind of the suspect, not the police." Moreover, the officer could have discovered that Roberson had requested counsel simply by examining the arresting officer's report.

The Court further clarified the *Edwards* rule in *Minnick v. Mississippi*, 498 U.S. 146 (1990). Minnick's interrogation was terminated when he requested counsel. Minnick subsequently met with counsel. Interrogation was later resumed at police initiative in the absence of Minnick's lawyer, and Minnick confessed to capital murder. The issue in this case was whether the protection afforded by *Edwards* is satisfied once a person meets with counsel. The Court said *Edwards* requires more. It requires that once counsel is requested, interrogation may not resume in the absence of counsel "whether or not the accused has consulted with his attorney." Consultation itself, said the Court, does not protect the suspect from "persistent attempts by officers to persuade him to waive his rights, or from the coercive pressures that accompany custody and that may increase as custody is prolonged."

As part of standard procedure in Cumberland County, Pennsylvania, a videotape recording was made as Inocencio Muniz was booked for drunk driving. Muniz was asked a number of questions including his name, address, and age. In addition, he was asked to calculate the date of his sixth birthday. The sobriety tests Muniz failed in the field were administered again and also taped. During the course of these tests, Muniz said a number of things. He was not given his *Miranda* warnings until the booking process was about to end. The question in *Pennsylvania v. Muniz*, 496 U.S. 582 (1990), was whether the tape could be used as evidence against Muniz. The Court's decision in this case hinged on whether the statements were testimonial and produced by actual police interrogation. The Court first ruled that Muniz's statements were admissible even though the "slurred nature of his speech was incriminating." The Court viewed the absence of the "physical ability to articulate words in a clear manner" to be nontestimonial. Revealing the "physical manner" of the way Muniz spoke the Court saw as analogous to requiring him to reveal the physical properties of his voice for a voice print. Second, the Court allowed use of Muniz's responses to questions about his name, height, weight, age, and so on. These were "routine" booking questions and were exempt from *Miranda* because they sought only basic biographical information needed to complete booking. Third, the Court allowed use of the tape showing the repeated sobriety tests and the statements made during them. Like slurred speech, the test performances were considered nontestimonial. Further, the statements made by Muniz were not elicited by the officer conducting the tests. The situation did not constitute an interrogation, thus Muniz's statements were voluntarily offered.

Davis v. United States, 512 U.S. 452 (1994), examined the issue of whether *Miranda* requires cessation of all police questioning when a suspect's request for counsel is ambiguous. Robert Davis, a member of the U.S. Navy, was questioned by Naval Investigation Service agents in connection with the death of a sailor. He was advised of his rights under *Miranda* and waived them prior to commencing the interview. About 90 minutes into the interview, he said, "Maybe I should talk to a lawyer." When the investigators asked him if he was requesting a lawyer, Davis indicated he was not. The interview continued following a short break and a readministration of the *Miranda* warnings. About an hour after the interview resumed, Davis formally requested a lawyer. At his military trial, Davis unsuccessfully sought to suppress statements made prior to his unambiguous request for counsel. His subsequent conviction was affirmed by the U.S. Court of Military Appeals, and the Supreme Court unanimously affirmed the conviction. Under *Edwards,* a subject who requests counsel is not to be questioned further until counsel has been made available, or the suspect reinitiates a conversation. *Edwards* provides a "second layer of prophylaxis" for *Miranda,* and is designed to prevent police from "badgering" a subject into waiving previously asserted Miranda protections. If, however, a suspect makes "ambiguous or equivocal" reference to counsel that a "reasonable officer in light of the circumstances would have understood only that the suspect might be invoking the right to counsel," cessation of questioning is not required. To commence the *Edwards* rule, counsel must be requested "unambiguously." That is, the suspect must state his or her desire to have counsel present "sufficiently clearly" that a reasonable officer would understand the statement to be an actual request for an attorney. If a statement is not sufficiently clear, *Edwards* does not require that officers stop questioning. A rule that would require cessation of questioning when counsel was not clearly discussed, said Justice O'Connor, would transform *Miranda* protections into "wholly irrational obstacles to legitimate police investigative activity"; it would "needlessly" keep police from interviewing a suspect in the absence of counsel "even if the suspect did not wish to have a lawyer present." The Court chose not to adopt a rule requiring officers to ask "clarifying questions" under these circumstances. Justice Souter, joined by Justices Blackmun, Stevens, and Ginsburg, concurred in the judgment to affirm Davis's conviction, but would have preferred a rule prohibiting further interrogation until it could be determined whether an ambiguous statement might be an actual request for counsel. Justice Souter said that the *Miranda* protections are designed to assure that an individual's right to "choose between speech and silence remains unfettered throughout the interrogation process." Requiring clarifying questions before proceeding further would have, in their view, better served the objectives of *Miranda*.

A confession made by a person within six hours of arrest is, by federal statute, admissible in a federal prosecution even if there is delay in presenting the person to a federal magistrate. *United States v. Alvarez-Sanchez*, 511 U.S. 350 (1994), considered when the clock begins to run when the defendant is in custody on state criminal charges. State authorities found counterfeit currency while executing a warrant to search a residence for evidence relating to state drug charges. Alvarez-Sanchez was arrested and booked on the state charges on a Friday evening. He remained in custody over the weekend. On Monday morning, local officials informed the Secret Service about the counterfeit currency. Shortly after, Secret Service agents took possession of the currency and began to interview Alvarez-Sanchez following the administration of *Miranda* warnings. Alvarez-Sanchez admitted that he knew the currency was counterfeit and was arrested. Congestion in the federal magistrate's docket prevented presentment until the following morning. Alvarez-Sanchez sought to suppress the statement made during the interview because of the delay between his arrest on state charges and his presentment on the federal charge. The Supreme Court unanimously ruled that the statement was admissible. The Court's resolution of this case hinged on whether terms of the federal law were triggered. Alvarez-Sanchez argued that he was under arrest for federal purposes during the interview at the Sheriff's Department, and that his incriminating statements to Secret Service agents constituted a confession governed by the six-hour rule. Because the statute applied to persons in custody of "any" law enforcement agency or officer, Alvarez-Sanchez argued that the six-hour time period begins whenever a person is arrested by state or local as well as federal officers. It was the Court's judgment that decisive weight could not be placed on the broad reference to "any" law enforcement agency or officer in isolation. The terms of the statute can apply only when there is some delay in presentment. There can be no delay in bringing a person before a federal magistrate until, at a minimum, there is "some obligation to bring the person before such a judicial officer in the first place." A duty to present a person to a federal magistrate, Thomas continued, "does not arise until the person has been arrested for a *federal* offense." If a person is arrested and held on state charges, the federal six-hour rule does not apply.

Self-Incrimination: Waiver of Miranda

North Carolina v. Butler, **441 U.S. 369 (1979),** considered whether waiver of the *Miranda* protections must be explicit. Butler was arrested and informed of his *Miranda* rights. He was given an "Advice of Rights" form, which he read and said he understood. He refused, however, to sign the waiver form, although he indicated he was "willing to talk." Butler subsequently tried to have statements made during the ensuing conversation suppressed. The case revolved around a determination of whether Butler had actually waived his rights. The Supreme Court decided that Butler's statements could be admitted. The Court said that although explicit waiver is usually the strongest proof of a valid waiver, it is not "inevitably either necessary or sufficient to establish a waiver." The Court said further: "[T]he question is not one of form, but rather whether the defendant in fact knowingly and voluntarily waived the rights delineated in *Miranda*." The burden of demonstrating the adequacy of a waiver rests with the prosecution, and the prosecution's "burden is great." However, "in at least some cases waiver can be clearly inferred from the actions and words of the person interrogated." Waivers must be evaluated in terms of the facts and circumstances of each case. The Court's judgment was that Butler made a knowing and voluntary waiver even though it was not explicit. The Court rejected the establishment of an "inflexible per se rule" requiring explicit waiver. The dissenters, Justices Brennan, Marshall, and Stevens, argued that an affirmative or explicit waiver is required to satisfy *Miranda*. The dissenting justices claimed that *Miranda* recognized that custodial interrogation is "inherently coercive," and that ambiguity must be "interpreted against the interrogator." They would have required a "simple prophylactic rule requiring the police to obtain express waiver." *See also Edwards v. Arizona*, p. 295; FIFTH AMENDMENT, p. 265; *Miranda v. Arizona*, p. 290; SELF-INCRIMINATION CLAUSE, p. 695.

Significance   The *Miranda* protections may be waived, but the waiver must be voluntary, knowing, and intelligent. Waiver may not be the product of coercion, trick, threat, persuasion, or inducement. Although the waiver need not be written or explicit, it cannot be presumed from silence under any circumstances. The burden rests with the prosecution to demonstrate that a waiver was freely, knowingly, and intelligently made. Determinations of the adequacy of a waiver are to be based on the "totality of the circumstances" of a particular case and may include such matters as the background and overall conduct of the defendant. *Butler* provides some latitude by not requiring a firm rule relative to explicit waiver. At the same time, it clarified and maintained the general protections afforded by *Miranda*. The latter was intended to draw a clear and bright line obviating the need for a case-by-case determination of voluntariness.

The governing role of a valid waiver is reflected in *Moran v. Burbine*, 475 U.S. 412 (1986). Burbine was arrested for breaking and entering. The police subsequently came to believe that he was involved in a murder in another community. Officers from the second community were notified, and they came to question Burbine about the murder. In the meantime, and unknown to Burbine, his sister was arranging for counsel on the breaking and entering charge. Neither Burbine's sister nor the public defender she obtained knew anything about the murder charge. Counsel contacted the police indicating that she was ready to represent Burbine if the police wished to question him. She was told he would not be questioned further until the next day. She was not told that police from the second community were present and ready to begin their questioning of Burbine. He was given *Miranda* warnings before each of three interview sessions, signed waivers prior to each interview session, and signed a confession to the murder. At no time was Burbine aware of his sister's arrangement of counsel or the attorney's telephone call. The Court allowed use of the confessions, finding the police followed "with precision" the *Miranda* procedure for obtaining the waivers. The failure to inform Burbine of the attorney's call did not deprive him of information essential to his ability to make a knowing and voluntary waiver. Events taking place outside his presence and unknown to him "can have no bearing on the capacity to comprehend and knowingly relinquish a constitutional right." As long as it could be shown that his waiver was uncoerced and that he knew he did not have to speak and could request counsel, the waiver was valid. The Court said *Miranda* would not be extended to require reversal of convictions if police are "less than forthright" in dealing with an attorney, or if they fail to inform the suspect of the attorney's unilateral efforts to contact him. The purpose of *Miranda* is to "dissipate the compulsion inherent in custodial interrogation" and thus protect the *suspect's* Fifth Amendment rights. A rule that focuses on how police treat an *attorney*—conduct that has no relevance to the matter of compulsion of the defendant—would "ignore both mission and its only source of legitimacy."

The Rehnquist Court dealt extensively with issues surrounding waiver of *Miranda*. In *Colorado v. Spring*, 479 U.S. 564 (1987), Spring was arrested on a stolen weapons charge. He was advised of his *Miranda* rights, and signed a statement saying that he understood and waived those rights. Authorities proceeded to ask Spring about the weapons charge but also about a murder, even though they had not told Spring they intended to do so. The interrogation produced a disclosure that Spring had shot someone, but there was no confession as such. At a subsequent interview, at which Spring was again advised of his rights, he admitted participation in the murder. The Court held that admission of Spring's statements was proper. Inquiry into whether a waiver is coerced, said Justice Powell, has two distinct dimensions: First, the relinquishment must be voluntary, "the product of free and deliberate choice." Second, the waiver must have been made with full awareness of the right being abandoned and the consequences of the decision to abandon it. The Court had no doubt that the waiver was voluntarily, knowingly, and intelligently made. Spring knew he could remain silent, and the Constitution, wrote Powell, does not require that a suspect know and understand every possible consequence of his Fifth Amendment waiver. The Court also rejected Spring's contention that failure to inform him of all the potential subjects of interrogation constituted illegal trickery or deception. Powell said it is difficult to see how mere silence on the subject matter of interrogation could cause a suspect to misunderstand the nature of his right to refuse to answer questions.

In *Colorado v. Connelly*, 479 U.S. 157 (1986), the Court ruled that a defendant diagnosed as a schizophrenic is not categorically unable to waive his *Miranda* rights. Connelly approached a Denver police office and said he had killed someone. He was immediately advised as per *Miranda*, but he replied he understood his rights and wished to discuss the murder. A detective was summoned, and on his arrival Connelly was once again advised of his *Miranda* rights. He was taken to police headquarters, where he told his story in detail. The following morning, Connelly became disoriented and said he had been ordered by the "voice of God" to confess. Subsequent psychiatric examination revealed that Connelly suffered from a psychosis that interfered with his capacity to make free and rational choices. A psychiatrist said that his psychosis had motivated his confession. It was also the psychiatrist's view, however, that Connelly's condition had not impaired his ability to understand his *Miranda* rights. The Supreme Court allowed the use of both the initial statements and the confession. Speaking for the Court, Chief Justice Rehnquist said that coercive police conduct was required to reach a finding that *Miranda* had been violated. Despite the significance of one's mental condition as a factor in the voluntariness calculus, the condition, "by itself and apart from its relation to official coercion," should never dispose of an inquiry into voluntariness. Coercive police conduct was seen as a necessary predicate to finding that a confession was not voluntary. In addition, mental illness will not invariably preclude a defendant from understanding and waiving his or her *Miranda* rights.

Connecticut v. Barrett, 479 U.S. 523 (1987), involved the arrest of a person on suspicion of sexual assault. Barrett was advised on three separate occasions of his *Miranda* rights, and each time Barrett signed a form acknowledging that he had been so advised. He proceeded to talk about the incident, but refused to sign a written statement in the absence of counsel. Barrett orally confessed to the assault. One of the police officers present at the time of the confession made written notes of Barrett's statements, and these were admitted into evidence. The Court permitted the used of the confession, finding that Barrett had made clear his willingness to talk. No evidence suggested that he was threatened, tricked, or cajoled into waiving his right to remain silent. Nothing in the rationale that underlies *Miranda* requires police to ignore the tenor or sense of a defendant's response to *Miranda*. That Barrett desired counsel prior to making a written statement had no bearing, since no written statement was taken. Barrett's limited requests for counsel were accompanied by affirmative announcements of his willingness to talk. That the police took the opportunity provided by Barrett to take his oral statement is "quite consistent" with the Fifth Amendment. *Miranda* gives the defendant a right to "choose between speech and silence, and Barrett chose to speak."

Brewer v. Williams, 430 U.S. 387 (1977), involved incriminating statements made by a defendant in the absence of his attorney. Williams was arrested, arraigned, and jailed in Davenport, Iowa, for abducting and murdering a young child in the city of Des Moines. Williams consulted with attorneys in both cities and was advised to make no statements to the police. As Williams was being transported from Davenport to Des Moines, he indicated unwillingness to be interrogated until his attorney was present, but said he would make a full statement at that time. Nonetheless, one of the officers, aware that Williams was a former mental patient and deeply religious, sought to elicit statements from Williams relative to the location of the child's body. The officer suggested to Williams that the child's parents were entitled to a "Christian burial" for their child. Williams eventually made a number of incriminating statements and directed the police to the location of the child's body. Williams was subsequently tried and convicted. Evidence relating to statements made during his transportation to Des Moines were admitted at his trial over his objections. The Supreme Court held that the evidence was inadmissible and set aside the conviction. The decision hinged on whether Williams had knowingly and intelligently waived his right to counsel. There was no dispute that the police officer had deliberately attempted to elicit information from Williams and that the "Christian burial speech" was "tantamount to interrogation." The defendant had relied heavily on advice of counsel throughout, had consulted with attorneys at both ends of his trip, and had specifically mentioned making a statement after completing the trip and consulting with his attorney. All of these were evidence of his unwillingness to waive his right to counsel. The officer elicited incriminating statements "despite Williams' express and implicit assertions of his right to counsel." Regardless of the "senseless and brutal" character of the offense, what had occurred was "so clear a violation" of Williams's constitutional protections that it "cannot be condoned." The dissenters were outraged. Chief Justice Burger called the result "intolerable."

Brewer v. Williams highlighted the relationship between assistance of counsel and the protection from self-incrimination. The Court established in *Miranda* that preservation of the privilege against self-incrimination is best accomplished by providing an accused with access to defense counsel. *Brewer* conveyed a reluctance by the Court to allow waiver of counsel in interrogation situations. *Brewer* also raised questions about what constitutes interrogation. The Court found the "Christian burial speech" intentionally designed to prompt incriminating responses. But *Brewer* does not fully define what constitutes an interrogation. The Court generally requires that *Miranda* safeguards apply when interactions occur that the police know may reasonably be expected to elicit an incriminating response. Thus warnings must be given whenever an officer, through any action verbal or otherwise, is likely to prompt an incriminating disclosure.

The Court has held firm on the counsel waiver issue. It will not accept a voluntary confession from a defendant after he or she has requested defense counsel and the counsel is not present for the confession. In *Oregon v. Bradshaw*, 462 U.S. 1039 (1983), the Court ruled, however, that a prisoner's question, "Well, what is going to happen to me now?" constituted initiation of further conversation that could yield admissible statements against him. The Court has frequently reiterated that once counsel is requested by an arrestee, interrogation cannot continue or be resumed in the absence of that counsel. The decisive issue is police-initiated action designed to elicit incriminating statements.

The question raised in *Illinois v. Perkins*, 496 U.S. 292 (1990), was whether *Miranda* applies to statements made by a suspect in custody on other matters to an undercover officer posing as a prisoner. With only Justice Marshall dissenting, the Court ruled that an officer can pose as a fellow inmate to elicit statements without a *Miranda* warning. The warning "mandated by *Miranda* was meant," said Justice Kennedy, to serve the privilege against self-incrimination during "incommunicado interrogation of individuals in a police-dominated atmosphere." On the other hand, conversations between suspects and undercover officers "do not implicate the concerns underlying *Miranda*." The "essential ingredients" of a "police-dominated atmosphere and compulsion are not present" when a suspect "speaks freely" to an officer "he believes to be a fellow inmate." When an individual believes he is in the company of cell mates and not the police, the "coercive atmosphere is lacking." The Court rejected the argument that *Miranda* warnings "are required whenever a suspect is in custody in a technical sense and converses with someone who also happens to be a government agent." *Miranda* forbids the use of coercion, not "mere strategic deception by taking advantage of a suspect's misplaced trust in one he supposes to be a fellow prisoner." "Ploys to mislead" a prisoner into a "false sense of security that do not rise to the level of compulsion or coercion to speak are not within *Miranda's* concerns." *Miranda* was not meant, Kennedy concluded, "to prevent suspects from boasting about their criminal activities in front of persons they believe to be their cellmates." As a result, Perkins spoke "at his own peril."

Self-Incrimination: Impeachment of Defense Witnesses

James v. Illinois, **493 U.S. 307 (1990),** determined that a *Miranda*-deficient statement could not be used to impeach defense witnesses other than the defendant. James was arrested as he sat under a hair dryer at his mother's beauty salon on a charge of involvement in a shooting. James indicated at the time of arrest that he was attempting to change his appearance. He also described the color and style of his hair prior to alteration. His statements were subsequently suppressed as the product of an improper arrest. At James's murder trial, several witnesses identified him. Each witness described the style and color of James's hair at the time of the shooting. These descriptions corresponded to James's own representation in the suppressed statement. James did not testify on his own behalf, but called a witness whose testimony differed as to James's hair. This witness testified that James's hair before the shooting was the same as it appeared when James emerged from the hair dryer. After determining that James's statements about his hair had been obtained voluntarily, the prosecution was allowed to use his prior statement to impeach the credibility of the defense witness, but the Supreme Court ruled that the statements could not be used for this purpose. Although prior statements that are otherwise inadmissible may be used to impeach the defendant, the Court refused to extend this practice to all defense witnesses. The truth-seeking rationale supporting the impeachment of defendants "does not apply with equal force" to other witnesses. The threat of criminal prosecution for perjury is far more likely to deter a witness from lying than to deter a defendant already facing conviction. Expanding the exception to all defense witnesses creates "different incentives affecting the behavior of both defendants and law enforcement officers." When police encounter opportunities to obtain illegal evidence after they have lawfully obtained enough evidence to support charging a suspect, excluding such evidence would leave officers with "little to lose and much to gain by overstepping the constitutional limits on evidence gathering." *See also* FIFTH AMENDMENT, p. 265; *Miranda v. Arizona*, p. 290; SELF-INCRIMINATION CLAUSE, p. 695.

Significance *Harris v. New York*, 401 U.S. 222 (1971), was the first post-*Miranda* case to consider whether statements made by a defendant in violation of *Miranda* could be used to impeach that defendant's own testimony at his trial. *Miranda* had established that criminal defendants must be informed of their right against self-incrimination and their right to assistance of counsel. While Harris was testifying at his own trial, he was asked during cross-examination whether he had made any statements immediately following his arrest. When he claimed he could not recall making any statements, the statements he had made were introduced into evidence for the purpose of impeaching Harris's credibility. The jury instruction attempted to differentiate between use of statements for impeachment purposes and their use as evidence of guilt. The jury was instructed it could not consider the statements as evidence of guilt. Harris was subsequently convicted, and the Supreme Court upheld his conviction. The Court said that *Miranda* is not an absolute prohibition against the use of statements taken without proper warnings. Rather, *Miranda* bars the prosecution from "making its case with statements" taken in violation of it. But "it does not follow from *Miranda* that evidence inadmissible against an accused in the prosecution's case in chief is barred for all purposes." Use of such evidence, however, must satisfy conditions of trustworthiness. Crucial to the outcome in *Harris* was the use of statements made in an adversary process, specifically impeachment of a witness through cross-examination. The "impeachment process here undoubtedly provided valuable aid to the jury in assessing petitioner's credibility." The Court felt that information was of more value than guarding against the "speculative possibility" that police misconduct would be encouraged. The Court emphasized the need to maintain the integrity of the trial itself. A defendant can testify in his own defense, but does not have "the right to commit perjury." Once the defendant takes the witness stand, the prosecution can "utilize the traditional truth-testing devices of the adversary process." Chief Justice Burger concluded the opinion by saying, "The shield provided by *Miranda* cannot be perverted into a license to use perjury by way of a defense, free from the risk of confrontation with prior inconsistent utterances."

Harris qualified *Miranda* and reflected the Burger Court's reluctance fully to embrace the *Miranda* holding, as well as its general unwillingness to disturb the dynamics of the adversary process. The basic thrust of *Harris* was that a jury ought to be given every opportunity to assess the credibility of the defense. The *Harris* rule cannot apply, however, when statements are obtained involuntarily. In *Mincey v. Arizona*, 437 U.S. 385 (1978), the Court ruled that interrogation of a defendant hospitalized in critical condition produced involuntary and untrustworthy responses. They could not be used even for impeachment purposes.

The Court has also held that postwarning silence cannot be used to impeach a defendant. In *Doyle v. Ohio*, 426 U.S. 610 (1976), two defendants offered exculpatory explanations at their trial, explanations not previously shared with police or prosecutors. They were cross-examined as to why they had withheld their stories until the trial. The Court concluded that "silence in the wake of these *[Miranda]* warnings may be nothing more than the arrestee's exercise of these *Miranda* rights." On the other hand, silence occurring previous to receiving *Miranda* warnings may be used for impeachment purposes on the grounds that the silence was not "induced by the assurances contained in the *Miranda* warnings." In *Wainwright v. Greenfield*, 474 U.S. 284 (1986), the Court ruled that a suspect's silence after receiving the *Miranda* warnings could not be used as evidence to counter his insanity defense. A unanimous Court said the source of unfairness is the assurance contained in the *Miranda* warnings that silence will carry no penalty. It is fundamentally unfair to promise a person that silence will not be used against him and then breach that promise by using silence to overcome a defendant's plea of insanity.

In *Oregon v. Elstad*, 470 U.S. 298 (1985), the Court concluded that a voluntary admission coming prior to *Miranda* warnings does not necessarily require suppression of a confession coming later. At the time of his arrest, Elstad incriminated himself before receiving any warnings. He made statements voluntarily, in the presence of his mother, and in an environment that could be characterized as noncoercive. He was subsequently taken to the sheriff's office and advised of his rights. Elstad waived his rights and confessed again. Although the initial statements were inadmissible, Elstad later argued that his sheriff's office confession was tainted by the statements made prior to receiving any warnings. The Supreme Court disagreed, saying that as long as the initial statements were voluntary, the later confession need not be suppressed. A defendant who responds to "unwarned yet uncoercive questioning is not disabled from waiving his warnings." In circumstances such as these, "thorough administration of *Miranda* warnings serves to cure the condition that rendered the unwarned statement inadmissible."

The Court extended *Harris* in *Michigan v. Harvey,* 494 U.S. 394 (1990). The prosecution, said the Court, "must not be allowed to build its case ... with evidence acquired in contravention of constitutional guarantees." Using such statements for impeachment purposes, however, "is a different matter." The Court said it has "consistently rejected" arguments that would allow an accused to turn the illegal method by which government evidence was obtained "to his own advantage, and provide himself with a shield against contradiction of his untruths." The Court ruled that the same rules apply in these Fifth and Sixth Amendment situations. The statements are inadmissible in the prosecutor's case-in-chief in both instances. At the same time, impeachment of a defendant's conflicting testimony should be allowed. Although a defendant may "sometimes later regret" the decision to make a statement, the Sixth Amendment "does not disable a criminal defendant from exercising his free will." The cases establishing "prophylactic rules that render some otherwise valid waivers of constitutional rights invalid" when they are the product of police-initiated interrogation should not be "perverted into a license to use perjury by way of a defense, free from the risk of confrontation with prior inconsistent utterances."

Decisions like *James* reiterate the proposition from *Miranda* and *Harris,* that the Fifth Amendment protects a defendant from involuntarily incriminating himself or herself, but does not protect perjured testimony.

Coerced Confession: Harmless Error

Arizona v. Fulminante, **499 U.S. 279 (1991)** Harmless error is error that does not affect the outcome of a criminal case. *Fulminante* extended harmless-error analysis as set forth in *Chapman v. California,* 386 U.S. 18 (1967), to coerced-confession situations. Fulminante was suspected of killing his stepdaughter in Arizona, although charges were not brought against him. He subsequently left Arizona for New Jersey where he was arrested on an unrelated federal charge. He was sentenced to a short term in a federal facility in New York. Rumored at the institution to be a child killer, Fulminante was subjected to abusive treatment by some of the inmates. Fulminante then met another inmate who offered to protect him from the other inmates in exchange for truth about the killing of the stepdaughter. Fulminante confessed to the murder. Unbeknown to Fulminante, the inmate to whom he confessed was an FBI informant. Fulminante unsuccessfully sought to suppress the confession at trial, and he was convicted, but the Arizona Supreme Court found the confession coerced and reversed his conviction. The U.S Supreme Court held that the harmless-error analysis can apply to coerced confessions. The Court had held in *Chapman* that a coerced confession situation could not be considered harmless. Chief Justice Rehnquist said in *Fulminante*, however, that the *Chapman* discussion of coerced confessions was "historical reference" rather than the adoption of a firm rule. More crucial, Rehnquist saw use of an involuntary confession as a "classic trial error," something "markedly different" from the two other constitutional violations referred to in *Chapman*—depriving defendants of counsel and trial before a biased judge. These latter violations are "structural defects in the constitution of the trial mechanism." Such defects affect the "framework within which the trial proceeds, rather than simply an error in the trial process itself." These are defects that cannot be subjected to harmless-error standards. In contrast, the admission of involuntary statements is a trial error "similar in both degree and kind" to erroneous admission of other kinds of evidence. Introduction of an involuntary confession is the kind of trial error, said Rehnquist, that can be "quantitatively assessed in the context of other evidence presented." When reviewing a case in which an involuntary statement is admitted, the appellate court is to review the remaining evidence to determine whether use of the statement was harmless beyond a reasonable doubt. Rehnquist acknowledged that the involuntary confession may have a "more dramatic effect" on a trial than other kinds of trial error. In such cases, the error is clearly not harmless. That eventuality, however, is not a reason for "eschewing the harmless error test entirely." Using harmless-error analysis, the Supreme Court agreed with the Arizona Supreme Court that Fulminante's confession was indeed coerced under the "totality of circumstances" standard. Furthermore, its admission at his trial was not harmless. The Supreme Court affirmed the Arizona court's ruling that a new trial on the murder charge was required. Justices White, Marshall, Blackmun, and Stevens disagreed. They felt the use of coerced confessions was "inconsistent" with the proposition that we do not use an "inquisitorial system of criminal justice." *See also* FIFTH AMENDMENT, p. 265; SELF-INCRIMINATION CLAUSE, p. 695.

Significance   The harmless-error concept is an analytic device used by appellate courts as they review actions of lower courts. Constitutional error in a criminal case does not automatically require reversal of a conviction. Some error made during a criminal trial may not be serious enough to affect the outcome of the trial. In other words, this kind of error is regarded as nonprejudicial to the rights of the defendant. Harmless-error analysis can be applied to a number of procedural errors. *Chapman* identified three categories of errors that could not be subjected to harmless-error analysis. The Supreme Court removed use of a coerced confession from that list in *Fulminante.* In order for an appellate court to preserve a conviction, it must be convinced beyond a reasonable doubt that the mistake or error was harmless. The *Fulminante* ruling leaves only two kinds of error, depriving the accused of counsel and trial before a biased judge, outside the reach of harmless-error analysis. By adding coerced confession to the categories that may be harmless error, the Rehnquist Court lowered the probability of a successful appeal by those convicted at trial.

Inevitable Discovery

Nix v. Williams, **467 U.S. 431 (1984),** decided that improperly obtained evidence may become admissible if it would have been inevitably discovered by lawful means. *Nix v. Williams* involved use at retrial of evidence derived from a conversation with the defendant conducted by police in the absence of counsel. Based on this improper interrogation, Williams's initial conviction was reversed in *Brewer v. Williams,* 430 U.S. 387 (1977). The critical disclosure during the improper conversation was the location of a murder victim's body. At the retrial, the state was permitted to use evidence pertaining to the condition of the body, articles of clothing worn by the victim, and results of various tests made on the victim's body. The Supreme Court upheld use of the evidence, saying that the victim's body would inevitably have been found in virtually the same condition as it was when Williams led authorities to it. Chief Justice Burger said the issue before the Court was whether to adopt the so-called ultimate or inevitable discovery exception to the exclusionary rule. The "admittedly drastic and socially costly course" of implementing the exclusionary rule is necessary to deter police from violations of constitutional and statutory protections. Accordingly, the prosecution is not to be put in a better position than it would have been without such improper conduct as may be excepted from the exclusionary rule. At the same time, the exclusionary rule has never been seen as an absolute bar to improperly obtained evidence. Burger noted the independent-source exception. While finding it not directly applicable in *Nix*, he saw its underlying rationale as wholly consistent with an inevitable discovery exception. When evidence is challenged as being the product of illegal governmental activity, judicial inquiry is not confined to the issue of misconduct alone. If the prosecution can show by preponderance of evidence that such information ultimately or inevitably would have been discovered by lawful means, then "the deterrence rationale has so little basis that the evidence should be admissible." The Court also concluded that the prosecution need not prove the absence of bad faith in originally obtaining the evidence. To do so would place the courts in a position of withholding from juries "relevant and undoubted truth" that would have been available without the misconduct. Suppression under such circumstances would do nothing whatever to promote the integrity of the trial process and would inflict a wholly unacceptable burden on the administration of criminal justice. Justice Brennan argued in dissent that "zealous efforts to emasculate the exclusionary rule" lose sight of the distinction between inevitable discovery and the independent-source exception. Independence of source requires a showing that evidence was gained by lawful means, while inevitably discovered evidence has not yet achieved independent-source status. *See also* FIFTH AMENDMENT, p. 265; SELF-INCRIMINATION CLAUSE, p. 695.

Significance   The Court established in *Nix v. Williams* that unlawfully obtained evidence may be used if it ultimately or inevitably would have been discovered legally. *Nix* is one of several later Burger Court decisions that ease the admission of evidence obtained through conversations with defendants. Most of the decisions have taken the form of exceptions to *Miranda v. Arizona*, 384 U.S. 436 (1966). In *Minnesota v. Murphy*, 465 U.S. 420 (1984), for example, the Court allowed the use of statements made by a probationer to his probation officer despite the probationer having received no warning about the statements' admissibility in a subsequent trial. The Court said that Murphy was not really in custody and thus did not require the *Miranda* warnings. Further, the obligation to report to his probation officer did not convert otherwise voluntary statements into compelled ones.

The Court fashioned a public-safety exception to *Miranda* in *New York v. Quarles*, 467 U.S. 649 (1984). The Court said that in some situations concern for public safety must take precedence over the need to administer *Miranda*. In *Quarles*, arresting police officers first inquired about the location of a weapon Quarles was known to be carrying. After the weapon was found, the officers administered the *Miranda* warnings. The Court said that *Miranda* did not need to be applied in all its rigor when police conduct is reasonably prompted by such a concern for public safety.

Finally, in *Berkemer v. McCarty*, 468 U.S. 420 (1984), the Court held that, although *Miranda* is required for custodial interrogation of a person accused of a misdemeanor traffic offense, the warnings are not required for the roadside questioning of a person. In the latter situation, the motorist is not in custody, the questioning is of short duration, and it is public enough to reduce the potential for police misconduct.

Physical Specimens

Schmerber v. California, **384 U.S. 757 (1966),** explored whether the privilege against self-incrimination extends to defendant-derived evidence of a noncommunicated nature. The privilege clearly covers communicated testimony. *Schmerber* involved a driving-while-intoxicated conviction in which critical evidence against the defendant came in the form of blood test results. The blood sample upon which the tests were performed was taken over Schmerber's objection. Schmerber challenged the conviction on search, self-incrimination, assistance of counsel, and general due process grounds. The Court rejected all of his contentions. The Court held that taking the blood sample "constituted compulsion for the purposes of the privilege." The critical question in *Schmerber* was whether the blood sample actually constituted making Schmerber "a witness against himself." The Court concluded that the scope of the self-incrimination protection did not extend far enough to reach Schmerber. The privilege applied only against compelling evidence against the accused "from his own mouth." The evidence must be testimonial—that is, the words or communications of the accused. The Court likened the blood sample to fingerprints and other means of identification. It said that making the suspect provide "real or physical evidence does not violate it (the privilege against self-incrimination)." The Court said that in Schmerber's case, "not even a shadow of testimonial compulsion upon or enforced communication by the accused was involved either in extraction or in chemical analysis." Schmerber's "testimonial capacities were in no way implicated." In the Court's view, Schmerber, "except as a donor, was irrelevant to the results of the test." Justice Black in dissent remarked that to say that "compelling a person to give his blood to help the State convict him is not equivalent to compelling him to be a witness against himself strikes me as quite an extraordinary feat." *See also* FIFTH AMENDMENT, p. 265; IDENTIFICATION PROCEDURES, p. 662; *Neil v. Biggers*, p. 313; SELF-INCRIMINATION CLAUSE, p. 695.

Significance   *Schmerber* is the definitive ruling on blood samples and self-incrimination. *Schmerber* held simply that blood samples, because they are not testimonial in character, are not covered by the privilege against self-incrimination. As long as the sample is not taken in a manner that "shocks the conscience," analysis conducted on the sample is admissible evidence. The Court has also permitted states to admit into evidence a person's refusal to submit to a blood-alcohol test. In *South Dakota v. Neville*, 459 U.S. 553 (1983), the Court held that because the offer of taking the test is "clearly legitimate, the action becomes no less legitimate when the State offers a second option of refusing the test, with attendant penalties for making that choice." In *California v. Trombetta*, 467 U.S. 479 (1984), the Court ruled that authorities are not required to preserve breath samples used to test for intoxication. Due process considerations do not require the samples as a necessary prerequisite to the introduction of breath-analysis test results at trial. The Court did not interpret *Trombetta* as an example of evidence being destroyed in a calculated effort to subvert due process. Failure to preserve the breath samples was a good faith action based on normal and established practice. More generally, the Court said that the need to preserve evidence is limited to that which is expected to play a significant role in the suspect's defense. In *Trombetta*, the defendants had "alternative means of demonstrating their innocence" beyond the samples themselves.

Use of test results based on urine, skin, and other samples obtained from a suspect's body are also covered under the *Schmerber* decision. This includes bullets. In *Winston v. Lee*, 470 U.S. 753 (1985), a suspect was compelled to have a bullet removed from his body. The Court found this to be an unreasonable search because it could not be justified against the risk created by having to administer a general anesthetic to perform the surgery. Extending *Schmerber*, the Court has held that samples of a person's handwriting or voice may be used for identification purposes. In *Gilbert v. California*, 388 U.S. 263 (1967), the Court said that although one's voice and handwriting are a means of communication, a sample of handwriting or a voice exemplar, independent of the content of what is written or said, is an "identifying physical characteristic" that is outside the protection of the privilege against compelled self-incrimination. Warren Court decisions such as *Schmerber* and *Gilbert* clearly distinguish protected testimonial incrimination from unprotected nontestimonial evidence. The Burger Court maintained that distinction. The only constraints on nontestimonial evidence stem from the Fourth Amendment and its guidelines governing seizure of evidence.

Identification Procedures

Neil v. Biggers, **409 U.S. 188 (1972),** clarified the criteria for admitting identifications in a trial. Direct confrontation by a witness is frequently used to identify persons suspected of criminal acts. Biggers was convicted of rape. The single most significant piece of evidence against him was the testimony of the rape victim. She had identified Biggers as two police officers walked him past her. This confrontation, or show-up, occurred seven months after the crime. A line-up for identification purposes was not used because the police could not assemble a sufficient number of other persons resembling the accused. The Supreme Court ruled that the show-up was adequate and upheld Biggers's conviction. The Court ruled that a defendant must demonstrate that the identification process was "so unnecessarily suggestive and conducive to irreparable mistaken identification" as to deny due process. That determination is to be made through examination of the "totality of the circumstances." The primary evil to be prevented is "a very substantial likelihood of irreparable misidentification." A confrontation may be suggestive, but not so suggestive as to make misidentification likely. The identification of Biggers was suggestive because he was the only person placed before the victim, but it was not too suggestive because other factors supported the reliability of the victim's identification. The Court noted several criteria that must be used in evaluating the reliability of the identification. The factors include: the opportunity of the witness to "view the criminal at the time of the crime"; the witness's "degree of attention"; how accurate the witness's "prior description" of the suspect had been; the "level of certainty demonstrated by the witness" at the confrontation; and the elapsed time between the crime and the identification. On the basis of these factors, the Court concluded that even though the show-up had been suggestive, the witness's identification had been reliable enough. *See also* FIFTH AMENDMENT, p. 265; IDENTIFICATION PROCEDURES, p. 662; *Schmerber v. California*, p. 312; SELF-INCRIMINATION CLAUSE, p. 695.

Significance *Neil v. Biggers* provides generally applicable standards by which the reliability of identifications can be assessed. The Supreme Court has never held that requiring a person to be viewed by a witness violates due process as such. It has, however, circumscribed confrontational identification processes in cases such as *Neil.* The *Neil* criteria are not always necessarily decisive, because occasionally the confrontation technique is so excessively suggestive as to be invalid. For example, the Court found in *Foster v. California*, 394 U.S. 440 (1969), that a line-up that contains only one person dressed in the manner described by a witness, only one person approximating the physical description provided by the witness, or only one person who appears in a second line-up who had also appeared in an earlier lineup are confrontations that made "identifications virtually inevitable." Such a confrontation is categorically prohibited. If the confrontation is not too suggestive, the reliability of the identification is evaluated further using the *Neil* criteria. The Court has determined that postindictment confrontations are a sufficiently critical stage in the criminal process that a suspect is entitled to assistance of counsel at that point. The presence of defense counsel at such proceedings deters the possibility of distorted or unnecessarily suggestive witness confrontations. The test from *Neil* balances the five factors through a consideration of the "totality of circumstances."

The Court extended the reliability criteria from *Neil* to photographic identifications in *Manson v. Brathwaite*, 432 U.S. 98 (1972).

Immunity

***Kastigar v. United States*, 406 U.S. 441 (1972),** determined the level of immunity from prosecution that is needed to satisfy self-incrimination requirements. Kastigar was subpoenaed to testify before a federal grand jury. He was granted "derivative use" immunity, which prohibits direct use of the compelled testimony or any information derived from that testimony to prosecute the witness. Kastigar argued that the derivative use immunity granted him was not coextensive with his jeopardy and refused to testify. He was then found to be in civil contempt and jailed, and the Supreme Court upheld the contempt ruling. Kastigar argued that only complete or transactional immunity would satisfy the protections of the Fifth Amendment. Transactional immunity prohibits prosecution for any transaction about which the person was compelled to testify. The Court disagreed. It found derivative use immunity to be "coextensive with the scope of the privilege against self-incrimination." The immunity "need not be broader" than the protection "afforded by the privilege." In the Court's view, "the privilege has never been construed to mean that one who invokes it cannot subsequently be prosecuted." If a subsequent prosecution does occur, the prosecution has the "affirmative duty to prove that the evidence it proposes to use is derived from a legitimate source wholly independent of the compelled testimony." The Court felt this protection was "substantial" and "commensurate with that resulting from invoking the privilege itself." Justices Douglas and Marshall would have required full transactional immunity. *See also* FIFTH AMENDMENT, p, 265; IMMUNITY, p. 662; SELF-INCRIMINATION CLAUSE, p. 695.

Significance *Kastigar v. United States* focused on the critical immunity issue of coextensiveness. The immunity granted a witness in exchange for testimony must cover or be coextensive with the vulnerability created by compelling the witness to testify. Prior to 1970 witnesses who were compelled to testify were granted transactional immunity. It insulates a witness from prosecution for *any transaction* about which the witness was required to testify regardless of how serious a crime is involved or how tangential the crime is to the primary issue under investigation. In 1970 Congress passed the Organized Crime Control Act, which authorized a more limited immunity. This immunity is confined to forbidding the use of the testimony itself or information derived from the testimony to prosecute the witness. It is called "derivative use," "use," or "testimonial" immunity. The key feature of such immunity is that a witness may be prosecuted subsequent to testifying, as long as the evidence used against him or her can be shown to be independent of the compelled testimony. The real significance of *Kastigar* is that it established a less rigorous definition of coextensiveness than had existed before. It approved limited immunity as sufficiently meeting the protections afforded by the privilege against self-incrimination. Although the testimony itself cannot be used directly or indirectly, compelled testimony may prompt investigation because authorities are aware of a witness's guilt. Immunity policy requires consideration of the balance between self-incrimination interests and the interest of public security served by gaining information about criminal activities. *Kastigar* shifts the balance point in favor of public security interests.

CHAPTER 5

The Sixth Amendment

Overview, 319

The Sixth Amendment, 323

OVERVIEW

The Sixth Amendment states:

> In all criminal prosecutions, the accused shall enjoy the right to a speedy and public trial, by an impartial jury of the State and district wherein the crime shall have been committed, which district shall have been previously ascertained by law, and to be informed of the nature and cause of the accusation; to be confronted with the witnesses against him; to have compulsory process for obtaining witnesses in his favor, and to have the Assistance of Counsel for his defence.

The provisions of the Sixth Amendment are aimed at providing a criminal defendant with a fair trial. The trial must occur without unnecessary delay. *Doggett v. United States*, 505 U.S. 647 (1992), reexamined the criteria by which speedy trial claims are evaluated. A defendant is also entitled to confront witnesses against him. *Pointer v. Texas*, 380 U.S. 400 (1965), held the Confrontation Clause applicable to the states and required that the defense have an opportunity to cross-examine witnesses. In *Coy v. Iowa*, 487 U.S. 1012 (1988), the Court examined the right to confront child witnesses who are the victims of sex offenses. *Rock v. Arkansas*, 483 U.S. 44 (1987), considered whether the Compulsory Process Clause enables a defendant to offer hypnotically refreshed testimony. Although not explicitly covered by the Sixth Amendment, the process for determining the competency of a criminal defendant to stand trial was addressed by the Court in *Medina v. California*, 505 U.S. 437 (1992).

The Sixth Amendment entitles a criminal defendant to trial by an impartial jury. Access to a jury trial is discussed in *Lewis v. United States*, 518 U.S. 322 (1996). What constitutes impartiality is a continuing issue before the Supreme Court. Several standards apply. Juries must be selected in a manner that does not systematically discriminate against any population group. *J.E.B v. T.B.*, 511 U.S. 127 (1994), held that the Equal Protection Clause of the Fourteenth Amendment precludes prosecutors from using the peremptory challenge of potential jurors in a discriminatory manner. Possible prejudice may be probed during the voir dire examination of prospective jurors, and as seen in *Lockhart v. McCree*, 476 U.S. 162 (1986), prospective jurors who would never impose the death penalty in capital cases can be excluded from service. A six-person jury in state trials was allowed in *Williams v. Florida*, 399 U.S. 78 (1970), and nonunanimous jury verdicts were upheld for state criminal trials in *Apodaca v. Oregon*, 406 U.S. 404 (1972).

The Sixth Amendment requires that trials be public. The main reasons for maintaining open trials are discussed in *Richmond Newspapers, Inc. v. Virginia*, 448 U.S. 555 (1980). Although criminal trials must remain open to the public, insulation from excessive media coverage may be necessary in order to protect the due process interests of a defendant. Such excessive media coverage as occurred in *Sheppard v. Maxwell*, 384 U.S. 333 (1966), requires strong judicial action.

The Sixth Amendment provides that the accused "have the Assistance of Counsel for his defence." A defendant may not be prevented from availing himself or herself of counsel. The key questions evolving from this clause are whether counsel is actually required in criminal cases as a condition of due process, and whether provisions of the clause bind state criminal proceedings. *Gideon v. Wainwright*, 372 U.S. 335 (1963), and *Argersinger v. Hamlin*, 407 U.S. 25 (1972), required counsel in state capital, felony, and misdemeanor trials, respectively. In *United States v. Monsanto*, 491 U.S. 600 (1989), the Court allowed the government to seize assets of indicted drug traffickers, including even those funds that had been intended to pay for privately retained counsel. *United States v. Wade*, 388 U.S. 218 (1967), is representative of a series of cases extending counsel to "critical stages" of the criminal process other than the trial itself. *Strickland v. Washington*, 466 U.S. 668 (1984), established a two-part test for examining the effectiveness of defense counsel. *Faretta v. California*, 422 U.S. 806 (1975), explored the right of self-representation.

Pleading guilty to a criminal charge effectively waives the Sixth Amendment protections inherent in the trial process. Pleading guilty also constitutes the most extreme form of self-incrimination. The Supreme Court has consistently upheld the constitutionality of plea bargaining as long as the plea is made knowingly and voluntarily. *Santobello v. New York*, 404 U.S. 257 (1971), focused on the performance requirements that apply to the prosecution in the plea process, and required that all promises made to a defendant as an inducement to plead guilty be fulfilled.

Until 1967 juvenile proceedings were viewed as civil in character, and generally unlike adult criminal prosecutions. *In re Gault*, 387 U.S. 1 (1967), dramatically altered the constitutional status of juvenile proceedings.

Although not grounded in Sixth Amendment claims, three other cases are discussed in this chapter: The first is *Morrison v. Olson*, 487 U.S. 654 (1988), the decision in which the Court upheld the portion of the Ethics in Government Act providing for the appointment of federal special prosecutors. Second, in *Printz v. United States*, 521 U.S. 898 (1997), the Court concluded that the federal government could not require state and local law enforcement officers to perform background checks on prospective handgun purchasers. Third, in *Jaffee v. Redmond*, 518 U.S. 1 (1996), the Court recognized the privileged status of patient-psychotherapist communications.

The Sixth Amendment   The Sixth Amendment mandates a fair trial for criminal defendants. Like the Fifth Amendment, the Sixth is based in traditions of English common law. Abuses of laws intended to safeguard the rights of criminal defendants were common in colonial America. Most of the constitutions of the first 13 states contained language designed to correct them. The Virginia Bill of Rights, written by George Mason, put the concern this way in Article VIII:

> In all capital or criminal prosecutions, a man hath a right to demand the cause and nature of his accusation, to be confronted with the accusers and witnesses, to call for evidence in his favour, and to a speedy trial by an impartial jury of twelve men of his vicinage, without whose unanimous consent he cannot be found guilty; nor can he be compelled to give evidence against himself.

The state constitutional ratifying conventions, with North Carolina taking the lead, insisted that the principle of trial by jury is one of the most fundamental rights accruing to the citizens of a democracy. It was not enough that the protection also appears in Article III, Section 2, of the Constitution: "The Trial of all cases, except in Cases of Impeachment, shall be by Jury; and such Trial shall be held in the state where the said Crimes shall have been committed."

The immediate cause of such deep concern was the British practice in colonial America of sending defendants to England for trial. Colonists believed to be guilty of violating the trade laws or stamp acts, for example, were tried by the British Admiralty Court in England without benefit of a jury. On 21 October 1774 the Continental Congress declared unequivocally that "the seizing of or attempting to seize any person in America in order to transport such person beyond the sea for trial of offences committed within the body of a county in America, being against the law, will justify, and ought to meet with, resistance and reprisal." In that part of the Declaration of Independence containing the litany of "repeated injuries and usurpations" suffered by the colonies, the following complaints appear: "For depriving us in many cases of the benefits of Trial by Jury; for transporting us beyond seas to be tried for pretended offences." The colonists also insisted that provisions of the Magna Carta be remembered on the subject of speedy trials. A person accused of a crime must not be kept in prison an unreasonable period of time *before* trial of the facts. It is essential to the guarantee that persons unjustly accused will not be incarcerated for a crime not committed.

The Founders were equally concerned that the Bill of Rights

embody the English common-law tradition holding that one accused of a criminal act should have available the bill of indictment containing the charges against him or her. The assumption implicit in this clause of the Sixth Amendment is that if a defendant is aware of the precise charges levied against him or her, an appropriate defense can be mounted. The Supreme Court has suggested that the Constitution is not specific on the process by which a defendant is to be informed, but there is no doubt of the right of the accused to demand such information. The Virginia ratifying convention stated simply, "A man hath a right to demand the cause and nature of his accusation."

A clause of the Sixth Amendment that did not originate in the English common-law tradition was the guarantee of compulsory process. Until 1787 it was well settled in the conduct of English trials that persons accused of felonies or treason were not allowed to introduce witnesses in their own behalf. After 1787 this general law was abolished in England, but there were restrictions on the number and kinds of witnesses who could be summoned. Not only did the constitutional ratifying conventions have this immediate precedent before them in 1789, they also took language from the Federal Crimes Act of 1790, which said in part that "all criminals shall have the same privileges of Witnesses as their Prosecutors."

The right of compulsory process is now an unchallenged part of American criminal procedure, as is the right of access to counsel. Prior to 1836 defendants in the English court system were allowed access to counsel only when the charge against them was treason. Even then the access was limited to arguing points of law with the permission of the judge. Blackstone said, "It is a settled rule at common law that no counsel shall be allowed a prisoner upon his trial, upon the general issue in any capital crime, unless some point of law shall arise to be debated." Blackstone then condemned the practice as inhumane to the treatment of English prisoners and defendants. As in the case of compulsory process, the American tradition was different, however. The Charters of Pennsylvania and Delaware also established a legal right to counsel, although it was limited to the right to retain counsel at one's own expense. This right was codified both in the Judiciary Act of 1789 and the Federal Crimes Act of 1790. Thus if a defendant could afford to retain counsel, his right to counsel was guaranteed.

Several twentieth-century Supreme Court decisions dramatically reinterpreted this tradition. In *Powell v. Alabama*, 287 U.S. 45 (1932), the Court determined that states were required to furnish counsel as an extension of the due process guarantee of the Fourteenth Amendment. In *Gideon v. Wainwright*, 372 U.S. 335 (1963), the Court said:

The right of one charged with a crime to counsel may not be deemed fundamental and essential to fair trials in some countries, but it is in ours. From the very beginning, our state and national constitutions and laws have laid great emphasis on procedural and substantive safeguards designed to assure fair trials before impartial tribunals in which every defendant stands equal before the law. This noble ideal cannot be realized if the poor man charged with crime has to face accusers without a lawyer to assist him. (372 U.S. at 344)

Three years later the Court said in *Miranda v. Arizona,* 384 U.S. 436 (1966), that as soon as an accused person is in custody and police interrogation has begun, he or she must be informed of the right to counsel in order to be afforded all the protections of due process. Thus the evolution of the Sixth amendment phrase "have the Assistance of Counsel for his defence" has made legal representation an absolute constitutional guarantee. *See also* BILL OF RIGHTS, p. 621; COMMON LAW, p. 631; *Gideon v. Wainwright,* p. 360; *Miranda v. Arizona,* p. 290.

Significance   The Sixth Amendment provides rights that differentiate the American system of jurisprudence from many others in the modern world. Yet the set of requirements mandating a fair trial represent one of the more interesting misunderstandings in the history of criminal procedure. It has been commonly agreed that the Magna Carta contained the linguistic structure for trial by jury. Evidence now suggests, however, that the concept of trial by jury was contemplated neither in form nor function at Runnymede. That part of Sixth Amendment guarantees emerged full blown in the Plymouth Colony in 1623, where it was required that all criminal facts to be adjudicated should be tried by a jury of 12 "honest men to be impaneled by authority, in form of a jury upon their oaths." The Plymouth tradition that these 12 persons should unanimously agree on a verdict survives in federal criminal procedures to this day, although the Supreme Court has ruled that in state actions a unanimous decision by the jury is not always necessary to convict a defendant.

Another early American tradition surviving intact is the principle that a trial for any criminal offense must take place in the district in which the alleged offense took place. Such a holding became the impetus for state and local court systems. Later interpretations of it have allowed for changes of venue depending on circumstances determined appropriate by the presiding judge. Similarly, later interpretations of what constitutes a fair trial and a proper jury have evolved according to the due process and equal protection standards of the Fourteenth Amendment. It is now Supreme Court doctrine that impartiality in the composition of a jury must reflect the socio-logical makeup of the trial district's population. By the same token, the idea of witness confrontation has evolved from the right of those accused of treason to confront witnesses against them under England's Treason Act of 1696, to modern rules of procedure that take strongly into account a trial's reliance on evidence and testimony brought by witnesses. The Supreme Court stated what continues to be the status of this clause of the Sixth Amendment in *Kirby v. United States*, 174 U.S. 47 (1899):

> A fact which can be primarily established only by witnesses cannot be proved against the accused except by witnesses who confront him at the trial, upon whom he can look while being tried, whom he is entitled to cross-examine, and whose testimony he may impeach in every mode authorized by the established rules governing the trial or conduct of criminal cases. (174 U.S. at 56)

The Sixth Amendment's guarantee of the right to counsel assures that all other provisions of the Amendment are monitored by persons with legal knowledge. The right to counsel has been extended to every corner and aspect of the criminal process: to the states, to the poor, and to persons immediately after being put in custody. In no other modern government have so many safeguards been assigned to the rights of persons accused of crimes.

Speedy Trial

***Doggett v. United States*, 505 U.S. 647 (1992)**   Doggett had been indicted on federal drug charges, but left the country before he could be arrested. He subsequently reentered the country and lived openly using his own name until his arrest—more than eight years after his indictment. The Court ruled that Doggett's speedy trial right had been violated. The government argued that Doggett had not shown "precisely" how he was prejudiced by the delay between his indictment and trial. The Court said, however, that "consideration of prejudice is not limited to the specifically demonstrable." While "bad faith" delay would make relief "virtually automatic," said Justice Souter, neither is negligence "automatically tolerable simply because the accused cannot demonstrate exactly how it has prejudiced him." Rather, it must generally be recognized that excessive delay "presumptively compromises the reliability of a trial in ways that neither party can prove or, for that matter, identify." Such presumptive prejudice is "part of the mix of relevant facts, and its importance increases with the length of delay." On this basis, the Court concluded that the negligent delay between Doggett's indictment and arrest "presumptively prejudiced his ability to prepare an adequate defense." When the government's negligence causes delay "six times as long as that generally sufficient to trigger judicial review," and when the presumption of prejudice, "albeit unspecified, is neither extenuated, as by the defendant's acquiescence, nor persuasively rebutted, the defendant is entitled to relief." *See also* SIXTH AMENDMENT, p. 323; SPEEDY TRIAL, p. 700.

Significance   *Klopfer v. North Carolina*, 386 U.S. 213 (1967), decided that the speedy trial provisions of the Sixth Amendment applied to the states. *Barker v. Wingo*, 407 U.S. 514 (1972), established criteria by which claims of denial of speedy trial might be evaluated. Defendant Barker was charged with murder and had a trial date set. Between the original trial of October 1958 and October 1963 Barker's trial was continued 17 times. Barker did not object to the first 11 continuances because he was on pretrial release through most of the period. When eventually tried, Barker was convicted and sentenced to life in prison. The Supreme Court unanimously upheld Barker's conviction. Before fashioning a speedy-trial test in the case, Justice Powell spoke of the unique character of the speedy-trial protection calling it "generically different" from other constitutional protections because there is a "societal interest in providing a speedy trial which exists separate from, and at times in opposition to, the interests of the accused." The speedy-trial concept is also "amorphous" and "vague," more so than other rights of the accused. Powell rejected specific timetables and an "on demand" approach as inflexible. Instead he devised a "balancing test" for evaluating speedy-trial claims. The test contains four elements and "compels courts to approach speedy trial cases on an *ad hoc* basis." The four factors identified are: (1) length of delay; (2) reasons offered by the government (prosecution) to justify the delay; (3) the defendant's assertion of his or her right to a speedy trial; and (4) prejudice to the defendant in terms of pretrial incarceration, anxiety, and impairment of the defense. Applying these criteria to Barker, the Court concluded that despite the lengthy delay, Barker's defense was not prejudiced. He was on release throughout most of the period, and he failed seriously to assert the right to a speedy trial. *Barker* provided a two-edged rationale for a speedy trial. The defendant must be protected from lengthy pretrial detention and diminution of the capacity to offer a defense, but the prosecutor's case must be similarly protected from erosion by delay. The Court rejected both the fixed-time and "demand-waiver" approaches in *Barker*, preferring a "balancing" or "totality of the circumstances" standard.

The Court has been quite specific on the issue of when the speedy-trial protection begins. *United States v. Marion*, 404 U.S. 307 (1971), examined a three-year delay between a criminal act and the filing of charges. The Court concluded that the speedy-trial guarantee does not apply "until the putative defendant in some way becomes an accused." *United States v. Lovasco*, 431 U.S. 783 (1977), also considered preindictment delay. In *Lovasco* the prosecution had a chargeable case within a month of the crime but did not seek indictment for an additional 17 months. The delay was attributed to an inability to finish the investigation of the case against Lovasco as well as several others. Compounding the situation was the fact that the defendant lost the testimony of two witnesses who died during the 18-month delay. Nonetheless the Court found for the prosecution and refused to find an investigative delay prior to indictment a fatal defect. The Court refused to require prosecutors to charge as soon as evidence might be minimally sufficient. The Court recognized that "reckless" preindictment delay or delay aimed at gaining an advantage did constitute a denial of due process. In *United States v. MacDonald*, 456 U.S. 1 (1982), a murder case that drew national attention, the Court found that the time between dismissed charges brought within the military system of justice and the subsequent filing of civilian charges is not subject to speedy-trial protection. The Court reiterated the *MacDonald* rationale in *United States v. Loud Hawk*, 474 U.S. 302 (1986), saying that the time when persons are free of all restrictions on their liberty is not to be included in the computation of delay. It is only the "actual restraints imposed by arrest and holding to answer a criminal charge that engages the protection of the Speedy Trial Clause." Thus the burden of demonstrating violation of the speedy-trial protection clearly rests with the defense, and cases such as *Marion*, *Lovasco*, and *MacDonald* reflect the Court's preference for limiting the stages or time periods to which the speedy-trial protection applies. In the meantime Congress has legislated a speedy-trial time period for federal courts. An accused must be brought to trial within 70 days of his or her first court appearance to answer criminal charges. That time period can be tolled for various reasons, usually consistent with defense requests. Some states have also enacted speedy-trial legislation, frequently allowing six months from the time of arraignment. The balancing test of *Barker* still applies, however. Indeed, the Rehnquist Court extended the scope of *Barker* by identifying a fair trial dimension in *Doggett*.

Confrontation

***Pointer v. Texas*, 380 U.S. 400 (1965),** decided that the Confrontation Clause, which requires that the accused "be confronted with the witnesses against him," was applicable in state criminal trials. Pointer was tried for robbery. His chief accuser provided a detailed account of the crime at a preliminary hearing, a proceeding at which Pointer was unrepresented by defense counsel. At the trial the prosecution used transcripts of the witness's preliminary hearing testimony because the witness had moved to another state. Pointer was convicted, but a unanimous Supreme Court reversed the conviction, saying that the right to cross-examine a witness was a central aspect of confrontation. Inclusion of the confrontation protection in the Sixth Amendment reflected the Framers' belief that "confrontation was a fundamental right essential to a fair trial." The major reason underlying the confrontation rule is to provide the defendant with an opportunity to cross-examine adverse witnesses. As for the practice in Texas of allowing use of a transcript, the Court said that the confrontation protection would have been satisfied had the statements been made at a "full-fledged hearing" at which Pointer had been represented by counsel with "a complete and adequate opportunity to cross-examine." Absent that condition, what occurred was an unconstitutional denial of the Sixth Amendment right of confrontation. No one experienced in criminal trials, said Justice Black, would "deny the value of cross-examination in exposing falsehood and bringing out the truth in the trial of a criminal case." *See also* CONFRONTATION CLAUSE, p. 633; *Coy v. Iowa*, p. 333; SIXTH AMENDMENT, p. 323.

Significance   *Pointer* extended the confrontation right to state trial proceedings for the first time. The Supreme Court held specifically that the right to confront and cross-examine witnesses is a fundamental right essential to a fair trial and is obligatory for state courts by virtue of the Fourteenth Amendment. *Pointer* is one of a series of cases in which the Warren Court extended to state criminal defendants rights long given to federal defendants. The right to confront historically has meant that witness and defendant must be present in the courtroom for the various stages of the judicial process. Though that expectation generally holds, it is not inflexible. A defendant may choose not to attend any or all of the proceedings. A defendant's courtroom behavior may also become sufficiently disruptive to justify his or her removal from the courtroom as a condition of continuing the trial, as occurred in *Illinois v. Allen*, 397 U.S. 337 (1970). The capability to cross-examine, however, remains the heart of the confrontation protection. Soon after *Pointer*, the Court reinforced its decision in *Bruton v. United States*, 391 U.S. 123 (1968). Bruton was tried in a federal court. A postal inspector gave testimony describing an oral confession by Bruton's codefendant. The confession implicated both the codefendant and Bruton. The trial judge instructed the jury that the confession was inadmissable hearsay and must be disregarded in deciding Bruton's guilt. The Supreme Court held that the jury instruction was insufficient protection for Bruton. The use of the codefendant's confession "added substantial, perhaps even critical, weight to the Government's case in a form not subject to cross-examination, since Evans [the codefendant] did not take the stand." Although conceding that some situations might be remedied by jury instructions, the Court found that that remedy was inadequate in Bruton's case. The introduction of the confession "posed a substantial threat" to Bruton's capability to confront. "In the context of a joint trial we cannot accept limiting instructions as an adequate substitute for the petitioner's constitutional right of cross-examination. The effect is the same as if there had been no instruction at all." The Court extended the *Bruton* doctrine to cases in which the defendant's own admissible confession corroborates that of the codefendant in *Cruz v. New York*, 481 U.S. 186 (1987). Prior to *Cruz*, the governing rule was that when a defendant had entered his own confession, the introduction of a codefendant's confession would seldom, if ever, be of substantial enough weight to establish a Confrontation Clause violation under *Bruton*. In *Cruz*, the Court extended the *Bruton* rule to confessions of nontestifying codefendants despite the use of the defendant's own confession.

State rules of evidence may also interfere with the right of cross-examination. In *Chambers v. Mississippi*, 410 U.S. 284 (1973), a murder defendant called a particular witness in order to introduce the witness's written confession to the crime. The witness repudiated his confession, at which point Chambers sought to cross-examine him as an adverse witness. The request was denied because of hearsay limitations and a state rule that a party may not impeach his or her own witness. With only Justice Rehnquist dissenting, the Supreme Court reversed Chambers's conviction. Justice Powell's opinion emphasized the "realities of the criminal process." Defendants must be able fully to explore testimony from all witnesses including their own because "in modern criminal trials defendants are rarely able to select their witnesses; they must take them where they find them." Impeaching his own witness may be crucial to a defendant's ability to put on a defense. In addition, such rules of evidence as the hearsay rule must allow exceptions and not "be applied mechanistically to defeat the ends of justice." *Chambers* clearly reflects the view that a trial is a productive fact-finding process only if reliable evidence can be fully considered. The Confrontation Clause is designed to ensure evidence reliability by providing for cross-examination and requiring a witness to testify under oath. Further, the testimony of witnesses in open court can be assessed in terms of the witnesses' demeanor, or manner. The Confrontation Clause entitles a defendant to examine and perhaps challenge the full range of evidence against him or her in an attempt to develop the best factual defense.

As seen in *Chambers*, the Burger Court has been generally unreceptive to attempts to limit the examination/cross-examination process. In *Davis v. Alaska*, 415 U.S. 308 (1974), the Court applied the *Chambers* decision to a case in which a defendant had been denied the opportunity to disclose and develop during cross-examination the juvenile record of a crucial prosecution witness. Although disclosure of the witness's status as a juvenile delinquent would conflict with the state's policy of preserving confidentiality of juvenile proceedings, the Court decided that disclosure of the witness's status was necessary to impeach the credibility of the witness. There are practical limits, however. In *Ohio v. Roberts*, 448 U.S. 56 (1980), the Court returned to a variation of the *Pointer* fact situation. After testifying at a preliminary hearing, a witness did not appear at the trial, despite several subpoenas. A state statute permitted use of preliminary hearing testimony of a witness who could not be produced at the trial. The defendant objected to the use of the transcript, despite the fact the witness had originally been called by the defense, because her preliminary hearing testimony had not been entirely favorable to his defense. The Supreme Court concluded that a sufficiently good faith effort had been made to locate the witness and that the prior testimony bore "sufficient indicia of reliability" to be used under these circumstances.

A different confrontation issue was addressed in *Delaware v. Fensterer*, 474 U.S. 15 (1985). Here an expert witness for the prosecution was unable to recall the basis for an opinion he offered in testimony. The Court said that this did not violate the defendant's right to confront the witness. The right to cross-examine is not denied "whenever the witness' lapse of memory impedes one method of discrediting him." The Confrontation Clause includes no guarantee that every witness "will refrain from giving testimony that is marred by forgetfulness, confusion, or evasion." To the contrary, the requirements of the Clause are generally satisfied when the defense has a full and fair opportunity to probe and expose these infirmities through cross-examination. *United States v. Owens*, 484 U.S. 554 (1988), involved the testimony of a witness whose memory loss precluded his fully explaining the basis of his previous out-of-court identification of the defendant. The witness, a federal prison counselor, was the victim of a brutal assault. He suffered a fractured skull that resulted in extensive memory impairment and was hospitalized for a lengthy period after the attack. During the hospital visit of an investigating agent, the victim described the incident, named the attacker, and identified his photograph. At the defendant's trial, the witness recalled identifying the accused, but admitted on cross-examination that he could not remember seeing his assailant or whether anyone visiting him in the hospital had suggested the accused had assaulted him. Defense counsel unsuccessfully sought to refresh the witness's memory with hospital records, one of which indicated that he attributed the assault to someone other than the accused. The defendant was convicted nonetheless. The Supreme Court held that the Confrontation Clause had not been violated. The Confrontation Clause guarantees only an "opportunity for effective cross-examination." It is not a guarantee that cross-examination will be successful. Here the defendant had a "full and fair" opportunity to point out the witness's impaired memory as well as other "facts tending to discredit his testimony."

Joint trials occur regularly and can occasionally raise confrontation problems. The Court held in *Bruton* that a confession from a nontestifying codefendant could not be used in a joint trial, unless the jury was instructed that the confession could be considered with regard only to the confessing defendant. Since *Bruton* the Court has permitted edited or redacted confessions to be admitted into evidence in joint trials when all references to a nonconfessing defendant are removed. Kevin Gray was jointly tried for murder with a codefendant named Anthony Bell. The trial court permitted Bell's confession to be read to the jury. The confession was edited to insert blank spaces or the word "deleted" in place of Gray's name. The jury was subsequently instructed by the judge to consider the confession against Bell only. Gray testified in his own defense and denied any involvement in the murder. The jury convicted both defendants, however. The U.S. Supreme Court concluded in *Gray v. Maryland*, 118 S.Ct. 1151 (1998), that the confession fell within the reach of the *Bruton* ruling. The Court held that a confession edited to remove only the nonconfessing codefendant's name may still be perceived by the jury as referring "directly to the existence of the nonconfessing defendant." Justice Breyer said that for a juror "who does not know the law" and may wonder to whom the blank might refer "need only lift his eyes to [the codefendant] ... to find what will seem the obvious answer," especially after the judge instructs the jurors "not to consider the confession as evidence against [the codefendant], for that instruction will provide an obvious reason for the blank." Furthermore, the "obvious deletion" may draw the jurors' attention to the removed name. By "encouraging the jury to speculate about the reference, the redaction may overemphasize the importance of the confession's accusation." The inferences at issue in this case, Breyer concluded, "involve statements that, despite redaction, obviously refer directly to someone, often obviously the defendant, and which involve inferences that a jury could make immediately, even were the confession the very first item introduced at trial." Justice

Scalia, joined by Chief Justice Rehnquist and Justices Kennedy and Thomas, dissented. It was their view that the jury was not left with an "unavoidable inference" that Bell's confession implicated Gray, and that the confession could be admitted with the appropriately limiting jury instructions.

***Coy v. Iowa*, 487 U.S. 1012 (1988),** examined the issue of whether placing a screen between the defendant charged with child molestation and the child victims violated the Confrontation Clause. Under provisions of a state law, a screen was used while the victims testified, which blocked Coy from their view although he was able to both see and hear them. The Supreme Court struck down the procedure. The Court said that it "never doubted" that the confrontation protection guarantees the defendant a "face-to-face meeting" with witnesses. The protection has been essential to fairness "over the centuries" because a witness may "feel quite differently" when he or she testifies while looking at the person whom he or she may harm by "distorting or mistaking the facts." The face-to-face confrontation, like the right to cross-examine, "ensures the integrity of the fact-finding process." The state, said the Court, cannot deny the "profound effect" the presence of the defendant may have on a witness, as it is the "same phenomenon used to establish the potential trauma that allegedly justified the extraordinary procedure" used in this case. That face-to-face presence "may unfortunately upset the truthful rape victim or abused child," the Court said, but it may also "undo the false accuser, or reveal the child to be coached by a malevolent adult." Constitutional protections simply "have costs," the Court observed. The state argued that the confrontation interest was "outweighed by the necessity of protecting victims of sexual abuse." The Court ruled that this was not enough. "Something more" than the "generalized finding" underlying the law is required when an exception to a constitutional protection is not "firmly rooted in our jurisprudence." The Court said that the exception created by the law "could hardly be viewed as firmly rooted." Because the state made no "individual findings" that the witnesses in this case "needed special protection," the judgment in this case could not be "sustained by any conceivable exception." *See also* CONFRONTATION CLAUSE, p. 633; *Pointer v. Texas*, p. 328; SIXTH AMENDMENT, p. 323.

Significance   As reflected in *Coy*, maintenance of the right to confront may exact a high price. This has been especially true in cases in which children have been the victims of criminal conduct. Another example is *Pennsylvania v. Ritchie*, 480 U.S. 39 (1987). Ritchie was prosecuted for several sex offenses against his minor daughter. He sought to obtain records on the daughter from a state child welfare agency in hope of finding information helpful to his defense. The agency refused to comply with a subpoena, citing a state statute intended to protect the confidentiality of such records. The law limited access to specific persons or agencies, including courts with appropriate jurisdiction. The trial judge in Ritchie's case refused to order disclosure. The Supreme Court did not agree that there was a confrontation violation, but ruled that Ritchie had a Due Process Clause right to have the records of the child welfare agency submitted to the trial court for review by the judge, with release of germane material to the defendant to follow. The Court found the state's interest in protecting the records to be considerable, but the interest of ensuring Ritchie a fair trial was also substantial.

In *Kentucky v. Stincer*, 482 U.S. 730 (1987), the Court ruled that a defendant charged with child molestation is not entitled to attend a pretrial hearing on the competency of child witnesses to testify. Stincer argued that the competency hearing was a stage of the trial and was therefore subject to the requirements of the Confrontation Clause. The Court replied that, because the functional purpose of the clause was to promote reliability by ensuring an opportunity for cross-examination, a more useful inquiry was whether exclusion of Stincer interfered with that opportunity. The Court saw no such interference. Once witness competency was determined, the witnesses were subject to full and complete cross-examination in the presence of the defendant. The Court found no indication that Stincer's presence at the competency proceeding "would have been useful in ensuring a more reliable determination as to whether the witnesses were competent to testify."

Maryland v. Craig, 497 U.S. 836 (1990), held that states could protect child abuse victims by allowing them to testify on closed-circuit television. Justice O'Connor said that neither *Coy* nor any other previous confrontation ruling established that defendants have an "absolute right to a face-to-face meeting" with witnesses. Although the Confrontation Clause "reflects a preference for face-to-face confrontation at trial, ... we cannot say that such confrontation is an indispensable element of the Sixth Amendment guarantee." The "central concern" of the Clause is to "insure the reliability of evidence ... by subjecting it to rigorous testing in the context of an adversary proceeding." Maryland's procedure of using closed-circuit television does prevent the child witness from seeing the defendant, but it "preserves all the other elements of the confrontation right": The child witness must be competent and testify under oath; the judge, jury, and defendant can view the witness's demeanor as he or she testifies; and the defendant "retains full opportunity for contemporaneous cross-examination." The presence of these other elements "adequately insures that the testimony is both reliable and subject to rigorous adversarial testing in a manner functionally equivalent to that accorded live, in-person testimony." The "critical inquiry" in *Craig* was whether use of the television procedure was needed to further an important state interest. The Court concluded that protection of minor victims of sex crimes from "further trauma and embarrassment is a compelling one." Further, the Court determined that the interest in the "physical and psychological well-being of child abuse victims may be sufficiently important to outweigh, at least in some cases, a defendant's right to face his or her accusers in court." The Court's preference for case-by-case determination of the need for use of such devices as closed-circuit television over the blanket legislative judgment at issue in *Coy* was clear. Justice Scalia dissented, seeing the confrontation protection as absolute. He said that the Court had "no authority" to "speculate" that where confrontation "causes significant emotional distress in a child witness," it might "disserve" the "truth-seeking goal" of the Confrontation Clause. For "good or bad," said Scalia, the "Sixth Amendment requires confrontation, and we are not at liberty to ignore it."

In *Idaho v. Wright*, 497 U.S. 805 (1990), the Court said that states may not utilize hearsay exceptions that permit doctors or other adults to testify about their conversations with abuse victims. At issue in this case was the testimony of a pediatrician who represented statements made to him by a three-year-old girl. The Court concluded that the statements could not be admitted because they "lacked the particularized guarantees of trustworthiness necessary to satisfy the requirement of the Confrontation Clause."

White v. Illinois, 502 U.S. 346 (1992), reexamined the issue of hearsay evidence in child abuse cases. White was convicted on several charges, including aggravated criminal sexual assault. The victim was the four-year-old daughter of a former girlfriend. The prosecution twice attempted to use the victim as a witness. The victim experienced "emotional difficulty on being brought to the courtroom," however, and left in both instances without testifying. The trial court was not asked to make a finding that the victim was unavailable to testify. Instead, the victim's statement about what happened was conveyed by five witnesses with whom the victim had talked within four hours of the incident. Over White's objection, the trial court found three of the witnesses qualified for the spontaneous declaration hearsay exception, while the other two qualified for the medical examination exception. White challenged his conviction on confrontation grounds, asserting that the prosecution was required to show the declarant unavailable to testify before introducing hearsay testimony. The Supreme Court unanimously rejected White's argument. Chief Justice Rehnquist reiterated the evidentiary rationale for allowing hearsay testimony that represents spontaneous declarations and statements made while receiving medical care. The context in which such statements occur provides "substantial guarantees of their trustworthiness." Those same factors that contribute to the statements' reliability "cannot be recaptured even by later in-court testimony." The restrictions that generally apply to hearsay statements reflect a preference for in-court testimony because it permits the opportunity for cross-examination. On the other hand, "where proffered hearsay has sufficient guarantees of reliability to come within a firmly rooted exception to the hearsay rule, the Confrontation Clause is satisfied."

Finally, there are the state "rape-shield" laws designed to protect complaining witnesses in sexual assault prosecutions. In essence, these laws make it difficult for rape defendants to introduce evidence of the victim's past sexual conduct. The Michigan rape-shield law allows a defendant to show that he had a past sexual relationship with the victim. In order to introduce evidence of that relationship, however, the defendant must notify the court and prosecution of his intent to do so within 10 days of the arraignment. If such notice is given by the deadline, a closed hearing is held to determine whether the evidence is relevant and not unduly prejudicial to the victim. The Court reviewed Michigan's rape-shield law in *Michigan v. Lucas*, 500 U.S. 145 (1991). Lucas sought to establish prior sexual involvement with the victim, but he failed to meet the 10-day deadline. As a result, the trial court excluded the evidence. A Michigan appellate court concluded that the law interfered with defendants' rights to effectively confront adverse witnesses and ruled that the Sixth Amendment categorically prohibits such exclusion. However, the Supreme Court disagreed. The Court ruled that exclusion of evidence on procedural grounds does not violate the Confrontation Clause in every instance. Rather, the right to confront may, in appropriate situations, "bow to accommodate other legitimate interests in the criminal trial process." Michigan's law, said Justice O'Connor, represents a "valid legislative determination that rape victims deserve heightened protection against surprise, harassment, and unnecessary invasions of privacy."

Compulsory Process

Rock v. Arkansas, **483 U.S. 44 (1987),** held that hypnosis-enhanced testimony could not be categorically prohibited. Rock was charged with shooting her husband. She twice underwent hypnosis to refresh her memory on details of the incident. The trial court ruled that hypnotically refreshed testimony could not be permitted as a matter of state law and limited Rock's testimony to repeating statements she made prior to hypnosis. The Court said the state rule that excluded all hypnotically refreshed testimony impermissibly interfered with Rock's right to testify on her own behalf. Although the right to present relevant testimony is not without limitation, restrictions "may not be arbitrary or disproportionate to the purposes they are designed to serve." The Arkansas rule did not allow a trial court to consider whether posthypnosis testimony may be admissible in a particular case. As a result, an accused's testimony is "limited to matters that he or she can prove were remembered *before* hypnosis." The Court concluded that the Arkansas rule operated to the detriment of any defendant who underwent hypnosis without regard to the reasons for it, the circumstances under which it took place, or any independent verification of the information it produced. Although hypnosis may be unreliable in some situations, it has been found effective in obtaining certain kinds of information. Arkansas did not justify, in the Court's view, exclusion of all testimony that the defendant was unable to prove to be the product of prehypnosis memory. "Wholesale inadmissibility" of the defendant's testimony in this way the Court found to be an "arbitrary restriction on the right to testify." In addition, hypnotically refreshed testimony is subject to verification by a variety of means, and any inaccuracies produced by the process can be reduced by the use of procedural safeguards and cross-examination. *See also* COMPULSORY PROCESS, p. 632; SIXTH AMENDMENT, p. 323.

Significance   The Court decided that the compulsory process provision of the Sixth Amendment, which gives the accused the right to obtain witnesses in his or her favor, applies to the states through the Fourteenth Amendment in *Washington v. Texas*, 388 U.S. 14 (1967). The issue in *Washington* was whether a state may prohibit "principals, accomplices, or accessories" in the same crime from being witnesses for each other. Washington, charged with murder, wished to use Charles Fuller, a coparticipant in the alleged crime, as a defense witness. Under Texas law, Fuller could testify for the prosecution, but not a codefendant. The Supreme Court unanimously reversed Washington's conviction. The Court held that the right of compulsory process for the defense "stands on no lesser footing than other Sixth Amendment rights" previously held applicable to the states. The Warren Court viewed the Clause as fundamental because, broadly defined, it is the "right to present a defense." The Court was unconvinced that codefendants typically would perjure themselves on behalf of other codefendants. If a witness is convicted and awaiting sentence, or simply awaiting trial, "common sense would suggest that he often has a greater interest in lying in favor of the prosecution rather than against it." The Court concluded that to think that "criminals will lie to save their fellows but not to obtain favors from the prosecution for themselves is indeed to clothe the criminal class with more nobility than one might expect to find in the public at large."

The compulsory process provision of the Sixth Amendment has not frequently been before the Supreme Court, but even the more conservative Courts tend to support defendant claims of interference with their defense. The Court prefers that juries consider as much relevant evidence as possible before making judgments. Two examples illustrate further: *Webb v. Texas*, 409 U.S. 95 (1972), involved judicial intimidation of a defense witness. The witness, serving a sentence on a prior criminal conviction, was admonished by the trial judge about the "dangers of perjury," how a perjury conviction would mean substantial supplement to his sentence, and would impair chances of parole. The witness decided not to testify, and Webb claimed that his only witness had been coerced into not testifying by the trial judge. The Supreme Court agreed. It cited the judge's "threatening" remarks as effectively driving the witness from the stand and denying Webb due process. In the other case, *Cool v. United States*, 409 U.S. 100 (1972), the Court again ruled for the defendant because the defense was impaired by an improper jury instruction. Defendant Cool relied on the testimony of a codefendant. The witness admitted his own guilt, and testified that Cool had nothing to do with the crime. The trial judge gave the jury a lengthy "accomplice instruction" to be used in evaluating the codefendant's testimony. The judge suggested that the testimony was "open to suspicion" and that unless the jury believed the testimony "beyond a reasonable doubt," it should be discarded. The Supreme Court concluded that "the clear implication of the instruction was that the jury should disregard [the codefendant's] testimony." An instruction of that kind "places an improper burden on the defense." Thus *Washington, Webb,* and *Cool* establish a firm expectation that the defense will be able to present a full and undeterred case.

The Court has upheld some limits on the right to compulsory process. The issue in *Taylor v. Illinois*, 484 U.S. 400 (1988), for example, was whether the Compulsory Process Clause permitted the defense to use surprise witnesses. Prior to Taylor's trial, the prosecution filed a discovery motion to obtain a list of defense witnesses. Taylor's response, as well as an amended answer, failed to list a particular witness. After the trial had begun, the defense attorney sought orally to amend the discovery answer to include the previously undisclosed witness. Defense counsel indicated that he had been unable to locate the witness earlier, and he had not included his name on the list. Subsequently, the witness disclosed, among other things, that defense counsel had come to his home prior to trial. The trial judge refused to allow the witness to testify on the grounds that the defense attorney had violated discovery rules. The Supreme Court ruled that disallowing the testimony of the undisclosed witness as a sanction for the discovery violation did not abridge the defendant's compulsory process rights. While noting that violations of the right may occur by imposition of discovery sanctions that preclude testimony by the witness, the right is not an "absolute bar to preclusion." In part this is because there is a "significant difference" between the right to compulsory process and other Sixth Amendment rights. Most Sixth Amendment protections "arise automatically" when the criminal process begins, whereas the compulsory process protection depends on defendant's initiative. The "very nature" of the right requires that its "effective use be preceded by deliberate planning and affirmative conduct." The adversary process "could not function effectively" without adherence to rules of procedure that govern "orderly presentation of facts and arguments."

Edward Scheffer, an airman in the U.S. Air Force, provided federal agents with a urine sample that subsequently tested positive for methamphetamine. He was tried and convicted by general court-martial on several drug charges, including illegal drug use. Shortly after providing the urine sample, Scheffer submitted to a polygraph examination. In the polygraph examiner's judgment, Scheffer's denial of drug use since enlisting in the Air Force was not deceptive. His motion to have the polygraph evidence admitted was denied on the basis of Military Rule of Evidence 707, which makes polygraph evidence inadmissible in court-martial proceedings. Scheffer was convicted on all charges. Over the single dissent of Justice Stevens, the Supreme Court ruled, in *United States v. Scheffer*, 118 S.Ct. 1261 (1998), that a defendant's right to present relevant evidence is subject to reasonable restrictions to accommodate other legitimate interests in the criminal trial process. The Court found Rule 707 to serve several legitimate interests including "ensuring that only reliable evidence" is introduced at trial, "preserving the jury's role" in determining credibility of evidence, and avoiding litigation that is "collateral to the primary purpose" of the trial. Justice Thomas said Rule 707 was neither "arbitrary nor disproportionate" in promoting these ends, nor does it "implicate a sufficiently weighty interest" of the defendant to raise a constitutional concern. State and federal governments have a legitimate interest in ensuring that reliable evidence is presented at trial. The exclusion of unreliable evidence, said Thomas, is the "principal objective of many evidentiary rules." The scientific community, he continued, "remains extremely polarized about the reliability of polygraph techniques." The Court concluded that the Rule 707 exclusion of all polygraph evidence is a "rational and proportional means of advancing the legitimate interest in barring unreliable evidence." The Court found that Rule 707 served a second legitimate governmental interest—preserving the jury's "core function of making credibility determinations in criminal trials." A fundamental premise of our criminal trial system, Thomas said, is that the "jury is the lie detector." In creating rules of evidence, jurisdictions may legitimately be concerned that juries "will give excessive weight to the opinions of a polygrapher." Finally, the rule did not preclude Scheffer from introducing any factual evidence, but only kept him from introducing "expert opinion testimony to bolster his own credibility." Scheffer also testified on his own behalf and conveyed his version of the facts to the court-martial members, leading the Court to conclude that Scheffer's defense was not "significantly impaired by the exclusion of polygraph evidence." Justice Stevens dissented, saying that the Court's decision rested on a "serious undervaluation" of Scheffer's right to present a defense and an "unrealistic appraisal of the importance of the governmental interests that undergird the Rule." Stevens also objected to the "blanket" rule of exclusion. No matter how reliable and how probative the results of any polygraph may be, the rule "categorically denies the defendant any opportunity to persuade the court that the evidence should be received for any purpose."

Competency to Stand Trial

Medina v. California, **505 U.S. 437 (1992),** held that states may require criminal defendants to carry the burden of proof to demonstrate incompetence to stand trial. Justice Kennedy said for the Court that historical practice is "probative of whether a procedural rule can be characterized as fundamental." Lack of "settled tradition" on this issue reflects the absence of any fundamental due process principle. Similarly, contemporary practice reveals that "there remains no settled view of where the burden of proof should lie." Expansion of constitutional rights of the accused "under the open-ended rubric of the due process clause invites undue interference with both considered legislative judgments and the careful balance that the Constitution strikes between liberty and order." A restrained interpretive approach to due process on criminal rights issues requires judges to give state procedural practices "substantial deference." On the substantive issue of allocating the burden of proof, it was the Court's judgment that only a "narrow class" of cases would be affected—those cases in which the evidence supporting competence and incompetence is equally strong. Once a state provides a defendant with access to procedures for making a competency evaluation, said Kennedy, there remains "no basis for holding that due process further requires the State to assume the burden of vindicating the defendant's constitutional right by persuading the trier of fact that the defendant is competent to stand trial." Justices Blackmun and Stevens dissented, and expressed strong reservations about the trial and conviction of a person "about whom the evidence of competency is so equivocal and unclear." *See also* DUE PROCESS CLAUSES, p. 641.

Significance The U.S. Supreme Court ruled in *Medina* that states could require defendants to demonstrate their incompetence to stand trial. *Cooper v. Oklahoma,* 517 U.S. 348 (1996), considered whether a state may require a defendant to show incompetence by satisfying the clear and convincing standard of proof. Cooper was unable to prove incompetency by this standard. He was subsequently tried, convicted, and sentenced for murder. The U.S. Supreme Court unanimously set aside the conviction. Justice Stevens's opinion was based on the premise that the criminal trial of an incompetent defendant violates due process. The "well-settled" standard for incompetence is that a defendant may not be tried unless he or she has "sufficient present capacity" to consult rationally with counsel and possesses a "rational as well as factual understanding of the proceedings" against him or her. Oklahoma argued that the clear and convincing standard reasonably accommodated the opposing interests of the state and the defendant, but the Court was unpersuaded. The Court found no evidence from "traditional and modern practice" to support Oklahoma's claim; only four states currently impose the "heavy burden" on defendants of demonstrating incompetence by the clear and convincing standard. The clear and convincing standard imposes a "significant risk" of an erroneous determination that the defendant is competent. Stevens termed as "dire" the consequences to the defendant of an erroneous competency determination. Such defendants would not be able to communicate effectively with counsel or rationally make "myriad smaller decisions" concerning their defense. By contrast, the injury suffered by the state when a defendant is erroneously determined to be incompetent is "modest." The Court concluded that the defendant's fundamental right to be tried only when competent outweighs a state interest in the "efficient operation of its criminal justice system."

On a related matter, the Court held in *Riggins v. Nevada,* 504 U.S. 127 (1992), that a state cannot require a defendant pursuing an insanity defense to take antipsychotic medication during his or her trial unless there exists "overriding justification." Justice O'Connor said that medicating the defendant might impair his or her defense. Under terms of *Washington v. Harper,* 494 U.S. 210 (1990), Riggins had a due process interest in avoiding involuntary administration of the medication. Once Riggins asserted that interest, Nevada was obligated to prove that the medication was "medically appropriate," and despite less intrusive alternatives, "essential for the sake of Riggins' own safety or the safety of others." In this case, however, the trial court permitted Riggins to be medicated without a determination of need or a review of possible alternatives. Riggins had contended that his trial rights had been violated because he was kept from effectively advancing an insanity defense. Although O'Connor did not directly embrace this contention, she did say that the trial court's error "may well have impaired the constitutionally protected trial rights *Riggins* invokes." It was "clearly possible," said O'Connor, that medicating Riggins could have impacted not only on his "outward appearance, but also the content of his testimony on direct and cross-examination, his ability to follow the proceedings, or the substance of his communication with counsel." Justice Thomas, joined by Scalia, were of the view that Riggins's "inability to introduce evidence of his mental condition as he desired did not render his trial fundamentally unfair."

Jury Trials

Lewis v. United States, **518 U.S. 322 (1996),** held that a defendant who is prosecuted in a single proceeding for multiple petty offenses does not have a right to a jury trial, even if the aggregated term of imprisonment exceeds six months. Justice O'Connor indicated that the Court has sought "objective indications" of the level of seriousness society regards an offense by considering the maximum penalty established by the legislature. Because the legislature is "far better equipped" to make such a judgment, the judiciary ought not to substitute its judgment for that of the legislature. The current standard is that if an offense carries a maximum prison term of six months or less, it is presumed to be "petty." Lewis contended that he was entitled to a jury trial because his potential penalty was greater than six months. He argued that the right to a jury trial should be determined on the basis of the aggregate potential prison term. The Court disagreed. The Sixth Amendment is reserved, said O'Connor, for defendants accused of "serious crimes." In this case, Congress categorized the offense of obstructing the mail as petty. The fact that Lewis was charged with two counts of a petty offense "does not revise the legislative judgment as to the gravity of that particular offense, nor does it transform the petty offense into a serious one." Because Lewis was not entitled to a jury trial, the Court did not consider whether the trial judge's "self-imposed limitation" on sentencing to six months or less may affect the right to a jury trial. Justices Kennedy and Breyer found that point significant and agreed that Lewis was not entitled to a jury trial here because he was not going to be imprisoned for longer than six months from the outset of the trial. They sharply disagreed, however, that a defendant convicted of multiple petty offenses in a single proceeding could receive an aggregated prison term of longer than six months without a jury trial. Kennedy characterized the ruling and its practical effect as "one of the most serious incursions on the right to jury trial in the Court's history." There is no limit to the length of sentence a judge can impose without a jury as long the prosecutor "carves up the charges into segments punishable by no more than six months apiece." Justices Stevens and Ginsburg said the right to a jury trial "attaches at the moment of prosecution." A judge may not deprive a defendant of a jury trial by making a pretrial determination that the aggregate sentence will not exceed six months. *See also* JURY, p. 673; SIXTH AMENDMENT, p. 323.

Significance   Jury trials are guaranteed to any defendant charged with a "serious" offense. The Warren Court saw the jury trial as "fundamental to the American scheme of justice," and extended the jury trial provision of the Sixth Amendment to the states in *Duncan v. Louisiana*, 391 U.S. 145 (1968). Justice White said in *Duncan* that the jury trial is granted to criminal defendants in order to "prevent oppression by the Government." The right is an "inestimable safeguard" against the corrupt or overzealous prosecutor and against the "compliant, biased, or eccentric judge." Two years later, the Court distinguished "serious" and "petty" offenses in *Baldwin v. New York*, 399 U.S. 66 (1970). The line was drawn at six months. Imprisonment for six months may result, said Justice White, in "quite serious repercussions affecting his career and his reputation." When the accused faces less than six months imprisonment, the disadvantages, "onerous through they may be, may be outweighed by the benefits which result from speedy and inexpensive nonjury adjudications."

Blanton v. City of North Las Vegas, 489 U.S. 538 (1989), considered whether the right to a jury trial extends to a first-offense driving-while-intoxicated charge for which the maximum detention was six months. The Court unanimously ruled that the penalty faced by first-offense defendants was not sufficiently severe to constitute a "serious" offense for jury trial purposes. The "most relevant criterion" for determining the seriousness of an offense is the "maximum authorized penalty fixed by the legislature." When an offense carries a maximum of less than six months, it is "presumed to be petty" unless it can be shown by the defendant that additional penalties, when viewed "in conjunction with the maximum authorized period of incarceration, are so severe that they clearly reflect a legislative determination that the offense in question is a serious one." Applying this standard to Blanton's first-offense driving-while-intoxicated charge, the Court saw no evidence that the state legislature saw the offense as "serious."

Jury Size

Williams v. Florida, **399 U.S. 78 (1970),** considered whether a jury of fewer than 12 persons satisfies the Sixth Amendment requirement that no state may deny trial by jury in a criminal case—a point settled by the Court in *Duncan v. Louisiana*, 391 U.S. 145 (1968). The Court found that Florida's trial of Williams with a jury of six persons was constitutionally sound. Justice White concentrated on three principles in the opinion of the Court. First, although the jury is deeply rooted in our legal history, White said he found nothing from historical evidence to suggest that the Framers intended that exactly 12 persons should always serve on a jury, or that the number 12 was an "indispensable component" of the Sixth Amendment. Second, juries should be large enough to promote group deliberation, and to be free from "outside attempts at intimidation." The Court found nothing to lead it to believe that this goal was "in any meaningful sense less likely to be achieved when the jury numbers six than when it numbers twelve." Third, juries must "provide a fair possibility for obtaining a representative cross section of the community." The Court found the difference between twelve and six to be "negligible" in this regard. As long as selection processes prevent arbitrary or discriminatory exclusions, the Court felt that "the concern that the cross section will be significantly diminished if the jury is decreased in size from twelve to six seems an unrealistic one." Justice Marshall dissented, arguing that the Fourteenth Amendment required a 12-member jury in cases in which a defendant such as Williams could be sent to prison for the remainder of his life upon conviction. *See also Apodaca v. Oregon*, p. 345; JURY, p. 673; SIXTH AMENDMENT, p. 323.

Significance   *Williams v. Florida* represented an unexpected departure from English common-law tradition, which clearly acknowledged a jury of 12 persons. When *Duncan v. Louisiana* established the fundamental character of the jury trial at the state level, it presumed state juries would have 12 jurors, as do federal juries. The rationale offered by the Court in *Williams* has been subjected to serious criticism, particularly as it relates to the deliberative and representational aspects of twelve- versus six-person juries. The Court did establish subsequently that six was the constitutionally acceptable minimum. In *Ballew v. Georgia*, 435 U.S. 223 (1978), the Court considered a conviction by a five-member jury in a state obscenity case. A unanimous Court, including all five members who had voted in the *Williams* majority eight years earlier, found a five-member jury to be constitutionally defective. The Court's opinion used as its rationale the reasons offered by critics of the Williams decision. The Court found that "effective group deliberation" and the ability adequately to represent a cross section of the community was seriously threatened by a five-member jury. Notwithstanding *Ballew*, the *Williams* decision provided the states with considerable latitude in the use of juries in criminal cases.

Jury Unanimity

Apodaca v. Oregon, **406 U.S. 404 (1972)**, upheld a state criminal conviction by less than a unanimous jury verdict. Apodaca was convicted by an eleven-to-one jury vote. The Court "perceived no difference" between the unanimous and nonunanimous jury. Both fulfilled the "interest of the defendant in having the judgment of his peers interposed between himself and the officers of the State." In response to the argument that nonunanimity detracted from the reasonable-doubt standard, the Court replied that the standard of reasonable doubt "did not crystallize in this country until after the Constitution was adopted." Thus it was not directly required by the Sixth Amendment. Apodaca also argued that nonunanimity diminished the representativeness of a jury and allowed convictions "to occur without the acquiescence of minority elements within the community." The Court rejected this argument by saying it is not necessary that every "distinct voice in the community" be represented on every jury. The Court also rejected the notion that minority viewpoints would not be adequately represented even when convictions were obtained. They "found no proof for the notion that a majority will disregard its instructions and cast its vote for guilt or innocence based on prejudice rather than the evidence." Justice Blackmun admitted "great difficulty" with the prospect of a seven-to-five conviction. A nine-to-three conviction was, however, "a substantial" enough majority for Blackmun. Justice Powell preferred the unanimity requirement at the federal level to honor the Sixth Amendment, but allowed the states some latitude to deviate from the unanimity requirement. Justices Brennan, Marshall, Douglas, and Stewart dissented, citing "diminution of verdict reliability" because juries not needing unanimity need not deliberate as fully, and possibly not deliberate at all. Justice Marshall, in a separate dissent, focused on the "beyond reasonable doubt" standard, feeling the doubts of the three impeached the verdict of the nine. *See also* JURY, p. 673; SIXTH AMENDMENT, p. 323; *Williams v. Florida*, p. 344.

Significance   *Apodaca* highlighted the level of confidence that can be achieved with jury decisions. Many contend that the reasonable-doubt standard is eroded by the nonunanimous verdict, and the increased likelihood of conviction it brings. Like the 12-person jury, the unanimity standard had been viewed as an integral part of the criminal process. It still is so in the federal courts. Taken together with *Williams v. Florida*, 399 U.S. 78 (1970), however, the Court left the jury trial a less effective right in state criminal proceedings. The Court later established that conviction in a state criminal case coming on a five-to-one vote is unsatisfactory. In *Burch v. Louisiana*, 441 U.S. 130 (1979), the unanimous view of the Court was that when a constitutional minimum of six jurors sit on a criminal case, nothing less than unanimity will suffice. *Apodaca* established that nonunanimous convictions on votes that may be split as much as nine to three are adequate, however. The sufficiency of margins less than nine to three for twelve-person juries, and split decisions from juries numbering more than six but fewer than twelve, remains to be defined. *Apodaca* and *Williams* opened doors regarding jury decision and size long thought to be locked shut. Many states have accepted the Court's invitation to alter their policies accordingly.

Jury Selection

***J.E.B. v. Alabama ex rel. T.B,* 511 U.S. 127 (1994)** The Supreme Court ruled in *Batson v. Kentucky*, 476 U.S. 79 (1986), that the state cannot use peremptory challenges to remove prospective jurors solely on the basis of race. The Court extended the *Batson* ruling to gender in *J.E.B. v. Alabama ex rel. T.B.* T.B. was a defendant in a paternity action. The state used nine of its ten peremptory challenges to remove male jurors. As a consequence, the case was tried by an all-female jury. The jury concluded that T.B. was the child's father. The Alabama appellate courts ruled that the *Batson* rule did not extend to gender-based discrimination, but the Supreme Court disagreed. Discrimination in jury selection, Justice Blackmun said, "whether based on race or on gender," causes harm to litigants, the community, and the individual jurors who are "wrongfully excluded from participation in the judicial process." The Court found virtually no support for the conclusion that gender alone is an accurate predictor of jurors' attitudes and refused to "condone the same stereotypes that justified the wholesale exclusion of women from juries and the ballot box." The state, Blackmun said, "seems to assume that gross generalizations that would be deemed impermissible if made on the basis of race are somehow permissible when made on the basis of gender." Since *Batson*, Blackmun continued, we have "reaffirmed repeatedly our commitment to jury selection procedures that are fair and nondiscriminatory." In this case, the Court reaffirmed what, "by now, should be axiomatic: Intentional discrimination by state actors violates the

Equal Protection Clause, particularly where, as here, the discrimination serves to ratify and perpetuate invidious, archaic and overbroad stereotypes about the relative abilities of men and women." Like race, gender is an "unconstitutional proxy for juror competence and impartiality." Justice O'Connor concurred that the Equal Protection Clause of the Fourteenth Amendment precludes exclusion from jury service on the basis of gender. The "blow against gender discrimination is not costless," however. She characterized *Batson* as "intrus[ive]" in the jury selection process, citing the "now routine" *Batson* "mini-hearings" in state and federal courts. She predicted that by further "constitutionalizing" jury selection procedures, the Court increases the number of cases in which jury selection, "once a sideshow, will become part of the main event." She suggested that "one need not be sexist to share the intuition that in certain cases, a person's gender and resulting life experience will be relevant to his or her view of [a] case." Individuals are not expected to ignore as jurors what they know as men or women. O'Connor's concern was that this ruling "severely limits a litigant's ability to act on this intuition, for the import of our holding is that any correlation between a juror's gender and attitudes is irrelevant as a matter of constitutional law." Justice Scalia, joined by Chief Justice Rehnquist and Justice Thomas, dissented. They understood the Court to find that peremptory challenges on the basis of any characteristic subject to heightened scrutiny are unconstitutional under the Equal Protection Clause. Such a conclusion can only be reached, said Scalia, by "focusing unrealistically upon individual exercises of the peremptory challenges and ignoring the totality of the practice." Because all groups are subject to the peremptory challenge, Scalia concluded, "it is hard to see how any group is denied equal protection." *See also* JURY, p. 673; SIXTH AMENDMENT, p. 323.

Significance   A number of jury selection decisions, including *J.E.B.*, do not raise Sixth Amendment questions. Rather, the Court's rulings are grounded in the Equal Protection Clause. Discussion of these cases appears in this chapter, however, because of the direct impact on the selection of trial juries for criminal cases, and because the issues in these cases parallel the ground rules for selecting a representative and impartial jury, ground rules that have developed from the Sixth Amendment.

   Batson v. Kentucky had its origin in *Norris v. Alabama*, 294 U.S. 587 (1935). The *Norris* case, an appeal growing out of the notorious Scottsboro trial, prohibited systematic exclusion of persons from jury service on the basis of race. *Norris* allowed discriminatory practice to be inferred from statistics showing an absence of racial minorities from juries. Thirty years later, the Court dealt with the use of peremptory strikes against claims of purposeful discrimination in *Swain v. Alabama,* 380 U.S. 202 (1965). *Swain* was brought to the Supreme Court because more subtle methods of discrimination, such as using strikes to remove minority jurors, had been designed following *Norris* to minimize the involvement of blacks and others in jury service. The Court's decision in *Swain* did not abandon the basic thrust of *Norris* in terms of systematic exclusion, but it made the burden of proving discriminatory practice much more difficult. Since *Swain,* challenges based on less severe underrepresentation than was present in *Swain* have prevailed in establishing a prima facie case of discrimination in more recent cases. Nevertheless, there remains no specific expectation that population ratios must be reflected in specific juries.

Cases such as *Taylor v. Louisiana,* 419 U.S. 522 (1975), and *Duren v. Missouri,* 439 U.S. 357 (1979), rejected certain state selection methods on the grounds that they systematically excluded women from jury service. But the Court has continued generally to defer to the states in the establishment and administration of techniques designed to draw juries and assure that they are a representative cross section of the community.

A significant change in policy on peremptory challenges occurred in *Batson* when the Court held that the Equal Protection Clause precludes racially discriminatory use of peremptory challenges of potential jurors by prosecutors. During Batson's burglary trial, the prosecutor used his peremptory challenges to remove all four black persons from the venire. Batson was subsequently convicted by an all-white jury. The Supreme Court used the *Batson* case to reexamine the element of *Swain* dealing with the burden of evidence that a defendant must demonstrate in support of any claim of discriminatory use of peremptory challenges, and shifted much of the burden previously resting with the defendant to the prosecution. The Court reaffirmed that exclusion of minorities from jury service was an evil that the Fourteenth Amendment was designed to cure, as purposeful racial discrimination violates a defendant's right to a venire of jurors who are "indifferently chosen." Beyond its impact on defendants, the Court introduced a theme maintained since then that such discrimination unlawfully denies minorities an opportunity to participate in jury service and "undermines public confidence in the fairness of our system of justice." Under *Swain,* a defendant was required to demonstrate an ongoing pattern of discrimination in order to set aside a conviction. The *Batson* Court viewed this requirement as a "crippling burden of proof," and one that left prosecutorial strikes "largely immune from constitutional scrutiny." Accordingly, the Court concluded that a defendant may establish a prima facie case of intentional discrimination based exclusively on a prosecutor's use of the peremptory challenges at the defendant's trial. Once a defendant establishes such a prima facie case, the burden shifts to the state to offer a neutral explanation for challenging black jurors. The explanation need not rise to the level justifying exercise of a challenge for cause. The Court reiterated its recognition that the peremptory challenge "occupies an important position in our trial procedures." At the same time, the practice has been used as a means of discrimination. By requiring trial courts to be sensitive to discriminatory use of the procedure, *Batson* "enforces the mandate of equal protection and furthers the ends of justice." Justice Marshall would have gone further. Citing "common and flagrant" abuses of the peremptory challenge, he urged elimination of this step from the jury selection process. Chief Justice Burger and Justice Rehnquist dissented, voicing a preference for the evidentiary standard established in *Swain*.

The Court has expanded *Batson* several times since 1986. The Court included selection of grand jurors within *Batson* in *Vasquez v. Hillery*, 474 U.S. 254 (1986). In that case the Court ruled that even if the grand jury's action is "confirmed in hindsight" by a conviction on the indicted offense, the confirmation "does not suggest that discrimination did not impermissibly infect the framing of the indictment and, consequently, the nature or existence of the proceedings to come." A conviction simply cannot be "understood to cure the taint attributable to a charging body selected on the basis of race."

Powers v. Ohio, 499 U.S. 400 (1991), focused on the race of the defendant claiming a *Batson* violation. The prosecution used peremptory challenges to remove seven black jurors from Powers's jury. Powers, a white murder defendant, unsuccessfully asserted a *Batson* objection at trial. On appeal, Powers contended that his own race was irrelevant to an attempt to file a *Batson*-based objection to the discriminatory use of peremptory challenges. Ohio countered that *Batson* should be confined to the circumstances of that case, and that the race of the objecting defendant is a relevant precondition for a *Batson* challenge. The Court rejected both state arguments. *Batson* was designed, said Justice Kennedy, to serve "multiple ends, only one of which was to protect individual defendants from discrimination in the selection of jurors." *Batson* recognized as well that discriminatory use of peremptory challenges harms the excluded juror and the community at large. Racial exclusion directly violates the "overriding command" of the Equal Protection Clause because race is unrelated to a person's fitness to serve as a juror and cannot be used as a "proxy for determining juror bias or competence."

Another aspect of *Batson* was examined in *Hernandez v. New York*, 500 U.S. 352 (1991). In *Hernandez*, the prosecutor used some of his peremptory challenges to remove the only Latino prospective jurors. Hernandez raised a *Batson* objection, but before the trial court ruled on whether a prima facie case existed, the prosecutor offered an explanation for their removal. Both of the removed jurors were bilinguals, and it was the prosecutor's impression that when he asked them whether they would accept the court translator as the final word on witness testimony, both "looked away" and hesitatingly said they "would try." The Supreme Court ruled that the exclusion of the Latino jurors was race neutral and affirmed Hernandez's conviction. Justice Kennedy attempted to keep the ruling narrow, saying that the exclusion of persons because they are bilingual may be neither "wise" nor constitutional in all cases. Kennedy considered discriminatory effect a relevant measure of impermissible conduct, but a constitutional violation requires a showing of intent in addition. Language is an unacceptable basis of exclusion of Hispanics as such. A general pattern of exclusion on the basis of language might constitute a pretext for unlawful discrimination. Kennedy, however, was satisfied with the trial court's finding that the basis for the prosecutor's peremptory strikes in this case was the "specific responses and demeanor" of the jurors and not the fact that they were Hispanic or bilingual.

The *Batson* rule was extended to civil juries in *Edmonson v. Leesville Concrete, Inc.*, 500 U.S. 614 (1991). Justice Kennedy said that racial discrimination in selecting a jury for a civil proceeding "harms the excluded juror no less than discrimination in a criminal trial." Although the conduct of private parties is often beyond the reach of the Constitution, Kennedy drew upon the concept of state action as the foundation for the ruling. State action exists when private parties make "extensive use of state procedures with the overt, significant assistance of state officials." Without government participation, the peremptory challenge system as well as the jury trial system of which it is a part "simply could not exist." By enforcing discriminatory use of peremptory challenges, a court has not only become party to the discrimination but has "elected to place its power, property, and prestige" behind any discrimination. The peremptory challenge, said Kennedy, is used in selecting an "entity that is a quintessential governmental body, having no attributes of a private actor."

The Court further extended the reach of *Batson* and the reasoning of *Edmonson* once again in *Georgia v. McCollum*, 505 U.S. 42 (1992), holding that—like the prosecution—criminal defendants also cannot exclude prospective jurors on the basis of race. Extension of *Batson* in this way, said Justice Blackmun, is designed to "remedy the harm done to the dignity of persons and the integrity of the courts" by race-based discrimination. Whether at the initiative of the state or the defense, if a court allows exclusion of jurors because of group bias, it becomes a "willing participant in the scheme that could only undermine the very foundation of our system of justice—our citizens' confidence in it." It was the Court's conclusion that racial exclusion of jurors by the defendant constituted state action. The jury system performs "critical governmental functions," functions that are both "unique and constitutionally compelled" in a criminal case. Whether exclusion of jurors results from actions of the prosecution or the defense, the "perception and the reality in a criminal trial will be that the court has excused jurors based on race, an outcome that will be attributed to the State."

Under Louisiana law, grand jury forepersons were selected by the judge before the remainder of the grand jury were randomly selected. A grand jury indicted Terry Campbell for second-degree murder. Campbell offered evidence that an African American had not been selected as a grand jury foreman for more than 16 years, even though more than 20 percent of the registered voters in the Parish were African American, and sought to quash the indictment on the grounds of racially discriminatory selection procedures. The motion was denied because Campbell, who was white, lacked standing to complain about the exclusion of racial minorities from serving as grand jury forepersons. Campbell was subsequently convicted and sentenced to life in prison without the possibility of parole. The Supreme Court ruled in *Campbell v. Louisiana*, 118 S.Ct. 1419 (1998), that the preconditions found in *Powers* for a litigant to assert the rights of a third party had been met here as well. A defendant such as Campbell suffers "serious injury in fact" because discrimination casts doubt on the integrity of the judicial process. In addition, the excluded juror and the criminal defendant have a "close relationship." They share a "common interest" in eliminating discrimination, and the defendant has an incentive to serve as an "effective advocate because a victory may result in overturning his conviction." Finally, a juror dismissed because of race probably will leave the courtroom possessing "little incentive to set in motion the arduous process needed to vindicate his own rights." Grand juries are used to initiate a prosecution and serve as a check against the wrongful exercise of power by the state and its prosecutors. The grand jury controls not only the initial decision to indict but also decisions such as how many counts to charge and whether to charge a greater or lesser offense. The integrity of these decisions "depends on the integrity of the process used to select the grand jurors." If that process is "infected with racial discrimination, doubt is cast over the fairness of all subsequent decisions."

Jury Selection: Voir Dire

Lockhart v. McCree, **476 U.S. 162 (1986),** determined that opponents of capital punishment may be excluded from juries in death penalty cases. McCree was tried for capital felony murder in a state proceeding. Prior to the guilt adjudication phase of a two-stage capital trial, the judge removed for cause all prospective jurors who indicated they could not impose the death penalty. A jury subsequently convicted McCree, but rejected the death penalty at the sentencing stage. Instead, it set punishment at life imprisonment without parole. McCree contended that the "death qualification" of the jurors remaining to determine his guilt or innocence deprived him of an impartial jury chosen from a representative cross section of the community, but the Supreme Court ruled against him. Justice Rehnquist pointed out several flaws in the evidence used by the lower courts to find that the death qualification produces conviction-prone juries. Even if the proposition could be demonstrated, Rehnquist said, the Constitution does not preclude use of death-qualified juries in capital trials. The fair cross-section requirement cannot be applied to limit use of either for cause or peremptory challenges or to require that petit juries (as distinct from jury panels or venires) reflect composition of the community at large. Further, the essence of a fair cross-section claim is the systematic exclusion of a distinctive group in the community. Groups defined solely in terms of shared attitudes that would substantially impair their functioning as jurors are not distinctive groups for fair cross-section purposes. Exclusion here did not occur for reasons completely unrelated to the ability of members of the group to function as jurors. This differentiated the *Lockhart* case from those in which exclusion of a distinctive group arbitrarily skewed the composition of a jury and denied defendants the benefit of community judgment. *See also* JURY, p. 673; SIXTH AMENDMENT, p. 323.

Significance   *Lockhart v. McCree* is one of the most recent of a series of decisions dealing with the troublesome issue of juror impartiality in capital cases. In *Witherspoon v. Illinois*, 391 U.S. 510 (1968), the Court found that a jury that is uncommonly willing to condemn a person to death may not be selected. Yet the Court refused to announce a blanket constitutional rule requiring the reversal of every jury selected in the Illinois fashion. The Court said simply that in this case the jury "fell woefully short of that impartiality to which petitioner was entitled under the Sixth and Fourteenth Amendments." Justice Stewart found it clear that imposing the death penalty by a "hanging jury" would deprive the defendant of his life without due process of law. *Witherspoon*, however, was decided before the states were required to use two-stage processes separately to adjudicate guilt and then consider sentence. Since 1976 opponents of the death penalty have typically been excluded from both stages. This produced several follow-up cases. While *Witherspoon* remains in effect to a degree, the modifications brought in later cases up through

Lockhart stem from the bifurcation requirement. In *Davis v. Georgia*, 429 U.S. 122 (1976), the Court voided the death sentence of a state prisoner whose sentence had been imposed by a jury from which one prospective juror had been excluded because of general reservations about the death penalty. In *Adams v. Texas*, 448 U.S. 38 (1980), the Court considered whether a state could exclude from a jury those persons unable to swear under oath that the extant possibility of the death penalty would not affect their deliberations. With only Justice Rehnquist dissenting, the Court decided that *Witherspoon* required reversal of the oath process. While still allowing exclusion of people who cannot be impartial, the Court was not satisfied that irrevocable opposition could be inferred from failure to swear to the impossibility of imposing the death penalty. The *Witherspoon* test for exclusion established that jurors could be excluded for cause only if they make it unmistakably clear they would automatically vote against the death penalty without regard to evidence. The Court modified this standard in *Wainwright v. Witt*, 469 U.S. 412 (1969), in which it held that a better criterion was whether a prospective juror's views would prevent or substantially impair performance of the juror function. *Wainwright* modified the *Witherspoon* automatic judgment language to say that in order to exclude for cause, a juror's bias need not be shown with unmistakable clarity. *Lockhart* clearly moved even further in the direction of allowing a death qualification for prospective jurors. *Lockhart* permitted the prosecution to have removed any prospective juror who indicates that he or she could not under any circumstances impose a death sentence.

In *Morgan v. Illinois*, 504 U.S. 719 (1992), the Court ruled that criminal defendants have a comparable right to remove prospective jurors who would automatically impose the death sentence upon conviction. Justice White said that a juror who will automatically rule for the death penalty "will fail in good faith to consider the evidence of aggravating and mitigating circumstances" as the jury instructions require. Because such a juror has already formed a judgment on sentence, presence or absence of either aggravating or mitigating circumstances is "entirely irrelevant." Accordingly, capital defendants must be permitted during voir dire to "ascertain whether his prospective jurors function under such misconception." Justices Scalia, Rehnquist, and Thomas disagreed. Scalia argued that because the Sixth Amendment does not require jury participation in capital sentencing proceedings, the "subsidiary requirement that the requisite jury be impartial" is not necessary either.

The voir dire process precedes peremptory challenges in the jury selection process. *Ristaino v. Ross*, 424 U.S. 589 (1976), considered the question of whether a defendant is constitutionally entitled to ask questions specifically directed toward racial prejudice during the voir dire examination of prospective jurors. The trial judge denied the defendant's motion to pose the question, and a black defendant was subsequently convicted in a state court of violent crimes against a white victim. The Supreme Court upheld the trial judge's decision. Justice Powell reasoned that the Constitution "does not always entitle a defendant to have questions posed during voir dire specifically directed to matters that conceivably might prejudice veniremen against him." Though circumstances might warrant specific questions about racial prejudice, these are matters to be handled through the exercise of "sound discretion" by the trial court, a function "particularly within the province of the trial judge." The mere fact that the victim and the defendant are of different races was not in itself something that was "likely to distort the trial." Therefore, the defendant was not entitled to voir dire questions pursuing race prejudice. *Ristaino* is representative of the Burger Court's view of what kinds of questions a defendant is entitled to pursue during a voir dire examination. The voir dire process refers to a series of questions posed to prospective jurors to determine their impartiality. A prospective juror found to be partial on the basis of his or her responses is excused from service on a given jury "for cause." The supervision of voir dire rests with the trial judge. *Ristaino* decided that a trial judge's discretion has been properly exercised when a defendant is denied the opportunity to probe the racial prejudice of prospective jurors simply because the defendant and victim of the crime are of different races. *Ristaino* underscored the requirement that a defendant must demonstrate unusual circumstances, such as the presence of a racial issue as an actual component of a particular case. A similar holding involving national origin was made in *Rosales-Lopez v. United States*, 451 U.S. 182 (1981), in which a Mexican defendant, on trial for illegally bringing Mexican aliens into the country, wished to ask potential jurors about possible prejudice toward Mexicans. In *Ham v. South Carolina*, 409 U.S. 524 (1973), by contrast, the Court concluded that questions relating to racial prejudice *were* appropriate given the defendant's high visibility in the civil rights movement in the locality of his trial. *Ristaino*, *Ham*, and *Rosales-Lopez* place the monitoring of the jury selection process, specifically the conduct of the voir dire examination, exclusively in the hands of the trial judge.

This rule was modified for capital cases in *Turner v. Murray*, 476 U.S. 28 (1986). The Court said that a capital defendant accused of an interracial crime is entitled to have prospective jurors informed of the race of the victim and questioned on the issue of racial bias during voir dire. The Court believed that the risk of racial prejudice infecting a capital sentencing proceeding is especially serious in light of the finality of the death sentence.

The Court has also held that a juror's failure properly to answer a question during voir dire does not require retrial. In *McDonough Power Equipment, Inc. v. Greenwood*, 464 U.S. 548 (1984), the Court said that unless a showing can be made that failure to disclose actually denied a party an impartial jury, at least in civil cases, the invalidation of a jury decision is not required. To mandate vacating the jury decision in such a circumstance would be "to insist on something closer to perfection than our judicial system can be expected to give."

Mu'Min v. Virginia, 500 U.S. 415 (1991), considered the outer limits of the voir dire examination in cases in which there is the possibility of prejudicial pretrial publicity. Mu'Min was charged with murder in a case that received substantial publicity. His attorney sought to have prospective jurors individually examined and proposed voir dire questions to probe the specific information to which members of the venire had been exposed. The trial court denied Mu'Min's motions and examined prospective jurors as a group and then in smaller groups of four. A jury was eventually empaneled, Mu'Min was convicted, and the Supreme Court affirmed the conviction. Chief Justice Rehnquist said that trial courts have historically been accorded wide discretion in conducting voir dire. The voir dire must "cover the subject" of the pretrial publicity, but need not do more. Rehnquist acknowledged that focused inquiries on the content of news reports might be revealing of a juror's "general outlook," and be helpful in making decisions about when to use peremptory challenges. At the same time, the Court was not convinced that such benefit should become the basis of a constitutional requirement. Constitutionally compelled questions must be more than merely "helpful" in assessing impartiality. The questions the Constitution requires are those that render a trial "fundamentally unfair" if they go unasked.

Pretrial Publicity

Sheppard v. Maxwell, **384 U.S. 333 (1966),** considered whether pervasive pretrial publicity, most of which was highly adverse to the defendant, deprived him of the fair trial mandated by the Sixth Amendment. Every stage of the *Sheppard* case was subjected to intensive media coverage, from inquest to indictment and through the trial itself. The general substance of the coverage given Sheppard was hostile. Jurors were subjected to continuous publicity. Sheppard was eventually convicted of the murder of his wife, but the Supreme Court reversed the conviction. The Court focused its discussion on the failures of the trial judge adequately to provide Sheppard with the "judicial serenity and calm to which he was entitled." Specifically, the trial judge should have more aggressively applied rules governing media in the courtroom, better insulated the witnesses from media coverage, limited the flow of information to the media from principles in the case, and admonished the media to monitor the accuracy of their reports. The Court found the failure properly to insulate the jury to be the most glaring error in the trial. Several jurors admitted hearing media broadcasts about the case while serving. The Court said Sheppard's trial turned into an avoidable "carnival," and deprived him of the fair trial to which he was entitled. *See also Richmond Newspapers, Inc. v. Virginia*, p. 357; SIXTH AMENDMENT, p. 323.

Significance   *Sheppard* focused on the tension existing between a defendant's right to a fair trial and the First Amendment right of a free press to cover newsworthy events. The press has always had some potential to jeopardize the fairness of criminal proceedings, but the increased capacity of the broadcast media to reach mass audiences has increased that potential dramatically. Virtually an entire community can be reached with information that may have a prejudicial effect on a particular case. The *Sheppard* case portrays these prejudicial effects at their worst. The result was that the Court did not even require Sheppard to identify any *actual* prejudice to him. Since the totality of the circumstances raised the *possibility* of prejudice, that provided a sufficient basis for granting him relief. Even with the excesses that occurred in *Sheppard*, the Court resisted placing direct restrictions on the press. Instead, the Court focused on the trial judge as the key figure in ensuring a fair trial. Justice Clark talked about the option of delaying a trial until publicity had subsided or of changing the venue of a case. He emphasized how the voir dire examination could have been used to determine whether prejudicial publicity existed, and suggested sequestering or isolating juries in particularly visible cases. The caution of the Court in addressing press behavior prompted initiatives elsewhere. The industry itself, through meetings with representatives of trial courts, fashioned media guidelines for covering criminal cases. Much of the press now voluntarily complies.

A subsequent decision, *Murphy v. Florida*, 421 U.S. 794 (1975), provided more clarity on the question of when reported information becomes prejudicial. The Court said in *Murphy* that prospective jurors need not be "totally ignorant" of a case. They need only be able to "reach a verdict based on the evidence presented in the court." The thrust of *Murphy* was reiterated in *Patton v. Yount*, 467 U.S. 1025 (1984), in which the defendant challenged the jury selection process for a retrial following his successful appeal. Although extensive publicity had attended the first trial, the Court felt that the four-year period between trials had greatly reduced "any presumption of prejudice" that existed at the time of the initial trial. The

Court said that when the matter of prejudice was examined, the relevant question was not whether the community remembered the case, but whether the jurors had such fixed opinions that they could not judge impartially. Press treatment of a case, especially one governed by self-imposed limits, does not necessarily mean the publicity is either prejudicial or adverse. The *Sheppard* case, however, clearly demonstrated the need for certain safeguards to ensure a fair trial for criminal defendants.

The Court considered restrictions on an attorney's public comments about pending cases in *Gentile v. State Bar of Nevada*, 501 U.S. 1030 (1991). A Nevada Supreme Court rule prohibited a lawyer from making "extrajudicial comment" to the media that he or she "knows or reasonably should know will have a substantial likelihood of materially prejudicing" a pending proceeding. The rule contained a "safe harbor" provision that indicated some kinds of statements that could be made "without fear of discipline notwithstanding other sections of the rule." Included in this subsection was language allowing a lawyer to state "without elaboration" the "general nature" of the defense. The Court struck down the rule as unlawfully vague because the rule failed to give attorneys "fair notice" of the content that is to be avoided.

Media Coverage of Criminal Proceedings

Richmond Newspapers, Inc. v. Virginia, **448 U.S. 555 (1980)** In *Richmond*, the Court would not permit closure of a trial to the public and media despite the defendant's request that this be done. With only Justice Rehnquist dissenting, the Court held that trial judges could not "summarily close courtroom doors" without interfering with First Amendment protections. The open trial serves a "therapeutic purpose for the community," especially in the instance of shocking crimes. Open trials offer protection against abusive or arbitrary behavior on the part of the state. In other words, they allow the criminal process to "satisfy the appearance of justice." While access to trials is not specifically provided by the First Amendment, it is implicit in the free press provision. The closure order in this case was defective because the trial judge made no specific finding to support such an order. Alternatives to closure were not explored, there was no recognition of any constitutional right for the press or the public to attend the proceeding, and there was no indication that insulating witnesses from media coverage of the trial could not have been handled otherwise. In a concurring opinion, Justice Brennan said that open trials "play a fundamental role in furthering the efforts of any judicial system to assure the criminal defendant a fair and accurate adjudication of guilt or innocence." The open trial is also the means by which a society becomes aware that it is governed reasonably. *See also Sheppard v. Maxwell,* p. 355; SIXTH AMENDMENT, p. 323.

Significance   *Richmond* makes clear that closing trials will not occur without some overriding and demonstrable defense interest. However, a trial may indeed be closed to the public and the press. Some fair trial options may be excessive from a free press standpoint. *Nebraska Press Association v. Stuart,* 427 U.S. 539 (1976), examined the propriety of a "gag order" on the media as a way of preventing prejudicial pretrial publicity in violation of the fair trial requirement of the Sixth Amendment. In this case Judge Stuart restrained the media from "publishing or broadcasting accounts of confessions or admissions made by the accused or facts 'strongly implicative' of the accused" until such time as a jury was impaneled. The crime itself was the murder of six persons. Compliance with the order, as modified by the Nebraska Supreme Court, was achieved. While noting also that the trial judge "acted responsibly, out of a legitimate concern, in an effort to protect the defendant's right to a fair trial," the Court viewed the judge's restraining order as excessive. The Court suggested that truly extraordinary prejudicial publicity must be present in order to consider an action as severe as prior restraint. Given that the gag is a denial of free press, the Court said it must review carefully whether the record justifies such an "extraordinary remedy." Included in such an examination are certain factors such as the "nature and extent" of the coverage, alternative measures and their likely impact on mitigating publicity, and the effectiveness of the gag order in preventing damaging and prejudicial publicity. The Court unanimously concluded that the record was not sufficient to justify a gag order.

Nebraska Press Association dealt with whether the press should be precluded from publishing what it already knows. This is a different problem from *Sheppard,* which focused on remedies *after* prejudicial pretrial publicity has occurred. Although *Nebraska Press Association* stopped just short of invalidating the gag rule altogether, it is clear that the preconditions for a gag order are virtually impossible to satisfy. The Court upheld a protective order issued against publication of all information obtained through the discovery process in the defamation case of *Seattle Times Corp. v. Rhinehart,* 467 U.S. 20 (1984). The Court said that limits on dissemination of information prior to trial implicates press protections "to a far lesser extent than would restraints in other contexts." The Court referred to rules authorizing discovery as "a matter of legislative grace," and said that a litigant has no First Amendment right to access information made available only for purposes of trying his suit. Restraints on discovered information are not limits on a traditionally public source of information.

Because there is opportunity to obtain information that could be damaging, prevention of such damage is sufficient justification for the authorization of protective orders.

Gannett Co. v. De Pasquale, 443 U.S. 368 (1979), posed the question of whether the media could be denied access to a pretrial suppression hearing. If the press is allowed to observe a judicial proceeding, it generally will be allowed to report what it observed. Because both the defense and prosecution agreed to close the proceeding in *Gannett*, the case really asked whether the public has an independent right to an open pretrial judicial hearing. The Court upheld the closed hearing, reasoning that pretrial suppression hearings as distinct from trials pose "special risks of unfairness." The objective of such hearings is to screen out unreliable or illegally obtained evidence. Pretrial publicity about such evidence could "influence public opinion" and "inform potential jurors of inculpatory information wholly inadmissible at the actual trial." As for the public's independent right to access, the Court stressed two points: First, public interest in the application of the Sixth Amendment does not create "a constitutional right on the part of the public." The public interest is protected by the participants in the adversary process. Thus the public has no claim that could displace the defendant's desire to close the proceeding. Second, the common-law tradition recognizes a difference between pretrial proceedings and trials. Pretrial proceedings, "precisely because of [a] concern for a fair trial, were never characterized by the degree of openness as were actual trials." Justices Blackmun, Brennan, Marshall, and White dissented. They concentrated on the benefits of open processes and what they considered to be unconstitutional limitations on the press. Justice Blackmun said that casting fair trial rights in terms of the accused is "not sufficient to permit the inference that the accused may compel a private proceeding simply by waiving that right." *Gannett* sidestepped the censorship question raised in *Nebraska Press Association*. The press was not prohibited from publishing information it already possessed in the *Gannett* case. Rather than consider infringement of the First Amendment rights of a free press, *Gannett* focused on whether a defendant's interest in closing a pretrial hearing supersedes the public's interest in an open proceeding. The decision clearly raised the prospect of all judicial proceedings, even trials, being closed at the initiative of the defense.

Chandler v. Florida, 449 U.S. 560 (1981), examined implementation of media coverage provisions in a trial in which the defendant objected to such coverage as a violation of the Sixth Amendment's requirement of a fair and impartial trial. The Florida Supreme Court, as part of the Florida Code of Judicial Conduct, developed provisions that permitted electronic media and still photographic coverage of trials. The rules conveyed authority over all media coverage to the presiding trial judge. The Supreme Court decided in *Chandler* that, absent a specific showing of prejudice, the Florida program was constitutional. Chief Justice Burger said that an absolute ban on broadcast coverage could not be justified because of potential risk. The Court preferred the Florida approach and was satisfied that leaving the judgment to the trial judge safeguarded a defendant's fair trial rights. The "mere presence" of the broadcast media does not "inherently" adversely affect the process. Rather, the burden is on the defendant to show that his or her case was influenced by the coverage. Chandler could demonstrate no specific adverse impacts of media coverage on his trial that were sufficient to constitute a denial of due process. *Chandler* reflected the Supreme Court's deference to the discretion of trial judges in managing problems relating to media coverage of criminal trials. Just as in *Gannett*, and *Richmond Newspapers*, the Court left critical assessments of possible adverse effects of coverage to the presiding judge. This approach was consistent with the Burger Court's preference for letting the "totality of circumstances" provide the basis for resolving questions of law. Courtroom coverage by electronic media has the potential to be most problematic in terms of fair trial standards. Yet in *Chandler* the Court refused to find such coverage inherently violative of due process as the Warren Court had in *Estes v. Texas*, 381 U.S. 532 (1965). *Chandler* placed the burden of proof with the defendant by requiring the accused to demonstrate prejudice. *Gannett* had allowed an accused simply to request closure. Absent a demonstration of adverse effect, a defendant cannot simply terminate coverage or achieve closure by request alone. The experiment in Florida warrants ongoing attention to determine whether benefits or any liabilities emerge as a result of more extensive media coverage. The Federal Judicial Conference prohibits the use of photography or reading devices in federal courts.

Assistance of Counsel

***Gideon v. Wainwright*, 372 U.S. 335 (1963),** ruled that states must provide indigent defendants with counsel in all felony cases. Gideon was charged with a property felony in Florida and was unable to secure his own defense counsel. He requested appointment of counsel, but the state trial court denied the request. Gideon was convicted and sentenced to five years' imprisonment. The Supreme Court unanimously reversed his conviction. Had Gideon been prosecuted for a federal felony-level offense, he would have had counsel appointed under provisions of *Johnson v. Zerbst*, 304 U.S. 458 (1938). The governing precedent in state cases, however, was *Betts v. Brady*,

316 U.S. 455 (1942), which required "special circumstances" in order to necessitate appointment of counsel. *Gideon* gave the Court an opportunity to reconsider *Betts,* and the Court concluded that denial of counsel to indigent noncapital felony defendants violated the basic concept of due process. The fundamental right to a fair trial "could not be realized if the poor man charged with a crime has to face his accuser without a lawyer to assist him." The right of an accused to defense counsel "may not be deemed fundamental and essential to fair trials in some countries," said Justice Black, "but it is in ours." From the beginning of our constitutional history, great emphasis has been placed on procedural and substantive safeguards "designed to assure fair trials before impartial tribunals in which every defendant stands equal before the law." This "noble ideal" cannot be realized "if the poor man charged with a crime has to face his accusers without a lawyer to assist him." The Court said that *Betts* "had departed from the sound wisdom upon which the Court's holding in *Powell v. Alabama* rested," that *Betts* was "an anachronism when handed down," and "should now be overruled." *See also Argersinger v. Hamlin,* p. 363; COUNSEL, ASSISTANCE OF, p. 635; *Faretta v. California,* p. 373; SIXTH AMENDMENT, p 323.

Significance *Gideon* confirmed a position on counsel in state felony trials that had been evolving since the day *Betts* was decided, and essentially took two forms. First, *Betts* required that trial courts find "special circumstances" before appointing counsel. Initially these special circumstances included capital cases, physical or mental handicap, or a very young defendant. Over time the Court broadened the concept of special circumstances and made denial of counsel impossible in most felony-level cases. Between the late 1940s and the *Gideon* decision, no state conviction was affirmed by the Supreme Court over claims of denial of counsel. The Court was clearly moving toward the position it enunciated in *Gideon.* Second, many states adopted a policy of requiring counsel in all felony cases on their own initiative. By the time *Gideon* was decided, almost half of them had already adopted the policy *Gideon* required, at least for the trial stage of criminal proceedings. Indeed, the attorneys general of 22 states submitted an amicus curiae brief to the Supreme Court on behalf of Gideon. Unlike some of the other Warren Court decisions dealing with rights of the accused, the holding was well received. It ended the uncertainties stemming from the special circumstances rule and established that all felony cases require counsel at the trial stage. With *Gideon* in place, the Court could move on two other critical questions: extending the counsel requirement to misdemeanors, and requiring counsel at other stages in the criminal process. *Gideon* reshaped policy on assistance of counsel, but it also provided the foundation for such decisions as *Miranda v. Arizona*, 384 U.S. 436 (1966). Gideon's lawyer on appeal was Abe Fortas, himself appointed a Supreme Court justice two years later. A popular book on the development of the case, *Gideon's Trumpet* by Anthony Lewis (New York: Vintage Books, 1964), is still widely read and highly regarded. The book was described by one reviewer as an account of "how one lonely man, a poor prisoner, took his case to the Supreme Court—and changed the law of the United States."

Powell v. Alabama, 287 U.S. 45 (1932), first raised the constitutional issue of whether the Due Process Clause of the Fourteenth Amendment required appointment of counsel in a state capital case. *Powell* arose out of the infamous "Scottsboro" trial in which nine black defendants were convicted of rape of two white women in Alabama in 1931. Powell and his codefendants were on trial for their lives in a wholly hostile environment. In addition, they were indigent and illiterate. Trial counsel was not named for the defendants until the morning of the trial. All nine defendants were found guilty, but the Supreme Court reversed the convictions. The Court determined that counsel was "fundamental" to due process, at least in capital cases. The trial judge in the Scottsboro case failed to give reasonable time and opportunity to secure counsel for the preparation of a defense. In a capital case in which the defendant is unable to employ counsel and is "incapable adequately of making his own defense because of ignorance, feeblemindedness, illiteracy or the like," a trial judge, whether requested to or not, must assign counsel for him or her as a necessary requisite of due process. The assignment obligation can only be fulfilled if counsel is assigned in time to allow the "giving of effective aid in the preparation and trial of the case." A criminal defendant requires "the guiding hand of counsel at every step in the proceeding against him." Although the Court did not indicate the stage of the proceedings at which counsel might be required, clearly it was required at the latest at the trial stage in a state criminal proceeding. *Powell* was a limited decision in that it involved only state capital cases and was bound by an unusual fact situation. Nonetheless, *Powell* had substantial impact on policy regarding assistance of counsel in two ways: First, it tied the Sixth Amendment Counsel Clause to the states through the Due Process Clause of the Fourteenth Amendment for the first time, albeit only for capital cases at the trial stage. Second, *Powell* changed the direction of Court policy on assistance of counsel. For some time prior to *Powell*, many argued that the Sixth Amendment merely allowed a defendant to have counsel—that the state could not keep a defendant from bringing counsel into court. *Powell* became the basis for establishing assistance of counsel as an indispensable requirement of fairness. It was only a matter of time until the Court examined the requirement of providing counsel in noncapital felonies. In *Johnson v. Zerbst,* 304 U.S. 458 (1938), the Court ruled that in all federal felonies counsel must be provided to indigent defendants. Although limited to federal cases, *Zerbst* extended *Powell* beyond capital cases and established that, without a knowing and voluntary waiver by the defendant, counsel must be appointed for federal criminal trials. *Zerbst* also took *Powell* to the threshold of application of a parallel counsel policy at the state level, accomplished in *Gideon.*

Argersinger v. Hamlin, 407 U.S. 25 (1972), extended the *Gideon v. Wainwright,* 372 U.S. 335 (1963), doctrine to indigent defendants at the misdemeanor level. *Gideon* required that all indigent felony defendants be provided counsel at state expense. Argersinger was convicted of an offense punishable by up to six months' imprisonment. He was indigent and unrepresented by counsel. In a unanimous decision, the Supreme Court found his trial and conviction to be constitutionally defective. The opinion of the Court stressed that there was no historical evidence to suggest that Sixth Amendment rights should be retractable in cases involving petty offenses. It was the Court's view that the legal issues of a case should be the criterion for assessing necessity of counsel—cases in which lesser terms of imprisonment result may not be any less complex than cases in which lengthy sentences may be imposed. The assembly-line character of misdemeanor proceedings also made assistance of counsel especially valuable. The basic holding of *Argersinger* is that absent a "knowing and intelligent waiver," no defendant may receive jail or prison time unless the accused was represented by counsel at his or her trial. Several members of the Court wrote concurring opinions addressing the decision's implementation problems, but the basic holding was unanimous and included all four appointees of President Nixon. *See also* COUNSEL, ASSISTANCE OF, p. 635; *Gideon v. Wainwright,* p. 360; SIXTH AMENDMENT, p. 323.

Significance   *Argersinger* revealed the tension between abstract principles and implementation considerations. On the one hand, the Court wished to extend *Gideon* as far as possible. On the other hand, the Court was faced with implementation of policy where the court system is most congested and where pressures for "assembly-line justice" are most acute. *Argersinger* fashioned a compromise. It recognized that the legal needs of misdemeanor defendants may be as complex as those facing defendants in felony cases. It also provided trial judges with the choice of not appointing counsel, although in refusing to do so, the trial judge must forfeit imprisonment as a sentence option. Despite the implementation problems, *Argersinger* fundamentally altered the process of justice in misdemeanor courts, often called city courts, municipal courts, or Justice of the Peace courts. It also produced important legislation at the state and local level. Many cities now appoint or contract with counsel to provide legal assistance to persons who desire to try misdemeanor charges. Some states have decriminalized most traffic offenses in order to avoid the consequences of *Argersinger.*

Argersinger was refined in *Scott v. Illinois,* 440 U.S. 367 (1979), in which the Supreme Court held that a state court does not have to appoint counsel when imprisonment is authorized for a particular offense, but is not actually imposed. *Argersinger* and *Scott* together require greater caution by state and local governments in criminal proceedings. Many local judges are loath to imprison for misdemeanor convictions when defense counsel is not present, unless the defendant was made aware of his or her right to counsel before tendering a guilty plea.

The *Scott* emphasis on actual incarceration was reinforced in *Lassiter v. Department of Social Services,* 452 U.S. 18 (1981), in which the Court held that counsel need not be provided to an indigent parent at a hearing that could result in termination of his or her status as a parent. The Court said an indigent litigant was entitled to counsel only when the litigant is threatened with the deprivation of physical liberty.

On a related matter, the Court held in *Ake v. Oklahoma,* 470 U.S. 68 (1985), that an indigent defendant seeking to utilize the insanity defense is entitled to court-appointed psychiatric assistance. Justice Marshall wrote that a trial or sentencing proceeding is fundamentally unfair if the state proceeds against an indigent without ensuring that he or she has access to advice that is "integral to the building of an effective defense." The impact of *Ake* is limited in that the great majority of states already provided such aid to indigent defendants.

Perry v. Leeke, 488 U.S. 272 (1989), considered whether a defendant could be barred from conversing with his attorney during a 15-minute recess in proceedings. The recess occurred after the defendant had testified on direct examination, but before cross-examination had taken place. When a defendant becomes a witness, rules that serve the "truth-seeking" function of trials are applicable to him as well as to witnesses generally. A judge must be able to determine if cross-examination is "more likely to elicit truthful responses" if it occurs without allowing a witness to consult with counsel. The Court was concerned with more than "unethical coaching" taking place. Effective cross-examination, said the Court, "often depends" on the ability to "punch holes" in testimony "at just the right time, in just the right way." Consultation with counsel after direct examination but before cross-examination gives a witness an "opportunity to regroup and regain a poise and sense of strategy that the unaided witness would not possess." The Court concluded that a trial judge's "unquestioned power" to refuse to declare a recess is akin to limiting consultation. *Federal Trade Commission (FTC) v. Superior Court Trial Lawyers Association*, 493 U.S. 411 (1990), focused on compensation for appointed counsel. The case examined whether a boycott by attorneys who frequently acted as appointed counsel for indigent criminal defendants constituted illegal price-fixing. This case was not decided on Sixth Amendment grounds, but bears directly on the provision of counsel to indigent defendants. The FTC had found the boycott to be a restraint of trade in violation of federal antitrust laws and attempted to enforce its finding. The attorneys, who were seeking increases in the rate of compensation for the court-appointed cases, countered that the boycott was meant to communicate a political message and was, therefore, expression protected by the First Amendment. The Supreme Court disagreed. Justice Stevens said that increasing rates of compensation from the presumably "unreasonably low" preboycott levels produced "better legal representation for indigent defendants." Those considerations, however, were not seen as primary in this case. Instead, the Court concluded that the boycott constituted a "horizontal arrangement among competitors" that was "unquestionably" a "naked restraint of price and output" in violation of antitrust law. The "social justifications" asserted for the restraint of trade "do not make it any less unlawful."

***United States v. Monsanto*, 491 U.S. 600 (1989),** upheld federal forfeiture provisions allowing seizure of assets, including those intended to retain private defense counsel. Under provisions of the Racketeer Influenced and Corrupt Organizations Act (RICO) and the Continuing Criminal Enterprise Act (CCE), the federal government may seize the proceeds of criminal activity. Congress expanded these forfeiture provisions in the Comprehensive Forfeiture Act of 1984, which focused on proceeds from organized crime activities and narcotics trafficking. The issues in *Monsanto* were whether forfeiture covers those assets intended to pay for defense counsel, and if so, whether such compelled forfeiture interferes with a defendant's Sixth Amendment right to counsel. When Monsanto was indicted for various crimes, including RICO and CCE violations, the government obtained a restraining order freezing his assets as a preliminary step in the forfeiture process. Monsanto was unable to secure private counsel because attorneys feared he could not pay their fees. Under terms of the 1984 law, proceeds from criminal activity belong to the government from the time the crime is committed. In addition, the forfeiture applies not only to proceeds still in the hands of the defendant but also proceeds that had been paid to third parties subsequent to the crime. The trial judge appointed counsel for Monsanto after finding that the restraining order had left him virtually indigent. The Supreme Court ruled assets intended to cover attorneys are not exempt from seizure, and that freezing Monsanto's assets did not unconstitutionally interfere with the right to counsel. Justice White saw the language in the Forfeiture Act as "plain and unambiguous." Congress could not have chosen "stronger words to express its intent that forfeiture be mandatory" under circumstances presented in these appeals. Neither does the statute contain any language that "even hints" that assets used for attorneys' fees are not included in the seizable property. By enacting the Forfeiture Act, said White, Congress "decided to give force to the old adage that 'crime does not pay.'" There is no evidence, he continued, that Congress "intended to modify that nostrum to read, 'crime does not pay, except for attorney's fees.'" On the constitutional issue of assistance of counsel, the Court said that "nothing in [the Act] prevents defendants from hiring the attorney of their choice," or disqualify any attorney from serving as a defendant's counsel." A defendant with nonforfeitable assets remains free to retain "any attorney of his choosing." There will be cases like these, however, in which a defendant is unable to retain an attorney of choice. "[I]mpecunious" defendants, said the Court, do not have the right to "choose their counsel." Compulsory forfeiture of assets, even if such forfeiture renders a defendant unable to privately retain counsel, is not unconstitutional because defendants are not entitled to "spend another person's money for services rendered by an attorney." Justices Blackmun, Brennan, Marshall, and Stevens viewed the Sixth Amendment as a bar to congressional interference with the right to counsel. Blackmun said the decision loses sight of the "distinct role of the right to counsel in protecting the integrity of the judicial process." Indeed, if Congress had set out to "undermine the adversarial system as we know it," it could not have "found a better engine of destruction" than to seize assets intended to pay for defense counsel. *See also* ASSET FORFEITURE, p. 617; COUNSEL, ASSISTANCE OF, p. 635; SIXTH AMENDMENT, p. 323.

Significance   *Monsanto* was one of two asset-seizure cases decided by the Rehnquist Court. The second case was *Caplin & Drysdale, Chartered v. United States*, 491 U.S. 617 (1989). Although the fact situation differed, the outcome was identical to *Monsanto*. A law firm's (Caplin & Drysdale) client (Christopher Reckmeyer) was indicted for various narcotics offenses and a CCE violation. The defendant owed the law firm in excess of $26,000 in fees before the indictment, and had made a payment (with two $5,000 checks) on the day prior to his being indicted. That same day before the indictments, the government obtained a court order restraining Reckmeyer from transferring any assets relating to the indictment charges. When the law firm attempted to deposit Reckmeyer's checks, they were returned unpaid under terms of the restraining order. Reckmeyer eventually pleaded guilty, was sentenced, and had virtually all his assets seized. Caplin & Drysdale filed a claim for the two $5,000 checks returned unpaid at the outset, plus additional fees amounting to almost $200,000. As in *Monsanto*, the Court ruled that the assets intended to compensate private counsel were subject to forfeiture. The decision upheld forfeiture of assets even though such action deprived the defendant of the capacity to select private counsel.

A defendant's choice of counsel was also an issue in *Wheat v. United States*, 486 U.S. 153 (1988). The Sixth Amendment generally entitles a defendant to select his or her counsel, but the right does not extend to a selection that creates a conflict of interest with the counsel's other clients. In *Wheat*, the Court reviewed a trial court's refusal, on motion by the prosecution, to allow a defendant to be represented by the same attorney as his codefendants. Two days prior to his trial for participation in an extensive drug distribution conspiracy, Wheat sought to substitute the counsel of his two code-fendants for his original attorney. Wheat and his codefendants were all willing to waive the right to conflict-free counsel. The trial court refused to allow the substitution on the grounds that the conflicts were "irreconcilable and unwaivable" because of the likelihood that Wheat would have to testify at the trial of the second codefendant while the third codefendant was likely to testify at Wheat's trial. The Supreme Court upheld the trial court's denial of the substitution of counsel. The Court noted that the Sixth Amendment right to choose one's own counsel is "circumscribed in ... important respects." In cases in which there is multiple representation, the trial court has a duty to take measures that are "appropriate to protect criminal defendants against counsel's conflicts of interest, including the issuance of separate representation orders."

Swidler & Berlin v. United States, 118 S.Ct. 2081 (1998), arose out of Special Prosecutor Kenneth Starr's investigation of the White House travel office and the dismissal of its employees. Vincent Foster, a deputy White House counsel in the Clinton administration at the time of the dismissals, met with James Hamilton, an attorney at Swidler & Berlin, to seek legal representation concerning the inves-tigations of the dismissals. Hamilton took several pages of notes during the meeting. Less than two weeks later, Foster committed suicide. At the request of the independent counsel, a grand jury issued subpoenas to Hamilton and Swidler & Berlin for the notes. Hamilton responded by arguing that the notes were protected by attorney-client privilege. The Supreme Court ruled that the notes were covered by lawyer-client privilege. The privilege is intended to "encourage full and frank communication" between attorneys and their clients and thereby "promote broader public interests in the observance of law and the administration of justice," said Chief Justice Rehnquist. The question in this case was whether the privilege "survives the death of the client." The special prosecutor argued that the privilege should not prevent disclosure "where the client has died and the information is relevant to a criminal proceeding." It was the Court's judgment that there are "weighty reasons that counsel in favor of posthumous application" of the privilege. Knowing that communications will remain confidential even after death "encourages the client to communicate fully and frankly with counsel." Although the "fear of disclosure and the consequent withholding of information from counsel," said Rehnquist, "may be reduced if disclosure is limited to posthumous disclosure in a criminal context, it seems unreasonable to assume that it vanishes altogether." Clients may be concerned about "reputation, civil liability, or possible harm to friends or family." Posthumous disclosure of such communications "may be as feared as disclosure during the client's lifetime." The Court found it quite plausible that Foster, "perhaps already contemplating suicide," may not have sought Hamilton's counsel had he not been assured the conversation was privileged. The independent counsel argued for a criminal case exception for the privilege, but the Court concluded that although the established exceptions are "consistent with the purposes of privilege, ... a posthumous exception in criminal cases appears at odds with the goals of encouraging full and frank communication and of protecting a client's interests." Justice O'Connor issued a dissent that was joined by Justices Scalia and Thomas. In their view, a criminal defendant's right to exculpatory evidence or a compelling law enforcement need for information may, "where testimony is not available from other sources, override a client's posthumous interest in confidentiality."

Assistance of Counsel: Critical Stages

United States v. Wade, **388 U.S. 218 (1967),** considered whether counsel must be present at a postindictment line-up session. Once the Supreme Court determined in *Gideon v. Wainwright*, 372 U.S. 335 (1963), that assistance of counsel was a fundamental element of due process at the trial stage of any felony prosecution, it followed that assistance of counsel at other stages in the criminal process would have to be evaluated. *Wade* is one of a number of cases that defined the stages critical enough to require assistance of counsel. Justice Brennan said that in addition to counsel's presence at trial, the accused is "guaranteed that he need not stand alone against the State at any stage of the prosecution, formal or informal, in court or out, where counsel's absence might derogate from the accused's right to a fair trial." The Court vacated Wade's conviction and ordered a new trial, saying that the postindictment process was "peculiarly riddled with innumerable dangers and variable factors which might seriously, even crucially, derogate from a fair trial." There exists "grave potential for prejudice, intentional or not, in the pre-trial lineup." The "vagaries" of eyewitness identification are "well known," Brennan continued, and the "annals of criminal law are rife with instances of mistaken identification." The presence of counsel "can often avert prejudice and assure a meaningful confrontation at trial." Further, improper influences may go undetected by a defendant who "experiences the emotional tension which we might expect in one being confronted with potential accusers." The accused also has limited ability to effectively "reconstruct at trial any unfairness that occurred at the lineup," which may deprive him or her of the "only opportunity meaningfully to attack the credibility of the witness' courtroom identification." The Court's conclusion was that there was "little doubt" that the line-up was a "critical stage," a stage at which Wade was entitled to aid of counsel. *See also Argersinger v. Hamlin*, p. 363; COUNSEL, ASSISTANCE OF, p. 635; CRITICAL STAGE, p. 636; *Gideon v. Wainwright*, p. 360; SIXTH AMENDMENT, p. 323.

Significance   *United States v. Wade* was one of a number of rulings examining the question of whether stages of the criminal process other than trial require assistance of counsel. The Warren Court approached the issue through the "critical stage" concept. A critical stage occurs at any point where advice of counsel may be essential to protecting a defendant's rights and where the final outcome is substantially affected. Within five years of *Gideon*, pretrial steps or proceedings such as custodial interrogation prior to charging, postcharge investigations, and preliminary hearings and identifications such as the line-up in *Wade* were found to be critical stages requiring assistance of counsel. These rulings came in *Miranda v. Arizona*, 384 U.S. 436 (1966); *Massiah v. United States*, 377 U.S. 201 (1964); and *White v. Maryland*, 373 U.S. 59 (1963), respectively. Even before *Gideon*, counsel provisions had been extended to arraignments in *Hamilton v. Alabama*, 368 U.S. 52 (1961). Expansion of the concept of critical stage also occurred with respect to posttrial proceedings. In *Douglas v. California*, 372 U.S. 353 (1963), the Court held that counsel was required for those appeals that are a matter of right. Counsel is required for juvenile proceedings under *In re Gault*, 387 U.S. 1 (1967), and at the sentencing stage of adult criminal proceedings. In *Mempa v. Rhay*, 389 U.S. 128 (1967), the Court said that an individual is entitled to counsel in a proceeding in which probation is revoked and a sentence is to be imposed. These cases demonstrate the exceptionally high priority assigned by the Warren Court to making legal counsel available to all persons at most stages of the criminal charge process. They reflect the Court's recognition that other constitutional protections are often best given fullest effect through defense counsel.

In *Pennsylvania v. Finley*, 481 U.S. 551 (1987), the Court ruled that a state law providing assistance of counsel for collateral postconviction proceedings need not require all the procedural protections established for trial and first appeals. The Court said the right to appointed counsel extends to the first appeal, the appeal of right, and no further. An attorney is not required for an indigent simply because an affluent defendant may retain one. The state's obligation is not to duplicate the legal arsenal that may be privately retained in a continuing effort to reverse a conviction. The state need only to assure that the indigent defendant has an adequate opportunity to present his or her claims fully in the context of the state's appellate process. The Court ruled in *Murray v. Giarratano*, 492 U.S. 1 (1989), that Sixth Amendment counsel protection did not require states to provide assigned counsel to indigent death-row inmates as they pursue postconviction review. Currently, states are required under the Sixth Amendment to provide counsel for an appeal of right, but have discretion over whether counsel is provided for additional proceedings. Giarratano claimed that those on death row are entitled to personal counsel assigned to assist them in seeking, for example, habeas corpus relief. The state did provide death-row prisoners with access to a law library, access to a "unit" attorney, and assignment of counsel after the formal filing of a petition. An indigent is entitled as a "matter of right" to counsel for an initial appeal from the "judgment and sentence of the trial court." The right to counsel at the various stages of the criminal process, on the other hand, do not "carry over to a discretionary appeal." The analysis from *Finley* "requires the conclusion" that no different rules should extend to capital cases.

Under a rule established in *Anders v. California*, 386 U.S. 738 (1967), court-appointed counsel wishing to withdraw from a frivolous appeal must submit a withdrawal motion accompanied by a brief that refers to "anything in the record that might arguably support the appeal." A Wisconsin court rule embraced this requirement, but further required that the brief include discussion of "why the issue lacks merit." The case of *McCoy v. Court of Appeals*, 486 U.S. 429 (1988), examined the Wisconsin variation on the *Anders* procedure. McCoy's court-appointed counsel concluded that appeal of McCoy's conviction would be frivolous, but was unwilling to include in his withdrawal brief the additional discussion required by Wisconsin. Counsel unsuccessfully challenged the requirement in the state courts on the grounds that it was incompatible with *Anders* and that it compels counsel to violate a client's right to assistance of counsel. The Court ruled the discussion requirement to be constitutional. In the Court's view, the rule "merely goes one step further than the minimal requirements stated in *Anders*." It serves the "same objectives" of *Anders* of assuring an appellate court that a review has been "diligently and thoroughly" researched, and it allows the reviewing court to "determine whether counsel's frivolous conclusion is correct."

Effectiveness of Counsel

Strickland v. Washington, **466 U.S. 668 (1984),** established a two-part test for examining the effectiveness of defense counsel performance. *Strickland* developed from a death penalty sentencing proceeding that followed guilty pleas to three capital murder charges. During the plea colloquy, Washington said he had no significant prior record and the crimes to which he was pleading were caused by extreme stress produced by his inability to provide for his family. Washington and his counsel discussed approaches to the sentencing hearing, and counsel decided it was inadvisable to call character witnesses or seek psychiatric examination. The decision reflected counsel's judgment that Washington was better off using his plea colloquy as evidence on these points because the state would be unable to cross-examine Washington or introduce its own evidence as to his mental state. Counsel also chose not to request a presentence report because it would have shown Washington's prior record to be extensive, rather than as "insignificant" as Washington had said in the statement accompanying his plea. Nevertheless, the trial judge sentenced Washington to death. Washington appealed on grounds of ineffective counsel, citing counsel's failure to request a presentence report, seek psychiatric examination, or present character witnesses. The Court said Washington had been effectively represented. Justice O'Connor said a fair trial is one in which "evidence subject to adversarial testing is presented to an impartial tribunal for the resolution of defined issues." The bench mark for assessing a claim of ineffectiveness is "whether counsel's conduct so undermined the proper functioning of the adversarial process" that the proceeding cannot be relied upon to produce a just result. Reversal on grounds of ineffective counsel requires the consideration of two elements: (1) that counsel performance is shown to be deficient, and (2) that the deficiency prejudiced the outcome. Counsel's representation must fall below an objective standard of reasonableness using prevailing professional norms. Judicial scrutiny of counsel performance should be highly deferential, and avoid second-guessing counsel's judgment. The courts should indulge a strong presumption that counsel's conduct falls within a wide range of reasonable professional assistance. Accordingly, strategic choices made after thorough investigation of plausible options are virtually unchallengeable. Despite the deference recommended, some cases require reversal because their result was prejudiced. The defendant must show that there is a reasonable probability that without the counsel's misrepresentation the result of a proceeding would have been different. Such a probability must be one sufficient to undermine confidence in the outcome of the proceeding. In examining Washington's case by these standards, the Court decided that had counsel offered the evidence Washington cited, it would "barely have altered" the profile on which the sentence was based. Justice Marshall dissented. He said the standards for effective counsel as defined here by the Court are so malleable they do not address the problem. *See also* COUNSEL, ASSISTANCE OF, p. 635; *Gideon v. Wainwright*, p. 360; SIXTH AMENDMENT, p. 323.

Significance   *Strickland v. Washington* emphasized that the most important factor in assessing the effectiveness of counsel is whether the integrity of the adversary process is maintained. So long as counsel is "reasonably effective" and there is no "reasonable probability" of a different outcome, the quality of assistance is presumed to be adequate. The matter of counsel effectiveness has long been troublesome, with no precise standards in place for cases in which ineffective counsel is claimed. The earliest recognized standard was the "mockery of justice" standard, but this criterion required demonstration of extraordinary ineffectiveness before a conviction could be set aside. The *Strickland* ruling displaced the "mockery of justice" standard with a somewhat more manageable standard, but ineffective counsel claims are infrequently successful, as in *Jones v. Barnes*, 463 U.S. 745 (1983). The Court held that counsel assigned to handle an appeal for a convicted defendant need not raise every issue suggested by the defendant. For courts to "second-guess reasonable professional judgments and impose on appointed counsel a duty to raise every 'colorable' claim suggested by a client" would not well serve the goal of vigorous and effective advocacy.

Similarly, in *United States v. Cronic*, 466 U.S. 648 (1984), the Court ruled that in assessing whether there had been a breakdown of the adversarial process, a court may not conclude by inference that circumstances surrounding representation constitute denial of effective assistance. Two years later, the Court unanimously ruled in *Nix v. Whiteside*, 475 U.S. 157 (1986), that an attorney does not deny a client effective assistance by insisting that the client testify truthfully. At a point at which the client indicated an intention to perjure himself at his trial, the attorney threatened to inform the trial court and withdraw as counsel. The Court said the attorney's duty to the client's cause is limited to "legitimate, lawful conduct compatible with the truth-seeking objective of a trial." The right to testify does not extend to testifying falsely, and the right to counsel "includes no right to have a lawyer who will cooperate with planned perjury." In *Evitts v. Lucey*, 469 U.S. 387 (1985), the Court added that effectiveness standards apply to a first appeal as well as to the trial stage of a criminal proceeding.

Following his death sentence for felony murder, Bobby Ray Fretwell appealed, arguing that his sentence was unconstitutional on the basis of a then-existing Eighth Circuit ruling, *Collins v. Lockhart*, 754 F.2d 258 (1985). Under *Collins*, a death sentence is unconstitutional if based on an aggravating circumstance that duplicates an element of the underlying felony. The Arkansas Supreme Court refused to consider whether *Collins* governed the sentence, however, because Fretwell had not asserted *Collins* at the sentencing hearing. Fretwell then sought federal habeas corpus review, claiming that his counsel had been "ineffective" by failing to raise a *Collins* objection. A U.S. district court agreed that Fretwell had suffered prejudice by the failure to raise the *Collins* objection. Although the court of appeals had overruled *Collins* subsequent to Fretwell's sentencing, it affirmed the district court reasoning that a *Collins* objection asserted at sentencing would have prevented Fretwell's death sentence. The Supreme Court reversed in *Lockhart v. Fretwell*, 506 U.S. 364 (1993). "The touchstone of an ineffective counsel claim," said Chief Justice Rehnquist, "is the fairness of the adversary proceeding." An analysis that focuses "solely on mere outcome determination, without attention to whether the result ... was fundamentally unfair or unreliable, is defective." To set aside a conviction or sentence solely because the result would have been different "but for counsel's error," Rehnquist continued, "may grant the defendant a windfall to which the law does not entitle him." Fretwell argued that, under terms of *Strickland v. Washington*, 466 U.S. 668 (1984), determination of whether he suffered prejudice ought to be based on the laws in effect at the time of trial. The Supreme Court disagreed. *Strickland* focused on the issue of whether counsel's performance was so defective as to "render the result of the trial unreliable or a proceeding fundamentally unfair." It was the Court's view that neither occurred in Fretwell's case.

Self-Representation

Faretta v. California, **422 U.S. 806 (1975),** considered the bases on which a trial court determines whether a defendant may represent himself or herself. By the mid-1970s it was clearly established that a person being tried on a criminal charge in either a state or federal court must be afforded the right of assistance of counsel. The trial judge had refused to allow Faretta to represent himself after quizzing him on several points of law, including the rules covering hearsay evidence. The Supreme Court held, however, that Faretta could constitutionally assist and defend himself. The Court, through Justice Stewart, recognized that self-representation may be an unwise course for a criminal defendant, but the Court said that it is "one thing to hold that every defendant, rich or poor, has the right to the assistance of counsel, and quite another to say that a State may compel a defendant to accept a lawyer he does not want." Free choice was crucial to the Court's decision. The choice of a defense belongs to the defendant, including the question of counsel. Although the defendant's choice may be "ultimately to his own detriment, his choice must be honored." A trial judge must make the defendant "aware of the dangers and disadvantages of self-representation" so that the record can reflect that the defendant made a choice with "eyes open." The criterion by which the determination is to be made is not technical. It makes no difference "how well or poorly Faretta had mastered the intricacies of the hearsay rule and the California code provisions." The decision rested with his "knowing exercise of the right to defend himself." The Court concluded that Faretta had been denied a constitutional right to "conduct his own defense." Chief Justice Burger and Justices Blackmun and Rehnquist dissented. They could find no Sixth Amendment right to represent oneself. The "spirit and logic" of the amendment required that the accused receive "the fullest possible defense." Burger did not agree with the freedom of choice argument of the Court, and suggested that the trial court retains discretion to reject a waiver of counsel. The chief justice was concerned that greater congestion of the courts would follow *Faretta*, and that the quality of justice would suffer. *See also* COUNSEL, ASSISTANCE OF, p. 635; *Gideon v. Wainwright*, p. 360; SIXTH AMENDMENT, p. 323.

Significance   *Faretta* established the rule that a defendant has a right to carry on his or her own defense without violating the "assistance of counsel" requirement of the Sixth Amendment. The case runs absolutely counter to many recent Supreme Court decisions that found "the guiding hand of counsel" to be indispensable to due process. *Faretta* not only recognized the option of self-representation but accorded it the status of a protected right on par with assistance of counsel. *Faretta* holds in addition that a defendant need not demonstrate even minimal levels of legal skill to exercise the right of self-representation. Like any other constitutional provision, the right to counsel may be waived voluntarily. More recently, the Court examined the issue of unsolicited participation by standby counsel as it relates to the right of self-representation. In *McKaskle v. Wiggins*, 465

U.S. 168 (1984), the Court said that the categorical silencing of stand-by counsel is not required as long as the defendant is able to retain control over the conduct of his or her own defense. The Court said that to determine whether *Faretta* rights have been preserved, "the primary focus must be on whether the defendant had a fair chance to present his case in his own way." As long as the jury perceives that the defendant is representing himself, even overzealous participation by standby counsel need not be absolutely barred.

Faretta also raised important questions about the quality of counsel. The Court examined the standard of competency that applies to a criminal defendant's decision to waive his or her right to counsel and plead guilty in *Godinez v. Moran*, 509 U.S. 389 (1993). The Court had ruled in *Dusky v. United States*, 362 U.S. 402 (1960), that an accused is competent to stand trial if he or she understands the proceedings against him or her and has the capacity "to consult with counsel and assist in the preparation of the defense." The Court ruled that if an accused is found competent to stand trial, he or she is also competent to discharge counsel and plead guilty to a serious crime, even capital murder. The Court acknowledged that the decision to plead guilty is a "profound one," but that decision is "no more complicated than the sum total of decisions that a defendant may be called upon to make during the course of a trial." Similarly, the Court did not see how the decision to waive the right to counsel "requires an appreciably higher level of mental functioning than the decision to waive any other constitutional right."

Plea Bargaining

Santobello v. New York, **404 U.S. 257 (1971),** considered the consequences of the prosecution failing to honor an agreement made during plea negotiations. Santobello was indicted for two felonies and agreed to enter a guilty plea in exchange for no sentence recommendation by the prosecuting attorney. At the sentencing hearing, delayed twice at defendant's initiative, a new prosecuting attorney appeared. Apparently ignorant of his colleague's promise, the new prosecutor recommended the maximum sentence, which Santobello received. The trial judge said, however, that he was not influenced by the prosecutor's recommendation. The Court concluded that Santobello's sentence must be vacated, while three justices felt that the defendant should be allowed to withdraw his guilty plea entirely. On the basic sentence question, the Court said that the condition of no sentence recommendation was an integral part of the bargain made with the prosecutor. The Court did not forgive the failure of one prosecutor to communicate the elements of the negotiation to his successor. The prosecutor's office has "the burden of 'letting the left hand know what the right hand is doing' or has done." The Court said further, "the breach of agreement was inadvertent," but that "does not lessen its impact." *Santobello* represented to the Court "another example of an unfortunate lapse in orderly prosecutorial procedures," presumably a product of excessively high caseloads. But while workload "may well explain these episodes, it does not excuse them." The plea process "must be attended by safeguards to insure the defendant what is reasonably due in the circumstances." The position of the Court was that when pleas "rest in any significant degree on a promise or agreement of the prosecutor, such promise must be fulfilled." *See also* PLEA BARGAINING, p. 686; SIXTH AMENDMENT, p. 323.

Significance   *Boykin v. Alabama,* 395 U.S. 238 (1969), first addressed some of the conditions that must be present for a guilty plea to be acceptable. An overwhelming majority of American criminal defendants plead guilty rather than face a trial. Defendant Boykin pled guilty to five counts of robbery and was sentenced to death by a jury. The record showed that the trial judge asked no questions of the defendant at the time of the plea, that the defendant did not address the court in any way, and that the defendant did not testify at his sentencing proceeding even though he was represented by counsel throughout. The Supreme Court found the plea insufficient. The Court focused on the trial judge's error of accepting the plea without an "affirmative showing that it was intelligent and voluntary." The Court held that a plea is "more than a confession, it is a conviction." Waiver of such rights as trial by jury, confronting one's accusers, and the protection from self-incrimination simply cannot be taken from a silent record. Justices Black and Harlan dissented primarily on the grounds that the record was merely silent, as opposed to showing that the plea was neither voluntary nor unknowing. *Boykin* established that the plea of guilty stands as a conviction equivalent to a jury finding, and involves the waiver of several constitutional protections. *Boykin* established minimum Sixth Amendment standards and federal-state uniformity regarding guilty pleas. Because of *Boykin,* no federal or state judge can accept a plea of guilty without questioning the defendant as to whether he or she understands the charge and the potential sentence that may result from pleading guilty to it, and whether promises or threats have been made to him or her. The defendant must be made aware that he or she is waiving many constitutional protections by pleading guilty.

The basis of *Boykin* was to ensure that the plea of guilty was the defendant's knowing and voluntary choice. Although *Boykin* does not require it, some jurisdictions place a summary of the case against a defendant in the record. In the absence of satisfactory responses to any of the judge's inquiries, a trial judge has the discretion of refusing to accept a guilty plea and having the case scheduled for trial. Today in federal courts a mandatory rule (Rule 11 of the Federal Rules of Criminal Procedure) stipulates the steps to be taken by the judge in considering a plea of guilty. The steps must comply with *Boykin*. Most state courts have similar code or rule requirements. Thus the plea process takes considerably more time than before *Boykin*, but on the other hand, the *Boykin*-type appeal rarely occurs anymore.

Soon after *Boykin* the Court considered whether pleas are acceptable if they are taken against the possibility of the imposition of the death penalty should a defendant be convicted on the same charge by a jury. The Court allowed such pleas to stand in *Brady v. United States*, 397 U.S. 742 (1970). Brady had been charged with kidnapping and demanded a jury trial. He changed his mind when a codefendant pled guilty to a comparable charge and became available to testify against him. Justice White said that knowledge and voluntariness are the two critical ingredients of an acceptable plea. If those two elements are present, motivation to avoid a possible death sentence was not a defect per se. After examining the "totality of the circumstances," the Court felt there was no evidence to suggest that Brady would have undergone a trial "but for" the capital punishment potential or that he "was so gripped by fear of the death penalty" that he could not make a rational decision. In addition, Brady was assisted by counsel throughout.

In *United States v. Jackson*, 390 U.S. 570 (1968), the Supreme Court held the death penalty provision of the Federal Kidnapping Act (the Lindbergh Law) unconstitutional on the grounds that it created incentives that tended to "discourage defendants from insisting on their innocence and demanding trial by jury." The *Brady* plea had been taken almost 10 years before *Jackson* and could have been handled by a determination that *Jackson* would not apply retroactively. The Burger Court, however, chose to modify *Jackson* by substituting the "totality of circumstances" standard. *Brady* had the effect of making challenges of pleas on the grounds of involuntariness much more difficult than under the Warren Court rule in *Jackson*. The *Brady* decision also dealt with the status of guilty pleas more generally. The Burger Court chose to comment positively on plea bargaining in *Brady*. Justice White said it would not find a plea deficient when "motivated by the defendant's desire to accept the certainty or probability of a lesser penalty rather than face a wider range of possibilities" through a jury trial. White itemized the benefits that accrue to both the defendant and the state through the process of plea bargaining. He suggested that it was this "mutuality of advantage" that explained the great frequency of dispositions of criminal cases by means of the plea. Although particular pleas may be suspect, the Burger Court clearly endorsed the practice of plea bargaining in *Brady*.

Santobello focused the problems attendant to congested court systems throughout the country, where over 90 percent of criminal cases are disposed of by means of the plea. The system requires nontrial dispositions in order to keep pace with case volume. The National Advisory Commission on Criminal Justice Standards and Goals strongly urged the abolition of plea bargaining in the early 1970s. *Santobello* addressed several important issues related to the Advisory Commission's recommendations. First, the Court established the basic expectation that where promises are instrumental in achieving a plea, the integrity of the bargaining process must be maintained and the promises honored. *Santobello* defined a performance standard for prosecutors. Second, *Santobello* permits a defendant in a criminal case to enforce a plea agreement against the government. Although *Santobello* involved only a prosecutorial recommendation, it raised the specter of a prosecutor offering to dismiss other counts against a defendant, and not prosecuting for similar offenses within a given time. The lower courts have frequently invoked *Santobello* when a defendant shows a plea agreement has been violated. It is not uncommon for courts to dismiss criminal proceedings when prosecutorial authorities have reneged on a plea. This kind of specific enforcement may be the most important aspect of *Santobello*. Third, *Santobello* gave the Court an opportunity to speak generally to the status of plea bargaining. The Court gave the practice a strong endorsement. It referred to plea bargaining as an "essential component of the administration of justice. Properly administered, it is to be encouraged." The Court itemized several reasons why plea bargaining should be regarded not only as essential but as "highly desirable." The advantages included finality, pretrial confinement, conservation of scarce resources, and enhancement of rehabilitative prospects. Taken with the positive language found in *Brady*, the *Santobello* language and decision can be viewed as foreclosing the possibility that the Court will call for the abolition of plea bargaining in the near future.

However, *Santobello* does not create an absolute right to have a plea bargain enforced. In *Mabry v. Johnson*, 467 U.S. 504 (1984), a defendant, following a successful appeal, accepted a plea proposal offered by the prosecutor rather than chance a retrial. The proposal was subsequently withdrawn on the ground that it had been mistakenly tendered. An alternative proposal was offered and rejected, and a new trial was held. After a mistrial was declared, the defendant accepted the second offer and was sentenced accordingly. The defendant then appealed again, arguing that the prosecutor was precluded from withdrawing the original offer once the defendant had accepted it. The Supreme Court disagreed. The Court said Johnson pled knowing what the prosecutor would recommend, he did so with the advice of competent counsel, and he was fully aware of the consequences. His plea was in no sense the product of governmental deception. It did not rest on an unfulfilled promise, and it "fully satisfied the test for voluntariness and intelligence."

Robert Hyde pled guilty to several counts of mail fraud and receipt of stolen property. In return, the prosecution dismissed additional charges. Hyde and the prosecution also agreed as to the applicable federal sentencing guidelines, although it was made clear that the final sentencing guidelines determinations resided with the court. Hyde then pled in open court, and the plea was accepted by the court. The court, however, took under advisement the matter of accepting the plea agreement itself. Before the court ruled on the agreement, Hyde sought to withdraw his plea on the grounds that it was made under duress, but the trial court refused to grant Hyde's motion. The Court ruled in *United States v. Hyde*, 520 U.S. 670 (1997), that a defendant may withdraw a plea only after demonstrating a "fair and just reason." The Federal Rules of Criminal Procedure allow the acceptance of pleas and plea agreements at different times. If a court does not accept a proposed plea agreement, the defendant may not withdraw his or her plea without meeting the "fair and just reason" requirement. Clearly a defendant cannot be bound by an agreement that is unacceptable to the trial court. The "necessary implication" is that if a trial court has neither rejected nor accepted the agreement, the defendant does not have the opportunity to withdraw his or her plea. Because the guilty plea is "one side of the plea agreement, the plea is obviously not wholly independent of the agreement." Nowhere in the rules, however, does it state that the plea agreement "must be treated identically."

Bordenkircher v. Hayes, 434 U.S. 357 (1978), weighed the question of how far a prosecutor may go in attempting to leverage a plea from a criminal defendant. After Hayes refused to plead to a particular felony indictment, the prosecutor carried out his threat to have him reindicted under Kentucky's habitual offender statute. The statute allowed the possibility of a mandatory life sentence. A jury subsequently convicted Hayes of the original charge and made an additional finding that he was eligible for a life term under the recidivist statute. Hayes appealed, claiming violation of due process, but the Supreme Court decided against Hayes. The Court acknowledged the breadth of prosecutorial discretion in the charging process and found little difference between charging initially and offering to drop the recidivist part of the subsequent charge. Further, the Court said the bargaining process must be able to entertain the whole range of options available that pertain to a particular case. In *Bordenkircher* the defendant was informed of what the prosecutor would do if he did not plead guilty, and because he was chargeable under the recidivist statute, the prosecutor had not acted improperly. The Court concluded that the prosecutor "openly presented the defendant with the unpleasant alternatives of foregoing trial or facing charges on which he was plainly subject to prosecution. In the 'give and take' of plea bargaining, there is no such element of punishment or retaliation so long as the accused is free to accept or reject the prosecutor's offer." Justices Brennan, Marshall, Blackmun, and Powell viewed the prosecutorial conduct as creating "a strong inference of vindictiveness." While expressing general deference to prosecutorial discretion, the dissenters thought the prosecutor had intended to discourage and penalize Hayes for pursuing his constitutional rights to a trial.

Bordenkircher extended substantial latitude to the prosecutor in plea bargaining situations and clarified the Court's ruling in *Blackledge v. Perry*, 417 U.S. 21 (1974). Perry was convicted of a misdemeanor. He pursued his statutory right to a retrial and was subsequently charged with a felony for the same conduct originally charged as a misdemeanor. The Court disallowed the substitute charge on the grounds that the recharging was motivated by vindictiveness. A retaliatory motive need not be shown. Rather, vindictiveness sufficient to "deter a defendant's exercise of the right to appeal" was seen as the determining factor in *Perry*.

In *Alabama v. Smith*, 490 U.S. 794 (1989), the Court considered whether the presumption of vindictiveness extended to a case in which a defendant sentenced on the basis of a subsequently withdrawn guilty plea was sentenced more harshly after a jury trial on the charges. The Court decided the presumption did not apply to *Smith* and allowed the enhanced sentence following the trial. The presumption was not designed, said the Court, to "prevent imposition of an increased sentence on retrial for some valid reason associated with the need for flexibility and discretion in the sentencing process." Rather, the presumption is to be used when there is a "reasonable likelihood" that an increase in sentence is the "product of actual vindictiveness" on the part of the sentencing judge. When no such likelihood exists, the defendant must demonstrate actual vindictiveness. In cases such as Smith's, considerably more information is typically available to the sentencing judge than after a guilty plea.

Joseph Libretti pled guilty to federal charges for drug distribution. As part of the plea agreement, Libretti agreed to forfeit all assets acquired with the proceeds of his criminal activities. The trial court was satisfied that there was both a factual basis for Libretti's plea and that Libretti understood that his plea included the forfeiture of all crime-tainted assets. Libretti was sentenced under terms of the plea agreement, but he then filed an appeal on the forfeiture order. He claimed that the trial court should have formally and separately determined that there was a factual basis for the property forfeiture as well as his plea to the drug charges. Further, he argued that the trial court should have explicitly indicated to him that his plea to the criminal charge included waiver of jury determination on the forfeiture issue. The Supreme Court rejected both contentions in *Libretti v. United States*, 516 U.S. 29 (1995). Justice O'Connor distinguished between an offense and a sentence imposed following a plea. A review of the statutory provisions definitively revealed that Congress intended that forfeiture of assets was to "operate as punishment for criminal conduct ... , not as a separate substantive offense." As a result, the trial court was required to find a factual basis only for the guilty plea, and not for the sentence. The Sixth Amendment does not entitle a defendant to a jury determination of a sentence including forfeitability, thus the trial court was not required to warn Libretti that his plea included waiver of jury consideration of any asset forfeiture. Rather, the trial court need only find that the defendant understands the "full consequences" of his or her plea for that plea to be valid.

An unusual convergence of double jeopardy, plea bargaining, and death penalty issues surfaced in *Ricketts v. Adamson*, 483 U.S. 1 (1987). Adamson was indicted for first-degree murder for his part in the killing of a newspaper reporter. Shortly after his trial began, Adamson and the prosecutor agreed that Adamson could plead guilty to second-degree murder in exchange for testifying against other persons involved in the crime. The agreement specified not only the actual time Adamson would spend in prison but also that the bargain was null and void if he refused to testify. Included as well was a specific provision that the original charge would automatically be reinstated if Adamson changed his mind. Adamson testified, those he testified against were convicted, and the trial court accepted the sentence proposed for Adamson. The convictions were eventually set aside on appeal, however, and remanded for retrial. The prosecutor sought Adamson's testimony at the retrial, but Adamson refused, saying that his obligation had ended when he was sentenced. The state then instituted new first-degree murder charges against Adamson and eventually secured a conviction. The Supreme Court ruled against Adamson. The Court was satisfied that the agreement covered any retrial and that Adamson was aware of the consequences of his breaching the agreement. Further, the Court said that double jeopardy need not be waived in the agreement. The agreement provided that any refusal to testify would automatically return the parties to the status quo ante, in which case Adamson would have had no double jeopardy defense to waive.

Gary Mezzanatto was charged with a federal drug offense. Mezzanatto and his counsel met with a federal prosecutor to explore how he might help himself by cooperating with federal authorities. The prosecutor insisted that Mezzanatto agree that anything he said during the meeting could be used for impeachment purposes should the case go to trial and Mezzanatto testify. Mezzanatto discussed this condition with counsel and agreed. The exploratory meeting did not produce an agreement and was ended by the prosecutor after Mezzanatto made statements that were inconsistent with other prosecution evidence. The case was eventually tried, and Mezzanatto testified in his own defense. He was confronted on cross-examination with contradictory statements from the pretrial meeting. Mezzanatto unsuccessfully attempted to have the use of the pretrial statements suppressed. The Supreme Court ruled in *United States v. Mezzanatto*, 513 U.S. 196 (1995), that the defendant could waive his self-incrimination rights under this circumstance. Justice Thomas concluded that the admission of plea statements for impeachment purposes "enhances the truth-seeking functions of trials and will result in more accurate verdicts." Mezzanatto made false statements either to the prosecutor during the plea discussion or to the jury during trial. Under any rule of evidence, suggested Thomas, making the jury aware of that inconsistency will "tend to increase the reliability of the verdict." In this case, Mezzanatto was represented by counsel at all stages, and his responses "made clear that he fully understood the nature and consequences of his guilty plea." Mezzanatto argued that waiver agreements should be prohibited because they invite prosecutorial "overreaching and abuse." The "mere potential" for abuse of prosecutorial bargaining power is an "insufficient basis for foreclosing negotiation altogether." The safeguard against such abuse is case-by-case inquiry into whether waiver agreements were the product of fraud or coercion.

Juvenile Justice System

In re Gault, **387 U.S. 1 (1967),** considered whether juvenile proceedings must meet due process standards. Gerald Gault, age 15, was found to have made a lewd telephone call and was committed to the state industrial school as a delinquent. He faced the possibility of having to remain there until he was 21 years of age. For an adult, the maximum punishment for such an offense would have been a $50 fine or confinement for not more than 60 days. Gault appealed the outcome, through his parents, claiming that: (1) he had been given inadequate notice of the charges; (2) the complainant had not testified; (3) he had not been offered counsel; (4) he had not been warned that any statements he made could be used against him; (5) no records had been made of the hearing; and (6) Arizona law permitted no appeal in a juvenile proceeding. With only Justice Stewart dissenting, the Supreme Court found for Gault. The Court recognized that juvenile and adult proceedings were intentionally made different. Justice Fortas declared, however, that the differences could not remain dissimilar with regard to basic constitutional protections. He suggested that the essential difference between Gault's case and adult criminal cases was that safeguards available to adults were discarded for the juvenile. Although some benefits derive from handling juveniles differently—i.e., more informally—there must be procedural protections. "Under our Constitution, the condition of being a boy does not justify a kangaroo court." The holding in *Gault* required that delinquency proceedings that may lead to detention must provide juveniles with access to counsel, with appointed counsel in instances of indigence, with adequate notification of charges with a right to confront witnesses, and with the privilege against self-incrimination. In his dissent Justice Stewart dwelt on traditional juvenile-adult procedural differences, urging that juvenile proceedings not become full-blown adversary proceedings. *See also* COUNSEL, ASSISTANCE OF, p. 635; SELF-INCRIMINATION CLAUSE, p. 695.

Significance   *Gault* challenged the longstanding view that juvenile proceedings are categorically different from adult criminal proceedings. A juvenile "conviction," for example, was not supposed to be viewed as a conviction by future employers and adult courts. Judges, however, usually had access to juvenile "convictions" when the former juvenile later found himself or herself before an adult court. For many years prior to *Gault*, juvenile courts were seen as places in which the state acted as *parens patriae* (benevolent parent) rather than as an adversary. Juvenile proceedings were civil in character and substantially more informal than adult criminal trials. They were viewed as being free from due process expectations in any strict sense. The characteristic of informality had been the strength of juvenile courts, but became the main source of problems as well. *Gault* was but one of a series of decisions by the Warren Court extending due process rights to categories of persons not previously enjoying them. *Gault* was actually the second Warren Court decision addressing due process in juvenile courts. The first case, *Kent v. United States*, 383 U.S. 541 (1966), preceded *Gault* by a year. *Kent* involved the waiver of jurisdiction by a juvenile court to allow transfer of a juvenile's case to adult court. The Court imposed several specific procedural requirements on the waiver process, including a hearing, representation by counsel, and access to all records and reports on the juvenile germane to the waiver. Although *Kent* was limited to a relatively few cases, it clearly conveyed the Court's interest in juvenile rights and procedural fairness in juvenile courts.

The effects of *Gault* are substantial. The procedural requirements of juvenile courts have now been formalized to the extent that many current proceedings bear little resemblance to juvenile court activities of 30 years ago. Although certain differences yet remain between juvenile and adult processes, the adjudicatory hearing in juvenile court contains most of the ingredients of the trial of an adult defendant.

In re Winship, 397 U.S. 358 (1970), examined the question of whether guilt must be proved beyond a reasonable doubt in juvenile proceedings. Using the "preponderance of the evidence" standard of proof as provided by state statute, a juvenile court found Winship guilty of having stolen money. The Supreme Court determined that proving guilt beyond a reasonable doubt was an essential element of due process, however, and must be used at the adjudicatory stage of any juvenile proceeding in which the juvenile is charged with an act constituting a crime if committed by an adult. Justice Brennan argued that a criminal defendant would be at "severe disadvantage" if guilt could be determined on the strength "of the same evidence as would suffice in a civil case." The reasonable doubt standard emphasizes the "necessity of reaching a subjective state of certitude of the facts" at issue. As for the need to extend the standard to juvenile proceedings, Brennan said that "civil labels and good intentions do not themselves obviate the need for criminal due process standards in juvenile courts." The dissent of Chief Justice Burger and Justice Stewart took issue with the notion that a juvenile proceeding was a "criminal prosecution." They said the *Winship* decision further eroded the differences between juvenile and criminal courts, and they registered unhappiness with "strait-jacketing" states with due process requirements in juvenile matters. They said that the juvenile justice process needed fewer rather than more "trappings of legal procedures and judicial formalism," concluding that the juvenile system must have "breathing room and flexibility" to survive. *Winship*, following soon after *Gault*, removed juvenile processes from the status of civil proceedings and drew them closer to adult criminal trials.

Some significant differences remained, however. One difference is illustrated in *McKeiver v. Pennsylvania*, 403 U.S. 528 (1971), in which the Court examined whether juveniles are entitled to jury trials in the adjudicative stage of delinquency proceedings. *Gault* and *Winship* had brought a number of process changes to the juvenile justice system, but the Supreme Court held that these process changes did not mean that all rights assured to an accused adult would automatically extend to juveniles. Jury trials were one of the excepted rights. The Court was clearly attempting to "strike a judicious balance" between "procedural orderliness" and the more informal approach of juvenile courts. The Court did not wish to remake juvenile proceedings into a "fully adversarial process" by making access to a jury a required element of the juvenile process. Such a policy might diminish the "idealistic prospect of an intimate, informal protective proceeding." Furthermore, the Court felt that use of a jury would not improve the fact-finding function of juvenile courts. Rather, it might "provide an attrition of the juvenile court's assumed ability to function in a unique manner." Justices Douglas, Black, and Marshall took issue with the Court's willingness to subordinate a constitutional protection such as the jury trial to the special objectives of the juvenile process. They felt that "where a state uses its juvenile court proceedings to prosecute a juvenile for a criminal act and to order 'confinement' until the child reaches 21 ... then he is entitled to the same procedural protection as an adult." *McKeiver* allowed the Burger Court to decide that the changes in juvenile rights brought by *Gault* and *Winship* would not remove all distinctions between adult and juvenile proceedings.

The Burger Court was not altogether unsympathetic to the basic formalizing of procedural requirements in juvenile processes. Soon after *McKeiver*, the Court held in *Breed v. Jones*, 421 U.S. 519 (1975), that juvenile proceedings counted for double jeopardy purposes. *Breed* involved a 17-year-old who was adjudicated in a juvenile court, but was later transferred to adult court for prosecution because he was "unfit for treatment as a juvenile." Jones appealed his adult court conviction, claiming he had been "in jeopardy" in his juvenile proceeding and that initiation of charges against him in the adult court was foreclosed by the double jeopardy prohibition. The Supreme Court agreed. The Court's holding rested primarily on its perception of jeopardy. The Court said it was "simply too late in the day" to think that a juvenile is "not put in jeopardy at a proceeding whose object is to determine whether he has committed acts that violate criminal law," a proceeding "whose potential consequences include both the stigma inherent in such a determination and the deprivation of liberty for many years." So, despite attempts to make juvenile proceedings different from trials of adults, the juvenile process resembles the adult process closely enough to create jeopardy. The Court also rejected the contention that the prosecution of Jones as an adult was merely a continuation of the prosecution begun at the juvenile level. While the Court agreed that the case "had not yet reached its conclusion" in the juvenile proceeding in that no sentence had been assigned, it determined the failure to sentence Jones had not in any way limited Jones's risk or jeopardy.

Independent Counsel

Morrison v. Olson, **487 U.S. 654 (1988),** upheld the federal independent prosecutor statute. The authorization for appointment of independent counsel is found in the Ethics in Government Act, which requires the attorney general to conduct preliminary investigations of particular high-level executive officers alleged to have engaged in criminal misconduct. If there is cause to believe "further investigation is warranted," the attorney general is obligated to refer the case to the U.S. Court of Appeals for the District of Columbia. The federal appellate court then appoints independent counsel. Once appointed, counsel may be removed by the attorney general only for "good cause," a decision subject to judicial review. The dispute in *Morrison v. Olson* began in 1982 as Congress sought certain documents from the Environmental Protection Agency concerning the "superfund" toxic waste law. On advice of Justice Department counsel, the documents were withheld. Olson, an assistant attorney general in the Office of Legal Counsel, testified before the House Judiciary Committee, which was investigating the matter. The Committee issued a report sometime later, suggesting that Olson had given false testimony during the inquiry. The Committee chair requested independent counsel to look into the actions of Olson and two other officials of the Office of Legal Counsel. Morrison was appointed following the preliminary investigation of the attorney general. As part of the inquiry into whether a conspiracy to obstruct the Judiciary Committee investigation had occurred, subpoenas were issued by a grand jury to obtain both testimony and documents from Olson and the others. In response, Olson asserted that Morrison had no authority to proceed because the independent counsel law was unconstitutional. The Supreme Court upheld the law under authority of the Appointments Clause of Article II. Under the Clause, the president nominates various "principal officers" of the government, but Congress has the authority to appoint "inferior" officers. The Court concluded that the independent counsel "clearly falls on the 'inferior officer' side of that line" because Morrison was subject to removal by the attorney general, an indication that she was "inferior in rank and authority." Second, the special prosecutor is empowered to "perform only certain, limited duties" and has no authority to "formulate policy" nor have administrative duties "outside those necessary to operate her office." Finally, the office is "limited in jurisdiction" and has "limited tenure." Chief Justice Rehnquist moved to the contention that the Clause did not permit "interbranch" appointments. While Congress possesses "significant discretion" to empower courts to make "interbranch" appointments, Congress could not vest the courts with power to appoint officers where "incongruity" exists between the "functions normally performed by the courts and the performance of their duty to appoint." There was, however, no "inherent incongruity" about a Court having the power to appoint prosecutorial officers. When Congress created the office of independent counsel, it was concerned with conflicts of interest that could occur when the executive branch was called upon to investigate its own officials. If it was necessary to remove the appointing authority from the executive, the "most logical place to put it was the Judicial Branch." Neither did the Court find that the law was incompatible with Article III provisions assigning the courts their judicial functions. The court's role in the independent counsel process is "passive" with the court having no supervisory power over the special prosecutor's performance. Particularly, the court is not entitled to approve or disapprove the content of any report or finding of either the attorney general or special counsel. Finally, the Court ruled that the law did not improperly encroach on executive power. Although the independent counsel cannot be removed at will, the Court did not find this factor decisive. The executive retains "sufficient control" over independent counsel to support the conclusion that Congress had not "unduly" interfered with the president's executive power. Important to its finding was the Court's observation that the law did not represent an attempt by Congress to "increase its own powers at the expense of the Executive Branch." *See also* SEPARATION OF POWERS, p. 697.

Significance *Morrison v. Olson* is not a Sixth Amendment case. Rather, it rests squarely on separation of powers considerations. It warrants mention because of its direct relationship to federal criminal justice processes and current attempts to implement more demanding ethics standards for government officials. The Court's ruling in *Morrison* represented a short-term loss for the Reagan administration and a number of former administration officials. The administration had strongly argued that the law was unconstitutional. Convictions of former Reagan advisers Lyn Nofziger and Michael Deaver in cases prosecuted by independent counsel became more secure in the wake of *Morrison*. The decision also applied to the ongoing investigation of the Iran-Contra affair and, most recently, Kenneth Starr's investigation of the Clinton White House. Starr's lengthy tenure as independent counsel was sufficiently controversial that its impact on the process was limited. Clinton's failure to postpone his grand jury appearance, however, may have added a measure of legitimacy to Starr's investigation and indirectly to the independent counsel function. While *Morrison* says that Congress can establish processes for investigations within the executive branch, the Court did not give Congress unlimited authority to designate areas subject to investigation by independent counsel. The exact dimensions of congressional authority and the limits that apply will continue to be clarified over the next several years.

Gun Regulation

Printz v. United States, **521 U.S. 898, 117 S. Ct. 2365 (1997)** Since 1968 the Gun Control Act has required that firearm dealers be licensed by the federal government. The Act also requires certification that persons who buy firearms from federally licensed dealers are not, among other things, convicted felons, undocumented aliens, users of controlled substances, or subject to any restraining order based on domestic assault. The Brady Handgun Violence Prevention Act enacted by Congress in 1993 amended the earlier Act by passing various implementation responsibilities on to state and local law enforcement officials. Specifically, local authorities were required to conduct background checks on those seeking to purchase handguns. Two county sheriff departments, one in Montana (Printz) and one in Arizona (Mack), challenged the background check provisions, contending that congressional action compelling state officers to execute federal laws is unconstitutional. The Supreme Court agreed. Justice Scalia termed "incontestable" the premise that the Constitution established a system of "dual sovereignty," and although the states "surrendered many of their powers to the new federal Government," they retained a "residuary and inviolable sovereignty." Scalia referred to the Court's decision in *New York v. United States*, 505 U.S. 144 (1992), in which the Court struck down a federal law that "unambiguously required the states to enact or administer a Federal regulatory program." The "whole effect" of the Brady Act was to "direct the functioning of the state executive, and hence to compromise the structural framework of dual sovereignty." The mandatory obligations imposed on chief law enforcement officers at the local level to perform background checks on prospective handgun purchasers "plainly runs afoul" of the rule that the federal government cannot "command the states' officers, or those of their political subdivisions, to administer or enforce a Federal regulatory program." Such commands are "fundamentally incompatible with our constitutional system of dual sovereignty." Justices Stevens, Souter, Ginsburg, and Breyer said in dissent that when Congress exercises the powers assigned to it by the Constitution, it may "impose affirmative obligations on executive and judicial officers of state and local governments as well as ordinary citizens." *See also* FEDERALISM, p. 649.

Significance *Printz* was the second recent ruling in which the Rehnquist Court limited federal commerce power on state sovereignty grounds. The Gun-Free School Zones Act of 1990 made it a crime to possess a firearm within 1,000 feet of a public or private elementary or secondary school. Alfonso Lopez was indicted under the Act for bringing a handgun into his high school in San Antonio, Texas. He unsuccessfully sought to have the indictment dismissed on the grounds that the Act exceeded federal authority to regulate inter-state commerce. The Supreme Court ruled in *United States v. Lopez*, 514 U.S. 549 (1995), that Congress had not established a close enough connection between firearms in local schools and interstate commerce. The Act, said Chief Justice Rehnquist, is a "criminal statute that by its terms has nothing to do with 'commerce' or any sort of economic enterprise, however broadly one might define those terms." The government contended that possession of a firearm in a local school zone substantially affects interstate commerce because violent crime affects the functioning of the national economy and impairs the educational process by threatening the learning envi-ronment. The Court focused on the implications of these arguments. If accepted, Rehnquist said, Congress could regulate not only all violent crime, but "all activities that might lead to violent crime, regardless of how tenuously they relate to interstate commerce." It is difficult, he continued, to "perceive any limitation on federal power, even in areas such as criminal law enforcement or education where States historically have been sovereign." Justice Breyer, joined by Justices Stevens, Souter, and Ginsburg, dissented. They saw the Act as falling "well within the scope of the commerce power as this Court has understood this power over the last half-century." Courts, said Breyer, must give Congress "a degree of leeway in determining the existence of a significant factual connection between the regulated activity and interstate commerce." The *Printz* ruling will not have long-term impact on the administration of federal gun regulations. By the end of 1998 the federal government will have the capacity to conduct its own background checks. More significant is the current Court's deference to state sovereignty in these kinds of cases.

Psychotherapist Privilege

Jaffee v. Redmond, **518 U.S. 1 (1996),** recognized a patient-psychother-apist privilege under federal law. Mary Lu Redmond, a Village of Hoffman Estates (Illinois) police officer, shot and killed Ricky Allen Sr. while on duty. A federal civil-rights action was filed by Allen's survivors against the Village and Redmond for wrongful death. During the trial, the plaintiffs attempted to compel disclosure of conversations between Redmond and her therapist, a licensed clinical social worker. The ther-apist refused to disclose the substance of all communications with Redmond. On appeal, the Court of Appeals for the Seventh Circuit reversed, ruling that the trial court had given the jury an improper instruction on the therapist privilege issue. The Supreme Court held in *Jaffee v. Redmond* that communications between a patient and a psychotherapist—including a licensed clinical social worker—are priv-ileged. The question before the Court, said Justice Stevens, was whether a privilege protecting confidential communications between a psychotherapist and a patient "promotes sufficiently important interests to outweigh the need for probative evidence." It was the Court's conclusion that it did. As with spousal and attorney-client privileges, the psychotherapist-patient privilege is "rooted in the imperative need for confidence and trust." Effective psychotherapy requires an "atmosphere of confidence and trust" in which the patient is willing to make candid disclosures. Because of the sensitive nature of the problems for which people need psychotherapy, disclosure of confidential communications made during therapy may cause "embarrassment or disgrace." The mere possibility of disclosure, Stevens continued, may "impede the development of the confidential treatment necessary for successful treatment." It is also necessary that an asserted privilege "serve public ends." Here, the privilege serves the public interest by "facilitating the provision of appropriate treatment for individuals suffering the effects of a mental or emotional problem." The mental health of our citizenry, no less than its physical health, is a "public good of transcendent importance." In a footnote to that conclusion, Stevens suggested that police officers engaged in the "dangerous and difficult tasks associated with protecting the safety of our communities" face those "stressful circumstances" that may produce psychological or emotional problems. The entire community may be affected if officers are not able to receive effective counseling after "traumatic" incidents, either because trained officers "leave the profession prematurely or because those in need of treatment remain on the job." By comparison, the possible evidentiary benefit that would result from denial of this privilege Stevens characterized as "modest." If the privilege is not recognized, confidential communications "would surely be chilled," especially when the circumstances that prompt the need for treatment will also prompt litigation. As a result, much of the evidence to which access is sought is "unlikely to come into being." This unspoken "evidence" will "serve no greater truth-seeking function than if it had been spoken and privileged." Stevens concluded by saying that the reasons for recognizing a privilege for treatment by psychiatrists and psychologists "apply with equal force to treatment by a clinical social worker." Justice Scalia, joined by Chief Justice Rehnquist, dissented. Scalia identified "occasional injustice" as the "purchase price" of a rule that "excludes reliable and probative evidence." The victim of the psychotherapist privilege is likely to be some individual who is "prevented from proving a valid claim—or (worse still) prevented from establishing a valid defense." *See also* COUNSEL, ASSISTANCE OF, p. 635; PRIVILEGE, p. 690.

Significance   A privileged communication consists of statements made by people within a protected relationship. The privilege protects these statements from compelled disclosure in a legal proceeding. The scope of particular privileged communications is largely defined by federal or state rules of evidence, although state law governs in most federal proceedings. Unlike most evidentiary rules, which intend to ensure the reliability or truthfulness of evidence, privileged communications are primarily designed to protect confidentiality, candor, and the effectiveness of counsel. Knowing that a disclosure cannot be compelled, a client may be forthcoming with his or her attorney, which in turn enhances the value of the attorney's counsel. Among the recognized privileged communications are those between husband and wife, attorney and client, doctor and patient, and clergy and penitent. No attorney can disclose privileged information, even after the end of the attorney-client relationship. A client or patient may waive the privilege and consent to disclosure of otherwise protected information.

CHAPTER 6

The Eighth Amendment

Overview, 395

The Eighth Amendment, 399

Overview

The Eighth Amendment states that "excessive bail shall not be required, nor excessive fines imposed, nor cruel and unusual punishments inflicted." The first clause of the Eighth Amendment provides protection from the imposition of disproportionate or inordinately high bail or fines for criminal offenses. Bail accomplishes pretrial release of a defendant by defining the conditions of the release and by specifying sanctions for "bail-skipping." The critical consideration is assuring the defendant's appearance at subsequent proceedings. Pretrial release allows a person charged with a crime to retain his or her freedom while awaiting trial. It is a significant component of the proposition that a person is presumed innocent until proven guilty. The Supreme Court has ruled that bail is excessive when it is set higher than an amount that reasonably can be expected to "assure the presence of the accused at trial."

Congress and state legislatures have attempted to define the perimeters of the Excessive Bail Clause of the Eighth Amendment. In 1966, for example, Congress passed the Bail Reform Act, which itemized criteria to be considered in making pretrial release judgments. Most state legislatures followed the 1966 act with reforms of their own, but for certain serious offenses and/or for defendants with previous and extensive criminal records, many state courts deny bail altogether.

The Bail Reform Act of 1984 provided for "preventive detention" of defendants determined likely to commit additional crime. This approach was upheld in *United States v. Salerno*, 481 U.S. 739 (1987). The Eighth Amendment also prohibits the imposition of "excessive fines." This provision was examined in the context of civil forfeiture proceedings in *Austin v. United States*, 509 U.S. 602 (1993).

The Supreme Court has established the following standards for its interpretation of the Cruel and Unusual Punishment Clause of the Eighth Amendment. Punishment cannot involve torture, be inordinately cruel, or be disproportionate or excessive relative to the offense. Punishment can be imposed only for bona fide criminal offenses. Chief Justice Earl Warren has said in *Trop v. Dulles*, 356 U.S. 86 (1958), that the Cruel and Unusual Punishment Clause draws its meanings from "evolving standards of decency that mark the progress of a maturing society." Thus, the interpretation of what constitutes cruel and unusual punishment is a fluid concept in which the status of a particular punishment, such as the death penalty, may change as society's values evolve and/or mature.

The Court initially considered the question of excessive and disproportionate punishment in a noncapital context in the case of *Robinson v. California*, 370 U.S. 660 (1962), in which the Court held that California's imposition of criminal penalties could not stand merely because competent authority had determined that a defendant was addicted to narcotics. The Court considered it cruel and unusual punishment to impose criminal penalties on someone whose only "offense" was addiction to narcotics. *Robinson* was especially important because it extended the clause to state actions. In *Harmelin v Michigan*, 501 U.S. 957 (1991), the Court considered the issue of proportionality for a prison sentence.

The dominant cruel and unusual punishment theme in recent years has been the clause's application to the death penalty. The constitutionality of such a penalty, including procedures by which it may be imposed and actual methods of execution, have all been examined by the Supreme Court. The Court held most state death penalty laws to be defective in 1972 because those with the authority to impose such a sentence could exercise complete discretion over the terms of capital punishment. Imposition of the death penalty constituted cruel and unusual punishment because its application was arbitrary, discriminatory, and capricious. In *Gregg v. Georgia*, 428 U.S. 153 (1976), the Court declared that capital punishment was not unconstitutional per se and could be used where sufficient "structure" was provided for its imposition.

The decision in *Woodson v. North Carolina*, 428 U.S. 280 (1976), invalidated the holding that made the death penalty mandatory for particular and specified offenses. One of the structural elements of new death penalty laws is the fashioning of aggravating circumstances, at least one of which must be present before a person may be sentenced to death. The Court said in *Maynard v. Cartwright*, 486 U.S. 356 (1988), however, that these aggravating circumstances must be precisely designed. It has been argued that another defect of the death penalty is that it falls inequitably to members of racial minorities. That issue was examined by the Court in *McCleskey v. Kemp*, 481 U.S. 279 (1987). Finally, the Court determined in *Stanford v. Kentucky*, 492 U.S. 361 (1989), that the Eighth Amendment permits the imposition of the death sentence on a person who commits the capital crime before reaching the age of 18.

The significance of the Cruel and Unusual Punishment Clause is illustrated by the Supreme Court extending its interpretation of the Clause to allow for review of all noncapital sentencing policies and penal objectives established by state legislatures, including the adequacy of prison facilities and confinement conditions. The Court found, for example, that the practice of double-celling prisoners in a maximum-security state prison did not violate the Cruel and Unusual

Punishment Clause. The Court has also held on numerous occasions that one of its ongoing functions is to review claims of violations of prisoners' rights through the Clause, and thus preside over the evolving standards of the Eighth Amendment.

This chapter concludes with two other issues related to punishment. One is the use of sentencing guidelines. In *Mistretta v. United States*, 488 U.S. 361 (1988), the Court upheld the process used to create the federal guidelines. The second issue involves federal review of state criminal cases through the habeas corpus process. The Rehnquist Court has significantly limited the relief available under federal habeas review in cases such as *Coleman v. Thompson*, 501 U.S. 722 (1991), *Teague v. Lane*, 489 U.S. 288 (1989), and *Herrera v. Collins*, 506 U.S. 390 (1993).

The Eighth Amendment protects the principle that one is presumed innocent until proven guilty and proscribes cruel and unusual punishments. The Eighth Amendment is divided into two clauses, the first saying, "excessive bail shall not be required, nor excessive fines imposed," the second adding, "nor cruel and unusual punishments inflicted." Like other provisions of the Bill of Rights, the Eighth Amendment originated in English common law. Centuries of English statutory law contributed to the tradition that individual liberties would be offended if an accused person was not afforded the opportunity to be "admitted to bail." The accused must be presumed innocent until trial of the facts and evidentiary proceedings prove otherwise. In 1679, for example, the Habeas Corpus Act required "persons imprisoned for bailable offenses to be set free on bail, so that the King's subjects could not longer be detained in prison in such cases where by law they are bailable." Section 20 of the Magna Carta had earlier stipulated that no excessive fines should be imposed upon subjects of the Crown. A major defect of English statutory law, however, was that for centuries no limit was set on the amount of bail a judge could demand. The resulting abuses in the bail system were not eliminated until passage of the English Bill of Rights after the Revolution of 1688. In 1689 the English Parliament was forced to adopt a Bill of Rights as the result of widespread abuses of individual liberties during the reign of the Stuarts. The Bill of Rights was directly the result of the cruel punishments imposed during the days of the infamous Court of Star Chamber. A major difference between the English and the American Bill of Rights was that the former had only legislative standing, while the latter had constitutional weight and status. The American authors of the Eighth Amendment also chose to substitute for the words "ought to" in the English Bill of Rights the imperative words "shall not" in the American Bill of Rights. The change made the amendment enforceable by the courts, not subject to future legislative caveats. The Virginia, North Carolina, and New York ratifying conventions urged the inclusion of the Eighth Amendment in the Bill of Rights, knowing implicitly of the violations of the safeguards purported to be contained in the English Bill of Rights through their study of Blackstone's *Commentaries*. Blackstone characterized the violations as "barbarous punishments." Punishments in the colonies during the years prior to the Revolutionary War were quite severe. *See also* BILL OF RIGHTS, p. 621; COMMON LAW, p. 631; CONSTITUTIONALISM, p. 634; MAGNA CARTA, p. 677.

Significance The Eighth Amendment assures that the amount of bail imposed on a criminal defendant is commensurate with the alleged offense. Presumption of guilt is not fixed before trial of the facts. The bail clause was codified in the Judiciary Act of 1789 and further elaborated in the Bail Reform Act of 1966. In *Stack v. Boyle*, 342 U.S. 1 (1951), Chief Justice Fred M. Vinson, writing for the Supreme Court majority, made the following statement concerning the established American tradition of bail admittance and imposition:

> From the passage of the Judiciary Act of 1789 to the present Rules of Criminal Procedure, federal law has unequivocally provided that a person arrested for a noncapital offense shall be admitted to bail. This traditional right to freedom before conviction permits the unhampered preparation of a defense, and serves to prevent the infliction of punishment prior to conviction.... Unless this right to bail before trial is preserved, the presumption of innocence, secured only after centuries of struggle, would lose its meaning. (342 U.S. at 5)

The second Clause of the Eighth Amendment illustrates the dynamic and evolutionary processes at work in American constitutional law. In *Weems v. United States*, 217 U.S. 349 (1910), the Supreme Court established that the Cruel and Unusual Punishment Clause of the amendment was to be interpreted in light of the social values of the time. Subsequent Courts have reiterated the *Weems* standard that the Eighth Amendment "is not fastened to the absolute but may acquire meaning as public opinion becomes enlightened by humane justice."

Noncapital Punishment

Robinson v. California, **370 U.S. 660 (1962),** invalidated a California statute that made narcotics addiction a crime. The question before the Warren Court in this case was whether the Eighth Amendment prohibition against cruel and unusual punishment precluded a state from making narcotics addiction a crime. Lawrence Robinson had been convicted in the Los Angeles Municipal Court of addiction to narcotics, a misdemeanor, and sentenced to 90 days in jail. Robinson was not under the influence of drugs at the time of his arrest, and the only evidence against him was the testimony of the arresting officer who observed scars and needle marks on Robinson's arms. The California courts upheld the conviction, and Robinson appealed to the United States Supreme Court. The Supreme Court struck down the California statute as one that punished an individual solely on the basis of a particular condition or status rather than for an overt criminal act. Justice Potter Stewart said that a statute that defines a chronic condition as an "offense" may render a person "continuously guilty of the offense." The statute subjected an individual to potential prosecution "at any time prior to [that individual's] reform." Further, the statute's focus on this "status of addiction" reached persons who might never have used or possessed narcotics nor have been engaged in any other "antisocial behaviors" in the state of California. The Court viewed narcotics addiction as similar to other illnesses, such as venereal disease and mental illness. The Court reasoned that legislation making an illness a criminal offense would "doubtless be universally thought to be an infliction of cruel and unusual punishment." The Court concluded that the 90-day jail sentence imposed on Robinson was not a problem in an "abstract" sense, but the particular penalty had to be considered in the context of the offense. Stewart wrote, "Even one day in prison would be cruel and unusual punishment for the 'crime' of having a common cold." The Court's emphasis, therefore, was not focused on the *method* of punishment so much as the *nature* of the "crime" for which the punishment was considered. The dissenters, Justices Clark and White, were critical of the Court's unwillingness to defer to California's initiative in responding to drug addiction. Clark said that the statute created something akin to "civil commitment," and would have permitted California to require some treatment for those "who have lost the power of self-control." In his concurring majority opinion Justice Douglas responded by observing that "the addict is a sick person [who] may, of course, be confined for treatment or for the protection of society. Cruel and unusual punishment results not from confinement, but from convicting the addict of a crime." *See also Coker v. Georgia*, p. 422; CRUEL AND UNUSUAL PUNISHMENT, p. 637; EIGHTH AMENDMENT, p. 399.

Significance *Robinson* extended the cruel and unusual punishment prohibition to the states through the Due Process Clause of the Fourteenth Amendment. It also established that the prohibitions envisioned in the Cruel and Unusual Punishment Clause contain limitations on the kinds of behavior and conditions that can properly be considered criminal. The decision in *Robinson* integrated the concepts of criminal intent and overt criminal acts into the Eighth Amendment: Criminal punishment requires criminal behavior. The broader immediate effect was to place in jeopardy all laws that focus on a particular condition or status. Vagrancy ordinances became suspect, for example, and many states decriminalized certain kinds of behavior in which the victim of the crime and the accused are the same person—the so-called victimless crime. Other states reduced from felonies to misdemeanors certain types of antisocial behavior. Still other states opened treatment facilities for alcoholics and drug abusers, while simultaneously abolishing the previously construed criminal nature of the condition.

Robinson also raised questions about the constitutionality of punishments that were the products of a nonpunishable condition or status. In *Powell v. Texas*, 392 U.S. 514 (1968), for example, the Court considered whether a chronic alcoholic could be convicted of public intoxication. The Court did not extend *Robinson* to include symptomatic behavior. The Court distinguished *Powell* from *Robinson*, saying that Powell was not being punished for his alcoholism, but for being drunk in public.

Excessive/Disproportionate Punishment

***Harmelin v. Michigan,* 501 U.S. 957 (1991),** held that a state may sentence someone to a life sentence without the possibility of parole for possession of more than 650 grams of cocaine. Harmelin had contended that the penalty was disproportionately heavy and, as a consequence, violated the Cruel and Unusual Punishment Clause of the Eighth Amendment. Michigan is the only state that provides the life-without-parole sentence for this drug offense. Five justices found no Eighth Amendment violation. These five justices were not in agreement, however, on how far this ruling should extend. The Court had previously ruled in *Solem v. Helm*, 463 U.S. 277 (1983), that a state recidivist law that imposed a life sentence without the possibility of parole for nonassaultive felonies was cruel and unusual on proportionality grounds—that is, that the punishment was excessive relative to the crime. Chief Justice Rehnquist joined Justice Scalia's opinion in *Harmelin*, which said that the Eighth Amendment "contains no proportionality guarantee." They were also of the view that *Solem* was wrongly decided and should be overruled. *Solem* had established three criteria by which sentence proportionality is to be examined: (1) inherent gravity of the offense, (2) sentences imposed in the same jurisdiction for the same offense, and (3) sentences imposed in other jurisdictions for the same crime. In Scalia's view, there are no "adequate textual or historical standards" by which this can be done; there is no "objective standard of gravity." Cross-jurisdictional comparisons were further flawed because without a "constitutionally imposed uniformity inimical to traditional notions of federalism, some state will always bear the distinction of treating particular offenders more severely than any other state." Diversity of policy and means of implementing policy is, continued Scalia, the "very *raison d'etre* of our federal system." The Eighth Amendment is "not a ratchet, whereby a temporary consensus on leniency for a particular crime fixes a permanent constitutional maximum, disabling the States from giving effect to altered beliefs and responding to changed social conditions." Scalia and Rehnquist also rejected Harmelin's contention that the Eighth Amendment contains a "required mitigation" doctrine that requires individualized sentencing in noncapital as well as capital cases. In their view, mandatory sentencing is prohibited only in death penalty situations. Justices Kennedy, O'Connor, and Souter did not find Harmelin's sentence to be excessive, but felt that the Eighth Amendment contains a principle of proportionality that applies to both capital and noncapital cases. Kennedy spoke for the three and preferred to reinterpret *Solem* rather than abandon it. The primary responsibility for prison terms "lies with the legislature," and courts should grant "substantial deference to the broad authority that legislatures necessarily possess in determining the types and limits of punishments for crimes." Kennedy said it was estimated that 650 grams of cocaine had a potential yield of 32,500 to 65,000 doses. Against those numbers, Kennedy characterized Harmelin's argument that his crime was nonviolent and victimless as "false to the point of absurdity." Harmelin's crime was seen as sufficiently severe that Michigan's legislature could rationally conclude the crime to be as "serious and violent as the crime of felony murder, ... a crime for which no sentence would be disproportionate." Comparison of Harmelin's crime and his sentence did not, said Kennedy, "give rise to an inference of gross disproportionality." As a result, Kennedy did not feel it necessary to conduct further comparative review. Justices White, Marshall, Blackmun, and Stevens dissented. They objected to the mandatory approach that did not permit a tailoring of the sentence to the individual's "personal responsibility and moral guilt." Possession of drugs, even in the large quantity involved in this case, said White, "is not so serious an offense that it will always warrant, much less mandate, life imprisonment without the possibility of parole." The dissenters also saw Michigan's penalty as substantially more severe than other jurisdictions. White pointed out that possession of the same amount of cocaine in Alabama would subject a defendant to a mandatory minimum sentence of only five years in prison. *See also* EIGHTH AMENDMENT, p. 399.

Significance   The disproportionality issue addressed in *Harmelin* has split the Court since the early 1980s. In *Rummel v. Estelle*, 445 U.S. 263 (1980), the Court assessed mandatory life sentences for repeat offenders. The Court decided in *Coker v. Georgia*, 433 U.S. 584 (1977), that the criteria used to assess Georgia's choice of the death penalty for rape were not directly applicable in a noncapital case. The Court said great deference ought to be extended to legislative judgments when prison sentences are involved. While Texas had the most extreme habitual offender statute in the country, it differed in degree rather than in kind from other states. Short of differences in kind, the Eighth Amendment should not be used to invalidate judgments that are "peculiarly" matters for the legislature. Two years later in *Hutto v. Davis*, 454 U.S. 370 (1982), the Court upheld the imposition of two consecutive 20-year prison terms and two $10,000 fines for the crime of possession and distribution of nine ounces of marijuana. Building on *Rummel* the Court said there was no way to "make any constitutional distinction between a term of years and a shorter or longer term of years." While expressing some concern about the severity of the sentence received by Davis, the Court refrained from finding for him. To have done so would be "invariably a subjective decision," and courts should be "reluctant to review legislatively mandated terms of imprisonment." *Rummel* and *Davis* seemed to suggest that Eighth Amendment challenges of prison sentences would not be successful. *Harmelin* reflects the deference that is characteristic of the Court in cases involving criminal penalties. The decision also suggests that it is unlikely that the Court will extend the proportionality analysis to many prison sentences.

Excessive Fines

***Austin v. United States*, 509 U.S. 602 (1993)** Federal law permits civil forfeiture of properties that are either used in or acquired with proceeds from illegal drug transactions. Richard Austin sold two grams of cocaine to an individual working with local police. The buyer had approached Austin at Austin's place of business. Austin left his shop, went to his trailer home that was located nearby, returned, and delivered drugs to the buyer. Austin eventually pleaded guilty to one state count of possession of drugs with intent to distribute. Following his sentencing, a federal civil forfeiture proceeding was initiated. Austin's trailer home and place of business were both confiscated without trial on the grounds that these properties had been used in the drug transaction. Austin unsuccessfully argued that the Excessive Fines Clause of the Eighth Amendment applied to civil forfeitures. A unanimous Supreme Court, however, held that the Excessive Fines Clause does apply and remanded the case for consideration of whether the forfeiture ordered in Austin's case was excessive. Justice Blackmun said that the general purpose of the Eighth Amendment was to "limit the government's power to punish." The Excessive Fines Clause more specifically limits the government's power to "extract payments, whether in cash or in kind, 'as *punishment* for some offense.'" The United States had argued that the civil forfeiture process is not limited by the Eighth Amendment. The issue according to Justice Blackmun, however, was not "whether forfeiture was civil or criminal, but rather whether it is punishment." Sanctions frequently serve more than one purpose. It is not necessary to "exclude the possibility that a forfeiture serves remedial purposes to conclude that it is subject to the limitations of the Excessive Fines Clause." All that must be shown is that the forfeiture "serv[es] in part to punish." The Court found the objective of punishment reflected several ways: in the legislative history of the law; in Congress's choice of linking forfeiture directly to drug offenses; and in the inclusion of an "innocent owner defense." Despite arguments by the United States that the law was remedial, the Court ruled that the government failed to show that the civil forfeiture process was exclusively remedial. A civil sanction that "cannot fairly be said *solely* to serve a remedial purpose, but rather can only be explained as also serving either retributive or deterrent purposes, is punishment, as we have come to understand the term." *See also* EIGHTH AMENDMENT, p. 399.

Significance   It is well established that the government may seize assets that are the proceeds of criminal activity. Seizure of assets has become a common approach when dealing with drug offenders. A number of constitutional issues have been prompted as a result, several of which have targeted the Eighth Amendment prohibition on excessive fines. Production and/or distribution of obscenity is one of the offenses falling under the forfeiture provisions of the Racketeer Influenced and Corrupt Organizations Act (RICO). RICO provides that persons convicted of two or more obscenity offenses may have all property directly or indirectly traceable to the convictions confiscated. Ferris Alexander was convicted in 1989 of 18 counts of obscenity offenses and three RICO violations stemming from them. In addition to prison terms, fines, and assessed costs, the trial court ordered Alexander to forfeit his entire business. Under the RICO forfeiture, Alexander lost almost $9 million in cash, plus the property and inventory connected to his business activities. Alexander challenged the RICO forfeiture as prohibited by the Eighth Amendment. The Supreme Court unanimously concluded that the forfeiture was a form of punishment for Eighth Amendment purposes in *Alexander v. United States*, 509 U.S. 544 (1993). The Excessive Fines Clause limits governmental power to "extract payments ... as punishment for some offense." The criminal forfeiture at issue here, said Rehnquist, "is clearly a form of monetary punishment no different, for Eighth Amendment purposes, from a traditional 'fine.'" Notwithstanding the *Austin* and *Alexander* rulings, the Court has generally deferred to government authority to seize assets connected to crimes, and the Excessive Fines Clause has not become a major impediment to the asset seizure strategy.

Hosep Bajakajian attempted to leave the country with more than $350,000 in cash without filing a currency-transport report. Bajakajian pleaded guilty to failing to file the report, and the government argued that the entire amount should be forfeited. The judge found the offense to be "minor," and set the amount of forfeiture at $15,000. The Supreme Court ruled in *United States v. Bajakajian*, 118 S.Ct. 2028 (1998), that when the government uses forfeiture primarily for punitive purposes, the amount seized may not be "grossly disproportional to the seriousness of the crime." The government argued it had an "overriding sovereign interest" in controlling property that enters and leaves the country. Full forfeiture of unreported currency, it was contended, supports that interest by serving to "deter illicit movements of cash" as well as providing the government with valuable information by which it might detect criminal activities associated with the money. The Court found deterrence to be a "traditional goal of punishment," and the forfeiture of currency does not "serve the remedial purpose of compensating the Government for a loss." The claimed loss of information about currency leaving the country, said Justice Thomas, "would not be remedied by the   Government's confiscation of [Bajakajian's] $357,144." The forfeiture in this case "does not bear any of the hallmarks" of traditional civil forfeitures against property. The government had not proceeded against the currency itself, but "instead sought and obtained a criminal conviction of [Bajakajian] personally"—the forfeiture served no remedial function, and was designed to punish the offender. The government argued that the money was the "instrumentality" of the crime because without the attempt to export the cash, there would have been no violation at all. Acceptance of the government's position, said Thomas, would "require us to expand the traditional understanding of instrumentality forfeitures." Instrumentalities historically have been treated as a form of "guilty property" that can be forfeited in civil proceedings against the property itself. In this case, the government has sought to punish Bajakajian by proceeding against him personally. As a result, the forfeiture is punitive, and the test for excessiveness of a punitive forfeiture "involves solely a proportionality determination." The amount of the forfeiture "must bear some relationship to the gravity of the offense that it is designed to punish." The standard the Court used is that a punitive forfeiture violates the Excessive Fines Clause "if it is grossly disproportional to the gravity of the defendant's offense." The Court concluded forfeiture of the entire $357,144 was excessive. Bajakajian's crime was "solely a reporting offense." He would have been able to transport the money out of the country as long as he reported it, thus his crime was "willful failure to report removal of currency from the United States." Further, his reporting violation was unrelated to other criminal activities. Under the Federal Sentencing Guidelines, he could not have been incarcerated for longer than six months nor fined more than $5,000. Such penalties in the Court's view "confirm a minimal level of culpability." The harm Bajakajian caused also "was minimal," affecting only the government in a "relatively minor way." Had his crime gone undetected, the government "would have been deprived only of the information that $357,144 had left the country." Forfeiture of the entire amount, Thomas concluded, "bears no articulable correlation to any injury suffered by the Government." Justice Kennedy, joined by Chief Justice Rehnquist and Justices Scalia and O'Connor, dissented. They thought it inappropriate that the Court substitute its view of the seriousness of the crime for the judgment made by Congress. The dissenters also felt that the Court underestimated the value of the reporting statute. Use of large sums of cash, said Kennedy, is "one of the few reliable signs of some serious crimes." Without full forfeiture, the fine upheld by the Court could become a "modest cost of doing business in the world of drugs and crime."

Excessive Bail/Preventive Detention

United States v. Salerno, **481 U.S. 739 (1987)** Congress enacted the Bail Reform Act of 1984, which authorized federal judges to order pretrial detention of persons accused of serious crimes if appearance could not be reasonably assured, and if the person was deemed sufficiently dangerous to others. The preventive detention provisions of the Act were upheld by the Supreme Court in *Salerno*. The Court rejected the contention that the Act was defective because it authorized punishment before trial. The history of the Act "clearly indicates that the Congress chose detention as a potential solution to the pressing societal problem of crimes committed by persons on release." Preventing danger to the community is a legitimate regulatory goal. Further, the incidents of detention are not excessive in relation to that goal. The Court then said unequivocally that the Due Process Clause did not prohibit pretrial detention as a regulatory measure. The government's regulatory interest in public safety can, under certain circumstances, outweigh an individual's liberty interest. The Court said that the Act narrowly focuses on the acute problem of crime by arrestees in a situation in which the governmental interest is overwhelming. In addition, the Act contains extensive procedural safeguards that both limit the circumstances under which detention may be sought for the most serious crimes and that further the accuracy of the likelihood-of-dangerousness determination. Finally, the Court said that the Act did not violate the Excessive Bail Clause. It simply permits bail to be set at an infinite amount for reasons not related to the risk of flight. Nothing in the Clause, said the Court, limits the government's interest in setting bail solely for the prevention of flight. When Congress has mandated detention on the basis of some other compelling interest—here public safety—the Eighth Amendment does not require release on bail. *See also* EIGHTH AMENDMENT, p. 399.

Significance   The Court's first consideration of preventive detention came in *Schall v. Martin*, 467 U.S. 253 (1984), which upheld the preventive detention of juveniles. *Schall v. Martin* examined a state statute that authorized pretrial detention of a juvenile as long as it could be shown that there was "serious risk" of the juvenile committing additional crimes if released. Martin brought suit, claiming the statute was unconstitutional on due process and equal protection grounds. A federal district court ruled the law violated the Due Process Clause and ordered the release of all juveniles detained under the statute. The Supreme Court found that the law did not violate the Due Process Clause. Justice Rehnquist said the Court needed to determine if legitimate state interests were served by preventive detention, and whether the procedural safeguards were adequate. The Court said that crime prevention is a "weighty social objective," and that a state's legitimate and compelling interest in protecting its citizenry from crime "cannot be doubted." That interest "persists undiluted in the juvenile context." The harm caused by crime is not dependent upon the age of the perpetrator, and the harm to society generally may be even greater, given the high rate of recidivism among juveniles. In addition, the juvenile's liberty interest may be subordinated to the state's "*parens patriae* interest in preserving and promoting the welfare of the child." Rehnquist argued that society has a legitimate interest in protecting a juvenile from the consequences of his criminal activity. This includes the potential injury that may occur when a victim resists and "the downward spiral of criminal activity into which peer pressure may lead the child." The Court saw the state interest as substantial and legitimate, a view "confirmed by the widespread use and judicial acceptance of preventive detention for juveniles." Rehnquist observed that "mere invocation of a legitimate purpose" will not justify particular restrictions and conditions of confinement amounting to punishment. The Court found the statute in question to have nonpunitive objectives, however. The detention specified was "strictly limited in time," and it entitled the juvenile to an expedited fact-finding hearing. The Court then addressed the procedural issue of whether there was "sufficient protection against erroneous and unnecessary deprivation of liberty." The Court found that the statute provided "far more predetention protection" than required for probable cause determinations for adults. Although the initial appearance was informal, full notice was given and stenographic records were kept. The juvenile was accompanied by a parent or guardian and was informed of his or her constitutional rights, including the right to remain silent and be represented by counsel. Finally, the Court rejected the contention that the statute's standard for detention—serious risk of additional criminal conduct—was "fatally vague." Prediction of future criminal conduct is a judgment based on "a host of variables which cannot be readily codified." Nonetheless, the decision on detention is based on "as much information as can reasonably be obtained at the initial appearance," and is not impermissibly vague. Justices Marshall, Brennan, and Stevens dissented. They saw the statute as a violation of due process because it allowed punishment before final adjudication of guilt. They felt the crime prevention interest was insufficient justification for the infringement of the detainee's rights.

Prior to *Schall*, the Court had let preventive detention statutes stand without review. While bail should have the effect of ensuring an appearance at subsequent proceedings, the policy of preventive detention is aimed at confining defendants who present a serious threat of additional criminal conduct. Although such a policy may be effective as a crime prevention strategy, it also runs counter to the presumption of innocence. For many, it constitutes imposition of punishment before adjudication of guilt. In *United States v. Montalvo-Murillo*, 495 U.S. 711 (1990), the Court considered whether failure to provide a timely detention hearing under the Bail Reform Act of 1984 required release of a person who would otherwise be detained. The Act provided that a detention hearing should occur "immediately" unless either side has "good cause" to obtain a continuance. Continuance on motion by the defendant is limited to five days, while a government initiated continuance may not exceed three days. For several reasons, Montalvo's detention hearing did not occur until 13 days after his arrest. Because the statutory time limit had elapsed, the trial court ruled that release was required. The Supreme Court disagreed. Although the time limits of the Act must be followed "with care and precision," the Act "is silent" on the issue of remedy for violation. Nothing in the Act "can be read to require, or even suggest, that a timing error must result in release of a person who should otherwise be detained." Automatic release "contravenes the object of the statute." The end of "exact compliance" with the letter of the Act "cannot justify the means of exposing the public to an increased likelihood of violent crimes by persons on bail, an evil the statute aims to prevent."

The *Salerno* reasoning was subsequently advanced in a case involving detention of individuals acquitted of crimes on grounds of mental illness. The issue in *Foucha v. Louisiana*, 504 U.S. 71 (1990), was whether a state can continue to confine such individuals, even if recovered, until they can demonstrate that they are no longer a threat to their own or others' safety. The Court did not find the *Salerno* rationale sufficient to save the Louisiana law under review. Justice White said that unlike the "sharply focused" pretrial detention policy at issue in *Salerno*, the Louisiana scheme of confinement is "not carefully limited." In addition, under the Louisiana law, individuals such as Foucha were not entitled to a hearing at which the state carries the burden of demonstrating a potential community threat. To the contrary, "the State need prove nothing to justify continued detention" while shifting the burden to the detainee to prove he or she is not dangerous. *Salerno* was further distinguished in that detention was "strictly limited in duration." On the other hand, because Foucha was found to have an "antisocial personality that sometimes leads to aggressive conduct, ... he may be held indefinitely." The Court concluded that by this reasoning a state could be permitted to hold indefinitely any other recovered insanity acquittee who could be shown to have a personality disorder that may lead to criminal conduct. The same could be true of "any convicted criminal, even though he has completed his prison term." If allowed, such a policy would be "only a step away from substituting confinement for dangerousness for our present system which ... incarcerates only those who are proved beyond reasonable doubt to have violated a criminal law."

Leroy Hendricks had a long history of sex offenses—five convictions for sexually molesting children. His most recent conviction came in 1984 through a plea agreement for which he was sentenced for a maximum of 20 years. Over the course of Hendricks's imprisonment, he earned sufficient early-release credit to be eligible for release in 1994. That same year, Kansas enacted its Sexually Violent Predator Act, which authorizes civil confinement for persons adjudged to be sexually violent predators. Under terms of the law, a person so confined may petition a court to review the continued confinement, but release from confinement may not occur unless the court finds the person no longer mentally ill or dangerous. Prior to Hendricks's release, the state sought authorization to continue his confinement under the Act. A jury found Hendricks to be a sexually violent predator, and he was committed to a mental health facility. A sharply divided Court upheld the law in *Kansas v. Hendricks*, 521 U.S. 346 (1997). There was consensus on Hendricks's substantive due process claim. The state court had concluded that the statute's definition of "mental abnormality" did not satisfy the "mental illness" requirement in the civil commitment context. The Supreme Court disagreed. The freedom from physical restraint has always been, said Justice Thomas, "at the core of the liberty protected by the Due Process Clause from arbitrary governmental action." That liberty interest, however, "is not absolute." An individual's constitutionally protected interests may be "overridden even in the civil context." Involuntary commitment statutes have been upheld generally "provided the confinement takes place pursuant to proper procedures and evidentiary standards." A finding of dangerousness by itself is ordinarily not enough to justify indefinite involuntary commitment, but when proof of dangerousness is combined with a mental "abnormality," the combination limits "involuntary civil confinement to those who suffer from a volitional impairment rending them dangerous beyond their control." In this case, Hendricks's admitted lack of volitional control, coupled with a prediction of future dangerousness, "adequately distinguishes" Hendricks from "other dangerous persons who are perhaps more properly dealt with exclusively through criminal proceedings." Hendricks's diagnosis as a pedophile, which qualifies as a "mental abnormality" under the Kansas law, said Thomas, "plainly suffices for due process purposes." Thomas then turned to Hendricks's double jeopardy claims. Categorization of proceeding as civil is a "question of statutory construction," and ordinarily the Court defers to the stated legislative intent. Although the civil label is "not always dispositive," Thomas said, the Court "reject[s] the Legislature's manifest intent" only when a party provides "clear proof" that the statutory scheme is "so punitive either in purpose or effect as to negate the State's intention to deem it 'civil.'" Hendricks "failed to satisfy this heavy burden" in the Court's view. Commitment under the Act did not implicate either of the "primary objectives" of criminal punishment: retribution or deterrence.

Death Penalty

Gregg v. Georgia, **428 U.S. 153 (1976),** determined that the death penalty is not categorically cruel and unusual punishment. The Supreme Court struck down all existing state capital punishment statutes in *Furman v. Georgia*, 408 U.S. 238 (1972). The principal defect was that the decision to impose or not the death penalty was arbitrary because the sentencer (judge and/or jury) possessed unlimited discretion. In other words, the states were using processes flawed by the absence of any guidelines to structure sentencer discretion. Many state legislatures responded to *Furman* by revising their capital punishment statutes to provide guidance to capital sentencers. In three cases, *Gregg v. Georgia*, 428 U.S. 153 (1976), *Proffitt v. Florida*, 428 U.S. 242 (1976), and *Jurek v. Texas*, 428 U.S. 262 (1976), the Supreme Court upheld statutes as revised by Georgia, Florida, and Texas. The Court said that the death penalty included in the revised statutes "does not invariably violate the Constitution." Justice Potter Stewart said that the Court may not "require the legislature to select the least severe penalty possible so long as the penalty selected is not cruelly inhumane or disproportionate." He found society willing to endorse

411

the death penalty because 35 state legislatures had provided for the death penalty after *Furman.* Thus contemporary standards were not offended. Justice Stewart said retribution was a sufficient legislative objective to support the statutes. He viewed capital punishment as an "expression of society's moral outrage at particularly offensive conduct." The Court also considered whether death was an excessive penalty in itself, deciding in Justice Stewart's words that when life has been taken, death is not invariably "disproportionate." It is "an extreme sanction, suitable to the most extreme crimes." As for the statutory flaws alleged in *Furman,* Justice Stewart concluded that the state statute revisions adequately remedied the defects. Arbitrariness was eliminated through several procedural revisions: All the statutes contained bifurcated trial-sentence processes, in which the guilt discrimination stage was separated from the sentencing stage. All required appellate review, and structured sentencer discretion through consideration of aggravating and mitigating circumstances. A sentencer could not consider imposing death in the absence of aggravating circumstances. The Court concluded that sentencer discretion had been adequately structured in the revised state statutes and that the *Furman* defects had been overcome. Justices Marshall and Brennan dissented, arguing that capital punishment was constitutionally offensive under any circumstances. Justice Marshall contended that a punishment may be excessive, and therefore cruel and unusual, even though there may be public support of it. *See also Coker v. Georgia,* p. 422; EIGHTH AMENDMENT, p. 399; *Woodson v. North Carolina,* p. 424.

Significance   *Gregg v. Georgia* clarified several issues regarding capital punishment. First, the Court held that death is a constitutionally permissible penalty for murder, given certain conditions. Second, *Gregg* acknowledged that retribution can serve as a sufficient basis for legislative decisions regarding penal policy. And third, *Gregg* determined that structuring sentencer discretion through the definition of aggravating and mitigating circumstances adequately remedied the problems cited in *Furman.* In *Furman* the Court invalidated statutes that allowed for unguided sentencer discretion. Justice Potter Stewart's concurring opinion emphasized the arbitrariness of unstructured discretion. He found the lack of statutory guidance a problem because it left an inordinate amount of discretion in the hands of the sentencer, and the resulting subjective judgments created cruel and unusual punishment. Justice Stewart found the death penalty in such cases to be cruel "in the same way that being struck by lightning is cruel." The recipients of the death penalty become a "capriciously selected, random handful." In his concurring opinion Justice Byron R. White cited the infrequency of the imposition of capital punishment as a factor in its diminished impact as a deterrent. He found the death penalty to be cruel by virtue of its occasional application. Justice William O. Douglas suggested the death penalty was not only capriciously imposed but was also imposed in a racially discriminatory manner. Justices William J. Brennen and Thurgood Marshall, as in *Gregg*, said capital punishment was unconstitutional on its face and not defensible under any circumstances. The dissenting opinions in *Furman* differed from the Court on three main points: First, the dissenters criticized what Justice Rehnquist characterized a majority's judgement as "an act of will" rather than a proper statement of law. Second, the dissenters maintained that capital punishment did not offend contemporary standards of humaneness. Third, the minority held that competent juries were capable of rendering reasonable decisions even in the absence of specific statutory guidance. The minority pointed to the infrequency of the imposition of the death penalty as a reflection of the proper exercise of "sensitivity and caution" by judges and juries. They saw discretion as an asset rather than a liability. *Furman* required the states to establish standards by which sentencers could or could not impose the death penalty. *Furman* also reversed the holding from *McGautha v. California*, 402 U.S. 183 (1971), that a multistage or bifurcated conviction and sentencing process was not required of the states. The Court believed unguided sentencer discretion to be the principal defect of many state statutes, and *Furman* signaled the states to make revisions accordingly. Two approaches for addressing the discretion issue seemed available after *Furman*. One was the provision of guidance to sentencers by a more careful definition of those offenses for which the death penalty might be imposed. The other was to remove sentencer discretion by imposing a mandatory death sentence as the automatic result of conviction for certain crimes. By 1976, 35 state legislatures had taken one or the other of these options in a thoroughgoing revision of *Furman*-flawed capital punishment statutes. *Gregg* upheld the approach that sought to structure or guide sentencer discretion.

Since *Gregg*, the Court generally has shown deference to state sentencing procedures. In *Spaziano v. Florida*, 468 U.S. 447 (1984), for example, the Court upheld a death sentence imposed by a judge following a jury's recommendation of a life sentence. The Court said that a defendant is not entitled to a jury determination of sentence. Neither is a jury's recommendation so final as to preclude override by the trial judge. Decisions such as *Spaziano* indicate that the Court feels the current death penalty statutes generally meet constitutional requirements. Although some nonuniform processes can be found state to state, the differences do not now constitute critical enough factors for the Court to interfere. Juries participate in the capital sentencing process of 33 states, and all but four of those states give the jury the final decision. The trial judge has the authority to override a jury's sentence recommendation in four states including Alabama, where juries render only an advisory verdict on the death penalty issue. The trial judge is then required to review the entire case record and independently examine the factors that are relevant to the death penalty decision. Alabama law requires that the trial judge only "consider" the jury recommendation on sentence.

Louise Harris was convicted of capital murder in Alabama. Notwithstanding the jury recommendation that she be sentenced to life imprisonment without the possibility of parole, the trial judge concluded that the aggravating evidence outweighed the mitigating evidence and sentenced Harris to death. Harris argued that the Eighth Amendment requires specification of the weight to be given to jury recommendations in capital cases, but the Supreme Court ruled against her in *Harris v. Alabama*, 513 U.S. 504 (1995). Central to the Court's ruling was a comparison of the Alabama process to that of Florida, another of the four states that permit judges to override the jury's sentence recommendation. The Florida statute requires judges to give jury recommendations "great weight," and provides that a jury recommendation of life imprisonment may not be overridden unless the facts supporting a death sentence "are so clear and convincing that virtually no reasonable person could differ." The Florida statute was upheld by the Court in *Spaziano*. The key question in *Harris* was "not the particular weight a State chooses to place upon the jury's advice, but whether the scheme adequately channels the sentencer's discretion so as to prevent arbitrary results." Justice O'Connor pointed out that the Court has neither mandated a specific method for balancing mitigating and aggravating factors nor has it required that states assign specific weight to factors in mitigation or aggravation. To require that "great weight" be given to a jury recommendation, one of the criteria to be considered by the sentencer, would "offend" these established principles and "place within constitutional ambit micromanagement tasks that properly rest within the State's discretion to administer its criminal justice system." The Constitution permits a trial judge, acting alone, to impose the death penalty. The Constitution, O'Connor concluded, is "thus not offended when a State further requires the sentencing judge to consider a jury's recommendation and trusts the judge to give it the proper weight." Justice Stevens, the lone dissenter, was concerned about the "complete absence" of standards to guide the judge's consideration of the jury's verdict. Furthermore, if retribution is the principal justification for the death sentence, Stevens argued that a jury, a representative cross section of a community, "should bear the responsibility to express the conscience of the community" in the death penalty situation. Judges, particularly those who are elected, may be "too responsive" to the "political climate." The jury system, on the other hand, provides "reliable insulation" against the "passions of the polity."

The Court did not find statistical evidence of racial bias in the implementation of Georgia's death penalty law sufficient to establish a constitutional violation in *McCleskey v. Kemp*, 481 U.S. 278 (1987). McCleskey claimed that Georgia's death penalty process was administered in a racially discriminatory manner. He supported his claim by submitting statistical data (known as the Baldus Study) based on more than 2,000 Georgia murder cases tried in the 1970s. The study revealed that blacks whose victims were white had the greatest possibility of receiving the death sentence. The Court ruled that the Baldus Study did not sufficiently demonstrate unconstitutional discrimination, however. In order for McCleskey to prevail, Justice Powell said, it was necessary to demonstrate that the decision makers in this specific case had acted with discriminatory purpose, and that Georgia's legislature had enacted or maintained the law because of an anticipated racially discriminatory effect. The Baldus Study did not show such intent. Further, the statistics did not show that Georgia's death penalty law was arbitrary or capricious, that race governed capital punishment decisions generally, or that race was a decisive factor in McCleskey's case. The likelihood of prejudice allegedly shown did not produce an unacceptable risk of racial prejudice. Justices Brennan, Marshall, Blackmun, and Stevens found the statistical evidence compelling, and that the Baldus Study had raised the probability that race influenced McCleskey's sentence. This outcome, said Brennan, was "intolerable by any imaginable standard." *McCleskey v. Kemp* was one of the most important capital punishment decisions since the Court conditionally upheld the death penalty in *Gregg*. In the years following *Gregg*, the Court focused on relatively narrow procedural questions and basically refined the general approach elucidated in *Gregg*. The Court's rejection of the race discrimination issues raised in *McCleskey* represented the last broad-based challenge to the death penalty entertained by the Rehnquist Court. It was apparent in *McCleskey* that the Rehnquist Court would not be receptive to further challenges to capital punishment. Changes in policies governing death sentences will emanate from state legislatures and state courts rather than the Supreme Court.

Nebraska law does not allow juries to consider lesser-included offenses when the defendant is charged with felony murder. Instead, Nebraska defines felony murder as a form of first-degree murder, but committed while perpetrating (or attempting to perpetrate) other specified felonies. The state does not have to prove a culpable mental state for the murder, as intent to kill is presumed "if the State proves intent to commit the underlying felony." Randolph Reeves was prosecuted for the murder of two women. The killings occurred after Reeves had sexually assaulted one of the murder victims. Reeves requested that the jury be instructed on both second-degree murder and manslaughter at his trial. The trial court refused, and Reeves was convicted of two counts of felony murder and subsequently sentenced to death. Reeves appealed, claiming that he was entitled to a new trial because the trial court had failed to include a lesser-included offense instruction to the jury as required by *Beck v. Alabama*, 447 U.S. 625 (1980). The Court found in *Hopkins v. Reeves*, 118 S.Ct. 1895 (1998), that the *Beck* ruling was "distinguishable in two critical respects." The Alabama law at issue in *Beck* prohibited instructions on offenses that state law clearly recognized as lesser-included offenses of the charged crime, and it did so only in capital cases. Alabama defined felony murder as a lesser-included offense of robbery—intentional murder. Thus, Alabama erected an "artificial barrier" that restricted its juries to a choice between conviction for a capital offense and acquittal. By contrast, the Nebraska court did not deny Reeves instructions on "any existing lesser-included offense of felony murder, because there were none; it merely declined to give instructions on crimes that are not lesser-included offenses." The Nebraska trial court neither "created an artificial barrier" for the jury nor did it treat capital cases differently from noncapital cases. In addition, the Court viewed the instructions Reeves proposed as introducing "another kind of distortion at trial." Nebraska proceeded against Reeves only on a theory of felony murder, a crime that under state law had no lesser-included homicide offenses. The state therefore "assumed the obligation of proving only that crime." To allow a defendant to be convicted on homicide offenses that are not lesser-included offenses of felony murder, therefore, would be to allow his jury to find beyond a reasonable doubt elements that the state had not attempted to prove, and indeed had ignored during the course of the trial. Justice Thomas suggested that this "can hardly be said to be a reliable result."

Death Penalty: Aggravation and Mitigation

Maynard v. Cartwright, **486 U.S. 356 (1988),** determined whether the term "especially heinous, atrocious, or cruel" was unconstitutional as being too vague to define aggravating circumstances that could lead to the death penalty in a murder case. The Supreme Court unanimously held that it was. Vagueness claims directed at aggravating circumstances assert that the challenged provision "fails adequately to inform juries what they must find to impose the death penalty."

This leaves both juries and appellate courts with the kind of "open-ended discretion" that was held invalid in *Furman v. Georgia*, 408 U.S. 238 (1972). Since *Furman* the Court has required that death penalty statutes "channel and limit" sentencer discretion in order to "minimize the risk of wholly arbitrary and capricious action." The Oklahoma aggravating circumstance instruction at issue in *Maynard* gave insufficient guidance to sentencers. To say that something is "especially heinous," said Justice White, merely suggests that the individual jurors should determine that the murder is "more than just heinous, whatever that means, and an ordinary person could honestly believe that every unjustified, intentional taking of human life is especially heinous." The notion that factual circumstances "in themselves" may characterize a murder as "especially heinous, atrocious, or cruel" is an approach that gives the sentencer impermissible discretion in the death penalty decision. *See also* EIGHTH AMENDMENT, p. 399; *Gregg v. Georgia*, p. 411.

Significance   The Court has established that states need to define aggravating circumstances that set the threshold for death penalty deliberations. *Lowenfeld v. Phelps*, 484 U.S. 231 (1988), for example, raised an additional procedural issue. The question was whether a death sentence based on but one aggravating circumstance was proper when that circumstance of aggravation was identical to an element of the crime for which the defendant was convicted. Lowenfeld had been convicted of three counts of first-degree murder, an element of which was his intent to "kill or inflict great bodily harm upon more than one person." At the sentencing phase of the trial, the only aggravating circumstance found by the jury was that he "knowingly created a risk of death or great bodily harm to more than one person." Lowenfeld asserted that the overlap allowed the jury to "merely ... repeat one of its findings in the guilt phase," and thus not to "narrow further" in the sentence stage the "class of death-eligible murderers." The Court rejected this contention. A constitutional scheme must "genuinely narrow" the class of persons eligible for the death penalty and must "reasonably justify" use of the comparatively more severe punishment. The narrowing function may be provided in two ways: by narrow legislative definition, or where broadly defined offenses are narrowed by jurors, by identifying aggravating circumstances. Use of aggravating circumstances is not an "end in itself," but a means of channeling jury discretion. This function can be performed by a jury finding at "either the sentencing phase of the trial or the guilt phase."

In *Dawson v. Delaware*, 503 U.S. 159 (1992), the Court vacated a death sentence on First Amendment association grounds. At Dawson's sentencing hearing, the prosecution read a stipulation referring to a white racist prison gang, known as the "Aryan Brotherhood," that had a chapter in the Delaware prisons. Evidence was subsequently introduced to show that Dawson had the name of the gang tattooed on his hand. The Court held that even though the First Amendment does not "erect a per se barrier to evidence concerning one's beliefs and associations," the narrowness of the stipulation left the reference to the gang irrelevant to Dawson's sentencing proceeding. The evidence about the Aryan Brotherhood was neither specifically tied to the murder committed by Dawson nor used to rebut any mitigating evidence offered by Dawson. The Court allowed that associational evidence might serve a legitimate purpose in representing a defendant's future dangerousness or in developing factors of aggravation. In this case, however, reference to the Aryan Brotherhood could do no more than represent "abstract beliefs" of the Delaware chapter of the gang and Dawson as an individual. The Court concluded that introduction of evidence about the prison gang and Dawson's membership was thus prohibited by the First Amendment.

Although the death penalty may not be cruel and unusual punishment as such, its utilization requires the application of extensive substantive and procedural safeguards. *Gregg v. Georgia*, 428 U.S. 153 (1976), revealed the Court's preference for leaving implementation of capital punishment to the guided discretion of judges and juries. The position taken by the Court in *Gregg* established the foundation for current judicial policy regarding the death penalty. *Barclay v. Florida*, 463 U.S. 939 (1983), gave notice to sentencers that they cannot depart from statutory guidelines in determining aggravating circumstances for imposing the death penalty, however. This is not to say that the Supreme Court will ignore statutory language that it deems vague and ambiguous. It struck down such language in *Godfrey v. Georgia*, 446 U.S. 420 (1980). In *Zant v. Stephens*, 462 U.S. 862 (1983), the Court underscored the jury's independence in determining aggravating circumstances when statutes are clear. The future dangerousness issue was also addressed by the Court in *Wainwright v. Goode*, 464 U.S. 78 (1983), in which it used *Barclay* to uphold a death sentence against challenge that the trial judge had improperly considered the nonstatutory aggravating circumstance of the defendant's future dangerousness. The Court said the critical question was whether consideration of this factor "so infects the balancing process between aggravating and mitigating circumstances fashioned by the capital punishment statute that the sentence needs to be reversed." The Court was satisfied that the independent reweighing of factors by the required review process for the death sentence did not take the future dangerousness factor into account, which meant that it did not violate the Eighth Amendment.

The Court examined the issue of sympathy as a factor in the

penalty phase of a capital murder trial in the case of *California v. Brown*, 479 U.S. 538 (1987). Just prior to the jury's deliberation of sentence, its members were instructed by the trial court to consider the aggravating and mitigating factors of the crime. The judge said that the jury "should not be swayed by mere sentiment, conjecture, sympathy, passion, prejudice, public opinion, or public feeling." The Supreme Court ruled that this instruction did not violate the Eighth Amendment. The Court felt it unlikely that jurors would focus on the term "sympathy" to the exclusion of the other terms accompanying it.

Sentencers (jury or judge) in state capital cases are often required to balance or weigh aggravating and mitigating factors that may exist in a specific case. The prosecution must show at least one aggravating factor in order to obtain a death sentence. The Court has reviewed a number of cases in which capital defendants have challenged the definition of certain aggravating factors on the grounds that the defining language is too vague or imprecise. Although many states require sentencers to weigh aggravating and mitigating factors, only California instructs sentencers to consider various undesignated factors "if relevant." In these situations, the sentencer is left to determine whether any of these factors constitute evidence of aggravation or mitigation. The consolidated cases of *Tuilaepa v. California* and *Proctor v. California*, 512 U.S. 967 (1994), allowed the Court to consider challenges to the wording of three aggravating factors used in California. Both Proctor and Tuilaepa challenged an open-ended factor requiring the sentencer to consider the "circumstances of the crime." Tuilaepa further challenged factors that required the sentencer to consider the "presence or absence of criminal activity ... which involved the use or attempted use of force or violence," and the age of the defendant at the time of the crime. The Court rejected these challenges, however. Justice Kennedy said the "circumstances of the crime" factor was consistent with settled principles of capital jurisprudence. Indeed, consideration of the circumstances of a particular crime is an "indispensable part" of the process of imposing the death sentence. The Court would be "hard pressed," said Kennedy, to "invalidate a jury instruction that implements what we have said the law requires." In the Court's view, the California factor instructs the jury to consider a "relevant subject matter and does so in understandable terms." Challenge of the factor that requires a sentencer to consider a defendant's previous criminal history similarly failed. The factor, Kennedy said, is phrased in "conventional and understandable terms." Both a "backward-looking and forward-looking inquiry" are permissible components of the sentencing process.

Jonathan Simmons was convicted by a South Carolina jury of capital murder. He had a history of prior violent crimes that would have made him ineligible for parole if he was sentenced to a term of incarceration for the murder. The prosecution indicated prior to jury selection that it would oppose any mention of parole, including during the voir dire process. At the sentencing proceeding following Simmons's conviction, the state sought the death penalty on the grounds that Simmons represented a continuing danger to society. Simmons requested a jury instruction that he would never be paroled if sentenced to life imprisonment. In support of this request, Simmons offered a statement from the South Carolina Department of Probation, Parole and Pardons confirming his ineligibility for parole. He also submitted findings from opinion polling data that reflected a widely held belief among the public that a person sentenced to life imprisonment would eventually become eligible for parole. The trial judge rejected the jury instruction requested by Simmons. The jury began its deliberation on sentence and soon thereafter specifically asked the judge whether a life sentence included the possibility of parole. Over defense objection, the judge instructed the jury not to consider parole or parole eligibility in its deliberations on sentence. Twenty-five minutes after receiving this instruction, the jury returned and sentenced Simmons to death. The Supreme Court invalidated the sentence in *Simmons v. South Carolina*, 512 U.S. 154 (1994). It was the Court's view that the Due Process Clause does not permit the execution of a prisoner on the basis of "information which he had no opportunity to deny or explain." Here, the sentencing jury could have reasonably believed that Simmons could be released on parole if he were not executed. To whatever extent this misunderstanding "pervaded the jury's deliberations," it had the effect of "creating a false choice" between sentencing Simmons to death or a period of incarceration. This "grievous misunderstanding was encouraged by the trial court's refusal to provide the jury with accurate information regarding [Simmons's] parole eligibility, and by the State's repeated suggestion that [he] would pose a future danger to society if he were not executed." Blackmun suggested that because this was a capital case, many issues that are "irrelevant" to the guilt-innocence determination "step into the foreground and require consideration at the sentencing phase." As the jury considered Simmons's future dangerousness, the actual duration of the defendant's prison sentence is "indisputably relevant." The state, said Blackmun, "raised the specter of [Simmons's] future dangerousness generally, but then thwarted all efforts by [Simmons] to demonstrate that, contrary to the prosecutor's intimations, he would never be released on parole and thus ... would not pose a future danger to society."

John Romano and a codefendant were together convicted of murder and sentenced to death. Romano was later convicted for a second murder. At the sentencing phase of the second trial, the state introduced the first murder conviction and death sentence as evidence of aggravation. The jury recommended the death penalty in the second case. In *Caldwell v. Mississippi*, 472 U.S. 320 (1985), the Court had ruled that a jury in a capital case must understand that it, rather than an appellate court, has the sole responsibility for determining the defendant's sentence. Romano appealed his second sentence on the ground that the jury's knowledge that he was already facing a death sentence diminished any sense of singular responsibility for the sentencing decision in the second trial. The case was made more difficult by the fact that following sentencing in the second case, Romano's conviction for the first murder was reversed by an Oklahoma appellate court on the grounds that he should have been tried separately from his codefendant. In *Romano v. Oklahoma*, 512 U.S. 1 (1994), the U.S. Supreme Court affirmed Romano's sentence in the second case nonetheless. Chief Justice Rehnquist said that to establish a *Caldwell* violation, a defendant must show that remarks to the jury "improperly describe the role assigned to the jury by local law." Romano contended that the evidence of his prior death sentence impermissibly undermined the sentencing jury's sense of responsibility in violation of the principle established in *Caldwell*. The Court disagreed. Here, said Rehnquist, the jury was not "affirmatively misled regarding its role in the sentencing process." The evidence presented to it was neither false at the time it was admitted nor did it directly pertain to the jury's sentencing role.

Douglas Buchanan was convicted of killing four members of his family in 1987. His attorney asserted four mitigating factors at his sentencing hearing: (1) that Buchanan had no prior criminal record; (2) his youth (he was 19 at the time of the murders); (3) impaired capacity; and (4) emotional distress at the time of the crimes. Buchanan asked that the jury at the sentencing hearing be instructed on each of these factors as well as more general instructions that the jury must "consider the circumstances" of the offense, Buchanan's "history and background," and any other factors that mitigate the offense. The trial judge did not give any of these instructions, but rather instructed the jury to consider "all of the evidence." The jury chose to impose the death penalty. The Supreme Court affirmed Buchanan's conviction in *Buchanan v. Angelone*, 118 S.Ct. 757 (1998). Although a sentencer may not be precluded from considering constitutionally relevant mitigating evidence, a state may "shape and structure the jury's consideration of mitigation so long as it does not preclude the jury from giving effect to any relevant mitigating evidence." The instruction Buchanan's sentencing jury received did not "foreclose the jury's consideration of any mitigating evidence." The direction to consider "all of the evidence" afforded the jurors sufficient opportunity to consider mitigating evidence. There were also two days of testimony relating to Buchanan's family background and mental and emotional problems. Rehnquist said that it was "not likely that the jury would disregard this extensive testimony in making its decisions, particularly given the instruction to 'consider all of the evidence.'"

Death Penalty: Proportionality

Coker v. Georgia, **433 U.S. 584 (1977),** held that the death penalty could not be imposed for the rape of an adult victim. The Court concluded in *Gregg v. Georgia*, 428 U.S. 153 (1976), that society did not endorse capital punishment for rape. Every death penalty state had to enact new capital punishment statutes after 1972. Thirty-two of the 35 states that chose to do so excluded rape of an adult victim as a capital crime. Before the statute was changed, Georgia juries typically had not imposed the death penalty in rape cases, suggesting that Georgia juries found the penalty disproportionate when it was available. Justice White argued that the death penalty was an excessive punishment for rape. Because the death penalty is unique in its "severity and irrevocability," it is excessive for a defendant "who does not take human life." The crime of rape "does not compare with murder." Dissents were offered by Chief Justice Burger and Justice Rehnquist who argued that states ought to be afforded extensive latitude and opportunity to deal with this particular crime. The chief justice concluded that it is not "constitutionally impermissible" for states to make the "solemn judgment" to utilize the death penalty to "combat the complete violation of a woman's dignity and personhood." *See also* EIGHTH AMENDMENT, p. 399; *Gregg v. Georgia*, p. 411; *Harmelin v. Michigan*, p. 402; *Woodson v. North Carolina*, p. 424.

Significance *Coker* produced a substantive limitation on the imposition of the death penalty. The Court attempted to establish in *Coker* a set of criteria by which excess could be evaluated. It suggested that public attitudes toward a particular offense were germane. These attitudes are reflected in legislative judgments about criminal penalties. Excess can therefore be judged in sentences that substantially depart from penalties thought to be appropriate in the majority of states. The Court found that Georgia was the only state in the Union to have authorized the death penalty for rape. Because 35 states had occasion to review their statutes following *Furman v. Georgia*, 408 U.S. 238 (1972), the Court concluded that Georgia's choice of punishment was at too great a variance from the norm. In addition, the Court found that Georgia juries rejected the death penalty in over 90 percent of rape case convictions, which the Court considered another indication of the excess of the law. Using the disproportionality rationale, the Court extended *Coker* to persons who aid and abet felony murder in *Enmund v. Florida*, 458 U.S. 782 (1982). The Court ruled that the Eighth Amendment precludes imposing the death penalty on a person who aids and abets a felony in which murder is committed by others, but who "neither took life, attempted to take life, nor intended to take life" himself or herself.

The Court discussed whether a punishment is disproportionately severe or excessive in *Harmelin v. Michigan*, 501 U.S. 957 (1991), as it upheld a life sentence without the possibility of parole for anyone convicted of possessing 650 or more grams of cocaine.

Comparative proportionality reviews are mandated by state law in a number of states. The Court ruled in *Pulley v. Harris*, 465 U.S. 37 (1984), that a state need not conduct a comparative proportionality review in capital punishment cases. Although such comparative reviews are performed in a number of states, the Court ruled in *Pulley* that the Eighth Amendment does not mandate them. Traditionally, the concept of proportionality had been used in conjunction with "an abstract evaluation of the appropriateness of a sentence for a particular crime." This involves comparing the gravity of the offense and the severity of the penalty to determine if the punishment was disproportionate or excessive. Harris asked the Court to consider whether his sentence was unacceptable because it was disproportionate to the punishment imposed on others convicted of the same crime. Harris argued that when the states redrafted their capital punishment laws after *Furman*, most of them required such a comparative review. Although such a comparative review was seen as an "additional safeguard against arbitrary or capricious sentencing," the Court did not see it as so critical that without the review the statute would not have passed constitutional muster.

The use of a victim impact statement (VIS) in capital cases has been before the Rehnquist Court three times. The Court ruled in *Booth v. Maryland*, 482 U.S. 496 (1987), that use of such evidence at the sentencing stage of a capital murder trial violated the Eighth Amendment. A VIS, required by state law, was based on interviews with the victim's family. It contained descriptions of the impact of the crime on the family, characterizations of the victim, and family opinions of the crime and the defendant. The Court said that the information contained in the VIS may be "wholly unrelated to the blameworthiness" of the defendant, however, and may cause the sentencing decision to turn on such factors as the degree to which the victim's family is willing and able to articulate its grief, or the relative worth of the victim's character. Use of family members' emotionally charged opinions could "serve no other purpose than to inflame the jury and divert it from deciding the case on the relevant evidence concerning the crime and the defendant." Similarly, the Court held in *South Carolina v. Gathers*, 490 U.S. 805 (1989), that evidence about the character of the victim could not be used in the sentencing phase of a capital case when that evidence does not directly bear on the crime itself. Gathers was convicted of murder. At the end of his argument to the jury during the sentencing stage of Gathers's murder trial, the prosecutor read from some of the religious materials that the victim was carrying at the time of the murder. The prosecutor characterized the victim based on inferences drawn from the fact that he was carrying the religious materials and other items, such as a voter registration card. The Court said that capital cases have "consistently recognized" that the death penalty be "tailored" to a defendant's "personal responsibility and moral guilt." Under the circumstances of this case, the Court said that the content of the various materials that the victim happened to be carrying when he was attacked was "purely fortuitous," and could not "provide any information relevant to the defendant's moral culpability."

Booth and *Gathers* were overruled by the Rehnquist Court in *Payne v. Tennessee*, 501 U.S. 808 (1991). The Court held in *Payne* that evidence reflecting the character of a murder victim and the crime's effects on his or her surviving family could be introduced at the sentencing stage of a murder trial. *Booth* "unfairly weighted the scales in a capital trial," said Chief Justice Rehnquist, by keeping the state from either offering a "glimpse of the life" that the defendant chose to end or from characterizing the "loss to the victim's family and to society." States have the authority to devise new methods for dealing with capital cases. Victim impact evidence is "simply another form or method of informing the sentencing authority about the specific harm caused by the crime in question." The Court in *Booth* was "wrong in stating this kind of evidence leads to the arbitrary imposition of the death penalty." To the contrary, victim impact evidence generally serves "entirely legitimate" purposes.

Death Penalty: Mandatory

Woodson v. North Carolina, **428 U.S. 280 (1976),** struck down the mandatory death sentence. Several states responded to *Furman v. Georgia*, 408 U.S. 238 (1972), by revising their capital punishment statutes to make the death penalty mandatory for certain offenses. The Supreme Court held that the mandatory approach was "unduly harsh and unworkably rigid." The Court said that allowing some discretion in sentencing was more compatible with "evolving standards of societal decency," a frequently used criterion in cruel and unusual punishment cases. The fact that juries possessing discretion infrequently imposed capital punishment suggested that capital punishment was viewed as "inappropriate" in a large number of cases. A second defect cited by the Court was that mandatory sentences did not remedy *Furman* flaws. The mandatory approach "papers over" the problem of jury discretion. There are no standards by which to determine "which murderer shall live and which shall die." Neither does the mandatory approach allow a review of arbitrary death sentences. The third flaw in the mandatory approach was its undifferentiating character. The statutes did not allow for the consideration of factors particular to the crime and the defendant. They precluded consideration of "compassion or mitigating factors." The statutes treated all convicted persons "as members of a faceless, undifferentiated mass to be subjected to the blind infliction of the penalty of death." The four dissenters were troubled by the Court's process focus. Justice Rehnquist felt that the Court should confine itself to a simple determination of whether a punishment is cruel, and the Court had already concluded in *Gregg v. Georgia*, 428 U.S. 153 (1976), that capital punishment was not a cruel and unusual punishment as such. *See also Coker v. Georgia*, p. 422; EIGHTH AMENDMENT, p. 399; *Gregg v. Georgia*, p. 411.

Significance   *Woodson* gave the Court an opportunity to choose between two alternative approaches to capital punishment. *Woodson* clearly reflected the Court's preference for retaining some discretion with sentencers in capital cases. To implement capital punishment reasonably, the sentencer must evaluate the specific details of a particular case against criteria defined by state legislatures. The mandatory approach precludes consideration of the factors that may make a case unique. The Court has since underscored the inadequacy of the mandatory approach. In striking down a Louisiana statute that called for capital punishment for the deliberate killing of a firefighter or police officer, the Court said in *Roberts v. Louisiana*, 431 U.S. 633 (1977), "It is incorrect to suppose that no mitigating circumstances can exist when the victim is a police officer." Neither can the scope of sentencer considerations be improperly restricted. In *Lockett v. Ohio*, 438 U.S. 586 (1978), the Court held that limiting a sentencer to a narrow range of possible mitigating circumstances was unsatisfactory. In *Eddings v. Oklahoma*, 455 U.S. 104 (1982), the Court remanded the case of a 16-year-old boy sentenced to death by a trial judge who determined that, as a matter of state law, he could not consider as a mitigating circumstance the youth's "unhappy upbringing and emotional disturbance." And in *Skipper v. South Carolina*, 476 U.S. 1 (1986), the Court held that a state could not withhold testimony representing a defendant's record of good behavior while in jail from the jury making a determination of a sentence in a capital case. Using a rationale similar to that in *Lockett* and *Eddings*, the Court said that the defendant's capacity to make a good adjustment to prison life reflected an aspect of his character relevant to the jury's sentencing decision. The Court came to the same conclusion in *Sumner v. Shuman*, 483 U.S. 66 (1987). Under Nevada law, a prisoner serving a life term without the possibility of parole could receive an automatic death sentence upon conviction of first-degree murder. The Court ruled that even under this circumstance, there could be no exception to the ban on mandatory capital punishment.

Three other Rehnquist Court rulings involved more specific mandatory actions by sentencing juries. Pennsylvania required the death penalty if a jury unanimously found aggravation in the absence of mitigation, or aggravation that outweighed mitigation. The Court upheld this method in *Blystone v. Pennsylvania*, 494 U.S. 299 (1990). The Court distinguished the approach from those in cases like *Woodson* by pointing out that the sentence was not automatically imposed upon conviction, but only after a consideration of aggravating and mitigating factors. An aggravating factor "serves the purpose of limiting the class of death-eligible defendants," while the mitigating factor satisfies the requirement that a capital sentencing jury be able to "consider and give full effect to all relevant mitigating evidence."

North Carolina had a death penalty law similar to Pennsylvania's, but it required that jurors find a mitigating circumstance unanimously before such factor could be weighed against aggravating circumstances. It also required a jury to unanimously find, beyond a reasonable doubt, that aggravating factors were sufficiently substantial to warrant the death penalty when considered along with any mitigating factors. The Court struck down these provisions in *McKoy v. North Carolina*, 494 U.S. 433 (1990), because the unanimity requirement precluded giving full effect to mitigating factors. Although the law allowed a jury to choose a penalty other than death in the absence of mitigation, it was required to make its choice based only on mitigating circumstances for which there was unanimity. As a result, one juror can prevent the others from giving effect to evidence they feel calls for a lesser sentence. Further, even if all the jurors agree there are *some* mitigating factors, "they cannot give effect to evidence supporting any of those circumstances unless they agree unanimously on the *same* circumstances."

California's death penalty statute also provided that a jury "shall impose" the death sentence in the presence of aggravating factors that outweigh any mitigating factors. In addition, the California law contained a list of specific factors that a capital jury was required to consider before determining sentence. The last of these factors [factor (k)] was a residual or "catch-all" factor that directed jurors to consider "any other circumstance which extenuates the gravity of the crime even though it is not a legal excuse for the crime." The Supreme Court upheld both provisions in *Boyde v. California*, 494 U.S. 370 (1990). The mandatory nature of the "shall impose" direction was seen as identical to the Pennsylvania law upheld in *Blystone*. It was the Court's judgment that the language did not foreclose "individual assessment" of Boyde's sentence nor interfere with jury consideration of all mitigating evidence.

Death Penalty: Juveniles

Stanford v. Kentucky, **492 U.S. 361 (1989),** upheld capital punishment for juveniles having reached the age of 16 before committing murder. *Thompson v. Oklahoma*, 487 U.S. 815 (1988), had held that the Eighth Amendment does not permit execution of a person who committed a capital crime before reaching the age of 16. Kevin Stanford and Heath Wilkins (in a companion case, *Wilkins v. Missouri*) were both convicted of murder and both were over the age of 16 at the time of the crime—Stanford was 17 years and four months of age while Wilkins was 16 years and six months old. The Court ruled that imposition of the death penalty on Stanford and Wilkins did not constitute cruel and unusual punishment. Justice Scalia's opinion closely paralleled the dissenters' reasoning in *Thompson*. Whether the execution of juveniles violates the Cruel and Unusual Punishment Clause requires determination of whether such action is contrary to "evolving standards of decency that mark the progress of a maturing society." In assessing these "evolving standards," the Court must look to "conceptions of modern American society" as reflected by "objective evidence" as opposed to "its own subjective conceptions." The "most reliable" reflection of "national consensus" are the actions of state legislatures and the Congress. The Court concluded that a "settled" consensus does not exist to prohibit execution of 16-year-olds as only 15 of the states that permit capital punishment so limit its use. The number of states restricting the death penalty decreases to 12 when the age is elevated to 17 years. This finding, said Scalia, does not "establish the degree of national agreement" necessary to "label" a punishment cruel and unusual. Neither does the jury conduct in cases involving 16- or 17-year-old defendants reveal a "categorical aversion" to the penalty. Scalia then turned to two other arguments advanced in the challenge to the juvenile death penalty. He rejected the relevance of 18 as the minimum legal age for such activities as "drinking alcoholic beverages and voting" to the capital punishment question. Such laws, he said, "operate in gross," and do not require individualized tests for application. The death sentence, by contrast, is highly selective, and "individualized consideration is a constitutional requirement." Scalia then addressed measures purporting to be "indicia" of national consensus. Scalia said that public opinion data and the positions of interest groups and professional associations are "too uncertain a foundation for constitutional law." He characterized "socioscientific or ethicoscientific" evidence or argument as similarly inadequate.

So long as these factors are given full consideration, the Rehnquist Court seems satisfied that these distinctions can be made by juries in capital cases. Two earlier cases illustrate further. The Court ruled in *Enmund v. Florida*, 458 U.S. 782 (1982), that a defendant could not be sentenced to death unless it could be shown that he or she killed, attempted to kill, or intended to kill. The ruling suggested that aiders and abetters could not be subjected to the death penalty because intent to kill was lacking. In *Tison v Arizona*, 481 U.S. 137 (1987), the Court rejected the *Enmund* framework, saying it dealt with two distinct subsets of felony murder: one in which a person is a minor actor and neither intended to kill nor was found to have any culpable mental state; and the other in which the felony murderer actually killed, attempted to kill, or intended to kill. The *Tison* case was in neither of these categories. The Tison brothers aided in their father's prison escape and were with him when he killed four persons taken captive. Though the brothers claimed surprise at the killings, neither attempted to aid the victims and both continued their participation in the escape. They were subsequently captured, tried, convicted, and sentenced to death. The issue before the Court in *Tison* was whether the death penalty is prohibited for a case between the extremes described in *Enmund* and a case in which a defendant's participation is major and whose mental state is one of reckless indifference to the value of human life. The Court said capital punishment was appropriate in this intermediate category. *Enmund*'s narrow focus on intent to kill was a "highly unsatisfactory means of definitively distinguishing the most culpable and dangerous murderers." Some nonintentional murderers may be among the most dangerous and inhumane of all, such as the person who tortures another without caring whether the victim lives or dies, or the robber who shoots someone in the course of a robbery and is utterly indifferent to the fact that killing may be an unintended consequence of the desire to rob. The Court ruled accordingly that "reckless disregard for human life implicit in engaging in criminal activities known to carry a grave risk of death represents a highly culpable mental state."

The Texas capital punishment law in effect until 1991 required that once a defendant was found guilty of murder, a jury had to find beyond a reasonable doubt that the killing was deliberate and that the defendant represented a "continuing threat to society" before a death sentence could be imposed. The statute did not define the factors that might be offered in mitigation on the death sentence question. The Supreme Court ruled in *Penry v. Lynaugh*, 492 U.S. 302 (1989), that special jury instructions were required under the Texas law to fully "give effect" to some mitigating evidence. The factors needing special instruction in Penry's case were his mental retardation and his extensive history of childhood abuse. It was the Court's judgment in *Penry* that the factors he wished to advance in mitigation might also suggest to a sentencing jury that he constituted a continuing threat to society. The *Penry* ruling thus required a special jury instruction when evidence offered in mitigation also supported the imposition of capital punishment.

The Supreme Court ruled in *Johnson v. Texas*, 509 U.S 350 (1993), that the Texas capital sentencing system allowed the jury to sufficiently consider the effect of Johnson's youth as a possibly mitigating factor. The Court did not dispute that Johnson's youth is a relevant mitigating factor that "must be within the effective reach" of a capital sentencing jury. A lack of maturity and an underdeveloped sense of responsibility are commonly found in the young, and these qualities "often result in impetuous and ill-considered actions and decisions." The issue in this case was whether this factor was allowed adequate consideration without special jury instruction. The adequacy of the instruction given, said Kennedy, is not determined by a "technical parsing of the language of the instructions, but instead approach the instructions in the same way that the jury would—with a 'common-sense understanding of the instructions in the light of all that has taken place at the trial.'" It was the Court's conclusion that there was "no reasonable likelihood" that the jury would have found itself "foreclosed" from considering the relevant aspects of Johnson's youth.

Thompson v. Oklahoma, 487 U.S. 815 (1988), ruled that a person may not be executed for a crime committed before he or she reaches 16 years of age. The Court said that the "contours" of the cruel and unusual punishment protection are determined by judges, who arc to be guided by the "evolving standards of decency that mark the progress of a maturing society." Measures of these "evolving standards" are present in recent legislative determinations on the issue as well as jury decisions in particular cases. The Court found "near unanimity" in all states and the District of Columbia "in treating a person under 16 as a minor for several important purposes." Most relevant" of these policies was the designation by every state for juvenile court jurisdiction at "16 years of age or younger." The Court concluded from this that it was offensive to "civilized standards of decency" to execute a juvenile. In addition to the judgments of legislatures and juries, the Court said that it needed to consider the juvenile's comparative culpability and then determine whether the death sentence for a juvenile "measurably contributes to the social purposes" of retribution and deterrence served by the penalty. The Court felt it so obvious that less culpability attaches to a crime committed by a juvenile that "extended explanation" was not deemed necessary. "Inexperience, less education, and less intelligence make the teenager less able to evaluate the consequences of his or her conduct" while being more likely to be "motivated by mere emotion or peer pressure" than an adult. The reasons juveniles are not "trusted with the privileges and responsibilities of an adult also explain why their irresponsible conduct is not as morally reprehensible as that of an adult." Given the lesser culpability, retribution serves no purpose in the context of juveniles and is "simply inapplicable" to the execution of a juvenile.

Prisoners' Rights: Cruel and Unusual Punishment/Conditions

Helling v. McKinney, **509 U.S. 25, 125 L.Ed. 2d 22, 113 S.Ct. 2475 (1993)** The question in *Helling* was whether the Eighth Amendment prohibition of cruel and unusual punishment applies to future health threats that may come from confinement with a heavy smoker. The Court ruled that the Eighth Amendment can extend to such future health risks. Justice White said that contemporary standards of decency "require no less" than for the treatment of a prisoner and the conditions of his confinement to be subject to Eighth Amendment scrutiny. An Eighth Amendment violation requires a showing of "deliberate indifference" by prison officials to the health needs of an inmate. The Court rejected Nevada's contention that the amendment does not protect against prison conditions that "merely threaten to cause health problems in the future." We have "great difficulty agreeing that prison authorities may not be indifferent to an inmate's current health problems," said White, "but may ignore a condition of confinement that is sure or very likely to cause serious illness and needless suffering the next week or month or year." The Court saw the situations as similar to one where an inmate could successfully complain about "demonstrably unsafe drinking water without waiting for an attack of dysentery." The Court saw nothing "novel" about applying the Eighth Amendment against future harm. It would be "odd," White said, "to deny an injunction to inmates who plainly proved an unsafe, life-threatening condition in their prison on the ground that nothing yet had happened to them." The Court remanded the case in order to give McKinney an opportunity to develop his Eighth Amendment claim, and White discussed some of the evidentiary requirements McKinney must meet. He must show that it is contrary to contemporary standards of decency for anyone to be exposed to environmental tobacco smoke (ETS), and that the prison authorities were "deliberately indifferent" to his complaints. Further, McKinney must show that he was exposed to an "unreasonably high level of ETS." Review of this objective factor must include the fact that he had been transferred to another detention facility, and that he is no longer the cell mate of a heavy smoker. Besides any statistical inquiry into the potential health risk caused by ETS exposure, McKinney also would need to demonstrate that the health risk he had claimed is "not one that today's society chooses to tolerate." Relevant to this subjective factor of deliberate indifference by prison officials are the current attitudes and conduct which may have "changed considerably" since the case was initiated. Justice Thomas was joined by Justice Scalia in dissent. Thomas was most concerned about the further expansion of the Eighth Amendment "beyond all bounds of history and precedent." The word *punishment* in the Eighth Amendment refers to the penalty imposed upon conviction of criminal charges. The word "does not encompass a prisoner's injuries that bear no relation to his sentence." *See also* EIGHTH AMENDMENT, p. 399.

Significance   The Supreme Court has fielded a growing number of prisoner petitions in recent years. These cases typically involve prison overcrowding or other factors that affect the conditions in detention facilities. The first major case in this area was *Bell v. Wolfish*, 441 U.S. 520 (1979), in which the Court upheld a variety of practices at a short-term custodial facility. Included in the permitted practices were "double-bunking," or the assignment of two detainees to a cell originally designed for a single occupancy, limiting receipt of hardcover books to those books mailed directly from publishers or bookstores, prohibiting receipt of all packages from outside the detention facility, strip and body cavity searches following contact visits, and unobserved cell searches. As in *Block*, the Court was highly deferential to the security and management interests of detention facility officials. The Court also noted a diminished privacy expectation for persons in such detention facilities. Two years after *Bell v. Wolfish*, the Court upheld in *Rhodes v. Chapman*, 452 U.S. 337 (1981), long-term double-celling against claims that it constituted cruel and unusual punishment. In *Whitley v. Albers*, 475 U.S. 312(1986), the Court ruled that the shooting of an inmate by a prison guard while the guard was trying to halt a prison riot was not cruel and unusual punishment either. The Court concluded that it is "obduracy and wantonness, not inadvertence or error in good faith" that characterizes conduct prohibited by the Cruel and Unusual Punishment Clause. The infliction of pain during an attempt to restore order is not prohibited by the Eighth Amendment "simply because it may appear in retrospect" that the measures taken may have been unreasonable, and hence unnecessary in the strict sense. The Court said the general requirement that a claimant establish the unnecessary and wanton infliction of pain should be applied with due regard for differences in the kind of conduct involved.

The Commonwealth of Kentucky promulgated regulations covering prison visitation. The regulations contained, among other things, nonexhaustive categories of visitors who may be prevented from making prison visits. Included on the list, for example, were those who presented a "clear and present danger" to prison security or a prison's "orderly operation." Individual penal institutions issued their own particular regulations as supplemental to the state regulations. One particular institution issued its own memorandum of policy which fully embraced the state regulations but also described additional processes under which visitors "may" have admittance refused or visiting privileges suspended. A class action was filed by a number of inmates after several visitors had been denied admission under the institution's regulations. Among other things, the inmates asserted that the regulations violated their due process rights under the Fourteenth Amendment. The Court ruled in *Kentucky Dept. of Corrections v. Thompson*, 490 U.S. 454 (1989), that no liberty interest was established through the policies. Liberty interests, said the Court, arise from two sources—the "Due Process Clause itself and the laws of the States." The Court said it could not "seriously be contended" that an "inmate's interest in unfettered visitation is guaranteed directly by the Due Process Clause."

In 1974 the Supreme Court had ruled in *Procunier v. Martinez*, 416 U.S. 396 (1974), that the censoring of prisoners' outgoing mail could be done only to advance a "substantial governmental interest." Because of the First Amendment implications of such actions by prison officials, *Martinez* required "heightened" judicial scrutiny. In *Thornburgh v. Abbott*, 490 U.S. 401 (1989), the Court refused to use the *Martinez* standard in reviewing restrictions on materials coming into a prison. Rather, the Court ruled that the reasonableness standard was sufficient in this situation. Under Federal Bureau of Prison regulations, wardens are authorized to reject certain publications if they are judged to be "detrimental to the security, good order, or discipline of the institution" or if they might "facilitate criminal activity." Publications may not be rejected solely on the basis of religious, philosophical, political, social, or sexual content or solely because the material may be "unpopular or repugnant." The Court distinguished incoming material from outgoing mail saying the problems associated with the latter were of a "categorically lesser magnitude." Materials received by a prison can circulate and become disruptive, thus a more deferential standard than *Martinez* is appropriate. The Court characterized the prison environment as "volatile" and said it was necessary to give prison officials "broad discretion to prevent ... disorder." The Court agreed that the process used to review materials would "raise grave First Amendment concerns outside the prison context," but was permissible for prisons given the primacy of protecting prison security. Justices Stevens, Brennan, and Marshall dissented saying that the Court was engaged in a "headlong rush to strip inmates of all but a vestige of free communication with the world beyond the prison gate."

The Supreme Court ruled in *Wilson v. Seiter*, 501 U.S. 294 (1991), that a showing of intent is required to win a suit based on the Cruel and Unusual Punishment Clause of the Eighth Amendment. Justice Scalia said the Eighth Amendment bars only cruel and unusual punishments. If the pain or discontent alleged by the prisoners was not "formally meted out as punishment" by statute or sentencing judge, "some mental element must be attributed to the inflicting officer before it can qualify." The Court then addressed the standard to be used in determining state of mind. Conduct must be "wanton," Scalia said, but wantonness does not have a "fixed meaning." Rather, it must be determined "with due regard for differences in the kind of conduct against which an Eighth Amendment objection is lodged." The Court concluded that wantonness of conduct depends on the "constraints facing the official" as opposed to effect upon the prisoner. In situations such as responding to a prison disturbance, actions of prison officials are balanced against "competing institutional concerns." Wanton conduct would be more difficult to demonstrate in a disturbance situation than in one where officials failed adequately to attend to medical needs. Unlike the emergency situation, the state would have no interest against which providing medical care might "clash." In the emergency situation, a finding of wantonness would require a showing of malicious and sadistic action designed to cause harm. Justices White, Marshall, Blackmun, and Stevens preferred to focus exclusively on effects of actions or inactions on prisoners. They saw intent as not very "meaningful" in prison condition cases. Poor conditions, in their view, might too easily be attributed to factors such as insufficient funding rather than "deliberate indifference" on the part of prison officials.

Physical mistreatment of prisoners by corrections officers constitutes cruel and unusual punishment under terms of the Eighth Amendment. The question in *Hudson v. McMillian*, 503 U.S. 1 (1992), was whether Eighth Amendment protection extended to excessive physical force situations where the injuries sustained by the prisoner are not serious. In reviewing the dismissal of Hudson's suit, the court of appeals had ruled that an excessive force claim requires a showing, among other things, of "significant injury." The Supreme Court disagreed. The "core judicial inquiry," said Justice O'Connor, is whether force is applied in a "good-faith effort to maintain or restore discipline, or maliciously and sadistically to cause harm." The extent of injury suffered by the defendant was seen by the Court as but one of several factors relevant to determining whether force was used in a wanton or unjustified manner. Such a determination is also based on whether force was necessary at all, the relationship of a perceived need for force and the amount of force actually used, whether the threat to which the prison officials responded was "reasonably perceived," and what, if any, effort was made to "temper the severity of a forceful response." If this were not so, the Eighth Amendment "would permit any physical punishment, no matter how diabolic or inhuman, inflicting less than some arbitrary quantity of injury." Such a result, concluded O'Connor, "would have been as unacceptable to the drafters of the Eighth Amendment as it is today." Justices Thomas and Scalia dissented saying that the use of force that causes only "insignificant harm" to a prisoner may be "immoral, it may be tortious, it may be criminal, and it may even be remediable under other provisions of the Federal Constitution, but it is not 'cruel and unusual punishment.'"

Demont Conner was a long-term prisoner in a maximum-security prison in Hawaii. As a condition of meeting with a counselor, Conner was subjected to a strip search. During the search, Conner angrily directed some comments at a correctional officer. In addition to losing his time with the counselor, disciplinary charges were filed against him. The facility "Adjustment Committee," the body authorized to determine if Conner had violated institutional disciplinary rules, did not allow Conner to call some staff members as witnesses at his disciplinary hearing. The Committee found Conner guilty of the disciplinary charges, and he was placed in disciplinary segregation (solitary confinement). Conner sought administrative appeal of the Committee's findings. He also filed suit claiming that the disciplinary process had violated his right to due process. Subsequent to commencement of the legal action but after Conner had served his 30 days in disciplinary segregation, a deputy administrator reversed the Committee's finding on the most serious disciplinary charge against Conner—obstruction of an officer in the performance of his duties—and ordered that all record of this finding be removed from Conner's file. The Court ruled in *Sandin v. Conner*, 515 U.S. 472 (1995), that the Due Process Clause afforded Conner no protection under these circumstances. Chief Justice Rehnquist was critical of the Court's recent receptivity to suits by prisoners seeking federal judicial intervention in the administration of prison facilities. Such intervention, he suggested "squanders" judicial resources with "little offsetting benefit to anyone." This approach also encourages prisoners "to comb regulations" looking for mandatory language "on which to base entitlements to various state-conferred privileges." While this may be "entirely sensible" when defining rights and remedies available to the general public, it is a "good deal less sensible" in the case of a prison regulation "primarily designed to guide correctional officers in the administration of a prison." Some of the Court's recent prison condition decisions had fostered "day-to-day involvement" of federal courts in prison management. Rehnquist acknowledged that States may occasionally create "liberty interests" that are protected by the Due Process Clause. These interests will be limited, however, to "freedom from restraint which ... imposes atypical and significant hardship on the inmate in relation to the ordinary incidents of prison life." Using this standard, the Court found no "dramatic departure" from the normal conditions of Conner's indeterminate sentence; his disciplinary confinement did not present the "significant deprivation in which a state might conceivably create a liberty interest." Comparing inmates in disciplinary segregation and those who were not, it was the Court's conclusion that segregating Conner for 30 days "did not work a major disruption in his environment." Indeed, the regime to which Conner was subjected as a result of the misconduct hearing was "within the range of confinement" normally expected for one serving an indeterminate term of 30 years to life. Justices Ginsburg, Stevens, Breyer, and Souter dissented. They felt the punishment not only severely altered the conditions of his incarceration, but also deprived him of privileges, diminished parole prospects, and stigmatized him.

The Supreme Court held in *Farmer v. Brennan*, 511 U.S. 825: (1994), that prison authorities can be held responsible for failing to adequately protect a prisoner from physical harm at the hands of other prisoners. Dee Farmer is a transsexual, a male who considered himself a female. He also looked like a female. At the time he was transferred to a federal maximum security facility in Terre Haute, Indiana, he had undergone treatment to change his sex, but had not yet had a "sex change" operation. He was placed in the general population of males at the Terre Haute facility, the current general practice of federal prison authorities. Within his first two weeks there, he was beaten and raped by another inmate. The question in this case was whether prison officials can be held liable if they knew or should have known that Farmer would be in danger when placed in the male population of a maximum security prison. The U.S. Supreme Court unanimously ruled for Farmer. Justice Souter said that the Constitution neither "mandate[s] comfortable prisons" nor "permit[s] inhumane ones." The Eighth Amendment places restraints on prison officials. The difficult task is the definition of the criteria against which prison officials' conduct is to be examined. Two requirements have emerged. The first is that the conduct of prison officials leads to "serious" harm. Second, the officials must have a "sufficiently culpable state of mind"; that they demonstrated a "deliberate indifference" to an inmate's welfare. Farmer's case focused on the test for deliberate indifference. Farmer sought to have the Court fashion an objective test with deliberate indifference defined similarly to the civil concept of "recklessness." The Court did not do so. Instead, the Court said that a prison official cannot be found liable under the Eighth Amendment for denying a prisoner "humane conditions of confinement" unless the official "knows of and disregards an excessive risk to inmate health or safety." The Eighth Amendment, said Souter, "does not outlaw cruel and unusual 'conditions'; it outlaws cruel and unusual 'punishments.'" An official's failure to alleviate a risk he or she should have perceived but did not "cannot under our cases be condemned as the infliction of punishment." At the same time, an Eighth Amendment claimant "need not show that a prison official acted or failed to act believing that harm actually would befall an inmate." It is enough, Souter continued, that the official acted or failed to act "despite his knowledge of a substantial risk of serious harm." Prison officials charged with deliberate indifference might show in response that they were unaware of underlying facts indicating substantial danger, or that they were aware of the underlying facts but concluded that any risk to the inmate was insubstantial or nonexistent. Prison officials might also free themselves from liability if they can show they "responded reasonably to the risk, even if the harm ultimately was not averted." The Court concluded that the record did not sufficiently represent Farmer's entitlement to judgment on the subjective knowledge issue.

Prisoners' Rights: Early Release

Lynce v. Mathis, **519 U.S. 433, 137 L.Ed. 2d 63, 117 S.Ct. 891 (1997)** Prison overcrowding is a problem that has arisen in most of the 50 states. Florida had enacted statutes that allowed prison officials, when necessary to meet overcrowded conditions, to grant additional early-release credit to inmates who were already earning such early-release incentives. Kenneth Lynce was one such inmate. Lynce was serving a 22-year sentence for several offenses including attempted first-degree murder. Over a period of several years, he had earned more than 1,800 days of overcrowding early-release credit. In 1992, however, the statute under which overcrowding credits could be earned was amended to exclude prisoners convicted of murder or attempted murder. The Florida Department of Corrections read the policy change to not affect credits granted previously. In the wake of publicity about the pending release of a convicted murderer, however, the Florida attorney general issued an opinion that the 1992 amendment was to apply retroactively. Acting on the basis of that opinion, the Department of Corrections revoked the over-crowding early-release credits previously granted to Lynce and other similarly situated prisoners. Lynce, in fact, was returned to confinement after having been out of prison for several months. The revocation of credits in his case extended his prison time by more than four years. The Supreme Court agreed with Lynce that retroactive application of the Florida law was unconstitutional on ex post facto grounds. The state argued that because the early-release credits had been issued as part of a process designed to alleviate overcrowding and not to serve as a part of Lynce's punishment, the Ex Post Facto Clause was not violated. It was the Court's view that the "subjective motivation" of the legislature in enacting the gain-time credits is not the relevant focus of review. The fact that the "generous gain-time provisions" in the initial 1983 statute were motivated by the interest of avoiding overcrowding "is not relevant to the essential inquiry demanded by the Ex Post Facto Clause," which is whether the cancellation of Lynce's 1,860 days of accumulated credits "had the effect of lengthening [Lynce's] period of incarceration." To the extent motive might be relevant, the Court saw the retrospective change in policy as intended to "prevent the early release of prisoners convicted of murder-related offenses who had accumulated overcrowding credits." Retroactive application of parole or other early-release provisions implicates the Ex Post Facto Clause because such credits are "one determinant of [Lynce's] term [and his] effective sentence is altered once this determinant is changed." Florida's 1992 law did more than simply "remove a mechanism that created an opportunity for early release" for a group of prisoners unlikely to secure early release otherwise. Instead, the 1992 law made ineligible for early release a "class of prisoners who were previously eligible—including some, like [Lynce], who had actually been released." *See also* FOURTH AMENDMENT, p. 193; *Helling v. McKinney*, p. 430.

Significance   Most states experience prison overcrowding and the early-release issues that appear in *Lynce*. Another case involving an ex post facto claim was *California Department of Corrections v. Morales*, 514 U.S. 499 (1995). Jose Morales was convicted of murder in California in 1970 and sentenced to life imprisonment. He was released to a halfway house early in 1980. Morales married Lois Washabaugh, who disappeared soon thereafter. Washabaugh was never seen again, although a hand, positively identified as hers, was eventually recovered. Morales pleaded no contest to the second-degree murder of his wife. He was sentenced to a term of 15 years to life, but under California law became eligible for parole in 1990. The Board of Prison Terms held a hearing in 1989 to consider Morales's suitability for parole. The Board found Morales unsuitable for parole. Under terms of the law in effect at the time Washabaugh was murdered, Morales would have been entitled to subsequent suitability review each year. In 1981, however, California amended its law and authorized the Board to defer subsequent suitability hearings for up to three years for a prisoner convicted on more than one offense involving the taking of a life. At the 1989 suitability hearing, the Board determined it was unlikely that Morales would be suitable for parole in the next year or two and set the next hearing for three years later. Morales petitioned for habeas corpus on the grounds that the 1981 amendment constituted an ex post facto law. The Supreme Court concluded that a retroactive law making parole hearings less accessible did not increase Morales's sentence and violate the Ex Post Facto Clause. The Clause incorporated a "term of art with an established meaning at the time of the framing of the Constitution." Consistent with this original understanding, said Justice Thomas, the Court has held that the Clause is directed toward laws that "retroactively alter the definition of crimes or increase the punishment for criminal acts." Since the California amendment did not change the definition of Morales's crime, the question in this case was whether the change away from annual parole hearings increased his punishment. The indeterminate sentence of 15 years to life was the same both before and after the amendment. In addition, the amendment neither changed the substantive formula for earning sentence reductions nor changed the criteria for fixing the initial date of parole eligibility. The amendment made only one change—the possibility that after the first parole hearing, the Board would not hold another hearing for another three years. The "evident focus" of the amendment was to "relieve the [Board] from the costly and time-consuming responsibility of scheduling parole hearings." Rather than change the sentencing range that applied to covered offenses, the amendment "simply 'alters the method to be followed' in fixing a parole release date under identical substantive standards." The critical determination was whether the change produced a sufficient risk of increasing the measure of punishment attached to Morales's crime. It was the Court's judgment that the amendment created "only the most speculative and attenuated possibility" of increasing the measure of punishment for Morales's crime, and such "conjectural effects are insufficient under any threshold we might establish under the Ex Post Facto Clause." Thomas also suggested that the amendment applied to only a class of prisoners for whom the likelihood of release on parole is "quite remote"; the narrow class of prisoners covered by the amendment could not "reasonably expect that their prospects for early release on parole would be enhanced by the opportunity of annual hearings." Justices Stevens and Souter dissented. The amendment's narrow focus on a "discrete class" of prisoners "implicates one of the principal concerns that underlies the constitutional prohibition against retrospective legislation—the danger that the legislature will usurp the judicial power and will legislate so as to administer justice unfairly against particular individuals." The provision of a parole hearing, concluded Stevens, is an "absolute prerequisite to release." For the three years during which Morales is denied his hearing, he is "absolutely deprived of any parole opportunity," and such "retroactive deprivation of the opportunity for early release constitutes ex post facto legislation."

Oklahoma established an early-release program in 1988 to be used whenever the state's inmate population exceeded 95 percent of the capacity of correctional facilities in the state. Qualified inmates were given conditional release to free space in the overcrowded facilities. Ernest Harper was serving a life sentence for a 1975 murder conviction. He was recommended for Oklahoma's preparole release program in 1990 by the Pardon and Appeal Board, a recommendation subsequently approved by the Department of Corrections. He agreed to a list of proposed conditions and was released from prison in October 1990. In March 1991 Harper was informed that the governor had denied his parole application and that he had to return to prison. The state did not contend that Harper violated any of the conditions of his release. Harper filed an unsuccessful habeas corpus petition claiming that he was entitled to a hearing on the revocation of preparole status. The Supreme Court unanimously ruled that terminating Harper's participation in the preparole program was "equivalent" to denying parole in *Young v. Harper*, 520 U.S. 143 (1997). The Court found that the prison overcrowding rationale for the program supported the conclusion that Oklahoma's early-release program differed from parole "in name alone."

Under Ohio law a capital punishment offender must be given a clemency hearing within 45 days of the scheduled execution. The Ohio Adult Parole Authority began its clemency investigation of Eugene Woodard following his conviction for murder and sentence of death. Woodard was informed that he could have a voluntary interview with members of the Parole Authority with his clemency hearing to follow a week later. Woodard challenged the process on self-incrimination and due process grounds, but the U.S. Supreme Court ruled against both his claims in *Ohio Adult Parole Authority v. Woodard*, 118 S.Ct. 1244 (1998). Chief Justice Rehnquist's opinion spoke to two inquiries made by the Court in this case—whether an inmate has a protected life or liberty interest in clemency proceedings, and whether giving inmates the option of voluntarily participating in an interview as part of the clemency process violates an inmate's self-incrimination right. The Court rejected the due process claim because pardon and commutation decisions "have not traditionally been the business of courts." The Due Process Clause is not violated where the procedures in question "do no more than confirm that the clemency and pardon power is committed, as is our tradition, to the authority of the executive." The procedural protection sought by Woodard would be "inconsistent with the heart of executive clemency, which is to grant clemency as a matter of grace, thus allowing the executive to consider a wide range of factors not comprehended by earlier judicial proceedings and sentencing determinations." A death-row inmate's petition for clemency is a "unilateral hope." The defendant "in effect accepts the finality of the death sentence for purposes of adjudication, and appeals for clemency as a matter of grace." Despite the Parole Authority's mandatory procedures, the "ultimate decision maker, the governor, retains broad discretion." The executive's clemency authority would cease to be a "matter of grace committed to the executive authority if it were constrained by the sort of procedural requirements" urged by Woodard. On the self-incrimination claim, Woodard argued that because there is only one guaranteed clemency review, his decision to participate was "not truly voluntary." He contended further that he may be forced to answer questions at the interview or, if he remains silent, his "silence may be used against him." The Court disagreed concluding instead that any testimony from Woodard at the clemency interview "would [not] be compelled within the meaning of the Fifth Amendment." Rehnquist said it was "difficult to see how a voluntary interview could 'compel' [Woodard] to speak." Justice Stevens was the only dissenter. He suggested that if a state adopts a clemency procedure "as an integral part of its system for finally determining whether to deprive a person of life, that procedure must comport with the Due Process Clause."

Keith Scott was paroled after serving 11 years of a 10- to 20-year sentence for third degree murder. Among the conditions on his release was that he could not own or possess firearms or other weapons. Violation of this or any of the other conditions could revoke his parole status. At the point Scott was released, he consented in writing that agents of the Board of Probation and Parole could search him, his property, and his residence without a warrant and that any evidence seized during such a search could be used against him at a parole revocation proceeding. Parole officers received information that Scott had been in the possession of firearms. The agents went to Scott's mother's home, where Scott had been living since his parole, to conduct a search. Several firearms were found in a room adjacent to Scott's bedroom. At a parole revocation hearing, Scott unsuccessfully sought to have the weapons suppressed on illegal search grounds. Even though Scott's stepfather testified the weapons were his and Scott testified that he was not aware of the existence of the guns, the Parole Board concluded Scott had violated the weapon possession condition and revoked his parole. The U.S. Supreme Court ruled in *Pennsylvania Board of Probation and Parole v. Scott*, 118 S.Ct. 2014 (1998), that the confiscated firearms need not be excluded at Scott's parole revocation hearing. Justice Thomas explained that a Fourth Amendment violation is "fully accomplished" by the illegal search or seizure, and the exclusion of evidence from a judicial proceeding cannot "cure the invasion of the defendant's rights which he has already suffered." Rather, the exclusionary rule is a "judicially created means" of deterring illegal searches and seizures. The rule does not prohibit the introduction of illegally seized evidence "in all proceedings or against all persons," but applies only in contexts where "remedial objectives are thought most efficaciously served." Because the rule is "prudential," it applies only where its "deterrence benefits outweigh its substantial social costs." Thomas said the Court would not extend application of the rule "beyond the criminal trial context." Application of the rule would "both hinder the functioning of state parole systems and alter the traditionally flexible, administrative nature of parole revocation proceedings." The rule would provide "only minimal deterrence benefits in this context," because application of the rule in the criminal trial context "already provides significant deterrence of unconstitutional searches." The rule precludes consideration of "reliable, probative evidence," and imposes "significant costs" as a result. It detracts from the truth-finding process and "allows many who would otherwise be incarcerated to escape the consequences of their actions." The costs of excluding reliable and probative evidence, Thomas continued, "are particularly high in the context of parole revocation proceedings." Parole is a "variation on imprisonment of convicted criminals." The state has an "overwhelming interest" in ensuring that a parolee complies with parole requirements and is returned to prison in the event of noncompliance. The exclusion of evidence establishing a parole violation hampers the state's ability to "ensure compliance with these conditions by permitting the parolee to avoid the consequences of his noncompliance." The costs of this result are "compounded by the fact that parolees (particularly those who have already committed parole violations) are more likely to commit future criminal offenses than are average citizens." Parole revocation does not deprive a parolee of the "absolute liberty to which every citizen is entitled, but only of the conditional liberty properly dependent on observation of special parole restrictions." In addition, most states have adopted informal parole revocation procedures, and traditional rules of evidence generally do not apply. Requiring the exclusionary rule would "significantly alter this process." Justice Souter, joined by Justices Stevens, Ginsburg, and Breyer, dissented. They saw the Court's ruling as resting on "selective" and "mistaken conceptions of the actual function of revocation" and the "objectives of those who gather evidence in support of petitions to revoke." The revocation proceeding "often serves the same function as a criminal trial," and while the probation officers serve as parolees' counselors, they also often serve as both "prosecutors and law enforcement officials in their relationship with probationers and parolees." If the police need the deterrence of an exclusionary rule to "offset the temptations to forget the Fourth Amendment," said Souter, "parole officers need it quite as much."

Sentencing Guidelines

Mistretta v. United States, **488 U.S. 361 (1988),** upheld the constitutionality of the Federal Sentencing Guidelines. *Mistretta* does not involve an Eighth Amendment claim, but instead involves a challenge of the Federal Sentencing Guidelines on separation of power and improper delegation of legislative power grounds. Since all federal sentencing is based on the Guidelines and accompanying commentary, and since the Eighth Amendment addresses criminal sentences, the discussion of *Mistretta* and subsequent cases on the Guidelines is included here. Troubled by the "serious disparities" produced under the federal indeterminate criminal sentencing system, Congress passed the Sentencing Reform Act of 1984. Among other things, the Act created the United States Sentencing Commission as an independent entity within the judicial branch. The Commission was empowered to promulgate binding sentencing guidelines creating a range of determinate sentences for all federal crimes. Mistretta pled guilty to conspiracy to distribute cocaine and was sentenced under the published Guidelines. Mistretta challenged the Guidelines, claiming that Congress had delegated excessive authority to the Commission, and that the Commission was established in violation of the separation of powers principle. The Supreme Court upheld the Guidelines and the process by which they were developed. The Court said that the determination of whether delegation is excessive is "driven by a practical understanding" that, given the complexity of problems facing Congress, it "cannot do its job absent an ability to delegate power under broad general directions." The Court ruled that delegation is not forbidden so long as Congress sets forth an "intelligible principle" by which the body given power to act must conform. In establishing the Commission, Congress offered specific goals it wanted criminal sentencing to achieve, and mandated the guideline approach to be used to regulate sentencing. The Court concluded that the Act set forth "more than merely an 'intelligible principle.'"

On the separation of power issue, the Court embraced Madison's "flexible understanding" of the concept. There is a "degree of overlapping responsibility" among the three branches, and the greatest security against accumulation of excessive authority in a single branch "lies not in a hermetic division" between the branches but in a "carefully crafted system of checked and balanced power within each branch."

The separation of powers issues in this case were manifest in three ways: The first was the location of the Commission within the judicial branch. Placement of the Commission, an independent body that does not exercise judicial power as such, in the judicial branch made it a "peculiar institution," but separation of powers are not violated, said the Court, by "mere anomaly." Congress's decision to create an independent rule-making body under the judicial branch is not unconstitutional unless Congress vested in the Commission "powers that are more appropriately performed by other branches or that undermine the integrity of the Judiciary." While judicial rule making falls into a kind of "twilight area," it has not been regarded historically as a function that cannot be performed by an entity within the judicial branch. Furthermore, location of the Commission within the judicial branch "simply acknowledges the role that the Judiciary has always played, and continues to play, in sentencing."

The second separation of power question stemmed from the requirement that three Commission members be federal judges. Mistretta argued that this undermined the integrity of the judicial branch by diminishing its independence and impartiality. The Court disagreed. Judicial participation in the promulgation of guidelines "does not affect their or other judges' ability impartially to adjudicate sentencing issues." The Commission was "devoted exclusively" to producing rules to "rationalize a process" that is "performed exclusively" by the judicial branch. This was seen as an "essentially neutral endeavor" and one in which participation of judges is "peculiarly appropriate."

Third was the issue of selection and removal of Commission members. The Court dismissed as "fanciful" the contention that the president's power to appoint federal judges to the Commission gave him or her inappropriate influence over the judicial branch or would interfere with the performance of its functions. Presidential appointment power for positions that may be attractive to judges does not, in itself, corrupt the integrity of the judiciary. The Court could not "imagine" that federal judges would "comport their actions to the wishes of a President for the purpose of receiving an appointment to the Sentencing Commission." *See also* EIGHTH AMENDMENT, p. 399; SEPARATION OF POWERS, p. 697.

Significance The Supreme Court approved of the process Congress chose to formulate sentencing guidelines in *Mistretta*. The Federal Sentencing Guidelines are an approach to reducing disparities in criminal sentences by confining judicial discretion. Sentence guidelines have been adopted in a number of states as well as for the federal courts. Guidelines may be mandated either legislatively as in the Sentencing Reform Act or by state supreme courts in the exercise of their supervisory authority over state judicial systems. *Mistretta* makes clear that procedures for developing these guidelines are virtually immune to challenge on delegation or separation of power grounds. Most guidelines provide sets of sentence ranges that vary by the seriousness of the offense and prior criminal record of the offender.

Giving effect to the Guidelines has produced many questions and a number of court decisions about federal criminal sentencing under them. The Guidelines are not binding. Rather, judges may impose a greater or lesser sentence than is suggested by the Guidelines, but must offer a written rationale for departing from the Guidelines. If a judge wishes to depart from the Guidelines, he or she must identify any factor(s) prompting departure from the recommended sentence. In *Williams v. United States*, 503 U.S. 193 (1992), the Court ruled that an appellate court may affirm an upward departure based on both valid and invalid factors. Williams contended that because the sentencing court had cited an invalid factor, he was entitled to an automatic remand of the case for resentencing. The Supreme Court disagreed. Remand may be avoided if the reviewing court is satisfied that the departure is reasonable, and that the same sentence would have been imposed in the absence of the invalid factor.

In the case of *Burns v. United States*, 501 U.S. 129 (1991), the Court ruled that a defendant is entitled to prior notice if the sentencing court is considering upward departure from the Guidelines on the basis of some factor not addressed in the presentence report.

In yet another Guidelines case, the Court ruled in *United States v. R.L.C.*, 503 U.S. 291 (1992), that the maximum sentence for a juvenile sentenced under the Juvenile Delinquency Act could not exceed the maximum sentence recommended by the Guidelines for the same offense by an adult. Defendants may also receive a sentence departing downward from that recommended in exchange for cooperation. Under terms of the Guidelines, judges do not have the authority to impose a more lenient sentence than recommended, absent a prosecutor's motion to do so. The question in *Wade v. United States*, 504 U.S. 181 (1992), was whether a court may review a prosecutor's reasons for not seeking a downward departure for a cooperating defendant. The Court unanimously concluded that federal courts may indeed "review a prosecutor's refusal to file a substantial-assistance motion and to grant a remedy if they find that the refusal was based on an unconstitutional motive."

Rodney King was seriously injured by police baton blows as several Los Angeles police officers attempted to take him into custody. A portion of the arrest was captured on videotape and received national exposure in 1991. Charges were subsequently brought against several officers, alleging that their actions had been both excessive and criminal. The officers were acquitted on state assault charges, but were later indicted by a federal grand jury for violating King's civil rights. Two officers, Stacey Koon and Laurence Powell, were convicted and sentenced under the Federal Sentencing Guidelines. The Guidelines set out a sentence range of 70 to 87 months' imprisonment. The district court judge reduced the sentence to 30 months because, among other things, King had provoked the initial use of force, and the officers were subject to other punishment, such as job loss and the threat of abuse during imprisonment. The consolidated cases of *Koon v. United States* and *Powell v. United States*, 518 U.S. 81 (1996), provided the Supreme Court with an opportunity to examine the extent to which federal judges have discretion to depart from the Guidelines and determine the standards to be used in reviewing sentencing decisions. The Supreme Court unanimously upheld the trial court's downward departure from the Guidelines in this case. The Sentencing Reform Act of 1984 mandated the guidelines approach to sentencing as a response to concerns about sentence disparity, but the Act did not "eliminate all the district court's discretion." The Act conveyed limited appellate jurisdiction to review federal sentences. Justice Kennedy acknowledged the concern about disparities, but concluded that by establishing limited review, the appellate courts were not to possess "wide-ranging" authority over district court sentencing decisions. Instead, trial court decisions to depart from the Guidelines are due "substantial deference." The trial court is in the best position to make sentencing decisions, and its sentencing judgment ought to be set aside, said Kennedy, only when an "abuse of discretion" occurs. The Court examined the specific factors cited by the trial court in reducing the sentences from the Guideline range, and unanimously concluded that the trial court was within its discretion to reduce sentences on the ground that King's conduct had significantly contributed to the officers' behavior. Five members of the Court found two additional factors to be valid reasons for reducing the sentences—the heightened risk that the officers would be attacked by other inmates in prison, and the officers had already faced state prosecution prior to the federal proceedings. The Court concluded that the trial court had abused its discretion, however, by reducing sentences on the grounds that the officers had lost their law enforcement jobs and were unlikely to engage in subsequent criminal conduct.

Federal criminal sentences are based on the Sentencing Guidelines as well as provisions of statute. These two sources may not produce the same sentence. Federal law permits offenders to be sentenced below the minimum levels defined by the applicable Guidelines or statute if they provide "substantial assistance" to the prosecution. Juan Melendez reached a plea agreement under which the prosecutor would recommend a sentence below the Sentencing Guideline minimum in exchange for Melendez's cooperation. The plea agreement was silent on sentence below the statutory mandatory minimum, however. The government requested a sentence under the Guideline minimum, but did not seek a downward departure from the statutory mandatory minimum of 10 years, and the court ruled it had no authority to sentence below that minimum. Melendez argued that the policy statements that accompany the Guidelines create a "unitary" motion system; a motion that attests to substantial assistance and requests a downward departure from the Guidelines also permits a downward departure from the statutory minimum. It was the judgment of the Court in *Melendez v. United States*, 518 U.S. 120 (1996), that such a unitary motion arrangement does not exist. Rather, a separate motion from the government is required before a district court can sentence below the statutory minimum.

Federal law provides that a minimum term of five years' imprisonment shall be imposed on anyone using or carrying a firearm while engaged in drug trafficking. The law also provides that any term of imprisonment imposed under this law shall not "run concurrently with any other term of imprisonment." Miguel Gonzales and two others were charged with several drug-related offenses under both state and federal law. They were tried, convicted, and sentenced under New Mexico law. While serving their state sentences, they were tried and convicted on the federal charges. Their federal sentences included the mandatory five-year firearm enhancement. While the drug-trafficking portion of their sentences was to run concurrently with the state sentences, the five-year enhancement was to begin upon completion of the state sentences. The question before the Court in *United States v. Gonzales*, 520 U.S. 1 (1997), was whether the language "any other term of imprisonment" should be "limited to some subset of prison sentences, namely, only federal sentences." The Court found nothing in the law to suggest that Congress meant sentences to run consecutively only to certain types of prison terms. Given this "clear legislative mandate," it is not for the courts to "carve out statutory exceptions based on judicial perceptions of good sentencing policy."

The question raised in *United States v. Dunnigan*, 507 U.S. 87

(1993), was whether a sentence drawn from the Federal Sentencing Guidelines could be enhanced if the court determined that the defendant had "willfully obstruct[ed] or imped[ed]" proceedings by perjuring himself or herself. The Supreme Court ruled that the enhancement provision for obstructing was designed to facilitate determination of the "appropriate type and extent of punishment." Commission of perjury, said Justice Kennedy, is of "obvious relevance ... because it reflects on a defendant's criminal history, on her willingness to accept the commands of the law and the authority of the court, and on her character in general." The Court rejected Dunnigan's contention that the sentence enhancement interfered with her right to testify. Kennedy referred to a number of cases holding that a "defendant's right to testify does not include a right to commit perjury."

In addition to the Guidelines, the Sentencing Commission fashioned policy statements and commentary to accompany the Guidelines. The question in *Stinson v. United States*, 508 U.S. 36 (1993), was whether federal judges are bound by the provisions of the commentary. Stinson pleaded guilty to a five-count indictment that included bank robbery and possession of a firearm. The presentence report contained a recommendation that he be sentenced as a "career offender" under the Guidelines. Among other things, the Guidelines required that the predicate offense for a career offender be a crime of violence. The district court saw Stinson's conviction for possession of a firearm as a crime of violence as it applied the career criminal provisions of the Guidelines. Following Stinson's unsuccessful appeal, the Guideline Manual was amended by the addition of language in the commentary to the section on career criminals specifically declaring unlawful possession of a firearm by a felon not to be a "crime of violence." Stinson sought retroactive application of the amendment to the commentary. The U.S. Court of Appeals for the Eleventh Circuit ruled that the commentary to the Guidelines is binding on the federal courts. A unanimous Supreme Court disagreed. Justice Kennedy said that, although the Sentencing Reform Act "does not in express terms authorize the issuance of commentary, the Act does refer to it." In this case, the commentary added by the amendment was "interpretive and explanatory of the guideline defining crime of violence." Commentary that functions in this way "controls" application of a particular guideline.

The Sentencing Commission revised its commentary to the Sentencing Guidelines in 1994. The change provided that sentences for repeat offenders would not include the statutory sentence enhancement for recidivists. The new commentary also provided that changes could apply retroactively—that sentencing judges could reduce sentences imposed prior to the changed language. George

LaBonte was sentenced at the maximum level under the Guidelines by a federal judge who also took into account his prior convictions. LaBonte sought resentencing following the adoption of the commentary amendment, and his sentence was reduced. The Supreme Court reinstated the original sentence in *United States v. LaBonte*, 520 U.S. 751 (1997). The Court found the 1994 revision to be inconsistent with the "plain and unambiguous" language of the sentencing provisions in place at the time LaBonte was originally sentenced. The phrase "maximum term authorized" must be read, said Justice Thomas, "to include all applicable statutory sentencing enhancements." The Court found "little merit" in LaBonte's contention that the "maximum term authorized" phrase referred only to the highest sentence for the offense, excluding enhancements of any kind. When Congress has enacted a base penalty for nonqualifying repeat offenders, and an enhanced penalty for qualifying repeat offenders, the maximum term authorized for the qualifying offender is "the enhanced, not the base term." Congress sought to distinguish the third-time offender from other categories of offenders, and the Sentencing Commission is not free to "ignore this distinction."

The Supreme Court held in *Baldasar v. Illinois*, 446 U.S. 222 (1980), that a trial court could not consider for sentencing purposes any previous misdemeanor conviction for which a defendant had not been represented by counsel. The Court revisited *Baldasar* in *Nichols v. United States*, 511 U.S. 738 (1994). Nichols pleaded guilty to federal felony drug charges. Under provisions of the Federal Sentencing Guidelines, his sentence was enhanced in part on the basis of a 1983 state misdemeanor conviction for driving under the influence (DUI). Nichols was unrepresented on the DUI conviction and was fined rather than incarcerated for the offense. Relying on *Baldasar*, Nichols objected to the inclusion of the DUI in the calculation of his criminal history score for the Guidelines. The sentencing judge rejected his arguments and sentenced Nichols to a term of imprisonment that was 25 months longer than it could have been had the DUI not been considered. The Supreme Court affirmed that judgment. The Court had held in *Scott v. Illinois*, 440 U.S. 367 (1979), that when no imprisonment was imposed, a defendant charged with a misdemeanor has no constitutional right to appointed counsel. Imprisonment is a penalty "different in kind" from fines or mere threat of imprisonment. That premise remains "eminently sound and warrants adoption of actual imprisonment as the line defining the constitutional right to appointment of counsel." The Court concluded that a "logical consequence" of the *Scott* decision was that uncounseled convictions valid under *Scott* may be used to enhance the sentence for a subsequent offense, even though that sentence entails imprisonment. Recidivist statutes do not change the penalty imposed on the earlier conviction. Instead, repeat-offender laws penalize only the last offense committed. Reliance on such a prior conviction is also "consistent with traditional understanding of the sentencing process," a process recognized as "less exacting" than the guilt adjudication process. Trial judges may generally conduct broad sentencing hearings "largely unlimited as to the kind of information he may consider, or the source from which it may come."

The Federal Armed Career Criminal Act mandates a 15-year minimum sentence for anyone with three prior felony or drug convictions upon conviction for possession of a firearm. Darren Custis was convicted in 1991 for cocaine possession and possession of a firearm by a convicted felon, a federal felony. The government sought to have his sentence enhanced under terms of the Act. Two of the prior convictions from Maryland and another from Pennsylvania were used to qualify Custis for a supplemented sentence. Custis objected to the use of the Maryland convictions on the ground, among others, that he was ineffectively represented by his lawyer. The Supreme Court ruled in *Custis v. United States*, 511 U.S. 485 (1994), that there was no right under the Act to challenge the prior convictions used for sentence enhancement. The Act focused on the "fact of the conviction" exclusively, without suggesting that a prior final conviction be subject to review for potential constitutional errors before it is to be counted. The Act provides that no conviction that has been "set aside" or for which a person has been pardoned "creates a clear negative implication," suggesting that any convictions that have not been set aside may be counted.

Federal Habeas Corpus Review

Coleman v. Thompson, **501 U.S. 722 (1991),** examined whether a state prisoner could pursue federal habeas corpus review before a state appellate court had concluded its review. Federal habeas corpus review of state criminal cases has become a significant criminal justice policy issue. By 1970 federal courts were processing more than 16,000 habeas petitions a year from state prisoners. Among other things, these cases presented important questions about federal and state sovereignty. Many of the cases that raised the most substantial policy questions involved federal habeas review of death sentences imposed in state proceedings. The cases discussed below treat issues that directly relate to rights of the accused and criminal sentences, thus they are included in this chapter.

Under *Fay v. Noia*, 372 U.S. 391 (1963), federal habeas corpus petitions could be granted even in cases in which state appellate review had not taken place, unless the petitioner had "deliberately bypassed" the state appellate courts. The Court overruled *Fay v. Noia* in

Coleman, finding that virtually any failure to satisfy state processes would constitute procedural default and preclude the prisoner from petitioning for federal habeas corpus review. The Court made it clear that the ruling reached cases in which failure to pursue state review was the result of "inadvertent error" by defense counsel. Coleman's petition for state review had been dismissed because it had not been filed within the prescribed time period. Justice O'Connor said that the case was "about federalism," and the respect federal courts owe state court processes. It was necessary to overturn *Fay v. Noia* because that decision was "based on a conception of federal-state relations that undervalued the importance of state procedural rules." *Coleman* held that federal courts can undertake habeas corpus review only if the petitioner can show cause why state processes were not completed. Under *Coleman*, mistakes of counsel acting as agents of the petitioner are insufficient cause. O'Connor said cause must be the consequence of something external to the petitioner, something that "cannot be fairly attributed to him." Justices Blackmun, Marshall, and Stevens dissented. Blackmun characterized the ruling as part of a "crusade" by the majority to limit the ability of state prisoners to access federal courts. He said that the Court had created a "byzantine morass of arbitrary, unnecessary, and unjustifiable impediments to the vindication of Federal rights." *See also* EIGHTH AMENDMENT, p. 399; HABEAS CORPUS, p. 658; *Herrera v. Collins*, p. 457; *Teague v. Lane*, p. 453.

Significance   The number of state criminal convictions reviewed under the federal habeas corpus process grew dramatically in the 1960s. It was the view of the Warren Court that federal courts must be available to maintain due process standards in state cases. The Burger and Rehnquist Courts did not share this view, and they began to reduce the access of state prisoners to federal courts. *Coleman* was the first of a number of significant habeas corpus rulings by the Rehnquist Court. Another significant habeas corpus question was considered in *McCleskey v. Zant*, 499 U.S. 467 (1991). Among the evidence against McCleskey was the testimony of a witness who occupied a jail cell next to him. He argued that his incriminating statements to the informant in the adjoining cell were elicited in violation of his Sixth Amendment right to counsel under *Massiah v. United States*, 377 U.S. 201 (1964). *Massiah* prohibits use of informants to elicit incriminating information after formal charges have been brought against a suspect. McCleskey filed a federal habeas corpus petition, but did not include a *Massiah* claim because the evidence available to McCleskey's counsel at the time suggested that such a claim would not be successful. Rather, McCleskey argued that Georgia administered its death penalty law in a racially discriminatory manner. The case reached the

Supreme Court, but the Court rejected McCleskey's discrimination claim in *McCleskey v. Kemp*, 481 U.S. 279 (1987). McCleskey then filed a second habeas corpus petition, this time asserting the *Massiah* claim. The issue was whether McCleskey's failure to include the *Massiah* issue in his first petition precluded his raising that claim in a second petition and whether the second submission constituted an "abuse of the writ." McCleskey's position was that such abuse could only occur as a result of deliberately abandoning a claim in the first petition or through inexcusable neglect. Georgia argued that the standard requires prisoners to include all claims of which they were aware in the first petition. Justice Kennedy said doctrines such as abuse of the writ are based on concerns about the "significant cost" of federal habeas corpus review. First, the writ "strikes at finality." Perpetual disrespect for the finality of convictions "disparages the entire criminal system." Second, habeas corpus review burdens scarce federal judicial resources by threatening the "capacity of the system to resolve primary disputes." Habeas corpus review may also give litigants "incentives to withhold claims for manipulative purposes." The Court sought to modify the abuse of writ doctrine to "curtail the abusive petitions that in recent years have threatened the integrity of the *habeas corpus* process." Under the new standard, habeas corpus petitions following the first one will be dismissed unless a prisoner can demonstrate cause for not asserting the claim earlier. The petitioner must demonstrate "some external impediment preventing counsel from constructing or raising a claim," and demonstrate that he or she suffered "actual prejudice resulting from the errors of which he complains." The burden of disproving abuse of the petition falls to the prisoner once the state describes the prior petition(s) and isolates claims raised for the first time.

Coleman and *McCleskey* established difficult hurdles for both initial and subsequent habeas corpus petitions of state prisoners. The Court continued to withdraw federal habeas corpus access from those convicted of state crimes in *Keeney v. Tamayo-Reyes*, 504 U.S. 1 (1992). Under standards that applied previous to *Keeney*, a state prisoner was entitled to habeas corpus review of evidence not adequately developed in state trial courts as long as the evidence was not deliberately withheld. The Court ruled in *Keeney* that federal habeas corpus review can take place only if "cause and prejudice" can be demonstrated. The prisoner must show cause for his or her failure to develop the evidence at trial and further demonstrate "actual prejudice resulting from that failure." The effect of the ruling was to make the standard for failing to develop a factual matter in a state court identical with the standard used to assert an appellate claim at the state level as required under *Coleman* and *McCleskey*. The new standard, said Justice White, "will appropriately accommodate concerns of finality, comity, judicial economy, and channeling the resolution of claims into the most appropriate forum."

Under the terms of *McCleskey v. Zant*, state prisoners are generally barred from submitting more than one petition for habeas corpus review. An exception exists if a prisoner can demonstrate "cause and prejudice." The petitioner must show that a "miscarriage of justice" would occur if the petition was not permitted. Meeting this standard essentially means that a prisoner must demonstrate "actual innocence." The question in *Sawyer v. Whitley*, 505 U.S. 333 (1992), was how this exception applies to cases in which a prisoner asserts that he or she was erroneously sentenced to death. The Court retained the "cause and prejudice" framework and held that the miscarriage exception should extend to any prisoners who can demonstrate legal ineligibility for the death sentence.

The more significant question of whether federal courts ought to make an independent examination of how state courts apply the Constitution to specific cases was raised in *Wright v. West*, 505 U.S. 277 (1992). The Court could not agree, however, on a response. Virginia, supported by the Bush administration, had argued that federal judges should not make such independent determinations. The Court was of the view that federal courts need not be so deferential to state judgments on constitutional questions.

Congress enacted the Anti-Terrorism and Effective Death Penalty Act in April 1996 (AEDPA). The law limited the authority of federal courts to consider habeas corpus petitions. The law was largely designed to restrict prisoner access to federal courts for the purpose of reviewing state criminal convictions. The law was prompted, among other reasons, by the view held by many members of Congress that then-current rules governing federal habeas corpus review led to protracted appellate proceedings in which guilty prisoners, particularly those on death row, could indefinitely delay implementation of sentences. The new law was challenged by Ellis Felker, a Georgia prisoner convicted of a 1981 rape and murder. Felker unsuccessfully filed a habeas corpus petition in 1993, but filed a second shortly after the new law was signed by President Clinton. Under terms of the new law, a second habeas petition could be considered only after permission to file the petition was granted by a federal appeals court. Felker failed to obtain the necessary permission. The Court upheld portions of the law in *Felker v. Turpin*, 518 U.S. 651 (1996). The Court considered two issues: (1) whether habeas corpus had been unconstitutionally "suspended" by the Act, and (2) whether the Court had been impermissibly denied appellate review by the "gate-keeping" function assigned to the courts of appeal. The Court ruled that the Act did not "suspend" the writ in violation of Article I, Section 9. The Court, said Rehnquist, has "long recognized" that the power to award the writ by any federal court "must be given by written law." Similarly, it established that "judgments about the proper scope of the writ are normally for Congress to make." The restrictions added by the Act on second habeas petitions are "well within the compass of this ... process, and we hold that they do not amount to a suspension" incompatible with Article I, Section 9. The Court further concluded that the new provisions imposed "new conditions on our authority to grant [habeas corpus] relief," but because the "gate-keeping" system applies only to second petitions filed with the district courts, the Supreme Court retained its jurisdiction to "entertain original habeas petitions." Although the statutory language did not directly apply to the Court's original jurisdiction, Rehnquist thought that the restrictions, although not binding as such, would "certainly inform our consideration" of original habeas corpus petitions.

The following year, the Court ruled in *Lindh v. Murphy*, 521 U.S. 320 (1997), that the AEDPA applied retroactively to all capital cases pending at the time of enactment, but that it should apply only prospectively to noncapital cases.

The Eighth Amendment prohibits the execution of a mentally incompetent prisoner. The issue of one's competency for execution may be raised, however, only after the setting of a date of execution. The AEDPA prohibits second federal habeas corpus petitions unless permission is secured from a panel of the federal appeals court of jurisdiction. The question in *Stewart v. Martinez-Villareal*, 118 S.Ct. 1618 (1998), was whether state death-row inmates who have previously filed federal habeas corpus petitions may file a subsequent petition on the execution competency issue. When Martinez-Villareal's counsel filed a habeas petition on the competency issue without the permission required by the AEDPA, the federal district court concluded it had no jurisdiction to hear the claim. The Supreme Court decided that Martinez-Villareal was not prevented by the AEDPA from raising his competency claim. Chief Justice Rehnquist acknowledged that the petitioner had once before sought relief on the competency question, but that did not "mean that there were two separate applications." Rather, there was only one application for habeas relief, and the district court "ruled (or should have ruled) on each claim at the time it became ripe." Martinez-Villareal brought his competency claim "in a timely fashion, and it has not been ripe for resolution until now."

***Teague v. Lane*, 489 U.S. 288 (1989),** held that new constitutional rules could not be applied retroactively in cases on collateral review—that is, cases before federal courts on habeas corpus petitions rather than on direct review. Frank Teague, an African American, was tried in Illinois in 1977 on several charges, including attempted murder. The prosecutor used all of the state's peremptory challenges to exclude African Americans from the jury, which left an all-white jury. Teague was convicted, and unsuccessfully raised equal protection claims on appeal. In *Batson v. Kentucky*, 476 U.S. 79 (1986), the Supreme Court changed the evidentiary standards for challenging race-based use of peremptory challenges. Teague sought to benefit from the *Batson* decision by filing a petition for habeas corpus in federal court. The Supreme Court ruled that the *Batson* rule could not be applied retroactively for anyone whose conviction became final before the decision. Justice O'Connor said a new rule is one that "breaks new ground or imposes a new obligation on the States of the Federal Government." A new rule is announced when the result was not "dictated by precedent existing at the time the defendant's conviction became final." Application of constitutional rules not in existence at the time a conviction becomes final "seriously undermines the principle of finality which is essential to the operation of our criminal justice system," O'Connor said. Without finality, the criminal law is "deprived of much of its deterrent effect." Considerations of federalism were substantial influences on the Court's ruling. The "costs" imposed on the states by retroactive application of new rules of constitutional law on habeas corpus "far outweigh the benefits of its application." The retroactivity rule announced in *Teague* is that habeas corpus cannot be used as "a vehicle to create new constitutional rules ... unless those rules would be applied retroactively to *all* defendants on collateral review through one of two exceptions." A new rule should be applied retroactively if it places a certain kind of conduct "beyond the power of the criminal law-making authority, or if it requires the observance of those procedures that are 'implicit on the concept of ordered liberty.'" *See also Coleman v. Thompson*, p. 449; EIGHTH AMENDMENT, p. 399; *Herrera v. Collins*, p. 457.

Significance The *Teague* "new rule" doctrine has generated a number of issues about federal habeas review. The primary effect of *Teague* has been to limit intervention by federal courts in state criminal cases. Cary Lambrix was convicted of two counts of capital murder. Under Florida law, a jury makes a sentence recommendation to the trial court in such cases. Lambrix's jury recommended the death penalty for both murders. Among the aggravating factors found by the jury were that the crimes were "especially heinous, atrocious or cruel," and that they were "cold, calculated and premeditated." The trial court agreed with the jury and imposed death sentences in 1984. The sentences became final following mandatory review by the Florida Supreme Court in 1986. While Lambrix's appeal was pending, the Supreme Court ruled in *Espinosa v. Florida*,

505 U.S. 1079 (1992), that the jury instructions for the two aggravating factors were unconstitutionally vague, and that trial courts could not remedy this insufficiency by reweighing the remaining factors. Lambrix's jury had received essentially the same instructions as those found defective in *Espinosa*. The "first and principal" task in reviewing a case such as Lambrix's, said Justice Scalia, is to "survey the legal landscape" as of the date a conviction becomes final to determine whether the rule announced later was "dictated by then-existing precedent." The Court ruled in *Lambrix v. Singletary*, 520 U.S. 518 (1997), that a reasonable jurist considering Lambrix's sentence in 1986 could have reached a conclusion different from the one *Espinosa* announced in 1992. Since the relief Lambrix was seeking would have required a "new rule" under *Teague*, the Court did not invalidate his death sentence.

Texas had a "special issue" statute that required jurors in murder cases to find unanimously that a defendant acted deliberately, was a future danger to society, and was not provoked by the victim in order for the death sentence to be imposed. Gary Graham was convicted of capital murder in 1981. The jury answered affirmatively on each of the "special issue" questions, and Graham was sentenced to death. Graham had argued at the sentencing phase of his trial that his youth—he was 17 at the time of the murder—and troubled childhood were mitigating factors. In 1989 the Supreme Court ruled in *Penry v. Lynaugh*, 492 U.S. 302 (1989), that a mentally retarded defendant was entitled to supplemental jury instructions before deliberation of the "special issue" questions in order to give his or her mitigating evidence "full effect." Graham argued that he should have received more extensive instructions. The Supreme Court held in *Graham v. Collins*, 506 U.S. 461 (1992), that he was not entitled to relief on federal habeas corpus grounds. The "new rule" principle adheres, said Justice White, "even if those good-faith interpretations are shown to be contrary to later decisions." Graham could prevail with his claim if the judges hearing his claim at the time his conviction became final "would have felt compelled by existing precedent, to rule in his favor." The Court thus concluded that neither *Penry* nor its predecessors "dictate[d] the ruling Graham seeks within the meaning required by *Teague*." Even "with the benefit" of *Penry*, the Court was not convinced that "reasonable jurists would be of one mind in ruling on Graham's claim today."

The case of *O'Dell v. Netherland*, 521 U.S. 151 (1997), considered whether the Court's ruling in *Simmons v. South Carolina*, 512 U.S. 154 (1994), announced a "new rule" under *Teague*. *Simmons* held that a capital defendant may, when a state argues future dangerousness as a rationale for the death penalty, inform the sentencing jury that he or she would be ineligible for parole under any circumstances if the death penalty was not imposed. O'Dell was convicted of capital murder and rape several years prior to the *Simmons* decision. The state obtained a death sentence against O'Dell, based in part on the contention that he posed a serious threat of future dangerousness. O'Dell attempted to rebut the future dangerousness issue by requesting that the trial judge inform the jury that if it chose life imprisonment instead of a death sentence, he would be ineligible for any form of early release. The trial court refused to inform the jury of the impossibility of O'Dell's early release. The jury subsequently recommended the death sentence, and the trial court imposed that sentence. While O'Dell was pursuing federal habeas corpus review, the Supreme Court made its ruling in *Simmons*. The Supreme Court ruled that *Simmons* announced a new rule and that O'Dell was not entitled to retroactive application of *Simmons*. The central inquiry is whether a state court considering a defendant's claim at the time a conviction became final "would have felt compelled by existing precedent to conclude that the rule [sought] was required by the Constitution." Justice Thomas suggested that *Simmons* was an "unlikely candidate for old-rule status" because there was insufficient consensus to produce an opinion supported by the majority of justices. The "array of views" expressed in *Simmons* suggests that the rule announced was "susceptible to debate among reasonable minds." O'Dell characterized the practice struck down in *Simmons* as a "shocking one," and contended that he had been denied the opportunity to make a "fair response to the prosecution's argument about future danger that he allegedly posed to the community." The Court disagreed. Justice Thomas said the "narrow right of rebuttal" that *Simmons* afforded to defendants in a "limited class of capital cases has hardly 'altered our understanding of the bedrock procedural elements essential to the fairness of a proceeding.'"

Coleman Gray was convicted of capital murder, and the state sought the death sentence. Under Virginia law, the state was required to prove the existence of at least one aggravating factor as a precondition for the death penalty. Several days prior to the sentencing hearing, the prosecution informed Gray that it would attempt, in part, to demonstrate aggravation by calling witnesses who would link him to the unsolved murders of two others. Gray objected, claiming insufficient time to prepare a response to all new evidence. The trial court admitted the evidence, nonetheless, and a jury sentenced Gray to death. At the evidentiary hearing on his habeas corpus petition, a police detective indicated that someone other than Gray had been a prime suspect, and that the detective had recommended that this other person be charged with the murders. The district court vacated Gray's sentence on two grounds: that the prosecutor had failed to inform the defense of this other suspect in violation of disclosure requirements set forth in *Brady v. Maryland*, 373 U.S. 83 (1963), and that notification of the intent to introduce the forensic evidence was offered too late. The Supreme Court reinstated Gray's death sentence in *Gray v. Netherland*, 518 U.S. 152 (1996). Unless Gray could demonstrate cause and prejudice for failing to assert this claim in the state courts, he had failed to exhaust state remedies, which constitutes a procedural default. Gray's notice of evidence claim was that due process entitled him to time to prepare and then be heard on the critical sentencing issues. Although a defendant has a right to be informed of the charges against him or her, the right to notice of evidence that the state uses to prove those charges "stands on quite a different footing." Whatever one might think of a notice-of-evidence rule, it has "none of the primacy and centrality" of the rule requiring assistance of counsel or other rules falling within the *Teague* "new rule" exception.

Gilmore v. Taylor, 508 U.S. 333 (1993), presented another issue arising out of the nonretroactivity rule set forth in *Teague*. Kevin Taylor was convicted of murder in an Illinois court and was sentenced to 35 years of imprisonment. He sought federal habeas corpus relief, claiming that the pattern jury instructions used at his trial violated his due process protections because the instructions allowed a jury to return a murder conviction without considering whether Taylor's mental state could support a voluntary manslaughter conviction instead. Subsequent to Taylor's conviction becoming final, the Court of Appeals for the Seventh Circuit ruled in another case that the pattern jury instructions used in Taylor's trial were unconstitutional. The Supreme Court ruled that a "new rule" had been established. The "new rule" doctrine "validates reasonable, good-faith interpretation of existing precedents made by state courts." Furthermore, the doctrine "effectuates the states' interest in the finality of criminal convictions and fosters comity between federal and state courts." Decisions prior to the Seventh Circuit's decision had established that jury instructions containing errors of state law "may not form the basis for federal habeas corpus relief." Although capital defendants are entitled to jury instructions that do not prevent consideration of "constitutionally relevant evidence," there is no counterpart to the "relevant evidence" rule for noncapital cases.

Herrera v. Collins, 506 U.S. 390 (1993) Leonel Herrera was convicted of murder in Texas in 1982 and sentenced to death. He unsuccessfully sought to have the conviction overturned at that time, including an attempt through federal habeas corpus review. Ten years after his conviction, Herrera filed a second habeas corpus petition, claiming that he was "actually innocent" of the murder. The claim of innocence was supported by affidavits suggesting that Herrera's brother, who had died during the 10-year interim, had committed the crime. The principal question in *Herrera* was whether his "actual innocence" claim, advanced in a second petition and based on new evidence barred by Texas law, entitled him to federal habeas corpus relief. The Supreme Court ruled that it did not. Herrera argued that the Eighth Amendment prohibits the execution of an innocent person. Though such a proposition has "elemental appeal," Chief Justice Rehnquist said that Herrera's claim must be assessed in light of the long history of the case. Rehnquist pointed out that Herrera was afforded every constitutional protection directed toward "assuring against the risk of convicting an innocent person." Herrera also received the additional procedural safeguards that apply to capital cases. All of these made it more difficult for the state to meet the presumption of innocence to which Herrera was entitled. At the same time, said Rehnquist, due process does not require that "every conceivable step be taken, at whatever cost, to eliminate the possibility of convicting an innocent person." Once a defendant has had a fair trial and been convicted, the "presumption of innocence disappears." Another approach would "all but paralyze" our criminal justice system. The "actual innocence" claim is not itself a constitutional claim, but instead is a "gateway through which a habeas petitioner must pass" before an otherwise barred constitutional claim may be examined on the merits. Herrera is "no longer innocent in the eyes of the law," said Justice O'Connor. He had a trial, the "paramount event for determining guilt," and he was found guilty. As a result, he does not appear before the Supreme Court as "an innocent man on the verge of execution." Rather, he is a "legally guilty one who, refusing to accept the jury's verdict, demands a hearing in which to have his culpability determined once again." Justice Blackmun, joined by Justices Stevens and Souter, dissented. The question is whether, in light of evidence not considered at the first trial, the result of the first trial "is sufficiently reliable for the State to carry out a death sentence." The dissenters did not find that level of reliability. *See also Coleman v. Thompson*, p. 449; EIGHTH AMENDMENT, p. 399; HABEAS CORPUS, p. 658; *Teague v. Lane*, p. 453.

Significance   The Supreme Court's modification of federal habeas corpus doctrine began in *Stone v. Powell*, 428 U.S. 465 (1976), in which it held that federal habeas corpus review is not available to state prisoners asserting search or seizure violations when the state has afforded them a "full and fair" review of the Fourth Amendment claims. The Court ruled in *Withrow v. Williams*, 507 U.S. 680 (1993), that the *Stone* restriction was limited to search and seizure issues and did not apply to claims based on violations of *Miranda v. Arizona*, 384 U.S. 436 (1966). The state of Michigan (and the United States as amicus curiae) argued that *Miranda*'s protections are not constitutional, but "merely prophylactic." As a consequence, they contended that federal habeas corpus review should not extend to *Miranda*-based claims. While accepting that *Miranda* is prophylactic in character, the Supreme Court rejected the conclusion on habeas corpus review. Characterizing *Miranda* protections as "prophylactic," said Souter, is a "far cry from putting *Miranda* on all fours with *Mapp* [*v. Ohio*, 367 U.S. 643 (1961)] or from rendering *Miranda* subject to *Stone.*" Souter pointed to two substantial differences between *Mapp* and *Miranda*. *Mapp* can neither remediate the extrajudicial Fourth Amendment violation nor improve on the reliability of evidence used at trial. On the other hand, *Miranda* safeguards a "fundamental trial right" by protecting a defendant's privilege against self-incrimination.

Doyle v. Ohio, 426 U.S. 610 (1976), held that *Miranda* warnings contain an implicit assurance that silence will carry no penalty. As a result, the prosecutor may not call attention to a defendant's choice to remain silent after the administration of *Miranda*, even in the course of cross-examination. The question before the Court in *Brecht v. Abrahamson*, 507 U.S. 619 (1993), was the standard to be used to determine if a *Doyle* violation entitled a defendant to federal habeas corpus relief. The Supreme Court held that a petitioner is entitled to federal habeas corpus relief if the *Doyle* violation "had substantial and injurious effect or influence in determining the jury's verdict." Chief Justice Rehnquist said direct review is the "principal avenue" for challenging a conviction. Although federal habeas corpus proceedings are important in protecting constitutional rights, their role compared to direct review is "secondary and limited." Federal courts are not, concluded Rehnquist, "forums in which to relitigate state trials." The standard chosen by the Court allows review of constitutional claims, but petitioners are not entitled to relief based on trial error unless they can show that the error resulted in "actual prejudice." The standard is "tailored" to the unique purpose of collateral review, and more likely to "promote the considerations under our recent *habeas* cases."

Robert O'Neal was convicted of aggravated murder, kidnapping, and robbery in Ohio. He filed a federal habeas corpus petition after failing to secure relief in the Ohio courts. O'Neal asserted, among other things, that the prosecutor had made improper remarks involving his complicity in the crime and that the judge had improperly instructed the jury in his case. The federal district court considered whether these errors actually affected the verdict—whether they had "substantial and injurious effect or influence" in determining the jury's verdict or were merely harmless. In the view of the district court, the record could support either finding. The Supreme Court ruled in *O'Neal v. McAninch*, 513 U.S. 432 (1995), that when there is

459

uncertainty as to whether error is harmful or harmless, the petitioner must win. Justice Breyer suggested that the conclusion that petitioners must prevail in cases in which there was grave doubt as to harmlessness was "consistent with the basic purposes underlying the writ of *habeas corpus*." Under these circumstances, a legal rule requiring issuance of the writ when a conscientious judge has grave doubt about the "substantial and injurious" effect of the asserted error will generally "avoid a grievous wrong."

Roy Heck filed a federal civil-rights action under United States Code § 1983 while direct appeal of his state manslaughter conviction was pending. Section 1983, based on provisions of the Civil Rights Act of 1871, enables persons to pursue damages for civil-rights violations. He was seeking damages for alleged unlawful acts on the part of various officials, acting under color of state law, that led to his arrest and conviction. Although he was not seeking release as such in his § 1983 action, his winning of the suit would require his release. As a result, a federal district court dismissed his § 1983 claim on the grounds that it was the functional equivalent of a habeas corpus petition. Under current rules, state prisoners are required to exhaust all state remedies before seeking federal habeas corpus relief, and Heck had not done so. The Supreme Court unanimously ruled in *Heck v. Humphrey*, 512 U.S. 477 (1994), that as a precondition to recovering damages for unlawful conviction, imprisonment, or other harm caused by unlawful actions that would render a conviction or sentence invalid, a § 1983 plaintiff must show that the conviction or sentence has been reversed on direct appeal, expunged by executive order, or invalidated by a federal court's issuance of a writ of habeas corpus.

The Congress chose death as the penalty for certain federal drug offenses in the Anti-Drug Abuse Act of 1988. The Act provides that capital defendants are entitled to "qualified legal representation" in "any post-conviction proceeding" falling under the federal habeas corpus statute. The question in *McFarland v. Scott*, 512 U.S. 849 (1994), was whether an unrepresented state capital defendant must file a federal habeas corpus petition in order to invoke the statutory right and to establish a federal court's jurisdiction to stay his or her execution. Frank McFarland was within four days of execution for murder in Texas when he petitioned a federal district court to appoint counsel and stay his execution long enough to allow counsel time to file a habeas corpus petition. The district court ruled against McFarland, concluding that because no postconviction proceeding had been initiated, McFarland was not entitled to appointed counsel. The district court also ruled that it had no jurisdiction to stay his execution. The Supreme Court held that a defendant need not file a formal habeas corpus petition in order to qualify for counsel. The Court also ruled that a formal petition for habeas corpus was not required for establishing a federal court's jurisdiction to stay an execution. An attorney's assistance prior to the filing of a capital defendant's habeas corpus petition is critical because the "complexity of our jurisprudence in this area" make its "unlikely" that capital defendants will be able to file successful petitions on their own. Requiring an indigent capital defendant to proceed without counsel in order to have counsel appointed would "expose him to substantial risk that his *habeas* claims would never be heard on the merits." Habeas corpus is an "extraordinary" remedy that should not be used to "relitigate" state trials. At the same time, criminal defendants are entitled to challenge their conviction or sentence through the process. By providing counsel to indigent capital defendants, Congress "recognized that federal *habeas corpus* has a particularly important role to play in promoting fundamental fairness in the imposition of the death penalty."

Thomas Thompson was convicted of rape and murder in a California court. Several years after Thompson filed his first federal habeas corpus petition, the U.S. Court of Appeals for the Ninth Circuit issued its mandate denying the writ. Two days before Thompson's scheduled execution, however, the Ninth Circuit, sitting en banc, recalled the mandate and granted habeas corpus relief. The Supreme Court ruled in *Calderon v. Thompson*, 118 S.Ct. 1489 (1998), that while the recall order did not violate terms of the Anti-Terrorism and Effective Death Penalty Act (AEDPA), the order was a grave abuse of discretion. The Ninth Circuit referred to "procedural misunderstandings" within the court as one reason it recalled its earlier mandate. The en banc court also concluded that the decision of the original panel "would lead to a miscarriage of justice." The Supreme Court acknowledged that courts of appeals have an "inherent power to recall their mandates," but that the power should be used only in extraordinary circumstances as a "last resort, to be held in reserve against grave, unforeseen contingencies." The Court concluded that the Ninth Circuit's recall of its mandate rested on the "most doubtful of grounds." Justice Kennedy reviewed the significant limits on federal habeas corpus authority—limits that reflect "enduring respect for the State's interest in the finality of convictions that have survived direct review within the state court system." Finality also serves to "preserve the federal balance." Kennedy said that a state's interests in finality are "compelling when a federal court of appeals issues a mandate denying federal *habeas* relief." Only with the assurance of "real finality" can the state execute its "moral judgment" in a case, and can the victims of crime "move forward knowing the moral judgment will be carried out." The Court found that the evidence in Thompson's case did not meet the "more likely than not" showing necessary to vacate his rape conviction or the "clear and convincing" showing necessary to vacate the death sentence.

CHAPTER 7

Equal Protection and Privacy

Overview, 467

The Equal Protection Clause, 473

The Right of Privacy, 476

OVERVIEW

The Fourteenth Amendment is familiar to most American citizens because of its due process of law language. Such language has been utilized by the Supreme Court frequently in extending protection afforded under the first nine amendments to the states, particularly in criminal procedure cases. Although it is clear that the Fourteenth Amendment was drafted with the slavery issue and the Civil War in mind, it was not utilized to any great extent by the Supreme Court for 50 years after its ratification in 1868. When it was used, it was generally in an economic context in relationship to corporations claiming due process for business purposes. The importance of applying the Due Process Clause in this context should not be underestimated. In *Santa Clara County v. Southern Pacific Railroad Co.*, 118 U.S. 394 (1886), the Court ruled that corporations are "persons" within the meaning of the Fourteenth Amendment. This view remains in effect, and affords corporations substantial insulation from government regulation.

Section I of the Fourteenth Amendment has the familiar phrase "nor shall any State deny to any person within its jurisdiction the equal protection of the laws." Equal protection is impossible to define precisely, but the phrase was intended to guarantee newly freed slaves equality of treatment and the enjoyment of basic civil and political rights. Like the Due Process Clause, however, considerable time passed before the Supreme Court began to interpret and apply the Equal Protection Clause against abridgement of civil and political rights.

The cases in this chapter are divided into three sections. The first section addresses the issue of racial discrimination, long a problem in American society. The persistence of the problem has required the courts to utilize the Due Process, Equal Protection, and Privileges and Immunities Clauses of the Fourteenth Amendment, the voting provisions of the Fifteenth Amendment, the Due Process Clause of the Fifth Amendment, the Interstate Commerce Clause, civil rights statutes passed by Congress under the Necessary and Proper Clause, and the enforcement clauses of the Thirteenth, Fourteenth, and Fifteenth Amendments in an orchestrated effort to redress the effects of prejudice in American society.

The language of the Fourteenth Amendment was, in part, directed toward the Supreme Court's decision in *Scott v. Sandford*, 60 U.S. 393 (1857). The Court ruled in that case that black people, their

467

slave status notwithstanding, were not citizens within the meaning of the Constitution. Even after ratification of the Fourteenth Amendment, the Court moved slowly to read full black citizenship into American jurisprudence. Indeed, in the *Civil Rights Cases*, 109 U.S. 3 (1883), the Court held that only discrimination that involved "state action" fell within the Court's constitutional purview. Neither could it address private discrimination. Even when state action was obviously involved, the Supreme Court insulated a large part of discrimination in the states by creating the separate-but-equal doctrine of *Plessy v. Ferguson*, 163 U.S. 537 (1896).

It took more than 75 years for the Supreme Court to modify its initial and largely negative response to the Fourteenth Amendment. The major decision was, of course, *Brown v. Board of Education (I)*, 347 U.S. 483 (1954), a decision that halted constitutional tolerance of segregation in public education. A substantial number of cases followed, including two decided recently by the Rehnquist Court. In *Board of Education v. Dowell*, 498 U.S. 237 (1991), the Court examined when a school district may be released from desegregation orders, and in *Freeman v. Pitts*, 503 U.S. 467 (1992), held that a federal court may withdraw its supervision of local school districts in stages.

The state action concept necessary for the Court to intervene was broadened over the years, but was accompanied by the need to demonstrate discriminatory intent. The Court's recent ruling in *Robinson v. Shell Oil Company*, 519 U.S. 337 (1997), provides a current illustration of an action brought under Title VII of the Civil Rights Act of 1964, which prohibits discriminatory conduct in the workplace.

City of Arlington Heights v. Metropolitan Housing Development Corp., 429 U.S. 252 (1977), extended the discriminatory intent requirement to challenges of local zoning ordinances affecting public housing. The Court upheld some state initiatives aimed at curbing racial inequalities. It determined that race could be a permissible consideration in university admission procedures in the case of *Regents of the University of California v. Bakke*, 438 U.S. 265 (1978). The Rehnquist Court narrowed the possibilities for affirmative action in *Adarand Constructors, Inc. v. Pena*, 515 U.S. 299 (1995). In *Patterson v. McLean Credit Union*, 491 U.S. 164 (1989), the Court examined the extent to which the private contract provisions of the Civil Rights Act of 1866 apply to current employment situations, and the limits of federal authority to protect civil rights.

The second section of equal protection cases treats an extension of coverage to classifications other than those based on race. Such an expansion of scope has been called the new equal protection. The Warren Court began to entertain the possibility that the Equal Protection Clause might apply to other classifications, but expanding the scope of the Clause meant that legitimate and illegitimate classifications had to be distinguished. An invalid classification impinges on fundamental rights, such as the right to vote. The reapportionment decisions of *Baker v. Carr*, 369 U.S. 186 (1962), and *Reynolds v. Sims*, 377 U.S. 533 (1964), are illustrative of such an invalid classification. *City of Mobile v. Bolden*, 446 U.S. 55 (1980), examined the racial impacts of redistricting, and *Davis v. Bandemer*, 478 U.S. 109 (1986), ruled that claims of political gerrymandering are justiciable. *South Carolina v. Katzenbach*, 383 U.S. 301 (1966), is included despite its Fifteenth Amendment foundation because it upheld the congressional initiative taken in the Voting Rights Act of 1965. The most recent decisions in this area have considered the convergence of constitutional and statutory provisions when redistricting plans have been challenged as prohibited racial gerrymanders. The foundation ruling came in *Shaw v. Reno*, 509 U.S. 630 (1993), in which the Court held that strict scrutiny standards would apply to race-based districting plans.

Shapiro v. Thompson, 394 U.S. 618 (1969), struck down a residency requirement for public assistance because it interfered with the fundamental right to unencumbered movement from state to state. If a fundamental right is involved, the Court imposes more stringent standards of review on the classification. Also deserving strict scrutiny are classifications that are said to be "suspect." Alienage was found to be such a classification in *Graham v. Richardson*, 403 U.S. 365 (1971). The Court struck down a state law disadvantaging illegitimate children in *Weber v. Aetna Casualty & Surety Co.*, 406 U.S. 164 (1972), although the standard of review for distinctions based on illegitimacy was not set at the more stringent level. Congress enacted the Age Discrimination in Employment Act to address the problem of age-based discrimination in the workplace. The Court considered the application of the law when "after-acquired" evidence supported termination of an employee in *McKennon v. Nashville Banner Publishing Co.*, 513 U.S. 352 (1995). In *San Antonio Independent School District v. Rodriguez*, 411 U.S. 1 (1973), the Court did not find that indigence-based classifications require the more stringent review, although indigence has long been considered a threat to due process requirements in a criminal justice context. Most troublesome for the Court has been the extent to which the Equal Protection Clause applies to gender-based classifications. It struck down single-sex education systems in *United States v. Virginia*, 518 U.S. 515 (1996). In *California Federal Savings & Loan Association v. Guerra*, 479 U.S. 272 (1987), the Court held that a state could enact a law requiring employers to grant maternity leave with guaranteed reinstatement. The problem of sexual harassment in the workplace has produced a number of significant rulings. *Harris v. Forklift Systems, Inc.*, 510 U.S.

17 (1993), examined the evidentiary requirements for legal action brought under Title VII of the Civil Rights Act of 1964. *Faragher v. City of Boca Raton*, 118 S.Ct. 2275 (1998), developed criteria to be used when assessing employer liability in sexual harassment cases. In *Grove City College v. Bell*, 465 U.S. 555 (1984), the Court held that Title IX prohibitions on sex discrimination apply to private institutions through the fact that enrolled students receive federal education grants. Earlier, in *Kahn v. Shevin*, 416 U.S. 351 (1974), the Court upheld a benevolent classification that favored women by providing a property tax exemption for widows, but not widowers.

The case of *Vlandis v. Kline*, 412 U.S. 441 (1973), altered the focus of equal protection issues by introducing the concept of irrebuttable presumptions. This approach raised the question of whether a classification makes a presumptive judgment and then precludes an affected person from addressing the classificatory judgment. Classification on the basis of sexual preference is reviewed in *Romer v. Evans*, 517 U.S. 620 (1996).

The final group of cases involves privacy rights. Although not an equal protection issue, the Equal Protection Clause is one of several clauses used by the Court in responding to privacy arguments. The concept of privacy is not explicitly addressed anywhere in the Constitution. The idea that certain aspects of life are simply beyond governmental intrusion evolved over time. In *Griswold v. Connecticut*, 381 U.S. 479 (1965), the Supreme Court established privacy as a constitutional value. The Court fashioned the right of privacy from several specific protections in the Bill of Rights and the Fourteenth Amendment.

Invasion of privacy was the basis of the Court's decision in *Roe v. Wade*, 410 U.S. 113 (1973), which struck down the prohibition of abortion. *Wade* entitled a woman to an abortion without governmental interference. This decision was reaffirmed in *Webster v. Reproductive Health Services*, 492 U.S. 490 (1989), despite significant pressure from the Reagan administration to reverse *Wade*. *Webster* recognized, however, greater state authority to regulate abortion, including substitution of a more stringent definition of viability than the standard contained in *Roe v. Wade*. The Court held in *Harris v. McRae*, 448 U.S. 297 (1980), one of several cases focusing on government subsidies of abortion, that government need not pay for abortions.

The scope of the right of privacy outside the abortion context remains unclear. Considerations of privacy led the Court to invalidate a housing ordinance limiting occupancy to single families in *Moore v. East Cleveland*, 431 U.S. 494 (1977), because the Court said the enactment interfered too greatly with family life. The right to privacy was also a factor as the Court addressed the troublesome question of termination of medical treatment. In *Cruzan v. Director of the Missouri Department of Health,* 497 U.S. 261 (1990), the Court ruled that a person had a qualified right to discontinue life-sustaining medical treatment. In a related ruling, the Court allowed states to enact bans on physician-assisted suicide in *Washington v. Glucksberg,* 117 S.Ct. 2258 (1997).

The **Equal Protection Clause** is a provision contained in the Fourteenth Amendment that prohibits unreasonable classifications. The Equal Protection Clause is one of the changes made in the Constitution after the Civil War. The Thirteenth Amendment outlawed slavery, the Fifteenth Amendment prohibited interference with the right to vote, but the Fourteenth Amendment provided the broadest adjustment to the Constitution. Section I ends with the phrase "nor shall any State deny to any person within its jurisdiction the equal protection of the laws." At the time the Equal Protection Clause was aimed at guaranteeing former slaves equal treatment under the law and certain basic civil rights. The Supreme Court made an effort to confine the language of the clause to blacks in the *Slaughterhouse Cases*, 83 U.S. 36 (1873). The *Slaughterhouse Cases* held that the Clause was to be used when state laws "discriminated with gross injustice and hardship" against "newly emancipated negroes." The Court said federal authority could be used only where racial discrimination occurred by action of a state because the coverage of the clause was aimed only at "that race and that emergency." After confining the clause to racial classifications, the Court set out in following years to define the nature of the protections afforded to blacks under the Clause. The early decisions were less than generous. In 1883 the Court struck down the Civil Rights Act of 1875, ruling that the Equal Protection Clause applied only to state action. The holding in the *Civil Rights Cases*, 109 U.S. 3 (1883), was consistent with the Court's position in the *Slaughterhouse Cases*. It placed private acts of discrimination outside the reach of the Equal Protection Clause and the courts. The Court categorically rejected the argument that the Clause authorized Congress to "create a code of municipal law for the regulation of private rights." The Fourteenth Amendment authorized only corrective, rather than general, legislation that "may be necessary and proper for counteracting such laws as the States may adopt."

Regulation of private discrimination, if it could occur at all, was left to state discretion and initiative. Soon thereafter a comprehensive network of state segregation statutes or Jim Crow laws was enacted. The Court found the segregative approach to be constitutional in *Plessy v. Ferguson*, 163 U.S. 537 (1896), using the separate-but-equal doctrine. The Court said that Jim Crow statutes only made a legal distinction between races and had "no tendency to destroy the legal equality of the two races." No constitutional provision could go further and "abolish distinctions based upon color, or to enforce social, as distinguished from political, equality, or a commingling of the two races upon terms unsatisfactory to either."

Little attention was paid to the equivalent-treatment-under-separate-circumstances idea until certain professional education cases came to the Court in the 1950s. Then the equality aspect of the separate-but-equal doctrine was carefully examined. Separate but equal was struck down in the landmark decision of *Brown v. Board of Education (I)*, 347 U.S. 483 (1954). The Court found that racial segregation imposed by law materially interfered with equal educational opportunity. Subsequently the Court used the Equal Protection Clause to require that affirmative steps be taken to desegregate when constitutional violations could be shown. The authority of the federal courts to mandate relief in such situations was extensively applied. The Supreme Court went on to hold that race can be a permissible consideration in university admission procedures and in establishing policies extending preferential treatment to those subjected to past discrimination. The state action requirement still provides some insulation for private discrimination, however, even though the Court has become more receptive to claims that private discriminators are acting closely enough to state authority to be reached. While softening the line of demarcation between private and state acts, the Court has kept purely private discrimination outside the scope of the Equal Protection Clause and has modified the nature of state action criteria by holding that prohibited behavior turns on discriminatory *intent* rather than discriminatory *impact*. *See also* CLASSIFICATION, p. 628; SEPARATE-BUT-EQUAL DOCTRINE, p. 696; STATE ACTION, p. 703.

Significance The Equal Protection Clause had a limited impact on public policy for many years. It was reserved exclusively for racial discrimination and was not always aggressively applied in that context. The Due Process Clause of the Fourteenth Amendment proved to be of greater policy significance than the Equal Protection Clause as a means of examining the reasonableness of state legislation. The character of equal protection began to change in the post–New Deal period, however, as the Court became more extensively involved with civil liberties questions. The Warren Court in particular began to consider application of the Equal Protection Clause to classifications in addition to race. The expanding scope of the clause is sometimes called the new equal protection. Because most legislation engages in some form of classification, the clause became an attractive vehicle for challenges. The Equal Protection Clause does not preclude the use of classifications. It merely requires that a classification be reasonable. The main problem of the new equal protection is that of distinguishing reasonable and permissible classifications from arbitrary and impermissible ones. Legislatures are generally afforded wide discretion in making classifications. Legislative classifications are typically evaluated by the rationality test, which is a standard reflecting the Court's understanding that the drawing of lines that create distinctions is peculiarly a legislative task as well as an unavoidable one. Classifications are presumed to be valid under this approach and need not produce perfect equality. Rather, if the legislative objective is legitimate, a classification may be used as long as it rationally relates to its objective. This doctrine places the burden of proof on the party claiming that the legislation has no rational or reasonable basis.

Under certain circumstances, a classification may be subjected to the strict scrutiny standard, a closer examination requiring a state to show more than reasonableness for a classificatory scheme. The state must demonstrate a serious need or a compelling interest that can only be addressed by use of the challenged classification. Thus the burden of proof shifts to the state in cases in which strict or close scrutiny is used. The strict scrutiny standard applies when the classification impinges on a fundamental right, understood as a right expressly protected, such as freedom of speech, religious exercise, or the right to vote. Or a fundamental right may be a right fashioned by implication, such as the right to cross state lines or the right to have an abortion. In *Shapiro v. Thompson*, 394 U.S. 618 (1969), the Court struck down a residency requirement for public assistance benefits because the classification inhibited movement of persons from state to state. The Court said that a classification that touches on the fundamental right of interstate movement is "patently unconstitutional." Similarly, interference with the fundamental right of an unimpaired and undiluted vote prompted the Court to develop the "one person, one vote" principle in legislative apportionment cases. The close scrutiny standard also applies if the classification is "suspect." A suspect class is one that is saddled with such disabilities, or is the recipient of such purposeful unequal treatment over time, or is a class that occupies such a politically powerless position, as to require extraordinary protection within the political process. Classifications based on race and alienage are considered to be inherently suspect. The racially conscious affirmative action policies upheld by the Court have demonstrated a compelling interest being served by the classification. If a classification is to be used in such situations, it must also be precisely drawn or carefully tailored, and it must employ the least drastic means possible to achieve its particular legislative objectives. The Court has struck down a number of gender-based classifications, but to date has not found gender to be a suspect class. Some members of the Court have suggested that gender receive heightened, although not strict, scrutiny. Neither are such classifications as age, illegitimacy, or wealth considered to be suspect, although the Court has required that indigent criminal defendants be entitled to appointed counsel and free transcripts for appeals. The new equal protection has dramatically altered the scope of the Equal Protection Clause, and it is likely that new ground will continue to be broken in this policy area.

The **Right of Privacy** is a protection drawn from several constitutional provisions placing certain aspects of life beyond the reach of governmental intrusion. The right of privacy was first acknowledged by the Supreme Court in *Griswold v. Connecticut*, 381 U.S. 479 (1965). The view that the Constitution afforded such protection had existed for some time, however. As early as 1928 in the wiretapping case of *Olmstead v. United States*, 277 U.S. 438 (1928), Justice Brandeis offered a classic dissent, stating that the Fourth and Fifth Amendments conferred the "right to be let alone." Brandeis regarded this as "the most comprehensive of rights and the right most valued by civilized men." Although Brandeis found the Fourth and Fifth Amendments to be a sufficient source for the right of privacy, the rest of the Court had more difficulty finding a constitutional mandate for the protection of privacy. Several additional possibilities have been suggested by individual justices in subsequent cases. The First Amendment has been cited, for example, as providing some insulation for privacy interests. In *Stanley v. Georgia*, 394 U.S. 557 (1969), a case involving privately possessed obscene materials, Justice Marshall said that regulation of obscenity cannot "reach into the privacy of one's own home." He added that "if the First Amendment means anything, it means that a state has no business telling a man, sitting alone in his own house, what books he may read or what films he may watch." In another obscenity case, *Paris Adult Theatre I v. Slaton*, 413 U.S. 49 (1973), Justice Brennan also looked to the First Amendment as a protection for "sexually oriented materials" for consenting adults. The First Amendment has also been used to protect the anonymity of a voluntary association. In *NAACP v. Alabama*, 357 U.S. 449 (1958), Justice Harlan cited the "vital relationship between freedom to associate and privacy in one's associations."

Justice Harlan argued in *Griswold* that the Due Process Clause of the Fourteenth Amendment also offered protection against invasions of privacy. In his view, the Connecticut prohibition on the distribution of contraceptives violated basic values "implicit in the concept of ordered liberty," thus contravening the protection of the Due Process Clause. Harlan said that while other constitutional provisions might be relevant in this instance, the Due Process Clause was sufficient in itself. It stands "on its own bottom" when a right as fundamental as privacy is concerned. The Due Process Clause must not, in Harlan's opinion, be limited to merely procedural safeguards. Rather, the Clause is a "rational continuum which includes a freedom from all substantial arbitrary impositions and purposeless restraints." The Connecticut birth control enactment failed due process muster because its substantive focus was an "intolerable and unjustifiable invasion of privacy in the conduct of the most intimate concerns of an individual's personal life."

Roe v. Wade, 410 U.S. 113 (1973), the landmark abortion decision, also grounded its privacy holding on due process considerations. Justice Brennan has seen privacy secured by the Equal Protection Clause of the Fourteenth Amendment in certain situations. *Eisenstadt v. Baird*, 405 U.S. 438 (1972), involved a state prohibition on the sale of contraceptives to unmarried persons. The Court struck down the statute. *Griswold* had already established that such regulation could not be applied to married persons because the right of privacy inhered in the marital relationship. *Eisenstadt* was based on the view that married couples were "two individuals with a separate intellectual and emotional make-up." Given that, if the "right of privacy means anything," it must mean that the "individual, married or single, is to be free from unwarranted governmental intrusion into matters so fundamentally affecting a person as the decision whether to bear or beget a child."

Finally, the Ninth Amendment has been mentioned as supporting a constitutional right to privacy. This amendment states that "the enumeration in the Constitution of certain rights shall not be construed to deny or disparage others retained by the people." In his concurrence in *Griswold*, Justice Goldberg argued for the recognition of privacy as a constitutionally protected right by saying that the Ninth Amendment "lends strong support" to the proposition that the liberty protected by the Fifth and Fourteenth Amendments "is not restricted to rights specifically mentioned in the first eight amendments."

The Court's approach in the pivotal *Griswold* decision drew indirectly from most of those arguments for privacy. Justice Douglas, author of the Court's opinion in *Griswold*, saw the issue as lying within a zone of privacy created by several fundamental constitutional guarantees. Douglas developed his right of privacy doctrine through the concept of penumbra. According to *Black's Law Dictionary*, a penumbra is an "implied power" that is "engrafted" on another. To Douglas, specific Bill of Rights guarantees have penumbras that are formed by "emanations from those guarantees that help give them life and substance." Douglas made reference to the right of association contained in the penumbra of the First Amendment as an illustration. When one draws together the right of association from the First Amendment, the quartering of soldiers prohibition from the Third Amendment, the unreasonable search and seizure protections from the Fourth Amendment, the self-incrimination privilege from the Fifth Amendment, and the retention language of the Ninth Amendment, a constitutional right of privacy emerges. *See also Cruzon v. Director of Missouri Department of Health*, p. 601; *Griswold v. Connecticut*, p. 586; *Roe v. Wade*, p. 588.

Significance   The right of privacy emanates from an aggregation of various Bill of Rights protections. *Griswold* provided the Supreme Court an opportunity to develop both the concept and the approach. *Griswold* sought to keep the Court from appearing to engage in the second-guessing of legislative policy choices. Justice Douglas declared that the Court does not sit as a superlegislature trying to determine the wisdom, need, and propriety of laws that touch economic problems, business affairs, or social conditions. He intentionally declined use of the Due Process Clause of the Fourteenth Amendment as a source of privacy protection in an attempt to avoid comparisons with the substantive due process predisposition of the Court in the early twentieth century. Nonetheless, the Connecticut statute was stricken because it operated "directly on an intimate relation of husband and wife and their physician's role in one aspect of their relationship." Douglas's efforts notwithstanding, the Court's holding in *Griswold* raised the possibility that the new right of privacy could be used indiscriminately to strike down legislative enactments. In his *Griswold* dissent, Justice Black argued that the only limit on the Court's use of a natural law due process philosophy in reviewing legislation would be the Court's own restraint. Black was concerned that the elevation of privacy to the status of a constitutional right was the creation of a means whereby the Court could substitute its views of appropriate social policy for the views of legislative bodies. There was a general concern that *Griswold* reflected the view that persons were entitled to freedom from regulation in a broad sense. These concerns touched on matters of fundamental proportion and consequence. Since *Griswold* the Court has both enlarged and confined the right of privacy doctrine. Cases such as *Eisenstadt* and *Wade* broadened the concept of privacy, taking it from interpersonal relationships to the level of individual choice. At the same time, however, the Court rejected the view that the right of privacy is unlimited or absolute in character. In *Wade,* the Court held that assertions of the right of privacy must be weighed against state regulatory interests. Accordingly a number of decisions since *Wade* have rejected claims of privacy infringement. Given their relatively recent origin, the evolution of right of privacy standards is still in a definitional phase.

Citizenship

***Scott v. Sandford,* 60 U.S. 393 (1857),** held that blacks were not citizens of the United States. *Scott v. Sandford* was one of the Supreme Court's first major rulings on civil liberties. It explored the nature of citizenship, the institution of slavery, and it was a factor in precipitating the Civil War. It also prompted response in the Fourteenth Amendment. Dred Scott was a black slave from Missouri who had been taken by his master to the free state of Illinois and then to the Louisiana Territory, an area designated "free" under terms of the Missouri Compromise of 1820. Scott ultimately returned to the slave state of Missouri where he brought suit, claiming that his residency in free areas had revoked his status as a slave. The Missouri Supreme Court held that Missouri law governed despite Scott's residence elsewhere. Scott then pressed his suit in federal court. The case could have been resolved simply by adhering to previous decisions and ruling that Scott's status was a matter of Missouri law. The Supreme Court chose to address the slave issue, however, largely because of the extremely powerful antislavery position argued in dissent by Justices Curtis and McLean. The remainder of the Court decided against Scott, with each member of the Court entering a separate opinion. In what is commonly viewed as the most significant statement, Chief Justice Taney said that Scott was not a citizen because he was black and a slave, and was not entitled to sue in federal court because he lacked citizenship. Taney contended that at the time the Constitution was written, blacks were regarded as "beings of an inferior order and altogether unfit to associate with the white race, either in social or political relations." Blacks were property. Taney invoked the concept of "dual citizenship" to foreclose Scott's claims. Federal citizenship is conferred only through federal action, he said, and no matter how extensive the privileges and immunities conferred elsewhere, they neither carried over to Missouri nor could they affect Scott's ineligibility for federal citizenship. The chief justice said no state can "introduce a new member into its political community created by the Constitution of the United States. It cannot make him a member of this community by making him a member of its own." Neither can a state "introduce any person, or description of persons, who were not intended to be embraced in this new political family, which the Constitution brought into existence, but here intended to be excluded from it." Scott's noncitizen status also flowed from his still being a slave. Taney asserted that Scott had never achieved free status under provisions of the Missouri Compromise because that enactment was unconstitutional. In the Court's view, Congress did not have the authority to designate certain territories as free. To do so would deprive slaveholders of their due process property rights. The two dissenters, Curtis and McLean, split from the Court on every issue in the case. Curtis in particular disputed Taney's proposition that blacks were not citizens at the time the Constitution was ratified. To Curtis, "it would be strange if we were to find in that instrument anything which deprived of their citizenship any part of the people of the United States who were among those by whom it was established." *See also The Civil Rights Cases,* p. 480; EQUAL PROTECTION CLAUSE, p. 473; FOURTEENTH AMENDMENT, p. 651.

Significance   The citizenship questions of *Scott v. Sandford* were rendered moot by adoption of the Fourteenth Amendment in 1868. Indeed, the first sentence of Section I reversed *Scott*. Although the Fourteenth Amendment was very narrowly interpreted initially, in the *Slaughterhouse Cases*, 83 U.S. 36 (1873), its provisions have since become the foundation for civil liberties and civil-rights protections in modern America. *Scott* provided the political impetus for a tragic Civil War fought over the extent to which federal authority could be brought to bear on the issue of slavery. Eventually it paved the way for public policy adjustments that gave the descendants of Dred Scott equal protection of the laws.

State Action

***Civil Rights Cases*, 109 U.S. 3 (1883),** limited the applicability of the Equal Protection Clause to situations in which the state is an actual party to the discriminatory conduct. The *Civil Rights Cases* were an aggregation of suits that challenged the constitutionality of the Civil Rights Act of 1875, passed on the authority conferred by the Fourteenth Amendment. The cases specifically challenged the power of Congress to regulate private acts of racial discrimination. The Civil Rights Act provided that all persons "shall be entitled to the full and equal enjoyment of the accommodations, advantages, facilities and privileges of inns, public conveyances and theaters." In addition to its prohibitions of private discriminatory behavior in public accommo-dations, the Act also assumed federal control over situations in which state and local governments failed to protect citizens from discrimi-nation by other private citizens. Over the vigorous dissent of Justice Harlan, the Court struck down the Act. Justice Bradley's opinion for the Court stressed that the Fourteenth Amendment did not extend to Congress an unlimited source of legislative power. The amendment was intended to "provide modes of relief against State legislation, or State action." The Fourteenth Amendment did not "invest Congress with power to legislate upon subjects which are within the domain of State legislation" or "authorize Congress to create a code of municipal law for the regulation of private rights." The Fourteenth Amendment authorized Congress to enact only corrective rather than general legislation that "may be necessary and proper for counteracting such laws as the States may adopt or enforce, and which, by the amend-ment, they are prohibited from making or enforcing." The Civil Rights Act of 1875 was defective in that it was not corrective, it referred to no state violation, and it impermissibly reached into the domain of local jurisprudence and laid down rules for the conduct of individuals. Justice Bradley expressed the fear that if Congress had authority to pass such legislation, it would be difficult "to see where it is to stop." Bradley said the Thirteenth Amendment could not provide authority for such legislation either. He indicated that "mere discrimination on account of race or color was not regarded as a badge of slavery." Justice Harlan felt that the Thirteenth Amendment was a sufficient power source, saying that "such discrimination practiced by corporations and individuals in the exercise of their public or quasi-public functions is a badge of servitude the imposition of which Congress may prevent under its power." Critical for Justice Harlan was the "public convenience" or accommodation nature of the enterprises covered by the Civil Rights Act. *See also* EQUAL PROTECTION CLAUSE, p. 473; FOURTEENTH AMENDMENT, p. 651; *Plessy v. Ferguson*, p. 481; STATE ACTION, p. 703.

Significance   The state action requirement established by the *Civil Rights Cases* remains to the present day, but discrimination in privately owned public accommodations now can be regulated. The Court eventually became receptive to assertions that a close relationship exists between state authority and discriminating activity. In *Burton v. Wilmington Parking Authority*, 365 U.S. 715 (1961), for example, the Court found that the state had become a party to discrimination by a restaurant that leased space in a municipal parking facility. The state had not required equal access to all patrons. Granting a liquor license to a racially exclusive private club, however, was held not to alter the club's private character in *Moose Lodge No. 107 v. Irvis*, 407 U.S. 163 (1972). Congress was also able to by-pass the state action requirement by regulating access to public accommodations by basing the Civil Rights Act of 1964 on its power to regulate interstate commerce. The Court upheld the public accommodations title of the statute, provisions of which looked very much like those of the Civil Rights Act of 1875.

In *United States v. Guest*, 383 U.S. 745 (1966), the Court upheld a federal indictment of private individuals for the violation of a murder victim's civil rights. While the Court found state action present, six members of the Court said Congress has the power to reach wholly private acts that violate Fourteenth Amendment protections. Neither the Burger nor the Rehnquist Courts have yet to take the additional step of abandoning the state action requirement altogether.

Separate But Equal

Plessy v. Ferguson, **163 U.S. 537 (1896),** addressed the question of state-mandated segregation and used the so-called separate-but-equal doctrine to uphold it. In the *Civil Rights Cases*, 109 U.S. 3 (1883), the Supreme Court limited the coverage of the Equal Protection Clause to situations in which the state was a party to acts of discrimination. A number of southern states simultaneously established comprehensive segregation through legislative enactments that required accommodations segregated by race. Louisiana enacted a statute that compelled all railroads operating within the state "to provide equal but separate accommodations for the white and colored races." Plessy, a black passenger on a railway car, was subjected to criminal penalties for his refusal to leave the white section. Plessy appealed his conviction on Thirteenth and Fourteenth Amendment grounds, but the Court rejected the appeal. Justice Brown began the Court's opinion by dismissing the Thirteenth Amendment contentions. A statute that implies merely a legal distinction between races "has no tendency to destroy the legal equality of the two races or reestablish a state of involuntary servitude." The Fourteenth Amendment claims were more difficult. The Fourteenth Amendment, in Brown's view, was intended to provide both races with equality before the law, but it was also *limited* to legal equality. The amendment was not designed "to abolish distinctions based upon color, or to enforce social, as distinguished from political, equality, or a commingling of the two races upon terms unsatisfactory to either." Statutory segregation does not necessarily imply the inferiority of either race to the other and is a policy option within the competency of the state legislatures in the exercise of their police power. Legislatures must have discretion to act with reference to "established usages, customs, and traditions of the people" as they reasonably attempt to promote the people's comfort and preserve public peace and good order. The Court categorically rejected the proposition that "social prejudices may be overcome by legislation, and that equal rights cannot be secured to the negro except by an enforced commingling of the two races." Such equality could only occur as the result of natural affinities, because the Constitution cannot put social inequality "upon the same plane." With that reasoning the Court established the separate-but-equal doctrine. The sole dissent in the case was entered by Justice Harlan, who argued that no superior, dominant, ruling class of citizens existed under the Constitution. The Constitution simply did not permit caste because it is "color-blind" and cannot tolerate classes among citizens. To segregate on the basis of race is "a badge of servitude wholly inconsistent with the civil freedom and the equality before the law established by the Constitution. It cannot be justified on any legal ground." Neither was Harlan impressed by the statute's requirement that equivalent facilities be provided. He said the "thin disguise of equal accommodations for passengers in railroad coaches will not mislead anyone, nor atone for the wrong done this day." *See also Brown v. Board of Education (I)*, p. 485; EQUAL PROTECTION CLAUSE, p. 473; FOURTEENTH AMENDMENT, p. 651.

Significance   The words of Justice Harlan's dissent in *Plessy v. Ferguson* were prophetic. For several decades the Court used the separate-but-equal doctrine without paying serious attention to whether facilities were actually equivalent. The only successful challenges to segregation in public carriers prior to 1954 typically involved interstate travelers who allowed, or forced, the Court to base its decisions on the impermissible burdens segregation imposed on the free flow of interstate commerce, as in *Morgan v. Virginia*, 328 U.S. 373 (1946). Following the Court's renunciation of the separate-but-equal doctrine in *Brown v. Board of Education (I)*, 347 U.S. 483 (1954), it added to the public education focus of *Brown* state-mandated segregation in transportation, public accommodations, and municipal facilities. Nonetheless, the separate-but-equal doctrine served as the rationale for constitutional segregation for the better part of six decades.

The Court began to disengage the separate-but-equal doctrine in the late 1940s. In *Sweatt v. Painter*, 339 U.S. 629 (1950), for example, the Court held that intangible factors may be considered in determining whether professional educational programs are comparable under the separate-but-equal doctrine. *Sweatt* involved a comparison of the educational facilities at two state law schools in Texas. The equivalence of segregated facilities had not been seriously examined by the Court for several decades following *Plessy*. Educational inequalities became the setting in which the deficiencies of the separate-but-equal doctrine were examined. Challenges were first directed at the advanced degree level. Sweatt was precluded from admission to the University of Texas Law School by statute because he was black. Sweatt's state court suit was postponed to give Texas time to establish a separate law school for blacks. Sweatt persisted in his effort to enter the white law school, however, even after a black law school was opened. The Supreme Court unanimously reversed the state court's finding that the facilities were equivalent. It ordered that Sweatt be admitted to the white law school. Sweatt had argued that the Court should reverse the separate-but-equal standard itself, but the Court chose to focus on the narrower issue of the institutional equivalence of the two law schools. Chief Justice Vinson began with obvious and easily measured items such as the size of the faculties, the breadth of course offerings, the capacity of the libraries, and opportunities for specialization. On the basis of these factors, the Court concluded there was not "substantial equality in the educational opportunities offered white and Negro law students by the State." More important to the Court, however, were the differences between the two schools "in qualities which are incapable of objective measurement." Vinson included among the "intangibles" such items as faculty reputation, the position and influence of alumni, tradition, and prestige. The black law school was also deficient because it provided law studies in an "academic vacuum." Pointing out that a black lawyer would be practicing in a real world with many white lawyers, witnesses, jurors, judges, and other officials, Vinson said that a black law school simply could not qualify as a proving ground for legal learning and practice because of its isolation. He concluded by saying, "it is difficult to believe that one who had a free choice between these law schools would consider the question close."

Sweatt was actually the last of a series of decisions involving segregation in higher education. The first, *Missouri ex rel. Gaines v. Canada*, 305 U.S. 337 (1938), was decided 12 years before *Sweatt*. Gaines had been denied admission to the University of Missouri Law School. Unlike Texas, Missouri had no alternative law school to offer Gaines. The all-white school proposed instead to underwrite Gaines's costs at a law school in an adjacent state. Gaines rejected the offer and continued his effort to gain entry to the University of Missouri. The Court ruled that Gaines was entitled to admission. The Court reaffirmed *Gaines* 10 years later in *Sipuel v. Board of Regents*, 332 U.S. 631 (1948). In another decision rendered on the same day as *Sweatt*, *McLaurin v. Oklahoma State Regents*, 339 U.S. 637 (1950), the Court said that a black graduate student could not be segregated within a state university.

Although the decisions involving graduate education had been focused narrowly, it was clear from cases such as *Sweatt* and *McLaurin* that the stage was being set for a full-scale reexamination of the separate-but-equal doctrine. Less than two years later, the Court agreed to examine segregation in elementary- and secondary-level public education. Mississippi's eight public colleges and universities were segregated by law for almost a decade after *Brown v. Board of Education (I)*. In 1962 James Meredith was admitted to the previously all-white University of Mississippi by force of a federal court order. Although both black and white students were subsequently admitted to each of the schools historically designated for students of either the black or white race, the numbers of cross-enrolled students were sufficiently low that each of the schools remained racially identifiable. A class action was brought by a number of black residents of Mississippi, charging both constitutional and statutory violations by the state through its perpetuation of a dual system of higher education. The federal government eventually intervened in the case and pursued its own appeal of the court of appeals ruling in the case of *United States v. Fordice*, 505 U.S. 717 (1992). The case gave the Supreme Court its first opportunity to examine the issue of desegregating educational institutions at the university level, and it found several aspects of Mississippi's system to be "constitutionally suspect." A state does not fulfill its constitutional obligations, said Justice White, "until it eradicates policies and practices traceable to its prior *de jure* system that continue to foster segregation." The adoption of race-neutral policies such as the "freedom of choice" approach does not "alone suffice to demonstrate that the state has completely abandoned its prior dual system." Attendance by choice is determined, White pointed out, "not simply by admissions policies, but also by many other factors." The case was remanded for specific reconsideration of admissions standards, the mission statements of each of the eight institutions, duplication of programs among the black and white universities, and whether Mississippi needed all eight institutions. Justice Scalia supported the judgment to remand the case, but separated himself from White's statement of the standard to be applied on remand.

School Desegregation

Brown v. Board of Education (I), 347 U.S. 483 (1954), overruled the separate-but-equal doctrine and held racial segregation in public schools to be unconstitutional. *Brown v. Board of Education (I)* was a Kansas case but had companion cases from Delaware, Virginia, South Carolina, and the District of Columbia. Each was premised on different facts and different local conditions, but all raised the common legal question of the constitutionality of racial segregation in public schools. After taking arguments in December 1952 the Court postponed a decision and ordered reargument of the issues in December 1953. During the intervening year, Earl Warren succeeded Fred M. Vinson as chief justice. The decision that came the following May was unanimous, and the opinion was written by the new chief justice. Warren considered whether those persons who proposed the Fourteenth Amendment intended it to apply to school segregation, but found the amendment's history to be elusive and the evidence generally inconclusive. Neither was the separate-but-equal doctrine helpful, because, unlike in *Sweatt v. Painter*, 339 U.S. 629 (1950), black and white public schools appeared substantially equal when tangible factors were used to evaluate them. Warren declared that resolution of the issue must come from an examination of "the effect of segregation itself on public education." This could not be done by turning the clock back to 1868, when the Fourteenth Amendment was adopted, or even to 1896, when *Plessy v. Ferguson* was decided. Rather, the Court was obliged to consider public education in the light of its full development and its present place in American life. The chief justice spoke of the importance of education, calling it the basis of good citizenship. He said it was instrumental in awakening a child to cultural values. It was the key to success in life. In fact, education was "perhaps the most important function of state and local government." Given the fundamental character of education, therefore, opportunity to acquire it must be made available to all on equal terms. The controlling question was whether segregation deprived minority children of equal educational opportunity. The Court concluded that it did. The basis of the Court's judgment was extensive psychological evidence that showed that segregation negatively affected the educational development of minority students. "To separate them from others of similar age and qualifications solely because of their race generates a feeling of inferiority as to their status in the community that may affect their hearts and minds in a way unlikely ever to be undone." The doctrine of separate but equal has no place in public education, the Court said. Separate educational facilities are "inherently unequal." *See also* DE JURE, p. 638; EQUAL PROTECTION CLAUSE, p. 473; FOURTEENTH AMENDMENT, p. 651; SEPARATE-BUT-EQUAL DOCTRINE, p. 696.

Significance   *Brown v. Board of Education* held that the Equal Protection Clause of the Fourteenth Amendment prohibits the segregation of public schools anywhere in the United States. In *Bolling v. Sharpe*, 347 U.S. 497 (1954), the companion to *Brown* from the District of Columbia, the Court reached the same conclusion using the Due Process Clause of the Fifth Amendment. The Court held that the concepts of equal protection and due process, both stemming from the American ideal of fairness, are not mutually exclusive. While the justices did not suggest that the two concepts are always interchangeable, they recognized that "discrimination may be so unjustifiable as to be violative of due process." Because segregation in the District's schools was not reasonably related to any proper governmental objective, black students "are burdened in a fashion which constitutes an arbitrary deprivation of their liberty in violation of the Due Process Clause." Having found constitutional violations in all of the five cases involving official, or *de jure*, segregation, the Court then separated the remedial questions and docketed them for later argument.

    Brown v. Board of Education II, 349 U.S. 294 (1955), addressed enforcement of the decision in *Brown I*. The broad implications of the decision were apparent immediately, however. Although *Brown I* had focused on segregation in public education, it had the effect of establishing a constitutional prohibition on race as a classification. Soon thereafter, the Court extended the *Brown* holding to other areas, such as transportation and municipal facilities. Yet the question of whether segregation that existed unofficially, or *de facto*, was subject to the same relief as segregation that existed officially, or *de jure*, remained unanswered for several years following *Brown I*.

    Brown II was devoted to implementation of the desegregation of public schools as mandated by the Court's decision in *Brown I*. The

Supreme Court chose to remand all five original cases back to the lower federal courts from which they had come because "full implementation may require solution of varied local school problems." The Court saw the primary responsibility for elucidating, assessing, and solving these problems resting with local school authorities. The role of the courts was defined as considering "whether the action of school authorities constitutes good faith implementation of the governing constitutional principles." Lower federal courts were to be guided by equitable principles in fashioning specific decrees. Recourse to equity law allowed courts practical flexibility in shaping their remedies and the facility for adjusting and reconciling public and private needs. While supervising courts could take into account the public interest in eliminating obstacles in making an orderly transition to school systems operated in accordance with the constitutional principles set forth in *Brown I*, the Court warned that in doing so, "the vitality of these constitutional principles cannot be allowed to yield simply because of disagreement with them." The Court did not specify a timetable as such. Rather, local authorities were expected to make a "prompt and reasonable start toward full compliance." Additional time might be available, presuming that school districts could establish "that such time is necessary in the public interest and is consistent with good faith compliance at the earliest practicable date." The Court said that constitutional violations must be relieved "with all deliberate speed."

Desegregation Orders: Public Schools

Freeman v. Pitts, **503 U.S. 467 (1992),** held that federal court supervision may be withdrawn in stages as local districts desegregate particular aspects of their operations. The DeKalb County, Georgia, schools had been under a desegregation decree since 1969. The school district filed for dismissal of the order in 1986, and a federal court determined that the school district had made sufficient good faith efforts to comply. A dual system of student assignment no longer existed. The Supreme Court concluded that lower federal courts could relinquish remedial control incrementally as particular district operations were found to be unitary in character. A district court "need not retain active control over every aspect of school administration" until a district has shown "unitary status in all facets of its system." Justice Kennedy said that in addition to remediating the violation, lower courts must also "restore state and local authorities to the control of a school system that is operating in compliance with the Constitution." Returning schools to local control at the "earliest practicable date is essential to restore their true accountability." Kennedy acknowledged that the potential for discrimination remains in our society, and that the state and its subdivisions must "ensure that such forces do not shape or control the politics of its school systems." Kennedy pointed to several criteria that lower courts must apply when considering partial withdrawal from supervision of a school district. They include: (1) whether there has been "full and satisfactory compliance with the decree in those aspects of the system where supervision is to be withdrawn"; (2) when retention of control is still needed to "achieve compliance with the decree in other facets of the school system"; and (3) whether the local district has shown to the public and those among the "once disfavored race" its good faith commitment to the "whole of the court's decree and to those provisions of the law and the Constitution that were the predicate for judicial intervention in the first place." The district court found that measures taken by the DeKalb schools had indeed achieved desegregation, at least for a period. The lower court held that the resegregation that had subsequently occurred was the result of population shifts unrelated to any misconduct by the school district. The Supreme Court agreed. A finding of racial imbalance in attendance zones was not itself a showing of school district noncompliance with the court order. "Racial balance," said Kennedy, "is not to be achieved for its own sake." It is pursued only in response to a constitutional violation. Once a *de jure* violation has been remedied, a district is "under no duty to remedy imbalance that is caused by demographical factors." Resegregation produced by private choices rather than state action "does not have constitutional implications." It is "beyond the authority and ... practical ability" of federal courts to try to "counteract these kinds of continuous and massive demographic shifts." To pursue such an end would require "ongoing and never-ending supervision by the courts of school districts simply because they were once *de jure*–segregated." Finally, Kennedy said that while vestiges of past discrimination are a "stubborn fact of history" that we cannot escape, neither should federal courts "overstate" history's consequences in fixing legal responsibilities. The vestiges of segregation under review by federal courts may be "subtle and intangible but nonetheless they must be so real that they have a causal link to the *de jure* violations being remedied." As *de jure* violations become "more remote in time," and as demographic changes occur, the likelihood a student assignment imbalance is a vestige of a previous *de jure* violation is lessened. Further, the causal link between any current imbalance and prior violations is "even more attenuated if the school district has demonstrated its good faith." Justice Souter said that as federal judges partially release school districts from their supervision, they must be sure that vestiges of prior discriminatory conduct do not "act as an incubator for resegregation" in other aspects of school operations. *See also Brown v. Board of Education (I),*

p. 485; EQUAL PROTECTION CLAUSE, p. 473; FOURTEENTH AMEND-
MENT, p. 651; SEPARATE-BUT-EQUAL DOCTRINE, p. 696.

Significance   Reactions to *Brown I* and *Brown II* were both intense
and varied. There was widespread support and applause for the end
of the separate-but-equal doctrine in public education. The
temperate character of the order in *Brown II* diffused potential opposition from a large middle population. Nonetheless, resistance developed. In some places the reactions were violent. The situation in
Little Rock, Arkansas, is illustrative. The state legislature passed a
state constitutional amendment registering opposition to the desegregation decisions and enacted legislation "relieving school children
from compulsory attendance at racially mixed schools." As school
was to begin in the fall of 1957 under a desegregation plan designed
by the Little Rock School Board, the governor of Arkansas, Orval
Faubus, sent units of the Arkansas National Guard to Central High
School in Little Rock and placed it "off limits" to black students.
Crowds gathered and violence was threatened. The school board
sought postponement of *Brown I* implementation because of
"extreme public hostility." In *Cooper v. Aaron*, 358 U.S. 1 (1958), the
Court unanimously found the situation "directly traceable" to
provocative actions by state officials and rejected the request to postpone. The Court firmly indicated that "constitutional rights of
respondents are not to be sacrificed or yielded to the violence and
disorder which have followed upon the actions of the Governor and
Legislature."

Another form of resistance in segregated areas was to close the
public schools altogether. One such attempt was made in Prince
Edward County, Virginia, a school district involved in one of the original suits decided in *Brown I*. Under a "freedom of choice" provision
of state law, local authorities closed the public schools. Education was
made available to white students through private schools financed by
means of a complex mixture of state monies and local tuition grants.
In *Griffin v. County School Board*, 377 U.S. 218 (1964), the Court
upheld a lower court injunction against this technique. The Court
said it had "no doubt of the power of the court to give this relief to
enforce the discontinuance of the county's racially discriminatory
practices." The most common form of resistance, however, was
simply to delay any change from the dual school system. The Court,
in *Green v. County School Board*, 391 U.S. 430 (1968), termed "intolerable" local plans that "at this late date fail to provide meaningful
assurance of prompt and effective disestablishment of a dual school
system." The following year, in *Alexander v. Holmes County Board of
Education*, 396 U.S. 19 (1969), the Court ended the "all deliberate
speed" aspect of *Brown II* and ordered operation of unitary school

systems "at once." The latter two cases clearly established an affirmative obligation for local authorities or federal district judges to desegregate public schools with no further delay.

Missouri v. Jenkins, 495 U.S. 33 (1990), examined the scope of remedial power of the federal judiciary in school desegregation situations. A federal district court found that the state of Missouri had maintained racially segregated schools in Kansas City and had failed to sufficiently address the effects of this discriminatory conduct. The school district had been unable to generate additional tax revenues for desegregation because of certain provisions of state law such as a two-thirds voter approval requirement for tax increases. The court approved a desegregation plan submitted by the school board, but the district had exhausted all available means of raising the needed funds. The court then ordered that the local property tax rate be raised to a level required to yield the necessary revenue to implement the desegregation plan for the 1987–1988 school year. The order was approved by the court of appeals for the first year, but the district court was directed to take a "less obtrusive" course for subsequent years. In particular, the appellate court recommended that the local school board ordered to impose any increase itself rather than the court taking action directly. The Supreme Court ruled that the order to increase the property tax rate was an "abuse of discretion" on the part of the district court. Before taking such a "drastic step," the district court was "obliged to assure itself that no permissible alternative would have accomplished the required task." Missouri contended that federal courts cannot set aside limits established by state law on local taxing authorities. The Supreme Court disagreed. It was "clear" to the Court, however, that a local taxing authority may be ordered to levy taxes in excess of the limit set by the state "where there is reason based in the Constitution for not observing the statutory limitation."

The Kansas City case was back before the Court five years later. In *Missouri v. Jenkins (Jenkins II)*, 515 U.S. 70 (1995), the Supreme Court was asked to find that the vestiges of unlawful segregation had been effectively addressed, and that a partially unitary status had been achieved. Such a finding would lead to ending the lower court's oversight of the school district's operations. The state and school district also pursued an alternate objective if the district court's oversight was not terminated. They contended that the district court had improperly relied on achievement test scores when it ruled that partial unitary status as to educational quality had not been attained. The state and school district argued that the court had again exceeded its remedial authority by ordering the expenditure of resources to improve student achievement as measured by standardized testing, and by ordering pay increases for school district teachers and support staff. The Supreme Court did not end the lower court's supervision of the school district, but did vacate the district court's remedial order. Drawing extensively from *Freeman*, Rehnquist indicated that "vestiges of segregation" must be both "real" and have a "causal link to the *de jure* violation being remedied." The basic task of the court is to determine whether the reduction in achievement by minority students "attributable to prior *de jure* segregation has been remedied to the extent practicable." The district court's "insistence on academic goals unrelated to the effects of legal segregation unwarrantably postpones the day when the [District] will be able to operate on its own." Although recognizing that the district court's "end purpose" was to remedy the violation as fully as practicable, the Court held that the lower court must also "restore state and local authorities to the control" of the system. Justice Thomas offered a lengthy and outspoken concurring opinion. In his view, federal courts have been permitted to exercise "virtually unlimited equitable powers to remedy this alleged constitutional violation." The exercise of this authority has "trampled upon principles of federalism and the separation of powers," and has allowed courts to "pursue other agendas unrelated to the narrow purpose of precisely remedying a constitutional harm." The "mere fact that a school is black," Thomas continued, does not mean that it is the "product of a constitutional violation." A "racial imbalance" does not itself establish a constitutional violation. The existence of one-race schools is not by itself an "indication that the State is practicing segregation." In order for a "vestige" of segregation to provide the basis for the exercise of remedial authority, it must be "clearly traceable to the dual school system."

Remedial Orders: Interdistrict Busing

Board of Education v. Dowell, **498 U.S. 237 (1991),** considered the terms under which a school district might be released from a busing order even though the district's schools may have become resegregated. Litigation in the *Dowell* case began in the early 1960s. A district court found that Oklahoma City was operating a "dual" (intentionally segregated) school system, and desegregation efforts were commenced. In 1972 the district court found those efforts inadequate, and an order including busing was issued. After the busing order had been in effect for five years, the school district sought to close the case. The district court concluded that the objective of achieving a "unitary" school district had been met and issued an order terminating the case. The original plaintiffs did not appeal. Then the demographics began to change, and the school district considered reassignment of students. It eventually adopted a Student Reassignment Plan (SRP) in 1984, in part to alleviate the burden on the bused black students. While some busing continued under the SRP, it was contended that the plan had the effect of resegregating the school district. The district court concluded that the prior decree should be vacated on the grounds that the underlying residential segregation was the result of "private decision making and economics, and that it was too attenuated to be a vestige of former school segregation." The court of appeals reversed, saying that an original decree must remain in effect until a school district can demonstrate a "grievous wrong evoked by new and unforseen conditions ... that impose[s] extreme and unexpectedly oppressive hardships." Applying this standard, the court of appeals ruled that conditions in the school district had not changed enough to justify modification of the initial decree. The Court ruled that decrees such as those in the Oklahoma City case are not intended to "operate in perpetuity." Local control is preferable because it allows citizens to participate in decision making and permits adaptation of school programs to local needs. Relinquishing federal authority by dissolving a desegregation decree should occur, said Chief Justice Rehnquist, "after the local authorities have operated in compliance with it for a reasonable period of time." Rehnquist then turned to the standard to be used in deciding whether to modify or dissolve a decree. Although courts should not accept at face value a district's profession that it would no longer discriminate in the future, compliance with previous court orders is a factor that is "obviously relevant." In addition to determining whether a school district had made good faith compliance with a prior desegregation decree, a court must also determine whether the "vestiges of past discrimination have been eliminated" as far as "practicable." *Brown v. Board Education I*, 347 U.S. 483 (1954), ruled that a racially segregated or "dual" school system violated the Equal Protection Clause. *See also Brown v. Board of Education (I)*, p. 485; EQUAL PROTECTION CLAUSE, p. 473; FOURTEENTH AMENDMENT, p. 651; SEPARATE-BUT-EQUAL DOCTRINE, p. 696.

Significance　　Under terms of *Brown v. Board of Education II*, 349 U.S. 294 (1955), a large number of American school districts have operated under the supervision of federal courts for the purpose of establishing "unitary" systems. In 1991 the Supreme Court ruled in *Board of Education v. Dowell* that a school district may achieve unitary status if the school district has complied in good faith with any desegregation order for a "reasonable period" of time. *Dowell* further said that school districts need address unlawful discrimination only as long as it is "practicable." *Swann v. Charlotte-Mecklenburg Board of Education*, 402 U.S. 1 (1971), was the first Supreme Court ruling to uphold a desegregation order that included intradistrict busing. *Swann* examined at length the scope and character of remedies to be used by federal judges in eliminating public school segregation under the Equal Protection Clause of the Fourteenth Amendment. In 1965 the Charlotte-Mecklenburg, North Carolina, school district was required to devise a desegregation plan. The plan, approved by a federal court, had a substantial number of black students still attending schools identifiable as "black." Finding the Charlotte-Mecklenburg plan inadequate, a federal district court had a plan of its own prepared by a court-appointed desegregation expert. The new plan involved extensive transportation of elementary level students and was adopted by the district court as part of its desegregation order. The school board appealed, arguing that the remedy was excessive, but a unanimous Supreme Court upheld the lower court's entire remedy, including the busing. Chief Justice Burger said that the controlling objective was the elimination of all vestiges of state-imposed segregation. Judicial authority may be invoked if local school authorities fail in their affirmative obligation to eliminate such discrimination. The scope of judicial authority to remedy past wrongs is broad, for breadth and flexibility are inherent in equitable remedies. Such power is not unlimited, however. It may be exercised "only on the basis of a constitutional violation." Remedial authority does not put judges automatically in the shoes of school authorities. Rather, federal judicial intervention begins only when local authority defaults. The Court found the use of racial population ratios a "useful starting point in shaping a remedy" rather than an inflexible requirement. As for alteration of attendance zones, the Court felt that "administratively awkward, inconvenient and even bizarre" arrangements may be required to eliminate dual school systems. Neighborhood schools can be maintained only where there is no constitutional violation. If attendance zones are to be altered, student transportation becomes essential. The Court concluded that local school boards may properly be required to "employ bus transportation as one tool of school desegregation."

The Court said in *Swann* that district courts would retain power to deal with future developments in districts under desegregation orders. The question of resegregation was addressed in *Pasadena City Board of Education v. Spangler*, 427 U.S. 424 (1976). The Court held that once a district has been desegregated, school authorities need not readjust pupil assignments to reflect population shifts. Unless it could be shown that official actions had caused resegregative shifts in population, continued court involvement would constitute impermissible pursuit of racial balance rather than creation of a unitary school system. The Court struck down a statute prohibiting assignment of students on account of race and involuntary busing to that end in *Swann*, a companion to the Charlotte-Mecklenburg case. Three years later in *Milliken v. Bradley (I)*, 418 U.S. 717 (1974), the

Court invalidated a busing order involving the Detroit school system and 53 suburban school districts. Chief Justice Burger said that a consolidation as extensive as this would "give rise to an array of other problems in financing and operating this new school system." The new "super" school district would require that the federal court become a *de facto* legislative authority to resolve many complex operational questions. The Court found a more fundamental flaw, however, in the scope of the district court's order: It exceeded the scope of the demonstrated violation. The Court held that before a consolidation or cross-district order could occur, it must be shown that a "constitutional violation within one district produces a significant segregative effect in another district." The Court concluded that without an interdistrict violation, and interdistrict effect, there is no constitutional wrong calling for an interdistrict remedy. This case returned to the Court three years later as *Milliken v. Bradley (II)*, 433 U.S. 267 (1977). The second case involved a decree that not only assigned pupils throughout the Detroit school district but also required a number of additional educational activities such as remedial reading, intensified student testing and counseling, and extensive in-service teacher training. The Court unanimously upheld the lower court order saying that despite the compensatory character of the remedy, it "does not change the fact that it is part of a plan that operates prospectively to bring about the delayed benefits of a unitary school system."

In *Keyes v. School District No. 1*, 413 U.S. 189 (1973), the Court held that actions undertaken in support of *de facto* segregated schools constituted *de jure* segregation. In two cases from Ohio, *Columbus Board of Education v. Penick*, 443 U.S. 449 (1979), and *Dayton Board of Education v. Brinkman*, 443 U.S. 526 (1979), the Court upheld systemwide busing as a remedy because both systems were officially segregated at the time *Brown I* was decided. Given the encompassing interpretation the Court put on the concept of *de jure* segregation in these cases, the need to determine the constitutionality of *de facto* segregation has diminished significantly.

Job Discrimination: Race

Robinson v. Shell Oil Company, **519 U.S. 337 (1997)** Title VII of the Civil Rights Act of 1964 prohibits discrimination in the workplace and protects a worker who files a discrimination complaint from retaliation by a current employer. *Robinson* examined whether Title VII similarly protects an employee from retaliation by an employer for whom the complainant no longer works. Charles Robinson filed a discrimination complaint after his discharge by Shell Oil Company, but a federal district court subsequently found in favor of Shell.

Several months later Robinson was being considered for a job with Metropolitan Life Insurance Company. Metropolitan contacted Shell requesting information on Robinson's performance while an employee with Shell. Robinson was rated below average on all but one of the performance categories contained in Metropolitan's questionnaire. Once again Robinson filed an employment discrimination claim against Shell contending that Shell gave him a negative recommendation as retaliation for his original discrimination complaint. Robinson's suit was dismissed on the grounds that Title VII provided protection against retaliation for current employees only, but the Supreme Court unanimously reversed the decision to dismiss. Justice Thomas said that the first step in a review of statutory language is to determine whether a provision has a meaning that is "plain and unambiguous." This is determined by considering the language itself, the "specific context" in which the language is used, and the "broader context" of the statute as a whole. Although the term *employee* at issue in this case might, at "first blush," seem to refer to those having an "existing employment relationship" with the employer in question, this first impression does not "withstand scrutiny in the context of Title VII." The law contains no "temporal qualifier" nor does Congress explicitly distinguish "current" from "former" employees in Title VII. In some provisions of Title VII use of the term "employee refers unambiguously" to a current employee, but that unambiguous meaning is determined by context. Resolution of the ambiguity of the term *employee* requires looking to the "broader context" provided by other sections of the law. The Court concluded that several sections of the statute "plainly contemplate that former employees will make use of the remedial mechanisms of Title VII." In particular, the law "expressly includes discriminatory discharge as one of the unlawful employment practices against which Title VII is directed." Because the law explicitly protects employees from retaliation for filing a charge under Title VII, and a charge alleging unlawful discharge would "necessarily be brought by a former employee, it is far more consistent to include former employees within the scope of employees protected by the law." The Court embraced Robinson's argument that the term *employees* includes former employees "because to hold otherwise would effectively vitiate" much of the protection afforded by Title VII. This position, Thomas noted, was also supported by the Equal Employment Opportunity Commission (EEOC). According to the EEOC, exclusion of former employees from the protection would "undermine the effectiveness" of Title VII by allowing the threat of postemployment retaliation to deter victims of discrimination from complaining to the EEOC, and would "provide a perverse incentive for employers to fire employees who might bring Title VII claims." *See also* CIVIL RIGHTS

ACT OF 1964, p. 626; EQUAL PROTECTION CLAUSE, p. 473; FOURTEENTH AMENDMENT, p. 651.

Significance   *Robinson* is the Court's most recent Title VII ruling on race discrimination in the workplace. One of the first was *Washington v. Davis*, 426 U.S. 229 (1976). *Davis* considered the question of whether statutory standards prohibiting racial discrimination in employment under Title VII of the Civil Rights Act of 1964 are the same as the constitutional standards for adjudicating claims of invidious racial discrimination. The Court held that the latter required not only a showing of impact but intent to discriminate on the basis of race as well. The Court has "never held that the constitutional standard is identical to the standards applicable under Title VII." A law, said Justice White, "neutral on its face and serving ends otherwise within the power of government to pursue" is not invalid because it may affect a greater proportion of one race than another. Although disproportionate impact is not irrelevant, it is not the sole touchstone of impermissible discrimination. The Court concluded that to apply the Title VII approach to constitutional adjudication involves a more probing judicial review of "seemingly reasonable acts of administrators than is appropriate under the Constitution." Justices Brennan and Marshall dissented, arguing that once discriminatory impact is demonstrated, the employer must prove how the challenged practice has a demonstrable relationship to successful performance of the job for which it was used.

Davis distinguished situations in which constitutional provisions such as equal protection are involved from those based upon federal civil-rights statutes. In *Griggs v. Duke Power Co.*, 401 U.S. 424 (1971), the Court held that once a plaintiff shows unequal or disproportionate impact, the employer must demonstrate a relationship between the challenged practice and job performance. The intent element was added five years later in *Davis*. In *Watson v. Fort Worth Bank and Trust*, 487 U.S. 977 (1988), the Court ruled that measures of "disparate impact" as distinct from demonstration of "disparate treatment" could be used in examining subjective employment criteria in job discrimination challenges. Watson, a black bank teller, was denied promotion four times. She brought suit in federal court and established a prima facie case of discrimination. The court, however, found that the bank had sufficiently justified its reasons for each denial, based on grounds other than racial discrimination. In so finding, the court refused to consider certain statistical evidence offered by Watson addressing the bank's subjective evaluations, and the effects of its decisions on blacks as a class. The Supreme Court, however, ruled for Watson and extended for the first time the disparate impact test of *Griggs* to subjective employment decisions. In other words, the *Watson* decision altered the evidentiary standards that apply in cases flowing from Title VII of the Civil Rights Act of 1964, and applied the disparate impact test to the discretionary judgments of supervisors. The Court basically agreed with Watson's contentions that subjective criteria are as likely to have discriminatory effects as objective tests, and that by confining disparate impact analysis only to objective criteria, employers could substitute subjective criteria and render *Griggs* a "dead letter."

Several Rehnquist Court rulings made job discrimination more difficult to demonstrate, however. One such decision was *Wards Cove Packing Company, Inc. v. Atonio*, 490 U.S. 642 (1989). *Wards Cove* involved Title VII complaints brought by nonwhite workers at two fish canneries in Alaska. Employment was divided into two classes: cannery and noncannery jobs. The cannery jobs were unskilled and were largely held by local and nonwhite employees. Noncannery jobs were skilled jobs, higher paying, and held by white workers hired at company offices in Washington and Oregon. The minority workers filed an action claiming that the company's practices unfairly divided the workforce on racial bases. The Court was highly critical of the data used by the lower courts to establish a prima facie case of disparate impact. To simply compare percentages of nonwhite workers in the two job classes the Court termed "nonsensical." The "proper" comparison is between the racial composition of the "at issue jobs" and the "qualified population in the relevant labor market." In the Court's view, the cannery workforce "in no way reflected the pool of *qualified* job applicants or the *qualified* labor force population" relevant with respect to the skilled noncannery jobs. Accordingly, the methods of recruiting workers or other employment practices "cannot be said to have disparate impact on nonwhites" if the absence of nonwhites holding such skilled jobs reflects a "dearth of qualified nonwhite applicants for reasons that are not the [employers'] fault."

Janet Scott-Harris, an African American, headed the Department of Health and Human Services in Fall River, Massachusetts. She attempted to terminate an employee who had been temporarily assigned to her office after the employee was repeatedly heard making racial slurs. The employee, however, was politically connected to City Councilwoman Marilyn Roderick and was suspended rather than dismissed. Mayor Daniel Bogan subsequently reduced the length of the suspension. This personnel matter arose during the time Mayor Bogan was preparing the municipal budget for the next year prior to submitting the budget proposal to the city council. Among other things, the budget proposed eliminated the DHHS and its only permanent employee, Ms. Scott-Harris. The budget proposal was subsequently adopted by the city council, an action which included an affirmative vote by Councilwoman Roderick. Scott-Harris commenced a § 1983 suit against the city, Bogan, and Roderick claiming that the elimination of her department and her position was both race-based and retaliation for her exercising her free speech rights in her attempt to terminate the employee. The Supreme Court held that both the Constitution and common law protects legislators from liability for their legislative activities. The Court had previously extended this immunity to both state and regional legislators and held that Congress had not intended the language of § 1983 to "impinge on a tradition so well grounded in reason and history." The Court extended that same immunity from § 1983 suits to local legislators in *Bogan v. Scott-Harris*, 118 S.Ct. 966 (1998). Regardless of the level of government, said Justice Thomas, "the exercise of legislative discretion should not be inhibited by judicial interference or distorted by the fear of personal liability." Restrictions on a legislator's freedom "undermines the public good by interfering with the rights of the people to representation in the democratic process." Further, the energy and time required to defend against lawsuits are of a particular concern at the local level where the "part-time citizen-legislator remains commonplace." Thomas suggested that the threat of liability may significantly deter service in local government, "where prestige and pecuniary rewards may pale in comparison to the threat of civil liability." Finally, the Court concluded that Bogan and Roderick's actions were legislative. Roderick's act of voting for the proposed ordinance was "quintessentially legislative." Mayor Bogan's introduction of the budget proposal and his signing of the ordinance following council adoption were "formally legislative" notwithstanding the executive character of his office; his actions were legislative here because they were "integral steps in the legislative process." Adoption of the budget ordinance reflected a "discretionary, policymaking decision implicating the budgetary priorities of the city and the services the city provides to its constituents." The budget ordinance involved the termination of a position that may have "prospective implications that reach well beyond the particular occupant of the office." When the city council eliminated Scott-Harris's department, it "certainly governed in a field where legislators traditionally have power to act."

Housing Discrimination

City of Arlington Heights v. Metropolitan Housing Development Corp., **429 U.S. 252 (1977),** held that discriminatory intent must be shown in order to establish an equal protection violation in a local government zoning decision affecting housing. The Metropolitan Housing Development Corporation (MHDC) wished to build racially integrated low- and middle-income housing in the Village of Arlington Heights. MHDC contracted to purchase a site, but the sale was contingent on having the tract rezoned from single-family to multiple-family dwelling. The Village refused to rezone, claiming the particular area had always been zoned for single-family use, and that the multiple-family classification had historically been reserved for locations adjacent to commercial areas. The zoning decision was challenged as racially discriminatory. The Court concluded that proof of racially discriminatory intent or purpose is necessary in order to find an equal protection violation. Justice Powell said that courts should generally defer to legislative and administrative judgments that balance numerous competing considerations. He stated, however, that race "is not just another competing consideration." When a discriminatory purpose is shown to be a motivating factor in a policy, judicial deference is no longer justified. Determining whether a discriminatory purpose exists demands sensitive inquiry. Certainly the "impact of the official action" is an "important starting point." Without a clear pattern, unexplainable on grounds other than race, other evidence must be considered. Historical background may be a useful source if it reveals a series of official actions taken for invidious purposes. Sequences of events leading to the challenged decision may be relevant. So, too, would be departures from normal procedural sequence or if factors usually considered important strongly favor a decision contrary to the one reached. Finally, courts might defer to legislative or administrative history, especially where there are contemporary statements by members of the decision-making body, minutes of its meetings, or reports. Although the decision impacted heavily on minorities in Arlington Heights, the Court did not find proof of discriminatory purpose as it examined the record using these criteria. *See also The Civil Rights Cases*, p. 480; EQUAL PROTECTION CLAUSE, p. 473; FOURTEENTH AMENDMENT, p. 651.

Significance   The Court did not find an Equal Protection Clause violation in *Arlington Heights* absent a showing of discriminatory intent. *Arlington Heights* followed from a long line of significant Fourteenth Amendment cases involving discrimination in housing. The Court ruled in *Shelley v. Kraemer*, 334 U.S. 1 (1948), that private restrictive covenants could not be enforced in state courts. Such covenants were agreements among private property owners not to sell or rent to various specified minorities, usually African Americans. *Shelley* assumed that court enforcement made the state a party to the discrimination. On the same state action grounds, the Court ruled in *Reitman v. Mulkey*, 387 U.S. 369 (1967), that a state could not repeal open-occupancy statutes by referendum without encouraging discriminatory conduct. The use of a century-old civil rights statute to justify federal proscription of private discrimination in conveying property was upheld in *Jones v. Alfred H. Mayer Co.*, 392 U.S. 409 (1968). In *James v. Valtierra*, 402 U.S. 137 (1971), the Court permitted a state constitutional provision requiring referendum approval of all low-income housing projects. As in *Arlington Heights*, the Court refused to hold that use of the referendum technique presumed discriminatory or prejudicial purpose. When discrimination is a motive, courts are able to construct broad remedies. In *Hills v. Gautreaux*, 425 U.S. 284 (1976), the Court approved a plan that made public housing available in suburban areas because violations to which the Department of Housing and Urban Development had been a party were found to exist both in Chicago and in adjoining areas. *Arlington Heights* is a pivotal case in that it took the Court in a new direction. After years of finding the requisite state action in housing cases, *Arlington Heights* elevated the need to show discriminatory purpose as well.

Despite a flurry of federal legislation immediately after the Civil War, civil rights policy was tied until the 1950s to the proposition that only overt state action violating specific federal rights could be reached by federal criminal sanctions. Like actions based on other civil rights laws, civil suits under the old civil rights laws were infrequent. Private actions under § 1983 of Title 42 of the U.S. Code, originally enacted in the Civil Rights Act of 1866, are of this kind. This law allows civil suits against persons violating, under color of law, the constitutional rights of others. Long dormant, § 1983 began to provide a basis for successful litigation in the early 1960s. In *Monroe v. Pape*, 365 U.S. 156 (1965), for example, the Court held that police brutality constituted deprivation of civil rights and could be redressed by a § 1983 action. After this decision, civil rights actions seeking damages or other relief became more numerous.

Prescribing the conduct of state and local officials under § 1983 has serious implications for federal-state relationships, as the Court pointed out in *Rizzo v. Goode*, 423 U.S. 362 (1976). In *Rizzo*, the Court restricted the intervention of federal courts into the internal disciplinary policies of a local police department. The Court deferred to principles of federalism in limiting judicial intervention when named municipal officials could not be tightly enough linked to alleged civil rights violations. The trend, however, has been to bring state and local governments under closer federal scrutiny. Illustrative is the decision of *Maine v. Thiboutot*, 448 U.S. 1 (1980). In this case, the Court held that § 1983 suits may be brought against state and local governments for alleged denial of *any* federal law. The controversy in *Thiboutot* arose over loss of certain benefits under the Aid to Families with Dependent Children provisions of the Social Security Act. Cases like *Thiboutot* proved to have a powerful impact on the old doctrine of dual federalism. Given the degree to which federal laws, especially those involving entitlement programs, intertwine with state and local governmental activities, officials responsible for these activities have become more and more subject to direct legal action.

Affirmative Action

Regents of the University of California v. Bakke, **438 U.S. 265 (1978)**, rejected use of quotas in university admission procedures, but permitted use of race as a factor in recruiting heterogeneous student bodies. *Bakke* represented the Supreme Court's first on-the-merits discussion of affirmative action. The troublesome constitutional question posed by affirmative action programs is whether preference may be extended to a particular racial or ethnic group in order to correct historical inequalities. The medical school at the University of California at Davis admitted 100 students annually. To assure minority representation within the student body, 16 places were reserved for minority applicants. Bakke, a white applicant, was twice denied admission, although his credentials were better than some of the minority applicants admitted under the affirmative action policy. Bakke brought suit, arguing that the race-driven quota system at Davis violated Title VI of the Civil Rights Act of 1964. The Act prohibited discrimination in programs receiving federal funding. The Court resolved the case by finding for both sides. In a five-to-four decision, the Court ruled that the *Davis* quota system was impermissible and ordered that Bakke be admitted. At the same time, the Court also held in a five-to-four vote that a state university may take race into account in attempting to assemble a diverse student body. Each issue split the Court into two blocs of four members each, with Justice Powell providing the decisive vote on each judgment. Powell joined Chief Justice Burger and Justices Rehnquist, Stewart, and Stevens on the quota question, but aligned himself with Justices Brennan, Marshall, White, and Blackmun on the issue of assigning weight to race or ethnicity for diversity purposes. Powell's opinion reflected skepticism about racial classifications generally, but categorically rejected the use of quota systems. The Fourteenth Amendment confers protection to individuals, he said. The "guarantee of equal protection cannot mean one thing when applied to one individual and something else when applied to a person of another color." Powell also rejected the view that race was not a suspect classification when applied to the white majority simply because the purpose of a classification might be benign. Individuals within that class "are likely to find little comfort in the notion that the deprivation they are asked to endure is merely the price of membership in the dominant majority and that its imposition is inspired by the supposedly benign purpose of aiding others." Noting that the white majority itself was composed of various minority groups, Powell feared that courts would forever be asked to assess the degree of discrimination each has suffered and the redress each was due. By "hitching the meaning of the Equal Protection Clause to these transitory considerations, we would be holding, as a constitutional principle, that judicial scrutiny of classifications touching on racial and ethnic background may vary with the ebb and flow of political forces." Powell did, however, recognize attainment of a diverse student body as a constitutionally permissible goal for an institution of higher education. Indeed, he said the nation's future depends upon leaders trained through wide exposure, which comes through a diverse student body. He referred to the Harvard admissions program, which assigns a plus to particular racial or ethnic backgrounds, but still treats each applicant as an individual in the admissions process. A majority of the justices saw the *Davis* program as educationally sound and sufficiently important to justify the use of race-conscious admissions programs, but without any admissions set asides for minorities. *See also Adarand Constructors, Inc. v. Pena*, p. 505; AFFIRMATIVE ACTION, p. 610; EQUAL PROTECTION CLAUSE, p. 473; FOURTEENTH AMENDMENT, p. 651.

Significance   *Bakke* was a compromise holding. While the Court rejected quotas as such, it still allowed universities to manipulate admissions to produce heterogeneous student bodies.

The Court had an opportunity to deal with the affirmative action issue four years earlier in *DeFunis v. Odegaard*, 416 U.S. 312 (1974). DeFunis argued that he had been denied admission to the University of Washington Law School because of a preferential admissions policy very much like that at issue in *Bakke*. DeFunis, however, had been admitted to the law school under court order and was actually close to graduation at the time the case was scheduled for argument. The Court decided the case was moot and did not address the equal protection question.

Following *Bakke*, a more positive affirmative action decision came from the Court in *United Steelworkers of America v. Weber*, 443 U.S. 193 (1979). The Court upheld a private and voluntary employee training program against a challenge based on Title VII of the Civil Rights Act of 1964. The program gave selection preference to black employees for training, although not to the total exclusion of white employees.

Several years later, the Court held in *Firefighters Local 1784 v. Stotts*, 467 U.S. 561 (1984), that federal judges may not ignore seniority rights in order to protect newly hired minority employees from layoffs forced by budget reductions. The Court said that Title VII exempts seniority systems unless the system is shown to have been designed to discriminate purposefully.

In *Local 28, Sheet Metal Workers International Association v. EEOC*, 478 U.S. 421 (1986), the Court sanctioned the use of affirmative action as a means of addressing past racial discrimination. This case involved a court-ordered minority membership target for a union local. The availability of race-conscious affirmative relief for violations of Title VII furthers the broad purposes underlying the statute. Such affirmative race-conscious relief may be the only means available to assure equality of employment opportunities and to eliminate those discriminatory practices and devices that have "fostered racially stratified job environments to the disadvantage of minority citizens."

In most situations, courts need only order an employer to cease discriminatory practices and make the appropriate award of relief to victimized individuals. In some cases, however, it may be necessary to require an employer or union to take affirmative steps to end discrimination effectively. If an employer or union has been involved with particularly longstanding or egregious discrimination, compelling it to hire or admit to membership qualified minorities roughly in proportion to the number of qualified minorities in the workforce may be the only effective way to ensure the full enjoyment of the rights protected by Title VII.

The *Sheet Metal Workers* decision was one of the important workplace affirmative action rulings made by the Burger Court. Another was *Wygant v. Jackson Board of Education*, 476 U.S. 267 (1986), in which the Court said that the remedy for past discrimination may make it necessary to take race into account even if "innocent persons may be called upon to bear some of the burden of the remedy." In a concurring opinion, Justice O'Connor said that addressing past discrimination is a "sufficiently weighty state interest to warrant the remedial use of a carefully constructed affirmative action program." The Court rejected the view advanced by the Reagan administration that racial preference in employment was to be used only to remedy specifically named victims. Despite the endorsement of affirmative action in general, however, the Court refused to allow the layoff of white teachers to preserve the employment of less senior black teachers. In order to do so, the racial preference required a showing of compelling state interest. Given the fact that the Jackson School District was not found to have discriminated against blacks in hiring teachers, the compelling interest test was not met.

Another affirmative action ruling came in *Local 93, International Association of Firefighters v. City of Cleveland*, 478 U.S. 501 (1986). The City of Cleveland had agreed to resolve employment discrimination suits brought by black and Hispanic fire fighters by promising to promote black and Hispanic workers one-for-one with whites, notwithstanding seniority and test performance. The Court ruled that Title VII does not preclude federal courts from approving such agreements. The Court saw such consent decrees as a preferred means of achieving voluntary compliance with Title VII.

At issue in *United States v. Paradise*, 480 U.S. 149 (1987), was the use of promotion quotas as a race-based remedy for past discrimination. A federal district court had found that the Alabama Department of Public Safety had systematically excluded blacks from employment as state police officers. An order was issued in 1972 calling for the end of such discrimination and establishing a hiring quota. A number of years later it was discovered that none of the blacks recruited under the quota had been promoted. The department agreed to fashion a plan to resolve the problem, but after two years no blacks had been promoted. A test was subsequently devised for promotions, but it was found to have an adverse impact on blacks. When the department failed to submit a satisfactory promotion plan, the court ordered that blacks and whites be promoted on a one-for-one basis until such time as acceptable promotion policies were in place. The Supreme Court upheld the one-for-one plan against the claim that the approach was race conscious and violated both the Equal Protection Clause and the Civil Rights Act of 1964. The remedy devised in this case was seen by the Supreme Court as effective, temporary, and flexible. Similarly, the Court upheld the use of an affirmative action plan giving preference to women in *Johnson v. Transportation Agency*, 480 U.S. 616 (1987). The Santa Clara County Transportation Agency designed an affirmative action plan that applied to employee promotions. The plan authorized the agency to consider the gender of a qualified applicant for promotion to positions within traditionally segregated job classifications. The Court upheld the plan. The Court drew heavily from the rationale in *Weber*, with Justice Brennan saying that the Court must be mindful of the consistent emphasis in both the Court and Congress on the value of voluntary efforts to further the objectives of the law when evaluating an affirmative action plan against Title VII's prohibition of discrimination. In this case, the agency identified a conspicuous imbalance in a traditionally segregated job class and undertook a "voluntary effort in full recognition of both the difficulties and the potential for intrusion on males and nonminorities."

In *Martin v. Wilks*, 490 U.S. 755 (1989), the Court ruled that settlements reached in race or gender discrimination cases may subsequently be challenged by persons affected by the settlements, but not party to them. *Martin* arose out of a suit brought against the City of Birmingham, Alabama. The suit claimed racial bias in the hiring and promotion of blacks. A settlement was eventually reached and a federal court embraced its provisions in a consent decree. The order was aimed at producing numbers of black fire fighters roughly reflecting the proportion of blacks in the workforce. Under the order, blacks and whites were to be hired and promoted in equal numbers until the result was achieved. A group of white fire fighters later sought to challenge employment decisions made pursuant to the consent decree. Such decrees were generally regarded as immune from subsequent legal challenge, but in a five-to-four decision, the Supreme Court ruled that attack on the decrees was not precluded.

Adarand Constructors, Inc. v. Pena, **515 U.S. 299 (1995)** The Surface Transportation and Uniform Relocation Assistance Act of 1987 provided that not less than 10 percent of the funds appropriated by the Act "shall be expended with small business concerns owned and controlled by socially and economically disadvantaged individuals." At issue in *Adarand* was "subcontractor compensation" language that gave preference in the form of a monetary bonus to prime contractors in federal highway construction projects who subcontract at least 10 percent of the work to "disadvantaged business enterprises" (DBEs). A prime contractor for a highway project was awarded the bonus because it chose a DBE to perform guardrail work even though Adarand submitted the lowest bid for the work. Adarand, owned and operated by a white male, did not qualify as a DBE. Adarand filed suit, claiming that the preference given DBEs violated the Equal Protection Clause. The Supreme Court concluded that Congress may not use race-based preference in federal construction projects. The central question was the scrutiny level to be used for remedial race-conscious initiatives of the federal government.

The Court had ruled in *Richmond v. J.A. Croson Co.*, 488 U.S. 469 (1989), that strict scrutiny is required for such initiatives by state and local governments. *Croson* did not establish review standard for the federal government, but Justice O'Connor noted three "instructive themes" about governmental racial classifications from *Croson:* (1) skepticism (any preference based on racial or ethnic criteria must "necessarily receive a most searching examination"); (2) consistency (all racial classifications reviewable under the Equal Protection Clause "must be strictly scrutinized"); and (3) congruence (equal protection analysis under both the Fifth and Fourteenth Amendment "is the same"). Taken together, these themes lead to the conclusion that a person of whatever race "has the right to demand that any governmental actor subject to the Constitution justify any racial classification subjecting that person to unequal treatment under the strictest judicial scrutiny." The problem according to O'Connor was the Court's decision in *Metro Broadcasting, Inc. v. FCC*, 497 U.S. 547 (1990), a ruling that came a year after *Croson*. *Metro Broadcasting* represented a "surprising turn" in which the Court "repudiated the long-held notion that 'it would be unthinkable that the same Constitution would impose a lesser duty on the Federal Government' than it does on a state to afford equal protection of the laws." By adopting intermediate scrutiny as the standard for "Congressionally mandated 'benign' racial classifications," *Metro Broadcasting* departed from prior cases in two ways. First, it "turned its back" on the *Croson* reasoning of why strict scrutiny of "all governmental racial classifications is essential." The purpose of strict scrutiny, said O'Connor, is to "'smoke out' illegitimate uses of race by assuring that the legislative body is pursuing a goal important enough to warrant use of a highly suspect tool." Further, *Metro Broadcasting* rejected the theme of congruence between the standards applicable to federal, state, and local racial classifications suggested by earlier equal protection decisions. All governmental action based on race should be subjected to "detailed judicial inquiry to insure that the personal right to equal protection of the laws is not infringed." Holding "benign" state and federal racial classifications to different standards "does not square" with this principle. The Court concluded that all race-based classifications, imposed by "whatever Federal, state or local governmental actor," must be reviewed under strict scrutiny—race-based classifications are constitutional only if they are "narrowly tailored measures that further compelling governmental interests." O'Connor noted that the "unhappy persistence" of discrimination against minorities is an "unfortunate reality," and government is "not disqualified from acting in response to it." When race-based action is necessary to further a compelling interest, such action is within constitutional limits if it satisfies the "narrow tailoring" test set out by the Court. Justices Scalia and Thomas concurred separately. It was Scalia's view that government can "never have a 'compelling interest' in discriminating on the basis of race in order to 'make up' for past racial discrimination in the opposite direction." He suggested that individuals who have been victimized by unlawful discrimination should be "made whole," but under the Constitution there can be no such thing as either a "creditor or a debtor race." Pursuit of racial entitlement even for the most "admirable and benign of purposes is to reinforce and preserve for future mischief the way of thinking that produced race slavery, race privilege and race hatred." Justice Thomas directed his concurring opinion to the premise "underlying" affirmative action initiatives as represented in the dissenting opinions of Justices Stevens and Ginsburg—that there is a "racial paternalism exception to the principle of equal protection." He saw a "moral" and "constitutional equivalence" between laws intended to "subjugate a race" and those that attempt to allocate benefits on the basis of race "in order to foster some current notion of equality." In Thomas's view, so-called benign discrimination is destructive. It conveys to many that because of "chronic and apparently immutable handicaps, minorities cannot compete with them without their patronizing indulgence." Race-conscious governmental policies "engender attitudes of superiority," or "provoke resentment among those who believe that they have been wronged" by the government's initiatives. These programs "stamp minorities with a badge of inferiority" and may cause minorities to "develop dependencies or to adopt an attitude that they are 'entitled' to preferences." Justice Stevens's dissent focused on the contention that there is "no significant difference" between a decision to "impose a special burden" and a decision to "provide a benefit." There is no "moral or constitutional equivalence between a policy that is designed to perpetuate a caste system and one that seeks to eradicate racial subordination." An interest in consistency, Stevens suggested, does not justify "treating differences as though they were similarities." He rejected Thomas's contention that attempts to subjugate were the equivalents of attempts to redress as "extreme." It is one thing to "question the wisdom" of affirmative action programs, but quite another to equate "well-meaning and intelligent" legislators who have supported affirmative action to "segregationists and bigots." *See also* AFFIRMATIVE ACTION, p. 610; CIVIL RIGHTS ACT OF 1964, p. 626; EQUAL PROTECTION CLAUSE, p. 473; *Regents of the University of California v. Bakke*, p. 501.

Significance   The first federal preference program was reviewed in *Fullilove v. Klutznick*, 448 U.S. 448 (1980), which allowed a portion of federal construction grant funds to be reserved or "set aside" for businesses owned and operated by racial minorities. The Public Works Employment Act of 1977, a forerunner of the federal program under review in *Adarand*, contained a minority business enterprise (MBE) section that required at least 10 percent of federal monies designated for local public works projects to be set aside for businesses owned by minorities. Implementation of the policy was designed to come through grant recipients who were expected to seek out MBEs and provide whatever assistance or advice that might be necessary to negotiate bonding, bidding, or any other historically troublesome process. The policy was challenged by a number of nonminority contractors, but was upheld by the Supreme Court. Chief Justice Burger said the MBE section must be considered against the background of ongoing efforts directed toward deliverance of the century-old promise of equality of economic opportunity. Burger noted that a program using racial or ethnic criteria, even in a remedial context, calls for close examination, "yet we are bound to approach our task with appropriate deference." The Court ruled that Congress had ample evidence to conclude that minority businesses had impaired access to public contracting opportunities, that their impaired access had an effect on interstate commerce, and that the pattern of disadvantage and discrimination was a problem that was national in scope. Racial or ethnic criteria may be used in a remedial fashion as long as the program is narrowly tailored to achieve the corrective purpose. The Court rejected the view that in developing remedies Congress must act in a wholly color-blind fashion. No organ of government has a more comprehensive remedial power than Congress. When Congress can prohibit certain conduct, Burger said, "it may, as here, authorize and induce state action to avoid such conduct." Justices Stewart, Rehnquist, and Stevens disagreed. It was their view that racial discrimination is invidious by definition, and that rule cannot be any different.

Fullilove upheld the use of set asides, or reserved funds, for minority business enterprises as a method of remedying past discrimination in the construction industry. A year before *Fullilove*, the Court had approved a preferential employment training plan in *United Steelworkers of America v. Weber*, 443 U.S. 193 (1979). The plan, a component of a collective bargaining agreement, sought to reduce racial imbalances in a corporation's skilled or craft workforce. The plan gave preference to unskilled black employees over white employees, even white employees with greater seniority, in admission to training programs that taught the skills needed to become a craft worker. The Court held that Title VII of the Civil Rights Act of 1964 did not categorically preclude private and voluntary affirmative action plans. To prohibit such plans would produce a result inconsistent with the intent of the Civil Rights Act. It would be ironic if Title VII, "triggered by a nation's concern over centuries of racial injustice," was interpreted as the "legislative prohibition of all voluntary, private, race-conscious efforts to abolish traditional patterns of racial segregation and hierarchy." *Fullilove* and *Weber* together adopted the proposition that compensatory policies for groups that have demonstrably been disadvantaged in the past could be implemented without violating the Equal Protection Clause.

The City of Richmond adopted an affirmative action plan requiring prime contractors receiving city construction contracts to subcontract at least 30 percent of the dollar value of the contract to businesses owned or controlled by one (or more) of a number of specified minorities. The plan was designed to "promote wider participation by minority business enterprises in the construction of public projects." The Court disallowed the plan in *City of Richmond v. J.A. Croson Company*, 488 U.S. 469 (1989). The principal defect was that Richmond failed to show past discrimination in the city's contract-letting practices or in the conduct of prime contractors toward minority subcontractors. The data on which the plan was based provided "no guidance for a legislative body to determine the precise scope of the injury it seeks to remedy"; it has no "logical stop-ping point." Using these kinds of data to define "identified discrimi-nation" would allow local government "license to create a patchwork of racial preferences based on statistical generalizations about any particular field of endeavor." The Court also refused to defer to the city's own designation of the plan as remedial. "Mere recitation of a 'benign' or legitimate purpose for a racial classification is entitled to little or no weight." Racial classifications are "suspect," and that means that "legislative assurances of good intention cannot suffice" in themselves. The Court made it clear that striking down the Richmond plan had absolutely no effect on the federal set-aside law upheld in *Fullilove* after which the Richmond plan had been fash-ioned. The Court made clear that a different standard applies to congressional action. While the Fourteenth Amendment bars state and local units from discriminating on the basis of race, Congress has a "specific constitutional mandate to enforce the dictates of the Fourteenth Amendment."

Rehnquist Court decisions typically have concluded that race-based affirmative action programs violate the Equal Protection Clause unless they address a "compelling state interest." The only interest that has been compelling enough to justify race-preference initiatives so far is remediation of demonstrated past discrimination. The ruling that deviated from this pattern was *Metro Broadcasting*, in which the Court ruled that Congress may mandate "benign" minority preference policies even if those measures "are not 'remedial' in the sense of being designed to compensate victims of past governmental or societal discrimination." At issue in *Metro Broadcasting* (and the companion case of *Astroline Communications Company v. Shurberg Broadcasting, Inc.*) were two policies established by the Federal Communications Commission (FCC). The first allowed the FCC to consider minority ownership as a factor in licensing decisions. Consideration of this factor enhances minority chances of obtaining new licenses. The second gave minority bidders preference in situa-tions in which current license holders were likely to lose their licenses—so-called distressed sale situations. Of "overriding" signifi-cance in cases such as this, said Justice Brennan, is that these minority preference programs "have been specifically approved—indeed mandated—by Congress." The Court based its decision on *Fullilove*, which required that minority preference programs need serve only "important governmental objectives" and be "substantially related" to achievement of those objectives. The Court reviewed the need for federal regulation of the "unique medium" of broadcast. The safe-guarding of the public's right to receive a diversity of views and information over the airwaves was seen as an "integral component of the FCC's mission." On that basis, the Court concluded that "enhancing broadcast diversity is, at the very least, an important governmental objective and therefore a sufficient basis for the commission's minority ownership policies." Justices O'Connor, Kennedy, Scalia, and Chief Justice Rehnquist disagreed on the different review standards for the federal government. "The Constitution's guarantee of equal protection," said O'Connor, "binds the Federal Government as it does the states."

Protection of Civil Rights

Patterson v. McLean Credit Union, **491 U.S. 164 (1989),** reiterated that provisions of the Civil Rights Act of 1866 could be used in legal actions against private racial discrimination. The Civil Rights Act of 1866 guaranteed blacks the right to "make and enjoy" contracts. For a long period of time, this language was thought to be applicable only against state action or public discrimination. In the case of *Runyon v. McCrary,* 427 U.S. 160 (1976), the Court extended the law to private discrimination. Since *Runyon* this provision has become a common basis of actions seeking damages for employment discrimination.

Brenda Patterson brought such an action against her employer, claiming racial harassment. *Patterson* eventually led the Court to reexamine *Runyon.* Although confirming that the law could be used in private actions, the Court ruled that the statute had limited application in the employment setting and did not extend to Patterson's racial harassment claim. Justice Kennedy suggested that departure from the doctrine of *stare decisis,* the practice of adhering to previously decided cases, demands "special justification," especially when the Court is asked to overrule a point of statutory construction. *Stare decisis* has "special force" in statutory construction because, unlike with constitutional interpretation, the "legislative power is implicated." The Court concluded that no such "special justification" had been demonstrated necessitating the overruling of *Runyon.* The most common reason for a court to shift position on a precedent is the "intervening development of the law." *Runyon,* said Kennedy, has not been "undermined by subsequent changes or development in the law." Kennedy noted that *Runyon* remains "entirely consistent with our society's deep commitment to the eradication of discrimination based on a person's race." The Court concluded that the "most obvious feature" of the 1866 statute is the restriction on its scope. If a discriminatory act does not involve "impairment" of one of its specific provisions, the law "provides no relief." The law cannot, said Kennedy, "be construed as a general proscription of racial discrimination in all aspects of contract relations," for it expressly prohibits discrimination only in the making and enforcement of contracts. The statute prohibits refusal to enter into a contract because of race, or make contracts on discriminatory terms. The right to make contracts does not extend, "as a matter of either logic or semantics, to conduct by the employer after the contract relation has been established." That limitation includes breaching the contract terms or imposing "discriminatory working conditions.Such postformation conduct does not involve the right to make a contract." Instead, performance of established contract obligations are involved, which are matters "more naturally governed by state contract law and Title VII" of the Civil Rights Act of 1964. Justices, Brennan, Marshall, Blackmun, and Stevens dissented and criticized the Court's interpretation of the law as "needlessly cramped" and based on a "most pinched reading of the phrase 'right to make a contract.'" Brennan said the Court's "formalistic" interpretation was "antithetical to Congress's vision of a society in which contractual opportunities are equal." *See also* CIVIL RIGHTS ACT OF 1964, p. 626; EQUAL PROTECTION CLAUSE, p. 473; FOURTEENTH AMENDMENT, p. 651; *Harris v. Forklift Systems*, p. 568.

Significance   *Patterson* limited the reach of the Civil Rights Act of 1866. It confined the "make and enjoy" contracts provision to those discriminatory employment decisions occurring before someone is hired. Once a person is employed, discriminatory treatment falls under the purview of Title VII of the Civil Rights Act of 1964. *Patterson* can be seen as a decision that narrows the scope of previous civil-rights rulings, but *Patterson* is perhaps more important for what it did not do: It did not overrule *Runyon*, but rather reaffirmed it.

The Civil Rights Act of 1871 enabled persons to recover damages for violations of their civil rights. *Jett v. Dallas Independent School District*, 491 U.S. 701 (1989), examined the relationship of the 1866 and 1871 statutes, and the standard to be used in judging the liability of a school district for damages. Jett, a white male, was a teacher, athletic director, and football coach at a largely black high school in Dallas, Texas. After a series of conflicts Jett had with the school's black principal, the principal recommended that Jett be relieved of his athletic duties. The school superintendent concurred in the recommendations and reassigned Jett to another school. Jett brought an action claiming that his reassignment was the product of racial discrimination on the part of the school district. The Supreme Court ruled against Jett, saying that school district liability exists only if the principal and superintendent had acted pursuant to a formal policy or "well-settled custom that amounted to official policy." It was the Court's view that Congress had limited the liability of public entities language of the 1871 act through the employee conduct language in § 1983 adaption of the 1866 law, and that Congress had not intended that such liability previously possible under § 1981 should remain. The statutory language on liability in the latter (1871) law, including the "official policy or custom" standard, modified the earlier (1866) law as well. Thus to recover damages, it must be shown that public employees who allegedly discriminate possess formally conveyed policy-making authority or have acted pursuant to official "custom or policy." Because most public entities have formally adopted antidiscrimination statements, the effect of *Jett* is to largely insulate local entities from damage awards.

David Lanier, a state chancery and juvenile court judge, was convicted of a number of counts of violating the civil rights of several women through the commission of sexual assault. The charges were brought under 18 U.S.C. § 242, which makes it a federal offense to willfully deprive a person of rights protected by the Constitution while acting "under color of state law." Lanier's convictions were reversed by a federal appellate court, which ruled that § 242 neither "mention[ed]" nor "contemplate[d] sex crimes," and that including such conduct went beyond the proper scope of the law. Accordingly, the Court of Appeals for the Sixth Circuit ruled that the district court should have dismissed the indictment for failure to pursue a federal crime covered under § 242. The government argued that Lanier's sexual misconduct unlawfully interfered with the "bodily integrity" of the victims in a way that was "shocking to the conscience." The Supreme Court ruled in *United States v. Lanier*, 520 U.S. 259 (1997), that criminal liability may be lawfully imposed for depriving someone of a constitutional right if "in light of pre-existing law the unlawfulness [is] apparent." When such unlawfulness is apparent, the fair warning requirement is satisfied. The court remanded the case to the trial court for adjudication under this standard.

Stacey Burns, a reserve deputy sheriff in Bryan County, Oklahoma, allegedly used excessive force in removing Jill Brown from a vehicle driven by her husband. Brown sustained serious injury during the incident. She subsequently brought a federal civil-rights action claiming that the county had violated her constitutional rights by hiring Burns. He had been hired and given authority to make forcible arrests notwithstanding an extensive record of prior misdemeanor arrests, including one for assault. It was Brown's contention that the hiring of Burns demonstrated "deliberate indifference" to her constitutionally protected rights. A federal district court found for Brown and set damages at a little over $800,000, but the Supreme Court reversed in *County Board of Commissioners v. Brown*, 520 U.S. 397 (1997). Justice O'Connor indicated that plaintiffs must identify a "municipal policy or custom" that caused the claimed injury. Locating such a policy, said O'Connor, "ensures that a municipality is held liable only for those deprivations resulting from the decisions of its duly constituted legislative body" or those officials whose acts "may fairly be said to be those of the municipality." A plaintiff must also show that, "through its deliberate conduct," the municipality was the "moving force" behind the alleged injury. When a plaintiff presents a claim premised on the inadequacy of an official's review of a prospective applicant's record, there is a "particular danger that a municipality will be held liable for an injury not directly caused by deliberate action." A court " must carefully test the link between the policymaker's inadequate decision and the particular injury alleged." The fact that inadequate scrutiny of an applicant's record would make a violation of rights more likely "cannot alone give rise to an inference that a policymaker's failure to scrutinize the record of a particular applicant produced a specific constitutional violation." The decision to hire this applicant could not have been "deliberately indifferent" unless, in light of the applicant's record, his "use of excessive force would have been a plainly obvious consequence of the hiring decision." Congress did not intend municipalities to be held liable unless "deliberate action attributable to the municipality directly caused a deprivation of federal rights." Justice Souter, in dissent, suggested that the decision to hire this applicant constituted a "policy choice attributable to Bryan County."

Ronnie McKnight, an inmate in a Tennessee corrections facility, filed a civil rights claim alleging that officers at the facility subjected him to physical abuse, thereby violating his Eighth Amendment rights. The management and operation of Tennessee prisons were provided by Corrections Corporation of America (CCA), a private contractor. The officers named in McKnight's suit were CCA employees. The officers sought to have McKnight's complaint dismissed on qualified immunity grounds, a kind of immunity typically afforded defendants who are public employees. The Supreme Court ruled in *Richardson v. McKnight*, 521 U.S. 399 (1997), that employees of private contractors are not entitled to the immunity that applies to government employees even though the private employees may perform public functions. A purely functional approach to the problem "bristles with difficulty," because in many places, government and private business may "engage in fundamentally similar activities." The purpose of the immunity doctrine is to protect the government's ability to "perform its traditional functions." The guards contended that those functions supported immunity whether the employee is public or private, but this "overlook[ed] certain important differences" that are critical in the immunity context. The most important concern—protecting the public from unwarranted timidity on the part of public officials—is "less likely present, or at least is not special, when a private company subject to competitive market pressures operates a prison." The marketplace pressures provide the private contractor with "strong incentives to avoid overly timid, insufficiently vigorous, unduly fearful, or 'nonarduous' employee job performance."

Cases such as *Patterson* involve the scope of legislative power to protect civil rights. Several recent rulings address the scope of judicial remedial power to protect civil rights. *Spallone v. United States*, 493 U.S. 265 (1990), considered whether a federal court could order city counsel members to vote a particular way on a desegregation matter. The City of Yonkers was found to have acted in a racially discriminatory manner when it located all its subsidized housing in a nonwhite section of the city. The city and its community development agency were then ordered to facilitate construction of subsidized housing throughout the city. An agreement, subsequently embraced in a consent decree, was reached between the parties. The order contained a provision that the city council would adopt regulations that all future housing constructed anywhere in the city included some portion of subsidized units. The legislation was also to include certain incentives to foster the development of such housing. Reaction from the residents of neighborhoods where such housing was to be built was both extensive and negative. Indeed, the opposition was sufficiently strong that the city council refused to adopt the legislation required under the consent decree. Instead, the council adopted a resolution adopted in direct defiance of the court decree that declared a moratorium on construction of all public housing. The court once again ordered the council to adopt the necessary legislation. The court gave the council only a few days to do so and indicated that failure to act would result in contempt sanctions against both the city and the council members who voted against the legislation. A resolution on intent to comply was defeated by a four-to-three council vote. Following a hearing, the court found the city and the four council members in contempt. Two council members eventually switched their votes in the face of escalating fines against the city. The fines ceased following the second vote, although $820,000 in fines were assessed against the city. While none of the council members was jailed, each paid $3,500 in fines. The Supreme Court refused to review the fines against the City, but consolidated the petitions from the four council members for review. The Supreme Court reversed the sanctions against the individual council members as an abuse of judicial discretion under "traditional equitable principles." The Court said the council members, as distinct from the city, were not parties to the original action nor were they found to be "individually liable" for any particular violations on which the remedial order was based. The original corrective order itemizing specific "affirmative steps" was directed only to the city. Furthermore, the Court said there was also a "reasonable probability" that sanctions against the city would have been sufficient to obtain the desired results.

James Smith, a deputy sheriff in Sacramento County, California, chased a motorcyclist and his passenger through residential streets of Sacramento at speeds reaching 100 miles per hour. The driver of the motorcycle lost control, causing the passenger—a minor—to be struck and killed by the patrol car. The parents of the young man who was killed sought damages through a § 1983 suit against Deputy Smith, the Sheriff's Department, and Sacramento County. The Supreme Court unanimously held in *Sacramento County v. Lewis*, 118 S.Ct. 1708 (1998), that police could only be held liable when their actions were taken "maliciously and sadistically for the very purpose of causing harm." The Court found "unsound" the argument that the liability issue here was grounded on an application of the "reasonableness standard governing searches and seizures." The Lewises' claim was not "covered by" the Fourth Amendment because neither a search nor seizure occurred. Rather, substantive due process analysis was determined to be the appropriate approach for resolving this case. The substantive component of the Due Process Clause is violated by executive action, said Souter, "only when it can properly be characterized as arbitrary, or conscience-shocking, in a constitutional sense." Souter said conduct "intended to injure in some way unjustifiable by any government interest is the sort of official action most likely to rise to the conscience-shocking level." Rules of due process are not "subject to mechanical application in unfamiliar territory," however. Deliberate indifference that "shocks in one environment may not be so patently egregious in another." Attention to the "markedly different circumstances of normal pretrial custody and high-speed law enforcement chases shows why the deliberate indifference that shocks in the one case is less egregious in the other." The deliberate indifference standard is applied "only when actual deliberation is practical." In the custodial situation of a prison, for example, forethought about an inmate's welfare is "not only feasible but obligatory under a regime that incapacitates a prisoner to exercise ordinary responsibility for his own welfare." A much higher standard than "deliberate indifference has to be shown for officer liability in a prison riot." In those circumstances, said Souter, liability should turn on whether force was applied in a "good faith effort to maintain or restore discipline or maliciously and sadistically for the very purpose of causing harm." The "analogy to sudden police chases would be hard to avoid." Just as purpose to cause harm is required for Eighth Amendment liability in a prison riot case, "so it ought to be needed for Due Process liability in a pursuit case." Accordingly, concluded Souter, "high-speed chases with no intent to harm suspects physically or to worsen their legal plight do not give rise to liability under the Fourteenth Amendment."

Reapportionment: Justiciability

***Baker v. Carr,* 369 U.S. 186 (1962),** held that legislative districting was justiciable, a matter properly before federal courts. *Baker v. Carr* abandoned the position that apportionment was a "political question" not subject to resolution by the judicial branch. By the middle of the twentieth century, extensive malapportionment existed for most state legislative districts as well as for Congress. Years of inattention to shifting populations had produced highly inequitable representation. Baker and others brought suit in federal district court in Tennessee, claiming that despite significant growth and shifts in the population of Tennessee, districts were still defined on the basis of a 1901 statute. The resulting population differences in legislative districts deprived them of political equality. Residents of more populous districts were less well represented because of population differences. The Supreme Court ruled that the federal courts possessed jurisdiction because the equal protection claim was not "so attenuated and unsubstantial as to be absolutely devoid of merit."

Precedent would seem to have foreclosed the Court from adjudicating *Baker* by virtue of the political question doctrine in *Colegrove v. Green,* 328 U.S. 549 (1946). The *Colegrove* decision held that the enjoining of an election because of malapportionment was beyond the competence of federal courts because apportionment was of a "peculiarly political nature and therefore not meet for judicial determination." Thus the *Colegrove* Court viewed the matter in separation-of-powers terms exclusively. For the judiciary to involve itself would "cut very deep into the very being of Congress. Courts ought not to enter this political thicket." In *Baker* Justice Brennan traced the history of the political question doctrine and concluded that its application revealed a definite pattern. "Prominent on the surface of any case held to involve a political question is found a textually demonstrable constitutional commitment of the issue to a coordinate political department." Guaranty Clause claims and the conduct of foreign affairs are particularly clear examples of this category. A second category of political question issues involved cases in which there was a lack of judicially discoverable and manageable standards for resolving such cases, or in which it was impossible to decide without an initial policy determination clearly outside judicial discretion. Brennan said the apportionment question fit neither of those categories. It was rather an equal protection problem containing claims of arbitrary and capricious action by the state of Tennessee. Justices Frankfurter and Harlan dissented. Justice Frankfurter, who had written the Court's opinion in *Colegrove,* felt that the *Baker* case was controlled by the political question doctrine and that the decision was a "massive repudiation of the experience of our whole past in asserting destructively novel judicial power." The Court must, in

Justice Frankfurter's view, maintain "complete detachment, in fact and in appearance, from political entanglements and by abstention from injecting itself into the clash of political forces in political settlements." *See also* APPORTIONMENT, p. 613; EQUAL PROTECTION CLAUSE, p. 473; POLITICAL QUESTION, p. 688; *Reynolds v. Sims*, p. 518; *South Carolina v. Katzenbach*, p. 531.

Significance   *Baker v. Carr* allowed the legislative districting questions to reach federal courts. *Baker* did not attempt to develop particular standards regarding reapportionment, but left in its wake a great deal of activity directed toward relieving malapportionment. The Court first introduced a redistricting standard in *Gray v. Sanders*, 372 U.S. 368 (1963). The voting practice at issue in *Gray* was the unit system, a technique by which statewide officials were nominated in Georgia. Each county was a separate unit. A candidate winning a majority of the votes in a county was awarded one unit, regardless of the population of the county, thus diluting or diminishing the value of votes in larger counties. Although the Court distinguished this process from legislative districting, it held that the Equal Protection Clause required persons to have an equal vote, thus the application of the "one man, one vote" standard in *Gray*. The following year the Court applied the one-person-one-vote standard to apportionment of congressional districts in *Wesberry v. Sanders*, 376 U.S. 1 (1964).

Apportionment of congressional districts to the states raises additional questions. In *Department of Commerce v. Montana*, 503 U.S. 87 (1992), the Court upheld the formula used to apportion districts across the 50 states. The method, known as the equal-proportions formula, was adopted by Congress in 1941 and was designed to minimize the percentage differences of people represented in each district when applied across all the states. Use of this formula resulted in Montana losing one of its two seats in the U.S. House of Representatives. This case was the Court's first examination of House district apportionment since the adoption of the one-person-one-vote districting standard. Congressional districts within a state must achieve virtual mathematical equality. Interstate equality of district populations is not possible, however, because districts cannot cross state lines.

The question in *Franklin v. Massachusetts*, 505 U.S. 788 (1992), was whether the Census Bureau properly counted federal employees stationed overseas as residents of states for apportionment purposes. These citizens, mostly members of the military, were not counted in the 1980 census, but were counted in the 1990 census. Massachusetts, which had fewer overseas residents than some other states, lost one of its U.S. House seats in the post-1990 census apportionment. The effect of this change caused Massachusetts to lose one of its seats. A three-judge panel had found the Census Bureau policy to be "arbitrary and capricious." A unanimous Supreme Court disagreed, saying that the decision to include overseas workers "does not hamper the underlying constitutional goal of equal representation." Indeed, the Court said that the change may "actually promote equality" to the extent that overseas employees may retain ties to their home states.

Reynolds v. Sims, **377 U.S. 533 (1964),** held that the one-person-one-vote principle applied to both houses of state legislatures. *Reynolds,* accompanied by several companion cases from other states, involved a challenge of the apportionment of Alabama house and senate districts. The boundaries for these districts had not changed since the 1900 census. The Court struck down the existing districts, as well as a proposal based on the "federal" analogy—that is, basing boundaries in only one of the two legislative houses on population. Chief Justice Warren saw the central question as whether there are any constitutionally cognizable principles that would justify departures from the basic standard of equality among voters in the apportionment of seats in state legislatures. The concept of equal protection requires the "uniform treatment of persons standing in the same relation to the governmental action" that is challenged. All voters, "as citizens of a State, stand in the same relation regardless of where they live." Because the achievement of fair representation is the "basic aim" of apportionment and districting, the Court concluded that the Equal Protection Clause "guarantees the opportunity for equal participating by all voters in the election of state legislators." The gravity of the issue was reflected in the observation that "the right of suffrage can be denied by a debasement or dilution of the weight of a citizen's vote just as effectively as by wholly prohibiting the free exercise of the franchise." Warren declared that legislators represent people, not trees or acres, and are "elected by voters, not farms or cities or economic interests." People must have an unimpaired capacity to elect representatives, and the weight of a citizen's vote cannot be made to depend on where he or she lives. Population is of necessity the starting point for the consideration of, and the controlling criterion for judgment in, legislative apportionment controversies. The Equal Protection Clause requires that a legislative vote is not "diluted" when compared with other citizens living elsewhere in the state. Further, it requires that both chambers of state legislatures be apportioned on the basis of population. The Court rejected the federal analogy approach calling it "inappropriate and irrelevant." Proposing such plans is often "little more than an after-the-fact rationalization offered in defense of maladjusted state apportionment arrangements." The Court found that electing both houses on the basis of population was compatible with the concept of bicameralism. It said the composition and complexion of the two houses would "differ substantially." Thus population-based representation, "as nearly of equal population as is practicable," became the rule, with only small deviations allowable for flexibility or to prevent gerrymandering. Justices Harlan, Stewart, and Clark dissented. They called the decision "profoundly ill-advised and constitutionally impermissible." All three felt that states ought to be able to choose any electoral legislative structure they think is best suited to the interests, temper, and customs of their people. The dissenters rejected the idea that equal protection requirements could only be met by "uncritical, simplistic, and heavy-handed application of sixth-grade arithmetic." *See also* APPORTIONMENT, p. 613; *Baker v. Carr*, p. 516; EQUAL PROTECTION CLAUSE, p. 473; *City of Mobile v. Bolden*, p. 519; *South Carolina v. Katzenbach*, p. 531.

Significance   *Reynolds v. Sims* established stringent population guidelines for the apportionment of districts in state legislatures. The extent to which the Warren Court would adhere to the one-person-one-vote standard was demonstrated in *Lucas v. Forty-Fourth General Assembly*, 377 U.S. 713 (1964), one of the companions to *Reynolds*. In *Lucas*, the Court rejected a plan with a 3.6-to-1 variance in one house and a 1.7-to-1 variance in the other house on equal protection grounds. The ruling was made despite approval of the plan in a statewide referendum. Chief Justice Warren said a citizen's constitutional rights "can hardly be infringed simply because the majority of the people choose to do so." The Burger Court permitted deviations of slightly more than 16 percent in *Mahan v. Howell*, 410 U.S. 315 (1973). The variance was permitted because it was done "to advance the rational state policy of respecting the boundaries of political subdivisions" and did not otherwise exceed constitutional limitations.

Following *Reynolds*, the Court was asked to consider whether the one-person-one-vote rule applied to local units of government. In *Avery v. Midland County*, 390 U.S. 474 (1968), the Court held that when local governments elect representatives from single-member districts, good faith attempts must be undertaken to make those districts equal in population. The considerations given to equal protection in apportioning legislative districts have been defined as carrying over to other electoral situations. In *Kramer v. Union Free School District*, 395 U.S. 621 (1969), the Court held that a state could not restrict participation in school district elections to district property owners and parents of children in the school system. Despite the controversy associated with the Warren Court's activism on this issue, the democratic premise underpinning *Reynolds* has been generally accepted since.

Reapportionment and Race

City of Mobile v. Bolden, **446 U.S. 55 (1980),** upheld a municipal at-large election process against claims that such a system diluted minority group voting influence. The Supreme Court found the at-large plan to be constitutionally acceptable. Critics of the at-large or multimember district approach argued that some elements of the electorate were left unrepresented. The Court noted that criticism of the at-large election was rooted in its winner-take-all aspect and its tendency to submerge minorities. The specific question posed in *Bolden* was whether the at-large scheme had been established for the purpose of reducing the impact of black voters. No finding was made by the trial court that black voters had been deprived of the privilege of voting or hampered in the registration process. The Court had previously found in such cases as *White v. Regester,* 412 U.S. 755 (1973), that the multimember election system was not unconstitutional per se. Constitutional violations occur in apportionment systems only "if their purpose were invidiously to minimize or cancel out the voting potential of racial or ethnic minorities." To demonstrate such a violation, a plaintiff must prove that the disputed plan was conceived or operated as a purposeful device to further racial discrimination. A showing that a particular group has not elected representatives in proportion to its members is not sufficient. The Court said that while black candidates in Mobile have been defeated, that fact alone does not prove a constitutional deprivation. The Court also rejected the relevance of discrimination by the city in the context of municipal employment and the dispensing of public services. Evidence of possible discrimination by city officials in other contexts is "tenuous and circumstantial evidence of the constitutional invalidity of the electoral system under which they attained their offices." The Burger Court concluded that past cases show "the Court has sternly set its face against the claim, however phrased, that the Constitution somehow guarantees proportional representation." Justices Brennan, Marshall, and White argued in dissent that a sufficient discriminatory impact had been shown for relief to be given. Justice Marshall said the Court's decision meant that "in the absence of proof of discrimination by the State, the right to vote provides the politically powerless with nothing more than the right to cast meaningless ballots." *See also* APPORTIONMENT, p. 613; *Baker v. Carr,* p. 516; *Reynolds v. Sims,* p. 518; VOTING RIGHTS ACT OF 1965, p. 709.

Significance   *City of Mobile v. Bolden* held that discriminatory intent must be demonstrated before an electoral system can be found to violate the Constitution. The more complex issue arises when an apportionment plan is intentionally designed to make more likely the electoral success of a minority. The Court upheld such a plan in *United Jewish Organizations, Inc. v. Carey,* 430 U.S. 144 (1977), in which district lines in New York were redrawn to enhance the possibility of electing racial minorities to the state legislature. The plan split a group of Hasidic Jews, formerly concentrated in a single state assembly and senate district, into two districts. Suit was brought claiming that voter reassignment had been based on race. The Court upheld the redistricting plan, finding that other voters in the county involved were not denied an opportunity to participate in the political process. The Court also held that considerations of race could be made in an attempt to comply with provisions of the Voting Rights Act of 1965, as in *South Carolina v. Katzenbach*, 383 U.S. 301 (1966). As long as reasonable considerations of race were directed toward the achievement of racial equality, they were permissible. The Rehnquist Court changed this standard in *Shaw v. Reno*, 509 U.S. 630 (1993), and decisions that followed *Shaw*.

Plans that actually disenfranchise remain clearly unconstitutional. In *Gomillion v. Lightfoot*, 364 U.S. 339 (1960), for example, the Court held that a plan that restructured the boundaries of a city so that most black residents were placed outside the city limits was in violation of both the Fourteenth and Fifteenth Amendments. The Voting Rights Act of 1965 also requires that any changes in voting procedures or conditions that impact on voting practices must be cleared by the attorney general of the United States before they can be implemented. The full impact of this requirement was seen in *City of Pleasant Grove v. United States*, 479 U.S. 462 (1987). Pleasant Grove, a nearly all-white city in Alabama, was denied preclearance to annex a then-uninhabited area on the ground that it had refused to annex adjacent black neighborhoods, despite petitions by the neighborhood residents. The Supreme Court said an annexation is subject to preclearance under the law. Even the annexation of vacant land on which residential development is anticipated must be precleared. In the Court's view, to allow a state to circumvent the preclearance requirement when annexing vacant land intended for white development would disserve congressional intent to reach the subtle, as well as the obvious, official actions that have the effect of denying voter groups representation based on their race. Pleasant Grove argued that there were no black voters in the city at the time the annexation decision was made, so the proposals did not deny or reduce existing black voter representation. The Court rejected this contention, saying it was based on an incorrect assumption that relevant provisions of the Act can only relate to present circumstances. Its provisions look not only at present effects but at future effects as well. Annexation cannot be used as a means of preventing integration. An obvious means of thwarting integration is to provide for the growth of a monolithic white voting block, thereby effectively diluting the black vote in advance. This is just as impermissible an objective as the dilution of present black voting strength.

The New York City Board of Estimate is a body with power relating to, among other things, city contracts, property, and finances. It is composed of eight members, each of whom serves by virtue of holding another elective office. The Board's membership includes the New York City mayor, city counsel president, and city comptroller. Each of these persons hold these positions by citywide election. The five other members of the Board are the borough presidents, elected respectively by residents of the Bronx, Brooklyn, Manhattan, Staten Island, and Queens. The Board does not establish the city's budget, but does participate with the city counsel in its preparation. On such matters as contracting, city property use, and franchising, the Board has exclusive power. For issues of exclusive jurisdiction, the mayor, city counsel president, and comptroller have two votes each. The five borough presidents have only one vote. Thus, if the three citywide members vote together, they have a majority regardless of what the borough presidents do. On matters relating to the budget, however, the mayor cannot vote. The consequence in this instance is that a coalition of borough presidents can always control budget issues. In *New York City Board of Estimate v. Morris*, 489 U.S. 688 (1989), the Court was asked to determine if the one-person-one-vote rule applied to this Board. The contention of the challengers was that the five boroughs were equally represented on the Board despite disparate borough populations. The Court struck down the Board of Estimate's structure on the basis of operative reapportionment requirements. The Court further required an equal population computational method be devised to take into account that voters in each borough vote for and are represented by both their borough president and citywide members.

A provision of the Missouri state constitution authorized creation of a board empowered to reorganize city and county governments in St. Louis. The constitutional provision limited membership on the board to owners of real property. The restriction was challenged as a violation of equal protection. A unanimous U.S. Supreme Court held in *Quinn v. Millsap*, 491 U.S. 95 (1989), that the board of property owners was within the reach of the Equal Protection Clause, and struck down the board as constituted at the time. The Clause "protects the right to be considered for public service without the burden of individually discriminatory disqualifications."

Gerrymandering

Davis v. Bandemer, **478 U.S. 109 (1986),** ruled that claims of political gerrymandering are justiciable. *Bandemer* focused on a challenge to Indiana's reapportionment plan devised after the 1980 census. The plan called for a mixture of single- and multimember districts to elect the state house of representatives. Members of the Democratic Party challenged the plan, alleging that it was intentionally disadvantageous to them and thus violated their right to equal protection of the laws. Results from the 1982 election showed a dilution of the Democratic vote. Democratic house candidates received 51.9 percent of the vote cast statewide, but won only 43 of the 100 seats in the house. The Supreme Court ruled that gerrymandering claims are justiciable even when the plan under challenge meets the one-person-one-vote standard. Justice White said that the case presented neither the "identifying characteristics" of a nonjusticiable political question nor issues for which there were no judicially discernible and manageable standards for decision. The suit claimed that "each political group in a state should have the same chance to elect representatives of its choice as any other political group." Even though the one-person-one-vote standard did not apply, the issue was one of representation, and "we decline to hold that such claims are never justiciable." Justice White said that an equal protection violation requires a threshold showing of discriminatory vote dilution. The mere fact that an apportionment plan makes it more difficult for a particular group in a particular district to elect the representatives of its choice does not render that scheme constitutionally infirm. Unconstitutional vote dilution, either on an individual district or statewide level, requires demonstration beyond a mere lack of proportional representation. Unconstitutional discrimination occurs "only when the electoral system is arranged in a manner that will consistently degrade a voter's or a group of voters' influence on the political process as a whole." The principal question in reviewing gerrymandering allegations is whether a particular group has been "unconstitutionally denied its chance to effectively influence the political process." A finding of unconstitutionality must be supported by evidence of "continued frustration of the will of a majority of the voters or effective denial to a minority of voters of a fair chance to influence the political process." Relying on a single election to prove unconstitutional discrimination was viewed as unsatisfactory. Chief Justice Burger and Justices Rehnquist and O'Connor maintained that partisan gerrymandering challenges were categorically nonjusticiable. *See also* APPORTIONMENT, p. 613; *City of Mobile v. Bolden*, p. 519; EQUAL PROTECTION CLAUSE, p. 473; GERRYMANDERING, p. 522; POLITICAL QUESTION, p. 688; VOTING RIGHTS ACT OF 1965, p. 709.

Significance   Although the Court refused to invalidate the Indiana redistricting plan, it ruled in *Bandemer* that gerrymandering is subject to constitutional challenge. The Court also heightened the chances of successful challenge of electoral practices and districting schemes in *Thornburg v. Gingles*, 478 U.S. 30 (1986). To better understand this ruling, it is necessary to backtrack *to City of Mobile v. Bolden*, 446 U.S.

55 (1980). In *Bolden,* the Court held that plaintiffs alleging the dilution of minority votes must demonstrate that a disputed practice or
plan was conceived or operated as a purposeful device to further
racial discrimination. The *Bolden* decision prompted amendment of
Section 2 of the Voting Rights Act in 1982. The amendment changed
the focus from intent to outcome in assessing discrimination in electoral processes. A unanimous Court ruled in *Gingles* that a Section 2
claim is not foreclosed simply because some minority candidates
have been successful. A plan that dilutes minority votes cannot be
defended on the ground that it "sporadically and serendipitously
benefits minority voters." The Court then fragmented on the criteria
to be used to assess Section 2 challenges. Writing for five members of
the Court, Justice Brennan offered a three-element standard for
establishing a violation: First, minority challengers must show that
they are large and geographically compact enough to constitute a
majority of voters in the district. Second, the challenging group must
show that it votes cohesively. Third, the minority group must be able
to demonstrate that a majority of whites usually vote to defeat the
minority's preferred candidates. If a challenging group cannot
respond to these criteria, the challenged plan or practice cannot be
found responsible for the inability of minority voters to elect their
candidates.

Gerrymandering: Race-Based

***Shaw v. Reno,* 509 U.S. 630 (1993)** Congressional districts were reap-
portioned following the 1990 census. The process resulted in a gain
of one congressional seat for North Carolina in the U.S. House of
Representatives. The North Carolina General Assembly fashioned a
plan establishing 12 congressional districts, one of which was a
majority-minority district, a district with enough minority voters to
probably ensure the election of a minority representative. The plan
was submitted to the Justice Department for preclearance as
required under Section 5 of the Voting Rights Act. A Section 5 objection was made by the Justice Department on the grounds that,
despite including one black majority district, the plan still underrep-
resented minority voting strength in the state. In response to the
objection, the general assembly revised the plan by adding a second
majority-minority district. The Justice Department approved the
revised plan containing these two majority-minority districts. A
minority candidate was elected in both of these districts in November
1992. A challenge to the revised plan was brought by the North
Carolina Republican Party and several white voters residing in the
state. They claimed that the plan was based on unconstitutional political gerrymandering. The district court rejected the challengers'

contention that race-conscious redistricting "to benefit minority voters is per se unconstitutional" and upheld the North Carolina plan containing the two majority-minority districts. The Supreme Court disagreed, concluding that the challengers' claim was one for which Equal Protection Clause relief could be granted. Justice O'Connor said that it was "unsettling how closely the North Carolina plan resembles the most egregious racial gerrymanders of the past." The challengers claimed a constitutional right to "participate in a 'color-blind' electoral process." Their objection to the redistricting plan was that it was so "extremely irregular on its face" that it could be viewed "only as an effort to segregate the races for purposes of voting, without regard for traditional districting principles and without sufficiently compelling justification." In the Court's view, the Equal Protection Clause could provide relief in such a situation. O'Connor referred to such traditional districting principles as compactness, contiguity, and political subdivision boundaries as "objective factors" that might provide the basis for setting aside claims of racial gerrymandering. Apportionment is an area in which, said O'Connor, "appearances do matter." A reapportionment plan that includes in a district individuals of one race, but who are otherwise "widely separated by geographical and political boundaries, and who may have little in common with one another but the color of their skin, bears an uncomfortable resemblance to political apartheid." Racial classifications of "any sort pose the risk of lasting harm to our society." Such classifications reinforce the belief that individuals should be judged on the basis of race. Racial classifications with respect to voting "carry particular dangers." Racial gerrymandering, even for remedial purposes, she concluded, "may balkanize us into competing racial factions; it threatens to carry us further from the goal of a political system in which race no longer matters." Justices White, Blackmun, Stevens, and Souter dissented. They contended that the Court had recognized districts with "bizarre" shapes as the basis for employing strict judicial scrutiny. Justice White observed that members of the white majority can "not plausibly argue that their influence over the political process has been unfairly canceled or that such had been the State's intent." Similarly, it was Blackmun's view that no Equal Protection Clause violation exists unless the redistricting plan has the effect of unduly minimizing a particular group's voting strength. He found it "particularly ironic" that the Court chose a case in which to recognize an "analytically distinct" constitutional claim that was a challenge by white voters to a plan under which North Carolina "has sent black representatives to Congress for the first time since Reconstruction." Justice Stevens saw drawing districts for the purpose of facilitating election of a second black member of Congress as justifiable. The difference between constitutional and unconstitutional gerrymanders has nothing to do with whether they are based on assumptions about the groups they affect, but whether their purpose is to "enhance the power of the group in control of the districting process at the expense of any minority group, and thereby to strengthen the unequal distribution of electoral power." *See also* APPORTIONMENT, p. 613; EQUAL PROTECTION CLAUSE, p. 473; FOURTEENTH AMENDMENT, p. 651; *Reynolds v. Sims*, p. 518; VOTING RIGHTS ACT OF 1965, p. 709.

Significance   The Court ruled in *Shaw v. Reno (Shaw I)*, that congressional districts created on the basis of "racial gerrymandering" violate the Equal Protection Clause. The Court remanded *Shaw I* to allow North Carolina to justify the intentional use of race in drawing new congressional district boundaries. The three-judge federal district court concluded that North Carolina's interest was compelling, and that the plan was sufficiently narrowly tailored to survive strict scrutiny, but the Supreme Court disagreed in *Shaw v. Hunt*, 517 U.S. 899 (1966) (*Shaw II*). *Shaw II* was a narrow case, because the Court's review was limited to application of the strict scrutiny standard as mandated by *Shaw I*. The fact situation remained the same with only the state's justifications for the plan under review. In order to meet the *Shaw I* standard under strict scrutiny, North Carolina had to demonstrate that the plan with two majority-minority districts both pursued a "compelling" state interest, and did so in a "narrowly tailored" way. North Carolina sought to sustain the plan by asserting three compelling interests: to eradicate the effects of past discrimination, and to comply with Sections 2 and 5 of the Voting Rights Act. Eradication of the effects of past racial discrimination may only rise to the "compelling" level if the discrimination is "identified" as such. A generalized assertion of past discrimination is insufficient. Further, the institution that distinguishes the specific from the generalized assertion of discrimination must have a "strong basis in evidence" that remedial action is required. It was the Court's conclusion that an interest in "ameliorating past discrimination did not actually precipitate the use of race in the redistricting plan." Chief Justice Rehnquist then addressed the justifications stemming from North Carolina's duty to comply with the Voting Rights Act. Section 5 requires the Justice Department to "preclear" any changes in election laws. Although the Justice Department urged creation of the second majority-minority district, the second district was not required under a "correct reading of Section 5." Citing *Miller v. Johnson*, 515 U.S. 900 (1995), Rehnquist said that North Carolina's first plan was sufficiently ameliorative. However, the majority-minority district was not required—notwithstanding the Justice Department's "preclearance demands." North Carolina also asserted that the plan was created to avoid liability under Section 2 of the Act. Section 2 prohibits the "dilution" of minority group voting strength. Rehnquist said that Section 2 liability is contingent on the "geographical compact[ness]" of the minority group. The Court concluded that such a "geographically compact population of any race" did not reside in one of the districts. As a result, the plan with two majority-minority districts could not serve as a remedy for any potential Section 2 violation. Vote dilution injuries suffered by members of a minority, said Rehnquist, are "not remedied by creating a safe majority-black district somewhere else in the State." Justices Stevens, Souter, Ginsburg, and Breyer disagreed. Justice Stevens took issue with the conclusion that race was the "predominant" factor underlying the plan. Legislative decisions are often the "product of compromise and mixed motives." Such mixed motives Stevens characterized as "endemic to the endeavor of political districting."

Shaw I did not categorically rule out the creation of majority-minority districts, but remanded the North Carolina plan to the district court for further consideration. A number of cases were filed after *Shaw*, and one of the first to reach the Court was *Miller v. Johnson*. It involved a challenge to a plan adopted by the Georgia legislature and approved by the Justice Department. Prior to 1990 one of Georgia's 10 districts was a majority-minority district. The 1990 census showed sufficient population increase to entitle Georgia to one additional seat in the U.S. House of Representatives. An 11-district plan was drawn up that contained three majority-minority districts. The plan was challenged, and a three-judge district court found "overwhelming" evidence of the state legislature's intention to "racially gerrymander" at least one of the new districts (the eleventh), and struck down the plan. The Supreme Court affirmed the lower court's decision. It was Georgia's contention that *Shaw I* required more than a showing of deliberate classification of voters by race. Regardless of purpose, it must also be shown that a district's "shape is so bizarre that it is unexplainable other than on the basis of race." Justice Kennedy suggested that Georgia's view of a constitutional violation "misapprehends our holding in *Shaw I*" and the equal protection decisions upon which *Shaw I* was based. *Shaw I* recognized a claim "analytically distinct" from a vote dilution claim. The latter asserts that the state purposefully sought to "cancel out" the voting potential of racial or ethnic minorities. An equal protection claim, on the other hand, occurs when the state uses race as a basis for separating voters into districts. Just as the state may not otherwise segregate on the basis of race, neither may it separate citizens into voting districts on the basis of race. The idea, said Kennedy, is a "simple one: 'At the heart of the Constitution's guarantee of equal protection lies the simple command that the Government must treat citizens as individuals, not simply as components of a racial, religious, sexual or national class.'" When a state assigns voters on the basis of race, it engages in the "offensive and demeaning assumption that voters of a particular race, because of their race, think alike, share the same political interests and will prefer the same candidates at the polls." The observations in *Shaw I* about the consequences of racial stereotyping were not meant to suggest that a district "must be bizarre on its face" as a threshold condition of a constitutional violation. Shape is relevant "not because bizarreness is a necessary element of the constitutional wrong," Kennedy continued, but because it "may be persuasive circumstantial evidence that race for its own sake, and not other districting principles, was the Legislature's dominant and controlling rationale in drawing its district lines." The Court had "little doubt" that Georgia's "true interest" in designing the Eleventh District was to design a third majority-minority district in order to satisfy preclearance requirements of the Justice Department under the Voting Rights Act. Compliance with federal antidiscrimination laws could not, in the absence of an interest in remedying past discrimination, provide the necessary compelling interest to validate the scheme. Kennedy suggested that trying to achieve equal opportunity to gain public office is a worthwhile objective, but that end is "neither assured nor well served ... by carving electorates into racial blocs." Justice O'Connor provided the critical fifth vote in the *Miller* case. The standard announced in this case, she said, "does not throw into doubt the vast majority of the Nation's 435 Congressional districts" where states have established district boundaries using "customary" districting principles. That is true even though race "may well have been considered in the redistricting process." Application of the new standard gives effect to *Shaw I*'s basic objective of making "extreme instances of gerrymandering subject to meaningful judicial review." Justice Ginsburg issued a dissent joined at least in part by Justices Stevens, Souter, and Breyer. It was their view that in *Shaw I* virtually every factor other than race was excluded. The record in this case did not demonstrate that race "similarly overwhelmed traditional districting practices in Georgia." Ginsburg was disturbed that a state can no longer avoid federal judicial oversight by giving "genuine and measurable consideration" to traditional districting practices. Instead, a federal case can be pursued whenever a plaintiff can plausibly allege that other factors "carried less weight than race." Finally, Ginsburg took issue with the Court's approach that strict judicial scrutiny is in order once it is determined that an apportionment is "predominantly motivated" by race. It matters "not at all" under this new approach whether the apportionment "dilutes or enhances minority voting strength." Justice Stevens also issued a separate dissent. The Constitution does not "mandate any form of proportional representation, but it certainly permits a State to adopt a policy that promotes fair representation of different groups."

Texas gained three congressional seats as a result of population increases measured in the 1990 census. The redistricting plan drawn by the Texas legislature after the census created some "irregularly" shaped majority-minority districts. In addition to enhancing the prospect of electing minorities to Congress, the plan had nonrace-based objectives, such as protecting incumbent members of Congress. A three-judge U.S. district court ruled that the three new majority-minority districts were unconstitutional under the Supreme Court's decision in *Shaw I. Bush v. Vera*, 517 U.S. 952 (1996), gave the Court an opportunity to further develop criteria applying to redistricting cases in which race plays a prominent but not exclusive role. The Court struck down the Texas plan although the majority was split on the rationale. Justice O'Connor spoke for Chief Justice Rehnquist and Justice Kennedy. She saw no need to "revisit" the discussion from *Shaw I*, but rather focused on the particulars of the Texas plan and whether it met the requirements of that framework. The Constitution does not "mandate regularity of district shape," O'Connor said, and the "neglect of traditional districting criteria is merely necessary, not sufficient." In her view, the decision to create a majority-minority district is not in itself unconstitutional. In order for strict scrutiny to apply, traditional districting criteria must be *"subordinated to race."* O'Connor saw evidence of subordinating other factors to race. One component of that evidence was the decision to create majority-minority districts. Another component was the use of a computer program that was "significantly *more* sophisticated with respect to race than with respect to other demographic data." When this evidence was taken together, the trial court had substantial reason to believe that race led to the "neglect of traditional districting criteria." The strict scrutiny standard, on the other hand, does not apply to districting plans in which "traditional considerations predominated over racial ones." Political gerrymandering, for example, is not subject to strict scrutiny. Similarly, protecting incumbents has been recognized as serving a "legitimate state goal." If district lines "merely correlate" with race as a result of basing the lines on party affiliation that also correlate with race, then there is "no racial classification to justify." And if the goal is otherwise constitutional political gerrymandering, O'Connor continued, the state may freely use a range of political data such as precinct voting patterns to achieve its objective "regardless of its awareness of its racial implications." On the other hand, if race becomes a "proxy for political characteristics, a racial stereotype requiring strict scrutiny is in operation." It was O'Connor's conclusion that the district court had ample grounds in this case to find that "racially motivated gerrymandering had a qualitatively greater influence" on this districting plan than politically motivated gerrymandering, and that political gerrymandering was essentially accomplished "by the use of race as a proxy." Despite using the racial data in "complex ways" and for "multiple objectives does not mean that race did not predominate over other considerations." Indeed, the trial court record reflected "intensive and pervasive" use of race both as a "proxy to protect the political fortunes of adjacent incumbents, and for its own sake in maximizing the minority population [in one of the three districts] regardless of traditional districting principles." Justices Scalia and Thomas concurred separately. They agreed that the three Texas districts were unconstitutional, but were of the view that race could never be constitutionally taken into consideration. Justices Stevens, Souter, Ginsburg, and Breyer dissented. It was their view that in determining whether to apply strict scrutiny to the Texas plan, the Court improperly ignored the "complex interplay" of political and geographical factors that led to the creation of these particular districts. Instead, the Court focused exclusively on the "role race played in the State's decision to adjust the shape of its districts." Stevens noted the "irrational[ity]" of assuming that a person is not qualified to vote simply because of skin color or other physical characteristics. At the same time, it is neither "irrational nor invidious" to assume that a black resident of a particular community is a Democrat "if reliable statistical evidence discloses that 97 per cent of the blacks in that community vote in Democratic primary elections." For that reason, Stevens felt it as reasonable for those drawing the district lines in Texas to sometimes use racial data as a proxy for making political judgments as assuming that "wealthy suburbanites ... are more likely to be Republicans than communists."

The Supreme Court held in *Miller* that the boundaries for Georgia's Eleventh Congressional District were drawn with race being the "predominant" factor. A second suit was brought following *Miller* challenging the boundaries of the Second District, and a district court ruled that the Second suffered the same constitutional deficiencies as the Eleventh. The district court received plans from the parties to this suit when the state legislature was unable to fashion a new statewide congressional districting plan. The district court opted for the plan submitted by the group led by Davida Johnson that had originally challenged the plan containing the majority-minority districts, although the court's plan did retain one majority-minority district (the Fifth). The consolidated cases were docketed for review, but the Court refused to stay use of the district court's plan, and the November 1996 elections were conducted with district lines created in that plan. The incumbent African American representatives from the majority-minority districts struck down in the courts were both able to win reelection in the new districts. The Supreme Court then affirmed the lower court in *Abrams v. Johnson,* 521 U.S. 74 (1997). Justice Kennedy referred to the contested Eleventh District from the Justice Department's original plan with three majority-minority districts (called the max-black plan by critics) as a "geographic monstrosity." The Eleventh District stretched from Atlanta to Savannah with its "core in the plantation country" in the middle of the state. The district was "lightly populated, but heavily black" that linked by "narrow corridors the black neighborhoods in Augusta, Savannah, and southern DeKalb County." The Court found "strong support" for the conclusion that "Justice Department pressure led the State to act based on an overriding concern with race." Under these circumstances, said Kennedy, "the trial court acted well within its discretion in deciding it could not draw two majority-black districts without itself engaging in racial gerrymandering." Justice Breyer, in a dissent joined by Justices Stevens, Souter, and Ginsburg, portrayed the redistricting process as reflecting a wide range of pressures brought to bear by "many different individuals and groups using subtle and unsubtle suggestions, promises or threats, of votes, support, publicity, and even lawsuits." It was the dissenters' view that the Justice Department's role and influence on redistricting was not "any less legitimate."

Voting Rights Act of 1965

South Carolina v. Katzenbach, **383 U.S. 301 (1966),** upheld the Voting Rights Act of 1965. The Act abolished devices such as the literacy test and accumulated poll taxes by which citizens had been disqualified from voting. The Act also provided for extensive federal supervision of elections and required that any new conditions of voter eligibility be reviewed by the attorney general before implementation. Provisions of the Act were triggered if less than 50 percent of citizens of voting age were registered to vote or where fewer than 50 percent of the voting age population had participated in the 1964 presidential election. Chief Justice Warren emphasized that the purpose of the Act was "to banish the blight of racial discrimination in voting, which has infected the electoral process in parts of our country for nearly a century." The Court deferred to Congress even though it had exercised power in an inventive manner. Referring to the stringent remedies and their implementation without prior adjudication, the Court said that litigation was inadequate when discrimination was widespread and persistent. Following nearly a hundred years of systematic resistance to the Fifteenth Amendment, Congress might well decide to "shift the advantage of time and inertia from the perpetrators of the evil to its victims." The targeted nature of the Act's coverage was a reasonable legislative option. Congress determined that voting discrimination "presently occurs in certain sections of the country and to limit its attention to the geographic areas where immediate action seemed necessary." In sum, the Court viewed the Act as an array of potent weapons marshaled to combat the evil of voting discrimination. They were weapons that constitute, "a valid means for carrying out the commands of the Fifteenth Amendment." Justice Black was the sole dissenter in *Katzenbach*, and was troubled by the federalism implications of the preclearance requirement. The "inevitable effect" of a law that forces any of the states to "entreat federal authorities ... for approval of local laws ... is to create the impression that the States treated in this way are little more than conquered provinces." *See also City of Mobile v. Bolden*, p. 519; FIFTEENTH AMENDMENT, p. 630; *Shaw v. Reno*, p. 524; VOTING RIGHTS ACT OF 1965, p. 709.

Significance In upholding the Voting Rights Act of 1965, the Court targeted voting practices involving non-English-speaking voters for the first time. The Act had provisions intended for the large Spanish-speaking Puerto Rican population in New York. They were upheld on equal protection grounds in *Katzenbach v. Morgan*, 384 U.S. 641 (1966). The Act had a five-year duration, but was extended in 1970, 1975, and 1982. The 1970 extension banned the use of literacy tests. The same extension also set the minimum voting age at 18 throughout the country. The Court held in *Oregon v. Mitchell*, 400 U.S. 112 (1970), however, that Congress could only establish age qualifications for federal elections. States retained control over state and local elections. Ratification of the Twenty-Sixth Amendment in 1971 superseded the Court's decision in *Oregon v. Mitchell*. Primary elections also have attained constitutional status. After several decisions to the contrary, the Court held in *United States v. Classic*, 313 U.S. 299 (1941), that the federal government could regulate primaries because of their integral role in the overall election process. In *Smith v. Allwright*, 321 U.S. 649 (1944), the Court found that political parties conducting racially exclusive primaries were acting as an agent of the state and thus were in violation of the Fifteenth Amendment. The Court also outlawed the poll tax for state elections in *Harper v. Virginia State Board of Elections*, 383 U.S. 663 (1966), holding that such a tax discriminated in an invidious fashion.

The question in *Chisom v. Roemer*, 501 U.S. 380 (1991), was whether the "results test" contained in the 1982 amendment to the Voting Rights Act protects the right to vote in state judicial elections. The Court ruled that judicial elections are covered by the Act as amended. Prior to 1982 Section 2 was not violated absent a showing of discriminatory intent. The 1982 amendment substituted the results standard. Congress established that a violation would occur if portions of the electorate had less opportunity than others to "participate in the political process and to elect representatives of their choice." The question in *Chisom* rested on whether judges are "representatives." The Court concluded that they are. Justice Stevens began the majority opinion by noting that the Voting Rights Act had been enacted for the "broad remedial purpose" of eliminating racial discrimination in voting. Accordingly, the Act should be interpreted in a manner that provides the "broadest possible scope in combatting racial discrimination." The Court pointed to the "extensive legislative history" of the 1982 amendment. Had Congress intended to exclude judicial elections from the coverage of the Act, such intent would have been made explicit. Furthermore, Congress had replaced the term "legislators" with the word "representative" in the amendment. This substitution indicated "at the very least," said Stevens, "that Congress intended the amendment to cover more than legislative elections." Finally, the Court felt the "fundamental tension between the ideal character of the judicial office and the real world of electoral politics cannot be resolved by crediting judges with total indifference to the popular will while simultaneously requiring them to run for elective office." When each of several judges of a court must live in separate districts and be elected by the voters of those districts, it "seems both reasonable and realistic to characterize the winners as representatives of that district." Justice Scalia issued a dissent that was joined by Chief Justice Rehnquist and Justice Kennedy. Scalia said that the Act is not "some all-purpose weapon for well-intentioned judges to wield as they please in the battle against discrimination." Scalia saw the term "representative" as going beyond popular election to include the notion of acting on behalf of the people. A prosecutor, for example, acts on behalf of "the People" while a judge represents "the Law." Judges often must rule against the people in upholding the law, which is why "we do not ordinarily conceive of judges as representatives."

Section 5 of the Voting Rights Act requires "preclearance" by the federal government when a state covered by the Act attempts to change any "practice or procedure with respect to voting." The issue before the Court in *Presley v. Etowah County Commission*, 502 U.S. 491 (1992), and a companion case, *Mack v. Russell County Commission*, was whether a shifting of authority away from an elected official to another body was subject to the preclearance requirement. Prior to 1986 members of the Etowah and Russell County Commissions had been elected at-large but required to live in different districts. Each commissioner individually controlled all county bridge and road maintenance expenditures within his or her district. In the early

1980s the at-large election process was found to impermissibly dilute minority electoral influence, and the counties were ordered to move to a single-member district system. The election conducted in 1986 brought about the election of one black commissioner in Etowah County and two in Russell County. During the same period, both counties transferred control over bridge and road funds from individual commissioners to the county commissions as a whole. This meant that funds over which individual commissioners previously had full control were now pooled into a single countywide fund with expenditures governed by majority vote. This reassignment of function was made without Justice Department approval, but the Supreme Court ruled that the reorganization of the county commissions was not covered by Section 5 of the Voting Rights Act, and thus did not require preclearance. Justice Kennedy spoke for the Court. He noted that the Court had given Section 5 "broad construction" in previous cases. Those prior decisions, however, had recognized for Section 5 purposes only those changes that had a "direct relation to voting and the election process." Although the restructuring of commissioners' authority had the "effect of altering" county commission practices, the change had "no connection to voting procedures" or the "substance of voting power." Rather, the change "concerns the internal operations of an elected body." Application of Section 5 to such situations, said Kennedy, would "work an unconstrained expansion of its coverage." Because virtually any governmental decision "implicates voting," Kennedy expressed concern that no workable standard could be found to define the reach of Section 5 if extended beyond voting itself. The Voting Rights Act is "not an all-purpose antidiscrimination statute." The changes requiring preclearance "must bear a direct relation to voting itself." The changes under review in these cases "affected only the allocation of power among governmental officials" and must remain outside the reach of the Act. Kennedy concluded by saying that if "federalism is to operate as a practical system of governance and not a mere poetic ideal, the States must be allowed both predictability and efficiency in structuring their governments." Justice Stevens, joined by Justices Blackmun and White, dissented. They felt that the reallocation of authority under the circumstances present in these cases had the "same potential for discrimination" as changes from district to at-large voting or the gerrymandering of district boundaries. In their view, the decision left states free to "evade" the requirements of Section 5, and to "undermine" the objectives of the Act "simply by transferring the authority of an elected official, who happens to be black, to another official or group controlled by the majority."

Section 2 of the Voting Rights Act essentially prohibits use of a qualification to vote or a "standard, practice, or procedure" that abridges the right to vote on the basis of race or membership in a language minority. Dilution of the voting strength of a minority (or minorities) violates Section 2. The test for determining whether minority voting strength has been illegally diluted was set forth by the Court in *Thornburg v. Gingles*, 478 U.S. 30 (1986). If a minority group can demonstrate that its voters are "sufficiently numerous and compact" that they would constitute a majority in a district of a multi-member body, Section 2 is violated. The case of *Holder v. Hall*, 512 U.S. 874 (1994), considered whether the *Gingles* criteria apply to single-official electoral situations. Bleckley County, Georgia, oper-ated with a single commissioner form of county government; that is, a single commissioner possessed all legislative and executive authority. In 1985 the state legislature authorized the county to move to a five-member commission, but the proposal was defeated in a referendum. Black voters filed an action claiming that the single-commissioner system was maintained to limit the political influence of the minority population of the county, which constituted 23 percent. A federal court ordered a five-member commission with one district created to facilitate the election of a minority commissioner, but the Supreme Court reversed. The size of a governing body is not subject to a vote dilution challenge under Section 2 of the Voting Rights Act. There is no "objective and workable standard, said Justice Kennedy, in cases where the "challenge is brought to the size of a governing authority; there is no reason why one size should be selected over another." In this case, the challengers to the single-commissioner structure offered no convincing reasons why the bench mark should be a five-member commission. Neither the fact that a five-member commission is most commonly found in use in Georgia counties nor that Bleckley County was authorized to expand its commission up to five members constituted convincing evidence in the Court's view. Justices Thomas and Scalia also voted to overturn the lower court. Their reasoning, expressed in Justice Thomas's concurring opinion of almost 60 pages in length, differed substan-tially from that of Justice Kennedy. They felt that the size of a governing body was not a "standard, practice, or procedure" within the meaning of Section 2. Section 2 of the Voting Rights Act covers only those practices that affect ballot access by minority voters. Districting systems and election processes that affect the "weight" given a vote, on the other hand, are "simply beyond the purview of the Act." They urged that *Gingles* be overruled because it interpreted Section 2 as reaching vote dilution. By allowing consideration of dilu-tive electoral practices, the Supreme Court has devised remedial mechanisms that "encourage federal courts to segregate voters into racially designated districts to ensure minority electoral success." In doing so, the Court has "collaborated on what may be called the racial 'Balkanization' of the Nation." Thomas said he no longer joined a reading of the Voting Rights Act that has produced "such a disastrous misadventure in judicial policymaking." Justices Blackmun, Stevens, Souter, and Ginsburg dissented. They concluded that the single-commissioner system had the effect of diluting minority voting strength. It was their view that the Voting Rights Act had to be interpreted to effectively confront "subtler, more complex means of infringing minority voting strength."

Congress enacted the National Voter Registration Act in 1993 to facilitate voter registration. It allowed people to register to vote while getting drivers' licenses (hence the Act became known as the motor-voter law) or doing other state business. The Act applies to registration for federal offices exclusively, although states could use the process for state and local election registration as well. In addition, the Act provided that once registered, voters could not be purged from the voter rolls for not voting. Prior to the effective date of the Act, the secretary of state of Mississippi distributed an instructional manual to state and local officials indicating that the Act's procedures had been modified to include registration for all Mississippi elections. Mississippi submitted these changes to the Justice Department for preclearance under Section 5 of the Voting Rights Act. The new procedures for this "provisional" plan were approved. The Mississippi legislature, however, refused to act on a bill that would have statutorily reflected these changes. The Mississippi secretary of state and attorney general then issued a memorandum indicating that voters registered under the Act were not registered to vote in state and local elections. Instead, the memorandum instructed election officials to keep those registered under the Act separate from state-registered voters by using state procedures and state eligibility criteria. The Justice Department then sought materials from the state for preclearance review of the decision to treat registrants under the Act separately from those registered for state and local elections. When Mississippi failed to provide the necessary documents, the Justice Department and several Mississippi voters, including Thomas Young, filed suit seeking to bar implementation of the dual-registration system without Justice Department approval. The Supreme Court unanimously concluded in *Young v. Fordice*, 520 U.S. 273 (1997), that there had been no change from the electoral procedures used prior to the effective date of the Act, and that instructions to the contrary from the Mississippi secretary of state were unauthorized. Mississippi had argued that the "provisional" plan had been precleared and had become part of the baseline against which subsequent changes must be considered. It was the Court's judgment, however, that the "provisional" plan was never "in force or effect." Failure to formally enact the provisional plan, in turn, created a new registration system that was "significantly different from" the system in effect in 1994.

Suits were filed in federal court early in 1992 by various parties, each claiming that the 1990 census had revealed defects in both federal and state legislative district lines in Florida. Some of the plaintiffs alleged excessive population variance while others claimed unlawful dilution of minority voting strength. The Florida Supreme Court modified the plan when the state legislature did not do so. The court's plan increased the number of African Americans in one particular Tampa-area state senate district, although it stopped short of creating a district where African Americans constituted a majority of the voting age population. The three-judge federal district court hearing the original suit adopted the plan drawn by the Florida Supreme Court. An African American was eventually elected to the state senate from the district. Another federal suit was initiated by several Florida voters, including Martin Lawyer III, claiming that the state senate district was racially gerrymandered. The district court attempted to resolve the dispute through mediation. The various parties (and intervenors) who met with the court-appointed mediator agreed, except for Lawyer, on a redrawn district. The lower court concluded that, although some evidence existed to support the racial gerrymandering claim, no constitutional violation had been demonstrated. The Supreme Court disagreed in *Lawyer v. United States Department of Justice*, 117 S.Ct. 2186 (1997). It was the Court's judgment that the lower court need not find the challenged plan unconstitutional before allowing modification of the plan through mediation. The state chose to participate in the negotiations through its designated representatives. The Court saw no reason to "burden" the state's choice of how to pursue its own redistricting policy by requiring a "formal adjudication of unconstitutionality." Lawyer's choice not to join the settlement "could not preclude other parties from settling their own disputes." Although a settlement agreement may not "impose duties or obligations on an unconsenting party or dispose of his claims, the agreement here did none of those things." The settlement did not "cut him off" from a remedy to which he was entitled, but rather granted him an "element of the relief he had sought."

The Republican Party of Virginia chose to select its candidate for the U.S. Senate in 1994 by means of a nominating convention rather than a primary election. The party established a $45 registration fee as a condition of participating as a convention delegate. The registration fee was challenged on the ground that the fee needed Justice Department approval under terms of Section 5. The Supreme Court found for the challengers in *Morse v. Republican Party*, 517 U.S. 347 (1996), and extended the reach of the Voting Rights Act to party nominating conventions. Justice Stevens emphasized that the party was acting under state authority at the nominating convention. Virginia election law provided that nominees of the two major political parties would automatically appear on the general election ballot. The law allowed the two parties to determine how their nominees were to be selected. The party was "delegated the power to determine part of the field of candidates from which the voters must choose." The two major parties, said Stevens, "have no inherent right" to decide who may appear on the ballot. Rather, Virginia law confers the privilege. If the party "chooses to avail itself of this delegated power over the electoral process, it necessarily becomes subject to the regulation." Stevens also concluded that a filing fee for delegates "operates in precisely the same fashion" as earlier covered practices. By limiting the opportunities for voters to participate in the convention, the fee "undercuts their influence" on the field of candidates who could appear on the ballot, and thus "weakens the effectiveness of their votes cast in the general election itself." Justices Scalia, Thomas, and Kennedy each wrote separate dissents. Justice Scalia, joined by Justice Thomas, saw the ruling as encroaching on the First Amendment right of association. "Any interference" with the freedom of a political party is "simultaneously an interference with the freedom of its adherents." Justice Thomas agreed that parties may sometimes be characterized as state actors, but the state action principle "does not reach to all forms of private political activity." Use of the Act in suits like this "trivialises" the goal of preventing covered states from "intentionally and systematically evading the guarantees of the Voting Rights Act by simply recasting their election laws."

Residency Requirements

Shapiro v. Thompson, **394 U.S. 618 (1969),** held that residency requirements for welfare eligibility impermissibly restricted the right to move freely from state to state. *Shapiro v. Thompson* was a pivotal case in the development of expanded equal protection coverage under the Fourteenth Amendment. Once the Court decided that the Equal Protection Clause might apply to other than racial classifications, the Court was forced to examine the scope of the protection afforded and the standards by which classifications might be assessed. It determined that legislative classifications that interfered with "fundamental rights" were "suspect" and demanded "close scrutiny" by the courts. *Shapiro* involved a woman trying to obtain support under the Aid to Families with Dependent Children (AFDC) public assistance program. She was denied assistance because she could not satisfy the state's one-year residency requirement. The Court found the residency requirement unconstitutional. Justice Brennan said the effect of the waiting period requirement was to create two classes of needy resident families indistinguishable from each other except that one is composed of residents who have resided in the state a year or more and the other is composed of residents who have resided less than a year. The purpose of the requirement was to deter migration of needy persons into the state, and thus preserve the fiscal integrity of state public assistance programs. But the Court said inhibiting migration is constitutionally impermissible. It is a long-recognized right of citizens "to be free to travel throughout the length and breadth of our land uninhibited by statutes, rules, or regulations which unreasonably burden or restrain this movement." The right of interstate travel was held to be a fundamental right, and a classification that would "chill" the assertion of such a right is "patently unconstitutional." Classifications such as this that touch on the fundamental right of interstate movement must be assessed by the stricter standard of whether they promote a compelling state interest, and the arguments submitted by the state were not compelling. Chief Justice Warren and Justices Harlan and Black dissented, with Harlan saying that the branch of the compelling-interest doctrine associated with fundamental rights, as distinct from the branch dealing with suspect classes, is "unfortunate, unnecessary, and unwise when extended beyond racial classifications." *See also* EQUAL PROTECTION CLAUSE, p. 473; FOURTEENTH AMENDMENT, p. 651; TRAVEL, RIGHT TO, p. 708.

Significance   *Shapiro v. Thompson* led to the elimination of many residency requirements when provision of public services is involved, and it reduced voting registration residency requirements to a short duration. Some residency requirements have survived, however. State university in-state versus out-of-state tuition differences were allowed in *Vlandis v. Kline*, 412 U.S. 441 (1973), and residency requirements prior to securing divorces were upheld in *Sosna v. Iowa*, 419 U.S. 393 (1975), for example. *Shapiro* was the first of a series of cases involving access to public assistance as a matter of right. *Shapiro* did not directly address the question of whether welfare was to be protected as a fundamental right. Soon after *Shapiro*, the Court again refused to address that problem in *Dandridge v. Williams*, 397 U.S. 471 (1970). It upheld a ceiling on monthly aid to be received by any one family. The policy was challenged as overbroad, but the Court said that the concept of overreaching "has no place in cases which establish social and economic regulations." Although some aid payment disparities may be produced, the imperfection of classifications does not necessarily produce equal protection violations as long as there is a reasonable basis for the regulation.

In *Jefferson v. Hackney*, 406 U.S. 535 (1972), the Court allowed Texas to reduce aid payment limits to AFDC recipients, as well as to those receiving Old Age Assistance, Aid to the Blind, and Aid for Permanently and Totally Disabled Persons. The recipients of AFDC were overwhelmingly African American and Hispanic, while the other categories of recipients were largely white. The Court held that the aid levels of the various programs need not be comparable.

In *Graham v. Richardson*, 403 U.S. 365 (1971), the Court invalidated a state law imposing limitations on access to welfare benefits on the basis of alienage. It also ruled in *Goldberg v. Kelly*, 397 U.S. 254 (1970), that welfare recipients are entitled to formal hearings before welfare benefits can be terminated. Although the Court has established some limits on the use of residency requirements and protected access to public assistance benefits, none of its cases has established residency as a suspect classification. Neither has welfare been established as a fundamental right, although the United States recognized the special position of various forms of welfare by signing the Universal Declaration of Human Rights in 1948.

The Court has also examined the issue of whether preference can be extended on the basis of residency. Generally, resident preference policies have been found to be defective on privileges and immunities grounds. In *Hicklin v. Orbeck*, 437 U.S. 518 (1978), the Court struck down an Alaska law reserving jobs in the oil and gas development industry for qualified state residents. Similarly, the Court said that a municipal ordinance requiring hiring preference for city residents on all city construction projects was subject to privileges and immunities limitations. This was true even though a state did not discriminate against citizens of another state. A political subdivision of a state cannot discriminate against state residents not living within the political subdivision, in this case a city.

Aid to Families with Dependent Children is a federal welfare program created under the Social Security Act of 1935. The program is jointly funded by the federal and state governments. AFDC is administered by participating states under regulations formulated by the states and approved by the federal Department of Health and Human Services. As long as states remain within limits set by federal law, they are generally able to define eligibility requirements and establish benefit levels. The Court considered challenges to two California welfare provisions in *Anderson v. Edwards*, 514 U.S. 143 (1995), and *Anderson v. Green*, 514 U.S. 557 (1995). The question in *Edwards* was whether federal welfare law prohibits a state from grouping all needy children (whether or not they are siblings) living in the same household under the care of one adult into a single "assistance unit" (AU). The consolidation of two or more units into a single unit under the California rule decreased the maximum per capita

AFDC benefits for which the effected children were eligible. Edwards's situation is illustrative. As the caretaker of her grand-daughter, Edwards was eligible for maximum aid benefits of $341 monthly. Subsequently, she became caretaker of her two grandnieces (who were siblings) who were initially grouped together into a separate unit. The maximum benefits for this two-person unit was $560 monthly. Edwards received the maximum of $901 monthly in AFDC benefits for the three girls because none of the children received any outside income. Under the new rule, the three girls were grouped together into a single AU and eligible for maximum monthly payments of $694, a reduction of $207 per month from the amount received for two separate units. The Court must be cognizant of the "cardinal principle," said Thomas, that federal law "gives each State great latitude in dispensing available funds." From this perspective, the Court concluded that California was not precluded from adopting the new rule. Edwards argued that the reduction of the granddaughter's per capita benefits was solely the result of the presence of the grandnieces, children who were "not legally responsible individuals" in relation to the granddaughter. Thomas dismissed this argument as "simply wrong." The presence of grandnieces was not solely responsible for the decline in per capita benefits for the granddaughter. To be sure, the grandnieces were part of Edwards's household. Equally important was that the application for AFDC assistance for the grandnieces came through Edwards. Had the grandnieces not applied for AFDC assistance or applied through a different caretaker relative living in that home, the California rule would not have affected the granddaughter's level of benefits. Proof of state residency as a condition for enrolling in a tuition-free public school was upheld in *Martinez v. Bynum*, 461 U.S. 321 (1983). Texas law permitted a public school district to deny admission to a minor living apart from parents or legal guardians if his or her presence in the district is for the "primary purpose" of attending the free public school. A uniformly applied residence requirement furthered the state interest of "assuring that services provided for the State's residents are enjoyed only by residents." The requirement "simply required" that persons establish residence before demanding the services that are restricted to residents. With such requirements, the "proper planning and operation of the schools would suffer significantly." The previous year, however, the Court held in *Plyler v. Doe*, 457 U.S. 202 (1982), that a state may not withhold funds to school districts to be used to educate students who are not legal residents in the United States. The Supreme Court concluded that whatever the status of a person under the immigration laws, an alien is nonetheless a "person" within the meaning of the Fourteenth Amendment.

Alienage

***Graham v. Richardson*, 403 U.S. 365 (1971),** prohibited a state classification based on alienage. *Graham v. Richardson* held that classifications based on alienage were "suspect," and, as a result, subject to "strict scrutiny" review. Richardson was a lawfully admitted resident alien who had become permanently and totally disabled. She applied for public assistance benefits under provisions of the Social Security Act, which offered financial assistance to persons with the disabilities she had. She met all the requirements for benefits except for a 15-year residency requirement for aliens. The Supreme Court unanimously ruled the requirement unconstitutional on Fourteenth Amendment grounds. Justice Blackmun suggested that states generally have been accorded broad discretion to classify, especially in the areas of "economics and social welfare." Yet "classifications based on alienage, like those based on nationality or race, are inherently suspect and subject to close judicial scrutiny." Aliens are a prime example of a "discrete and insular minority" for whom such heightened judicial solicitude is appropriate. The Arizona requirement was defective because it created two classes of needy persons, indistinguishable except with respect to whether they are or are not citizens of the United States. Arizona sought to justify its classification on the basis of "a special public interest in favoring its own citizens over aliens in the distribution of limited resources such as welfare benefits." The Court disagreed that such a special interest existed, even though Arizona had "a valid interest in preserving the fiscal integrity of its programs." But a state cannot accomplish even valid purposes by invidious distinctions, and "the saving of welfare costs cannot justify an otherwise invidious classification."

The fiscal integrity rationale was found no more compelling in *Graham* than in *Shapiro v. Thompson*, 394 U.S. 618 (1969). Unlike *Shapiro*, however, the justification is "particularly inappropriate where the discriminated class consists of aliens." Aliens, like citizens, pay taxes and may be called into the armed forces. Unlike the short-term residents involved in *Shapiro*, aliens may live within a state for many years, work in the state, and contribute to the economic growth of the state. Thus no special public interest approach can apply to distribution of tax benefits to which aliens have contributed on an equal basis with residents of the state. Finally, the Court held that the federal government has overriding and superior authority in this field. Federal power is preemptive of state regulation, and Congress "has not seen fit to impose any burden or restriction on aliens who become indigent after their entry into the United States." *See also* CLASSIFICATION, p. 628; EQUAL PROTECTION CLAUSE, p. 473; FOURTEENTH AMENDMENT, p. 651; *Shapiro v. Thompson*, p. 538.

Significance   *Graham v. Richardson* found alienage to be a suspect classification when used by states as the basis for denial of welfare benefits. In *Sugarman v. Dougall*, 413 U.S. 634 (1973), the Court used the *Graham* rationale to strike down a state civil service statute precluding aliens from competing for state civil service jobs. Alienage does not retain suspect status in all contexts, however. In *Mathews v. Diaz*, 426 U.S. 67 (1976), the Court unanimously upheld a Social Security Act provision denying Medicare supplemental medical insurance to aliens unless they had been admitted for permanent residence and had resided in the United States for at least five years. The Court deferred to the federal government's comprehensive authority regarding immigration and citizenship and evaluated the classification using the less stringent rationality test.

Alienage classifications are also subject to the rational standard test rather than the compelling state interest test associated with strict scrutiny when vital governmental functions are involved. In *Foley v. Connelie*, 435 U.S. 291 (1978), the Court upheld a New York regulation limiting state police appointments to citizens. Suggesting that it would be inappropriate to require every statutory exclusion of aliens to clear the high hurdle of strict scrutiny, the Court held that the police function is a basic function of government and the right to govern may be reserved to citizens.

In *Ambach v. Norwich*, 441 U.S. 68 (1979), the Court upheld a statute preventing a noncitizen from becoming certified to teach in the public schools. Using the rational basis test, the Court held that a state could restrict the performance of those functions that go to the heart of representative government to persons who have become part of the process of self-government. The same approach was used in *Cabell v. Chavez-Salido*, 454 U.S. 432 (1982), to uphold a California law requiring "peace officers," including deputy probation officers, to be citizens. It is clear that the Supreme Court subjects to strict scrutiny any restriction on aliens that affects their economic interests, but it uses a less stringent standard when the restriction involves political activity.

Lorelyn Miller was born out of wedlock in the Philippines. Her mother was a Filipino and her father was an American citizen. At the age of 22 Miller unsuccessfully applied for American citizenship. Her father then obtained a paternity decree from a Texas court, and the daughter reapplied for citizenship. The application was again denied, this time because the paternity decree did not satisfy that provision of federal law requiring that a child born out of wedlock and outside the United States to an alien mother and an American father "must be legitimated before age 18 in order to acquire citizenship." Miller and her father brought suit in federal court in Texas seeking a judgment declaring her to be a U.S. citizen. They argued that citizenship of an out-of-wedlock, foreign-born child of an alien father and an American mother is established at birth, and that the law's different treatment of citizen fathers and noncitizen mothers violated the Equal Protection Clause. The Supreme Court acknowledged in *Miller v. Albright*, 118 S.Ct. 1428 (1998), that different citizenship qualifications had been established for the two classes of children, but six justices concluded that the distinction was neither "arbitrary nor invidious." Justice Stevens, joined by Chief Justice Rehnquist, found a "vast difference" between the burdens imposed on the respective parents of potential citizens born out of wedlock in a foreign land—the female citizen's burdens were "obvious[ly] more severe." Requiring reliable proof of a biological relationship between the potential citizen and its citizen parent is an "important governmental objective." Male and female parents are "undeniably differently situated" in this respect. The blood relationship to the birth mother is "immediately obvious" and is easily documented. The relationship to the birth father, on the other hand, may often be "undisclosed and unrecorded." Surely the fact that the statute allows 18 years for the father to provide evidence that is "comparable to what the mother provides immediately after birth cannot be viewed as discriminating against the father or his child." Justice Stevens suggested that the statute also served two other important purposes unrelated to the determination of paternity—the interest in "encouraging the development of a healthy relationship between the citizen parent and the child" while the child is a minor, and the related interest in "fostering ties between the foreign-born child and the United States." Stevens and Rehnquist also concluded that the gender equality principle was only "indirectly" involved in this case. Lorelyn Miller was not a citizen for reasons other than the gender of her father. Even if her mother had been a citizen and her father had been the alien, she would not qualify for citizenship because her mother had never been in the United States. Furthermore, it is not merely the sex of the citizen parent that determines whether the child is a citizen. It is, instead, an "event creating a legal relationship between parent and child—the birth itself for citizen mothers, but post-birth conduct for citizen fathers and their offspring." Justices O'Connor and Kennedy said that the law was unconstitutional under the standard of "heightened scrutiny" that applies to gender-based differences of treatment. The victim of gender discrimination here was the father and not his daughter. In their view, he ought to have been able to transfer citizenship in a manner similar to that of a citizen mother. The sex discrimination claim, however, could not be advanced by the daughter because she did not have standing to introduce her father's claim. Justices Scalia and Thomas would have dismissed the daughter's suit on the grounds that only Congress, not the courts, could define conditions of citizenship. Justices Ginsburg, Breyer, and Souter argued that the daughter could assert claims on behalf of her father as well as for herself. They saw both the father and the daughter as victims of discrimination "solely on the ground of the parent's gender."

The Supreme Court upheld the current United States policy of intercepting vessels attempting to illegally transport Haitians to the United States in *Sale v. Haitian Centers Council, Inc.*, 509 U.S. 155 (1993). Interception typically occurs before the vessels reach U.S. territorial waters. The Haitian passengers are summarily returned to Haiti without determination of whether they might qualify as refugees. The policy was challenged on the grounds that it violated the 1980 amendments to the Immigration and Nationality Act and Article 33 of the United Nations Protocol Relating to the Status of Refugees. With only Justice Blackmun dissenting, the Supreme Court ruled that neither the Act nor the U.N. Protocol were violated. Justice Stevens spoke for the Court. Aliens residing illegally in the United States may be deported following a formal hearing. Aliens arriving at the border are subject to removal following a less formal exclusion hearing. In either situation, the alien may seek asylum as a political refugee. Provisions of the Act afford hearings only to aliens who reside in or have arrived at the border. For a number of years, the interdiction policy challenged in this case prevented Haitians, among others, from getting to "our shores and invoking those protections." Under terms of the Act when enacted in 1952, the attorney general was given authority to stop deportation proceedings for any alien "within the United States" who would be deported to a country where the alien would be persecuted "on account of race, religion or political opinion." The Act was amended in 1980 and the phrase "within the United States" was removed. The word "return" was added to the phrase "deport or return." It was the Court's judgment that addition of the word "return" was intended to clarify Congress's intention to prevent summary return of two kinds of aliens, those who had been admitted to the United States and were subject to deportation, and "excludable aliens" who were in the country or at the border but had never been admitted. It was the Court's view that removal of the phrase "within the United States" was simply an effort to protect the latter category in the same way "deportable aliens" are already protected. Like the relevant sections of the Act, the Court concluded that the United Nations Protocol is "completely silent with respect to the Article's possible application to actions taken by a country outside its own borders." In spite of the "moral weight" of the argument that a nation be prevented from repatriating refugees to their "potential oppressors," the text and negotiating history of Article 33 "affirmatively indicate that it was not intended to have extraterritorial effect." Justice Blackmun strongly disagreed. The Haitians did not claim a right to admission to the country. Rather, all they sought was for the United States to "cease forcibly driving them back to detention, abuse and death. That is a modest plea, vindicated by the Treaty and the statute. We should not close our ears to it."

Illegitimacy

Weber v. Aetna Casualty & Surety Co., **406 U.S. 164 (1972),** struck down a state classification based on legitimacy as a violation of the Equal Protection Clause of the Fourteenth Amendment. *Weber v. Aetna Casualty & Surety Co.* examined the classification of illegitimacy and held that a state handling claims for workers' compensation benefits may not disadvantage the unacknowledged illegitimate child of a deceased worker. Henry Stokes died from employment-related injuries. At the time of his death, Stokes was living with four legitimate minor children, one unacknowledged minor, and Willie Mae Weber, the mother of the unacknowledged minor. Stokes's wife had been committed to a mental institution prior to his death. After Stokes's death, a second illegitimate child of Stokes and Weber was born. The Louisiana workers' compensation law placed unacknowledged illegitimate children in a class of "other dependents," a class of lower status than that of "children." The "other dependents" class could recover workers' compensation benefits only if the higher class of survivors did not exhaust the maximum benefits. The four legitimate offspring of Stokes were awarded the statutory maximum, leaving nothing to the two unacknowledged illegitimate children.

The Supreme Court ruled that this statutory scheme violated the Equal Protection Clause of the Fourteenth Amendment. Justice Powell's opinion declared the statute to be unacceptable even though it was limited to unacknowledged illegitimate children and did not prohibit recovery altogether. The less favorable position into which the unacknowledged illegitimate child was placed was said to be unconstitutional because "such a child may suffer as much from the loss of a parent as a child born within wedlock or any illegitimate later acknowledged." Louisiana law precluded acknowledgment of the illegitimate child even if the father had wished to do so. Powell observed that "the burdens of illegitimacy, already weighty, become doubly so when neither parent nor child can legally lighten them." He suggested that the Court's inquiry into such cases turned on two questions: What legitimate state interest does the classification promote, and what fundamental personal rights might the classification endanger. The Court did not take issue with Louisiana's interest in protecting legitimate family relationships, but it did not feel that the challenged statute promoted that interest. "Persons will not shun illicit relations because their offspring may not one day reap the benefits of workmen's compensation." While illegitimacy has been socially condemned through the ages, Justice Powell thought that visiting this condemnation on the head of an infant is illogical and unjust. Penalizing the illegitimate child is simply an ineffectual way of deterring the parent. Justice Rehnquist felt that the Court was engaged in a highly subjective review of what constituted legitimate state interests and how those interests might be advanced in relation to fundamental personal rights. He would have deferred to Louisiana's distinction between legitimate and unacknowledged illegitimate children. *See also* CLASSIFICATION, p. 628; EQUAL PROTECTION CLAUSE, p. 473; FOURTEENTH AMENDMENT, p. 651; RIGHT OF PRIVACY, p. 476.

Significance   *Weber* said that a state could not deny equal benefit recovery opportunities to unacknowledged illegitimate children. But the Supreme Court has never been able to determine conclusively the exact character of illegitimacy as a classification or the level of scrutiny it deserves. The Court has scrutinized the problem more closely than the rationality test would require, but it has never found illegitimacy to be a suspect class deserving the strictest scrutiny. Examples of the Court's crisscrossing path in dealing with this classification follow.

In *Levy v. Louisiana*, 391 U.S. 68 (1968), the Court struck down a law that denied unacknowledged illegitimate children opportunity to recover damages for the wrongful death of their mothers. The statute was viewed as sufficiently arbitrary that impermissible discrimination could be found by use of standards less demanding than strict scrutiny. In *Labine v. Vincent*, 401 U.S. 532 (1971), however, the Court upheld a state succession law that denied illegitimate children equal inheritance rights to those of legitimate children. The Court said a state had the power to protect and strengthen family life as well as to regulate the disposition of property. *Weber* was next in the sequence and resembled more closely the approach taken in *Levy*. *Mathews v. Lucas*, 427 U.S. 495 (1976), then held that a requirement demanding proof of dependency by illegitimate children seeking social security death benefits was a rational means of protecting against survivor benefits being paid to children who were not dependent. The Court noted in *Lucas* that statutory classifications based on illegitimacy fall into "a realm of less than strict scrutiny." Claiming that such less-than-strict scrutiny was not "toothless," the Court a year later struck down an Illinois statute that precluded illegitimate children from inheriting property from their fathers in *Trimble v. Gordon*, 430 U.S. 762 (1977). Using a rationale closely resembling that of *Weber*, the Court found the classification too remote from a legitimate state purpose to pass review. Finally, in *Pickett v. Brown*, 462 U.S. 1 (1983), the Court disallowed a statute barring paternity suits brought on behalf of illegitimate children more than two years after their birth. The Court unanimously concluded that the state infringed upon the illegitimate child's opportunity to secure support and that the two-year period did not sufficiently advance the state's interest in preventing litigation of stale and possibly fraudulent claims.

Age

McKennon v. Nashville Banner Publishing Co., **513 U.S. 352 (1995)**
Christine McKennon was fired by the Nashville Banner Publishing Company after 39 years of service as a secretary. She was 62 years of age at the time of her discharge. The *Banner* claimed that her termination was part of a larger plan to downsize the workforce. McKennon contended that her discharge was prompted by considerations of her age. She sought relief under the Age Discrimination in Employment Act (ADEA) of 1967. Prior to trial, McKennon was deposed by counsel for the *Banner*. It was discovered that prior to her discharge, McKennon had copied and taken several confidential company documents. On the basis of this after-acquired evidence, McKennon's suit was dismissed on the ground that her misconduct justified the termination even though the *Banner* conceded that age discrimination motivated the firing. The question before the Court in *McKennon* was whether an employee fired in violation of the ADEA is barred from any relief if the employer subsequently discovers evidence of misconduct that would have led to lawful discharge. The Court unanimously ruled that McKennon was still entitled to relief under ADEA. Justice Kennedy spoke for the Court. The Court assumed that McKennon's age was the sole reason for her initial discharge, and that the discharge was unlawful under the ADEA. The Court further presumed that the misconduct revealed by the deposition was sufficiently serious that her discharge would necessarily follow its disclosure. The Court ruled that "after-acquired" evidence did not provide a complete defense for an employer; in other words, after-acquired evidence of misconduct that would have resulted in termination does not necessarily prevent an employee from relief under the ADEA. In the Supreme Court's view, McKennon's misconduct did not render "irrelevant" the question of whether she was the victim of discrimination. The ADEA violation, said Kennedy, "cannot be so altogether disregarded." The objectives of the ADEA are furthered when "even a single employee establishes that an employer has discriminated against him or her." Unlike other cases in which two or mixed motives are involved, this case came to the Court on the

assumption that an unlawful motive was the sole basis for the termination. The *Banner* could not have been motivated by knowledge it did not have, and it "cannot now claim that the employee was fired for the nondiscriminatory reason." Even though the *Banner* violated the ADEA, the Court considered how the after-acquired evidence of McKennon's misconduct affected the matter of remedy. The employee's wrongdoing "must be taken into account ... lest the employer's legitimate concerns be ignored." Under the ADEA, the employee's misconduct is relevant in order to "take due account of the lawful prerogatives of the employer in the usual course of its business and the corresponding equities that it has arising from the employee's wrongdoing." Resolution of the backpay issue must recognize that an ADEA violation occurred that must be "deterred and compensated" without undue infringement on the employer's rights. If an employer learns about any misconduct on the part of the employee that would lead to legitimate termination, the Court cannot require the employer to ignore the information. The beginning point in the fashioning of remedial orders should be calculation of backpay from the date of unlawful discharge to the date the new information was discovered. A court can then take into account "extraordinary equitable circumstances" that affect the legitimate interests of either party. An absolute rule barring any recovery of backpay, however, "would undermine the ADEA's objective of forcing employers to consider and examine their motivations, and of penalizing them for employment decisions that spring from age discrimination." *See also* CLASSIFICATION, p. 628; EQUAL PROTECTION CLAUSE, p. 473; FOURTEENTH AMENDMENT, p. 651.

Significance   The first important ruling on age classification came in *Massachusetts Board of Retirement v. Murgia*, 427 U.S. 307 (1976), in which the Court upheld a mandatory retirement age of 50 for uniformed police officers against Fourteenth Amendment challenge. The rationality test is typically used in reviewing age-based classifications. Key to the Court's holding in the case was the criteria used to assess the mandatory retirement policy. Murgia argued that age was a "suspect class" and entitled to a "strict scrutiny" review, a more stringent review than that associated with the rationality test. The Court disagreed and held that Murgia did not belong to a suspect class. The Court upheld the mandatory retirement law and determined that the strict scrutiny approach should be used only when the classification impermissibly interferes with the exercise of a fundamental right or operates to the particular disadvantage of a suspect class. In the Court's view the Massachusetts policy involved neither situation. It reviewed the mandatory retirement policy by using the rational basis standard. Under this standard, the legislature's actions are presumed to be valid, and "perfection in making the necessary classification is neither possible nor necessary." The legislature sought "to protect the public by assuring the physical preparedness of its uniformed police." Given the fact that physical ability generally declines with age, the Court found the mandatory retirement policy rationally related to the state's objective. It concluded that although the choice of policy by Massachusetts may not be the best means, and that it was possible that a more just and humane system could be devised, under the rational basis test the enactment did not deny equal protection. Justice Marshall would have preferred a flexible standard that would have examined more carefully the means chosen by Massachusetts.

Soon after *Murgia*, the Court upheld a mandatory retirement policy for Foreign Service officers in *Vance v. Bradley*, 440 U.S. 93 (1979). Again the Court found a retirement policy rationally related to the legislative goal of assuring the professional capacity of persons holding critical public service positions. In this case, Foreign Service officers have to undergo special rigors associated with overseas duty.

Not all age discrimination suits have been unsuccessful, however. In *Trans World Airlines, Inc. v. Thurston*, 469 U.S. 111 (1985), the Court unanimously held that an airline's policy of not permitting the automatic transfer of age-disqualified captains to other positions with the company was a violation of the Age Discrimination in Employment Act of 1967. The *Thurston* decision was soon followed by two other important rulings on the same federal law. In *Western Air Lines, Inc. v. Criswell*, 472 U.S. 400 (1985), the Court unanimously held that an airline could not require mandatory retirement of flight engineers at age 60. Unlike the situation of pilots and copilots, in which age was considered a bona fide occupational qualification, the Court felt that flight engineers could be individually assessed rather than subjected to blanket early retirement rules. In *Equal Employment Opportunity Commission v. Wyoming*, 460 U.S. 226 (1983), the Court ruled that state and local governments are not immune from provisions of the Age Discrimination in Employment Act. This Act prohibits employer discrimination against any employee or potential employee because of age. The Court made it clear, however, that the judgment did not compel a state to abandon policies that can demonstrate age as a bona fide occupational qualification. Central to the decisions in both *Murgia* and *Bradley* was the conclusion that compulsory retirement would enable good job performance by limiting the age of employees. Both cases sought to maximize the physical capabilities of persons performing certain lay functions. The Missouri state constitution establishes 70 as the mandatory retirement age for state judges. The Court upheld the mandatory retirement provision in *Gregory v. Ashcroft*, 501 U.S. 452 (1991), against challenges brought by a number of state judges subject to the requirement. The judges asserted that the requirement violated both the ADEA and the Equal Protection Clause of the Fourteenth Amendment. The Court ruled on Tenth Amendment grounds that there was no ADEA violation. Justice O'Connor said that the authority of the people of a state to set qualifications of government officials "lies at the heart of representative government." Making such a decision is one of the "most fundamental sort for a sovereign entity." Because congressional interference with Missouri's decision would "upset the usual constitutional balance of federal and state powers," courts must be certain that congressional intent to do so is "unmistakably clear." No such level of certainty existed here. The Court also rejected the Equal Protection Clause challenge. In order to overturn the mandatory requirement provision, it must be demonstrated that the classification is so unrelated to a legitimate objective as to be irrational. The Court said that it is quite rational that the people of a state could conclude that the risk of mental and/or physical deterioration at age 70 is sufficiently great, in the absence of effective alternatives, to warrant mandatory retirement. The Court saw the interest in maintaining a capable judiciary as not only legitimate but "compelling."

The case of *Hazen Paper Company v. Biggins*, 507 U.S. 604 (1993), involved another action arising from the Age Discrimination in Employment Act. Thomas Biggins was fired by Hazen Paper after almost 10 years of employment. He was 62 when terminated, and was just short of the time in service needed for his pension benefits to vest. A jury found a "willful" violation of the ADEA and awarded damages to Biggins. The central question considered by the Supreme Court was whether interference with the vesting of pension benefits violates the ADEA. In a disparate treatment case such as this, said Justice O'Connor, liability "depends on whether the protected trait (age in the case of ADEA) actually motivated the employer's decision." Regardless of the employer's decision-making process, a disparate treatment claim "cannot succeed unless the employee's protected trait actually played a role in that process and had a determinative influence on the outcome." When, however, an employer's decision is motivated by factors other than age, the "problem of inaccurate and stigmatizing stereotypes disappears." This is true "even if the motivating factor is correlated with age, as pension status typically is." The Court saw age and years of service as "analytically distinct"; an employer could "take account of one while ignoring the other." Thus, the Court concluded that it is "incorrect to say that a decision based on years of service is necessarily 'age-based.' A decision to fire an older employee solely because of years of service would "not constitute discriminatory treatment on the basis of age," said O'Connor.

The ADEA protects any worker 40 years of age or older from employment discrimination based on age. James O'Connor was terminated at the age of 56 by his employer and replaced. The employee given his job, however, was within the age scope of ADEA. The question in *O'Connor v. Consolidated Coin Caterers Corp.*, 517 U.S. 308 (1996), was whether an age discrimination claim can be made when a protected worker is replaced by a younger worker who also falls within the class protected by the ADEA—a worker whose age is 40 or older. A lower court dismissed O'Connor's case because no age discrimination could be inferred when the replacement employee is 40 years of age or older, but the Supreme Court disagreed. The ADEA does not prohibit discrimination against employees "because they are age 40 or older." Rather, the law bans discrimination against employees "because of their age." Although the ADEA defines the protected class as those who are 40 or older, the fact that a person in the protected class loses to another person in the protected class is "irrelevant," so long as the employee has lost out because of age. There can be "no greater inference of age discrimination (as opposed to '40 or over' discrimination)," said Scalia, "when a 40-year-old is replaced by a 39-year-old than when a 56-year-old is replaced by a 40-year-old." The ADEA prohibits discrimination on the basis of age rather than class membership. The fact that a replacement is "substantially younger than the plaintiff is a far more reliable indicator of age discrimination than is the fact that the plaintiff was replaced by someone outside the protected class."

Title II of the Older Workers Benefit Protection Act of 1990 (OWBPA) requires that waiver of any ADEA claim must be both knowing and voluntary. Delores Oubre received a poor performance evaluation from Entergy Operations in 1995. She was given the choice of improving her performance or accepting a voluntary severance proposal. Oubre was given 14 days to make her choice. Oubre agreed to the severance proposal and accepted payment in excess of $6,000 in exchange for a signed blanket promise not to raise any claims for damages in the future. The release failed to comply with the ADEA requirement that an employee must be given at least 21 days to consider a severance offer. Oubre filed an age discrimination complaint with the Equal Employment Opportunity Commission (EEOC) followed by an ADEA claim in federal district court. Entergy argued that Oubre had validated the agreement—including the nonconforming provisions in the release—by retaining the severance payment. The Supreme Court disagreed in *Oubre v. Entergy Operations, Inc.*, 118 S.Ct. 838 (1998), ruling that because the release did not comply with statutory requirements, it could not bar Oubre's ADEA claim. Entergy had based its arguments on state contract law and the doctrine of equitable estoppel, which bars someone from "shirking the burdens of a voidable transaction" as long as the benefits received under it are retained. The Court found this argument insufficient to overcome the specific directives contained in the OWBPA. Justice Kennedy said the statutory command "is clear: an employee may not waive an ADEA claim unless the waiver or release satisfies the OWBPA's requirements." The OWBPA implements congressional policy through a "strict, unqualified statutory stricture on waivers, and we are bound to take Congress at its word." Congress imposed specific duties on employers who seek release from certain claims created by statute. Congress "delineated these duties with precision and without qualification." The text of OWBPA "forecloses" the defense asserted by Entergy, "notwithstanding how general contract principles would apply to non-ADEA claims." A decision favoring the employer in this case, said Kennedy, "would frustrate the statute's practical operation as well as its formal command." In many instances, a discharged employee will likely have spent some or all of the monies received and will be unable to return the severance payment. These realities might "tempt employers to risk noncompliance with the OWBPA's waiver provisions," knowing that their severance payments would be difficult for the discharged employee to repay and relying on ratification that would result from failure to return the payment. "We ought not to open the door to an evasion of the statute by this device."

Wealth

San Antonio Independent School District v. Rodriguez, 411 U.S. 1 (1973), approved a state system for financing public education using locally levied property taxes. *San Antonio Independent School District v. Rodriguez* raised two provocative questions: (1) whether public education is one of the fundamental rights that a state can limit only by showing a compelling interest, and (2) whether indigence constitutes a suspect classification under the evolving equal protection standards of the Fourteenth Amendment. The *Rodriguez* case involved a challenge of the funding mechanisms for public education in Texas. A portion of the educational costs was provided by state appropriations, with local districts supplementing these revenues by locally levied property taxes. Suit was brought asserting that this funding approach created inequities among school districts because some were disadvantaged by low or limited property tax bases. It was argued that the differences in property tax yields produced impermissible disparities in per pupil expenditures.

The Court distinguished *Rodriguez* from prior cases involving indigence. Typically, indigents are unable to pay for a particular benefit so that "an absolute deprivation of a meaningful opportunity to enjoy that benefit occurs." Even in the poorest Texas school districts, however, children were receiving some kind of public education. This led the Court to conclude that the Texas system "does not operate to the particular disadvantage of any suspect class." Further, striking down the educational financing system in Texas would require it to intrude in an area in which it had traditionally deferred to state legislatures. The Court said that it was impossible to devise a scheme of taxation that would be completely free of discriminatory impacts. Although the Texas system "provides less freedom of choice with respect to expenditures from some districts than for others, the existence of some inequality in the manner in which the state's rationale is achieved is not alone a sufficient basis for striking down the entire system." Insofar as wealth was concerned, the Equal Protection Clause "does not require absolute equality or precisely equal advantages." The Court also concluded that the importance of a service performed by the state does not determine whether it must be regarded as fundamental for Equal Protection Clause purposes. While noting the historical importance of public education, the Court did not regard education as a fundamental right. Justices Brennan, Marshall, Douglas, and White were critical of the Court's "rigidified approach to equal protection analysis." The dissenters would have deemed education a fundamental right and found the Texas financing system invidiously discriminatory. *See also* CLASSIFICATION, p. 628; EQUAL PROTECTION CLAUSE, p. 473; FOURTEENTH AMENDMENT, p. 651.

Significance   *Rodriguez* upheld a school financing system that produced disparities in local tax yields against claims that such inequities constituted impermissible economic discrimination. *James v. Valtierra*, 402 U.S. 137 (1971), contained quite a different income-related issue. In *Valtierra*, the Court had upheld a state constitutional requirement that all low-income housing projects be approved by local referendum. The Court said that a procedure that disadvantages a particular group does not always deny equal protection.

At the same time, a wealth classification that interferes with a fundamental right is typically invalidated. In *Harper v. Virginia State Board of Elections*, 383 U.S. 663 (1966), the Court declared a state poll tax unconstitutional because it discriminated against the poor. The Court said that the qualification to vote should have no relation to wealth.

The impacts of indigence have also been recognized with respect to ensuring procedural protections for those accused of crimes. The vulnerability of indigents in this context is seen in *Tate v. Short*, 401 U.S. 391 (1971), in which the Court held that an indigent person could not be jailed as a substitute for payment of penal fines. Even earlier, the Court required states to provide legal counsel for indigent felony defendants.

M.L.B. had her parental rights to three minor children terminated in a Mississippi Chancery Court on a finding that she was an unfit mother. Parental rights were then awarded to her ex-husband and his new wife. M.L.B. filed notice to appeal on the grounds that the judgment of the trial court was not supported by "clear and convincing" evidence. State law required that the party attempting to obtain reversal of a court judgment provide a transcript from the trial. The cost of preparing such a record in this case exceeded $2,300. M.L.B. could not pay the fee, and was subsequently notified that she had 14 days to pay the fee or have her appeal dismissed. She then filed a motion seeking to have the fee waived, but the motion was denied because Mississippi law did not provide for waiver of fees for appeals arising out of civil judgments. The Supreme Court ruled in *M.L.B. v. S.L.J.*, 519 U.S. 102 (1996), that states must allow indigents to appeal orders to terminate parental rights even if they cannot pay required fees. Justice Ruth Bader Ginsburg said that choices about "marriage, family life, and the upbringing of children" are among the associational rights ranked as being of "basic importance in our society." These rights are "sheltered" by the due process and equal protection provisions of the Fourteenth Amendment against the state's "unwarranted usurpation, disregard, or disrespect." Ginsburg suggested that the loss of a parent's relationship with children is of "such magnitude and permanence" as to make it "barely distinguishable from criminal condemnation." In this case, M.L.B. was endeavoring to defend against the state's "destruction of her family," and to "resist the brand associated with a parental unfitness adjudication." Like an accused defending against criminal conviction, M.L.B. sought to be "spared from the State's devastatingly adverse action." Ginsburg carefully distinguished termination of parental rights and the loss of custody. The latter does not "sever the parent-child bond," while parental status termination is "irretrievably destructive of the most fundamental relationship." Furthermore, the risk of error is "considerable." Only a transcript can reveal the sufficiency, or insufficiency, of the evidence to supporting judgments. Justice Thomas, joined by Chief Justice Rehnquist and Justice Scalia, dissented. He was critical of Ginsburg's use of precedent requiring waiver of fees in the preparation of transcripts in criminal cases. Thomas was also troubled by the prospect of this case becoming more broadly applicable. The "inevitable consequence will be greater demands on the states to provide free assistance to would-be appellants in all manner of civil cases that cannot ... be distinguished from the admittedly important interest at issue here."

Gender

***United States v. Virginia*, 518 U.S. 515 (1996)** Virginia Military Institute (VMI) was a male-only state college. The United States sought to open the school to women in 1990. A U.S. district court found, however, that VMI provided an educational experience that could not be obtained if women were included in the student body. Accordingly, the court found that the use of gender was necessary to achieve a legitimate state interest. The same district court later found acceptable a plan to establish such a program for women at another institution—the Virginia Women's Institute for Leadership (VWIL) program located at Mary Baldwin College, a private liberal arts school for women. The Supreme Court disagreed. Justice Ginsburg, speaking for six of the seven justices in the majority, suggested that neither the "goal of producing citizen-soldiers nor V.M.I.'s implementing methodology is inherently unsuitable to women." Admission to the institution was characterized as "desirable," and yet Virginia chose to "preserve exclusively for men" the advantages and opportunities afforded by a VMI education. When seeking to defend gender-based government action, the burden rests entirely on the state to demonstrate an "exceedingly persuasive justification." The justification for gender-based classification must be "genuine, not hypothesized or invented *post hoc* in response to litigation." Furthermore, the justification, said Ginsburg, "must not rely on overbroad generalizations about the different talents, capabilities, or preferences of males and females." Gender classification may not be used to "create or perpetuate the legal, social and economic inferiority of women." Virginia attempted to justify VMI's male-only policy on two grounds. First, Virginia contended that single-sex education has "important educational benefits" and that maintaining the single-sex option contributes to "diversity in educational approaches." Ginsburg agreed that diversity among public educational institutions "can serve the public good," but concluded that Virginia had not demonstrated that VMI was either established or maintained "with a view to diversifying, by its categorical exclusion of women, educational opportunities within the state." While single-sex education may afford "pedagogical benefits," such benign justifications advanced in defense of categorical exclusions will not "be accepted automatically." Providing diversity of educational options was not served by VMI's plan to afford a "unique education benefit only to males." However well this plan served the "State's sons, it makes no provision whatever for her daughters. That is not *equal* protection." Second, Virginia argued that VMI's method of training provided benefits that could not be made available, "unmodified," to women. Education, Ginsburg responded, is surely not a "one size fits all business." The issue, however, is not whether men or women should be "forced to attend V.M.I." Rather, the question was whether Virginia could "constitutionally deny to women who have the will and capacity, the training and attendant opportunities that V.M.I. uniquely affords." Ginsburg pointed to the successful entry of women into the federal military academies and their participation in the nation's military. She concluded that Virginia's justification for excluding all women from "citizen-soldier training for which some are qualified" does not meet the "exceedingly persuasive" standard. The Court also rejected the program offered through VWIL. A remedial action must "closely fit the constitutional violation." It must be designed to place persons unlawfully denied an opportunity or advantage in a position that they would have occupied without the discriminatory classification. In this case, the violation was the categorical exclusion of women from an "extraordinary" educational opportunity provided to men. Virginia chose, said Ginsburg, "not to eliminate, but to leave untouched, V.M.I.'s exclusionary policy." Instead, Virginia proposed for women a separate program, "different in kind ... and unequal in tangible and intangible facilities," a program "fairly appraised as a 'pale shadow' of V.M.I." Ginsburg concluded by saying that generalizations about "the way women are, estimates of what is appropriate for *most women,* no longer justify denying opportunity to women whose talent and capacity place them outside the average description."

Chief Justice Rehnquist was among the majority, but he issued a separate opinion that focused on the inadequacies of VWIL in comparison to the program at VMI. He also rejected the argument advanced by Virginia that the male-only program at VMI pursued the interest of educational diversity. Rehnquist responded that the diversity "benefitted only one sex." The single dissent came from Justice Scalia. He was highly critical of the Court's rejection of the "long tradition" of publicly supported men's military institutions. He saw the Court as "embark[ing] on a course of inscribing one after another of the current preferences of society ... into our basic law." This ruling, Scalia continued, "enshrines the notion that no substantial educational value" is to be served by an all-men's military academic so that the decision of the people of Virginia to establish and maintain such an institution denies equal protection to women "who cannot attend that institution but can attend others." Justice Thomas did not participate in this case as his son was a student at VMI. *See also California Federal Savings & Loan Association v. Guerra,* p. 561; CLASSIFICATION, p. 628; EQUAL PROTECTION CLAUSE, p. 473; *Harris v. Forklift Systems, Inc.,* p. 568.

Significance The Burger Court first utilized the Equal Protection Clause to invalidate a gender-based classification in the early 1970s. Although the Court continued generally to find that sex discrimination is constitutionally forbidden, it did not find consensus on the standard of review to be applied. A pivotal case was *Frontiero v. Richardson*, 411 U.S. 677 (1973). *Frontiero* involved a female air force lieutenant who sought higher housing and medical allowances by having her husband declared a dependent. Such benefits were automatically granted with respect to the wife of a male member of the uniformed services. Frontiero argued that the policy was discriminatory in two ways. From a procedural standpoint, only female members were required to demonstrate spouse dependency. As a matter of substance, a male member received benefits even if he provided less than half of his wife's support. A similarly situated female did not receive such benefits. With only Justice Rehnquist dissenting, the Court invalidated the statutory provisions. The eight-justice majority was fragmented, however, on the standard by which gender classification ought to be evaluated. Justices Brennan, Douglas, White, and Marshall viewed sex classifications, like those of race, alienage, and national origin, to be inherently suspect and therefore subject to close judicial scrutiny. Justice Brennan noted a long history of sex discrimination, rationalized by an attitude of romantic paternalism that, "in practical effect, put women not on a pedestal, but in a cage." Sex is an "immutable characteristic determined solely by the accident of birth." To impose special disabilities on women because of their sex runs counter to the concept that legal burdens should bear some relationship to individual responsibility. What gives sex classification its suspect status, argued Justice Brennan, is that the "sex characteristic frequently bears no relation to ability to perform or contribute to society." The result is that women are often invidiously relegated to inferior legal status without regard to actual capabilities. Policies achieving nothing more than administrative convenience through different treatment by gender represent "the very kind of legislative choice forbidden by the Equal Protection Clause." Chief Justice Burger and Justices Powell, Stewart, and Blackmun agreed that the benefit policy was unconstitutionally discriminatory, but refused to go so far as to label gender an inherently suspect class. They resolved the case using the less stringent rational basis test. Justice Powell said an expansion to suspect status had far-reaching implications, but it was also preemptive and premature given current consideration of the Equal Rights Amendment. The Equal Rights Amendment (ERA) was proposed in 1972 and provided that "equality of rights under the law shall not be denied or abridged by the United States or any State on account of sex." A seven-year ratification deadline was initially set, but was later extended for three years. The deadline expired in 1982 with the ERA having failed to secure the necessary ratification by three-fourths of the states.

The Court had been urged by the Clinton administration, among others, to elevate gender to the level of strict scrutiny in the Virginia Military Institute case, *United States v. Virginia*, a position the Court was within one vote of taking in *Frontiero v. Richardson* in 1973. Instead, in the VMI case Justice Ginsburg referred to the state's need to show an "exceedingly persuasive" justification as "skeptical scrutiny."

Until the 1970s the Court found no constitutional defect in sex-based classifications. In *Goesaert v. Cleary*, 335 U.S. 464 (1948), the Court upheld a law denying a bartender's license to all women except the wives or daughters of bar owners, saying that states were not precluded from drawing "a sharp line between the sexes." *Reed v. Reed*, 404 U.S. 71 (1971), however, struck down an Idaho law giving preference to males over females in administering estates. Using the rationality test, the Court unanimously concluded that the Equal Protection Clause does not permit states to place persons into different classes on the basis of criteria wholly unrelated to the objective of the statute. In *Stanton v. Stanton*, 421 U.S. 7 (1975), the Court carried the holdings of *Reed* and *Frontiero* to a Utah statute that set the age of majority at 21 for males and 18 for females. The case involved a divorce decree ordering child support payments for a son through age 21 and a daughter only through age 18. While again refusing to find sex an inherently suspect class, the Court held that the statute contained nothing rational relative to the provision of child support.

In *Craig v. Boren*, 429 U.S. 190 (1976), the Court struck down an Oklahoma statute that permitted females to buy 3.2 percent beer at age 18 while prohibiting males to do so until age 21. The Court said gender classifications must serve important governmental objectives and be substantially related to reaching those objectives, and the Oklahoma statute did not survive those criteria. Most important was that *Boren* established a "heightened" level of scrutiny for gender. Although not comparable to strict scrutiny, the intermediate level of review was substantially more stringent than the rationality test of the minimum scrutiny standard.

In *Personnel Administrator v. Feeney*, 442 U.S. 256 (1979), the Court upheld a state policy extending preferential status to military veterans for state employment. It found no discriminatory intent in the advantage given veterans over nonveterans, a class composed of both men and women, despite the policy's adverse impact on women. In *Parham v. Hughes*, 441 U.S. 347 (1979), the Court upheld a Georgia statute that permitted fathers of legitimate or legitimated children to sue for the wrongful death of a child only if the mother is deceased, and the father first legitimated the child as a condition of maintaining the wrongful death suit. The Court found the policy to be a rational means for dealing with the matter of proving paternity. The Court also held that the policy did not reflect any overbroad generalizations about men as a class.

In *Rostker v. Goldberg*, 453 U.S. 57 (1981), the Court ruled that Congress constitutionally could exclude women from registering for a possible military draft without violating the due process limitations of the Fifth Amendment. *Rostker* involved the Military Selective Service Act and the power it gave the president to require "every male citizen" and male resident aliens of appropriate age to register for potential conscription. Justice Rehnquist said that congressional judgments warrant particular deference when the issue involves raising and regulating the armed forces. Congressional authority is at its "apogee" in this policy area. Against that background, the Court turned to the issue of gender-based registration. Unlike previous sex discrimination cases, this one involved an enactment in which the legislative body "did not act unthinkingly or reflexively."

The decision to exempt women from registration was not the accidental by-product of a traditional way of thinking about women. On the contrary, the policy was considered at great length, and Congress clearly expressed its purpose and intent. The Court upheld the classification primarily because males and females are not similarly situated with respect to combat duty. Indeed, women are statutorily restricted from such duty. By viewing the draft of combat troops in time of national emergency and registration for that draft as part of the same function, the Court found a basis for distinguishing the situations of males and females. Justice Rehnquist said that the Constitution "requires that Congress treat similarly situated persons similarly, not that it engage in gestures of superficial equality." Justice White pointed out in dissent that a draft could recruit personnel for both combat and noncombat needs. In his view women should not have been excluded for that reason alone.

In a similar ruling, the Court upheld a statutory rape law prohibiting sexual intercourse with a female under 18 years of age in *Michael M. v. Superior Court*, 450 U.S. 464 (1981). The Court ruled that statutes cannot make overbroad generalizations based on sex that are entirely unrelated to any differences between men and women. The statute was permissible because it addressed a substantial inequity between men and women based on "the harmful and inescapably identifiable consequences of teenage pregnancy." Further, the risk of pregnancy "constitutes a substantial deterrence to young females" to engaging in sexual activity. The statute creating criminal sanctions for males "serves roughly to equalize the deterrent on the sexes."

Gender: Employment

California Federal Savings & Loan Association v. Guerra, **479 U.S. 272 (1987),** upheld a state law requiring employers to grant maternity leave and job reinstatement to women employees. California Federal Savings & Loan (Cal Fed) refused to reinstate Lillian Garland following her pregnancy disability leave. Garland then sought to invoke state law by filing a complaint with the state agency authorized to enforce the law. Cal Fed brought an action in U.S. district court claiming that the state law was inconsistent with and preempted by Title VII of the Civil Rights Act of 1964 as amended by the Pregnancy Disability Act of 1978 (PDA). The PDA declared that discrimination on the basis of pregnancy constituted illegal gender discrimination. The PDA also required that pregnant women be treated the same as any other disabled employee. Cal Fed asserted that the PDA therefore prohibited the preferential treatment of pregnant women, but the Supreme Court disagreed. The central question was whether Title VII, as amended by the PDA, preempted California law. Federal law may supersede state law by stating so in express terms or when the scheme of federal regulation is sufficiently comprehensive to support the inference that Congress left no room for supplementary state regulation. A third alternative in areas in which Congress has not completely displaced state regulation holds that federal law may preempt state law to the extent that the latter actually conflicts with federal law. This third basis for preemption was involved in *Guerra.* Upon examination of the Civil Rights Act of 1964, the Court found that Congress had assigned importance to the role of state antidiscrimination laws in achieving Title VII objectives. The provisions added by the PDA accomplished the same purpose. The PDA was intended to illustrate how discrimination against pregnancy is to be remedied. Congress intended the PDA to be a "floor beneath which pregnancy disability benefits may not drop—not a ceiling above which they may not rise." In addition, the Court found it significant that Congress was aware of state laws similar to California's, but apparently did not consider them inconsistent with the PDA. In the Court's view, Title VII as amended by the PDA and California's pregnancy disability leave statute shared a common goal. Both sought to promote equal employment opportunity. By requiring reinstatement after pregnancy leave, the California law ensured that women would not lose their jobs because of pregnancy disability. By taking pregnancy into account, California's leave statute allowed both men and women to have families without losing their jobs. The state law did not compel employers to treat pregnant workers better than other disabled employees. Rather, it established benefits that employers must, at a minimum, provide to pregnant workers. Chief Justice Rehnquist and Justices White and Powell dissented. They felt that Title VII clearly prohibited the preferential treatment of pregnant workers, which preempted the California law. *See also* CLASSIFICATION, p. 628; EQUAL PROTECTION CLAUSE, p. 473; *Harris v. Forklift Systems, Inc.*, p. 568; PREEMPTION DOCTRINE, p. 689.

Significance   The decision in *Guerra* hinged on whether the law gave pregnant women preferential treatment in violation of the provisions of Title VII of the Civil Rights Act of 1964 as amended by the Pregnancy Disability Act of 1978. If the state statute was in conflict with the federal law, it would be invalidated by application of the preemption doctrine, a rule grounded in the Supremacy Clause of Article VI. The Court concluded that there was no substantive conflict between the state law and the federal enactments—thus the doctrine was inapplicable. The *Guerra* decision also broadened the scope of protections available to pregnant employees.

Pregnancy as an employment disability had not always fared so well. In *Geduldig v. Aiello*, 417 U.S. 484 (1974), for example, the Court allowed a state disability insurance program to exempt coverage of wage losses for normal pregnancies. Rather than finding impermissible gender classification, the Court held that the relevant classes were divided on the basis of pregnancy, and the nonpregnant class consisted of both men and women. Two years later the Court upheld an employee benefit plan that excluded from its coverage pregnancy-related disabilities in *General Electric Company v. Gilbert*, 429 U.S. 125 (1976). The *Gilbert* decision prompted Congress to enact the PDA. Indeed, as Justice Marshall said in *Guerra*, when Congress amended Title VII with the PDA, it "unambiguously expressed its disapproval of both the holding and the reasoning of the Court in the *Gilbert* decision." *Guerra* seems compatible with the sentiments of Congress as embodied in the 1978 amendments. In addition to approving state initiatives on the matter of leave and reinstatement rights in connection with pregnancy, the *Guerra* decision enhanced the likelihood of federal legislation similar to that of the California statute reviewed in this case.

In *Wimberly v. Labor & Industrial Relations Commission*, 479 U.S. 511 (1987), a decision less favorable to the interests of pregnant employees, the Court unanimously held that states may deny unemployment benefits to women who left their jobs because of pregnancy as long as the state disqualified "all persons who leave for reasons not causally connected to the work." For a state to apply such a law, it is not necessary to know that the employee left because of pregnancy. All that is relevant is that she stopped work for a reason "bearing no causal connection to her work or her employer." Coupled with the *Guerra* decision, *Wimberly* gives the states a great deal of discretion in establishing policy about how pregnancy is to be managed in the workplace.

County of Washington v. Gunther, 450 U.S. 907 (1981), allowed the Court to clarify the relationship between two federal enactments treating sex-based wage discrimination. Title VII of the Civil Rights Act of 1964 bars employment discrimination, while the Equal Pay Act of 1963 prohibits wage differentials based on sex for persons performing equivalent work. Title VII contained a reference to the Equal Pay Act through a provision known as the Bennett Amendment, which exempted from the Equal Pay Act differences in wage stemming from seniority, merit, or work quantity. The question in *Gunther* was whether the Bennett Amendment made Title VII and the Equal Pay Act coextensive relative to wage discrimination, or whether Title VII provided broader protection than situations in which unequal pay for equal work were involved. Gunther, a female guard at a county jail, brought suit under Title VII claiming wage disparity between male and female guards for substantially similar, but not identical, work. The Court ruled that the Bennett Amendment permitted Title VII litigation to go beyond equal pay for equal work claims. Justice Brennan's opinion stressed that the objective of the Bennett Amendment was to make the two statutes compatible by specifying some affirmative defenses that would apply in situations in which pay disparities existed for equal work. To confine Title VII to the equal work standard of the Equal Pay Act would mean that a woman who was discriminatorily underpaid could obtain no relief, no matter how egregious the discrimination might be, unless her employer also employed a man in an equal job in the same establishment at a higher rate of pay. The Court rejected the view that Congress had intended the Bennett Amendment "to insulate such blatantly discriminatory practices from judicial redress under Title VII." Rather, Title VII was used by Congress "to strike at the entire spectrum of disparate treatment of men and women resulting from sex stereotypes." The dissenters, Chief Justice Burger and Justices Stewart, Powell, and Rehnquist, felt that the intent of Congress in Title VII was to make claims of gender-based wage discrimination contingent on a showing of equal work.

In *Geduldig v. Aiello*, the Court had allowed a state disability insurance program to exempt coverage of wage losses from normal pregnancies. Rather than finding a classification by gender, the Court held that the two classes were divided on the basis of pregnancy, and the nonpregnant class consisted of both men and women. Three subsequent cases, however, found the Court moving away from the *Geduldig* position. In *Newport News Shipbuilding & Dry Dock Co. v. EEOC*, 462 U.S. 669 (1983), the Court struck down a health plan that did not provide the same pregnancy coverage for wives of male employees as it provided for female employees.

In *Los Angeles Department of Water & Power v. Manhart*, 435 U.S. 702

(1978), the Court held that requiring female employees to make higher contributions to retirement programs than men violated Title VII, despite the statistical probability that a woman would collect more retirement benefits because of greater longevity. The counterpart to *Manhart* came in *Arizona Governing Committee for Tax Deferred Annuity & Deferred Compensation Plans v. Norris*, 463 U.S. 1073 (1983), in which the Court invalidated an employer-sponsored retirement plan that provided smaller benefits to women by using sex-based actuarial tables reflecting greater longevity for women. The Court said that the classification of employees on the basis of sex was no more permissible at the pay-out stage of a retirement plan than at the pay-in stage.

In *Hishon v. King & Spalding*, 467 U.S. 69 (1984), the Court unanimously held that law firms may not discriminate on the basis of gender in making decisions on promotion to partnership. The law firm had contended that such promotion decisions as this were exempt from the job discrimination provisions of Title VII, and that the right of association insulated partnership decisions. The Court disagreed on both points. A similar decision came in *Price Waterhouse v. Hopkins*, 490 U.S. 228 (1989). Hopkins was an officer at Price Waterhouse, a national accounting firm. She was proposed for partnership, but the decision was postponed for a year. At the end of the year, her partnership was never reconsidered. She resigned the firm and filed suit under Title VII of the Civil Rights Act of 1964, claiming gender discrimination. The Supreme Court ruled that Price Waterhouse bore the burden of proof, but need only establish its case by a preponderance of the evidence. Title VII, said the Court, "eliminates certain bases for distinguishing among employees while otherwise preserving employers' freedom of choice."

The issue before the Court in *Lorance v. AT&T Technologies, Inc.*, 490 U.S. 900 (1989), was the timing of job discrimination actions under Title VII. Prior to the collective bargaining agreements of 1979, seniority at AT&T Technologies was based on plantwide service and could be transferred upon promotion to other positions. Lorance and several other women were promoted to the more skilled position of "tester." The 1979 agreements entered subsequent to Lorance's promotion provided that seniority in tester positions was dependent exclusively on time as a tester. The women, all of whom were promoted between 1978 and 1980, were notified of workforce reductions requiring their demotions in 1982. They were demoted because they were least senior under the new seniority rules, but would not have been least senior if their years of plantwide service were considered. The women filed charges contending that the new system was adopted to protect incumbent male testers. The Supreme

Court ruled that the 300-day filing limitation for Title VII actions dates from the adoption of the discriminatory system, not when its effects become manifest. The Court's rulings in *Hopkins* and *Lorance* were overturned by provisions of the Civil Rights Act enacted by Congress in October 1991.

The Court held in *University of Pennsylvania v. EEOC*, 493 U.S. 182 (1990), that universities can be compelled to disclose previously confidential peer reviews in cases in which discrimination is charged in the making of tenure and promotion decisions. Title VII of the Civil Rights Act of 1964 prohibited employment discrimination and empowered the Equal Employment Opportunity Commission (EEOC) to investigate claims of such discrimination. The EEOC was given the power to subpoena needed documents as part of its enforcement authority. Here, the EEOC requested materials relating to an allegedly discriminatory tenure decision. The Court unanimously declined to protect the peer review process. The Court said that the process was not entitled to privileged status unless it "promotes sufficiently important interests to outweigh the need for probative evidence." Justice Blackmun, speaking for the Court, noted a particular reluctance to recognize a privilege in an area in which Congress itself had thoroughly considered the possibility and chosen against it. He referred to congressional judgment to extend Title VII to educational institutions and provide the EEOC with broad subpoena power. The Court agreed that the role of universities is significant and that confidentiality is important to the peer review process, but concluded that the "costs that ensue from disclosure, however, constitute only one side of the balance." The costs associated with racial and gender discrimination are "a great if not compelling governmental interest." Often, peer review documents are indispensable in determining the presence of illegal discrimination. "Indeed, if there is a 'smoking gun' to be found that demonstrates discrimination in tenure decisions, it is likely to be tucked away in peer review files."

A year later, the Supreme Court ruled in *United Auto Workers v. Johnson Controls, Inc.*, 499 U.S. 187 (1991), that women may not be excluded from jobs that might endanger a developing fetus or a fetus a woman might conceive in the future. Johnson Controls manufactures batteries, and one of the primary ingredients of the batteries is lead. Exposure to lead carries health risks, including the risk of endangering a fetus. Johnson Controls first established a fetal protection policy in 1977, in which it suggested that women who expected to have a child should not choose a job that would include exposure to lead. The company changed its policy in 1982 to one that excluded all women "capable of bearing children" from jobs that could expose them to lead. An exception was made for women who could medically document that they could no longer bear children. A class action was brought claiming the policy violated Title VII of the Civil Rights Act of 1964. The lower courts found the policy to be justified as both a "business necessity" and a "bona fide occupation qualification (BFOQ)." The Supreme Court disagreed. Under the terms of Johnson Controls' policy, fertile men were given a choice as to whether they wished to assume reproductive health risks for a particular job. Women did not have the same choice. A unanimous Supreme Court found the bias in Johnson's policy "obvious." The policy, said Justice Blackmun, "excludes women with childbearing capacity from lead exposed jobs and so creates a facial classification based on gender." The policy concerns itself only with the "harms that may befall the unborn offspring of its female employees." Johnson's use of the words "capable of bearing children" is an explicit classification based on potential for pregnancy. The Pregnancy Disability Act of 1978 (PDA) provides that such a classification must be regarded, for Title VII purposes, in the "same light" as explicit sex discrimination. Johnson's choice to treat all female employees as potentially pregnant "evinces discrimination" on the basis of gender. The lower court's assumption was that because Johnson's objective of protecting women's unconceived offspring was "ostensibly benign," the policy did not constitute sex-based discrimination. The Supreme Court rejected this argument. Absence of a malevolent motive "does not convert" a facially discriminatory policy into a neutral policy with a discriminatory effect. Whether an employment practice involves disparate treatment through explicit facial discrimination, said Blackmun, "does not depend on why the employer discriminates but rather on the explicit terms of the discrimination." Unless pregnant employees differ from others in their "ability or inability to work," they must be treated the same. The Court acknowledged the health risks, especially late in pregnancy, but said Congress decided that an employer must take into account "only the woman's ability to get her job done." Women as capable of doing their jobs as their male counterparts "may not be forced to choose between having a child and having a job."

The Court has also faced some intriguing gender issues in connection with the right of association. In *Roberts v. United States Jaycees,* 468 U.S. 609 (1984), the Court upheld the application of a state antidiscrimination law that forced an organization to accept women into its membership. The Court concluded that the state's interest in promoting gender equality prevailed over the organization's expression and association interests.

In a decision similar to *Roberts,* the Court upheld a state law that required all-male, nonprofit clubs to admit women to membership in *Board of Directors of Rotary International v. Rotary Club of Duarte*, 479 U.S. 929 (1986). The Court ruled that application of the state law was appropriate and did not interfere with the freedom of private association. Constitutional protection is afforded only those associations that are sufficiently intimate or private. A number of factors are germane in determining whether a particular association warrants protection, including organization size, purpose, selectivity, and whether others are excluded from critical aspects of the relationship. Rotary Clubs were found not to qualify for protection because of their potentially large size, their high membership turnover, the inclusive nature of club membership, the public character of their service activities, and the encouragement of nonmember participation and media coverage of their activities. The Court also concluded that even if there were some slight infringement on the association rights of members, such an infringement is justified by the state's compelling interest in eliminating discrimination against women and in assuring them equal access to public accommodations, as well as the acquisition of leadership skills and business contacts.

The balance between regulations designed to combat discrimination and the associational rights of private clubs was again considered in *New York State Club Association v. City of New York*, 487 U.S. 1 (1988). New York adopted a human rights law in 1965 that prohibited discrimination of virtually all kinds. The law specifically exempted clubs and institutions of a "distinctly private" nature. A 1984 amendment to the law provided that a club would not be considered "distinctly private" and therefore exempt from the original law if it has "more than four hundred members, provides regular meal service and regularly receives payment ... directly or indirectly from or on behalf of nonmembers for the furtherance of trade or business." Benevolent orders and religious corporations were not included in the narrowed exemption language of the 1984 amendment. The New York State Club Association, a nonprofit consortium of private clubs and associations, facially challenged the amendments on First and Fourteenth Amendment grounds but was unsuccessful. A unanimous Supreme Court upheld the constitutionality of the amended law. A number of the large clubs were clearly subject to antidiscrimination regulation under the holding in *Roberts*. The Court did not find any infringement on club members' rights. Absent evidence demonstrating special circumstances, the Court was satisfied that large clubs could "effectively advance their desired viewpoints without confining their memberships to persons having the same sex, for example, or the same religion." Neither was there evidence to demonstrate that the law actually impaired the "ability to associate or to advocate public or private viewpoints."

Gender: Sexual Harassment

Harris v. Forklift Systems, Inc., **510 U.S. 17 (1993)** Title VII of the Civil Rights Act of 1964 prohibits discrimination in the workplace on the basis of such factors as race and gender. The Supreme Court ruled in *Meritor Savings Bank v. Vinson,* 477 U.S. 57 (1986), that actions can be brought under Title VII when sexual harassment is sufficiently severe as to "alter the conditions of the victim's employment and create an abusive working environment." Teresa Harris filed a sexual harassment claim against her employer, but was unsuccessful in the lower courts because she had not demonstrated that she suffered psychological injury from the employer's conduct. The Court granted review in *Harris* to determine whether proof of psychological injury was the appropriate standard by which to qualify sexual harassment as actionable under Title VII. A unanimous Court reaffirmed the standard contained in *Meritor* that "takes a middle path between making actionable any conduct that is merely offensive and requiring the conduct to cause a tangible psychological injury." Conduct that is not pervasive enough to create an "objectively hostile work environment," or an environment that a "reasonable person would find hostile or abusive," is outside the reach of Title VII. Similarly, if the victim does not "subjectively perceive the environment to be abusive," there is no conduct that has actually altered the victim's working conditions and no Title VII violation. On the other hand, said O'Connor, Title VII "comes into play before the harassing conduct leads to a nervous breakdown." An abusive workplace environment, even one that does not "seriously affect employees' psychological well-being," can and often will "detract from employee's job performance, discourage employees from remaining on the job, or keep them from advancing in their careers." Even without regard to what O'Connor characterized as "tangible effects" of workplace discrimination, conduct that is so severe as to create an abusive workplace environment "offends Title VII's broad rule of workplace equality." The Court said that the lower courts erred in Harris's case by "needlessly focus[ing] the factfinder's attention on concrete psychological harm," an element not required under Title VII. Certainly conduct that seriously affects an employee's psychological well-being violates Title VII, but the statute, said O'Connor, "is not limited to such conduct." As long as the workplace environment is reasonably perceived as hostile or abusive, there "is no need for it also to be psychologically injurious." O'Connor acknowledged that there is no "mathematically precise" test to apply to claims of sexual harassment. Determination of whether a workplace environment is hostile or abusive requires examination of "all the circumstances." Psychological harm, like any other relevant factor, may be taken into account, "but no single factor is required." Justice Scalia concurred, but expressed concern about the imprecision of the standard contained in O'Connor's opinion. As a practical matter, he suggested, the ruling "lets virtually any unguided jury decide whether sex-related conduct engaged in (or permitted by) an employer is egregious enough to warrant an award of damages." He favored an inquiry that would focus more attention on job performance, but agreed that Title VII cases should not be confined to that consideration. *See also* CIVIL RIGHTS ACT OF 1964, p. 626; EQUAL PROTECTION CLAUSE, p. 473; *Faragher v. City of Boca Raton*, p. 569; *Grove City College v. Bell*, p. 574.

Significance   The *Harris* ruling left several questions unresolved. The issue in *Landgraf v. USI Film Products*, 511 U.S. 229 (1994), was whether provisions of the Civil Rights Act of 1991 applied retroactively to cases already in progress prior to the effective date of the law. Under Title VII of the 1964 Civil Rights Act, victims of job discrimination were able to obtain job reinstatement and backpay, or an order prohibiting future discriminatory conduct. The 1991 Act added trial by jury in employment discrimination cases, and it provided the opportunity to obtain compensatory and punitive damages. Barbara Landgraf brought a Title VII action claiming that she had been forced from her job because of unlawful sexual harassment. The trial court found that her employer had taken sufficient corrective action that Landgraf's resignation was unrelated to any unlawful harassment. The Act became law while Landgraf's case was on appeal, but the Supreme Court ruled that Landgraf was not entitled to benefit from provisions of the new law. Justice Stevens said that the Court starts with a "presumption against statutory retroactivity." There was, however, no conflict between the presumption and statutory language that "unambiguous[ly]" provided for retroactivity. The presumption could be set aside only if there was "clear evidence" that Congress intended retroactive application. Absent such clear evidence, the Court had no legal basis except to apply statutory language prospectively. Requiring clear evidence of intent assures that Congress has "affirmatively considered the potential unfairness of retroactive application and determined that it is an acceptable price to pay for the countervailing benefits." No such clear evidence of congressional intent for retroactivity was found here. In dissent, Justice Blackmun indicated that provisions of the Act ought to apply to cases pending when the law took effect even without specific legislative instruction to do so. In his view, the retroactivity presumption should not apply to remedial legislation that "does not proscribe any conduct that was previously legal."

Faragher v. City of Boca Raton, **118 S.Ct. 2275 (1998),** developed guidelines by which liability resulting from sexual harassment can be determined. Beth Faragher, a lifeguard employed by the city of Boca Raton,

Florida, was subjected to sexual harassment by David Silverman and Bill Terry. Both men held supervisory positions over lifeguards in the Parks and Recreation Department. Faragher reported the illegal conduct to another supervisor in the department, but without result. Prior to leaving her job, another female employee reported similar problems with the same two men to the city's personnel director. Following an investigation, the two men were disciplined. Although the city had a sexual harassment policy, it had not been distributed to employees of the Parks and Recreation Department. Until the coworker reported the misconduct, the city had no formal complaint process in place. The Supreme Court concluded in *Faragher v. City of Boca Raton* that an employer is vicariously liable for sexual harassment committed by a supervisor, but is entitled to offer as a defense the reasonableness of its conduct and that of the victim. Boca Raton had adopted a sexual harassment policy prior to the incidents of harassment, but it "completely failed to disseminate its policy among employees of the marine safety section, with the result that Terry, Silverman, ... and many lifeguards were unaware of it." In implementing Title VII, the Court found that "it makes sense" to hold an employer vicariously liable for some "[mis]conduct of a supervisor made possible by the abuse of his supervisory authority." There is a sense, said Justice Souter, in which a "harassing supervisor is always assisted in his misconduct by the supervisory relationship." Indeed, the "agency relationship" affords contact with an employee, and the victim "may well be reluctant to accept the risks of blowing the whistle on a superior." Further, an employee "generally cannot check a supervisor's abusive conduct the same way she might deal with abuse from a co-worker." The Court then set some criteria by which to determine when an employer is liable for misconduct that leads to a hostile work environment. An employer is liable for harassment by a supervisor "with immediate authority over the employee." No affirmative defense is available, said Souter, when the supervisor's "harassment culminates in a tangible employment action," such as termination, demotion, or undesirable reassignment. When no "tangible employment action is taken," a defending employer may raise an affirmative defense that comprises two "necessary elements": (1) that the employer exercised "reasonable care to prevent and correct promptly any sexually harassing behavior," and (2) that the victim "unreasonably failed to take advantage of any preventive or corrective opportunities provided by the employer or to avoid harm otherwise." Justices Scalia and Thomas dissented. It was their view that an employer could not be held vicariously liable for a supervisor creating a hostile work environment without an "adverse employment consequence." They also disagreed with the Court's conclusion that Boca Raton should be liable as a matter of law "merely because the city did not disseminate its sexual harassment policy." *See also* CIVIL RIGHTS ACT OF 1964, p. 626; EQUAL PROTECTION CLAUSE, p. 473; *Harris v. Forklift Systems, Inc.*, p. 568.

Significance   The Rehnquist Court made several important sexual harassment rulings in 1998. Kim Ellerth was sexually harassed by a corporate official, Theodore Slowik, from the point of her interview for a position with Burlington Industries until the time she quit some 14 months later. Throughout the time of her employment, Burlington had a sexual harassment policy in effect. Ellerth chose not to use the formal procedure for fear of losing her job. Following her resignation, Ellerth filed a sexual harassment complaint. The Supreme Court ruled in *Burlington Industries, Inc. v. Ellerth*, 118 S.Ct. 2257 (1998), that an employee who refuses "unwelcome and threatening sexual advances of a supervisor" may recover damages under Title VII even in the absence of "adverse, tangible job consequences." The Court thought it "prudent to import the concept of a tangible employment action for resolution of the vicarious liability issue" presented in this case. A tangible employment action "constitutes a significant change in employment status," and would take such form as a denial of a raise or a promotion. A tangible employment action typically "inflicts direct economic harm," and, as a rule, only a person with supervisory authority "can cause this sort of injury." Tangible employment actions are the "means by which the supervisor brings the official power of the enterprise to bear on subordinates." It is for these reasons that a tangible employment action taken by a supervisor, said Justice Kennedy, "becomes for Title VII purposes the act of the employer." The Court reiterated the guidelines set forth in *Faragher*. If no tangible employment action is taken, a defending employer may undertake an affirmative defense subject to proof by a preponderance of the evidence. The defense, said Kennedy, "comprises two necessary elements": (1) that the employer exercised "reasonable care to prevent and correct promptly any sexually harassing behavior," and (2) that the plaintiff employee "unreasonably failed to take advantage of any preventive or corrective opportunities provided by the employer or to avoid harm otherwise." Although proof that an employer had an antiharassment policy with a complaint procedure in place is not necessary in every instance as a matter of law, the need for a policy suitable to employment circumstances "may appropriately be addressed in any case when litigating the first element of the defense." Demonstration of an employee's failure to take reasonable care to avoid harm is not limited to showing failure to use any complaint process; a demonstration of such failure will "normally suffice to satisfy the employer's burden under the second element of the test." The Court concluded, however, that no affirmative defense is available "when the super-visor's harassment culminates in a tangible employment action." Because Ellerth had not alleged a tangible employment effect, Burlington was still subject to vicarious liability, but was entitled to an opportunity to assert the affirmative defense to liability. Justices Thomas and Scalia dissented. It was their view that if a supervisor creates a hostile work environment, he "does not act for the employer." Creation of a hostile work environment, said Thomas, is "neither within the scope of his employment, nor part of his apparent authority." The dissenters contended that a hostile work environment is "antithetical" to the interest of the employer, and an employer should be liable "only if the employer knew ... about the hostile work environment and failed to take remedial action."

Title IX of the Educational Amendments prohibits sex discrimina-tion, including sexual harassment by recipients of Title IX funding. Frank Waldrop was a teacher at Lago Vista High School in Texas, and Alida Gebser was assigned to Waldrop's class for ninth grade. During much of the year Waldrop found ways to be alone with Gebser, although sexual contact did not begin until the spring of Gebser's ninth-grade year. The two had sex on a regular basis for almost a year before it was discovered and stopped. None of the sexual acts occurred at the school. The school district fired Waldrop and his teaching license was revoked by the state of Texas. Gebser and her mother filed suit in a state court, alleging that state law as well as Title IX had been violated. The Supreme Court held in *Gebser v. Lago Vista Independent School District*, 118 S.Ct. 1989 (1998), that a sexual harass-ment victim can collect damages from a school district only if a school official with authority to take action knew of the misconduct and with "deliberate indifference" failed to intervene. The Court ruled that Congress had not "contemplated unlimited recovery" against a Title IX recipient if the recipient was "unaware of discrimination in its programs." Taking Gebser's position would amount, said Justice O'Connor, to "allowing unlimited recovery of damages under Title IX where Congress had not spoken on the subject of either the right or the remedy." O'Connor distinguished Title IX from Title VII. Title IX conditions an offer of federal funding on a promise by the recipient not to discriminate, in what amounts essentially to "a contract between the Government and the recipient of funds." The "contex-tual framework" distinguishes the two titles. Title VII applies to all employers without regard to federal funding. Title VII "aims centrally to compensate victims of discrimination"; to "make persons whole for injuries suffered through past discrimination." Title IX, by contrast, focuses on protecting individuals from discriminatory practices carried out by recipients of federal funding. It is "sensible to assume" that Congress did not envision a recipient's liability in damages if it was unaware of the discriminatory conduct. O'Connor concluded by saying that there is no question that a "student suffers extraordinary harm when subjected to sexual harassment and abuse by a teacher." She characterized such behavior as "reprehensible," and said that the teacher's conduct "undermines the basic purposes of the educational system." The issue in this case, however, was whether the independent misconduct of a teacher is attributable to the school district that employs him. Until Congress speaks directly on the subject, she said, "we will not hold a school district liable in damages under Title IX for a teacher's sexual harassment of a student absent actual notice and deliberate indifference." Justices Stevens, Souter, Ginsburg, and Breyer dissented. Justice Stevens voiced concern that the Court had set a standard for damages that was too difficult for harassment victims to meet, and that as long as school officials could remain ignorant of such misconduct, school districts could effectively immunize themselves from liability.

Joseph Oncale filed a Title VII complaint against his employer alleging sexual harassment on the part of his coworkers. Justice Scalia called the precise details of this case "irrelevant," but generally reviewed events. Oncale worked on an oil platform in the Gulf of Mexico and was "forcibly subjected to sex-related, humiliating actions" involving physical assault "in a sexual manner" and threat of rape. A U.S. district court ruled that Oncale, a male, had no Title VII cause of action for misconduct by male coworkers, but the U.S. Supreme Court unanimously reversed in *Oncale v. Sundowner Offshore Services, Inc.*, 118 S.Ct. 998 (1998). Justice Scalia said that Title VII "evinces a congressional intent to strike at the entire spectrum of disparate treatment of men and women in employment." When a workplace is "permeated with discriminatory intimidation, ridicule, and insult that is sufficiently severe or pervasive to alter the conditions of the victim's employment and create an abusive working environment, Title VII is violated." Title VII's prohibition of discrimination on the basis of gender, Scalia continued, "protects men as well as women." The Court saw no justification in the language of Title VII for a "categorical rule excluding same-sex harassment claims." Male-on-male sexual harassment in the workplace was not the "principal evil" Congress was concerned with when it enacted Title VII, but statutory prohibitions "often go beyond the principal evil to cover reasonably comparable evils." Thus, the statutory term *sexual harassment* must be interpreted as including any kind of sexual harassment that meets the statutory requirements. The "critical issue" in the text of Title VII is whether members of one sex are "exposed to disadvantageous terms or conditions of employment to which members of the other sex are not exposed." Scalia was careful to note that there is another requirement that prevents Title VII from expanding into a "general civility code." The statute does not reach "genuine but innocuous differences" in the ways men and women "routinely interact" with members of the same and opposite sex. Rather, Title VII forbids only behavior "so objectively offensive as to alter the conditions of the victim's employment." Conduct that is not severe or pervasive enough to create an "objectively hostile or abusive work environment" is beyond the purview of Title VII, and inquiry in harassment cases requires "careful consideration of the social context" in which the behavior occurs.

Gender: Title IX

Grove City College v. Bell, **465 U.S. 555 (1984),** held that Title IX prohibitions against sex discrimination apply to private institutions through the fact that enrolled students receive federal education grants. *Grove City* also limited the scope of Title IX by ruling that the statute's language does not apply to an educational institution in its entirety, but only to the specific programs through which federal aid is received. Title IX of the Educational Amendments of 1972 prohibits sex discrimination "in any education program or activity receiving Federal financial assistance." There is also a provision that permits any federal agency administering assistance programs to secure compliance by terminating federal aid if compliance is not forthcoming. Grove City College, a private institution, accepted no federal assistance directly, nor did it administer any federal student grants. It did enroll a number of students who received federal educational grants. When the college refused to sign an assurance of compliance with Title IX, the Department of Education sought to terminate the grants awarded to students of the college on the grounds that Grove City was a recipient of federal assistance, however indirectly. The Supreme Court unanimously ruled that Title IX did apply to Grove City through the student grant program. The Court qualified the holding, however, by saying that receipt of the grant by some students did not require application of Title IX on an institution-wide basis. Rather, the holding affected only the college's financial aid program. The decision resolved two important questions about the scope and reach of Title IX and the regulations established by the Department of Education pursuant to Title IX. First, the Court rejected Grove City's contention that by its refusal to accept direct federal and state assistance, it had preserved its institutional autonomy from Title IX. The Court found that when students finance their education with federal Basic Educational Opportunity Grants, a centerpiece element of the Educational Amendments of 1972, an institution's programs are drawn into the coverage of Title IX. Congress had recognized discrimination in the administration of financial aid in education, and it sought to address the problem with grants-in-aid. The Court said it would be "anomalous" to find that one of the primary components of the comprehensive package of federal aid was not intended to trigger coverage under Title IX. The linchpin of Grove City's argument was the direct-indirect distinction, but the Court saw no support in the text of the law for such a distinction. The Court said that the language of the relevant section of Title IX was "all inclusive terminology" covering all forms of federal educational aid, direct or indirect. The Court also noted that Title IX was patterned after Title VI of the Civil Rights Act of 1964. Title VI envisioned the initiation of coverage with receipt of federal aid, and because Congress approved identical language when Title IX was adopted, the Court had no reason to believe that those who voted for Title IX intended a different result. The Court read the appropriate sections of the law as subject to program-specific applications. It rejected the view that "Grove City itself is a 'program or activity' that may be regulated in its entirety." In addition to what it saw as clear program-specific language, the Court said there was no evidence that the aid received by Grove City students resulted in diversion of funds from the college's student aid fund to other uses. Neither did the Court find the student aid analogous to a nonearmarked direct grant that an institution might use for whatever purpose it desired. The purpose of the grant was to enable students to get an education, not to increase institutional revenues. Although the student grants ultimately found their way into Grove City's general operating budget, that did not create regulatory authority to follow federally aided students from classroom to classroom, building to building, or activity to activity. Thus, although Grove City could be required to execute an Assurance of Compliance for its student aid program, under threat of termination of student grants, it could not be required to apply Title IX provisions institution wide. Justices Brennan, Marshall, and Stevens dissented on the second point. Justice Brennan said that the decision "conveniently ignored controlling indicia of congressional intent." He referred to the "absurdity" of the decision's practical effect. He feared the decision permits gender discrimination in mathematics classes, for example, even though affected students are supported by federal funds. "If anything about Title IX were ever certain," it is that discriminatory practices "were meant to be prohibited by the statute" on an institution-wide basis. *See also* CIVIL RIGHTS ACT OF 1964, p. 626; EQUAL PROTECTION CLAUSE, p. 473.

Significance　The Burger Court's decision in *Grove City College v. Bell* limited the scope of Title IX and reversed a decade of interpretation that held that the law reached entire institutions. The Court's judgment on this point essentially upheld a Reagan administration initiative that began to confine Title IX administratively. As recently as 1982 the Court had opted not to make restrictive interpretations of Title IX. In *North Haven Board of Education v. Bell*, 456 U.S. 512 (1982), for example, the Court held that Title IX prohibited sex discrimination in the employment practices of institutions receiving federal assistance. In doing so, the Court upheld an agency-ordered termination of funds to a school district, even though the language of Title IX does not explicitly extend to employment situations. In 1988 Congress enacted legislation "reaffirming" judicial and executive branch interpretations and enforcement practices that existed before the *Grove City* ruling. The effect of this legislation was to reinstate the "broad coverage" of the original antidiscrimination provisions of Title IX. The Court ruled in *Franklin v. Gwinnett County Public Schools*, 503 U.S. 60 (1992), that Title IX could serve as the basis of actions by school and college students seeking damages for various forms of sex discrimination. Franklin had filed a lawsuit against Gwinnett County schools claiming that she had been subjected to ongoing sexual harassment by a teacher. Her complaint was dismissed on the ground that a damage remedy is not available under Title IX. In a unanimous decision, the Supreme Court disagreed. Although Title IX does not specify damages as a remedy, Justice White said that it presumes "availability of all appropriate remedies unless Congress has expressly indicated otherwise." It had been urged by the Gwinnett County schools, supported by the Bush administration, that Title IX remedies be confined to backpay or injunctions directed at ending any violations. Such a limitation on remedies would have left Franklin "remediless," said White, in that she was no longer a student in the school system and the teacher was no longer employed by the school system. The Court also noted that Congress had clearly indicated intent not to limit the remedies available under Title IX by subsequent adoption of language amending Title IX.

Gender: Benevolent Purpose

Kahn v. Shevin, **416 U.S. 351 (1974),** upheld a state statute that provided a property tax exemption to widows, but not widowers. *Kahn v. Shevin* explored the fact that not all gender-based classifications convey disabilities to women. A number of enactments use gender as a "benevolent" classification, and *Kahn* allowed such a preferential policy. A Florida statute provided widows with an annual $500 exemption on property taxes. No similar benefit existed for widowers. The Supreme Court found the classification permissible. Justice Douglas wrote the brief opinion of the Court. He noted that "the financial difficulties confronting the lone woman in Florida or in any other State exceed those facing the man." Whether the cause was overt discrimination or "the socialization process of a male dominated culture," a woman finds the job market inhospitable. Douglas referred to data showing income disparities between males and females. This disparity was likely to be exacerbated for the widow. Unlike the male, the widow will be thrust into "a job market with which she is unfamiliar, and in which, because of her former economic dependency, she will have fewer skills to offer." The tax exemption was designed to further the policy of "cushioning the financial impact of spousal loss upon the sex for whom that loss imposes a disproportionately heavy burden." The Court differentiated this situation from that of *Frontiero v. Richardson,* 411 U.S. 677 (1973), in which benefits were granted on a gender basis solely for administrative convenience. The differentiation that favored females over males in granting the tax exemption in *Kahn* was a reasonable rather than an arbitrary distinction. States are to be permitted large leeway in making such classifications. Justices Brennan, White, and Marshall dissented. They argued that gender-based classifications are suspect and require more justification than the state offered. The dissenters also felt that the statute was "plainly overinclusive," and that the state should have been required to prove that its interests could not have been served by a more precisely tailored statute or by use of feasible and less-drastic means. For the dissenters, Florida could have advanced the interest of ameliorating the effect of past economic discrimination against women without categorically excluding males or including widows of substantial economic means. *See also* BENEVOLENT CLASSIFICATION, p. 621; CLASSIFICATION, p. 628; EQUAL PROTECTION CLAUSE, p. 473.

Significance   *Kahn v. Shevin* upheld a benevolent classification that conveyed favorable treatment to a designated class. A benevolent classification can survive equal protection scrutiny if the legislative objective is legitimate, and the classification reasonably pursues that end. In *Califano v. Webster,* 430 U.S. 313 (1977), the Court allowed a provision of the Social Security Act that permitted women to exclude more low-earning years than men in calculating an average wage for use in the benefit formula. The objective of the provision was "the permissible one of redressing our society's longstanding disparate treatment of women." The Court also upheld a gender-based differential requiring mandatory discharge of naval officers who failed to be promoted within a specified period of time in *Schlesinger v. Ballard,* 419 U.S. 498 (1975). Women were permitted four more years to gain promotion because women officers were not "similarly situated" to men. They had fewer opportunities to gain the needed professional service required for promotion.

Nevertheless, the Court has found some benevolent gender classifications actually to be punitive and therefore invalid. In *Weinberger v. Wiesenfeld*, 420 U.S. 636 (1975), for example, the Court found that social security survivor benefits for widows with minor children discriminated against women in that their compulsory social security contributions produced less protection for their survivors than the comparable contributions of men. Using the same reasoning, the Court set aside dependency requirements in the federal Old-Age, Survivors, and Disability Insurance Benefits Program in *Califano v. Goldfarb*, 430 U.S. 199 (1977). From the perspective of the two wage earners, the Act "plainly disadvantages women contributors as compared with similarly situated men." Congress repealed the dependency requirement following *Goldfarb*, but adopted a pension offset provision to soften the fiscal impact on the Social Security Trust Fund. The offset reduced benefits, but Congress exempted certain persons from the offset requirement if they had retired or were about to retire at the time the offset policy was adopted. Although the exemption protected the financial interests of these people, it also had the effect of extending the gender classification invalidated in *Goldfarb*. The Court unanimously upheld the exemption in *Heckler v. Mathews*, 465 U.S. 728 (1984).

In another social security benefits ruling, the Court held in *Bowen v. Owens*, 476 U.S. 340 (1986), that Congress could extend survivor benefits to widowed spouses who remarry while denying the same benefits to a surviving spouse who had been divorced from the decedent. The Court concluded that Congress had discretion to concentrate limited federal resources in places in which the need was greatest. Because divorced spouses did not enter remarriage with the same level of dependency on the wage earner's account as widowed persons, the Court reasoned it was acceptable for Congress to treat these groups differently after remarriage.

In *Orr v. Orr*, 440 U.S. 268 (1979), the Court voided an Alabama statute authorizing alimony payments to women but not to men. Justice Brennan suggested that benevolent gender classification carries "the inherent risk of reinforcing stereotypes about the proper place of women." Even compensatory objectives must be carefully tailored. Here the state's purpose could be as well served by a gender-neutral classification as by one that classified by gender. The latter carries with it the baggage of sexual stereotypes.

Americans with Disabilities Act

Bragdon v. Abbott, **118 S.Ct. 2196 (1998).** The Americans with Disabilities Act (ADA) was designed to eliminate discrimination against disabled persons in places of public accommodation. Sidney

Abbott disclosed that she was HIV-infected on a patient information form at a dentist's office. The dentist, Dr. Randon Bragdon, examined Abbott and found that she needed to have a cavity filled. He indicated, however, that it was his policy to fill cavities of persons with infectious diseases at a hospital. Bragdon said he would charge the same fee as if the work had been done in his office, but told Abbott she would have to cover hospital costs. She refused the offer and brought suit for violation of the ADA.

The Supreme Court ruled in *Bragdon v. Abbott* that HIV-infected persons are covered by the ADA even if they present no symptoms. In order to determine whether HIV infection met the disability definition of the Act, the Court engaged in a three-step inquiry: (1) to determine whether HIV infection is a "physical impairment"; (2) to identify the "life activity" upon which the claimant relies; and (3) to determine whether the impairment "substantially limited the major life activity." Justice Kennedy said that in light of the "immediacy with which the virus begins to damage the infected person's white blood cells and the severity of the disease, we hold that it is an impairment from the moment of infection." HIV infection must be regarded as a "physiological disorder with a constant and detrimental effect on the person's hemic and lymphatic systems from the moment of infection," thus the HIV infection meets the statutory definition of a physical impairment "during every stage of the disease." The statute, however, is not operative unless the impairment "affects a major life activity." Kennedy suggested that because of the "pervasive and invariably fatal course of the disease, its effect on major life activities of many sorts might have been relevant to our inquiry." The Court found that HIV infection had "profound impact on almost every phase of the infected person's life, but focused on reproduction because Abbott had argued from the outset of the case that the HIV infection impaired her ability to reproduce and bear children. Kennedy said that the Court had "little difficulty" concluding that reproduction is a major life activity. Although conception and childbirth are not impossible for an HIV-infected person, they are "dangerous to the public health." The disability definition, said Kennedy, "does not turn on personal choice." When significant limitations result from the impairment, the definition is met "even if the difficulties are not insurmountable." The Court concluded that Abbott was disabled in terms of the ADA, and remanded the case for further consideration of the dentists's contention that Abbott's disability posed a significant health risk to him. Chief Justice Rehnquist, joined by Justices O'Connor, Scalia, and Thomas, dissented. They did not find reproduction a major life activity under the ADA. Although the dissenters did not deny that reproductive decisions are "important in a person's life," fundamental importance "of this sort, is not the common thread linking the statute's listed activities." Rather, the common thread, said Rehnquist, is that the "activities are repetitively performed and essential in the day-to-day existence of a normal functioning individual." Even presuming that reproduction is a major life activity, however, the dissenters did not agree that an "asymptomatic HIV infection substantially limits that activity." Although a person infected with HIV may not choose to engage in sexual activity, bear a child if she becomes pregnant, or perform the tasks necessary to rear a child, the dissenters found "no support in language, logic, or case law for the proposition that such voluntary choices constitute a 'limit' on one's own life activities." *See also* EQUAL PROTECTION CLAUSE, p. 473.

Significance   Disabilities present distinctive and difficult equal protection questions. The issue of physical qualifications for professional training programs is an example. Frances Davis sought admission to a registered nursing program at a state community college despite a hearing disability. She was denied admission and filed suit under the Rehabilitation Act, which prohibits discrimination against an "otherwise qualified handicapped person, solely by reason of his handicap." The Court unanimously held in *Southeastern Community College v. Davis*, 440 U.S. 980 (1979), that an educational institution may impose reasonable physical qualifications for admission to a clinical training program.

The Court ruled in *School Board of Nassau County v. Arline*, 480 U.S. 273 (1987), that the Rehabilitation Act also prohibits discrimination against persons with contagious diseases. The Act provides that no "otherwise qualified" person can be excluded from any program receiving federal funding simply because of a handicap. Among the ways *handicap* is defined includes one who has a "record of impairment" that limits one or more major life activities. Subsequent administrative regulations have included work as a major life activity. Arline, a teacher, had been hospitalized for tuberculosis in 1957 before the disease went into remission. In 1977 and 1978 Arline suffered relapses and was suspended with pay at the end of the school year. She was then discharged because of the continued recurrence of the disease. Arline failed to obtain relief under state law and brought suit under the Rehabilitation Act. The Supreme Court concluded that Arline had established a record of impairment since her initial hospitalization. The school district argued that this was irrelevant and that Arline was dismissed because of the threat her continued employment posed to others. The Court rejected the contention that the contagious effects of Arline's disease could be distinguished from the physical effects of the disease. It would be unreasonable to allow an employer to use a distinction between the effects of a disease on others and the effects on the patient to justify discriminatory treatment.

The Rehnquist Court decided a second Americans with Disabilities Act case in addition to *Bragdon* in 1998. A Pennsylvania trial court sentenced Ronald Yeskey to prison for 18 to 36 months. The court recommended that Yeskey be assigned to the "boot camp" program, which would have made him eligible for release after six months provided he successfully completed the program's requirements. The Pennsylvania Department of Corrections did not place Yeskey in the program, however, because of his high blood pressure. Yeskey brought an action against the department in federal district court claiming that failure to assign him to the program or an equivalent alternative violated the ADA. The ADA prohibits denial of a qualified person from an opportunity to take advantage of a benefit offered by a public agency. Yeskey claimed he was denied an opportunity for a substantially shortened sentence by the department's failure to assign him to the boot camp program. The Supreme Court unanimously ruled in *Pennsylvania Department of Corrections v. Yeskey*, 118 S.Ct. 1952 (1998), that the ADA covers state prisoners. Exercising ultimate control over the management of state prisons is a "traditional and essential State function." When such functions are involved, Congress must make an "unmistakably clear" intention to "alter the usual constitutional balance between the States and federal Government" before the courts will interpret a federal law in a manner that will "reserve rather than destroy" the sovereign powers of the states. Further, the Court rejected Pennsylvania's attempt to invoke the doctrine of "constitutional doubt," which requires that courts interpret statutes to avoid "grave and doubtful constitutional questions." That doctrine enters in only when a statute is "susceptible of two constructions." The Court concluded that the text of the ADA was not "ambiguous." The fact that a statute could be "applied in situations not expressly anticipated by Congress does not demonstrate ambiguity." Rather, said Justice Scalia, "it demonstrates breadth."

Irrebuttable Presumptions

Vlandis v. Kline, **412 U.S. 441 (1973),** invalidated a classification based on residency because it constituted an irrebuttable presumption. *Vlandis* examined whether equal protection issues may be assessed by using a framework in which a classification is presumed to exist, while those affected by the classification are prohibited from disputing their status. Connecticut required nonresident state university students to pay higher tuition and higher fees than state residents. If the legal address of a married student was outside the state at the time of application for admission to the university, such a person would forever remain a nonresident student. Similarly, if an unmarried person had a legal address outside Connecticut at any time during the year prior to seeking university admission, that person would permanently and irrebuttably retain nonresident status. At issue in the case was not the residency classification per se, but rather the "conclusive and unchangeable presumption" attached to it. Kline and others claimed that they had a constitutional right to controvert that presumption of nonresidence by presenting evidence that they were bona fide residents. Connecticut sought to justify the presumption through its interest in equalizing the cost of public higher education between state residents and nonresidents.

The Court ruled that rather than ensuring that only its bona fide residents receive their full subsidy, the Connecticut presumption also ensured that some bona fide residents, like Kline, did *not* receive their full subsidy. They could never do so while they remained students. The Court also refused to allow Connecticut to turn its classification into a policy that "favors with the lower rate only its established residents, whose past tax contributions to the State have been higher," because the statutory provisions are "so arbitrary as to constitute a denial of due process of law." Finally, the Court rejected Connecticut's justification of administrative convenience and certainty. Such an interest "cannot save the conclusive presumption from invalidity where there are other reasonable and practicable means of establishing the pertinent facts on which the State's objective is premised." Thus *Vlandis* held that irrebuttable presumptions are prohibited when the presumption is not necessarily or universally true, and when there are reasonable alternative means of making the crucial determination.

Chief Justice Burger and Justices Rehnquist and Douglas dissented, taking issue with application of the language of strict scrutiny to a Due Process Clause issue. The dissenters also felt Connecticut should be free to pursue a policy that favored established state residents. *See also* CLASSIFICATION, p. 628; EQUAL PROTECTION CLAUSE, p. 473; IRREBUTTABLE PRESUMPTION, p. 667.

Significance   *Vlandis* struck down a state residency requirement because it was based on a conclusive or irrebuttable presumption. A provision of the Food Stamp Act was likewise invalidated in *United States Department of Agriculture v. Murry*, 413 U.S. 508 (1973). The Act withheld food stamp eligibility from households with an 18-year-old "who is claimed as a dependent child for Federal tax purposes by a taxpayer who is not a member of an eligible household." The Court ruled that the provision created a conclusive presumption that such a household is not in need, and that the presumption was not a rational measure of need.

In *Cleveland Board of Education v. La Fleur*, 414 U.S. 632 (1974), the Court struck down a requirement that pregnant teachers take an unpaid leave at least five months prior to their child's expected date of birth and not return to work until the semester following the child's attaining an age of three months. The Court noted the failure of the regulation to make individual determinations of a teacher's capacity to continue teaching. The rule served no legitimate purpose, and it unnecessarily penalized the female teacher for asserting her right to bear children.

An irrebuttable presumption is not categorically prohibited, however. In *Weinberger v. Salfi*, 422 U.S. 749 (1975), the Court upheld a duration-of-relationship requirement for survivor benefits under social security. By law, benefits are denied to wives and stepchildren in cases in which the marriage occurred less than nine months prior to the death of the wage earner. The Court ruled that Congress could reasonably conclude that a broad prophylactic rule could protect against the possibility of persons entering marriage simply to claim benefits upon the anticipated early death of the wage earner. The restriction also obviated the necessity for large numbers of individual determinations. Further, it protected large numbers of claimants who satisfy the rule from the uncertainties and delays of administrative inquiry into the circumstances of their marriages.

In *Massachusetts Board of Retirement v. Murgia*, 427 U.S. 307 (1976), the Court upheld a mandatory retirement age against arguments that individual fitness determinations were a more reasonable approach.

A slightly different kind of presumption was reviewed in *Michael H. v. Gerald D.*, 491 U.S. 110 (1989). Under provisions of California law, a child born to a married woman living with her husband, absent a showing of sterility, is conclusively presumed to be an issue of the marriage. The statute permitted only limited rebuttal to this presumption and only by the husband or wife. A challenge to the law was brought by a man (Michael H.) who fathered a child (Victoria D.) during an affair with a married woman (Carole D.) who, at the time of the affair, was separated from her husband (Gerald D.). The husband and wife later reconciled. Test results demonstrated to a certainty in excess of 98 percent that the plaintiff (Michael H.) was the child's father. The law was also challenged on behalf of the child who wished a father-child relationship with both Michael and Gerald. The law makes "irrelevant for paternity purposes" whether a child conceived or born into an existing marriage was fathered by anyone but the husband. The presumption not only expresses substantive policy but "furthers it, excluding inquiries into the child's paternity that would be destructive of family integrity and privacy."

The Court then turned to the substantive issue of whether Michael had a constitutionally protected liberty interest in his relationship with Victoria. Michael contended that the state's interest in protecting the union of Gerald and Carole was insufficient to justify termination of his parental relationship. Considerations of substantive due process hinge on a liberty interest being "fundamental," and that it be an interest "traditionally protected by our society." The legal issue in this case, said the Court, "reduces to whether the relationship between persons" in the situation of Michael and Victoria has been treated as a "protected family unit under the historic practices of our society," or whether on any other basis it has been accorded "special protection." The Court ruled that "it is impossible to find that it has." Indeed, the Court found the reverse to be true. Rather, "our traditions have protected the marital family against the sort of claim Michael asserts."

Sexual Orientation

Romer v. Evans, **517 U.S. 620 (1996)** The voters of Colorado passed a constitutional amendment (Amendment 2) that repealed all state or local laws prohibiting discrimination on the basis of sexual orientation and banned the passage of any such laws or ordinances in the future. Soon after the passage of the amendment, it was challenged in the Colorado courts by several individuals and some of the local governmental units that had policies repealed by the amendment. The Supreme Court held that the amendment was unconstitutional. The Court found that Amendment 2 did more than rescind ordinances that prohibit discrimination on the basis of sexual orientation. It prohibited all "legislative, executive, or judicial action at any level of state or local government designed to protect the named class." The state's defense of the amendment was that Amendment 2 put gays and lesbians "in the same position as all other persons." According to its proponents, the measure did no more than deny homosexuals "special rights." Kennedy termed this reading of Amendment 2 as "implausible," and characterized the changes in legal status resulting from Amendment 2 as "sweeping and comprehensive." By state mandate, homosexuals are "put in a solitary class" with regard to transactions and relations in both the private and public spheres. Amendment 2, said Kennedy, "withdraws from homosexuals, but no others, specific legal protection from the injuries caused by discrimination, and it forbids reinstatement of these laws and policies." The amendment "imposes a special disability upon those persons alone." Amendment 2 failed the "conventional inquiry" regarding equal protection that a classificatory scheme must bear a "rational relation to some legitimate end." The amendment has the "peculiar" property of imposing a "broad and undifferentiated disability on a single named group," said Kennedy. The "sheer breadth" of the amendment is so "discontinuous" with the justification offered for it that the amendment seems "inexplicable by anything but animus toward the class." Indeed, the Court could not find any "identifiable legitimate purpose" for the amendment. The Court also rejected Colorado's contention that Amendment 2 was designed to protect other persons' rights to association, and the rights of landlords and employers who have "personal or religious objections" to homosexuality. No state has the authority to "deem a class of persons a stranger to its laws." Justice Scalia offered a scathing dissent that was joined by Chief Justice Rehnquist and Justice Thomas. Scalia called Amendment 2 a "modest attempt...to preserve traditional sexual mores against the efforts of a politically powerful minority to revise those mores through the use of the laws." Scalia referred to the "cultural debate" currently taking place to determine whether "opposition to homosexuality is as reprehensible as racial or religious bias." The Court, said Scalia, "has no business imposing upon all Americans the resolution favored by the elite class from which the members of this institution are selected, pronouncing that 'animosity' toward homosexuality is evil." Scalia was also critical of Kennedy's opinion for not mentioning the "most relevant" case on the issue of homosexual rights, *Bowers v. Hardwick*, 478 U.S. 186 (1986). In *Bowers* the Court upheld a Georgia law that criminalized sodomy, finding that the Constitution does not prohibit "making homosexual conduct a crime." If it is constitutional for a state to criminalize homosexual conduct, Scalia said, "surely it is constitutionally permissible for a state to enact other laws merely disfavoring homosexual conduct." It follows, he concluded, that it is permissible for a state to adopt a provision merely prohibiting all levels of state government from "bestowing special protections upon homosexual conduct." *See also Bragdon v. Abbott*, p. 578, CLASSIFICATION, p. 628, EQUAL PROTECTION CLAUSE, p. 473.

Significance   The Court has reviewed very few cases involving homosexual rights as such. Even *Romer* was resolved on political rights grounds. The right of privacy is commonly limited to traditional marital relationships. In *Doe v. Commonwealth's Attorney*, 425 U.S. 901 (1976), the Court summarily affirmed a three-judge district court dismissal of a privacy challenge to the use of a state sodomy statute against homosexuals. The lower court found that homosexuality was "obviously no portion of marriage, house, or family life," and that a state may impose criminal sanctions on conduct "even when committed in the home, in the promotion of morality and decency." A more thorough discussion can be found in the controversial ruling of *Bowers v. Hardwick*, the case that Justice Scalia used as the basis of his dissent *Romer*. In *Bowers*, the Court upheld a state law that criminalized consensual sodomy. The Court said that homosexuals had no right to engage in sodomy. The Court rejected the contention that the previous right of privacy cases insulated private sexual conduct between consenting adults from state regulation. Neither does the fact that the conduct occurred in the privacy of a home immunize otherwise illegal conduct. Victimless crimes such as possession and use of illegal drugs, said the Court, "do not escape the law when they are committed at home." The same is true for sexual conduct. It would be difficult to limit the asserted right to homosexual conduct "while leaving exposed to prosecution adultery, incest, and other sexual crimes even though they are committed in the home. We are unwilling to start down that road."

The Court indirectly addressed the issue of AIDS in *School Board of Nassau County v. Arline*, 480 U.S. 273 (1987). The principal issue in *Arline* was whether a school district could discharge a teacher whose tuberculosis recurred. The Court ruled that the Rehabilitation Act, which provides that no "otherwise qualified handicapped shall be excluded from participating in any program receiving federal funds solely on the basis of handicap," prevented ending her employment, despite the threat her disease might pose for others. The decision had implications for persons suffering from AIDS. Although Justice Brennan's opinion in *Arline* did not discuss AIDS as such, two footnotes to the opinion made reference to AIDS. One responded to the contention that some carriers of a disease may not suffer any physical impairment. Discrimination solely on the basis of contagiousness may not be handicap discrimination. The second footnote indicated that a person who poses a significant risk of communicating an infectious disease to others in the workplace may become unqualified for her or his job if reasonable accommodation would not eliminate that risk. HIV infection was discussed more directly in *Bragdon v. Abbott*, 118 S.Ct. 2196 (1998).

PRIVACY
Origin

Griswold v. Connecticut, **381 U.S. 479 (1965)**, struck down a state birth control regulation as an impermissible invasion of privacy. The Constitution contains no expressed right of privacy, but in *Griswold* the Court fashioned such a right out of various provisions of the Bill of Rights. The Court was presented with the occasion to consider the privacy issue through review of a Connecticut statute that made it a crime to use birth control devices or provide counsel on their use. Griswold was arrested and convicted for violation of the statute. The Supreme Court voided the statute in a seven-to-two decision, although members of the majority differed in their views about the source of the privacy protection. The opinion of the Court was offered by Justice Douglas. He disclaimed that the Court should act as a "super-legislature," making determinations about the "wisdom, need, and propriety of laws that touch economic problems, business affairs, or social conditions." At the same time, said Douglas, the Connecticut statute "operates directly on an intimate relation of husband and wife and their physician's role in one aspect of that relation." The Court could intervene because "various guarantees create zones of privacy." These zones are formed by emanations from "penumbras" of specific Bill of Rights guarantees. Justice Douglas developed the freedom of association as an example. The Court protected the privacy of association as a right peripheral to the First Amendment. The protection of association comes from a First Amendment penumbra under which expression is broadly protected from governmental interference. The emanations that cast the penumbras draw from Bill of Rights guarantees and give them life and substance. The several guarantees involved with privacy include: the First Amendment; the privacy of the home, which comes from the Third and Fourth Amendments; the self-incrimination provision of the Fifth Amendment; and the Ninth Amendment. Justices Harlan and White used the Due Process Clause of the Fourteenth Amendment to find that "the enactment violates basic values implicit in the concept of ordered liberty." Justices Black and Stewart dissented. Justice Black noted the absence of a specific constitutional provision and accused the Court of engaging in wholly inappropriate substantive second-guessing. He said the Court does not possess the power "to measure constitutionality by our belief that legislation is arbitrary, capricious or unreasonable, or accomplishes no justifiable purpose, or is offensive to our own notions of civilized standards of conduct." Justice Black compared the Court's approach to that of the substantive due process cases of an earlier era and felt it "no less dangerous when used to enforce this Court's views about personal rights than those about economic rights." *See also Moore v. East Cleveland*, p. 599; RIGHT OF PRIVACY, p. 476; *Roe v. Wade*, p. 588.

Significance   *Griswold* defined privacy as a constitutionally protected right. The key questions remaining after *Griswold* were the scope of the protection and the criteria for application of the right. Initially the Court enlarged upon the privacy protection defined in *Griswold*, particularly as it affected procreation. In *Eisenstadt v. Baird*, 405 U.S. 438 (1972), the Court struck down a Massachusetts statute limiting distribution of contraceptives to married persons. Justice Brennan argued that "if the right of privacy means anything, it is the right of the individual, married or single, to be free from unwarranted governmental intrusion into matters so fundamentally affecting a person as the decision whether to bear or beget a child." *Eisenstadt* became the cornerstone of the highly controversial abortion decision of *Roe v. Wade*, 410 U.S. 113 (1973). In a related case, the Court invalidated a New York law prohibiting contraceptive sales to minors in *Carey v. Population Services International*, 431 U.S. 678 (1977). Boundaries began to appear in the mid-1970s as the Court talked of privacy rights as attaching to such matters as marriage, procreation, and the family. Outside those contexts, claims of invasion of privacy have been generally unsuccessful.

Abortion

***Roe v. Wade*, 410 U.S. 113 (1973),** held that criminal abortion statutes impermissibly encroach upon a woman's right of privacy. *Roe v. Wade* was by far the most controversial outgrowth of the privacy doctrine begun in *Griswold v. Connecticut*, 381 U.S. 479 (1965). *Wade* involved a Texas statute that made it a crime to perform an abortion except when preserving the mother's life. It was typical of many nineteenth-century criminal abortion laws. Justice Blackmun's opinion surveyed criminal abortion laws and reviewed the states' rationale for them. The objectives of these statutes were to discourage illicit sexual conduct, protect pregnant women from the hazardous abortion procedure, and protect prenatal life. In Blackmun's view, only the final justification, protection of prenatal life, offered any possibility of providing a sufficient state interest that might override a pregnant woman's privacy right. It was, however, a very limited interest because the language and meaning of the Fourteenth Amendment applies "only postnatally." The term *person* as used in the Amendment "does not include the unborn." Furthermore, the privacy protection is broad enough to encompass a woman's decision whether or not to terminate her pregnancy. It might appear, therefore, that the woman's choice was to be absolutely insulated from regulation. That is not quite so, for there comes a time in every pregnancy when the state's interests "become sufficiently compelling to sustain regulation of the factors that govern the abortion decision." Justice Blackmun established a timetable for these interests based upon the three trimesters of a pregnancy. During the first trimester, a state has no interest whatsoever. Throughout the second trimester, the state could regulate the conditions under which abortions occur. The pregnant woman, in consultation with her physician, was still free to determine, without regulation by the state, whether or not to terminate the pregnancy. The state's interest in protecting potential life begins with the final trimester when the fetus becomes viable or has the capability of meaningful life outside the mother's womb. This approach allowed Justice Blackmun to suggest that the Court need not resolve the difficult question of when life begins. When doctors, philosophers, and theologians "are unable to arrive at any consensus, the judiciary is not in a position to speculate as to the answer." Justices White and Rehnquist dissented, as neither saw any consideration of privacy that could justify striking down the Texas statute. *See also Griswold v. Connecticut*, p. 586; *Harris v. McRae*, p. 596; RIGHT OF PRIVACY, p. 476; *Webster v. Reproductive Health Services*, p. 589.

Significance   *Roe v. Wade* established a woman's right to have an abortion. *Doe v. Bolton*, 410 U.S. 179 (1973), was a companion case to *Wade*, in which a Georgia law was also invalidated. The Georgia enactment was less than five years old at the time the Court reviewed it, and was thought to be a prototype of modern abortion regulation, but the Court found the statute overly restrictive in several ways. First, the statute required that all abortions take place in certified hospitals, even during the first trimester. Second, a committee of hospital staff persons was required to approve the procedure. Third, the judgment of the woman's physician needed confirmation by at least two other physicians. The statute was also flawed because of a residency requirement.

Since *Roe* the Court has sustained increasing regulation of abortion. In *Harris v. McRae*, 448 U.S. 297 (1980), for example, the Court said that federal Medicaid funds could not be used to cover abortion costs. In *Colautti v. Franklin*, 439 U.S. 379 (1979), the Court held a Pennsylvania viability statute unconstitutional because it subjected physicians to possible criminal prosecution if certain specified techniques were not used when a fetus "is" or "may be" viable. The Court felt the requirement was too vague. It subjected physicians to threat in the absence of intent. The statute was also seen as having a "chilling effect" on the willingness of physicians to perform abortions. More comprehensive regulation was permitted in *Webster v. Reproductive Health Services*, 492 U.S. 490 (1989). The critical question for the last decade has been how long the basic premises of *Roe v. Wade* will be retained by the Court.

Abortion Regulation

Webster v. Reproductive Health Services, **492 U.S. 490 (1989),** provided the Court with an opportunity to fully reconsider *Roe v. Wade*, 410 U.S. 113 (1973). The Court rendered a decision in *Webster* that substantially modified *Roe*, but did not explicitly overrule it. The origin of the case was a Missouri statute enacted in 1986. Several components of the statute were challenged in federal court by a number of doctors and nurses and two nonprofit medical corporations, one of which was Reproductive Health Services (RHS). The challenged provisions included: (1) a preamble stating that life begins at conception, and that the "unborn" have life interests requiring protection; (2) a requirement that before performing an abortion on any woman who a physician had "reason to believe" was 20 or more weeks pregnant, the physician had to determine whether the fetus was "viable" by performing specified medical examinations and tests; (3) an informed-consent requirement that included information on abortion alternatives; and (4) prohibitions on use of public funds, public facilities, or public employees in "performing or assisting" an abortion. This prohibition included public employees counseling pregnant women to have nontherapeutic abortions.

The Supreme Court allowed the restrictions, but did not explicitly reverse *Roe*. The opinion of the Court was delivered by Chief Justice Rehnquist. The Court did not rule on the preamble because it was seen as an "abstract proposition" rather than an operating regulation. Because the preamble did not restrict the activities of RHS in "some concrete way," the Court concluded RHS had no standing to challenge the preamble language. This ruling was a rejection of RHS's argument that the preamble was an "operative part" of the statute intended to "guide the interpretation of other provisions of the Act." The Court allowed the ban on the use of public funds, facilities, and employees. Increased costs and possible delays were attributed to the regulation by RHS. The Supreme Court used much of the same analysis as can be found in the Medicaid cases such as *Maher v. Roe*, 432 U.S. 464 (1977), and *Harris v. McRae*, 448 U.S. 297 (1980), and recognized the state's decision to "encourage childbirth over abortion." Chief Justice Rehnquist said that policy preference "places no governmental obstacle in the path of a woman who chooses to terminate her pregnancy." Missouri's refusal to allow public employees to perform abortions or to allow abortions to be performed in public facilities leaves a pregnant woman "with the same choices as if the State had chosen not to operate any public hospitals at all." Having already ruled that state refusal to fund abortions (in *Maher* and *Harris*) does not violate *Roe v. Wade*, it "strains logic to reach a contrary result for the use of public facilities and employees."

Rehnquist then turned to the most critical aspect of the decision, the viability testing requirements. Rehnquist said the statute required physicians to perform "only those tests that are useful to making subsidiary findings as to viability." Key, however, was the presumption of viability at 20 weeks, which had to be directly rebutted by viability test results before an abortion could be performed. The *Roe v. Wade* decision was based on a concept of trimesters. Under *Roe*, the interests of the fetus are not recognized until the final trimester, which occurs about 24 weeks into the pregnancy. A problem, said Rehnquist, was the "rigid trimester analysis of the course of a pregnancy enunciated in *Roe*." The Court simply should not function as the "country's *ex officio* medical board with powers to approve or disapprove medical and operative practices and standards." Thus, a loosening of the "web of legal rules" developed through application of *Roe* could be performed. More important, the Court did not see "why the State's interest in protecting potential human life should come into existence only at the point of viability," and that there should be a "rigid line allowing state regulation after viability but prohibiting it before viability." The Court acknowledged that the tests "increase the expense of abortion and regulate the discretion of the physician in determining viability of the fetus." Nonetheless, the Court was "satisfied" that the viability testing requirement "permissibly furthers the State's interest in protecting potential human life" and is constitutional. Justice O'Connor agreed that the viability testing requirement was constitutional, but came to that conclusion because she did not see the requirement as incompatible with *Roe v. Wade*. Justice Scalia was also among the majority, but said in his concurring opinion that *Roe* had been effectively overruled. Indeed, he was critical of Rehnquist for not acknowledging that result. By hanging on to *Roe*, Scalia said the Court "needlessly" prolonged its "self-awarded sovereignty over a field where it has little proper business" since responses to most of the critical questions are "political and not juridical."

Justices Blackmun, Brennan, Marshall, and Stevens dissented. Blackmun, the author of the *Roe v. Wade* opinion, was most outspoken in criticizing the decision. He was very troubled by the viability testing and what it meant to the *Roe* trimester framework. He was even more troubled by Rehnquist's decision to uphold viability testing because it "permissibly furthers the State's interest in protecting potential human life." The "newly minted" standard is "circular and totally meaningless." *See also* RIGHT OF PRIVACY, p. 476; *Roe v. Wade*, p. 588.

Significance   *Webster* signaled state legislatures that the Court would be receptive to additional restrictions on abortion. *Thornburgh v. American College of Obstetricians & Gynecologists*, 476 U.S. 747 (1986), reaffirmed a woman's constitutional right to an abortion. *Thornburgh* involved a challenge to a state abortion control statute. The authors of the statute did not dispute the fact that the law was designed to discourage elective abortions. Suit was brought by an organization of obstetricians and gynecologists as well as various individuals. They alleged that the statute was incompatible with *Roe v. Wade*.

The challenged provisions of the statute fell into three main categories. The first required that all women give informed consent before an abortion. This required the woman be told of the comparative risks of abortion and full-term pregnancy, the medical assistance benefits available for full-term pregnancies, the legal recourse for obtaining support from the father, and the possible detrimental physical and psychological effects of having an abortion. The woman was also to be told of the characteristics of the fetus in two-week gestational increments.

The second category of regulations involved reporting. All physicians were required to report a variety of information about the woman, the abortion, and the nonviability of the fetus. Although these reports were not to be deemed public records, they were accessible for public inspection and copying.

Third, the law required all physicians performing abortions after a point when the fetus could be viable to exercise the degree of care required to preserve the fetus. The attendance of a second physician was mandated in all instances in which viability was possible.

Despite the numerous attempts to restrict the exercise of a woman's right of choice, Justice Blackmun said that the constitutional principles that provided the basis for *Roe* "still provide the compelling reason for recognizing the constitutional dimensions of a woman's right to decide whether to end her pregnancy." The states are not free, under the guise of protecting maternal health or potential life, to intimidate women into continuing pregnancies. Close analysis of the statute's provisions showed that they wholly subordinated constitutional privacy interests and concerns with maternal health in an effort to deter a woman from making a decision that, with her physician, was hers to make. Blackmun characterized the informational requirements as "poorly disguised elements of discouragement for the abortion decision." He called the provision requiring dissemination of specific printed materials an "out-right attempt to wedge" the state's antiabortion message into the privacy of the patient-physician dialogue. The reporting requirements were found impermissible because they "raise the spectre of public exposure." The decision to terminate a pregnancy is an intensely private one that must be protected in a way that assures anonymity. A woman and her physician would necessarily be more reluctant to choose an abortion if there existed a possibility that her decision and her identity would become known publicly. The second physician attendance requirement when possible fetus viability exists was struck down because it addressed no medical emergency. It simply chilled the performance of late abortions. Blackmun concluded by saying that the Constitution recognizes that a certain private sphere of individual liberty will be kept largely beyond the reach of government. Few decisions are more "personal and intimate, more properly private, or more basic to individual dignity and autonomy" than the abortion decision.

The statute reviewed in *Thornburgh* closely resembled the law struck down in *Akron v. Akron Center for Reproductive Health, Inc.*, 462 U.S. 416 (1983). The Akron ordinance required that all abortions performed after the first trimester occur in a hospital, and that unmarried minors under 15 years of age have parental consent or a court order to obtain an abortion. Further, attending physicians must convey specific statements about the fetus as a "human life," about fetal viability, and about the physical and emotional complications that may result from an abortion in an effort to ensure that the patient's consent is "informed."

Between *Akron* and *Thornburgh*, the Reagan administration strongly urged the overruling of *Roe v. Wade*. Although reversal did not happen in *Thornburgh*, the majority in favor of retaining *Roe* reduced to five to four. Most enactments imposing restrictions on abortions reviewed by the Court before *Akron* were invalidated. In *Planned Parenthood of Central Missouri v. Danforth*, 428 U.S. 52 (1976), for example, the Court rejected spousal consent, or parental consent in the case of an unmarried minor, for all abortions. The Court said that a state cannot delegate a veto power that the state itself is absolutely and totally prohibited from exercising.

The Court reiterated its position on consent requirements in *Bellotti v. Baird*, 443 U.S. 622 (1979), by rejecting a parental consent requirement because it provided no process by which the minor's own capacity to make the decision could be examined. Several abortion regulations received the Court's approval, however. In *H.L. v. Matheson*, 450 U.S. 398 (1981), the Court upheld a parental *notification* provision if the patient were a minor, although parental *consent* for the abortion was not required. Regulations in the two companion cases to *Akron* were also upheld. In *Planned Parenthood Association v. Ashcroft*, 462 U.S. 476 (1983), statutory provisions involving parental consent, mandatory pathological examination of all abortion tissue, and attendance of a second physician for abortions after 12 weeks were upheld. The Missouri consent section was approved because, unlike *Akron*, it contained a process by which a minor could be determined mature enough to make the decision, thus bypassing parental or judicial consent.

Two other cases involving parental notification were decided in 1990. A Minnesota statute required notification of both biological parents when a minor daughter sought an abortion, but the Court struck down this requirement in *Hodgson v. Minnesota*, 497 U.S. 417 (1990). The statute contained contingency language that if a court enjoined enforcement of the notification requirement, the statute would be amended automatically to provide a judicial by-pass as an alternative to parental notification. This alternative allowed a minor to petition a court for permission to obtain an abortion without notifying her parents. The Court upheld this alternative with Justice O'Connor providing the decisive vote. The Ohio statute required notification of only one parent. It also contained judicial by-pass language, but the Court upheld the one-parent notice requirement in *Ohio v. Akron Center for Reproductive Services*, 497 U.S. 502 (1990).

The defect with the Minnesota statute absent the judicial by-pass arose from the fact that only about half of Minnesota's minors resided with both biological parents. Justice Stevens spoke of the "particularly harmful effects" of the two-parent notification requirement on "both the minor and custodial parent when parents were divorced or separated." In addition, the Court concluded that the requirement "does not reasonably further any legitimate state interest." The principal justification for notification was that it "supports the authority of a parent who is presumed to act in the minor's best interest and thereby assures that the minor's decision to terminate her pregnancy is knowing, intelligent, and deliberate." To the extent "such an interest is legitimate," it could be "fully served" by the notification of one parent who can then seek counsel from the other parent or anyone else. The state has no legitimate interest in questioning the one parent's judgment on whether to seek wider counsel. The Court concluded that the two-parent requirement actually "disserves" any state interest in protecting a minor in "dysfunctional families." Two-parent notice in such situations is "positively harmful to the minor and her family." As in cases involving judicial hearings as an alternative to securing parental consent for an abortion, the Court found the by-pass alternative constitutionally sufficient for notification as well. The judicial by-pass feature allows a minor to demonstrate she is fully capable of making the abortion decision.

The Court decided the Ohio case without actually ruling on whether the judicial by-pass provision was necessary in the one-parent notice situation. Rather, it upheld the one-parent notification requirement as a "rational way" for a state to assist a pregnant minor who is considering abortion. "It would deny all dignity to the family," said Justice Kennedy, "to say that the State cannot take this reasonable step ... to ensure that, in most cases, a young woman will receive guidance and understanding from a parent."

Several provisions of the Pennsylvania Abortion Control Act were before the Court in *Planned Parenthood of Southeastern Pennsylvania v. Casey*, 505 U.S. 833 (1992). The Act required a woman seeking an abortion to give "informed consent." To that end, the woman had to be provided with certain information at least 24 hours before an abortion. A minor had to obtain the informed consent of one of her parents. As in parental consent requirements upheld by the Court in previous cases, judicial by-pass was allowed if the minor did not wish to seek or could not secure parental consent. Further, the Act required a married woman to inform her husband of the intended abortion. Finally, the Act established certain reporting requirements for facilities that perform abortions.

As with several other cases in recent years, most notably *Webster*, this case provided the Court with an opportunity to reconsider the basic question of whether an abortion is constitutionally protected; that is, whether to overturn the ruling of *Roe v. Wade*. A coalition of five justices—Blackmun, Stevens, O'Connor, Kennedy, and Souter— said "the essential holding of *Roe v. Wade* should be retained and once again reaffirmed." These same five justices struck down the portion of the Act requiring notification of the husband. Over the dissents of Blackmun and Stevens, the other seven justices upheld the remaining four restrictions contained in the Pennsylvania law. Justices O'Connor, Kennedy, and Souter issued a decisive joint opinion. They identified three underlying principles from *Roe v. Wade* that must be retained: First, women have a right to an abortion at any time before fetal viability and must be free to obtain it "without undue interference from the States." Prior to viability, they said, a state's interests are not strong enough to support either a prohibition on abortion or to impose any "substantial obstacle to the woman's effective right to elect an abortion." Second, they confirmed a state's power to regulate abortions after fetal viability as long as the regulation "contains exceptions for pregnancies which endanger a woman's life or health." Third, a state has a legitimate interest in protecting a woman's health and the "life of the fetus that may become a child" from the "outset" of the pregnancy. These principles, they concluded, "do not contradict one another; and we adhere to each."

The three justices referred to abortion as a "unique act," and a state is not entitled to "proscribe it in all instances." This is because the liberty of a woman "is at stake in a sense unique to the human condition and so unique to the law." The right is qualified, however. Women must be able to "make the ultimate decision," although the right to an abortion does not permit her to be "insulated from all others in doing so." As a result, regulations that only create a structural mechanism by which the state, or the parent or guardian of a minor, may "express profound respect for the life of the unborn" are permissible if they do not create a "substantial obstacle to the woman's exercise of the right to choose." Similarly, regulations intended to foster the health of a pregnant woman "are valid if they do not constitute an undue burden."

Justice Blackmun expressed strong support for the reaffirmation of *Roe*, and acknowledged as an "act of personal courage and constitutional principles" the positions taken by O'Connor, Kennedy, and Souter. At the same time, he expressed a "fear for the darkness as four Justices anxiously await the single vote necessary to extinguish the light." He noted his age (83), and said he and his vote could not "remain on this Court forever." He predicted a serious confirmation battle for that vote upon his decision to step down.

Chief Justice Rehnquist, in dissent, said that *Roe* was "wrongly decided" and should be overruled. Following what he called a "newly minted variation on *stare decisis*," Rehnquist said that the Court had retained only the "outer shell" of *Roe*.

To Justice Scalia, the question in *Casey* was not whether the "power of a woman to abort her unborn child is a 'liberty' in the absolute sense; or even whether it is a liberty of great importance to many women." Scalia acknowledged both as true. Rather, he maintained, the "issue is whether it is a liberty protected by the Constitution of the United States." His answer was, "I'm sure it is not." His conclusion was not based on "anything so exalted" as his own concept of existence or the "mystery of life." Instead, it was based on two simple facts: "the Constitution says absolutely nothing about it, and the longstanding traditions of American society have permitted it to be legally proscribed."

Medicaid Abortion Funding

***Harris v. McRae*, 448 U.S. 297 (1980),** held that federal Medicaid funds could not be used to cover abortion costs. The restriction, known as the Hyde Amendment, limited federal funds for abortions to those cases in which the mother's life was jeopardized by a full-term pregnancy or for rape or incest victims, provided "such rape or incest has been reported promptly to a law enforcement agency or public health service." The Supreme Court upheld the Hyde Amendment against equal protection and due process challenges. The Court concluded that the right to have an abortion as established in *Roe v. Wade*, 410 U.S. 113 (1973), carried with it no entitlement to federal funding to cover an abortion's costs. The funding limitation imposed no restriction on access to abortions, and while indigence may make it more difficult, perhaps impossible, for some women actually to have abortions, the enactment did not create or affect the indigence. The Hyde Amendment merely reflected a value choice favoring childbirth over abortion. It placed no governmental obstacle in the path of a woman who chooses to terminate her pregnancy. By means of unequal subsidization of abortion and other medical services it encourages alternative activity. The Hyde Amendment leaves an indigent women with at least the same range of choice in deciding whether to obtain a medically necessary abortion as she could have had if Congress had chosen to subsidize no health care costs at all. The freedom to be protected from governmental interference in such personal decisions as abortion does not also confer an entitlement to such funds as may be necessary to realize all the advantages of that freedom. Finally, the Court concluded that the Hyde Amendment was rationally related to a legitimate governmental objective. The incentives that make childbirth a more attractive alternative bear a direct relationship to the legitimate congressional interest in protecting potential life. That abortion was singled out for more extensive restriction than other medical services was viewed as rational in that abortion is inherently different from other medical procedures because no other procedure involves the purposeful termination of potential life. Justices Brennan, Marshall, Blackmun, and Stevens dissented. Justice Brennan referred to the Hyde Amendment as "a transparent attempt by the Legislative Branch to impose the political majority's judgment of the morally acceptable and socially desirable preference on a sensitive and intimate decision that the Constitution entrusts to the individual." The Amendment "both by design and in effect serves to coerce indigent pregnant women to have children that they would otherwise elect not to have." *See also Griswold v. Connecticut*, p. 586; RIGHT OF PRIVACY, p. 476; *Roe v. Wade*, p. 588.

Significance　*Harris v. McRae* was not the Court's first experience with restrictions on public monies for covering the costs of abortions. It was the most extensive, however, in that it included therapeutic abortions. In *Maher v. Roe*, 432 U.S. 464 (1977), the Court upheld a Connecticut restriction on funding for elective or nontherapeutic abortions while subsidizing childbirth. *Maher* provided the foundation of *McRae*.

The Court decided two other cases on the same day as *Maher*, both of which upheld limitations on funding for abortions. In *Beal v. Doe*, 432 U.S. 438 (1977), it held that the federal Medicaid program did not require a participating state to bear costs of nontherapeutic abortions. The extent to which the Court was irreconcilably split on these cases can be seen in the harsh dissent offered by the usually mild-mannered Justice Blackmun. In *Beal* he remarked that "there is another world out there, the existence of which the Court, I suspect, either chooses to ignore or fears to recognize." He felt the Court's decision was punitive and tragic for the indigent. Implicit is the condescension that she may go elsewhere for her abortion. "I find such condescension disingenuous and alarming, almost reminiscent of 'let them eat cake.'" The other companion to *Maher*, *Poelker v. Doe*, 432 U.S. 519 (1977), allowed a municipality to provide subsidized hospital services for childbirth while excluding services for nontherapeutic abortions.

Title X of the Public Health Service Act of 1970 authorized federal funding for public and private nonprofit agencies providing family planning services. The Act specified that none of the funds appropriated under Title X could be used for programs in which "abortion is a method of family planning." Until 1988 this phrase was interpreted as precluding Title X grantees from actually performing abortions, as opposed to providing information about abortion as an option. In 1988 the secretary of Health and Human Services issued new regulations that imposed significant conditions on grant recipients. First, Title X projects could not counsel about abortion or provide referrals for abortions. Instead, pregnant clients had to be referred to agencies providing "appropriate" prenatal services. Recipient agencies were explicitly forbidden from referring a client to an abortion provider even on specific request. Second, a Title X project could not engage in activities that "encourage, promote or advocate abortion as a method of family planning." Finally, recipient agencies had to be organized in such a way as to be wholly independent from any abortion-related activities. Activities supported by federal funds were required to take place in separate facilities and use personnel independent from any agency personnel involved in providing abortion services. A number of Title X grantees and physicians associated with recipient agencies sought to prevent implementation of the new regulations.

The Supreme Court ruled in *Rust v. Sullivan*, 500 U.S. 173 (1991), that the secretary's regulations were permitted under terms of the Act, and that the regulations did not violate the First or Fifth Amendment rights of recipient agencies or their clients. Chief Justice Rehnquist said that the secretary's interpretation of the meaning of Section 1008 of the Act must be accorded substantial deference not only because his agency administers the statute, but because the evidence as to congressional intent is "ambiguous." The principal First Amendment contention of the challengers was that because Title X funds speech in a way that is not "evenhanded with respect to views and information about abortion, it invidiously discriminates on the basis of viewpoint." Rehnquist agreed that the secretary's regulations represented a value choice preferring childbirth to abortion, but he said that the government may make that policy decision and "implement that judgment by the allocation of public funds." Unequal subsidization, however, is not unconstitutional. When government believes it in the public interest to fund a program to "encourage certain activities" but does not fund an alternate program, government has not "discriminated on the basis of viewpoint; it has merely chosen to fund an activity to the exclusion of the other." When government appropriates public funds to establish a program, it is entitled to define the limits of that program. Furthermore, the regulations do not require Title X recipients to forego abortion-related speech. Instead, the regulations "merely require that the grantee keep such activity separate and distinct from Title X activities." The Court also found that the regulations did not interfere with the patient-physician relationship or a woman's right to have certain options discussed by her physicians. Access to abortion-related information remained "unfettered outside the context of the Title X project." Justices Blackmun, O'Connor, Marshall, and Stevens dissented. Blackmun said that the regulation was "viewpoint suppression of speech solely because it is imposed on those dependent on the Government for economic support." The purpose and result of the regulations is to "deny women the ability voluntarily to decide their procreative destiny."

Definition of Family

Moore v. East Cleveland, **431 U.S. 494 (1977),** ruled that a municipality did not have authority to restrict, through a zoning ordinance, the occupancy of a private home to persons defined as family. *Moore* involved an ordinance that limited occupancy of a dwelling unit to members of a "single family." The zone of privacy issue involved in the case had provided the basis for numerous challenges of legislation since *Griswold v. Connecticut*, 381 U.S. 479 (1965). Most successful applications of the invasion of privacy approach have been in situations in which matters of family were involved in some way. In the East Cleveland ordinance, *family* was defined very narrowly to include essentially parents and children. Moore lived in her home with her son and two grandsons. She was found in violation of the ordinance because the grandsons were cousins rather than brothers. Although the Court could not agree on common language, a five-justice majority found the ordinance unconstitutional. Justice Powell characterized the ordinance as "slicing deeply into the family itself." He said such an enactment compels the Court to act aggressively. "When a city undertakes such an intrusive regulation of the family, the usual judicial deference to the legislature is inappropriate." Such posture was demanded because the Court had long recognized that freedom of personal choice in matters of marriage and family life is one of the liberties protected by the Due Process Clause of the Fourteenth Amendment. Powell acknowledged that the family is not beyond regulation, but governmental interests in doing so must be very carefully examined, as well as the means chosen to advance those interests. The interests asserted by East Cleveland were served only marginally by the ordinance. Powell noted the risk involved when "the judicial branch gives enhanced protection to certain substantive liberties without the guidance of more specific provisions of the Bill of Rights." Although history counsels caution and restraint as a general rule, it does not counsel abandonment. Nor does it require what the city urges; that is, cutting off any protection of family rights at the first convenient boundary, the boundary of the nuclear family. Justice Brennan concurred and said that the zoning power "is not a license for local communities to enact senseless and arbitrary restrictions which cut deeply into private areas of protected family." He also charged that the ordinance was the imposition of "white suburbia's preference in patterns of family living," a preference reflecting "cultural myopia" and insensitivity to the concept of the extended family. Justices Stewart, White, and Rehnquist disagreed that the ordinance interfered with an aspect of family life deserving constitutional protection. *See also Griswold v. Connecticut*, p. 586; RIGHT OF PRIVACY, p. 476.

Significance   *Moore* set aside an ordinance that attempted to restrict occupancy of a home to persons within the ordinance definition of family. Prior to *Moore*, the Court had upheld a zoning ordinance in *Belle Terre v. Boraas*, 416 U.S. 1 (1974), that limited land use to single-family dwellings. The ordinance defined family more broadly than the enactment in *Moore*, and the Court deferred to the permissible legislative objectives of regulating population density and preventing congestion and noise.

In *Zablocki v. Redhail*, 434 U.S. 374 (1978), the Court found that the right of privacy precluded interference with a person's desire to marry. A Wisconsin statute required any person under an order to pay child support to obtain authorization to marry. Permission was contingent on showing that support obligations were current and that the children involved "would not likely thereafter become public charges." Redhail was denied a marriage license because he had failed to make support payments for a previously fathered child. The Court held the statute unconstitutional because it barred certain classes from ever marrying. They were "coerced into foregoing the right to marry."

The right of privacy was limited to traditional marital relationships in *Doe v. Commonwealth's Attorney*, 425 U.S. 901 (1976). The Court summarily affirmed a three-judge district court dismissal of a privacy challenge to the use of a state sodomy statute against homosexuals. The lower court found that homosexuality was "obviously no portion of marriage, house, or family life," and that a state may impose criminal sanctions on conduct "even when committed in the home, in the promotion of morality and decency."

The refusal to extend the right of privacy to homosexual conduct was amplified in the controversial ruling of *Bowers v. Hardwick*, 478 U.S. 186 (1986). In this case, the Court upheld a state law criminalizing consensual sodomy. The Court said that homosexuals had no right to engage in sodomy. In addition, the Court said that none of the previous right of privacy rulings involving family relationships, marriage, and procreation "bear any resemblance to the claimed constitutional right of homosexuals to engage in acts of sodomy that is asserted in this case."

Right to Terminate Medical Treatment

Cruzan v. Director of Missouri Department of Health, **497 U.S. 261 (1990),** ruled that a person has a right to discontinue life-sustaining medical treatment. At the same time, the Court ruled that a state can require maintenance of the treatment in the absence of "clear and convincing" evidence that the person would want the treatment stopped. Nancy Cruzan was injured in an automobile accident in 1983. From that time forward she remained in a "persistent vegetative" state and was administered food and water through a tube in her stomach. Cruzan's parents, acting as legal guardians, requested that the life-sustaining feedings be stopped. The hospital refused to stop the feedings, and the Cruzans initiated legal action. A state trial court found that a person had a right to refuse procedures that were "death prolonging." Cruzan, of course, was incompetent to stop the feedings herself. The issue became whether statements uttered by Cruzan prior to the accident constituted sufficient evidence of her desire to discontinue medical treatment under the postaccident circumstances. The Missouri Supreme Court ruled that Missouri's "living will" statute favored "preservation of life" in the absence of "clear and convincing" evidence for withdrawal of treatment. The "clear and convincing" standard is the highest standard of evidence used in a civil proceeding. Applying that standard, the Missouri Supreme Court decided that Cruzan's preaccident statements were "unreliable" for determining her intent.

The issue before the U.S. Supreme Court was whether any federal constitutional provision precludes a state from using the standard Missouri had adopted. It was the Court's view, based on Fourteenth Amendment due process grounds rather than the right of privacy, that a "competent person has a constitutionally protected liberty interest in refusing unwanted medical treatment." Chief Justice Rehnquist said that "does not end our inquiry," however. Whether constitutional rights have been violated requires that liberty interests be weighed against the "relevant state interests." The problem in this case was that Nancy Cruzan was herself incompetent to "make an informed and voluntary choice." Rather, the right "must be exercised for her ... by some sort of surrogate." Missouri recognized actions by surrogates, but also had "established a procedural safeguard to assure that the action of the surrogate conforms as best it may to the wishes expressed by the patient while competent." The Court held that Missouri's proof by clear and convincing evidence in such cases was not forbidden by the Constitution. This procedural requirement was established in furtherance of the state's interest in the "protection and preservation of human life, and there can be no gainsaying this interest." Furthermore, the state had an even "more particular interest" in situations like Cruzan's. The choice between "life and death is a deeply personal decision of obvious and overwhelming finality." Accordingly, Missouri may "legitimately seek to safeguard the personal element of this choice through the imposition of heightened evidentiary requirements." Rehnquist concluded by focusing on the issue of surrogate decision making. He characterized the Cruzans as "loving and caring parents." Were the Constitution to require states to "repose a right of 'substituted judgment' with anyone, the Cruzans would surely qualify." But, he said, the Court does not think the Fourteenth Amendment "requires the state to repose the judgment on these matters with anyone but the patient herself." Family members may possess a "strong feeling—a feeling not at all ignoble or unworthy, but not entirely disinterested, either— that they do not wish to witness the continuation of the life of a loved one which they regard as hopeless, meaningless, and even degrading." There is no automatic assurance that the view of the close family members "will necessarily be the same as the patient's would have been had she been confronted with the prospect of her situation while competent." That being the case, the Court concluded that Missouri could reasonably defer to the patient's own wishes rather than those of close members by imposing a clear and convincing standard of evidence.

Justices Brennan, Marshall, Blackmun, and Stevens dissented. The decision, said Brennan, "robs a patient of the very qualities protected by the right to avoid unwanted medical treatment." The state's "general interest" in life "must accede" to Nancy Cruzan's "particularized and intense interest in self-determination in her choice of medical treatment. There is simply nothing legitimately within the state's purview to be gained by superseding her decision." *See also* RIGHT OF PRIVACY, p. 476; *Washington v. Glucksberg*, p. 603.

Significance   *Cruzan* was the Supreme Court's first on-the-merits response to the so-called right to die issue. In 1976 the Burger Court had declined to review the New Jersey case involving Karen Ann Quinlan. Unlike *Cruzan*, the *Quinlan* case involved discontinuation of the use of life-support machinery as opposed to discontinuing administration of food and fluids. It may prove to be of consequence that the Court in *Cruzan* did not distinguish between feeding and other kinds of medical treatment. What is clear from *Cruzan* is that persons who provide for discontinuation of any form of treatment in "living wills" can effectively protect their wishes. Currently most states have living will laws, although they vary substantially, and the *Cruzan* case makes it almost certain that every state will soon have such a law. Living wills convey a person's instructions on how physicians and family are to handle life-sustaining treatment decisions, in the event the person becomes incapable of making that decision. Had Nancy Cruzan documented her wishes in a living will, her treatment could have been terminated by her parents because the will would have provided a "clear and convincing" expression of her preference under the circumstances.

The Reagan administration had sought to intervene in cases involving treatment of seriously handicapped infants. The asserted statutory basis for such intervention was the Rehabilitation Act of 1973. The Court said in *Bowen v. American Hospital Association*, 476 U.S. 610 (1986), also known as the Baby Doe case, that the act did not give the secretary of Health and Human Services authority to offer unsolicited advice to those persons faced with the "difficult treatment decisions concerning handicapped children." Intervention under the Act could not occur without evidence that a hospital had refused treatment requested by a child's parents.

Physician-Assisted Suicide

Washington v. Glucksberg, **117 S.Ct. 2258 (1997)** The state of Washington made assisting in a suicide a felony. A combination of physicians, including Harold Glucksberg, and terminally ill patients brought suit in federal court claiming violation of a right of competent terminally ill patients to choose suicide. The Supreme Court unanimously upheld the criminal prohibitions on assisted suicide in *Glucksberg*. Chief Justice Rehnquist observed that it is a crime to assist in a suicide in "almost every state, indeed, in almost every Western democracy." The state bans on assisted suicide are not "innovations." Rather, they are longstanding expressions of the states' "commitment to the protection and preservation of all human life." Opposition to suicide or the assisting with it are "consistent and enduring themes of our philosophical, legal, and cultural heritages." Rehnquist then focused on the due process claims in *Glucksberg*. The Due Process Clause provides "heightened protection against government interference with certain fundamental rights and liberty interests." At the same time, the Court has "always been reluctant to expand the concept of substantive due process because the guideposts for responsible decision making in the uncharted area are scarce and open-ended." Inquiry into the place of assisted suicide in our nation's traditions shows a "consistent and almost universal tradition that has long rejected the asserted right, and continues explicitly to reject it today, even for terminally ill, mentally competent adults." To allow assisted suicide, Rehnquist said, "we would have to reverse centuries of legal doctrine and practice and strike down the considered policy choice of almost every state." The Court thus concluded that the asserted right to assistance in committing suicide is "not a fundamental liberty interest protected by the Due Process Clause." The Constitution also requires that Washington's ban on assisted suicide be "rationally related to legitimate government interests." This requirement "unquestionably" implicates a number of state interests. First, Washington has an "unqualified interest in the preservation of human life." Second, all admit that suicide is a serious public health problem, especially among persons in "otherwise vulnerable groups." The state thus has an interest in "preventing suicide and in studying, identifying, and treating its causes." Legal physician-assisted suicide could make it more difficult for the state to protect "depressed or mentally ill persons, or those who are suffering from untreated pain, from suicidal impulses." Third, physician-assisted suicide could "undermine the trust that is essential to the doctor-patient relationship by blurring the time-honored line between healing and harming." Fourth, the state has an interest in protecting vulnerable groups "including the poor, the elderly, and disabled persons from abuse, neglect and mistakes." The state's interest goes beyond protecting the vulnerable from the "real risk of subtle coercion and undue influence in end-of-life situations." It extends to protecting disabled and terminally ill people from "prejudice, negative and inaccurate stereotypes and social indifference." Washington's ban on assisted suicide reflects and reinforces its policy that "the lives of terminally ill, disabled and elderly people must be no less valued than the lives of the young and healthy and that a seriously disabled person's suicidal impulses should be interpreted and treated the same way as anyone else's." Finally, said Rehnquist, the state may "fear that permitting assisted suicide will start it down the path to voluntary and perhaps even involuntary euthanasia." If suicide becomes a protected constitutional right, then "every man and woman in the United States must enjoy it." The "expansive reasoning" provides "ample support" for the state's concerns that the Ninth Circuit's decisions cannot be limited to "competent, terminally ill adults who wish to hasten their deaths by obtaining medication prescribed by their doctors."

Several justices, including the chief justice, suggested that this ruling did not foreclose continued discussion of the issue. Rehnquist said that the decision "does not absolutely foreclose" subsequent claims by terminally ill people that they have a right to physician assistance in expediting their deaths. Rehnquist noted the "earnest and profound debate" in which Americans are engaged about the "morality, legality, and practicality" of physician-assisted suicide. Our ruling, said Rehnquist, "permits this debate to continue, as it should in a democratic society." *See also Cruzan v. Director of Missouri Department of Health*, p. 601; *Griswold v. Connecticut*, p. 586; RIGHT OF PRIVACY, p. 476.

Significance   The Supreme Court decided a second physician-assisted suicide case with *Glucksberg*. Under New York law, it is a felony to assist someone to commit suicide. Several physicians, including Timothy Quill, and terminally ill patients unsuccessfully challenged the law in federal district court. The Court of Appeals for the Second Circuit, however, found an equal protection violation in New York's policy criminalizing physician-assisted suicide while, at the same time, allowing withdrawal of life-sustaining treatment. The Court was similarly unpersuaded by the equal protection claims raised in the New York case, *Vacco v. Quill*, 138 L.Ed. 2d 834 (1997). Generally, said Rehnquist, "laws that apply even-handedly to all unquestionably comply with the equal Protection Clause." Neither the state's ban on assisting suicide nor its laws permitting patients to refuse medical treatment "treat anyone differently ... or draw distinctions between persons. *Everyone*, regardless of physical condition, is entitled, if competent, to refuse unwanted lifesaving medical treatment; *no one* is permitted to assist a suicide." The Court found the distinction between assisting suicide and withdrawing life-sustaining treatment as "widely recognized and endorsed in the medical profession and in our legal traditions, both important and logical—it is certainly rational."

CHAPTER 8

Legal Words and Phrases

Abstention   A policy designed to reduce conflict between federal and state courts. Abstention allows a federal court to withhold exercise of its jurisdiction on a federal constitutional issue until a state court has rendered a judgment on such state law as may have a bearing on the federal question. Abstention is regarded as essential to the operation of a dual court system in which both federal and state judges have an obligation to uphold the federal Constitution. *See also* FEDERALISM, p. 649.

Significance   The doctrine of abstention maintains that a federal court should not assume jurisdiction in a case until the uncertainties of state law are addressed by the appropriate state courts. Abstention by the federal court may prevent or minimize conflict by limiting federal court interference in matters that pertain primarily to state law. Abstention also permits a federal court to relinquish its jurisdiction if the federal court determines that the central issue in a case has been appropriately resolved at the state level.

Adversary Proceeding   A legal process that involves a real contest between two opposing parties. In an adversary proceeding, formal notice is served on the party against whom an action has been filed to allow that party an opportunity to respond. An adversary proceeding is different from an ex parte proceeding, in which only one party appears. An adversary proceeding also differs from a summary proceeding, in which no significant fact dispute exists and in which the court may hasten and simplify the resolution of an issue. *See also* ADVISORY OPINION, p. 609; CASE OR CONTROVERSY, p. 622.

Significance   An adversary proceeding forces a plaintiff and defendant in a legal action to contest each other with evidence gathered in support of their respective cases. The system is generally regarded as the most effective means of the evaluation of evidence. The adversary system also features a diffusion of power among its principal participants, such as judge, prosecutor, jury, and defense counsel. Each actor helps to produce a check and balance effect, thus safeguarding against arbitrary or abusive judgments.

Advisory Opinion   A response by a judge or court to a legal question posed outside a bona fide case or controversy. An advisory opinion is a reply to an abstract or hypothetical question and indicates how the court would respond to the issue in an actual case. An advisory opinion has no binding effect unless it is legally accepted by the requesting body. *See also* CASE OR CONTROVERSY, p. 622; DECLARATORY JUDGMENT, p. 638; SEPARATION OF POWERS, p. 697.

Significance   An advisory opinion may not be rendered by a federal court because of the constitutional provision limiting the jurisdiction of federal courts to actual cases or controversies. The limitation is designed to preserve separation of powers and keep the judiciary from certain political entanglements that might adversely affect the judicial branch. Several states allow the rendering of an advisory opinion in order to clarify state legislation without the necessity of possibly burdensome litigation.

Affirmative Action   A policy designed to remedy the effects of past discrimination. Affirmative action programs are typically used in employment or educational situations and give preference or advantage to a particular group that has suffered previous discrimination. Racial minorities and women are most commonly targeted, although some programs focus on such groups as veterans or the handicapped. The constitutional question raised by affirmative action is whether preference can be justified because of its remedial or compensatory character. Those critical of affirmative action see it as reverse discrimination—remediating past discrimination through new discrimination. *See also Adarand Constructors, Inc. v. Pena*, p. 505; BENEVOLENT CLASSIFICATION, p. 621; CLASSIFICATION, p. 628; EQUAL PROTECTION CLAUSE, p. 473; *Regents of the University of California v. Bakke*, p. 501.

Significance   The issue of affirmative action has been before the Court on numerous occasions. The first important decision came in *Regents of University of California v. Bakke*, 438 U.S. 265 (1978). The Court upheld the use of race-conscious admissions policies for a state university graduate program, although it disallowed the allocation of seats on a quota basis. The Court found that recruitment of a diverse or heterogeneous student body was a substantial enough interest to allow race-conscious admissions. More extensive reverse discrimination was permitted in *United Steelworkers of America v. Weber*, 443 U.S. 193 (1979), in which the Court allowed a private employer to give preference to unskilled black employees over white employees for training programs designed to elevate the unskilled workers to craft levels. The Court permitted the preferential treatment because prior racial discrimination had demonstrably disadvantaged black workers in the past. The use of "set asides" was upheld by the Court as a remedial solution in *Fullilove v. Klutznick*, 448 U.S. 448 (1980). A set aside reserves a certain percentage of federal funds for minority businesses. The Court determined that Congress may allow narrowly tailored corrective actions to redress historical disadvantages. The Court struck down a local "set aside" program in *Richmond v. J.A.*

Croson, Inc., 408 U.S. 469 (1989), on the grounds that it was not "narrowly tailored." In *Croson*, the Court had applied strict scrutiny as it reviewed the Richmond plan. The federal program reviewed in *Fullilove*, however, had been reviewed using the far less demanding rationality or minimum scrutiny test. The use of different standards for state and federal affirmative action programs came to an end in *Adarand Constructors, Inc. v. Pena*, 515 U.S. 299 (1995), as the Court ruled that all race-based classifications, whether of federal or state origins, must be reviewed under strict scrutiny. This means that race-based classifications are constitutional only if they are "narrowly tailored measures that further compelling governmental interests."

Aggravating Circumstances   Elements that increase the severity of a criminal act. Aggravating circumstances go beyond the legal aspect of a particular crime. The presence of such a circumstance is required to distinguish guilty persons who may be sentenced to death. For a death sentence to be imposed for murder in most states, at least one aggravating circumstance must be shown beyond a reasonable doubt. This is done to isolate the most grievous offenses. An aggravating circumstance may be a substantial history of serious assaultive criminal convictions, a capital offense committed during the course of another capital offense, or a crime especially heinous or involving torture or "wantonly vile" acts. *See also* CRUEL AND UNUSUAL PUNISHMENT, p. 637; *Gregg v. Georgia*, p. 542; *Maynard v. Cartwright*, p. 416.

Significance   An enumeration of aggravating circumstances provides structure and guidance to sentencers in death penalty cases. Such an enumeration is required by the Supreme Court's ruling in *Furman v. Georgia*, 408 U.S. 238 (1972). Distinct from an aggravating circumstance is a *mitigating* circumstance, a factor that diminishes or reduces a convicted person's culpability. The presence of at least one mitigating circumstance may preclude imposition of capital punishment. Typical mitigating circumstances are youth, no prior criminal history, and emotional disturbance or duress.

Amendment Process   The process for amending the U.S. Constitution is described in Article V. Constitutional amendments can be initiated when two-thirds of both houses of Congress propose an amendment, or when a constitutional convention is convened and recommends a change. Such a convention can be called only after two-thirds of the states call for it. All of the amendments to the Constitution have been initiated by congressional resolution. Before a proposed amendment may take effect, the legislatures or specially called conventions in three-fourths of the states must give their approval. *See also* POLITICAL QUESTION, p. 688.

Significance   Principal responsibility for changing the Constitution rests with Congress. The Court has historically viewed issues arising out of the amendment process as falling under the "political question" doctrine. That is, the Court generally defers to congressional judgment on changing the Constitution. When Congress specified a time limit for ratification of the Eighteenth Amendment, the Court upheld the action in *Dillon v. Goss*, 256 U.S. 368 (1921). When Congress failed to establish a similar restriction on the amendment proposing prohibition of child labor, the Court refused in *Coleman v. Miller*, 307 U.S. 433 (1939), to establish a time limit itself. The Court also held in *Coleman* that a state legislature can reconsider a decision to reject an amendment and vote to ratify as long as any established time period has not expired.

Amicus Curiae   A third party submitting a brief to a court expressing views on a legal question before the court. An *amicus curiae*, literally meaning "friend of the court," is not an actual party to an action. The amicus participant is an interested third party who attempts to provide the court with information or arguments that may not have been offered by the actual parties. The amicus participant typically represents an interest group. It is not unusual, for example, to have amicus briefs from the NAACP or ACLU in civil-rights or civil liberties cases. Government entities may also act as amicus participants. Indeed, the federal government, represented by the solicitor general, frequently appears as an amicus participant on questions that relate to federal policy. *See also* BRIEF, p. 622.

Significance   Amicus curiae participation is a common court-related interest group activity. It typically occurs in cases with substantial public interest ramifications. As the Supreme Court considered whether a woman has a constitutional right to an abortion in *Roe v. Wade*, 410 U.S. 113 (1973), amicus briefs were submitted by 36 pro-choice and 11 antiabortion organizations. Some of the groups filed jointly. Amicus arguments tend to focus on the broader implications of a particular case. Submission of an amicus brief is not a matter of right, however. With the exception of amicus participation by an agency of the federal government, an amicus brief may be filed only with the consent of both parties in an action, on motion to a court, or by invitation of a court.

Appeal   A request to an appellate or superior court to review a final judgment made in an inferior or lower court. Appellate jurisdiction is the power placed in appeals courts to conduct such a review. It empowers the superior court to set aside or modify the lower court decision. An appeals court has several options in reviewing a lower court decision. It may affirm, which means the lower court result is correct and must stand. It may reverse or vacate, which means it sets aside the lower court ruling. Vacated judgments are often remanded to the lower court for further consideration. If an appellate decision overrules a precedent, it supersedes the earlier decision and nullifies the authority of that decision as precedent. A party seeking appeal is typically referred to as the appellant or petitioner, while the party against whom an action has been filed is the appellee or respondent. Appellate jurisdiction is distinguished from original jurisdiction. In the former, some other court or agency must render a judgment in a case before an appeal can be sought. *See also* CERTIORARI, p. 623; EQUITY JURISDICTION, p. 644; JUDICIAL REVIEW, p. 669; ORIGINAL JURISDICTION, p. 685.

Significance   Appeals courts are generally structured on two levels. One is an intermediate court that handles cases initially, and the other is a superior or supreme court. Appellate jurisdiction is conveyed through constitutional or statutory mandate. Federal appellate jurisdiction is granted by Article III of the Constitution, which says that the Supreme Court possesses such jurisdiction "both as to law and fact, with such exceptions and under such regulations as the Congress shall make." Appeals may be undertaken as a matter of right when the appellate court, typically an intermediate appeals court, must review a case. Other appeals occur at the discretion of the appeals court. The writ of certiorari is a discretionary route of access to the appellate jurisdiction of the United States Supreme Court. Review as a matter of right is subject to some discretion by the Supreme Court, as in the writ of appeal. The party seeking the appeal has a right to review, but the Court may reject the appeal for want of a substantial federal question.

Apportionment   The allocation of the number of representatives that a political unit may send to a legislative body. Apportionment is based upon population, and it is a requirement of equal protection that legislatures have districts of substantially equal populations. Prior to 1962 the Supreme Court had considered legislative apportionment to be a political question, a matter not subject to resolution by the judicial branch. In *Baker v. Carr*, 369 U.S. 186 (1962), however, the Court held apportionment to be a justiciable issue. *See also Baker* *v. Carr*, p. 516; GERRYMANDERING, p. 656; JUSTICIABILITY, p. 674; POLITICAL QUESTION, p. 688; *Reynolds v. Sims*, p. 518; *Shaw v. Reno*, p. 524; VOTING RIGHTS ACT OF 1965, p. 709.

Significance Apportionment evolved to the one-person-one-vote rule, although *Baker* itself did not establish that standard. *Baker* created a relatively stringent expectation of population equivalence for single-member legislative districts. The one-person-one-vote standard now applies to all levels of government, including local units. The need to design legislative districts with close to equal populations has not been disputed seriously since the early 1970s. The current apportionment controversy involves the extent to which race can be considered when legislative district lines are drawn. Under terms of the Voting Rights Act of 1965, several states developed districting plans that attempted to include high concentrations of minority voters in particular districts. The objective was to create districts in which African Americans or Hispanics would actually constitute a majority that, in turn, would probably result in the election of a minority candidate to office. In *Shaw v. Reno*, 509 U.S. 630 (1993), the Court ruled that strict scrutiny must be applied when reviewing challenges to districting plans containing majority-minority districts. This means that a state must demonstrate that a race-conscious districting plan serves a compelling interest and is as narrowly tailored as possible in pursuit of that interest. In *Miller v. Johnson*, 515 U.S. 900 (1995), the Court held that compliance with the Voting Rights Act could not, in the absence of an interest in remedying past discrimination, provide the necessary compelling interest.

Arraignment A pretrial proceeding at which an accused person is formally charged. During an arraignment, the accused is given a copy of the information or indictment against him or her, and is asked to respond to the charges. The options available at the arraignment are to plead guilty, not guilty, or *nolo contendere. Nolo contendere* expresses a wish not to contest the charges. The accused may also stand mute, which is entered as a plea of not guilty. In some jurisdictions, an arraignment occurs as the initial step in the court system. In this situation, a formal response to the charge(s) is not required. Rather, the defendant is more fully informed of constitutional protections. Counsel may be appointed if the defendant is indigent, and the question of pretrial release is considered. *See also* BAIL, p. 619; COUNSEL, ASSISTANCE OF, p. 635.

Significance Arraignment is one of several steps in the criminal justice process. It is designed to safeguard an accused against arbitrary or vindictive actions by the state. An arraignment must occur within a short period of time following an arrest. The constitutional protections to which the accused is entitled are reiterated at the arraignment, and his or her bail status may also be reviewed. In some jurisdictions a brief proceeding called an arraignment occurs prior to formal charging. This first appearance or presentment allows the rights of the accused to be reviewed and the pretrial release question to be addressed. A formal hearing to charge must still occur in jurisdictions that define arraignment in this way.

Articles of Confederation   The first constitution of the United States. The Articles governed the united colonies from 1781 until they were replaced by the new Constitution, which was written at the Philadelphia Convention in 1787. Writing of the Articles was commenced by the Second Continental Congress at the point independence from Britain was declared. The government created under the Articles was called upon to respond to national needs, such as the prosecution of the war of independence. The Articles were submitted to the states for ratification in late 1777, and the process was not completed until 1781. The issue that split the Continental Congress was essentially the same question that later split the Philadelphia Convention—the division of power between the national and state governments. The Articles that were eventually ratified set out a loose confederation of states over which the central or national government had only limited power. Because there was provision only for a weak executive and no judiciary, most of the powers of the central government were vested in the Congress. The enumerated powers of Congress included the determination of each state's share of the costs of operating the central government, but Congress had no authority to actually collect tax revenues and had only minimal authority to settle interstate disputes. The weakness of the central government ultimately caused the Articles to be superseded by the present Constitution, which was ratified by all the states and replaced the Articles in 1789. *See also* CONSTITUTIONALISM, p. 634; FEDERALISM, p. 649.

Significance   The Articles of Confederation created the United States from the 13 British colonies and enabled the newly independent nation to survive the War of Independence and its aftermath. It is argued that the Articles were fatally flawed from the outset because the states retained too much power relative to the national government. Indeed, the states had virtual veto power over many central government functions including taxation, and the inability of the national government to compel the states to pay their respective shares of the Revolutionary War debt was its undoing. The question of centralizing or decentralizing government power was the forefront issue at the Philadelphia Convention and has remained a central political issue in the United States ever since.

Assembly, Right to   A fundamental right provided by the First Amendment to the U.S. Constitution. The right of assembly holds that the people are entitled "peaceably to assemble, and to petition the government for redress of grievances." It includes the right to protest governmental policies as well as to advocate particular, even distasteful, views. The right to assemble generally involves "speech plus." This is expression with an associated action component, such as a demonstration or a march. While the people have a right peaceably to assemble, the government also has a legitimate function to maintain order. The two interests may collide. The right of assembly does not provide absolute protection. In the words of Justice Black, the right of assembly does not include expression whenever, however, and wherever one pleases. The government can impose regulations on the time, place, and manner of assembly, provided that substantial interests, such as preventing threats to public order, can be shown. Thus certain locations, such as jail grounds, may be constitutionally placed off-limits for demonstrations. Similarly, the right to assemble does not protect such actions as inciting breaches of the peace, the obstruction of traffic, or seizure of a local public library. Time, place, and manner regulations must be evenhandedly applied and must be wholly unrelated to the content of the expression involved. *See also Adderley v. Florida*, p. 149; *Carroll v. President and Commissioners of Princess Anne County*, p. 153; FREE SPEECH CLAUSE, p. 654; *PruneYard Shopping Center v. Robins*, p. 152; *Schenck v. Pro-Choice Network*, p. 155; SPEECH PLUS, p. 700.

Significance   The right to assemble is fundamental for people in a democratic society. As in matters involving free expression, restrictions on the right to assemble are suspect. They must be content neutral. As long as demonstrators do not interfere with normal business operations, they may access such private property as a shopping center. *PruneYard Shopping Center v. Robins*, 447 U.S. 74 (1980), placed the protection for assembly such as this under applicable state constitutional provisions. Assembly that requires prior governmental approval or permit is also suspect, although content-neutral permit systems are likely to be constitutionally acceptable if they are confined to reasonable time, place, and manner restrictions. The Court recently permitted restrictions on protesters at abortion clinics. In *Schenck v. Pro-Choice Network*, 519 U.S. 357 (1997), the Court upheld a restraining order that prohibited protesters from coming within 15 feet of clinic entrances and driveways. In doing so, the Court concluded that the governmental interests of ensuring public safety and order, maintaining the free flow of traffic, protecting private property, and protecting a woman's right to utilize pregnancy-related services of a clinic were sufficiently strong to justify the restrictions on the protesters.

Asset Forfeiture   Government seizure of property that was used in the commission of a crime or was purchased with the proceeds of criminal activity. Federal and state criminal statutes often have forfeiture provisions through which assets can be confiscated from those convicted of criminal conduct. The underlying rationale for the seizure of assets is that individuals should not profit from their crimes, and that title to assets tainted by criminal acts reverts to the state. *See also* DUE PROCESS CLAUSES, p. 641.

Significance   Asset forfeiture is a civil rather than a criminal process. This distinction is important because it allows the government to pursue both criminal penalties and asset forfeiture without violating the prohibition against double jeopardy. Civil forfeiture is a "remedial civil sanction" and does not constitute a punishment even though it has some characteristics in common with punitive sanctions. Chief Justice Rehnquist said in *United States v. Ursery*, 518 U.S. 267 (1996), that forfeiture has some "important noncriminal goals" such as "encouraging" property owners to take care of managing their property and ensuring that owners will not "permit that property to be used for illegal purposes." Two constitutional limitations apply to the forfeiture process. First, the Court held in *Austin v. United States*, 509 U.S. 602 (1993), that to the extent that it also has punitive purposes, it may be subject to limits stemming from the Eighth Amendment's Excessive Fines Clause. Second, the Court ruled in *United States v. Good Real Property*, 510 U.S. 43 (1993), that legal action that can result in the loss of property must comply with the procedural protections afforded by the Due Process Clauses of the Fifth and Fourteenth Amendments.

Association, Right to   The legal right of a group of people acting together to advance a mutual interest or achieve a common objective. The right of association is not expressly protected by the First Amendment. Rather, it is derived from safeguards for expression and assembly contained in the First Amendment. The utility of association as a means of achieving political and social goals was acknowledged by the Supreme Court in *NAACP v. Alabama*, 357 U.S. 449 (1958). The Court said, "Effective advocacy of both public and private points of view, particularly controversial ones, is undeniably enhanced by group association." Given the fundamental role of associational activity, government bears an obligation to ensure that interference with such activity does not occur. The Court struck down a state membership disclosure requirement in *NAACP v. Alabama* because the regulation adversely affected the ability of the NAACP and its members "to pursue their collective effort to foster beliefs which they admittedly have a right to advocate." Associational activity was also protected in *Baird v. State Bar of Arizona*, 401 U.S. 1 (1971), in which the Court held that applicants for admission to the bar may not be compelled to disclose organizational memberships. *See also* FREE SPEECH CLAUSE, p. 654; *Keyishian v. Board of Regents*, p. 160; LOYALTY OATH, p. 677; *NAACP v. Alabama*, p. 159; OVERBREADTH DOCTRINE, p. 686.

Significance   The right of association may have positive effects in a democracy, but regulation may still be imposed. The most troublesome association cases have involved statutory attempts to proscribe subversive organizations and prohibit criminal syndicalism. Syndicalism refers to the takeover of the means of industrial production by workers. Criminal syndicalism involves the advocacy of, or participation in, unlawful acts to achieve political change. Many states had criminal syndicalism statutes that were upheld initially because association itself was seen as concerted action threatening public security. Representative of such cases is *Whitney v. California*, 274 U.S. 357 (1927), in which the Taft Court allowed the punishment of a political party member for the party's unlawful advocacy. The Warren Court rejected this approach because such laws were directed at "mere abstract teaching" or advocacy that is not necessarily related to unlawful acts. Decisions such as *Keyishian v. Board of Regents*, 385 U.S. 589 (1967), found "mere membership" in a subversive organization to be insufficient grounds for exclusion from public employment. The Court said that laws that sanction membership unaccompanied by specific intent to further the unlawful goals of the organization violate constitutional limitations. The right of association is most often protected from regulation by means of the overbreadth doctrine, which cautions that restrictive statutes tend to trap association members indiscriminately. Associational protection has also been applied to organizational involvement in the electoral process. Indeed, the Supreme Court has rejected efforts to regulate campaign expenditures on associational expression grounds. The Court also recognized the right of a private association to exclude unwanted participants from its activities. The South Boston Allied

War Veterans Council annually organizes a parade that generally has been open to community participants. However, the Council excluded a gay rights organization from marching in the parade. In *Hurley v. Irish-American Gay, Lesbian & Bisexual Group*, 515 U.S. 557 (1995), the Supreme Court ruled that a parade is an expressive activity, and a private organizer of a parade has the "autonomy" to choose the content of its own message.

Bad Tendency Test   A standard used by the Supreme Court to evaluate the reasonableness of restrictions on speech and press. The bad tendency test permits restriction of expression if the expression tends to involve a danger of "substantive evil" or if it could lead to unlawful ends. In *Gitlow v. New York*, 268 U.S. 652 (1925), the Court said that a state may reasonably "extinguish the spark without waiting until it has enkindled the flame or blazed into the conflagration." It may also "suppress the threatened danger in its incipience." *See also* CLEAR AND PRESENT DANGER TEST, p. 629; FREE SPEECH CLAUSE, p. 654.

Significance   The bad tendency test is one of the standards developed by the Supreme Court for reviewing restrictions imposed on free speech and press. It is the least favorable standard the Court has utilized to judge expression. It presumes the constitutionality of restrictive regulations, and sometimes has been characterized as the approach designed to "kill the serpent in the egg."

Bail   Monetary security used to ensure the future appearance of an accused at proceedings to adjudicate criminal charges. In exchange for posting bail, an accused is released from custody pending completion of the adjudicative process. If the accused appears at all required proceedings, whatever security has been posted is returned, regardless of the outcome of the case. Bail is forfeited by failure to appear. Although pretrial release may be denied for certain serious offenses, the Eighth Amendment prohibits excessive bail. "Excessive" has been held to mean the imposition of pretrial release conditions beyond that necessary to ensure subsequent appearances. *See also* EIGHTH AMENDMENT, p. 399.

Significance   Bail is closely related to the assumption of the American legal system that accused persons are innocent until they are proved guilty. Pretrial release is one way of acting out this assumption. If an accused person is to be released before trial, such release may be accomplished in one of several ways. He or she may post an amount of money set by a judicial officer. In some jurisdictions a partial payment or a deposit is sufficient. Property may be used in lieu of money. In the event the accused cannot raise the full amount of bail, or does not possess property that might serve as collateral, a bail bondsman may be used. For a nonreturnable fee, a bail bondsman guarantees to the court that the bail levied against the accused will be covered if the accused fails to appear. An alternative approach to pretrial release involves release on personal recognizance. Instead of posting money or property, an accused may be released because there are factors—such as family or work—that minimize the likelihood of flight. Release on recognizance is limited to persons charged with less serious offenses. Releasing an accused before trial is consistent with the presumption of innocence and the view that bail is simply and exclusively a guarantee of a later appearance rather than the imposition of punishment. Some jurisdictions use bail as a method of detaining defendants thought to be dangerous and likely to commit additional crimes.

Balancing Test   An approach to judicial decision making in which free speech interests are weighed against other societal interests to determine if restraint of speech is warranted. The balancing test presumes that constitutionally protected rights are not absolute. It assesses the extent to which governmental authority may be exercised to protect society from substantial damage. *See also* BAD TENDENCY TEST, p. 619; CLEAR AND PRESENT DANGER TEST, p. 629; FREE SPEECH CLAUSE, p. 654.

Significance   Some approaches to constitutional interpretation do not vary on the basis of circumstances. A literal approach will always lead to the conclusion that speech is protected from federal regulation because the First Amendment says "Congress shall make no law ... abridging the freedom of speech." By contrast, a balancing approach views each specific case as presenting competing governmental and individual interests that must be weighed against one another. The conclusions the Court reaches in this way will necessarily vary. There will be occasions when the government interest will outweigh an individual's free speech interests. A person who urges that draft laws be disobeyed may find such a position protected speech during peacetime. The same speech, however, may be restricted during a time of war because the government's interest in maintaining the nation's security probably will be given overwhelming weight. The balancing approach may begin with both sides having equivalent weight, but it may also begin with some preference or advantage assigned to one or the other interest as when a national emergency of some kind exists.

Benevolent Classification   A preferential classification of persons conveying favorable treatment or an advantage for a particular group. Other classifications may convey disabilities to a designated group in terms of regulation, for example. *See also* AFFIRMATIVE ACTION, p. 610; CLASSIFICATION, p. 628; *Kahn v. Shevin*, p. 576.

Significance   A benevolent classification can pass equal protection scrutiny only if the legislative objective is not unnecessarily discriminatory. The objective is usually to implement an ameliorative policy designed to remedy past inequities as a form of affirmative action. An example of a benevolent classification was a Florida property tax exemption for widows but not for widowers. The exemption was intended to soften the financial impact of the death of a husband because such a loss imposes a disproportionately heavy burden on women.

Bill of Rights   The enumeration of individual rights protected against government violation. The American Bill of Rights is part of the U.S. Constitution and includes the first 10 amendments, which were ratified in 1791. The Bill of Rights is broader than the first 10 amendments, however. A number of rights were included in the text of the Philadelphia Constitution of 1787, such as the prohibition of suspension of habeas corpus, and the prohibition on bills of attainder and ex post facto laws in Article I. Individual rights are also protected by provisions of amendments added to the Constitution after the Civil War. The Thirteenth Amendment prohibits slavery, and the Fifteenth Amendment prohibits race discrimination with respect to voting rights, for example. Many of the provisions contained in the Bill of Rights were founded in natural law concepts advanced by such political philosophers as John Locke and drew substantially from provisions in state constitutional provisions respecting individual rights. The absence of a bill of rights was raised by opponents of constitutional ratification. Following ratification, James Madison proposed a bill of rights soon after the first Congress was convened. Twelve amendments were proposed to the states, all but two of which were ratified within two years. *See also* CONSTITUTIONALISM, p. 634; INCORPORATION, p. 665; LOCKE, JOHN, p. 676; NATURAL LAW AND NATURAL RIGHTS, p. 679.

Significance   One purpose of constitutionalism is the protection of individuals from arbitrary governmental actions. The Supreme Court has established itself as the final authority on individual rights in the United States. Although the process of judicial review has generally worked well as a means for the Court to monitor compliance with Bill of Rights provisions, there have been occasions when the Court has permitted governmental interests to prevail over individual rights, especially during times of national emergency. The Court upheld, for example, convictions of those critical of the draft during World War I and supported indiscriminate detention of Japanese Americans during World War II. On the other hand, a significant expansion of constitutional rights occurred through a process known as incorporation. Beginning in the 1920s the Court began to attach specific provisions of the federal Bill of Rights to the states through the Due Process Clause of the Fourteenth Amendment. The entire Bill of Rights has not been incorporated, but most of the itemized protections, those "implicit in the concept of ordered liberty," have been made operative at the state level.

Brief   A written document presented to a court in support of a party's position on a legal question. A brief contains a statement of the facts, applicable law, and arguments drawn from the facts and law urging a judgment compatible with the interests of the party submitting the brief. In a law school context, a brief is a short outline of a case studied by the student and prepared for recitation and review. *See also* AMICUS CURIAE, p. 612.

Significance   A brief is the medium through which legal arguments are placed before courts. Briefs are generally submitted by the parties themselves, although third-party briefs from amicus curiae ("friends of the court") may also be submitted. If a brief is compelling enough, it may secure the court's judgment and favorable ruling.

Case or Controversy   A properly asserted legal claim made in a manner appropriate for judicial response. A case or controversy may be decided by federal courts under Article III of the Constitution. For a case to constitute a bona fide controversy sufficient to satisfy Article III requirements, it must possess several elements. It must involve parties who are truly contending or adverse. There must exist a recognizable legal interest arising out of a legitimate fact situation. The issue must be capable of judicial enforcement by judgment. The case must be justiciable. A person bringing a claim or petitioning a court is known as a party or a litigant. The initiating party to a legal action is also called a plaintiff or a petitioner. The party against whom such action may be brought is a defendant or a respondent. Cases are named for the parties involved. The designation *et al.* ("and others") is used after the first named party in a suit in which there are several plaintiffs or defendants who are not individually listed in the name of the case. Cases designated *in re* are proceedings that are not wholly adversarial, such as a juvenile case *in re*, or "in the matter of," John Doe. The phrase *ex rel.* may be made when a legal action is initiated by the state at the instigation of a party with a private interest in the result. *See also* ADVISORY OPINION, p. 609; JUSTICIABILITY, p. 674; STANDING, p. 701.

Significance   A case or controversy is a justiciable case. In *Aetna Life Insurance Co. v. Haworth*, 300 U.S. 227 (1937), the Supreme Court described a justiciable case as one in which the controversy is "definite and concrete, touching the legal relations of parties having adverse legal interests." Such a controversy must also be "real and substantial, admitting of specific relief through a decree of a conclusive character." A true case or controversy is opposite from a hypothetical or abstract question upon which a court might render an advisory opinion.

Certiorari   A writ or order to a court whose decision is being challenged to send up the records of the case so that a higher court can review the lower court's decision. *Certiorari* means "to be informed" and is granted to the losing party by the Supreme Court if four justices agree that the writ should be issued. Until 1891 the Court was formally obliged to take all appeals that came through the federal court system or that concerned a federal question and were appealed from the highest state courts. In 1890 the Court had to deal with some 1,816 cases, a near physical impossibility for the justices. Congress addressed the problem of an overcrowded docket in the Everts Act of 1891, in which Congress created three-judge circuit courts of appeals as intermediaries between the federal district courts and the Supreme Court. The Act restricted the means of appeal to the Supreme Court by introducing discretionary certiorari power. Through certiorari the Court could decline to hear certain cases if a given number of justices felt they were not sufficiently important. Denial of a certiorari petition means the decision of the lower court is upheld. Despite the Everts Act, the Court's workload continued to expand. It was occasioned by major increases in population, a more extensive governmental administrative apparatus, and the widespread use of the writ of error, by which cases came to the Court by assertion of legal error committed by a court below. The Judiciary Act of 1925 largely did away with the writ of error and gave the Court even wider discretion in broad classes of cases by reaffirming the writ of certiorari. In the years following the Judiciary Act of 1925, the proportion of certiorari petitions granted by the Court never exceeded 22 percent. Certiorari is one of four ways by which cases come before the Supreme Court. The others are appeal, the extra-ordinary writ, and certification. Certification is a process through which a lower court requests a higher court to resolve certain issues in a case while the case is still pending in the lower court. *See also* APPEAL, p. 613.

Significance   The certiorari power is the Supreme Court's principal means of keeping abreast of its work. It can also be an effective administrative tool in the hands of a skillful chief justice. When Charles Evans Hughes became chief justice in 1930, for example, he read and summarized all certiorari petitions coming to the Court. He weeded out some as easily disposable and put them on a separate list before the Saturday conference of the justices. In conference Chief Justice Hughes attempted to average only about three and one-half minutes for discussion of each certiorari petition. Because his preparation far exceeded that of the other justices, his views on whether to grant certiorari petitions were seldom challenged. Thus a chief justice, as chief administrative officer of the Court, can restrict access to the Court by controlling review of certiorari petitions. He or she can also direct the Court's attention to policy areas he or she thinks are important, as when Chief Justice Hughes expanded the Court's scrutiny of *in forma pauperis* petitions to the point at which habeas corpus arguments by prisoners became an important part of the Court's docket. *In forma pauperis* means "in the manner of a pauper" and refers to permission extended to an indigent to proceed with a legal action without having to pay court fees and other costs associated with litigation. The scope of the Supreme Court's certiorari jurisdiction is much broader than that afforded by any other means of access to the Court, including the writ of appeal. The writ of certiorari extends to any civil or criminal case in the federal courts of appeal regardless of the parties, the status of the case, or the amount in controversy. Any state court decision that involves the construction and application of the federal Constitution, treaties, or laws, or the determination of a federal title, right, privilege, or immunity falls within the Court's certiorari jurisdiction. Certiorari allows the Supreme Court to enter the policy-making process at virtually any point it chooses.

Child Benefit Doctrine   An approach to establishment of religion questions that allows indirect aid to religious institutions by focusing on individuals as aid recipients rather than a church or denomination. Child benefit theory has permitted transportation and textbooks to be provided to students of nonpublic schools, although the Establishment Clause prohibits government from aiding institutional religion as such. In *Everson v. Board of Education*, 330 U.S. 1 (1947), the Supreme Court held that provision of certain "general governmental services," such as police and fire protection, sewer and water services, and transportation, are the kinds of services "indisputably marked off from the religious function." The Court said religion would be unnecessarily handicapped if such services were not permitted. *See also* ESTABLISHMENT CLAUSE, p. 644; *Everson v. Board of Education*, p. 32; *Mueller v. Allen*, p. 38.

Significance   Child benefit reasoning has been effectively used to place certain governmental programs outside Establishment Clause restraints. The theory reflects a position on church-state relations that has been termed "benevolent neutrality" or "accommodationist." Child benefit is relevant to the Court's consideration of secular purpose and primary effects, two of the components of the current standard for establishment. In *Mueller v. Allen*, 463 U.S. 388 (1983), the Court reviewed a state income tax deduction for costs associated with elementary and secondary education—a deduction for expenses incurred at either public or private schools. Justice Rehnquist said in *Mueller* that the Establishment Clause did not necessarily prohibit a governmental program that in "some manner aids" a church-affiliated school. The Court saw a secular purpose served by assisting parents to meet the rising costs of education. Neither did the policy have a primary effect of advancing religion. No assistance was directly transmitted to nonpublic schools. Rather, assistance was "channeled" through individual parents and only got to parochial schools as a consequence of "numerous private choices of individual parents of school-age children."

Chilling Effect   The consequence of a policy or practice that discourages the exercise of a legal right. A chilling effect comes about when persons perceive the possibility of sanctions or reprisals if they exercise rights. A convicted person may not be sentenced more heavily after retrial, for example, because he or she successfully appealed the initial conviction. The possibility of a heavier sentence would have a chilling effect because it would penalize persons pursuing their constitutional right to appeal. It would also inhibit persons in prison from filing appeals. *See also* FREE SPEECH CLAUSE, p. 654; OVERBREADTH DOCTRINE, p. 686; PRIOR RESTRAINT, p. 690.

Significance   Chilling effect problems are often encountered in relation to First Amendment rights. In *Pittsburgh Press Co. v. Pittsburgh Commission on Human Relations*, 413 U.S. 376 (1973), for example, the Supreme Court said that a special problem of prior restraint on expression is that it induces excessive caution by speakers who wish to steer clear of restricted areas. A self-imposed regulation of expression occurs. Laws that are vague and create uncertainties about what can be said chill free expression.

Citizenship   One's status as a person who is entitled to all the rights and privileges guaranteed and protected by the Constitution of the United States. Citizenship is conferred by Congress. Since the Civil Rights Act of 1866, all persons born or naturalized in the United States are citizens of the United States. The Fourteenth Amendment reiterated that language in Section 1. The term "dual citizenship" typically refers to a person's status as a citizen of the United States and the state in which he or she resides, or to the holding of citizenship in two countries. American law allows citizens to maintain citizenship in both the United States and another country. This dual citizenship requires a person to take an oath of allegiance to the United States. Otherwise, American citizenship is forfeited if a person lives for three years in a country that also recognizes the person's citizenship of that country. *See also* PRIVILEGES AND IMMUNITIES CLAUSES, p. 690.

Significance   Citizenship is elaborated in two privileges and immunities clauses of the United States Constitution. The Constitution requires, among other things, that citizens of a particular state have parity with citizens of all other states. The *Slaughterhouse Cases*, 83 U.S. 36 (1873), emphasized the distinct character of federal and state citizenship. The *Slaughterhouse Cases* held that privileges and immunities conferred by state citizenship were outside federal reach through the Fourteenth Amendment. Such an interpretation took a very narrow view of the substance of federal citizenship. It covered only such things as interstate travel and voting. Although subsequent decisions have extended the meaning of citizenship in the Fourteenth Amendment, the decision in the *Slaughterhouse Cases* is still controlling in that it precludes use of privileges and immunities language in protecting citizens from regulations imposed by state government.

Civil Rights Act of 1964   A federal law designed to eliminate racial discrimination. The Civil Rights Act of 1964 was the most comprehensive legislation of its kind since Reconstruction. The Act contained several key policy thrusts, including the Title II provisions dealing with public accommodations. The provisions of Title II are very similar to those of the Civil Rights Act of 1875, which was struck down in the *Civil Rights Cases*, 109 U.S. 3 (1883). Title II prohibits discrimination in hotels, motels, restaurants, theaters, and other public halls and arenas.

Title III enables the Justice Department to undertake suits to desegregate noneducational public facilities. Title IV was aimed at school segregation. It authorizes greater federal involvement in achieving desegregation of local school districts. Title V broadened the power of the Civil Rights Commission to include all situations in which equal protection has been denied. Title VI authorizes the withholding of federal funds from any state or local program that discriminates in education or anywhere else. The threatened loss of federal revenue for school districts failing to desegregate became an effective means for encouraging compliance. Title VII prohibits employment discrimination. It established the Equal Employment Opportunity Commission to enforce the title. Federal court litigation has increased dramatically since passage of the Civil Rights Act of 1964. The civil-rights focus has since turned to issues of employment discrimination based on race, gender, and age. The Act settled the issue of equality in public accommodations to the extent that litigation in that subject area has virtually stopped. *See also* EQUAL PROTECTION CLAUSE, p. 473.

Significance   The Civil Rights Act of 1964 was the most comprehensive civil-rights law enacted since the Reconstruction period after the Civil War. The Act was tied to congressional regulatory power stemming from authority to protect interstate commerce and all that affects it. The Civil Rights Act of 1875, which contained many similar provisions was struck down by the Supreme Court in the *Civil Rights Cases*. The 1875 statute had been based upon legislative power presumed to flow from Section 5 of the Fourteenth Amendment. The adverse ruling in the *Civil Rights Cases* and the political circumstances in the mid-1960s led Congress to base the 1964 law on the commerce power, a choice the Court upheld in *Heart of Atlanta Motel, Inc. v. United States*, 379 U.S. 241 (1964). Title VII, which prohibits discrimination in the workplace, has provided the basis for most litigation in recent years. In 1989 the Court issued several decisions that made it more difficult for job discrimination plaintiffs to demonstrate discriminatory actions by employees under Title VII. The Civil Rights Act of 1991 reversed those Supreme Court decisions. Title VII has also provided the basis for sexual harassment claims. In *Harris v. Forklift Systems, Inc.*, 510 U.S. 17 (1993), the Court said that a Title VII violation occurs when discriminatory conduct creates a "hostile" or "abusive" working environment.

Class Action   A suit brought by several persons on behalf of a larger group whose members share the same legal interest. A class action is indicated when a group is so large that individual suits are impractical. Group suits have been used frequently in recent years and are often the means by which civil-rights, consumer, and environmental questions are litigated. A class action is sometimes called a representative action. It can be brought in either federal and state courts. It must be certified by a trial court at the outset—that is, a trial court must give permission for the suit to proceed—and all class members must be made aware of the suit and given an opportunity to exclude themselves. Certification involves a determination that the asserted class actually exists and that those persons bringing the action are members of the class.

Significance   A class action provides economy and efficiency in the adjudication of an issue. It significantly reduces the possibility of conflicting judgments resulting from numerous individual suits. Several limitations apply to a class action. In *Zahn v. International Paper Co.*, 414 U.S. 291 (1973), the Supreme Court held that in order to use federal diversity jurisdiction for class actions, each member of the class must have suffered an injury amounting to at least $10,000 in value. The Court also said in *Eisen v. Carlisle & Jacquelin*, 417 U.S. 156 (1974), that the initiators of a class action must notify, at their own expense, all members of the class. The impact of these decisions has been to reduce the number of large consumer and environmental suits. The more numerous smaller class actions have not been adversely affected.

Classification   A division of the population into two or more groups for purposes of allocating a benefit or imposing a restriction. To be permissible, a legislative enactment that classifies people must not be arbitrary or impose such disabilities as to be in violation of the Due Process or Equal Protection Clauses. *See also* AFFIRMATIVE ACTION, p. 610; BENEVOLENT CLASSIFICATION, p. 621; EQUAL PROTECTION CLAUSE, p. 473.

Significance   A classification is typically evaluated by the Supreme Court through the rational basis test, a deferential and relaxed standard. Classifications in legislative enactments are presumed to be valid under this test if they pursue legitimate government objectives and rationally relate to achieving those objectives. The Supreme Court may, however, place legislative classifications under closer examination or "strict scrutiny." Close or strict scrutiny transfers the burden of proof to the state and demands more than a showing of reasonableness. A compelling state interest must be demonstrated in these instances and a critical need established for the classification at issue. The state must also show that its compelling interest cannot be served through other than classificatory means. The strict scrutiny standard applies when the classification affects a fundamental right such as the right to vote, to speak freely, or to travel freely between and among the states. Classifications are also subjected to strict scrutiny if they touch a "suspect" class. Such a class is one that has been so damaged by long-term and purposeful discrimination that extraordinary protection for it is required. Classifications based on race and alienage are inherently suspect.

Clear and Present Danger Test   A standard used to determine if a particular expression is protected by the First Amendment. The clear and present danger test was first articulated in *Schenck v. United States*, 249 U.S. 47 (1919), a case involving an Espionage Act prosecution for obstruction of military recruitment. The Supreme Court upheld Schenck's conviction, saying that expression is a conditional freedom that must be evaluated in a situational context. Each situation must be reviewed to determine whether expression occurs in such a way and is of "such nature as to create a clear and present danger that it will bring about the substantive evil which legislatures are empowered to prevent." If speech is linked closely enough to illegal acts, it may be restricted. *See also* BAD TENDENCY TEST, p. 619; FREE SPEECH CLAUSE, p. 654; *Schenck v. United States*, p. 79; SLIDING SCALE TEST, p. 698.

Significance   The clear and present danger test presumes that free speech is not an absolute right. The test is designed to justify interference with speech only when the government can show that the speech creates a danger both substantial and immediate. In this respect clear and present danger is a more demanding test for restrictive enactments than the bad tendency test. The test is driven at least in part by context. Justice Holmes's conclusion that a clear and present danger existed in the *Schenck* case was based on Schenck's admitted intention to affect those subject to the draft. Holmes allowed, however, that under different circumstances such as peacetime, Schenck's expression would not have created a clear and present danger.

Collateral Estoppel   A legal principle that prohibits relitigation of an issue once a final judgment on the facts has been made. Collateral estoppel is derived from the doctrine of *res judicata*, which means "a matter already decided." Collateral estoppel had its origin in the civil process, but has been extended to criminal cases as it relates directly to the fundamental double jeopardy issues of "sameness." *See also* DOUBLE JEOPARDY, p. 640; *United States v. Foster*, p. 274.

Significance   In *Ashe*, six persons were robbed while they were playing poker. Ashe was separately charged with armed robbery of each of the six players. Ashe was tried for robbing one of the victims, but the jury found the evidence "insufficient" to convict. Several weeks later Ashe was tried for the robbery of another of the victims and was convicted. The Supreme Court reversed the conviction concluding that the only issue in dispute in the first trial was the identification of Ashe as the robber. Simply substituting one victim for another "had no bearing whatever" on the question of whether Ashe was the robber since the basic fact issue of the two trials was identical. The *Ashe* decision clarified the same offense criterion traditionally involved in double jeopardy cases. The collateral estoppel doctrine thus prevents prosecution of different offenses if previously resolved issues of fact are introduced in a second prosecution.

Commercial Press   Expression that promotes business transactions through the advertisement of products or services. As a category of expression, commercial press (or speech) has been subjected to extensive regulation. Beginning in the 1970s, however, the Supreme Court departed from its previous commercial speech position to substantially expand First Amendment protection. The test that now applies in commercial speech cases examines whether the speech truthfully represents legal activities, whether the government has a substantial regulatory interest, and whether the regulation directly advances the governmental interest and does so in the least restrictive way. *See also Central Hudson Gas & Electric Co. v. Public Service Commission*, p. 117.

Significance   Commercial press was made a distinct category of expression in *Valentine v. Chrestensen*, 316 U.S. 52 (1942), and it was initially excluded from First Amendment protection. The Court essentially maintained this position until the Burger Court changed the criteria by which commercial press is evaluated. The Burger Court's departure from prior commercial press doctrine began in *Bigelow v. Virginia*, 421 U.S. 809 (1975), when it ruled in favor of a Virginia newspaper that carried advertising about abortion services available in New York. The Court concluded that the ad contained "factual materials of a clear public interest." The following year the Court upheld the advertising of prescription drug prices by pharmacies in *Virginia State Board of Pharmacy v. Virginia Citizens Consumer Council, Inc.*, 425 U.S. 748 (1976), even though the advertisement had content that was exclusively commercial. The standards for commercial press were clarified in *Central Hudson Gas & Electric Co. v. Public Service Commission*, 447 U.S. 557 (1980). The four-part

Hudson test has been retained to the present, and the Court has ruled against government regulations in most instances since then. A recent example can be seen in *44 Liquormart, Inc v. Rhode Island*, 517 U.S. 484 (1996), in which the Court struck down a state law that prohibited all media advertising of liquor prices and prohibited all retail liquor outlets from posting price information visible from outside their premises. At the same time, some regulation of commercial press has been allowed. In *Florida Bar Association v. Went For It, Inc.*, 515 U.S. 618 (1995), the Court upheld regulations fashioned by the Florida Bar Association that prohibited attorneys in the state from sending direct-mail solicitations to accident victims or their survivors for a 30-day period following an accident. Similarly, in *Glickman v. Wileman Bros.*, 521 U.S. 457 (1997), the Court upheld "marketing orders" that imposed an assessment on fruit growers to help underwrite the costs of "generic" advertising initiatives for selected agricultural commodities.

Common Law   A body of principles that derive their authority from court judgments that embrace common customs and usages. Common law consists of all such principles that do not have their origin in legislative enactment and, as such, is distinct from statutory or administrative law. The tradition of common law evolved because the English legal profession strongly resisted the establishment of a statutory system. Students of law in Britain were trained more in the pragmatic applications of law than in documentary systems of law enforcement. The legal profession was not so much interested in anticipating the adjudication of infractions of statutes as it was in maintaining the precedent-setting value of settled controversies. This reliance on the value of precedent may be the greatest legacy of the English common-law system. *See also* JURISPRUDENCE, p. 672; *STARE DECISIS*, p. 703.

Significance   Common law is based on prevailing usage. Use of common law invests judges with substantial flexibility in fashioning responses to specific case needs, although precedent established by judges reduces this flexibility. Once a decision is made, its root principles are drawn upon in subsequent cases of a similar kind, thus making the particular legal principle common to other related situations. Common law forms the basis of many legal processes in the states. Although there is no federal common law as such, federal judges do utilize state common law in diversity of citizenship cases. Common law must yield to statutory law when conflicts between the two exist, but statutory law is generally founded upon common-law principles. As a result, few major substantive conflicts arise. Furthermore, courts tend to interpret statutory law using common-law traditions, which further diminishes the likelihood of incompatibility between statutes and common-law principles.

Community Standards   A criterion used in the evaluation of obscenity. The community standards test was first introduced in *Roth v. United States*, 354 U.S. 476 (1957). The Warren Court said in *Roth* that "community" should refer to national standards. National norms were perceived as being less restrictive and more permissive than community norms, which were defined by local standards. Defining standards in national terms also made criteria for adjudicating obscenity issues more uniform. It also places the Supreme Court at the center of the process of determining what constitutes obscenity. *See also* FIRST AMENDMENT, p. 29; *Miller v. California*, p. 137; OBSCENITY, p. 682; *Roth v. United States*, p. 135.

Significance   Community standards criteria have been a major source of disagreement in the Supreme Court's treatment of obscenity. The Burger Court abandoned the Warren Court approach in *Miller v. California*, 413 U.S. 15 (1973), saying that to require obscenity prosecutions to use national standards was "an exercise in futility." The Court said that the nation is simply too big and diverse to expect that fixed and uniform standards can be formulated. Rather, the standards should be drawn from each local community and applied in concert with "limiting instructions on the law." The Court rejected as neither realistic nor constitutionally sound a requirement that would have "the people of Maine or Mississippi accept the standards of Las Vegas or New York City." Defining community standards in local terms created the prospect of a more restrictive and diverse approach to the regulation of obscenity.

Compulsory Process   The Sixth Amendment right of a person accused of a crime to have witnesses in his or her favor. Compulsory process protects the defendant's right to present a defense, which includes calling witnesses who may not want to appear voluntarily. A defendant may subpoena a party and compel him or her to testify. A subpoena is the command of a court requiring a person to appear at a legal proceeding and offer testimony on a particular matter. A subpoena *duces tecum* is an order for physical items, such as papers or records, to be produced at such a proceeding. *See also Rock v. Arkansas*, p. 336; SIXTH AMENDMENT, p. 323.

Significance   Compulsory process was extended to the states in *Washington v. Texas*, 388 U.S. 14 (1967), in which the Supreme Court determined that the right was fundamental. The compulsory process provision of the Sixth Amendment has been interpreted more broadly than the right to subpoena witnesses. It has been held to prevent a state from denying access to certain categories of witnesses, such as coparticipants in an alleged crime. Similarly, it prevents a state from creating situations in which the testimony of a defense witness is diminished in value by a judicial action or jury instruction. The compulsory process protection establishes a substantial expectation that the defense will be able to present a full and unimpaired alternative version of the facts.

Confrontation Clause   The Sixth Amendment entitlement that an accused person must be confronted with the witnesses against him or her. The Confrontation Clause is often thought to be synonymous with the right to cross-examine accusers or adverse witnesses, but cross-examination is only one element of the Clause's broader objective of fully exposing reliable evidence to the fact-finding process. The Confrontation Clause requires that witnesses be brought to open court and placed under oath and thereby under threat of prosecution for perjury. Their testimony, as well as their manner and demeanor, is assessed there. *See also Coy v. Iowa,* p. 333; *Pointer v. Texas,* p. 328; SIXTH AMENDMENT, p. 323.

Significance   The Confrontation Clause entitles an accused person to challenge the evidence against him or her in an attempt to present the best factual defense possible. An accused person is therefore given the opportunity to be present at all proceedings against him or her, and a relatively unrestricted examination/cross-examination process can be utilized. The Supreme Court found the right of confrontation to be a fundamental right and has applied it to the states through the Fourteenth Amendment in *Pointer v. Texas,* 380 U.S. 100 (1965).

Consent Search   The right to waive Fourth Amendment protections and submit to a search by representatives of the government. The state must show that consent has been voluntarily given before evidence from the search can be used at a trial. The Supreme Court has determined that the voluntariness issue cannot be resolved by any infallible touchstone, but can only be resolved by looking at the totality of circumstances. In doing so, two competing concerns must be accommodated. One is the legitimacy of the need for the search, and the other is the need to assure the absence of coercion in gaining consent. *See also Ohio v. Robinette,* p. 239; THIRD-PARTY SEARCH, p. 706.

Significance   Consenting to a search means waiving a constitutional protection. The Supreme Court has established that the burden of proving the voluntariness of consent rests with the prosecution and cannot be inferred from silence. The Court has not gone so far as to require that persons be informed that they may withhold consent, although a number of states have done so. Assuming consent is voluntary, a person may limit his or her consent to particular places to be searched and specific items to be searched for. Once granted, consent may be withdrawn. Even uncoerced consent cannot purge taint stemming from an impermissible action occurring prior to consent. If a person is illegally detained, for example, any subsequent search is flawed.

Constitutionalism   The limiting of government power through a compact between the people and the state. A constitution allocates power to government and establishes the boundaries of government's power. Among the limitations contained in the American Constitution are separation of powers, division of powers between the national and state levels, checks and balances, and the Bill of Rights. *See also* BILL OF RIGHTS, p. 621; FEDERALISM, p. 649; SEPARATION OF POWERS, p. 697.

Significance   The roots of modern constitutionalism go back to Greece and Rome. Plato advanced a theory of constitutionalism by stressing that government must be guided by law. Aristotle distinguished between a nation's basic governmental structure, its laws, and its changeable policies. He clarified the fundamental and largely permanent nature of constitutions. Aristotle's description of the "mixed" constitution introduced the concepts of separation and balancing of government powers. The Romans advanced the practice of constitutionalism by giving "government by law" a written and codified foundation. A number of political thinkers provided a transition to the modern period of constitutionalism. Development of social contract theory was evolved through the writings of Thomas Hobbes, John Locke, and Jean-Jacques Rousseau. Locke and the Baron de Montesquieu helped define the doctrine of separation of powers. American political thinkers such as Thomas Jefferson, Alexander Hamilton, and James Madison wrote extensively of the American experience with constitutionalism. The final historical phase of modern constitutionalism was its democratization, beginning in the United States with Andrew Jackson and Abraham Lincoln, and in Great Britain with the Reform Act of 1832.

Contempt   Any act that obstructs the administration of justice by a court or that brings disrespect on a court or its authority. Contempt may be direct in that it occurs in the presence of the court and constitutes a direct affront to the court's authority. While some due process protections apply to contempt, it is generally a summary order through which penalties of fine or imprisonment may be directly imposed by the court. Contempt may be indirect in that the behavior demonstrating contempt may occur outside the courtroom. It is necessary to distinguish between criminal and civil contempt. Criminal contempt is an act of obstruction or disrespect typically occurring in the courtroom. A party who acts in an abusive manner in court is in criminal contempt. He or she may receive a fine and/or imprisonment for up to six months summarily imposed. Civil contempt results from failure to comply with the order of a court. Civil contempt is designed to coerce compliance with an order to protect the interests of the party on whose behalf the order to judgment was issued. Civil contempt ends when the desired conduct or compliance occurs. A legislative contempt power also exists. It may be used if a disturbance is created within a legislative chamber or if persons subpoenaed to appear before legislative committees fail to testify. Congressional contempt is not summarily imposed, however. It is handled through the standard criminal process with a trial occurring in a federal district court if an indictment has been secured from a grand jury. *See also* JURISDICTION, p. 671.

Significance   The contempt power provides courts with leverage to maintain courtroom decorum appropriate for judicial proceedings. Contempt enables a court to punish disruptive or disrespectful conduct, and it serves as a deterrent to such conduct. The contempt power also permits courts to compel compliance with a court order, backstopping the authority of all such orders.

Counsel, Assistance of   A protection of the Sixth Amendment that entitles any accused person to have "assistance of counsel for his defense." The assistance of counsel provision in its early construction was confined to preventing the government from keeping an accused from securing his or her own counsel. There was no expectation that counsel was required or would be provided in the instance of a defendant's indigence. The Supreme Court has gradually expanded the coverage of the counsel language, however, to require the appointment of defense counsel in all federal and state felony cases, and finally in all misdemeanor cases involving confinement to jail as a possible sentence. Juvenile delinquency proceedings also require the appointment of counsel. *See also Argersinger v.*

Hamlin, p. 363; CRITICAL STAGE, p. 636; *Gideon v. Wainwright*, p. 360; *United states v. Wade*, p. 368.

Significance   The assistance of counsel doctrine has developed around two points. First, the aid provided by counsel is invaluable in criminal cases, and due process requires "the guiding hand of counsel" for an accused charged with a criminal offense. Justice Black remarked in *Gideon v. Wainwright*, 372 U.S. 335 (1963), that lawyers are necessities, not luxuries. Second, a defendant should not be denied assistance of counsel because of his or her indigence. Any person who is charged with a criminal offense and who is not able to afford counsel cannot have a fair trial unless counsel is provided. The right to counsel has also been extended to various critical stages of the criminal process both before and after trial. A critical stage is defined as any step in the criminal process at which the advice of counsel may be essential to protecting the rights of an accused person, or at which the defendant's overall fate is substantially affected. Currently recognized as critical stages are custodial interrogations, preliminary hearings, arraignments, postindictment lineups, sentencing and probation revocation hearings, and appeals. Assistance of counsel is also a part of the civil trial process. Although such assistance is not constitutionally mandated for civil trials, federal appellate courts have held that less strict adherence to evidentiary rules and less formal discovery compliance ought to be applied by trial courts when one of the parties is unrepresented by counsel. An indigent dependant may waive appointment of counsel in favor of self-representation.

Critical Stage   The point in a criminal proceeding at which an accused person is entitled to assistance of counsel. A stage in the criminal process is considered to be "critical" if there exists the possibility that a criminal defendant's constitutional rights may be at risk. A critical stage also exists if something occurs that may ultimately impact on the outcome of a criminal prosecution. If a stage or step in the criminal process does either of these things, the defendant is entitled to legal counsel. *See also* COUNSEL, ASSISTANCE OF, p. 635; *Gideon v. Wainwright*, p. 360; *United States v. Wade*, p. 368.

Significance   Critical stage assistance is essential to protecting the rights of an accused person and may substantially affect the criminal process as a whole. Critical stage was defined only in terms of the trial itself until 1963. Assistance of counsel was not needed at other stages in the criminal process. Once trial assistance was mandated for all felony prosecutions in *Gideon v. Wainwright*, 372 U.S. 335 (1963), however, it was inevitable that other stages in the criminal process would be recognized as critical as well. Soon after *Gideon*, such stages as custodial interrogations, postindictment investigations, preliminary hearings, and postindictment identifications were found to be critical. Even prior to *Gideon*, counsel requirements had been extended to arraignments. The critical stages of posttrial proceedings have been defined as sentencing, probation revocations, and appeals. The large number of recognized critical stages reflects the high priority assigned to assistance of counsel by the Supreme Court. An accused must have access to legal counsel throughout the criminal process to satisfy due process requirements.

Cruel and Unusual Punishment   A criminal penalty that is excessive or is incompatible with societal standards of decency. The Cruel and Unusual Punishment Clause is located in the Eighth Amendment. As society matures, its values change, thus the status of a particular punishment may change as society's values change. Currently the Supreme Court has said that punishments that involve torture or cruelty are prohibited, as are punishments that are degrading. *See also* EIGHTH AMENDMENT, p. 399; *Gregg v. Georgia*, p. 411; *Harmelin v. Michigan*, p. 402; MANDATORY SENTENCE, p. 678; *Robinson v. California*, p. 400.

Significance   The cruel and unusual punishment doctrine holds that punishments must "comport with human dignity." They cannot be imposed upon a status or condition, and they must be proportionate to the offense. The death penalty, a punishment unique in terms of its severity and irrevocability, does not invariably offend the cruel and unusual punishment prohibition. Procedural flaws may make the imposition of the death penalty impermissible, however. It may not be imposed without a two-stage, or bifurcated, trial and sentencing process. The sentencer must be provided with sufficient guidance for making a determination of death. He or she must specify aggravating circumstances in assessing the gravity of a particular offense, and the sentencer must consider any and all mitigating circumstances. A mandatory sentence of death is not permitted because it does not allow for the consideration of mitigating circumstances. The Court has also said that the Cruel and Unusual Punishment Clause includes protection from penalties that may be "excessive" or "disproportionate," penalties that are more extensive than the underlying crime may justify. It was on this basis that the Supreme Court invalidated the death penalty for the crime of rape, at least where the victim was an adult. The Court has generally stayed away from reviewing prison sentences on disproportionality grounds, but suggested in *Solem v.*

Helm, 463 U.S. 277 (1983), that review of sentences for noncapital crimes can occur. The Court established three criteria in *Solem* by which sentence proportionality is to be examined: (1) gravity of the offense; (2) correlation with sentences imposed within the same jurisdiction (state) for the same offense; and (3) correlation with sentences imposed in other states for the same offense.

De Jure   A Latin term meaning "by right." A de jure action flows directly from an official action or pronouncement. De jure segregation, for example, is segregation mandated by law. Officially mandated classifications, both racial and other, meet the state action condition for application of the Fourteenth or Fifteenth Amendments. De jure is the opposite of de facto as a legal qualifier. De facto means "in fact," and is a condition that has status as a function of its existence or through established practice. *See also* CLASSIFICATION, p. 628; STATE ACTION, p. 703.

Significance   The terms *de jure* and *de facto* may be used in a variety of contexts to modify or qualify a condition. They have often been used in describing conditions of racial segregation. De jure segregation is intended and specifically sanctioned by law. Such legally sanctioned segregation was struck down by the Supreme Court in *Brown v. Board of Education*, 347 U.S. 483 (1954). De facto segregation occurs without formal assistance of government. In its de facto form, segregation has social and economic causes outside the established constitutional system and, therefore, are more difficult to remedy through the Equal Protection Clause.

Declaratory Judgment   A form of relief invoked when a plaintiff seeks a declaration of his or her rights. A declaratory judgment does not involve monetary damages but is an assessment of a party's rights prior to a damage occurring. It differs from a conventional action in that no specific order is issued by the court. It differs from an advisory opinion in that parties have a bona fide controversy in a declaratory judgment proceeding, although actual injury has not yet occurred. The federal courts are empowered to render declaratory judgments by the Federal Declaratory Judgment Act of 1934. In a declaratory judgment proceeding there must be a real controversy, but the plaintiff is uncertain of his or her rights and seeks adjudication of them. As in injunctive relief, a declaratory judgment request is a petition for a court to exercise its powers of equity. No jury is permitted. The judge is asked to declare what the law is regarding the controversy. *See also* ADVISORY OPINION, p. 609.

Significance   Declaratory judgment actions are a comparatively recent development in American jurisprudence because the traditional concept was that courts could only act when a plaintiff was entitled to a coercive remedy. A plaintiff may find it necessary, however, to determine if he or she is bound by contractual language that the plaintiff believes to be void or unenforceable for some reason. If the plaintiff should fail to comply, he or she is risking suit for breach of contract and consequential damages. The declaratory judgment procedure is helpful to all parties because it circumvents the necessity of a possible breach and the lengthy litigation that such action invites. Contract and patent disputes frequently require declaratory judgments. Courts are reluctant to issue them on broad public policy issues.

Diversity Jurisdiction   The authority of federal courts to hear civil actions involving parties from different states. Diversity jurisdiction is provided for in Article III of the Constitution. Diversity jurisdiction lies wholly within the control of Congress and is conveyed as inferior courts are established. Diversity jurisdiction was first conferred upon lower federal courts in the Judiciary Act of 1789, but a $50 controversy had to exist before the federal courts could enforce their jurisdiction. The amount in controversy was raised to $50,000 in 1958. *See also* CASE OR CONTROVERSY, p. 622; ORIGINAL JURISDICTION, p. 685.

Significance   Diversity jurisdiction is periodically debated in Congress among those who would abolish it altogether, those who would reduce it dramatically, and those who would retain it as it is. Proponents of abolition point to the cost to federal taxpayers, the intervention of federal courts in state law matters, and the redundancy and uncertainty that exist when a dual system of courts addresses the same issues. Opponents of change argue the possibility of home party bias against nonresidents, the value of two-system interaction, and the multiplicity of civil actions, which the federal courts for procedural reasons are better equipped to handle. Diversity jurisdiction exists when there is a diversity of citizenship among the parties to a suit or when there is an interstate aspect to a legal action. Suits below the dollar threshold and that involve no substantial federal issue are left to state courts. Diversity jurisdiction was established for the federal courts because state courts might be biased against litigants from out of state. The political interests of the Federalists were well served by having federal court jurisdiction touch on state and local matters. Diversity of citizenship cases constitute a large portion, about 30 percent, of the current civil caseload in federal courts. The potential for substantial conflict between

federal and state law litigated in federal courts under diversity jurisdiction was minimized by the Supreme Court's decision in *Erie
Railroad Co. v. Tompkins*, 304 U.S. 64 (1938), in which the Court held
that state statutory or common law is always to be applied in diversity cases.

Double Jeopardy   A Fifth Amendment provision that no person
shall be "subject for the same offense to be twice put in jeopardy of
life or limb." Double jeopardy precludes the state from successively
subjecting a citizen to the ordeal of prosecution for a given offense.
The ban on double jeopardy was extended to the states by the
Warren Court in *Benton v. Maryland*, 395 U.S. 784 (1969). The
Double Jeopardy Clause was seen by the Court in *Benton* as representing "a fundamental ideal in our constitutional heritage." The
Clause does not prevent both federal and state levels of government
from prosecuting persons for the same criminal act on the basis of
dual sovereignty, however. Bank robbery, for example, is both a
federal and a state crime if the bank has federal insurance coverage.
Successive prosecutions at the state and local levels are precluded
because local units of government are subordinate instrumentalities
of the state. In a jury trial jeopardy commences when the jury is
sworn. In a nonjury trial jeopardy commences when the first witness
is sworn. Cases dismissed prior to the commencement of jeopardy in
either type of proceeding may be reinstated. The Double Jeopardy
Clause does not apply to cases in which a defendant successfully
appeals following a conviction and has the conviction set aside on
grounds other than insufficiency of evidence. Reprosecution in such
situations is limited to a charge no greater than the equivalent of the
original conviction that prompted the appeal. However, a sentence
may be more severe following successful reprosecution without
violating the Double Jeopardy Clause if multiple punishments have
been imposed. *See also* COLLATERAL ESTOPPEL, p. 629; *Department of
Revenue v. Kurth Ranch*, p. 283; IMPLICIT ACQUITTAL, p. 663; *Schiro v.
Farley*, p. 279; *United States v. Foster*, p. 274.

Significance   A double jeopardy determination is frequently made
difficult by what constitutes *sameness*. Sameness is usually resolved by
precluding prosecutions for two offenses in which the same evidence
is required to prove guilt. A "same transaction test," which views
offenses in terms of similar actions by the defendant, may also be
used. The "same evidence" test determines sameness by comparing
the elements the prosecution must prove to convict. If the same
evidence or elements could be used to convict on two charges, the
offenses are the same. If, on the other hand, there is one distinct

element for a second offense, the offenses are not the same. Thus by adding premeditation to a murder prosecution, the offenses of first- and second-degree murder are distinguished. The "same conduct" approach focuses on whether the prosecution intends to show a second offense on the basis of the same conduct used to convict on a first. Under this approach, if a person was fined for driving while impaired, a subsequent prosecution for injuring another driver could not be established on the basis of that impaired driving offense. The same evidence standard is currently the standard preferred by the Rehnquist Court.

Neither approach clearly delineates sameness, however. The doctrine of collateral estoppel is held to be part of the double jeopardy protection and provides some assistance in solving the sameness problem. It forbids reprosecution in cases in which an accused has been acquitted on the basis of a decisive fact issue relitigated in the second trial. Another double jeopardy problem is created by the declaration of a mistrial after jeopardy has attached. If the defendant makes the mistrial motion, ordinarily there is no double jeopardy issue. But if the prosecution makes the motion, or if the judge grants a mistrial without a motion, an ambiguous situation is created. In the latter two situations, double jeopardy may occur on a reprosecution unless the mistrial was beyond the court's control. The Rehnquist Court has made a number of important double jeopardy rulings in recent years. In *United States v. Foster*, 509 U.S. 688 (1993), the Court abandoned the "same conduct" test for sameness, returning to the "same evidence" test used previously. The Court has also had to respond to a number of claims asserting that the double jeopardy protection contains a prohibition against multiple punishment. As in *Department of Revenue v. Kurth Ranch*, 511 U.S. 767 (1994), such claims have not received favorable response from the Court.

Due Process Clauses   Constitutional provisions designed to ensure that laws will be reasonable both in substance and in means of implementation. Due process language is contained in two clauses of the Constitution of the United States. The Fifth Amendment prohibits deprivation of "life, liberty, or property, without due process of law." It sets a limit on arbitrary and unreasonable actions by the federal government. The Fourteenth Amendment contains parallel language aimed at the states. Due process requires that actions of government occur through ordered and regularized processes. There are two kinds of due process: The first is *procedural due process*, which focuses on the methods or procedures by which governmental policies are executed. It guarantees fairness in the processes by which government imposes regulations or sanctions. Procedural due process requires that a person be formally notified of any proceeding in which he or she is a party, and that he or she be afforded an opportunity for an impartial hearing. Additional procedural rights have been enumerated in the Bill of Rights. Through the process of incorporation, most Bill of Rights protections have been applied to the states through the Due Process Clause of the Fourteenth Amendment. *Substantive due process* represents the second kind of due process. It involves the reasonableness of policy content. Policies may deny substantive due process when they do not rationally relate to legitimate legislative objectives or when they are impermissibly vague. *See also* FOURTEENTH AMENDMENT, p. 651; INCORPORATION, p. 665; PROCEDURAL DUE PROCESS, p. 692; SUBSTANTIVE DUE PROCESS, p. 705.

Significance   Due process is an evolving concept that undergoes continuing adjustment and refinement. The two due process clauses provide the Supreme Court an ongoing opportunity to consider and define the legal contours of fairness. The heart of the matter is reasonableness. If the substance of a government policy or the procedures used to implement it are adjudged to be arbitrary and unreasonable, the Court can nullify the policy or practice under the due process clauses.

Editorial Privilege   Refers to the freedom of publishers to make editorial judgments. Editorial privilege is a benefit (privilege) possessed by a person or a class of persons that provides an advantage over other persons or classes. In some instances a privilege exempts one from some obligation because his or her office or function would be impaired. If the editorial process is confidential, for example, a plaintiff in a libel action may not be able to inquire of a publisher about the source of information used by the publisher. Neither could the plaintiff in a libel suit inquire about the information-gathering process itself or the bases upon which journalistic judgments were made, including a publisher's state of mind. In *Herbert v. Lando*, 441 U.S. 153 (1979), the Supreme Court rejected the position that editorial privilege shields the editorial process from access by a plaintiff seeking to demonstrate malice in a libel action. *See also* LIBEL, p. 675; NEWSPERSON'S PRIVILEGE, p. 681; *New York Times Co. v. Sullivan*, p. 106.

Significance   Editorial privilege tends to protect publishers from successful libel actions. The privilege safeguards the freedom of the press by allowing substantial latitude in the making of editorial judgments. *Lando* shows that editorial privilege is limited, at least in theory. It remains to be seen whether representatives of the press would actually make disclosures that would establish malice or reckless disregard in libel cases. The Court has generally been unwilling to recognize privileged status. The press has often claimed that it should have greater access to locations or information than ordinary citizens. Journalists have also claimed a right to keep news sources confidential. Neither of these claims has been supported by the Supreme Court.

Electronic Surveillance   The observing or monitoring of a person by electronic means. Electronic surveillance includes telephone wiretaps and a wide variety of mechanisms that permit eavesdropping. Electronic surveillance did not fall within the purview of the Fourth Amendment until recently, because neither physical entry onto private property had occurred, nor had seizure of tangible items taken place. In the late 1960s the Supreme Court reinterpreted the Fourth Amendment to create a protection for personal privacy, and this reinterpretation extended Fourth Amendment coverage to electronic surveillance. Congress subsequently enacted the Omnibus Crime Control Act of 1968, which incorporated certain proscriptions on surveillance fashioned by the Court from its review of Fourth Amendment requirements. The Act mandates use of an application procedure to obtain prior approval for electronic surveillance. The process closely resembles that used in obtaining a warrant. An unapproved emergency surveillance may occur for up to 48 hours provided a threat to national security is involved. *See also Katz v. United States*, p. 203; WARRANT, p. 710.

Significance   Electronic surveillance constitutes a substantial threat to personal privacy. Modern technology is advanced enough that many sophisticated forms of intrusion yield thorough results. Although the Supreme Court has not forbidden such surveillance altogether, its use is extensively regulated. The various means of executing an authorized surveillance need not be separately approved by judicial officers.

En Banc   A decision or proceeding made or heard by the entire membership of a court. En banc distinguishes cases having full participation from the more typical use of only a fraction of a court's membership to hear a particular case. En banc is sometimes used in reference to state and federal intermediate appellate courts, which generally assign only three members of the larger panel to hear appeals. *See also* APPEAL, p. 613.

Significance   The United States Supreme Court and a state's highest appellate tribunal always sit en banc. An en banc court in United States court of appeals cases is usually ordered only in highly controversial cases or in cases in which reconsideration on a major point of law is sought following a ruling by a three-judge panel.

Equity Jurisdiction   The power of a court to grant relief or a remedy to a party based on perceptions of fairness that supplement common-law doctrines. Relief is assistance extended by a court to an injured or aggrieved party justified by these considerations, while a remedy is the specific means, such as an injunction, by which a court intervenes to protect a legal right or interest through its equity jurisdiction. In *Brown v. Board of Education (II)*, 349 U.S. 294 (1955), for example, the Supreme Court mandated that lower federal courts issue relief decrees that were to be shaped by equitable principles. The Court characterized equity as having a practical flexibility in its approach to constructing remedies. The lower courts were to reconcile public and private needs with decrees framed by perceptions of fairness and justice. A *show cause* proceeding is a process that applies rules of equity in the exercise of equity jurisdiction. A show cause order may be issued by a court to require a party to appear and explain why an action should not take place. Anyone opposed to the action has an opportunity to express his or her position and produce evidence in support of his or her interest. If the affected party does not appear or present acceptable reasons, the proposed show cause action will take place. The burden of proof is on the party required to show cause. *See also* APPEAL, p. 613; COMMON LAW, p. 631; INJUNCTION, p. 667.

Significance   Equity jurisdiction in the United States is placed in the same courts that possess jurisdiction over statutory and common law. In Great Britain, by contrast, courts of equity are structurally separate courts. Considerations of equity in American courts protect against injustices occurring through proper but too rigid application of common-law principles or where gaps exist in the common law.

Establishment Clause   The portion of the First Amendment that forbids Congress from enacting any law respecting an establishment of religion. The Establishment Clause in its most narrow construction holds that no official or state church can be established in the United States and that no particular religion can be preferred by government action. A still more rigorous construction would have an absolute separation of church and state. The Supreme Court has generally steered a course near, but not quite reaching, the latter position. *Everson v. Board of Education*, 330 U.S. 1 (1947), provided definitions on the subject as well as a linkage of the establishment prohibition to the states. *Everson* said that the Establishment Clause erected a wall of separation between church and state that precluded government from aiding all religions or preferring one religion over another. Neither could government aid religion in preference to nonreligion, nor participate in the affairs of any religious organization. A closely related position is defined as the concept of governmental neutrality toward religion. The neutrality position does not prohibit all interaction of church and state. Rather, it only forbids governmental policies that aid or handicap religion. Yet another interpretation of the Establishment Clause accommodates certain governmental contact with religion. This position allows what Chief Justice Burger has termed "benevolent neutrality" in *Walz v. Tax Commission of New York City*, 397 U.S. 664 (1970). Benevolent neutrality presumes that government need not act as an adversary of religion to avoid establishment prohibitions. *See also* CHILD BENEFIT DOCTRINE, p. 624; *Engel v. Vitale*, p. 54; *Everson v. Board of Education*, p. 32; *Lemon v. Kurtzman*, p. 35.

Significance The Establishment Clause has been interpreted in recent years to mean that government should not be prevented from providing benefits to people simply because they have religious beliefs. Government's provision of such services as fire protection should not constitute an establishment of religion under this view. The Supreme Court has also developed a construct known as the child benefit doctrine for establishment challenges to various educational aid programs. Under the child benefit doctrine, textbooks distributed to nonpublic school students are viewed as benefiting individual students rather than institutional religion. Contemporary establishment cases are generally evaluated using three criteria. These standards are often called the *Lemon* standards, because they were first applied in *Lemon v. Kurtzman*, 403 U.S. 602 (1971). First, government policy must have a secular legislative purpose. The prayer and Bible-reading programs struck down by the Court in the early 1960s were seen as having spiritual rather than secular purposes. Second, no enactment can have as its principal or primary effect the advancement or inhibition of religion. Third, no statute may foster an excessive entanglement of government and religion. The entanglement criterion was crucial in several school-aid cases because the Court felt government would be placed in a continuously monitoring relationship with religious institutions. Church and state would be brought into an impermissible pattern of regular and close interaction. The Court saw heated debate over various aid programs creating such ongoing divisiveness in American communities that undesirable entanglement was the inevitable result. The three-pronged *Lemon* test remains the operative standard for religious establishment, but not without substantial criticism. Several of the Rehnquist Court justices, including Chief Justice Rehnquist and Associate Justices Scalia and Thomas, would prefer moving to a test that focuses on government coercion that compels individuals to support or participate in any religion or its exercise. Justices O'Connor, Stevens, and Souter apply the purpose and primary effect elements from the *Lemon* test by determining whether the government intends to endorse religion and whether any governmental action conveys a message of endorsement. The Court's recent establishment decisions suggest declining support for the *Lemon* standard, and it may be substantially modified or even abandoned altogether in the near future.

Exclusionary Rule   A court-fashioned rule of evidence that prohibits the use in criminal trials of items gained from an unconstitutional search or seizure. The exclusionary rule was designed to give effect to the Fourth Amendment prohibition against unreasonable searches and seizures. The rule is highly controversial and is not explicitly required by the Fourth Amendment. Until 1914 common law provided that evidence obtained in violation of the Fourth Amendment could still be used in a criminal trial. *Weeks v. United States*, 232 U.S. 383 (1914), broke from that tradition and established the exclusionary rule in federal criminal cases. The Supreme Court said that without the rule, the Fourth Amendment is of no value, and "might as well be stricken from the Constitution." The Court refrained, however, from taking a parallel step for state criminal trials. In *Wolf v. Colorado*, 338 U.S. 25 (1949), the Court chose to leave the states free to choose whether the rule would operate in their courts. In 1949 the Court did not see the rule as essential enough that it must be extended to the states. *Mapp v. Ohio*, 367 U.S. 643 (1961), overruled *Wolf* and applied the rule to state trials. Since *Mapp* the Court has had occasion to consider the exclusionary rule quite often. Although the Court has chosen to retain the rule, dissatisfaction with it is apparent through either of two responses: First, the rule will not be extended beyond the trial setting. The Burger Court rejected extension of it to grand jury proceedings in *United States v. Calandra*, 414 U.S. 338 (1974). The Court also allowed illegally obtained evidence to be used in a civil tax proceeding in *United States v. Janis*, 429 U.S. 874 (1976). Second, the Court is willing to limit the coverage of the rule. It allowed otherwise inadmissible evidence to be used in impeaching a defendant's trial testimony in *Oregon v. Hass*,

420 U.S. 714 (1975), and it limited habeas corpus access to the federal courts in state search cases in *Stone v. Powell*, 428 U.S. 465 (1976). In 1984 the Court fashioned a "good faith" exception to the exclusionary rule in *United States v. Leon*, 468 U.S. 897 (1984). The Court said that evidence seized by police in "reasonable, good faith reliance" on a search warrant may be used at trial even if the warrant is subsequently found to be defective. *See also* FOURTH AMENDMENT, p. 193; *Mapp v. Ohio*, p. 205.

Significance   The exclusionary rule is justified in many ways. It is seen by some as an indispensable doctrine for making operational the personal protections guaranteed by the Fourth Amendment. The rule creates disincentives for police misconduct in the search context by making the products of such searches inadmissible. Others argue that the exclusionary rule protects the integrity of the courts by keeping the judicial process free of illegally seized evidence. Criticisms of the rule are numerous and substantial, however. Many regard it as excessive because it goes beyond Fourth Amendment provisions. Using the rule often is seen as too high a social cost because it may result in criminal conduct going unpunished. Further, it tends to defeat the best test of evidence, which is its reliability. The rule often allows suppression of reliable evidence because the means of obtaining it were flawed. In sum, critics of the exclusionary rule argue that instead of sanctioning police officers, the rule rewards criminal defendants. The rule is clearly threatened as political pressures mount to modify it. The exclusionary rule survives because its detractors have not been able to find an adequate alternative.

Exigent Circumstance   An exception to the warrant requirement because the special demands of a situation make normal warrant expectations impractical or impossible. Exigent circumstance searches include searches of automobiles, for example. The exigency or emergency is created by the unforeseen need to search and the fleeting opportunity to accomplish the search because of the vehicle's mobility. A stop and frisk encounter is also an exigent circumstance. In *Michigan v. Tyler*, 436 U.S. 499 (1978), the Supreme Court also permitted a warrantless search of a fire scene under the exigent circumstance exception. The Court held that a burning building "clearly presents an exigency of sufficient proportions" to permit a reasonable warrantless entry. It would defy reason to require a warrant or consent to be secured before entering a burning building. Once on the premises to fight the fire, police and fire officials are entitled to gather visible evidence. A hot pursuit chase may also create sufficient exigency to allow a warrant exception. The exigent circumstance doctrine takes cognizance of the impossibility of completing the warrant process in certain situations in which making a search or an arrest may need to be immediate. But authorities bear a heavy burden when attempting to show an urgent need to justify a warrantless arrest or search. When the arrest or search takes place inside a person's residence, searches are "presumptively unreasonable." In *Welsh v. Wisconsin*, 466 U.S. 740 (1984), the Court held that it would be virtually impossible to demonstrate exigency for a warrantless home arrest when the underlying offense is minor. *See also* HOT PURSUIT, p. 661; *Michigan v. Tyler*, p. 216; WARRANT, p. 710; WARRANTLESS SEARCH, p. 711.

Significance   The exigent circumstance doctrine provides the basis for an exception to the warrant requirement for searches and arrests. It is necessitated by situational demands that make the normal processes impossible. The exception reflects the opinion that Fourth Amendment protections are not absolute, yet it places the burden of justifying an exigent circumstance on law enforcement officers.

Fairness Doctrine   A Federal Communications Commission policy that requires the holder of a broadcast license to afford a reasonable amount of air time to issues of public significance and to replies by persons of differing viewpoints from those expressed by the station. The fairness doctrine is enforced by the Federal Communications Commission through its licensing authority. *See also* FREE PRESS CLAUSE, p. 653; *Turner Broadcasting v. FCC (II)*, p. 128.

Significance   The fairness doctrine has been upheld by the Supreme Court against First Amendment challenge in *Red Lion Broadcasting Co. v. FCC*, 395 U.S. 367 (1969). The Court distinguished the broadcast medium from the print medium, saying that the fairness doctrine was necessary for broadcasting because of the scarcity of access to the airwaves and because licensees could otherwise monopolize the medium. Like the "equal time" doctrine for political candidates, the FCC has largely abandoned the rule as part of a more general trend toward deregulation of broadcasting.

Federal Question   A federal question triggers jurisdiction for federal courts to hear cases involving issues related to the United States Constitution, federal laws, or treaties. A federal court has authority to entertain federal questions through powers conferred in Article III of the Constitution. *See also* JURISDICTION, p. 671.

Significance   A federal question must be shown by parties wishing to access the federal courts. Their case or controversy must be within the power of the federal courts to adjudicate. An exception can occur when citizens of two different states are adversaries in a legal action. The Supreme Court frequently refuses to review cases because it believes a substantial federal question is not present.

Federalism   A political system in which a number of political units are joined into a larger political unit that has authority to act on behalf of the whole. A federal system or federation preserves the political integrity or sovereignty of all the entities comprised in the federation. Common usage equates the term *federal* with the central or national government even though the term *federal government* technically includes both levels of government. Authority is divided in a federalist system such that the national level of government retains ultimate power on at least some policy issues. Similarly, the constituent units (or states or provinces) must retain ultimate authority over at least one issue. If one level is completely without such authority, a federalism does not exist. Federal systems are regarded as "weak" if the central government has control over very few policy questions, and a "strong" system is one in which the central government possesses authority over most significant policy issues. The United States is considered a "strong" Federalist system currently. In contrast, the constitutional arrangement under the Articles of Confederation after the Revolutionary War was "weak" federalism. Authority may be shared by the two levels and exercised concurrently, but the Supremacy Clause of the U.S. Constitution requires that conflicts arising from the exercise of federal and state power are resolved in favor of the central government. Powers not assigned to the national government are "reserved" for the states by the Tenth Amendment. *See also* ARTICLES OF CONFEDERATION, p. 615; *THE FEDERALIST*, p. 650; REPUBLICANISM, p. 693; SEPARATION OF POWERS, p. 697.

Significance   Federalism is one structural device the Framers of the Constitution utilized to minimize concentration of governmental power. The separation of powers principle assigns government functions to three branches of government (legislative, executive, and judicial). Federalism overlays the functional separation of powers with a territorial division of power. The degree to which a political system should be centralized or decentralized is an ongoing political issue, and the division of authority between the national government and the states continually is subject to modification. Among the consequences of federalism is that laws and policies may differ from state to state as federalism invites the possibility of diverse or nonuniform policies at the state level as each exercises its sovereign power as it sees fit.

The Federalist   A collection of essays written to promote ratification of the Constitution. The 85 essays comprising *The Federalist* were written by Alexander Hamilton, James Madison, and John Jay under the pen name of Publius and appeared from October 1787 through March 1788. Through these essays, the authors sought to respond to the principal objections of those who opposed ratification. Federalism and separation of power were the most important points of contention. Hamilton and Madison tried to reassure those concerned that the new central government would diminish state sovereignty. At the same time, more than half of the essays argued that there must be a stronger national government than existed under the Articles of Confederation. Madison and Hamilton also argued strongly for a representative or republican form of democracy, suggesting that the size of the nation made it unsuitable for direct democracy. It was also Madison's contention that a republican form of government would minimize the potentially destructive influence of "factions" or special interests that often surface in democratic systems. *See also* ARTICLES OF CONFEDERATION, p. 615; FEDERALISM, p. 649; SEPARATION OF POWERS, p. 697.

Significance   The *Federalist* was not intended as a comprehensive discussion of political philosophy or government. Rather, the objective was securing ratification of the constitutional system developed at the Philadelphia Convention in 1787. Although Hamilton and Madison differed on some aspects of the proposed constitution, such as judicial review, they both were agreed that the proposed governmental system would address most of the deficiencies of the national level of government under the Articles of Confederation. They were also satisfied that there existed sufficient safeguards against the arbitrary exercise of governmental power. The *Federalist* also provides an account of the thinking of those who met in Philadelphia to fashion a new system of government.

Fifteenth Amendment   A post–Civil War amendment added to the Constitution in 1870. The Fifteenth Amendment provides that "the right of the citizens of the United States to vote shall not be denied or abridged by the United States or by any State on account of race, color, or previous condition of servitude." A second section of the amendment empowered Congress to pass appropriate enforcement legislation. The Fifteenth Amendment did not extend the right to vote per se, but prohibited racial discrimination that affects exercising the right to vote. *See also* FOURTEENTH AMENDMENT, p. 651; *South Carolina v. Katzenbach*, p. 531; THIRTEENTH AMENDMENT, p.707.

Significance   The Fifteenth Amendment left control over voting to the states, which placed qualifications for voting within the purview of state legislatures. Early decisions of the Supreme Court acknowledged that federal power could be exercised if citizens were denied the opportunity to vote in state elections on the basis of race. It was not until the Second World War, however, that the Supreme Court used the Fifteenth Amendment to reach the more sophisticated discriminatory techniques used in several states, such as the white primary and qualifying tests. Congressional initiatives based on the Fifteenth Amendment did not appear until the Voting Rights Act of 1965. The Voting Rights Act abolished such devices as the literacy test and poll tax, by which people had been disqualified from voting since Reconstruction. The Act also provided for extensive federal supervision of elections and required that any new voter eligibility criterion be reviewed by the attorney general prior to its implementation. The Supreme Court unanimously upheld the Voting Rights Act in *South Carolina v. Katzenbach*, 383 U.S. 301 (1966), saying that an aggressive and inventive legislative approach was appropriate given nearly a century of systematic resistance to the Fifteenth Amendment. The Court's ruling in *Katzenbach* clearly established broad federal power over voting practices in the United States.

Fourteenth Amendment   A post–Civil War amendment added to the Constitution in 1868. The Fourteenth Amendment was designed to expand the basis of federal civil-rights authority. The amendment was also aimed at forcing Southern compliance with newly established political rights for blacks. The provisions of Section 1 constitute the heart of the amendment. It begins by declaring that "all persons born or naturalized in the United States, and subject to the jurisdiction thereof, are citizens of the United States and the State wherein they reside." This language reversed the citizenship holding in *Scott v. Sandford*, 60 U.S. 393 (1857). The privileges and immunities provision follows. This provision was intended to combat the effects of the Black Codes and allow federal authority to be used to protect and advance the civil rights of black citizens. The *Slaughterhouse Cases*, 83 U.S. 36 (1873), neutralized this thrust through use of the dual citizenship concept. Dual citizenship allowed the Supreme Court to ascribe civil and political rights of major consequence to the states. Section 1 also says that "no state shall deprive any person of life, liberty, or property without due process of law." The Due Process Clause ultimately allowed the Court to apply most Bill of Rights guarantees to the states in a process known as incorporation. The Clause also enabled the Court to engage in a substantive review of state policies, particularly those regulating private property rights. Section 1 concludes by saying that "no state shall deny to any person within its jurisdiction the equal protection of the laws." The function of this provision is to prohibit unjustified classifications that might discriminate unreasonably. Section 5 empowers Congress "to enforce by appropriate legislation, the provisions of this article." Early attempts to do so were unsuccessful because the Court held that congressional power might be used only in a remedial fashion in cases in which the state was itself an active participant in impermissible discrimination. The state action requirement survives, although the scope of federal legislative power conferred by the Fourteenth Amendment has been expanded considerably. *See also* CLASSIFICATION, p. 628; DUE PROCESS CLAUSES, p. 641; EQUAL PROTECTION CLAUSE, p. 473; INCORPORATION, p. 665; PRIVILEGES AND IMMUNITIES CLAUSES, p. 690; STATE ACTION, p. 703.

Significance The Fourteenth Amendment brought a federal presence to the protection of civil rights, but early interpretations of the amendment preserved a dominant role for the states in this policy area. Only recently has the amendment produced major changes, primarily through expanded construction of the Due Process and Equal Protection Clauses. The Fourteenth Amendment has become the cornerstone of civil-rights policy and the principal means by which Bill of Rights guarantees have been extended to the states.

Free Exercise Clause The Clause of the First Amendment that restricts Congress from passing any law interfering with religious exercise. The Free Exercise Clause restrains government from compelling worship or belief and from making any right or privilege contingent on religious belief. Since *Cantwell v. Connecticut*, 310 U.S. 296 (1940), the Free Exercise Clause has applied to the states through the Fourteenth Amendment. The Clause presents problems of differentiation stemming from actions that flow out of beliefs. While belief is an absolute right, associated conduct may be regulated under certain circumstances. Most government enactments are of wide scope and are not aimed at any particular religious group. *See also Employment Division v. Smith*, p. 68; ESTABLISHMENT CLAUSE, p. 644; *Sherbert v. Verner*, p. 61; *Wisconsin v. Yoder*, p. 64.

Significance   Free Exercise Clause cases typically involve conflicts between laws serving a wide and secular purpose on the one hand, and the religious interests of individuals on the other. Religion may not be used to exempt a person from compliance with secular law designed to safeguard the public's safety or health. The Supreme Court said in *Reynolds v. United States*, 98 U.S. 145 (1878), the Mormon polygamy case, that "to permit professed doctrines of religious beliefs to prevail over the law of the land would permit every citizen to become a law unto himself." A classic illustration of the secular regulation approach to free exercise interpretation is seen in the first compulsory flag salute case, *Minersville School District v. Gobitis*, 310 U.S. 586 (1940). Through Justice Frankfurter, the Court held that religious protections do not preclude legislation of a general secular nature as long as the legislation does not take direct aim at a sect. Justice Frankfurter said that even conscientious scruples cannot relieve an individual from obedience to general law. Modification of the secular regulation criterion came in the *Sunday Closing Law Cases*, 366 U.S. 421 (1961), when the Warren Court attempted to provide further protection for religious exercise. The Court said that enactments must use the least restrictive means possible when pursuing secular objectives. A state must show that it could not have achieved a secular objective through an alternative method that imposes less of a burden on religious exercise. The full impact of this modification is seen in *Sherbert v. Verner*, 374 U.S. 398 (1963), in which the Court ruled against a state unemployment compensation benefit system because it failed to demonstrate a compelling government interest that could be achieved by less burdensome means. Although less antithetical to religious exercise than the unmodified secular purpose test standing alone, the new approach raised the prospect of favoring religious preference. Such a course is laden with Establishment Clause difficulties because greater protection afforded religious practice means greater advantage for religion, an outcome precluded by the establishment prohibition. The Rehnquist Court abandoned the *Sherbert* test in *Employment Division v. Smith*, 494 U.S. 872 (1990), by ruling that government need not show a compelling interest when a challenged policy is generally applied. The *Smith* standard makes public policy far less vulnerable to successful challenge on religious exercise grounds.

Free Press Clause   A Clause of the First Amendment prohibiting Congress from enacting any law abridging the freedom of the press. The Free Press Clause restrains both the federal government and the states from imposing prior restraint on the print media. A *prior* or *previous restraint* is a restriction on publication before it takes place or before published material can be circulated. Such restraint typically occurs through licensure or censorship procedures. The First Amendment prohibits prior restraint because restriction of expression before it can occur constitutes a threat both to free speech and to free press. Exceptions to the prohibition may be justified if publication threatens national security, incites overthrow of the government, is obscene, or interferes with the private rights of other persons. The basic dimensions of prior restraint were established in *Near v. Minnesota*, 283 U.S. 697 (1931), and in *New York Times Co. v. United States*, 403 U.S. 713 (1971), the Pentagon Papers case. *See also* FREE SPEECH CLAUSE, p. 654; LIBEL, p. 675; *Near v. Minnesota*, p. 100; *New York Times Co. v. Sullivan*, p. 106; *New York Times Co. v. United States*, p. 101; OBSCENITY, p. 682; PRIOR RESTRAINT, p. 690.

Significance   The Free Press Clause protects the information-gathering function of the press, although an absolute right of access and confidentiality of sources does not exist. Freedom of the press occasionally collides with the fair trial interests of criminal defendants. Some limitations may therefore be imposed on the press to minimize prejudicial pretrial publicity. The press cannot be barred from criminal trials, however, and it cannot be restrained from reporting what is observed there except under extraordinary circumstances. The broadcast media are permitted to cover criminal proceedings provided they do so with no adverse consequences to the accused. Several forms of published expression remain unprotected by the Free Press Clause. Obscenity, for example, has consistently been held to be subject to government regulation. Another area outside Free Press Clause protection is libel, which is printed material falsely and maliciously defaming a person. Despite its unprotected character, libel has been narrowly defined by the Supreme Court, especially when public officials are concerned. Debate on controversial public issues cannot be inhibited by threats of libel actions. Finally, the Court has held that commercial speech is not fully protected. Commercial speech is advertising intended to promote the sale of a product or a service. The broadcast medium is affected by a First Amendment interest, but is subject to government licensure regulation anyway because of the difficulty of access to the airwaves and the limited electromagnetic spectrum available for use.

Free Speech Clause   A Clause in the First Amendment that protects against governmental interference with expression. The Free Speech Clause generally prohibits Congress from making any law that abridges the freedom of speech, and has been extended to the states through the Due Process Clause of the Fourteenth Amendment. In the case of *Schenck v. United States*, 249 U.S. 47 (1919), the Supreme

Court held that the First Amendment did not convey unlimited protection for expression despite the absolute-sounding language of the Clause. Because the Free Speech Clause does not protect all speech under all circumstances, it has become necessary to establish categories of expression and boundaries for when kinds of expression can be regulated. *See also* ASSEMBLY, RIGHT TO, p. 616; ASSOCIATION, RIGHT TO, p. 617; BAD TENDENCY TEST, p. 619; BALANCING TEST, p. 620; CLEAR AND PRESENT DANGER TEST, p. 629; PURE SPEECH, p. 692; SPEECH PLUS, p. 700; SYMBOLIC SPEECH, p. 706.

Significance The Free Speech Clause protects "pure speech" more than any other form of expression. Pure speech is communication that has no action element. In order for pure speech to be restricted, it must create a clear and present danger. If the expression advocates unlawful acts, for example, and involves a substantial and immediate danger of a kind the government is empowered to prevent, the expression loses its protection. Advocacy of abstract principles, such as overthrow of the government, is typically protected because it is not seen as having a sufficiently close connection to illegal acts. This kind of expression is virtually always unrestricted. A less rigorous standard than clear and present danger is the bad tendency test, which allows regulation if there is a chance that substantive evil will occur as a consequence of the speech. Another way of evaluating expression is through use of a balancing test. This standard weighs the expression interest against societal interests in an effort to determine if restriction of speech is warranted in a particular case. A form of balancing is a sliding-scale formulation in which the gravity of the threat is weighed against the likelihood of the threat coming to pass. Once speech has gone beyond its pure form to require action, the conduct becomes a possible object of regulation even though the expression itself may be protected. This is called "speech plus," which may take such forms as picketing, demonstrating, or symbolic speech. Such situations draw not only on the Free Speech Clause but on the First Amendment right to assemble as well. These kinds of expression may be subject to time, place, and manner restrictions, provided the restrictions are even handedly applied and are content neutral. Symbolic expression—that is, gestures or images that are substitutes for words—are recognized as having the same character of expression. Symbolic expression may be regulated only if the surrogate action is itself unlawful or subject to regulation. For example, the Warren Court upheld the criminal sanctions against persons who burned draft cards as a symbolic protest against the Vietnam War and military conscription.

Fundamental Right   Protection extended to a right expressly stated or implied in the Constitution. A fundamental right occupies a preferred position in American jurisprudence. It receives demanding review by the courts. If classificatory legislation affects a fundamental right, for example, the legislation is subject to the standards of strict scrutiny. The state must demonstrate that a compelling need is served by any enactment impinging on a fundamental right. *See also* PREFERRED POSITION DOCTRINE, p. 689; RIGHT, p. 694.

Significance   A fundamental right may be expressly provided in the Constitution or it may have evolved to constitutional status. Fundamental rights include the right to interstate travel, participation in the political process, opportunity to adjudicate legal issues, privacy, personal autonomy, and abortion. Such services as education, public welfare assistance, and public medical care have not been viewed by the Supreme Court as fundamental rights.

Gag Order   An order issued by a court directed to media representatives prohibiting the reporting of a court proceeding. A gag order is an injunction intended to minimize publicity that might prejudice a criminal trial. Except in extreme circumstances, the Supreme Court has limited the use of such orders as impermissible prior restraints. A gag order may also be issued to prevent a disruptive litigant from interfering with a court proceeding. The order might go so far as to bind and literally gag an unruly litigant, as in *Illinois v. Allen*, 397 U.S. 337 (1970). A gag order may be issued against the lawyers and litigants in a case, prohibiting them from discussing certain aspects of the case with the media. Sometimes a gag order results in sealing portions of a file or the transcripts of certain testimony in a trial in order to protect infants, mentally ill persons, or a patent or trade secret. *See also* INJUNCTION, p. 667; PRIOR RESTRAINT, p. 690.

Significance   A gag order is used to prevent prejudicial pretrial publicity. It is an extreme measure and constitutes a substantive encroachment on freedom of the press. Other alternatives, such as change of venue or delay in the commencement of a criminal prosecution, are more accepted means of protecting the fair trial rights of an accused person.

Gerrymandering   Drawing boundary lines for a legislative district to the advantage of some interest. Gerrymandering has typically occurred during redistricting when state legislatures draw district boundaries for

Congress and state legislative districts with the majority party attempting to ensure or expand its majority status. *See also* APPORTION-MENT, p. 613; *Davis v. Bandemer,* p. 522; *Shaw v. Reno,* p. 524.

Significance   Gerrymandering is a common political practice, and most redistricting plans engage in boundary manipulation for partisan advantage, at least to some degree. Gerrymandering was most extensive before the Supreme Court fashioned the one-person-one-vote standard for legislative districting. This standard required legislative districts of equal populations. Even with population-based districting, gerrymandering can still occur. The Supreme Court ruled in *Davis v. Bandemer,* 478 U.S. 109 (1986), that claims of political gerrymandering can be reviewed by federal courts. The ruling that gerrymandering may be challenged on constitutional grounds is significant in cases involving vote dilution claims brought by minorities under provisions of the Voting Rights Act of 1965. More importantly, the Court has held in cases such as *Shaw v. Reno,* 509 U.S. 630 (1993), that "racial gerrymandering" is highly suspect. That is, districting plans drawn to enhance the chances of minority candidates being elected can occur only if a compelling state interest is advanced by the race-based districting.

Grand Jury   An investigative body that makes accusations rather than determines guilt. The grand jury typically evaluates information brought to it by a prosecutor. If it determines that probable cause exists, it returns an indictment against an accused person. The indictment signifies that the grand jury feels a trial on specific charges is warranted. In English law the grand jury had the function of protecting persons from being tried arbitrarily. An American grand jury ranges from 12 to 23 persons with selection occurring under guidelines that require neutral and nondiscriminatory processes, as described in *Alexander v. Louisiana,* 405 U.S. 625 (1972). Grand juries operate in secret as a protection for persons it may not ultimately indict. Witnesses appear before grand juries under subpoena. Failure to provide information desired by a grand jury may result in a witness being cited for contempt, as in *Branzburg v. Hayes,* 408 U.S. 665 (1972). Upon hearing all testimony relating to a particular person, the grand jury determines by a simple majority vote whether to indict. Although grand juries may function through their own initiative, they are usually guided and sometimes dominated by a prosecutor. The latter determines which witnesses will appear and which evidence will be developed. The prosecutor has virtually complete discretion in grand jury proceedings through control of relevant information. Grand juries usually indict persons whom prosecutors want to be indicted. A person need not appear before a grand jury to be indicted. Witnesses who do appear usually are not permitted counsel at the proceeding itself, although out-of-room consultation during the proceeding is often permitted. A witness must be advised of his or her rights against self-incrimination, but the Court indicated in *United States v. Washington*, 431 U.S. 181 (1977), that this warning may be quite general. The Fifth Amendment mandates grand juries in the federal system, but the requirement has not been extended to the states. In *Hurtado v. California*, 110 U.S. 516 (1884), the Supreme Court held that California's use of the information process instead of the grand jury did not deny due process. *Hurtado* gave the states the opportunity to determine their own procedure for bringing criminal charges. Thirty-two states have elected to use the grand jury, at least for some portion of their criminal proceedings. Only eight states use it for all cases. Decisions subsequent to *Hurtado* have enhanced the investigative power of grand juries. An alternative accusatorial process to grand jury indictment is the information. This procedure allows a prosecutor to submit charges and supporting evidence directly to the trial court of appropriate jurisdiction. *See also Costello v. United States*, p. 270.

Significance The grand jury function is completely different from the guilt adjudication function. As a result, grand jury proceedings have been freed from some of the rigorous procedural and evidentiary standards used at trials. In *Costello v. United States*, 350 U.S. 359 (1956), for example, the Court ruled that the trial restrictions on hearsay evidence did not apply to grand juries. The relaxation of procedural constraints was intended to maximize the opportunity for a grand jury to consider as much evidence as possible before making its decision to charge. Flexibility designed to enhance the investigative power of grand juries has some costs, however. Procedural protections of witnesses are less extensive than at the trial stage, and a heightened potential for misconduct exists relative to contempt and immunity practices. The state of Michigan permits a one-person grand jury. This person is always a trial judge, and he or she functions in the same manner as a grand jury composed of laypersons.

Habeas Corpus A Latin term meaning "you have the body." Habeas corpus was a procedure in English law designed to prevent governmental misconduct, especially the improper detention of prisoners. Its primary purpose was to force jailers to bring a detained person before a judge who would examine the justification for the detention. If the judge found the person improperly held in custody, he could order the prisoner's release by issuing a writ of habeas corpus. A writ is an order from a court requiring the recipient of the order to do what the order commands. In American law the preliminary hearing functions as a point of examination into the propriety of pretrial detention as well as into the charges brought against an accused person. Article I, Section 9, of the United States Constitution provides that the "privilege of the Writ of *Habeas Corpus* shall not be suspended, unless when in Cases of Rebellion or Invasion the Public Safety may require it." President Lincoln attempted to suspend the writ early in the Civil War, but it was determined in *Ex parte Merryman,* 17 Fed.Cases 144, No. 9487 (1861), that suspension was entirely a congressional prerogative. Congress subsequently authorized President Lincoln to suspend the writ of habeas corpus at his discretion. This action was challenged and was eventually heard by the Supreme Court in *Ex parte Milligan,* 71 U.S. 2 (1866). A unanimous Court said that the president could not suspend habeas corpus under any circumstances. The Court held that Congress did not have the power to do so either. There has been no subsequent attempt to suspend habeas corpus in the United States. *See also* FEDERALISM, p. 649; FOURTEENTH AMENDMENT, p. 651.

Significance   Habeas corpus today involves federal court review of state criminal convictions. After the Fourteenth Amendment was ratified, Congress enlarged habeas corpus to include persons already convicted and in custody in the states. These prisoners could apply for a writ of habeas corpus if they believed a violation of the Constitution or federal statutes had occurred in their cases. The allegations of violations were limited to jurisdictional issues at the time, but this apparently insignificant change began a transformation of the traditional concept of habeas corpus. It eventually turned habeas corpus into a virtual substitute for the conventional appeals process. Several Supreme Court decisions initially expanded the habeas corpus remedy. *Frank v. Mangum,* 237 U.S. 309 (1915), held that habeas corpus review existed when states failed to provide an effective means for convicted prisoners to pursue alleged violations of their federal constitutional rights. *Brown v. Allen,* 344 U.S. 443 (1953), held that federal courts could reexamine a prisoner's constitutional allegations if the defendant had exhausted state corrective processes. In *Fay v. Noia,* 372 U.S. 391 (1963), the Court determined that even if all state processes are not utilized, a defendant could access the federal courts through a habeas corpus petition. The number of state prisoners seeking habeas corpus relief in the early 1940s was slightly over 100 annually. By the early 1970s there were over 15,000 applications per year. The Burger Court was critical of this trend and expressed strong disapproval of habeas corpus being taken "far beyond its historical bounds and in disregard of the writ's central purpose" in *Schneckloth v. Bustamonte,* 412 U.S. 218 (1973). The Burger Court then held in *Stone v. Powell,* 428 U.S. 465 (1976), that the habeas corpus remedy is not available to state prisoners—at least to those pursuing Fourth Amendment search violations—when the defendant had been afforded a full and fair opportunity to press the allegations in a state court. The Rehnquist Court has continued to reduce the access of state prisoners to federal habeas review. In *Coleman v. Thompson,* 501 U.S. 722 (1991), the Court overruled *Fay v. Noia,* holding that virtually any failure to exhaust state processes would constitute procedural default and preclude petitioning for federal review. In *McCleskey v. Zant,* 499 U.S. 467 (1991), the Court ruled that any second or later habeas corpus petitions must be dismissed unless a prisoner can demonstrate a reason beyond his or her control for not including the claim in the first petition. The net effect of these and other recent habeas corpus decisions has been to substantially limit federal review of state criminal cases.

Hate Speech   Hostile expression directed towards persons because of their race, ethnicity, gender, sexual orientation, or other similar characteristics. Hate speech is a particular form of offensive speech with no value as expression because it insults, injures, and by its very utterance may incite an immediate breach of peace. In *Chaplinsky v. New Hampshire,* 315 U.S. 568 (1942), the Court referred to such speech as "fighting words" because of the inherent likelihood of provoking violent reaction. *See also* FREE SPEECH CLAUSE, p. 654; OFFENSIVE SPEECH, p. 684; *R.A.V. v. City of St. Paul,* p. 90.

Significance   Hate speech has been targeted recently for regulation by many public bodies. While the Court has had some experience with offensive speech over the years, hate speech regulations are relatively new. The Court's first hate speech case as such was *R.A.V. v. City of St. Paul,* 505 U.S. 377 (1992). The city of St. Paul made it a misdemeanor to engage in speech or conduct likely to "arouse anger, alarm, or resentment in others on the basis of race, color, creed, religion or gender." The Court unanimously struck down the ordinance on First Amendment grounds because it prohibited speech on the basis of its content. Expression containing "abusive invective" was seen as permissible under the ordinance unless it addressed "one of the specified disfavored topics." The First Amendment does not allow government to impose restrictions on speakers in a selective manner because selectivity of this kind "creates the possibility that the city is seeking to handicap the expression of particular ideas." A year after *R.A.V.,* the Court reviewed a different approach to hate speech in *Wisconsin v. Mitchell,* 509 U.S. 476 (1993). Wisconsin authorized longer sentences for those criminal offenders who selected their victims on the basis of "race, religion, color, disability, sexual orientation, national origin or ancestry." A unanimous Court concluded that the sentence enhancement punished only conduct and not speech. The Wisconsin law selected hate-motivated crimes for enhanced penalty because such crime inflicts greater "social harm." The Court concluded that a state may attempt to redress such harm "over and above mere disagreement with offenders' beliefs or biases."

Hearsay   A statement by a witness repeating the words of another person rather than testifying on the basis of direct knowledge. Hearsay evidence brings statements made out of court into a legal proceeding. Hearsay is generally prohibited because the party whose out-of-court statement is offered cannot be subjected to tests of credibility through cross-examination. *See also* CONFRONTATION CLAUSE, p. 633.

Significance   The hearsay rule is designed to ensure that testimony coming before a court is reliable. Assertions that occur in open court and survive direct confrontation by the opposing party are regarded as credible, and the hearsay rule protects this method of screening evidence. There are exceptions to the hearsay rule, but before a court allows hearsay it must be convinced of both the reliability of hearsay testimony and the compelling need to use it. A "dying declaration" is typically not excluded under the hearsay rule because persons who believe death is imminent have little to gain by lying, and if the person actually dies, is obviously unavailable as a witness. Similarly, testimony about a person's "excited utterance" may be admitted because a statement made by someone who is genuinely startled minimizes the chance that intentional deception is involved.

Hot Pursuit   An exception to the rule that a law enforcement officer has authority to make arrests only within his or her jurisdiction. The hot pursuit doctrine allows an officer to arrest a fleeing suspect who has gone beyond the officer's assigned area of authority. *See also* EXIGENT CIRCUMSTANCE, p. 647; WARRANT, p. 710; WARRANTLESS SEARCH, p. 711.

Significance   Hot pursuit is established both in common law and by statute. Attempts to go after a suspect after an unreasonable interruption, however, are not permitted under the hot pursuit rule. Hot pursuit also permits police officers to chase a fleeing suspect onto private premises without having a warrant. Such a chase constitutes an exigent circumstance that relieves an officer of normal warrant requirements, at least prior to making a search or arrest.

Identification Procedures   Police methods used to determine if a witness to a crime can identify the offender. Identification procedures usually involve direct confrontation in a line-up. Identification may also be made from photographs. Such procedures are permissible as long as they are not unnecessarily suggestive and conducive of mistaken identification. *See also* CRITICAL STAGE, p. 636; *Neil v. Biggers*, p. 313; SELF-INCRIMINATION CLAUSE, p. 695.

Significance   Identification procedures are admissible in criminal cases under a totality of circumstances doctrine, with the reliability of the identification being the key consideration. Reliability rests upon the opportunity of the witness to observe the criminal at the time of the offense, the attentiveness of the witness at that time, the accuracy of the witness's description of the suspect, the witness's level of certainty at the time of confrontation with the suspect, and the amount of time between the incident and the identification. Without sufficient reliability, identification testimony may not be used. Recent Supreme Court decisions have declared postindictment line-ups to be a critical stage in the criminal process requiring assistance of counsel for the defendant.

Immunity   Part of the privilege against self-incrimination granted by the Fifth Amendment to the U.S. Constitution. Immunity prevents a person from involuntarily becoming a witness against himself or herself. The government generally cannot compel a person to disclose incriminating evidence. When a prospective witness is granted immunity, however, he or she cannot be prosecuted based upon the compelled testimony, thus satisfying Self-Incrimination Clause concerns. Once immunized from prosecution, a person must testify or be found in contempt of court. *See also Kastigar v. United States*, p. 315; SELF-INCRIMINATION CLAUSE, p. 695.

Significance   Immunity was first considered by the Supreme Court in the late nineteenth century. In *Counselman v. Hitchcock*, 142 U.S. 547 (1892), the Court held that the federal immunity statute was defective in that it left a witness vulnerable to prosecution based on evidence derived from compelled testimony. Four years later, in *Brown v. Walker*, 161 U.S. 591 (1896), the Court was asked to determine whether immunity could shield a witness beyond the prevention of actual prosecution. The Court decided that disgrace or impairment of reputation, which were possible consequences of involuntary testimony, were outside the coverage of the self-incrimination privilege. They need not be addressed when granting immunity. The matter of personal disgrace arose again in the mid–twentieth century during the investigations conducted into political subversion and national security. In *Ullmann v. United States*, 350 U.S. 422 (1956), the Court upheld provisions of the Immunity Act of 1954, which authorized immunity for testimony in national security cases. *Ullmann* reiterated the view from *Brown* that self-incrimination protects only against the danger of prosecution, not against the danger of loss of reputation and effects that may result. Immunity is typically used to obtain evidence from one person leading to the conviction of another. It allows information to develop that is not readily available through other investigative techniques. Given the frequent use of immunity, a critical question revolves around how extensive it must be to satisfy the self-incrimination protection. It clearly must extend to direct use of the testimony itself, known as use immunity, but it must go further. *Counselman* held that a witness must be protected from prosecution based on evidence derived from compelled testimony, known as derived use immunity. Even derived use immunity is limited, however. It does not prevent prosecution of a witness for a crime about which he or she may have involuntarily testified, provided the evidence used in the prosecution was developed wholly apart from the witness's testimony. Transactional immunity is the most inclusive form of immunity. It prevents prosecution for any matter or transaction about which the witness testifies. In *Kastigar v. United States*, 406 U.S. 441 (1972), the Court determined that derivative use immunity satisfied the prohibition against self-incrimination and that transactional immunity "affords the witness considerably broader protection than does the Fifth Amendment privilege." Derived use immunity is coextensive with the protection to which a person is entitled under the Fifth Amendment. *Kastigar* did require, however, that if a witness is subsequently charged, the prosecution must bear the burden of demonstrating that the evidence is independent of the witness's compelled testimony. Grants of immunity also apply across jurisdictions. When the Supreme Court made the self-incrimination protection applicable to the states in *Malloy v. Hogan*, 378 U.S. 1 (1964), it also looked at federal-state reciprocity on grants of immunity. In *Murphy v. Waterfront Commission*, 378 U.S. 52 (1964), it ruled that a witness granted immunity to testify at a state or federal proceeding could not be prosecuted at the other level based on the compelled testimony.

Implicit Acquittal   Prohibits charging a criminal defendant with a more serious offense on retrial than the charge upon which he or she was convicted at the first trial. Implicit acquittal acknowledges that a criminal defendant remains in continuing jeopardy if the defendant has obtained a reversal of a criminal conviction. Implicit acquittal applies to the level of charge for the retrial. If the initial judgment was to a lesser-included offense, retrial must be limited to that lesser-included offense. Double jeopardy absolutely bars reprosecution following an acquittal on a charge, but if a jury chooses to convict a defendant for a lesser-included offense, the jury has implicitly acquitted on the more serious charge. The Supreme Court said in *Price v. Georgia*, 398 U.S. 323 (1970), that a defendant's "jeopardy on the greater charge had ended when the first jury was given a full opportunity to return a verdict on that charge and instead reached a verdict on the lesser charge." *See also* DOUBLE JEOPARDY, p. 640; *Schiro v. Farley*, p. 279.

Significance   Implicit acquittal addresses a complex double jeopardy question. The double jeopardy prohibition clearly bars reprosecution on a charge already found inadequate by a jury. The implicit acquittal doctrine precludes a reprosecution at a level more serious than the original conviction on the ground that a jury consciously rejected conviction at that level, thus implicitly acquitting the accused of that charge. The Supreme Court has applied the implicit acquittal doctrine to the sentencing process in cases in which sentence is determined through a proceeding that resembles a trial on guilt or innocence. A two-stage sentencing procedure is used in capital punishment situations for that reason.

Implied Power   Authority not expressly conveyed in the Constitution or in statutes but inferred as stemming from expressly authorized grants of power. Implied power necessarily flows from expressed power and provides the means for the achievement of expressed power.

Significance   Implied power was first treated by the Supreme Court in *McCulloch v. Maryland*, 17 U.S. 316 (1819). At issue was the authority of Congress to establish a national bank, clearly not one of the enumerated powers of Article I of the Constitution. Chief Justice Marshall nonetheless upheld creation of the bank on implied power grounds. The Court decided that the Necessary and Proper Clause of Article I, Section 8, gave Congress wide discretion in the selection of methods by which it could carry out its policy judgments. Chief Justice Marshall said that if the objective sought by Congress is itself permissible, any means plainly adopted to that end were also permitted unless specifically prohibited by the Constitution. *McCulloch* thus established broad implied power as an aspect of legislative power. Inherent power is distinguished from implied power in that inherent power is authority beyond that expressly conferred or reasonably inferred. Implied power must be drawn from expressly granted power by reasonable inference.

In Camera   Means "in chambers" but refers to any kind of proceeding in which a judge conducts court business in private. In camera proceedings are held in a judge's chambers or any other location closed off to spectators.

Significance   In camera refers to the private review of written materials by a judge. The materials may be in the possession of one party who does not want to disclose them to an opposing party. The judge reviews the materials to determine if they are legally admissible. If they are, the materials are then disclosed to the other side.

Incorporation   Refers to the issue of whether the federal Bill of Rights acts as a limitation on state governments. Incorporation was originally defined in *Barron v. Baltimore*, 32 U.S. 243 (1833). Through Chief Justice Marshall, the Supreme Court held that the Bill of Rights constrained only "the government created by the instrument," the federal government, and not the "distinct governments," the states. *Barron* was controlling until ratification of the Fourteenth Amendment in 1868. The Fourteenth Amendment reopened the question of incorporation because it clearly directed its proscriptions to the states. Several schools of thought developed about how to resolve the matter. The most sweeping recommendation was to apply all Bill of Rights provisions to the states through the Due Process Clause of the Fourteenth Amendment. The clause prohibits a state from denying liberty without due process. Those advocating total incorporation viewed the term *liberty* as an all-inclusive shorthand for each of the rights enumerated in the Bill of Rights. The approach was vigorously advocated by the first Justice John Marshall Harlan (1877–1911) and by Justice Hugo L. Black, but it has never prevailed. A second opinion rejected any structural linkage of due process to the Bill of Rights and held simply that the Due Process Clause requires states to provide fundamental fairness. Due process is assessed under this standard by criteria of immutable principles of justice, or, as suggested by Justice Benjamin N. Cardozo in *Palko v. Connecticut*, 302 U.S. 319 (1937), by elements that are "implicit in the concept of ordered liberty." Application of such standards would occur on a case-by-case basis. The third opinion is a hybrid of the first two and is known as selective incorporation. The selective approach resembles the fundamental fairness position in that it does not view as identical those rights contained in the Bill of Rights and those rights fundamental to fairness. Unlike the fundamental fairness approach, however, the selective view holds that rights expressly contained in the Bill of Rights, if adjudged fundamental, are incorporated through the Fourteenth Amendment and are applicable at the state level regardless of the circumstances of a particular case. If the self-Incrimination privilege of the Fifth Amendment were determined to be fundamental, it would apply to all state cases. In making that connection, whatever substantive doctrine had been developed by the Court about the self-incrimination privilege would also apply to state cases. For example, if prior to incorporation of the Self-incrimination Clause the Court had found the practice of prosecutorial comment on a defendant's failure to testify in his or her own defense was prohibited, that specific rule would also be applied in state cases. The selective approach created an honor roll of Bill of Rights provisions, some viewed as fundamental and wholly incorporated and a few others as less important and not worthy of incorporation. *See also* BILL OF RIGHTS, p. 621; FEDERALISM, p. 649; *Palko v. Connecticut*, p. 268.

Significance Incorporation focuses on the degree to which Bill of Rights guarantees apply to the states. The question assumed important status soon after ratification of the Fourteenth Amendment and remained unresolved for many years. The Supreme Court finally settled on the selective incorporation approach, which allowed the Warren Court to apply most Bill of Rights safeguards to the states. The Warren Court added many provisions to the list developed under the preceding fundamental fairness doctrine. The only Bill of Rights provisions that have not been incorporated are the grand jury requirement of the Fifth Amendment and the Excessive Bail and Fine Clause of the Eighth Amendment. It is possible, though unlikely, that the Court might recognize a right not explicitly contained in the Bill of Rights to be extended to the states as a matter of "fundamental fairness." The Ninth Amendment provides that the enumeration of rights in the Bill of Rights should not be "construed to deny or disparage others retained by the people." This language could also provide the basis for the Court identifying rights not explicitly contained in the Bill of Rights. The Ninth Amendment was used by some justices in *Griswold v. Connecticut*, 381 U.S. 479 (1965), to recognize a right of privacy.

Informant A person who provides information to authorities about criminal violations. Informant data are used to further an investigation and may be offered to support an attempt to establish probable cause in the warrant process. Because the information obtained from an informant is typically represented by another person through an affidavit, it is hearsay information. Hearsay may be used if the informant is reliable, the information is credible, and some corroborative evidence exists to support the substance of the informant's data. Additional supportive evidence may be required when the informant is unnamed or anonymous. *See also* HEARSAY, p. 661; PROBABLE CAUSE, p. 691; WARRANT, p. 710.

Significance   An informant generally provides information for such considerations as money or favored treatment in reference to his or her own criminal conduct. In *Illinois v. Gates*, 462 U.S. 213 (1983), the Burger Court moved to a totality of the circumstances approach in determining probable cause when informants are used. The Court wanted to create more flexibility for warrant-issuing magistrates. The use of informants is a common-law enforcement technique, and the *Gates* decision reinforces that tradition.

Injunction   An order prohibiting a party from acting in a particular way or requiring a specific action by a party. An injunction allows a court to minimize injury to a person or group until the matter can otherwise be resolved, or an injunction may prevent injury altogether. An injunction was used in *New York Times Co. v. United States* and *United States v. The Washington Post Co.*, 403 U.S. 713 (1971), commonly refered to as the *Pentagon Papers Cases*, to keep the *New York Times* and the *Washington Post* from publishing sensitive Defense Department documents. Failure to comply with an injunction is a contempt of court. Once issued, an injunction may be annulled or quashed. *See also* EQUITY JURISDICTION, p. 644.

Significance   An injunction may be temporary or permanent. Temporary injunctions, known as interlocutory injunctions, are used to preserve a situation until the issue is resolved through normal processes of litigation. A permanent injunction may be issued upon completion of full legal proceedings. School segregation cases such as *Brown v. Board of Education (I)*, 347 U.S. 483 (1954), characteristically were cases in which injunctions were sought. An injunction is an example of a court exercising its equity jurisdiction as opposed to its legal jurisdiction.

Irrebuttable Presumption   A judgment about an issue of fact that is presumed final and unchangeable. An irrebuttable presumption is often used in equal protection litigation. In such cases, the Supreme Court considers whether a classification presumes correctly that a condition is true and whether it justifiably denies anyone affected by the classification presumptive relief. California law provided, for example, that a child born to a married woman living with her husband, absent a showing of sterility, is conclusively presumed to be a child of the marriage. The Court upheld the law in *Michael H. v. Gerald D.*, 491 U.S. 110 (1989), concluding that the presumption not only set substantive state policy but also excludes "inquiries into the child's paternity that would be destructive of family integrity and privacy." *See also Vlandis v. Kline*, p. 581.

Significance   An irrebuttable presumption is not always illegal, but the Court has generally struck down those presumptions when the presumed fact is not universally true or when there exist reasonable alternative means of making the critical determination. In *Massachusetts Board of Retirement v. Murgia*, 427 U.S. 307 (1976), however, the Court upheld a presumptive mandatory retirement age for uniformed police officers against arguments that individual fitness determinations were a more reasonable approach. It was the conclusion of the court that physical ability declines as people grow older, and that a state could reasonably conclude that the mandatory retirement policy advanced the interest of having physically capable uniformed police officers.

Irreparable Injury   A wrong or damage that has no sufficient remedy. An irreparable injury is the kind of injury for which monetary compensation is not adequate, or it is an injury that cannot be corrected or repaired. The possibility of an irreparable injury is one of the conditions precedent to granting an injunction. Plaintiffs often aver to the court that the type of injury they have suffered, or will suffer if the court does not intervene, is, or will be, irreparable. *See also* EQUITY JURISDICTION, p. 644; INJUNCTION, p. 667.

Significance   Irreparable injury must be demonstrated before many courts will grant injunctive relief. A potential irreparable injury might be media disclosure of military secrets or an unauthorized disposal of chemical waste into the environment. A case can be made in either instance to enjoin such activity because recovery from the harm caused if the activity is allowed to proceed might be impossible.

Judicial Activism   A judicial role orientation based on the view that appellate courts, particularly the U.S. Supreme Court, ought to fully assert independent review of the substantive and procedural policy decisions of the other branches. A judicial activist is less inclined to defer to the policy judgments of the elected branches of government. Instead, the judicial activist finds it appropriate for courts to intervene extensively into policy making. As a result, a judicial activist is more likely to find that legislative and executive actions exceed constitutional limits and invalidate those actions. The judicial activist is more likely to make rulings that are incompatible with the policy decisions of elected officials than a judge who subscribes to the judicial self-restraint orientation. *See also* JUDICIAL SELF-RESTRAINT, p. 670; JUSTICIABILITY, p. 674; PREFERRED POSITION DOCTRINE, p. 689.

Significance   All appellate judges have views about the appropriate role for themselves individually and the courts on which they sit. The role view influences the way appellate judges decide cases. A judicial activist will find more issues appropriate for judicial response than will the self-restraintist judge and is more willing to depart from prior decisions. An example of judicial activism of this kind is the Warren Court's ruling in *Baker v. Carr*, 369 U.S. 186 (1962), that legislative apportionment is a justiciable issue. The ruling not only set aside previous decisions to the contrary but set the stage for the Warren Court to then formulate the one-person-one-vote districting standard. The Warren Court's ruling in *Griswold v. Connecticut*, 381 U.S. 479 (1965), also illustrates judicial activism. In *Griswold*, the Court struck down a state law that prohibited the use of birth control devices or provide counsel on their use. The ruling was based upon the Court's conclusion that a right to privacy existed through several Bill of Rights provisions. Activism need not coincide with a liberal policy orientation. Classic examples of activism can be found in the 1930s as the Hughes Court struck down many New Deal initiatives in the interest of preserving laissez-faire economic doctrine, particularly when policies might impinge on individual rights. The "preferred position" doctrine advocates judicial activism and heightened judicial vigilance over the other institutions of government, when actions of those institutions impinge upon individual rights.

Judicial Review   The power of a court to examine the actions of the legislative and executive branches and declare them unconstitutional. Judicial review may also find a statute or action compatible with the federal Constitution or state constitutions. The power of judicial review was discussed extensively at the Constitutional Convention of 1787, but it was not included in the Constitution as an expressly delegated judicial function. The Supreme Court first asserted the power of judicial review in *Marbury v. Madison*, 5 U.S. 137 (1803). *See also* JUDICIAL ACTIVISM, p. 668; JUDICIAL SELF-RESTRAINT, p. 670.

Significance   Judicial review was established in *Marbury* when the Supreme Court determined that a section of the Judiciary Act of

1789 unconstitutionally expanded the original jurisdiction of the Court. The Court asserted that it must, under such circumstances, be able to void enactments that conflict with the Constitution—in other words, that the Supreme Court must act as the guardian of the Constitution. Chief Justice Marshall considered judicial review to be "the very essence of judicial duty." The arguments for judicial review became so firmly rooted in American jurisprudence that the doctrine has become one of the principal means by which courts participate in the shaping of public policy.

Judicial Self-Restraint   A role orientation that suggests that courts and judges should not intervene in the policy judgments of the elected branches of government unless absolutely necessary. Frequent use of the power of judicial review is largely incompatible with the self-restraint orientation. As a result, judicial self-restraint is sometimes manifest by a court's refusal to review certain controversial issues. The Warren Court's reluctance to entertain challenges to the U.S role in the Vietnam conflict is an example of such restraint. The self-restraint orientation is more frequently seen in the practice of confining rulings to narrow grounds rather than broad constitutional grounds. Justice Louis Brandeis offered some self-restraint ground rules in his concurring opinion in *Ashwander v. Tennessee Valley Authority*, 297 U.S. 288 (1936). Known as the Ashwander Rules, Brandeis counseled the Court, among other things, not to "anticipate" constitutional questions or "formulate a rule of constitutional law broader than is required by the precise facts to which it is to be applied." *See also* JUDICIAL ACTIVISM, p. 668; JUSTICIABILITY, p. 674.

Significance   Judicial self-restraint holds that courts should defer to the policy judgments made by the elected branches of government. Judges who adhere to the philosophy of restraint impose a more restrictive definition of justiciability and adhere more strictly to judicial precedent. Self-restraint does not necessarily coincide with a conservative policy orientation. Exercise of self-restraint by deferring to a legislative enactment mandating establishment of a minimum wage or an aggressive Equal Employment Opportunity Commission program, for example, might yield a liberal policy result. Judicial self-restraint is a perception of the judicial role that limits the exercise of judicial power and views the legislative and executive branches as the appropriate sources of major policy initiatives. Among the leading advocates of judicial self-restraint in the history of the Supreme Court are Justices Felix Frankfurter and the second Justice John Marshall Harlan (1955–1971).

Jurisdiction   The power of a court to act, including its authority to hear and to decide cases. Jurisdiction defines the boundaries within which a particular court may exercise judicial power. Judicial power is specifically conveyed through the definition of jurisdiction. The jurisdiction of federal courts is described in Article III of the Constitution in the case of the Supreme Court, and in acts of Congress in the case of the lower federal courts. A limitation on jurisdiction is that it may extend only to those issues specified by Article III as lying within the judicial power of the United States. Federal judicial power may extend to cases in law and equity stemming directly from the federal Constitution, federal statutes, treaties, or those cases falling into the admiralty and maritime category. Federal judicial power also extends to cases involving specified parties. Regardless of the substance of the case, federal jurisdiction includes actions in which the federal government itself is a party, between two or more states, between a state and a citizen of another state, between citizens of different states, between a state and an alien, between a citizen of a state and an alien, and when foreign ambassadors are involved. State constitutions and statutes usually define the jurisdiction of state courts. They often do so in terms of the amount of money in controversy in civil actions and the maximum punishment allowed in criminal actions. Jurisdiction also refers to the location of the parties and the court. A court located in a particular county may be the only court that has jurisdiction in a lawsuit involving two residents of that county, or it may be the only court that has jurisdiction to hear a criminal case when the crime has occurred within that county. The concept of location of jurisdiction is technically a question of venue, however, and not one of jurisdiction. If the power of a court is questioned on the basis of location, it is usually because the court lacks the proper venue. If an issue is properly before a court, a judgment may be rendered. A judgment is the final ruling of a court on a matter properly before it. The judgment of a court may also be called its decision or decree. Judgment on occasion also refers to the reasoning underlying a decision, but more typically the rationale of a decision is called the opinion. One such judgment may be to dismiss, which is to dispose of a case with no further consideration of it. A court may also issue a stay, which suspends some action or proceeding until a further event transpires. *See also* APPEAL, p. 613; DIVERSITY JURISDICTION, p. 639; EQUITY JURISDICTION, p. 644; ORIGINAL JURISDICTION, p. 685.

Significance   Jurisdiction conveys authority to courts to act in particular cases. Federal court jurisdiction is defined in provisions of the Constitution and federal statutes. Jurisdiction routes particular kinds of issues or parties to the appropriate judicial forum. Although the authority of courts may overlap to some degree, the lines of differentiation are usually quite clear. The independence of federal and state court jurisdictions was designed to maintain the respective sovereignty of the two levels of government.

Jurisprudence   The science and philosophy of law. Jurisprudence includes the examination of legal ideas, theories, and analyses based on methods of inquiry developed in the disciplines of anthropology, philosophy, political science, psychology, and sociology. Jurisprudence had its genesis in the thinking of Plato and Aristotle. Neither distinguished between legal theory and social theory, arguing that no polity could exist without law. Several centuries later, Roman thinkers saw jurisprudence as the science of knowing what is right and wrong. Jurisprudence can thus be viewed as the repository of thoughts and the body of sources from which the law emanates. Many Western legal thinkers have devoted attention to the rules that should govern the behavior of individuals in relation to each other and to the state. Jurisprudence has been classified into schools of thought. While each category may assert claims of independence from each other, there is some overlap among jurisprudential schools. Indeed, the evolution of the various schools is dialectic in character as one view reacts to that which has come earlier. Nonetheless, identification of several broadly distinctive categories is useful. The view that was first to appear was *natural law*. According to natural law jurisprudence, laws that govern all things have their origin in nature. Natural law is common to all persons at all times and in all places. As a consequence, if a law enacted by government violates one of the fundamental natural laws, the man-made law is immoral and invalid. *Legal positivism* sees law as separate from the moral abstractions of natural law. Rather, positivists focus on the concept of state sovereignty, enacted laws, and their purely logical application. *Sociological jurisprudence* rejected the abstractions and mechanistic logic of positivism and held that law and legal processes can only be understood as part of society. Closely akin to sociological jurisprudence is *legal realism*. Realists recognize the salience of social factors, but they go further and focus more tightly on the responses to these social forces by those functioning in the legal process. Within the more general category of legal realism fall *political* and *behavioral jurisprudence*. *See also* COMMON LAW, p. 631; NATURAL LAW AND NATURAL RIGHTS, p. 679.

Significance   Jurisprudence is the amalgam of philosophical thought, historical and political analysis, sociological and behavioral evidence, and legal experience. The study of jurisprudence fosters the view that ideas about law do not develop in an intellectual vacuum. Rather, they evolve from critical thinking in a number of disciplines. Jurisprudence enables people to understand how law has ordered both social institutions and individual conduct. It also allows a fuller appreciation of the scope of the responsibility held by those who make law, administer law, and render equitable decisions about the law.

Jury   A group of citizens called to render a judgment on various issues of fact in a legal proceeding. A jury in its most common form is the *grand jury* and the *petit* or *trial jury*. The grand jury hears evidence and determines whether a person must stand trial on a criminal charge. A petit jury makes an actual determination of guilt in a criminal or civil trial. Article IV of the Constitution mandates jury trials in criminal cases. The right is repeated in the Sixth Amendment, which entitles the accused to "a public trial, by an impartial jury." The Seventh Amendment preserves the right of jury trial in civil cases in which the amount in controversy exceeds $20. In 1968 the Supreme Court extended the jury trial provision in criminal cases to the states, because trial by jury is "fundamental to the American scheme of justice." Selection of jurors must conform to constitutional and statutory guidelines. Juries must be selected in ways that do not systematically exclude any segment of the population, although no particular jury needs to reflect proportionately a community's population. The *venire* or *jury pool* from which a particular jury is to be drawn is created by random selection from a master list of registered voters within a political jurisdiction. Once the venire has been established, a *voir dire* examination is conducted to determine if the potential jurors are impartial. Jurors whose responses to questions during voir dire are not acceptable are excused *for cause*. A prospective juror in a criminal case may have been the victim of the same offense that is at issue in the case where the person may sit as a juror. A prospective civil juror may have been a party to a suit similar to the case where he or she may serve as a juror. In either instance, there is reason to think the prospective juror may not be impartial, and the person is excused "for cause."

Following voir dire, counsel for either party may exclude jurors through a *strike* or *peremptory challenge*. No reason need be given for exclusions on this basis, but each party has only a limited number of peremptory challenges. Juries are typically composed of 12 persons, but states are permitted to use juries of as few as six persons in criminal or civil cases. Federal civil juries may be smaller than 12 people, but in criminal proceedings juries must consist of 12 citizens. State juries need not resolve fact issues by a unanimous decision, even in criminal cases. Margins of at least nine to three are constitutionally permissible in state criminal cases, although unanimity is required if the jury is as small as six. Unanimity is required in all federal criminal jury decisions. *See also Apodaca v. Oregon*, p. 345; GRAND JURY, p. 657; *Williams v. Florida*, p. 344.

Significance   A jury is guaranteed in criminal cases by the Sixth Amendment. The jury system, like many other elements of the American legal process, was inherited from the English. The expectation that selected citizens should participate in making judgments about other citizens is deeply ingrained in the legal traditions of both countries. The jury fosters citizen involvement in the justice system, and, specific case deviations notwithstanding, it brings a common-sense element into the legal process. Jury trials are conducted in the open, and thus deter abusive or arbitrary conduct on the part of the state and its officers. Jury trials also allow criminal processes to satisfy the appearance of justice.

Justiciability   Refers to a question that may properly come before a court for decision; that is, the appropriateness of the issue for judicial action. Justiciability differs from jurisdiction in that the latter involves the question of whether a court possesses the power to act. Justiciability presumes that the power to act exists, but it focuses on whether it is proper or reasonable to exercise that power. A court may have jurisdiction over a case, but it may find the question involved to be nonjusticiable. The Supreme Court's refusal to intervene on the legislative reapportionment issue on the basis of the "political question" doctrine is an example of a nonjusticiable issue. *See also* ADVISORY OPINION, p. 609; CASE OR CONTROVERSY, p. 622; JURISDICTION, p. 671; POLITICAL QUESTION, p. 688; STANDING, p. 701.

Significance   Justiciability considerations come in the form of real or bona fide cases as opposed to controversies raising abstract or hypothetical issues. A justiciable issue satisfies all the requirements of *standing*, and it is not more appropriately resolved by the legislative or executive branches. Justiciability allows the courts to limit or expand the extent to which judicial power is exercised. It directly affects the functional relationship of the courts to the legislative and executive branches.

Knock and Announce   A common-law rule that requires police officers to knock and announce their intentions before entering a residence to execute an arrest or search warrant. The Supreme Court concluded in *Wilson v. Arkansas*, 514 U.S. 927 (1995), that the rule "forms a part of the reasonableness inquiry under the Fourth Amendment." At the same time, the Court said that the Fourth Amendment's "flexible requirement of reasonableness" should not be read to "mandate a rigid rule of announcement that ignores countervailing law enforcement interests." *See also* FOURTH AMENDMENT, p. 193; *Richards v. Wisconsin*, p. 243; WARRANT, p. 710.

Significance   The *Wilson* ruling suggested that announcement was a general expectation for a reasonable search, but not an indispensable one. "Countervailing" police interests might outweigh the need for announcement, but the Court was not specific in *Wilson* about what those countervailing police interests might be. One such interest was examined in *Richards v. Wisconsin*, 520 U.S. 385 (1997). Wisconsin had a policy that categorically excepted searches in felony drug cases from the knock and announce requirement. The question in *Richards* was whether a blanket or categorical exception to the announcement rule was permissible after *Wilson*. Police sought to enter Richards's motel room to perform a warrant-authorized search for cocaine. The Court ruled that the announcement requirement could "give way" in situations that presented a threat of physical violence or when officers had reason to believe that evidence would be destroyed. Felony drug investigations may frequently involve these circumstances, but the Court concluded that an automatic exception was not justified. In some situations, the government interest in preserving evidence and maintaining safety may not outweigh the privacy of a person subjected to no-knock entry. The blanket exception "insulates" those cases from review by the courts. Applying these considerations to the *Richards*'s facts, the Court concluded that officers had reason to believe that Richards might destroy evidence if given opportunity to do so, thus the evidence seized in this case was not suppressed at trial.

Libel   The use of false and malicious material that injures a person's status or reputation. Libel has consistently been held to be a category of unprotected speech, and relief from libel may be pursued through civil proceedings. Libel laws may not inhibit debate on public issues, however, even if the debate includes vigorous and unpleasant attacks on the government and/or public officials. In such situations, statements must be made in print with reckless disregard of their falsehood and with actual malice before actionable libel occurs. Plaintiffs in libel proceedings may inquire into the editorial processes of defendant publications as a means of establishing state of mind as an ingredient of malice. Oral defamation is called slander. *See also* EDITORIAL PRIVILEGE, p. 642; FREE PRESS CLAUSE, p. 653; *New York Times Co. v. Sullivan*, p. 106.

Significance   Libel actions afford private citizens much greater insulation from adverse comments than they do public officials. The category of public officials has been expanded by the Supreme Court to include public figures. A *public figure* is a private citizen who may be in the midst of doing a public thing, or he or she may simply be a private person who attracts wide public attention. The Court has made it more difficult for public figures to win libel suits because they generally enjoy substantially greater access to the channels of effective communication and thus have a greater opportunity to counteract false statements than do purely private citizens. In addition, the public figure has voluntarily invited greater risk of closer public scrutiny—he or she has opted for life in the so-called fishbowl.

John Locke   A British political philosopher whose writings provided the foundation for the American Revolution and constitutionalism movement. Locke's most significant works were his *Two Treatises on Government.* Locke used the *First Treatise* to argue against the divine right of kings. The *Second Treatise* contained Locke's own political theory. Like other political thinkers of his time, such as Thomas Hobbes, Locke believed that human beings begin outside a civil society, in a "state of nature." Hobbes, however, thought people were hostile and lawless in this state of nature. Locke, on the other hand, thought people were aware of natural law. Central to natural law were the precepts of the individual's right to life, liberty, and property. In order to guarantee that everyone obeys the law of nature, people enter into a contract that starts them down the path to civil society. Consent to majority rule limits individual freedoms, but in exchange, individuals gain the protection of written law and the exercise of governmental enforcement authority. Once the initial contract is entered, the particulars about government powers and restraints are developed in more detail. *See also* CONSTITUTIONALISM, p. 634; NATURAL LAW AND NATURAL RIGHTS, p. 679; SOCIAL CONTRACT, p. 699.

Significance   Locke's thinking was central to the political philosophies of many early American political leaders, such as Thomas Jefferson and Alexander Hamilton. Jefferson borrowed heavily from Locke's *Second Treatise* as he wrote the Declaration of Independence. The discussion of natural law and natural rights, the inherent equality of human beings, popular consent as the basis of government, and the right of people to cast off unjust government are all grounded in the thinking of Locke. Themes from the *Second Treatise* can also be seen in the Constitution framed in Philadelphia in 1787—including separation of powers, primacy of the legislative branch, and majority rule.

Loyalty Oath   A declaration of allegiance to the state. A loyalty oath is usually not voluntary but is required for public employment. It may demand that persons offer a disclaimer of support for foreign governments or ideologies. *See also Keyishian v. Board of Regents*, p. 160; OVERBREADTH DOCTRINE, p. 686.

Significance   Loyalty oaths have not been categorically banned by the Supreme Court, but they are subject to limits. A loyalty oath cannot compel an individual to pledge that he or she will never become a member of a given organization at some time in the future, for example. Neither may a loyalty oath be overbroad or vague. The loyalty oath is not generally regarded as an effective means of instilling allegiance in citizens.

Magna Carta   Known as the "Great Charter" issued by King John at Runnymede in 1215, the Magna Carta became the statutory basis for English civil liberties. The Magna Carta was divided into more than 60 sections or clauses and covered a large number of issues, which included rights of various classes of the British population. The Magna Carta was important to British constitutionalism, and a number of its provisions remain a part of English law. Some of the language of the Magna Carta found its way into the American federal Constitution of 1787 and many of the early state constitutions. It stands as evidence of the importance of written law, limits on the state, and the right of rebellion. *See also* CONSTITUTION-ALISM, p. 634.

Significance   The Magna Carta was an attempt to articulate a constitutional basis for ensuring a balanced relationship between the sovereign and his subjects. The Magna Carta is one of the components of the English "living" constitution. A "living" constitution does not draw its authority from a written document as such, but rather is based on statutes, common law, and conventions. Besides the Magna Carta, a number of statutes, such as the Statute of York (1322), the Petition of Right (1628), the Bill of Rights (1689), the Reform Act (1832), and the Parliament Acts of 1911 and 1949 provide the basis for the English constitution. The English constitutional tradition also looks to common law as a source of its authority. Many of the most important principles of the English constitution are those decisions of courts applying the principles of common law. Indeed, most of the civil liberties and rights of British citizens are not found in statute, but rather in the body of common law. The living constitution relies on customs, convention, and usages considered practical for the efficient operation of government that have no foundation in statutory law.

Mandamus   An extraordinary writ issued by a court under its equity jurisdiction to require a public official to perform a specified official act. Mandamus is an affirmative command calling for an action to occur. A command preventing an action from occurring is an injunction.

Significance   A writ of mandamus can be issued only to compel performance of a nondiscretionary or ministerial function in an instance in which the plaintiff has a legal right to the performance of the function. A mandamus may be directed by a higher court to a lower court to require an action that a party has a legal right to expect. Failure to comply with a command issued through a writ of mandamus constitutes contempt of court.

Mandatory Sentence   A punishment that is legislatively set by statute and must be imposed by a sentencing judge. It is intended to promote incarceration of convicted criminals by precluding suspended sentences or probation. The policy does not permit consideration of the circumstances surrounding a particular offense or the background of the offender. For this reason the Supreme Court has invalidated mandatory death sentences on cruel and unusual punishment grounds. Mandatory death sentences are flawed because they do not allow consideration of "compassion or mitigating factors." The Court's major objection is the undifferentiating character of the mandatory process. Statutes that mandate the death penalty treat all persons as "members of a faceless, undifferentiated mass to be subjected to the blind infliction of the death penalty." *See also* CRUEL AND UNUSUAL PUNISHMENT, p. 637; *Harmelin v. Michigan*, p. 402; *Woodson v. North Carolina*, p. 424.

Significance   A mandatory sentence is used in many jurisdictions for noncapital offenses. It is often justified as a device that promotes uniformity in sentencing and as a warning to potential offenders that certain kinds of criminal conduct will bring automatic terms of incarceration. Mandatory sentences may also discourage what is perceived by legislators as judicial leniency. Mandatory sentencing is opposed by many judges and lawyers because it requires that offenders and situations be treated equally whether they are comparable or not. Opponents argue that flexibility and discretion are at the heart of the sentencing process.

Mayflower Compact   The social compact signed by the first settlers of the Plymouth Colony in what is now Massachusetts. The compact was signed by the adult males aboard the ship *Mayflower* before landing at Plymouth and contained such civil society provisions as majority rule. *See also* SOCIAL CONTRACT, p. 699.

Significance The Mayflower Compact was not a constitution in itself. The compact was, instead, a social contract that provided the foundation for the governance of the Plymouth Colony. The principal concept of the compact was the consensual formation of a civil society to be governed by "just and equal" laws, which would be enacted later. Perhaps the most important legacy of the Mayflower Compact was the institution of the town meeting of Plymouth Colony's member towns. The town meeting was later described by Thomas Jefferson as the "wisest invention ever devised by the wit of man for the perfect exercise of self-government and for its preservation."

Mootness (Moot Question) A case for which the courts can no longer provide a party any relief because the dispute has been resolved or has ceased to exist. A moot case is no longer a real controversy, and Article III of the Constitution requires that cases before courts be bona fide controversies. *See also* ADVISORY OPINION, p. 609; JUSTICIABILITY, p. 674; STANDING, p. 701.

Significance Mootness is the absence of an active question, which renders a matter nonjusticiable. When the Supreme Court refused to address the reverse discrimination issue in *De Funis v. Odegaard*, 416 U.S. 312 (1974), on mootness grounds, it said that the controversy was no longer definite and concrete. The case no longer touched "the legal relations of parties having adverse interests." Exceptions to the mootness threshold involve situations in which time is too limited to litigate an issue fully, and in which a likelihood exists that the question will reoccur. Abortion cases qualify for an exception to the mootness rule, for example, because no appellate court can ever get and decide an abortion case prior to the pregnancy involved running to full term. The Court observed in *Roe v. Wade*, 410 U.S. 113 (1973), that appellate review would forever be foreclosed by mootness because a pregnancy would not last beyond the trial stage. Saying that the law should not be that rigid, the Court acknowledged the need for the exception if issues are "capable of repetition, yet evading review." However, if the courts responded routinely to cases that had become moot, they would constantly be engaged in rendering advisory opinions.

Natural Law and Natural Rights A jurisprudential view that laws that govern all things have their origin in nature. The natural law concept is that such laws are both eternal and unchanging. Natural law asserts that fundamental rules of governing are derived from basic characteristics of human nature. Natural law jurisprudence has produced in volume more writing than any view of law. Early manifestations of natural law can be seen in the works of Aristotle and Roman political thinkers such as Cicero. The most systematic framework for natural law theory was developed by Thomas Aquinas in the thirteenth century. Natural law is opposite from the positivistic theories of private and public morality. Natural law and natural rights doctrine presume that everyone has rights in a "state of nature" and that government is created to protect those rights. As a consequence, if law is created by government that violates a fundamental natural law, the man-made rule is invalid. *See also* JURISPRUDENCE, p. 672; SOCIAL CONTRACT, p. 699.

Significance   The development of natural law and natural rights was an attempt to clarify how people should deal with arbitrary governmental conduct. The concept of natural law provided the foundation for social contract theory that, in turn, was to become a key element in American political thought. John Locke's *Second Treatise on Government*, for example, provided the theoretical basis for the American Revolution and constitutional movement. Natural law also underlies many acts of civil disobedience. If one believes that a man-made law is immoral, the person has an obligation to conduct acts of civil disobedience to heighten social consciousness on the issue. The question is whether human rights are grounded "in nature," and if so, whether such a view can be defended without a carefully defined justification. In the absence of such justification, the notion of human rights as products of natural law may provide a rationale for self-serving conduct and a circumstance approaching anarchy in which people claim a right to do whatever they please, regardless of the social consequences.

Neutral Magistrate   A judicial officer with the power to issue a warrant based on probable cause. In theory, a neutral magistrate has no interest in the outcome of a case, and possesses sufficient training and qualifications to be able to make inferences from evidence presented. *See also Coolidge v. New Hampshire*, p. 196; PROBABLE CAUSE, p. 691; WARRANT, p. 710.

Significance   A neutral magistrate may be a judge, as in lower state courts, or a lawyer with at least five years' experience, as in federal courts. A federal magistrate is appointed by federal district judges and has wide judicial powers. The warrant-issuing role is an important one because the Supreme Court has said that Fourth Amendment protections are null if warrant judgments are made only by prosecutors or police officers. The Court has also ruled that searches are unreasonable if not authorized by a neutral magistrate.

Newsperson's Privilege   Status that enables journalists to freely gather news to report to the public. The press argument is that without such privilege, the press capacity to gather and report the news is impaired. The privilege includes the capacity to withhold disclosure of news sources or the substance of information obtained from news sources. The newsperson's privilege means that journalists are free from the obligation to testify about their news sources in court because their press function would thereby be impaired. The privilege also includes the right to access places where ordinary citizens are not allowed to go. *See also Branzburg v. Hayes,* p. 113; EDITORIAL PRIVILEGE, p. 642; GRAND JURY, p. 657; PRIVILEGE, p. 690.

Significance   The newsperson's privilege is based in the First Amendment. The doctrine was limited by the Supreme Court's holding in *Branzburg v. Hayes,* 408 U.S. 665 (1972), that newspersons are obligated to disclose information and sources to grand juries. In response to *Branzburg,* a number of states passed shield laws that established a special privilege for newspersons even before grand juries.

Ninth Amendment   One of the Bill of Rights amendments. It provides that the enumeration of rights in the Constitution should "not be construed to deny or disparage others retained by the people." Some argue that the amendment is an open-ended invitation for courts to identify and protect rights not enumerated in the Bill of Rights. This stems from a natural rights view that it is impossible exhaustively to list the rights retained by the people against governmental encroachment. A counterposition is that the "retained rights" language of the Ninth Amendment referred to those common-law rights in existence at the time the Constitution and Bill of Rights was written. *See also* NATURAL LAW AND NATURAL RIGHTS, p. 679.

Significance   The Supreme Court has not had frequent occasion to examine the meaning of the Ninth Amendment. As a result, the exact meaning of the amendment is not clear. Until the 1960s the amendment was regarded as having minimal application. In *United Public Workers v. Mitchell,* 330 U.S. 75 (1946), for example, Justice Reed suggested that "retained" rights were rights that remained following the delegation of power to the federal government. Under this view, the Ninth Amendment could not refer to rights that were incompatible with formally conveyed power. When the Court considered the state law prohibiting the counseling of married couples about methods of contraception in *Griswold v. Connecticut*, 381 U.S. 479 (1965), however, Justice Goldberg based his conclusion that the Constitution protects a right of privacy on the Ninth Amendment. This view suggests that the amendment could be used to limit even delegated power.

Obiter Dictum   Remarks contained in a court's opinion that are incidental to the disposition of the case. *Obiter dictum* or *obiter dicta*, sometimes simply called dictum or dicta, are normally directed at issues upon which no formal arguments have been heard. The positions represented by *obiter dicta* are therefore not binding on later cases. Dicta are not considered to be precedent and should be distinguished from the *ratio decidendi*, which provides the basis of the court's ruling. *See also* STARE DECISIS, p. 703.

Significance   *Obiter dicta* can be found in *Myers v. United States*, 272 U.S. 52 (1926), for example, in which the Supreme Court held that Congress could not require Senate consent for presidential removal of postmasters. Postmasters are generally viewed as executive branch subordinates serving exclusively at the pleasure of the president. Chief Justice Taft offered the opinion, however, that removal power was incident to the power to appoint, as distinguished from the power to advise and consent. As a general proposition presidents could remove anyone appointed by them, including members of quasi-judicial agencies such as regulatory commissions. *Myers* did not require disposition of that question to settle the case. Thus, the remarks of the chief justice went beyond those necessary to resolve a case or controversy and were therefore dicta.

Obscenity   Content that offends accepted standards of decency. Obscenity is not protected expression under the First Amendment because it is "utterly without redeeming social importance or value." Because it falls outside the scope of the First Amendment, a carefully constructed definition of obscenity is essential to distinguish between protected expression and unprotected obscenity. Central to the identification of obscenity is its appeal to what the Supreme Court has described as "prurient interest"; that is, material that prompts "lustful thoughts." *See also* COMMUNITY STANDARDS, p. 632; FREE SPEECH CLAUSE, p. 654; *Miller v. California*, p. 137; PRIOR RESTRAINT, p. 690; *Roth v. United States*, p. 135.

Significance   The definition of obscenity was substantially redefined in *Roth v. United States*, 354 U.S. 476 (1957). Prior to *Roth*, the operative standard came from an English case, *Regina v. Hicklin*, 3 Q.B. 360 (1868). Under the *Hicklin* test for obscenity, isolated excerpts of a work that might "deprave and corrupt those whose minds are open to such immoral influences and into whose hands material of this sort might fall" could be banned. The *Hicklin* test allowed extensive regulation of expression, and it was for this reason that the Warren Court sought to change the standard. The *Roth* revision of the standard focused on "whether to the average person, applying contemporary community standards, the dominant theme of the material taken as a whole appeals to prurient interest." Within a decade the Warren Court modified the *Roth* standard by refining elements within the definitions. In *A Book Named "John Cleland's Memoirs of a Woman of Pleasure" v. Attorney General*, 383 U.S. 413 (1966), the Court described obscenity in terms of "patent offensiveness," and elevated the role of the social value criterion. Obscenity was still seen as "utterly without redeeming social value," but the Court placed a severe burden on the prosecutors of obscene material by asking for proof of the absence of social value. The Court held in addition that each of the elements of the obscenity definition were to be applied independently. The social value dimension could not be weighed against or canceled by either the patent offensiveness or prurient appeal of obscene materials. The outcome of these changes was to put all but hard-core pornography outside the reach of obscenity statutes. The Burger Court modified the standard again in *Miller v. California*, 413 U.S. 15 (1973), when it defined as obscene "works which, taken as a whole, appeal to prurient interest in sex," and which "portray sexual conduct in a patently offensive way." Obscenity must also lack "serious literary, artistic, political, or scientific value." The Burger Court removed the social value criterion as an insurmountable obstacle to prosecution, and it defined community standards in local terms. Obscenity may also be evaluated in contextual terms. Material may be found obscene if pandering is involved, for example. Pandering occurs when a person attempts commercially to exploit the sexual content of material offered for sale. Even if materials survive scrutiny under the *Miller* standards, they may become illicit through pandering. Under the provisions of *Miller*, many communities now attempt to regulate obscenity at the local level. The regulations frequently take the form of zoning ordinances or censorship techniques. Although censorship is not inherently unconstitutional, it does suggest prior restraint, and is very carefully examined by the Court. Regulation of the commercial exhibition of obscenity has been allowed, even when the exhibition is confined to consenting adults. The Court has also held that privately possessed obscenity, with the exception of child pornography, is beyond the control of government.

Offensive Speech   Expression that is objectionable and distasteful to a listener because it contains noxious language. Offensive speech is a form of pure speech in that no additional conduct is necessary. The Supreme Court has held that offensive speech is generally protected expression. In *Cohen v. California*, 403 U.S. 15 (1971), the Court said that government cannot function as the guardian of public morality and excise epithets and other offensive speech from public discourse. A state does not possess the power "to cleanse public debate to the point where it is grammatically acceptable to the most squeamish among us." The Court said that wide latitude must be afforded to ostensibly offensive speech. *See also Cohen v. California*, p. 89; FREE SPEECH CLAUSE, p. 654; LIBEL, p. 675; OBSCENITY, p. 682; PURE SPEECH, p. 692.

Significance   Offensive speech standards are influenced by the fact that words are often chosen as much for their emotive as their cognitive value. Some offensive speech is not protected, as in the case of obscenity, libel, and fighting words. *Fighting words* are words that are inherently insulting or likely to incite breach of the peace. Indeed, attempts to punish offensive speech typically take the form of prosecution for breach of the peace. Expressions of this kind are not protected by the First Amendment because they are of such slight value as to be outweighed by the public interest in maintaining order.

Opinion of the Court   The statement of a court that specifies its decision in a case and expresses the reasoning upon which the decision was based. The opinion of the court summarizes the principles of law that apply in a given case and represents the views of the majority of a court's members. Occasionally the opinion of a court may reflect the views of less than a majority of its members and is then called a plurality opinion. Trial courts also issue opinions, both written and oral. *See also OBITER DICTUM*, p. 682.

Significance   The opinion of the court is the means by which the legal principles of a decision are transmitted. The opinion of the court contains the *ratio decidendi*, which is the rationale for the judgment and the principal item of precedential value. The opinion of the court is not the only statement that may be issued in a particular case, however. A *concurring opinion* may be issued by a member of a court who agrees with the outcome of a case but who uses different reasons for reaching that decision. In *Coker v. Georgia*, 433 U.S. 584 (1977), for example, the Supreme Court ruled that the death penalty could not be imposed for the offense of rape. The majority felt that the death penalty was excessive for the specific crime involved. Justice Brennan agreed that Coker's sentence ought to be vacated but expressed in a concurring opinion that the death penalty is a cruel and unusual punishment under any circumstance. A *dissenting opinion*, on the other hand, is an opinion by a member of a court who disagrees with the decision of the majority of the court, and hence also disagrees with the majority opinion. A dissent may be joined by other members of a court's minority. It may focus on only one element of a court's decision and may be a disagreement in part. A dissenting opinion that attracts other members of a court may serve as an encouragement to litigants to bring subsequent cases raising similar legal arguments. A court may also issue a per curiam opinion. *Per curiam* is a Latin term meaning "by the court." It is an opinion that is either unsigned or authored by the judges collectively. A per curiam opinion is sometimes used to announce a court's holding summarily without discussion of the rationale. Individual members of a court frequently enter individual concurring or dissenting opinions on such occasions. See, for example, *Furman v. Georgia*, 408 U.S. 238 (1972), and *New York Times Co. v. United States*, 403 U.S. 713 (1971). Opinions are occasionally important for what they do not say. *Sub silentio* means "under silence" and refers to something that occurs without notice being taken of it. Sometimes an appeals court will overrule a precedent without explicitly acknowledging the precedent it overruled. The precedent is therefore replaced *sub silentio*.

Original Jurisdiction   The authority of a court initially to hear and determine a legal question. Original jurisdiction is vested with trial courts rather than appellate courts, although Article III of the Constitution extends very limited original jurisdiction to the United States Supreme Court. Various trial courts are assigned specific original jurisdiction defined in terms of subject matter or party. Original jurisdiction in civil cases is often divided on the basis of the monetary value of the action. In criminal matters, certain courts may be assigned misdemeanor cases while others adjudicate felonies. A *misdemeanor* is a minor criminal offense generally punishable by imprisonment in local jails and/or a fine. A *felony* is a criminal offense for which punishment may be death or imprisonment for more than a year. Because the United States district courts are the only trial courts of broad jurisdiction, they have original jurisdiction over both federal felonies and misdemeanors. *See also* APPEAL, p. 613; DIVERSITY JURISDICTION, p. 639; EQUITY JURISDICTION, p. 644; JURISDICTION, p. 671.

Significance   Original jurisdiction establishes which court will first respond to a case or controversy. Original jurisdiction is particularly important because comparatively few cases are appealed from courts that first hear them.

Overbreadth Doctrine   A doctrine requiring that enactments proscribing certain activity must not touch conduct that is constitutionally protected. Overbreadth refers to a statute that may fail adequately to distinguish between those activities that may be regulated and those that may not. *See also* CHILLING EFFECT, p. 625; FREE SPEECH CLAUSE, p. 654; *Schaumburg v. Citizens for a Better Environment,* p. 92.

Significance   The overbreadth doctrine is illustrated in *Schaumburg v. Citizens for a Better Environment,* 444 U.S. 620 (1980), in which the Supreme Court struck down a local ordinance that required all organizations soliciting contributions door-to-door to use at least 75 percent of their receipts for charitable purposes. The purpose of the ordinance was to prevent fraudulent solicitations. The Court objected to the approach because it imposed a direct and substantial limitation on organizations such as environmental education groups, the principal activities of which are typically research, advocacy, and public education. Although such organizations obviously do not meet the ordinance definition of charitable, their activities are constitutionally permissible. The Village's ordinance in *Schaumburg* was simply too inclusive or overbroad. A similar ordinance was invalidated in *Coates v. Cincinnati,* 402 U.S. 611 (1971), because the ordinance prohibited an assembly of three or more persons on public sidewalks. It subjected such assembled persons to arrest if their behavior annoyed a police officer or passerby. The ordinance made criminal what the Constitution says cannot be a crime. Neither may an enactment suffer from vagueness. Regulations must convey standards of conduct that persons of "reasonable intelligence" can understand. Enactments that do not clearly convey required or prohibited conduct may be invalidated as vague. Restrictions that are either overbroad or vague may have a "chilling effect" on expression or some other protected activity by prompting a speaker to be overly cautious in order to avoid saying (or doing) anything unlawful.

Plea Bargaining   A process whereby the prosecutor and the accused negotiate a mutually acceptable settlement in a criminal case. Plea bargaining usually involves a defendant pleading guilty to a charge in exchange for a lessening of the charge, a reduction in the number of counts charged, and/or a favorable sentencing recommendation. A proposed settlement must be accepted by the trial judge assigned to the case before it takes effect. Plea bargaining accounts for the disposition of approximately 90 percent of all criminal cases in the United States. *See also* JURY, p. 673; *Santobello v. New York*, p. 375.

Significance Plea bargaining has been clearly endorsed by the Supreme Court. Benefits accrue to both prosecution and accused and produce a mutuality of advantage sufficient to prompt the high plea rate. In *Santobello v. New York*, 404 U.S. 257 (1971), the Court spoke of plea bargaining as "an essential component of the administration of justice," and a practice to be encouraged if it is properly handled. Plea bargaining moves cases through the courts, relieving docket pressure that could not be handled through any other means. It is desirable because it produces prompt and largely final dispositions without lengthy pretrial confinement, with diminished chances of additional criminal conduct by those on pretrial release, and with enhanced rehabilitative prospects. The procedures by which pleas are made are carefully prescribed. The Federal Rules of Criminal Procedure set forth the steps by which pleas are to be entered in federal courts, and most states have established similar guidelines. At minimum, no plea can be taken without a trial judge inquiring into the voluntary nature of the plea. If a plea is determined to be freely and intelligently offered, all elements of the settlement agreement must be honored. The Supreme Court has determined that a plea to avoid the death penalty is not necessarily involuntary, nor is a prosecutorial threat to charge an accused with a more serious or additional offense prohibited as long as the greater or supplementary charge is legally sufficient.

Police Power Authority conveyed by the Reserve Clause of the Tenth Amendment to the effect that powers not delegated to the federal government or otherwise prohibited are "reserved to the States respectively, or the people." The police power gives the states broad authority to regulate private behavior in the interest of public health, safety, and general welfare. It enables states and their respective local units of government to enact and enforce policies deemed appropriate to serve the public good. Pursuit of these policies may include the creation of a police force. *See also* DUE PROCESS CLAUSES, p. 641; FEDERALISM, p. 649.

Significance The police power is comprehensive, and substantial discretion is possessed by the states for its exercise. The federal government has no police power as such, although it can use the power to regulate interstate commerce to reach some individual conduct. It is limited by various provisions of the United States Constitution and the constitutions of the states, however. It must conform to the requirements of due process.

Political Question   An issue that is not justiciable or that is not appropriate for judicial determination because of its political, rather than legal, character. A political question is one in which the substance of an issue is primarily political or involves a matter directed toward either the legislative or executive branch by constitutional language. *See also Baker v. Carr*, p. 516; JUSTICIABILITY, p. 674; SEPARATION OF POWERS, p. 697.

Significance   The political question doctrine is sometimes invoked by the Supreme Court, not because the Court is without power or jurisdiction, but because the Court adjudges the question inappropriate for judicial response. In the Court's view, to intervene or respond would be to encroach upon the functions and prerogatives of one of the other two branches of government. It would constitute a breach of the principle of separation of powers. In *Luther v. Borden*, 48 U.S. 1 (1849), the Court was asked to rule on the status of Dorr's Rebellion in Rhode Island. In 1841 Rhode Island was still operating under the terms of a charter in effect before independence. A group of citizens challenged the charter government by calling a convention and writing a new constitution. Elections were conducted under the new constitution, and Thomas Dorr was elected governor. Throughout the period, the charter government sought to maintain control and attempted to prosecute supporters of the Dorr government as insurrectionists. When the case reached the Supreme Court, one of the issues was whether the charter government was "republican" as required by Article IV. The Court refused to address this issue, holding instead that the Guaranty Clause of Article IV had committed the issue to Congress rather than the Supreme Court. Chief Justice Taney said it is the duty of the Court "not to pass beyond its appropriate sphere of action, and to take care not to involve itself in discussions which properly belong to other forums." Justice Brennan was more precise in characterizing a political question in *Baker v. Carr*, 369 U.S. 186 (1962), the first case in which the Court held legislative apportionment to be a justiciable issue. Justice Brennan described a political question as one with "a textually demonstrable constitutional commitment of the issue to a coordinate political department; or a lack of judicially discoverable and manageable standards for resolving it." He added that such questions typically require "a policy determination of a kind clearly for nonjudicial discretion." On such matters the Court cannot undertake "independent resolution without expressing lack of respect due coordinate branches of the government."

Preemption Doctrine   A doctrine that holds that federal laws supersede or *preempt* state laws in certain policy areas. The preemption doctrine is grounded in the Supremacy Clause of Article VI. *See also* FEDERALISM, p. 649; SMITH ACT, p. 698.

Significance   The preemption doctrine was said to have three criteria in *Pennsylvania v. Nelson*, 350 U.S. 497 (1956): First, federal regulation must be so pervasive as to allow reasonable inference that no room is left to the states. Congress may state explicitly such a preemptive interest, or the courts may interpret the intent of Congress fully to occupy the field. Second, federal regulation must involve matters in which the federal interest is so dominant as to preclude implementation of state laws in the field. Third, the administration of federal laws must be endangered by conflicting state laws. The policy area involved in *Nelson* was the regulation of seditious activity. Specifically, the question was whether the federal Smith Act prohibited enforcement of the Pennsylvania Sedition Act, which proscribed the same conduct. On the basis of the criteria described, the Supreme Court concluded that Pennsylvania's statute had to give way.

Preferred Position Doctrine   A doctrine holding that legislative enactments that affect First Amendment rights must be scrutinized more carefully than legislation that does not. The preferred position doctrine says that certain legislative activity deserves priority consideration because it affects fundamental rights such as free speech. Any enactment that impinges on the First Amendment must serve a compelling state interest. The burden is clearly on the state to demonstrate justification for limiting a preferred position freedom. *See also* BALANCING TEST, p. 620; FREE SPEECH CLAUSE, p. 654.

Significance   The preferred position doctrine is attributed to Justice Harlan Fiske Stone who said in a footnote to his opinion in *United States v. Carolene Products Co.*, 304 U.S. 144 (1938), that a lesser presumption of constitutionality exists when legislation "appears on its face to be within a specific prohibition such as those of the first ten amendments." Bolder articulation of the doctrine soon followed in such First Amendment cases as *Murdock v. Pennsylvania*, 319 U.S. 105 (1943), and *Thomas v. Collins*, 323 U.S. 516 (1945).

Prior Restraint   A restriction placed on a publication before it can be published or circulated. Prior restraint typically occurs through licensure or censorship or by a full prohibition on publication. Censorship requirements involve a review of materials by the state for objectionable content. The materials that satisfy the standards of the censor may be distributed or exhibited while materials found unacceptable may be banned. *See also* FREE PRESS CLAUSE, p. 653; *Kingsley Books v. Brown*, p. 147; *Near v. Minnesota*, p. 100; *New York Times Co. v. United States*, p. 101.

Significance   Prior restraint poses a greater threat to free expression than after-the-fact prosecution because government restrictions are imposed in a manner that precludes public scrutiny. The First Amendment therefore prohibits prior restraint in most instances. Prior restraint may be justified if the publication threatens national security, incites overthrow of the government, is obscene, or interferes with the private rights of others. Prior restraint is otherwise heavily suspect.

Privilege   An extraordinary right or exemption that is assigned to persons or occupants of particular positions. A privilege is a benefit possessed by a person or class that affords an advantage over others who do not share the benefit. A privilege may confer special authority as in the instance of those to whom government assigns a franchise, or relieve a person or class from liability or regulation that would apply in the absence of the privilege. *See also* EDITORIAL PRIVILEGE, p. 642; NEWSPERSON'S PRIVILEGE, p. 681.

Significance   A privilege is often attached to a person or class that must have substantial freedom to act in order to perform a particular function. Thus executive privilege is protection afforded presidential communications so that presidential advisers and a president may fully and candidly discuss and consider policy options. Similarly, lawyers' conversations with clients are confidential to encourage full and frank communication between attorneys and their clients. Other protected or privileged communications include those between doctor and patient, psychotherapist and patient, newspersons and news sources, priest and penitent, and husband and wife.

Privileges and Immunities Clauses   Clauses that protect benefits flowing from one's status as a citizen. A privilege is a benefit or an advantage. An immunity frees a person from an obligation. Certain privileges and immunities exist for a person by virtue of his or her citizenship. The United States Constitution contains two references to privileges and immunities. Article IV, Section 2, provides that the "Citizens of each State be entitled to the Privileges and Immunities of citizens in the several States." The purpose of this Clause was to ensure that out-of-state citizens receive the same treatment as a state's own citizens. It protected parity across the states. The Fourteenth Amendment also provides that "No State shall make or enforce any law which shall abridge the privileges or immunities of the United States." This section of the Fourteenth Amendment was a specific response to the Black Codes in many Southern states that had the effect of restoring pre–Civil War conditions of slavery. *See also* CITIZENSHIP, p. 626; DUE PROCESS CLAUSES, p. 641; EQUAL PROTECTION CLAUSE, p. 473; FOURTEENTH AMENDMENT, p. 651.

Significance   The Privileges and Immunities Clauses were severely limited by the *Slaughterhouse Cases*, 83 U.S. 36 (1873), in which the Supreme Court distinguished between federal and state citizenship. The Court placed most key civil and political rights within the state citizenship category. That limited the privileges and immunities of federal citizenship to such rights as interstate travel, protection while abroad, and participation in federal elections. The protections afforded by federal citizenship through the Fourteenth Amendment have expanded substantially over the years since the *Slaughterhouse Cases*, but the expansion has taken place under the Due Process and Equal Protection Clauses rather than the Privileges and Immunities Clauses.

Probable Cause   The foremost element required in making a lawful arrest or conducting a legal search. Probable cause is the level of evidence required to convince a neutral third party, typically a judge or magistrate, to issue a warrant. The level of evidence needed for probable cause is not as substantial as that required to prove guilt. This is sometimes called making a prima facie case. *Prima facie* means "at first sight" and refers to a case or claim that may be sufficient without further support or evaluation. *See also Draper v. United States*, p. 194; WARRANT, p. 710.

Significance   Probable cause relates to reasonable inferences rather than technical judgments based on rigid requirements. In *Draper v. United States*, 358 U.S. 307 (1959), the Supreme Court spoke of "probabilities" that focus closely enough on a person or location to allow a neutral magistrate to authorize an arrest or search. The standard established in *Draper* holds that probable cause exists when trustworthy information known to authorities is sufficient to encourage a person of reasonable caution to believe that an offense has been or is being committed. The standard can be met by providing evidence such as direct observation of a criminal act by a law enforcement officer, indirect observation through informants, physical evidence, or accounts provided by witnesses.

Procedural Due Process   A procedural review that focuses on the means by which governmental actions are executed. Procedural due process guarantees fairness in the ways government imposes restrictions or punishments. It demands that before any deprivation of liberty or property can occur, a person must be formally notified and provided an opportunity for a fair hearing. *See also* DUE PROCESS CLAUSES, p. 641; SUBSTANTIVE DUE PROCESS, p. 705.

Significance   Procedural due process must be accorded persons accused of crimes. It includes access to legal counsel, the ability to confront witnesses against one, and a trial by jury. Constitutional protection against loss of liberty or property is guaranteed in two constitutional amendments: the Fifth, which is directed at the federal government, and the Fourteenth, which is directed at the states.

Pure Speech   Expression or communication that occurs without any additional action or conduct on the part of the speaker. Pure speech is a conversation or a public address. Its content does not affect its character. *See also* FREE SPEECH CLAUSE, p. 654; OFFENSIVE SPEECH, p. 684; SPEECH PLUS, p. 700; SYMBOLIC SPEECH, p. 706.

Significance   Pure speech produces its effect, if any, only from the opinions, views, or positions communicated. It is the form of expression least subject to restriction. Pure speech is distinguished from speech plus or symbolic speech that require some kind of action beyond or instead of the language itself.

Remedial Power (Federal)   The power of the federal government to correct or relieve constitutional or statutory violations. Remedial power is typically exercised by the Congress, but may be undertaken by courts as well. Remedial statutes provide a means by which legal wrongs may be corrected or relief obtained. Federal law, for example, provides that anyone who violates another person's civil rights may be sued for damages. Another example of remedial legislation is the Public Works Employment Act of 1977. The law required that at least 10 percent of federal monies designated for local public works projects be set aside for minority businesses. The law was intended to relieve historical discrimination in the construction industry. Federal courts also possess remedial authority. If a court finds a constitutional or statutory violation, it may order the violator to take specified steps to end the illegal conduct or compensate the victim in some way. When federal courts found discriminatory practices in the public schools, they had the power to fashion remedial orders to end the discrimination. Court-ordered busing of students is a remedial measure used by courts to end dual or segregated public schools. *See also* EQUITY JURISDICTION, p. 644; JURISDICTION, p. 671.

Significance   Federal remedial authority has been used extensively to address legal violations. Protection of civil rights has been one area in which such remedial power has been used. There has been a difference of view among Supreme Court justices about the extent to which federal remedial authority is appropriate, particularly when that intervention might move into areas traditionally governed by the states. Public education provides an interesting example. The Court mandated the end of segregated public schools in *Brown v. Board of Education (I)*, 347 U.S. 483 (1954). A number of lower federal courts issued extensive remedial orders. More recently, however, the Rehnquist Court has sought to scale back federal judicial intervention. In *Board of Education v. Dowell*, 498 U.S. 237 (1991), Chief Justice Rehnquist said that remedial decrees "are not intended to operate in perpetuity." Supervision of school districts by federal courts is not to extend beyond the time "required to remedy the effects of past discrimination." Once that happens, control is to be relinquished to local authorities.

Republicanism   A political system based on representation in government by delegates chosen by the people. The principle of representation makes government a reflection of a given culture or society, and limits the power that any individual or group may wield over others. There are three theories of representation. *Mandate theory* has a representative doing what his or her constituency wants. A representative under this theory is called a delegate or agent. *Independent theory* suggests that a representative should act as a trustee doing what he or she feels is right. A combination of the two theories has a representative attempting to balance both the constituents' and representatives' interests. A republic is distinguished from a pure democracy in which the people make policy decisions directly rather than through elected representatives. *See also* CONSTITUTIONALISM, p. 634; NATURAL LAW AND NATURAL RIGHTS, p. 679.

Significance   Republicanism provides the theoretical basis for the American constitutional system. The framers of the Constitution combined the thought of John Locke with their own experience under the English constitution and common law to form the concept of limited government by consent of the governed. The constitutional founders were convinced that the best model for government was one in which legislative supremacy, majority rule, popular sovereignty, and representation prevailed. Article IV, Section 4 of the Constitution provides that the national government shall guarantee to each state a "republican form of government."

Right   A power or privilege to which a person is entitled. A right confers control of action upon an individual and provides protection for that action. *See also* BILL OF RIGHTS, p. 621; NATURAL LAW AND NATURAL RIGHTS, p. 679.

Significance   A right is legally conveyed by a constitution, statutes, or the common law. It may be absolute, such as one's right to believe, or it may be conditional so that the acting out of one's beliefs will not injure other members of a political community. Rights within constitutional systems are called natural, civil, or political. A *natural right* is derived from the nature of man and flows from natural law. It is not dependent on man-made law. A *civil right* grows out of the political community, attaching to one's citizenship. Thus every person has the right to a jury trial or equal treatment before the law. A *political right* protects a person's capacity to participate in his or her own governance by voting and by seeking political office.

Second Amendment   A constitutional amendment contained in the Bill of Rights that provides: "A well regulated militia, being necessary to the security of a free State, the right of the people to keep and bear arms, shall not be infringed." There is much current debate about whether this language protects an individual's right to bear arms and precludes Congress from passing gun control laws. The more authoritative interpretation seems to be that the guarantee was included to convince the states that the national government would not disarm state militias. *See also* BILL OF RIGHTS, p. 621.

Significance   The Second Amendment is seen as a limitation on federal, but not state, authority. Although federal regulation of guns has been minimal, the Court has upheld provisions of a federal law requiring registration of certain kinds of guns, such as sawed-off shotguns and machine guns that were often used by those working in organized crime. In *United States v. Miller*, 307 U.S. 174 (1939), the Court ruled that the Second Amendment was only intended to protect a citizen's right to own those kinds of weapons ordinarily used to arm a militia, and concluded that a sawed-off shotgun was not standard issue for members of a militia. While challenges to gun control laws have been entertained by lower federal courts, the Supreme Court has confined itself to weapon possession restrictions and not complete prohibition of possession. Discussion of bans on rapid-fire assault weapons may give the Court an opportunity to address criminalization of possession itself. In 1997 the Court struck down in *Printz v. United States*, 521 U.S. 898 (1997), provisions of the Brady Handgun Violence Prevention Act that required local authorities to conduct background checks on those seeking to purchase handguns. The *Printz* ruling, however, was decided on federalism grounds and not on Second Amendment grounds. The Court concluded that states retain sovereignty that precludes the Congress from requiring them to "enact or administer a Federal regulatory program" involuntarily.

Self-Incrimination Clause   The Fifth Amendment provision that no person "shall be compelled in any criminal case to be a witness against himself." The Self-Incrimination Clause covers testimony at the trial of an accused person or statements made prior to the trial that may have the effect of implicating the person in a crime. It requires the prosecution to demonstrate guilt without assistance from the accused. *See also Carter v. Kentucky*, p. 287; IDENTIFICATION PROCEDURES, p. 662; IMMUNITY, p. 662; *Kastigar v. United States*, p. 315; *Miranda v. Arizona*, p. 290; *Neil v. Biggers*, p. 313.

Significance   The privilege against self-incrimination was fully recognized in Great Britain by the early eighteenth century and was established in common law by the time the American Constitution was written. As the Supreme Court said in *Murphy v. Waterfront Commission*, 378 U.S. 52 (1964), the Self-Incrimination Clause reflects "many of our fundamental values and most noble aspirations." Those values and aspirations include "our unwillingness to subject those suspected of crime to the cruel trilemma of self-accusation, perjury or contempt." The privilege against self-incrimination represents a society's preference for an accusatorial rather than an inquisitorial system of criminal justice. It extends only to criminal prosecutions, however, and does not prevent compelled testimony that may damage a witness's reputation or create adverse economic or social consequences. The Supreme Court resisted early attempts to make the Self-Incrimination Clause applicable to the states through the

Fourteenth Amendment. In *Twining v. New Jersey*, 211 U.S. 78 (1908), the Court concluded that the privilege did not rank "among the fundamental and inalienable rights of mankind," but rather it constituted "a wise and beneficent rule of evidence." The Court said it may be "a just and useful principle of law," but it need not be required at the state level. The Warren Court reversed *Twining* in *Malloy v. Hogan*, 378 U.S. 1 (1964). It declared "the *Twining* view of the privilege has been eroded," and that it was "incongruous" to have different standards dependent upon whether the right was asserted in a state or a federal court. The contemporary significance of the self-incrimination protection was underlined not only by the Warren Court's decision to apply the privilege to the states but by the Court's decision to extend the privilege to pretrial situations such as custodial interrogations. It did so in *Miranda v. Arizona*, 384 U.S. 436 (1966). *Miranda* required that all detained persons be advised of their constitutional rights prior to interrogation. Voluntary confessions are not prohibited by *Miranda*. Even statements taken improperly may be used to impeach a defendant's trial testimony. The privilege against self-incrimination has been confined to communicative or testimonial evidence. Accordingly, it prohibits comment on a defendant's refusal to testify, but the prohibition does not extend to such defendant-derived evidence as blood samples or to involuntary identification procedures such as line-ups. The Self-Incrimination Clause may be satisfied by granting immunity to a witness, thereby protecting the witness from having compelled testimony used in a subsequent prosecution against him or her.

Separate-But-Equal Doctrine   The doctrine of a Supreme Court holding in *Plessy v. Ferguson*, 163 U.S. 537 (1896), that a legal distinction between the black and white races does not destroy the legal equality of the two. Separate-but-equal theory was a reaction to the Equal Protection Clause of the Fourteenth Amendment, which prohibits discriminatory state conduct. Following ratification of the Fourteenth Amendment, many southern states enacted statutes requiring racial segregation in a variety of situations. The states argued that such segregation did not constitute impermissible discrimination. In *Plessy*, the Supreme Court agreed and permitted state-mandated segregation as long as separate facilities were equal for both races. *See also Brown v. Board of Education (I)*, p. 485; EQUAL PROTECTION CLAUSE, p. 473; *Plessy v. Ferguson*, p. 481; STATE ACTION, p. 703.

Significance   The separate-but-equal formula was articulated in reference to a state statute that required all railroads operating in Louisiana to provide "equal but separate accommodations." The

Supreme Court said that the separate-but-equal concept provided both races with equality under the law. For several decades following *Plessy*, the standard was maintained with little attention paid to the actual equivalence of facilities. Renunciation of the doctrine began in the mid–twentieth century with several graduate education decisions. Separate but equal was abandoned totally in the context of public education in *Brown v. Board of Education (I)*, 347 U.S. 483 (1954). Soon after *Brown*, segregation was invalidated in transportation, public accommodations, and municipal facilities as well.

Separation of Powers   The doctrine and practice of dividing the powers of government among several coordinate branches to prevent the abusive concentration of power. The distribution of powers embodied in the U.S. Constitution distinguishes functionally between government and people, and between legislative, executive, and judicial branches. While the Constitution creates three separate branches, it also assigns overlapping responsibilities that make the branches interdependent through the operation of a system of checks and balances. *See also* CONSTITUTIONALISM, p. 634; FEDERALISM, p. 649; REPUBLICANISM, p. 693.

Significance   The principle of separation of powers is designed to limit the abusive exercise of governmental authority by partitioning power and then assigning that power to several locations. The structural distribution of authority creates different points of access as each branch tends to respond to different kinds of political stimuli. The key factor, however, is that none of the branches dominates the processes of government for a protracted period of time. The separation of powers may create fragmentation or disunity for government if there exists sufficient interbranch conflict. Such conflict can often be found when the executive and legislative branches are controlled by different political parties.

Seventh Amendment   Provides that the right to trial by jury will be preserved for federal suits at common law. This means that the amendment applies if the civil suit involves a private right that meets the jurisdiction requirements to be heard by an Article III federal court (as distinct from an administrative court created under provisions of Article I). The amendment further provides that judgments of civil juries will be reviewed by federal courts according to common-law principles. *See also* COMMON LAW, p. 631; EQUITY JURISDICTION, p. 644.

Significance   Issues arising out of the Seventh Amendment are exceptionally rare because it applies only to those cases in which federal law permits common-law principles to be used. In *Lorillard v. Pons*, 434 U.S. 575 (1974), however, the Court ruled that the amendment applies to actions enforcing statutory rights as well as actions arising under common law. The Court ruled in *Colegrove v. Battin*, 413 U.S. 149 (1973), that civil juries covered by the amendment can be of any size as long as they are not smaller than six persons. The Seventh Amendment is one of the few remaining provisions of the Bill of Rights that has not been extended to the states through the Fourteenth Amendment, thus states are not required to have juries in civil trials.

Sliding Scale Test   A standard for evaluating expression to determine if the expression is to be afforded First Amendment protection. The sliding scale test is a modification of the clear and present danger test. This test presumes that the right to free expression is conditional and may be regulated if the government's interest in regulation is substantial enough. *See also* BALANCING TEST, p. 620; CLEAR AND PRESENT DANGER TEST, p. 629; *Dennis v. United States*, p. 82.

Significance   The sliding scale test was first used by the Supreme Court in *Dennis v. United States*, 341 U.S. 494 (1951). The Court held in *Dennis* that inquiry must be made into "whether the gravity of the evil, discounted by its improbability, justifies such invasion of free speech as is necessary to avoid the danger." If the threat posed is severe enough, such as the violent overthrow of the government, a response is required even if the attempted overthrow is doomed from the outset. If the evil is less grave, its probability of success must be greater before regulation is allowed. The sliding scale test is a comparative judgment determination applied on a case-by-case basis.

Smith Act   The first federal legislative regulation of expression and association since the Alien and Sedition Acts of 1798. The Smith Act, formally known as the Alien Registration Act of 1940, required aliens living in the United States to register with the federal government. Any alien found to be associated with a subversive organization could be deported. The principal thrust of the statute, however, was its restriction on certain kinds of political expression by American citizens. The Smith Act prohibited advocacy of the violent overthrow of any government in the United States and the publication of any materials advocating forcible overthrow. It also prohibited the organization of any group dedicated to revolution. *See also*

CLEAR AND PRESENT DANGER TEST, p. 629; *Dennis v. United States*, p. 82; SLIDING SCALE TEST, p. 698.

Significance   The Smith Act was upheld in *Dennis v. United States*, 341 U.S. 494 (1951). The Supreme Court used a sliding scale test to determine that Congress had the authority to prevent an evil as extensive as forcible overthrow of the government. In the years following *Dennis*, successful prosecutions under the Smith Act became less and less likely as the Court further required that evidence of "knowing and active" participation in criminal conduct aimed at violent overthrow be demonstrated.

Social Contract   A theoretical justification for the consensual basis of human society and government. Social contract theory involves two concepts: the governmental contract and the social contract itself, each of which extends far back into history. The concept of governmental contract holds that the relation between a people and its rulers arises from a mutual agreement between both parties. The concept of a social contract holds that the establishment of any society beyond the family comes from a mutual agreement among all the individuals of the society. This theory has three main versions, each distinguished by its account of the relationship between the social contract and morality. The first version states that individuals in the state of nature preceding the contract are already subject to a moral natural law. John Locke subscribed to this view. The second version states that individuals in the state of nature are not yet under any moral law. It is the social contract that serves as the foundation of morality rather than morality serving as the basis of the contract. Thomas Hobbes and Jean-Jacques Rousseau are representative of those who held this view. The third version holds that the social contract is preceded by and founded on moral law, but the moral law itself is the result of an original contract with all other human beings. Immanuel Kant and John Rawls represented this view.   *See also* LOCKE, JOHN, p. 676; NATURAL LAW AND NATURAL RIGHTS, p. 679.

Significance   Social contract theory as a legitimating idea for government enjoys almost universal recognition, even in totalitarian regimes where the contract is often violated in practice. The American colonists felt the need for such a legitimating idea, and it is evident in the Constitution of 1787. Contract theory was developed as a response to the theory of the divine right of kings. Social contract theory was widely attractive, and it directly led to placing limits on the authority of monarchs. The theory provided the impetus for the revolutions in England, France, and the United

States. The primary justification used by Thomas Jefferson in the Declaration of Independence was the violation of the contract by the British. Many of the component propositions of social contract theory remain embedded in modern democratic theory and continue to serve as the basis for individual rights and limited government.

Speech Plus   Expression that requires additional action or conduct. Speech plus refers to such forms of expression as picketing, marching, demonstrating, and symbolic speech. These situations raise difficult First Amendment questions. Although expression carries free speech protection, conduct associated with expression may be subject to regulation. *See also Adderley v. Florida*, p. 149; FREE SPEECH CLAUSE, p. 654; *PruneYard Shopping Center v. Robins*, p. 152; PURE SPEECH, p. 692.

Significance   Speech plus takes normally protected speech out of bounds when it involves a demonstration in such places as the grounds of a county jail. If the conduct associated with speech is subject to regulation, the regulation comes at the expense of the expression. Cases that raise such First Amendment issues include access to private shopping malls; permit requirements; court injunctions; and time, place, and manner restrictions. Expressive activity in schools is subject to greater regulation because the students are minors and because school authorities are accorded great latitude in safeguarding students and the educational environment. Speech plus is distinguished from pure speech, which necessitates no additional conduct.

Speedy Trial   A safeguard of the Sixth Amendment that provides a criminal defendant with the right to a "speedy and public trial." The speedy-trial provision of the federal Constitution was made applicable to the states through the Fourteenth Amendment in *Klopfer v. North Carolina*, 386 U.S. 213 (1967). A speedy trial is intended to keep an accused from protracted pretrial detention, and it protects against the diminution of a criminal defendant's ability to offer a defense. Speedy trial also ensures that the prosecutor's case will not erode because of delay, given what Justice Powell has called a "uniquely two-edged sword" character to the right. The speedy-trial protection begins at the time a person is either arrested or formally accused, whichever comes first. Delay occurring before charging or arrest is evaluated after formal charges are made and focus on the sufficiency of the government's reasons for delay that might advantage the prosecution and the prejudice suffered by the defendant. *See also Doggett v. United States*, p. 326.

Significance   Speedy-trial challenges that would establish fixed time limits for trials or would depend on a formal demand by the accused for a speedy trial have been rejected by the Supreme Court. The Court developed a balancing test for speedy trials in *Barker v. Wingo*, 407 U.S. 514 (1972). The four components are (1) length of delay, (2) sufficiency of reasons for the delay, (3) assertion of the right to a speedy trial by the accused, and (4) injury or prejudice suffered by the accused through pretrial incarceration, anxiety, and/or impairment of the ability to present a defense. In addition to these guidelines established by the Court, both federal and state legislation exists to govern the speed by which a criminal case progresses through the courts. Defense-initiated requests for postponements are not considered delays covered by the speedy-trial protection.

Standing   The requirement that a real dispute exists between the prospective parties in a suit. Standing is necessary for a federal court to proceed with a case. The concept has several important components. Federal judicial power extends to cases or controversies through Article III of the Constitution. This has been interpreted to mean that bona fide disputes must exist if judicial resolution is to be sought. The federal courts are thus unable to respond to hypothetical or friendly suits, and they cannot render advisory opinions. The adversary system demands that litigants in a suit be true adversaries. Test cases have often been used to raise certain issues and satisfy the demands of the standing requirement. A test case is a legal action designed to obtain a court's judgment on a legal question and thereby have a principle or right established or clarified. Developing a test case is a common strategy of interest groups. The National Association for the Advancement of Colored People (NAACP), for example, orchestrated various test cases involving different aspects of racial segregation in an effort to obtain favorable judgments in the courts. Standing means that the plaintiff bringing suit must have suffered direct injury, and the injury must be protected by constitutional or statutory provisions. This means suits cannot be brought by a third party or someone indirectly related to the legal injury. Further, each suit must specify the remedy being sought from the court. The burden rests with the plaintiff to define the relief that the court might order. Standing also relates to the timing of a suit. A federal court must find a suit *ripe*, which means all other avenues of possible relief must have been exhausted. Similarly, a case cannot access federal courts if it has been resolved or if events have made pursuit of the original remedy inappropriate. A case that is too late is considered moot because there is no longer an adversarial situation. Exceptions are made when the limited duration of a situation or condition interferes with the litigation of the issues. Abortion cases are examples of the need for such an exception. *See also* CASE OR CONTROVERSY, p. 622; JUSTICIABILITY, p. 674.

Significance   Standing is discussed in several important Supreme Court decisions. The matter was first raised in *Massachusetts v. Mellon*, 262 U.S. 447 (1923). Plaintiff Frothingham attempted to enjoin the implementation of a federal program claiming injury by virtue of paying federal taxes. The Supreme Court denied standing and suggested that Frothingham's injury was shared by millions of others. The injury was therefore "comparatively minute and indeterminate." A plaintiff seeking judicial review of a federal statute must be able to show "direct injury as the result of its enforcement, and not merely that he suffers in some indefinite way in common with people generally." Inability to establish such injury prevents consideration of the constitutional issue regardless of how real and pressing the issue may be. The *Mellon* precedent lasted as an absolute barrier to judicial review of congressional spending legislation by taxpayers until *Flast v. Cohen*, 392 U.S. 83 (1968). The Court held in *Flast* that a taxpayer could achieve standing by showing a nexus between the taxpayer and the challenged program. The case involved a challenge of federal aid to private elementary and secondary schools. The Warren Court found the relationship among the federal taxing power, the payment of federal taxes, and First Amendment protections adequate to produce standing. The decision immediately raised questions about judicial review of congressional spending initiatives. It distinguished between the *Mellon* direct injury requirement and the litigant who might be acting on behalf of broader public rights. The Burger Court has shown, however, that access is still difficult. In *United States v. Richardson*, 418 U.S. 166 (1974), the Court refused to allow a taxpayer to inquire into Central Intelligence Agency appropriations. The Court said that allowing "unrestricted taxpayer standing would significantly alter the allocation of power at the national level." A second case, *Schlesinger v. Reservists Committee to Stop the War*, 418 U.S. 208 (1974), challenged the military reserve status of more than a hundred members of Congress. The Court denied standing, saying that to allow such a challenge by someone who has no concrete injury would require the Court to respond to issues in the abstract. The Court said that this would create the potential for abuse of the judicial process and distortion of the role of the judiciary. Standing too easily granted would open the courts to an arguable charge of government by the judiciary.

Stare Decisis Latin for "let the decision stand." *Stare decisis* holds that once a principle of law is established for a particular fact situation, courts should adhere to that principle in similar cases in the future. The case in which the rule of law is established is called a precedent.

Significance *Stare decisis* creates and maintains stability and predictability in the law. It creates a large body of settled usages that define common law. Precedents may be modified or abandoned if circumstances require, but the expectation is that rules from previously adjudicated cases will prevail.

State Action A requirement that limits application of the Equal Protection Clause to situations in which discriminatory conduct occurs under state authority. The state action requirement was first established by the Supreme Court in the *Civil Rights Cases*, 109 U.S. 3 (1883). It placed private discrimination outside the reach of the Fourteenth Amendment. The Court held that the amendment was intended to provide relief against state enactments rather than to empower Congress "to legislate upon subjects which are within the domain of state legislation" or "create a code of municipal law for the regulation of private rights." *See also City of Arlington Heights v. Metropolitan Housing Development Corp.*, p. 498; *The Civil Rights Cases*, p. 480; CLASSIFICATION, p. 628; EQUAL PROTECTION CLAUSE, p. 473; SEPARATE-BUT-EQUAL DOCTRINE, p. 696.

Significance State action requires a judgment about whether certain kinds of conduct occur "under color" of state law. A court must determine if discriminatory action is situated closely enough to state authority to be treated as though it were an overt act of the state. A sufficient nexus between challenged action and state authority is generally not difficult to demonstrate, although some private discrimination remains insulated from regulation. While softening the distinctions between private and state authorized discrimination, thus expanding the reach of the Equal Protection Clause, recent cases have required that discriminatory *intent* must be shown in addition to injurious impact in order to establish a constitutional violation.

State Constitutions Fundamental laws of the American states. States constitutions are not required under the U.S. Constitution, which only requires a "republican" form of government in the states. The original states all had state constitutions at the time the Constitution of 1787 was written, however. State constitutions are changed more frequently than the U.S. Constitution. About a third of the states have adopted new constitutions during the second half of the twentieth century, and upwards of 5,000 amendments have been made to state constitutions. *See also* CONSTITUTIONALISM, p. 634; FEDERALISM, p. 649; REPUBLICANISM, p. 693.

Significance　　The state constitutions reflect the deeply held commitment to written law. Constitutions from the original 13 states were very instructive to the delegates at the Philadelphia Convention. State constitutions served as guides through most of the nation's rapid territorial, economic, and population expansion. State constitutions allocate government power, but also limit that power and protect individual rights. State constitutions tend to be more lengthy and detailed than the U.S. Constitution and often contain specific limitations on the taxing power.

Statute　　A written law enacted by a legislative body. A statute declares, requires, or prohibits something. *See also* JUDICIAL REVIEW, p. 669.

Significance　　A statute is the most common means by which government regulates conduct. It must be enacted by a legislative body properly exercising the authority conveyed to it. A statute is inferior to constitutional provisions, and if a statute is incompatible with a constitutional command, the statute is void. Federal statutes are regularly compiled and found in the United States Code.

Stop and Frisk　　A limited detention of a suspicious person accompanied by a cursory weapons search. A stop and frisk is a warrantless stop for which probable cause to arrest does not exist. The stop, however, is based on an officer's reasonable suspicion that a crime is occurring or is about to occur. A stop and frisk is intended to be protective but it is nonetheless "an intrusion upon the sanctity of the person," and is extensively circumscribed. *See also* PROBABLE CAUSE, p. 691; *Terry v. Ohio*, p. 231; WARRANTLESS SEARCH, p. 711.

Significance　　Stop and frisk is discussed at length in *Terry v. Ohio*, 392 U.S. 1 (1968), which held that the overriding consideration for it must be the discovery of weapons in suspicious situations. The major importance of *Terry* is that it distinguishes stops from arrests and frisks from full searches. Under *Terry*, even situations lacking probable cause may be subjected to the preventive action of a temporary stop and a cursory weapons search. Custodial arrest with a full search may follow if the frisk yields a weapon. Random stops to request identification are not permissible. The *Terry* rationale was used to extend stop and frisk to the passenger compartment of a stopped car. In *Michigan v. Long*, 463 U.S. 1032 (1983), the Court held that *Terry* need not be restricted to a preventive search of the person of a detained suspect. A search of the passenger compartment is permitted if law enforcement agents have "an articulable and objectively reasonable belief that the suspect is potentially dangerous." *Long* allows a police officer to act upon reasonable suspicion to discover weapons that may be used to harm the officer or others.

Substantive Due Process   A substantive review focusing on the content of government policy. Substantive due process is distinguished from procedural due process, which attends to the means by which policies are executed. Judicial review of the reasonableness of legislative enactments allows the Court actively to intervene in policy judgments more than it could if review were confined to procedural considerations. *See also* DUE PROCESS CLAUSES, p. 641; PROCEDURAL DUE PROCESS, p. 692.

Significance   Substantive due process represents considerable monitoring power in the hands of the courts. In *Meyer v. Nebraska*, 262 U.S. 390 (1923), for example, the Supreme Court struck down a statute prohibiting the teaching of a foreign language to any student below the ninth-grade level, public or parochial. Justice McReynolds said that the statute was "arbitrary and without reasonable relation to any end within the competency of the State." The use of substantive due process to invalidate economic regulations is illustrated by *Lochner v. New York*, 198 U.S. 45 (1905). *Lochner* involved an attempt to limit the workweek of bakers to 60 hours. The Court held that there was "no reasonable ground for interfering with the liberty of a person or the right of free contract by determining the hours of labor in the occupation of a baker." The Court made a substantive judgment that the regulation of work hours for bakers was sufficiently unreasonable to constitute a denial of due process of law. Substantive due process review also occurs when statutes are stricken for reason of vagueness. When the Court voided a city ordinance that prohibited public annoyance by assemblies of three or more persons standing on public sidewalks in *Coates v. Cincinnati*, 402 U.S. 611 (1971), it did so because the ordinance was arbitrary. It conveyed no discernible standard of conduct. Another example of substantive due process enforcement is the striking down of state statutes prohibiting abortion.

Symbolic Speech   The use of action or gesture as a surrogate for words. Symbolic speech is generally protected by the First Amendment because of its expressive character. It may be restricted, however, if the substituted action is not permitted. *See also* FREE SPEECH CLAUSE, p. 654; PURE SPEECH, p. 692; SPEECH PLUS, p. 700; *Texas v. Johnson*, p. 85; *Tinker v. Des Moines Independent Community School District*, p. 84.

Significance   Symbolic speech was protected in *Tinker v. Des Moines Independent Community School District*, 393 U.S. 503 (1969), in which the Supreme Court upheld the wearing of armbands by high school students as a protest against American involvement in Vietnam. The Court found that the armbands were passive expression of opinion that closely resembled pure speech. School authorities may regulate symbolic expression by students on school grounds in a more restrictive manner than occurs with symbolic expression by adults. Most restrictions on symbolic speech are invalidated in order to ensure free political debate, but limits have been applied. The Court upheld a conviction for draft card burning in *United States v. O'Brien*, 391 U.S. 367 (1968), for example, saying that although the action was communicative, the Court could not accept a limitless variety of conduct labeled speech whenever a person intended to express an idea.

Third Amendment   A prohibition against the government housing soldiers in private homes during peacetime without the owner's consent. Lodging soldiers in private homes during times of war can occur "in a manner to be prescribed by law." *See also* RIGHT OF PRIVACY, p. 476.

Significance   The Third Amendment was included in the Bill of Rights because those drafting the amendments were well aware of the British practice of housing troops in private residences during the period preceding the War of Independence. The federal government has never sought to quarter troops, thus the amendment has never appeared before the Supreme Court as such. Justice Douglas included the amendment, however, in the list of constitutional protections that implied the existence of a right to privacy in his majority opinion in *Griswold v. Connecticut*, 381 U.S. 479 (1965).

Third-Party Search   A search involving an indirectly affected third party offering consent to the search of a suspect's premises. Third-party consent may legally be granted even though the consenting party is not directly suspected of criminal conduct. The third party must share common authority over the place to be searched, but he or she may not give permission to search areas exclusively used by the nonconsenting party. *See also* CONSENT SEARCH, p. 633; PROBABLE CAUSE, p. 691; WARRANT, p. 710; *Zurcher v. Stanford Daily*, p. 201.

Significance   Third-party search consent is separable from a title to property. Landlords may not consent to the search of tenants' rooms, for example. The third party involved in a third-party search is frequently a spouse or a roommate. Another third-party situation involves the search of a location despite the fact that the occupant is not a suspect. A warrant may be issued to search any premises as long as a neutral magistrate concludes there is probable cause to believe evidence pertaining to a crime is located there. In *Zurcher v. Stanford Daily*, 436 U.S. 547 (1978), the Supreme Court upheld a warrant-authorized third-party search of a newspaper office. Evidence germane to criminal investigations becomes more likely as computer-based record keeping by third parties develops. In *Zurcher* the Court rejected the policy option of using the subpoena to obtain evidence from third-party sources. Thus the premises of those not under active investigation are subject to search provided warrant conditions are met. Confiscation of evidence by private citizens is usually allowed, but minors may not turn over evidence found in the rooms of parents or guardians.

Thirteenth Amendment   A post–Civil War constitutional amendment providing that "Neither slavery nor involuntary servitude, except as a punishment for crime whereof the party shall have been duly convicted, shall exist within the United States, or any place subject to their jurisdiction." The Thirteenth Amendment gave legal effect to the Emancipation Proclamation of 1863. It also fundamentally altered the federal-state relationship in that it conferred on the federal government authority over a policy area previously residing exclusively in the states. A state could no longer permit slavery through the exercise of its own authority. The Thirteenth Amendment does not preclude military conscription, criminal sentences involving hard labor, or other similar requirements of involuntary service. The amendment was designed to apply to black persons in the particular context of the Emancipation Proclamation. Section 2 of the amendment empowered Congress "to enforce this article by appropriate legislation." *See also* FOURTEENTH AMENDMENT, p. 651; STATE ACTION, p. 703.

Significance   The Thirteenth Amendment gave Congress comprehensive power to legislate against racial discrimination and the denial of civil rights. Such power was incident to the power to outlaw slavery. Consistent with this view, Congress passed the Civil Rights Act of 1866, which clarified the citizenship status of freed slaves and protected certain rights such as entering into contracts and holding and conveying real property. Early Supreme Court construction of the amendment defined slavery very narrowly, however, and placed private discrimination outside the amendment's reach. Congress therefore had no occasion to exercise the limited authority conferred by Section 2. In 1968 the Supreme Court substantially modified its previous interpretations and found that the amendment empowered Congress to do more than simply abolish the institution of slavery. In *Jones v. Alfred H. Mayer Co.*, 392 U.S. 409 (1968), a case in which a litigant attempted to utilize provisions of the Civil Rights Act of 1866 against a discriminatory housing developer, the Court said that the Thirteenth Amendment had granted Congress power "to determine what are the badges and the incidents of slavery" and to respond accordingly. As construed in *Jones,* the Thirteenth Amendment became a foundation stone upon which civil-rights policy was established, particularly when the policy turns on what constitutes a badge or vestige of slavery. The correction of such badges and vestiges is now clearly located within the prerogatives of congressional power.

Tort   A private or civil injury to a person or property. A tort action must include the legal obligation of a defendant to a plaintiff, violation of that obligation, and a cause and effect relationship between the defendant's conduct and the injury suffered by the plaintiff.

Significance   A tort is any civil wrong, with the exception of breach of contract. A lawsuit alleging the negligence of an automobile driver is a tort action, for example. An assault is a tort. So is a trespass. A constitutional tort involves an action or inaction that allegedly violates the Constitution of the United States or federal statutes such as liability that may arise out of the action of governmental agencies that may violate a person's rights.

Travel, Right to   A fundamental right drawn implicitly from the Constitution of the United States. The right to travel freely from state to state is spread among all American citizens. Although several origins of the right have been suggested, the Supreme Court has settled on the Commerce Clause as the principal source. The Court has held that the power to regulate interstate commerce encompasses people as well as commodities. *See also* FUNDAMENTAL RIGHT, p. 656; *Shapiro v. Thompson*, p. 538.

Significance   The right to travel not only precludes denial of movement from state to state, but it also prohibits state policies that may inhibit interstate travel. In *Shapiro v. Thompson*, 394 U.S. 618 (1969), for example, the Court struck down a state residency requirement for welfare eligibility. The purpose of the enactment was to deter migration of welfare-eligible persons into a state. The Court categorically condemned any interference with the right to movement, saying that all citizens must be free to travel throughout the country. They must be "uninhibited by statutes, rules, or regulations which unreasonably burden or restrain this movement." A state must demonstrate a compelling interest before imposing any regulation that affects the right to travel.

Virginia Plan   One of the two plans presented to delegates at the Constitutional Convention in Philadelphia in 1787. The Virginia Plan was presented by Edmund Randolph and called for the establishment of a central government with substantially more power than that possessed by the central government under the Articles of Confederation. The Virginia Plan called for the creation of a bicameral national legislature, a strengthened executive branch headed by a single chief executive, and an independent federal court system, among other things. The Virginia Plan was countered by a proposal known as the New Jersey Plan, which more closely reflected the states' rights position of some of the Convention delegates. *See also* ARTICLES OF CONFEDERATION, p. 615; CONSTITUTIONALISM, p. 634; SEPARATION OF POWERS, p. 697.

Significance   The proposals contained in the Virginia Plan provided the foundation for the Constitution ultimately sent to the states for ratification. The Federalists, who supported the provisions of the Virginia Plan, prevailed at the Philadelphia Convention and a strengthened central government was established. While sovereignty was shared with the states under the proposed constitution, the central government possessed the authority to pass federal laws that applied directly to the people rather than indirectly through the states.

Voting Rights Act of 1965   The Voting Rights Act was adopted in 1965 and renewed and amended in 1970, 1975, and 1982. The Act contained a number of provisions designed to eliminate discriminatory voting practices. The Act authorized federal registrars to register voters in states or counties where less than half of those of voting age were already registered voters. The Act also prohibited the use of literacy and other tests that had been used as a means of furthering discriminatory ends. The 1970 extension of the Act attempted to lower the voting age to 18, but the Supreme Court ruled in *Oregon v. Mitchell*, 400 U.S. 112 (1970), that Congress could not lower the voting age for state and local elections by statute. The Twenty-Sixth Amendment was ratified the next year and accomplished through the amendment process what Congress had not been able to do by statute. The 1970 Act also limited residency requirements for voters to 30 days; voters could not be disqualified by states for failure to reside in-state for a period greater than 30 days. The reenactment of the Act in 1975 expanded the reach of the Act to all or parts of 10 more states and prohibited the disqualification of voters by virtue of their inability to read English. The most far-reaching change required federal approval of any changes in election laws in the states covered by the Act. The 25-year extension of the Act in 1982 added significant language prohibiting the dilution of minority voting strength. *See also* FIFTEENTH AMENDMENT, p. 650; *Shaw v. Reno*, p. 524; *South Carolina v. Katzenbach*, p. 531.

Significance The Voting Rights Act of 1965 and the subsequent amendments of it constitute the most comprehensive federal voting rights law. Passage of the Act in 1965 had substantial impact on the balance between federal and state authority. Prior to 1965 the states possessed virtually exclusive power over elections. The initial Act sent federal registrars into those states covered by the law, and significant numbers of minority voters were registered for the first time. The expanded electorate, in turn, had direct influence on the outcomes of federal, state, and local elections. The vote dilution and federal preclearance provisions of Sections 2 and 5, respectively, also have had substantial impact on election processes. Most recently the Supreme Court has considered the intersection of the Act and the Equal Protection Clause of the Fourteenth Amendment. In *Shaw v. Reno*, 509 U.S. 630 (1993), and rulings stemming from that decision, the Court said that legislative redistricting plans based "predominantly on race" must be subjected to strict judicial scrutiny. That means, among other things, that a state wishing to establish race-conscious district boundaries must demonstrate that a compelling state interest is the objective. Compliance with the antidiscrimination terms of the Voting Rights Act, however, will not meet the compelling interest standard by themselves.

Warrant An order issued by a court authorizing the arrest of a person or the search of a specified location. The warrant requirement in criminal cases is found in the Fourth Amendment, following the assertion of the people's right to be secure against unreasonable searches and seizures. *See also Coolidge v. New Hampshire*, p. 196; *Draper v. United States*, p. 194; NEUTRAL MAGISTRATE, p. 680; PROBABLE CAUSE, p. 691; WARRANTLESS SEARCH, p. 711; *Ybarra v. Illinois*, p. 197.

Significance   A warrant authorizes an official government intrusion into personal security. It must be obtained from an appropriate authority, who is generally a neutral magistrate. A request for a warrant must establish probable cause that the person to be arrested is linked to a criminal act or that the location to be searched likely contains particular seizable items. The warrant must describe in detail the person to be arrested or the items to be sought in a search.

Warrantless Search   An exception arising out of an exigent circumstance in which a police officer may be unable to seek a warrant. A warrantless search for evidence is allowed if it is conducted incident to a lawful arrest, for example. A warrantless search is permitted to allow removal of weapons from the arrestee or prevent the concealment or destruction of evidence. A search incident to arrest is confined to the area within the arrestee's immediate control. *See also Chimel v. California*, p. 214; CONSENT SEARCH, p. 633; EXIGENT CIRCUMSTANCE, p. 647; HOT PURSUIT, p. 661; STOP AND FRISK, p. 704; WARRANT, p. 710.

Significance   An exigency may be presented in an unforeseen stop and frisk situation, as in *Terry v. Ohio*, 392 U.S. 1 (1968). It may be presented in the search of an automobile, as in *Chambers v. Maroney*, 399 U.S. 42 (1970), or in a hot pursuit. Items may be seized if they are in the plain view of the officer and if the seized items were discovered in a place where the officer was entitled to be. Finally, a warrantless search may occur when a person voluntarily waives his or her Fourth Amendment rights and consents to the search.

APPENDIX A

Constitution of the United States

Preamble

We the People of the United States, in Order to form a more perfect Union, establish Justice, insure domestic Tranquility, provide for the common defence, promote the general Welfare, and secure the Blessings of Liberty to ourselves and our Posterity, do ordain and establish this Constitution for the United States of America.

Article I

Section 1. All legislative Powers herein granted shall be vested in a Congress of the United States, which shall consist of a Senate and House of Representatives.

Section 2. The House of Representatives shall be composed of Members chosen every second Year by the People of the several States, and the Electors in each State shall have the Qualifications requisite for Electors of the most numerous Branch of the State Legislature.

No Person shall be a Representative who shall not have attained to the age of twenty-five Years, and been seven Years a Citizen of the United States, and who shall not, when elected, be an Inhabitant of that State in which he shall be chosen.

Representatives and direct Taxes shall be apportioned among the several States which may be included within this Union, according to their respective Numbers, which shall be determined by adding to the whole Number of free Persons, including those bound to Service for a Term of Years, and excluding Indians not taxed, three-fifths of all other Persons. The actual Enumeration shall be made within three Years after the first Meeting of the Congress of the United States, and within every subsequent Term of ten Years, in such Manner as they shall by Law direct. The Number of Representatives shall not exceed one for every thirty Thousand, but each State shall have at Least one Representative; and until such enumeration shall be made, the State of New Hampshire shall be entitled to chuse three, Massachusetts eight, Rhode-Island and Providence Plantations one, Connecticut five, New York six, New Jersey four, Pennsylvania eight, Delaware one, Maryland six, Virginia ten, North Carolina five, South Carolina five, and Georgia three.

When vacancies happen in the Representation from any State, the Executive Authority thereof shall issue Writs of Election to fill such Vacancies.

The House of Representatives shall chuse their Speaker and other officers; and shall have the sole Power of Impeachment.

Section 3. The Senate of the United States shall be composed of two Senators from each State, chosen by the Legislature thereof, for six Years; and each Senator shall have one Vote.

Immediately after they shall be assembled in Consequence of the first Election, they shall be divided as equally as may be into three Classes. The seats of the Senators of the first Class shall be vacated at the Expiration of the second Year, of the second Class at the Expiration of the Fourth Year, and of the third Class at the Expiration of the sixth Year, so that one-third may be chosen every second Year; and if Vacancies happen by Resignation, or otherwise, during the Recess of the Legislature of any State, the Executive thereof may make temporary Appointments until the next Meeting of the Legislature, which shall then fill such Vacancies.

No Person shall be a Senator who shall not have attained to the Age of thirty Years, and been nine Years a Citizen of the United States, and who shall not, when elected, be an Inhabitant of that State for which he shall be chosen.

The Vice President of the United States shall be President of the Senate, but shall have no Vote, unless they be equally divided.

The Senate shall chuse their other Officers, and also a President pro tempore, in the Absence of the Vice President, or when he shall exercise the Office of President of the United States.

The Senate shall have the sole Power to try all Impeachments. When sitting for that Purpose, they shall be on Oath or Affirmation. When the President of the United States is tried the Chief Justice shall preside: And no Person shall be convicted without the Concurrence of two-thirds of the Members present.

Judgment in Cases of Impeachment shall not extend further than to removal from Office, and disqualification to hold and enjoy any Office of honor, Trust or Profit under the United States: but the Party convicted shall nevertheless be liable and subject to Indictment, Trial, Judgment and Punishment, according to Law.

Section 4. The Times, Places and Manner of holding Elections for Senators and Representatives, shall be prescribed in each State by the Legislature thereof; but the Congress may at any time by Law make or alter such Regulations, except as to the Places of chusing Senators.

The Congress shall assemble at least once in every Year, and such Meeting shall be on the first Monday in December unless they shall by Law appoint a different Day.

Section 5. Each House shall be the Judge of the Elections, Returns and Qualifications of its own Members, and a Majority of each shall constitute a Quorum to do Business; but a smaller Number may adjourn from day to day, and may be authorized to compel the Attendance of absent Members, in such Manner, and under such Penalties as each House may provide.

Each House may determine the Rules of its Proceedings, punish its Members for disorderly Behaviour, and, with the Concurrence of two-thirds, expel a Member.

Each House shall keep a Journal of its Proceedings, and from time to time publish the same, excepting such Parts as may in their Judgment require Secrecy; and the Yeas and Nays of the Members of either House on any question shall, at the Desire of one-fifth of those Present, be entered on the Journal.

Neither House, during the Session of Congress, shall, without the Consent of the other, adjourn for more than three days, nor to any other Place than that in which the two Houses shall be sitting.

Section 6. The Senators and Representatives shall receive a Compensation for their Services, to be ascertained by Law, and paid out of the Treasury of the United States. They shall in all Cases, except Treason, Felony and Breach of the Peace, be privileged from Arrest during their Attendance at the Session of their respective Houses, and in going to and returning from the same; and for any Speech or Debate in either House, they shall not be questioned in any other Place.

No Senator or Representative shall, during the Time for which he was elected, be appointed to any civil Office under the Authority of the United States, which shall have been created, or the Emoluments whereof shall have been encreased during such time; and no Person holding any Office under the United States, shall be a Member of either House during his Continuance in Office.

Section 7. All Bills for raising Revenue shall originate in the House of Representatives; but the Senate may propose or concur with amendments as on other Bills.

Every Bill which shall have passed the House of Representatives and the Senate, shall, before it become a Law, be presented to the President of the United States; If he approve he shall sign it, but if not he shall return it, with his Objections to that House in which it shall have originated, who shall enter the Objections at large on their Journal, and proceed to reconsider it. If after such Reconsideration two-thirds of that House shall agree to pass the Bill, it shall be sent, together with the Objections, to the other House, by which it shall likewise be reconsidered, and if approved by two-thirds of that House, it shall become a Law. But in all such Cases the Votes of both Houses shall be determined by Yeas and Nays, and the Names of the Persons voting for and against the Bill shall be entered on the Journal of each House respectively. If any Bill shall not be returned by the President within ten Days (Sunday excepted) after it shall have been presented to him, the Same shall be a Law, in like Manner as if he had signed it, unless the Congress by their Adjournment prevent its Return, in which Case it shall not be a Law.

Every Order, Resolution, or Vote to which the Concurrence of the Senate and House of Representatives may be necessary (except on a question of Adjournment) shall be presented to the President of the United States; and before the Same shall take Effect, shall be approved by him, or being disapproved by him, shall be repassed by two-thirds of the Senate and House of Representatives, according to the Rules and Limitations prescribed in the Case of a Bill.

Section 8. The Congress shall have Power To lay and collect Taxes, Duties, Imposts and Excises, to pay the Debts and provide for the common Defence and general Welfare of the United States; but all Duties, Imposts and Excises shall be uniform throughout the United States;

To borrow Money on the credit of the United States;

To regulate Commerce with foreign Nations, and among the several States, and with the Indian Tribes;

To establish an uniform Rule of Naturalization, and uniform Laws on the subject of Bankruptcies throughout the United States;

To coin Money, regulate the Value thereof, and of foreign Coin, and fix the Standard of Weights and Measures;

To provide for the Punishment of counterfeiting; the Securities and current Coin of the United States;

To establish Post Offices and post Roads;

To promote the Progress of Science and useful Arts, by securing for limited Times to Authors and Inventors the exclusive Right to their respective Writings and Discoveries;

To constitute Tribunals inferior to the supreme Court;

To define and punish Piracies and Felonies commited on the high Seas, and Offences against the Law of Nations;

To declare War, grant Letters of Marque and Reprisal, and make Rules concerning Captures on Land and Water;

To raise and support Armies, but no Appropriation of Money to that Use shall be for a longer Term than two Years;

To provide and maintain a Navy;

To make Rules for the Government and Regulation of the land and naval Forces;

To provide for calling forth the Militia to execute the Laws of the Union, suppress Insurrections and repel Invasions;

To provide for organizing, arming, and disciplining the Militia, and for governing such Part of them as may be employed in the Service of the United States, reserving to the States respectively, the Appointment of the Officers, and the Authority of training the Militia according to the discipline prescribed by Congress;

To exercise exclusive Legislation in all Cases whatsoever, over such District (not exceeding ten Miles square) as may, by Cession of Particular States, and the Acceptance of Congress, become the Seat of the Government of the United States, and to exercise like Authority over all Places purchased by the Consent of the Legislature of the State in which the Same shall be, for the Erection of Forts, Magazines, Arsenals, dock-Yards, and other needful Buildings;

—And

To make all Laws which shall be necessary and proper for carrying into Execution the foregoing Powers, and all other Powers vested by this Constitution in the Government of the United States, or in any Department or Officer thereof.

Section 9. The Migration or Importation of such Persons as any of the States now existing shall think proper to admit, shall not be prohibited by the Congress prior to the Year one thousand eight hundred and eight, but a Tax or duty may be imposed on such Importation, not exceeding ten dollars for each Person.

The Privilege of the Writ of Habeas Corpus shall not be suspended, unless when in Cases of Rebellion or Invasion the public Safety may require it.

No Bill of Attainder or ex post facto Law shall be passed.

No capitation, or other direct, Tax shall be laid, unless in Proportion to the Census of Enumeration herein before directed to be taken.

No Tax or Duty shall be laid on Articles exported from any State.

No Preference shall be given by any Regulation of Commerce or Revenue to the Ports of one State over those of another; nor shall Vessels bound to, or from, one State, be obliged to enter, clear or pay Duties in another.

No Money shall be drawn from the Treasury, but in Consequence of Appropriations made by Law; and a regular Statement and Account of the Receipts and Expenditures of all public Money shall be published from time to time.

No Title of Nobility shall be granted by the United States: And no Person holding any Office of Profit or Trust under them, shall, without the Consent of the Congress, accept of any present, Emolument, Office, or Title, of any kind whatever, from any King, Prince, or foreign State.

Section 10. No State shall enter into any Treaty, Alliance, or Confederation; grant Letters of Marque and Reprisal; coin Money; emit Bills of Credit; make any Thing but gold and silver Coin a Tender in Payment of Debts; pass any Bill of Attainder, ex post facto Law, or Law impairing the Obligation of Contracts, or grant any Title of Nobility.

No State shall, without the Consent of the Congress, lay any Imposts or Duties on Imports or Exports, except what may be absolutely necessary for executing its inspection Laws: and the net Produce of all Duties and Imposts, laid by any State on Imports or Exports, shall be for the Use of the Treasury of the United States; and all such Laws shall be subject to the Revision and Control of the Congress.

No State shall, without the Consent of Congress, lay any Duty of Tonnage, keep Troops, or Ships of War in time of Peace, enter into any Agreement or Compact with another State, or with a foreign Power, or engage in War, unless actually invaded, or in such imminent Danger as will not admit of delay.

Article II

Section 1. The executive Power shall be vested in a President of the United States of America. He shall hold his Office during the Term of four Years, and together with the Vice President, chosen for the same Term, be elected, as follows.

Each State shall appoint, in such Manner as the Legislature thereof may direct, a Number of Electors, equal to the whole Number of Senators and Representatives to which the State may be entitled in the Congress: but no Senator or Representative, or Person holding an Office of Trust or Profit under the United States, shall be appointed an Elector.

The Electors shall meet in their respective States, and vote by Ballot for two Persons, of whom one at least shall not be an Inhabitant of the same State with themselves. And they shall make a List of all the Persons voted for, and of the Number of Votes for each; which List they shall sign and certify, and transmit sealed to the Seat of the Government of the United States, directed to the President of the Senate. The President of the Senate shall, in the Presence of the Senate and House of Representatives, open all the Certificates, and the Votes shall then be counted. The Person having the greatest Number of Votes shall be the President, if such Number be a Majority of the whole Number of Electors appointed; and if there be more than one who have such Majority, and have an equal Number of Votes, then the House of Representatives shall immediately chuse by Ballot one of them for President; and if no Person have a Majority, then from the five highest on the list the said House shall in like Manner chuse the President. But in chusing the President, the Votes shall be taken by States, the Representation from each State having one Vote; a quorum for this Purpose shall consist of a Member or Members from two-thirds of the States, and a Majority of all the States shall be necessary to a Choice. In every Case, after the Choice of the President, the Person having the greatest Number of Votes of the Electors shall be the Vice President. But if there should remain two or more who have equal Votes, the Senate shall chuse from them by Ballot the Vice President.

The Congress may determine the Time of chusing the Electors, and the Day on which they shall give their Votes; which Day shall be the same throughout the United States.

No Person except a natural born Citizen, or a Citizen of the United States, at the time of the Adoption of this Constitution, shall be eligible to the Office of President; neither shall any Person be eligible to that Office who shall not have attained to the Age of thirty-five Years, and been fourteen Years a Resident within the United States.

In Case of the Removal of the President from Office, or of his Death, Resignation, or Inability to discharge the Powers and Duties of the said office, the Same shall devolve on the Vice President, and the Congress may by Law provide for the Case of Removal, Death, Resignation or Inability, both of the President and Vice President, declaring what Officer shall then act as President, and such Officer shall act accordingly, until the Disability be removed, or a President shall be elected.

The President shall, at stated Times, receive for his Services, a Compensation, which shall neither be encreased nor diminished during the Period for which he shall have been elected, and he shall not receive within that Period any other Emolument from the United States, or any of them.

Before he enter on the Execution of his Office, he shall take the following Oath or Affirmation:—"I do solemnly swear (or affirm) that I will faithfully execute the Office of President of the United States, and will to the best of my Ability, preserve, protect and defend the Constitution of the United States."

Section 2. The President shall be Commander in Chief of the Army and Navy of the United States, and of the Militia of the several States, when called into the actual Service of the United States; he may require the Opinion, in writing, of the principal Officer in each of the executive Departments, upon any Subject relating to the Duties of their respective Offices, and he shall have Power to grant Reprieves and Pardons for Offenses against the United States, except in Cases of Impeachment.

He shall have Power, by and with the Advice and Consent of the Senate, to make Treaties, provided two-thirds of the Senators present concur; and he shall nominate, and by and with the Advice and Consent of the Senate, shall appoint Ambassadors, other public Ministers and Consuls, Judges of the supreme Court, and all other Officers of the United States, whose Appointments are not herein otherwise provided for, and which shall be established by Law: but the Congress may by Law vest the Appointment of such inferior Officers, as they think proper, in the President alone, in the Courts of Law, or in the Heads of Departments.

The President shall have Power to fill up all Vacancies that may happen during the Recess of the Senate, by granting Commissions which shall expire at the End of their next Session.

Section 3. He shall from time to time give to the Congress Information of the State of the Union, and recommend to their Consideration such Measures as he shall judge necessary and expedient; he may, on extraordinary Occasions, convene both Houses, or either of them, and in Case of Disagreement between them, with Respect to the Time of Adjournment, he may adjourn them to such Time as he shall think proper; he shall receive Ambassadors and other public Ministers; he shall take Care that the Laws be faithfully executed, and shall Commission all the Officers of the United States.

Section 4. The President, Vice President and all Civil Officers of the United States, shall be removed from office on Impeachment for, and Conviction of, Treason, Bribery, or other high Crimes and misdemeanors.

Article III

Section 1. The judicial Power of the United States, shall be vested in one supreme Court, and in such inferior Courts as the Congress may from time to time ordain and establish. The Judges, both of the supreme and inferior Courts, shall hold their Offices during good Behaviour, and shall, at stated Times, receive for their Services, a Compensation, which shall not be diminished during their Continuance in Office.

Section 2. The judicial Power shall extend to all Cases, in Law and Equity, arising under this Constitution, the Laws of the United States, and Treaties made, or which shall be made, under their Authority; to all Cases affecting Ambassadors, other public Ministers and Consuls;—to all Cases of admiralty and maritime Jurisdiction;—to Controversies to which the United States shall be a Party;—to Controversies between two or more States;—between a State and Citizens of another State;—between Citizens of different States;—between Citizens of the same State claiming Lands under Grants of different States, and between a State, or the Citizens thereof, and foreign States, Citizens or Subjects.

In all Cases affecting Ambassadors, other public Ministers and Consuls, and those in which a State shall be Party, the supreme Court shall have original Jurisdiction. In all the other Cases before mentioned, the supreme Court shall have appellate Jurisdiction, both as to Law and Fact, with such Exceptions, and under such Regulations as the Congress shall make.

The Trial of all Crimes, except in cases of Impeachment, shall be by Jury; and such Trial shall be held in the State where the said Crimes shall have been committed; but when not committed within any State, the Trial shall be at such Place or Places as the Congress may by Law have directed.

Section 3. Treason against the United States, shall consist only in levying War against them, or in adhering to their Enemies, giving them Aid and Comfort. No Person shall be convicted of Treason unless on the Testimony of two Witnesses to the same overt Act, or on Confession in open Court.

The Congress shall have Power to declare the Punishment of Treason, but no Attainder of Treason shall work Corruption of Blood, or Forfeiture except during the Life of the Person attainted.

Article IV

Section 1. Full Faith and Credit shall be given in each State to the public Acts, Records, and judicial Proceedings of every other State. And the Congress may by general Laws prescribe the Manner in which such Acts, Records and Proceedings shall be proved, and the Effect thereof.

Section 2. The Citizens of each State shall be entitled to all Privileges and Immunities of Citizens in the several States.

A Person charged in any State with Treason, Felony, or other Crime, who shall flee from Justice, and be found in another State, shall on Demand of the executive Authority of the State from which he fled, be delivered up, to be removed to the State having Jurisdiction of the Crime.

No Person held to Service or Labour in one State, under the Laws thereof, escaping into another, shall, in Consequence of any Law or Regulation therein, be discharged from such Service or Labour, but shall be delivered up on Claim of the Party to whom such Service or Labour may be due.

Section 3. New States may be admitted by the Congress into this Union; but no new State shall be formed or erected within the Jurisdiction of any other State; nor any State be formed by the Junction of two or more States, or Parts of States, without the

Consent of the Legislatures of the States concerned as well as of the Congress.

The Congress shall have Power to dispose of and make all needful Rules and Regulations respecting the Territory or other Property belonging to the United States; and nothing in this Constitution shall be so construed as to Prejudice any Claims of the United States, or of any particular State.

Section 4. The United States shall guarantee to every State in this Union a Republican Form of Government, and shall protect each of them against Invasion; and on Application of the Legislature, or of the Executive (when the Legislature cannot be convened) against domestic Violence.

Article V

The Congress, whenever two-thirds of both Houses shall deem it necessary, shall propose Amendments to this Constitution, or, on the Application of the Legislatures of two-thirds of the several States, shall call a Convention for proposing Amendments, which, in either Case, shall be valid to all Intents and Purposes, as Part of this Constitution, when ratified by the Legislatures of three-fourths of the several States, or by Conventions in three-fourths thereof, as the one or the other Mode of Ratification may be proposed by the Congress; Provided that no Amendment which may be made prior to the Year One thousand eight hundred and eight shall in any Manner affect the first and fourth Clauses in the Ninth Section of the first Article that no State, without its Consent, shall be deprived of its equal Suffrage in the Senate.

Article VI

All Debts contracted and Engagements entered into, before the Adoption of this Constitution, shall be as valid against the United States under this Constitution, as under the Confederation.

This Constitution, and the Laws of the United States which shall be made in Pursuance thereof; and all Treaties made, or which shall be made, under the Authority of the United States, shall be the supreme Law of the Land; and the Judges in every State shall be the supreme Law of the Land; and the Judges in every State shall be bound thereby, any Thing in the Constitution or Laws of any State to the Contrary notwithstanding.

The Senators and Representatives before mentioned, and the Members of the several State Legislatures, and all executive and judicial Officers, both of the United States and of the several States, shall be bound by Oath or Affirmation, to support this Constitution; but no religious Test shall ever be required as a Qualification to any Office or public Trust under the United States.

Article VII

The Ratification of the Conventions of nine States, shall be sufficient for the Establishment of this Constitution between the States so ratifying the Same.

AMENDMENTS
Amendment I

(First ten amendments ratified Dec. 15, 1791.)
Congress shall make no law respecting an establishment of religion, or prohibiting the free exercise thereof; or abridging the freedom of speech, or of the press; or the right of the people peaceably to assemble, and to petition the Government for a redress of grievances.

Amendment II

A well regulated Militia, being necessary to the security of a free State, the right of the people to keep and bear Arms, shall not be infringed.

Amendment III

No Soldier shall, in time of peace be quartered in any house, without the consent of the Owner, nor in time of war, but in a manner to be prescribed by law.

Amendment IV

The right of the people to be secure in their persons, houses, papers, and effects, against unreasonable searches and seizures, shall not be violated, and no Warrants shall issue, but upon probable cause, supported by Oath or affirmation, and particularly describing the place to be searched, and the persons or things to be seized.

Amendment V

No person shall be held to answer for a capital, or otherwise infamous crime, unless on a presentment or indictment of a Grand Jury, except in cases arising in the land or naval forces, or in the Militia, when in actual service in time of War or public danger; nor shall any person be subject for the same offence to be twice put in jeopardy of life or limb; nor shall be compelled in any criminal case to be a witness against himself, nor be deprived of life, liberty, or property, without due process of law; nor shall private property be taken for public use, without just compensation.

Amendment VI

In all criminal prosecutions, the accused shall enjoy the right to a speedy and public trial, by an impartial jury of the State and district wherein the crime shall have been committed, which district shall have been previously ascertained by law, and to be informed of the nature and cause of the accusation; to be confronted with the witnesses against him; to have compulsory process for obtaining witnesses in his favor, and to have the Assistance of Counsel for his defence.

Amendment VII

In Suits at common law, where the value in controversy shall exceed twenty dollars, the right of trial by jury shall be preserved, and no fact tried by a jury, shall be otherwise reexamined in any Court of the United States, than according to the rules of the common law.

Amendment VIII

Excessive bail shall not be required, nor excessive fines imposed, nor cruel and unusual punishments inflicted.

Amendment IX

The enumeration in the Constitution, of certain rights, shall not be construed to deny or disparage others retained by the people.

Amendment X

The powers not delegated to the United States by the Constitution, nor prohibited by it to the States, are reserved to the States respectively, or to the people.

Amendment XI (Ratified Feb. 7, 1795)

The Judicial power of the United States shall not be construed to extend to any suit in law or equity, commenced or prosecuted against one of the United States by Citizens of another State, or by Citizens or Subjects of any Foreign State.

Amendment XII (Ratified June 15, 1804)

The Electors shall meet in their respective states and vote by ballot for President and Vice-President, one of whom, at least, shall not be an inhabitant of the same state with themselves; they shall name in their ballots the person voted for as President, and in distinct ballots the person voted for as Vice-President, and they shall make distinct lists of all persons voted for as President, and of all persons voted for as Vice-President, and of the number of votes for each, which lists they shall sign and certify, and transmit sealed to the seat of the government of the United States, directed to the President of the Senate;—The President of the Senate shall, in the presence of the Senate and House of Representatives, open all the certificates and the votes shall then be counted;—The person having the greatest number of votes for President, shall be the President, if such number be a majority of the whole number of Electors appointed; and if no person have such majority, then from the persons having the highest numbers not exceeding three on the list of those voted for as President, the House of Representatives shall choose immediately, by ballot, the President. But in choosing the President, the votes shall be taken by states, the representation from each state having one vote; a quorum for this purpose shall consist of a member or members from two-thirds of the states, and a majority of all the states shall be necessary to a choice. And if the House of Representatives shall not choose a President whenever the right of choice shall devolve upon them, before the fourth day of March next following, then the Vice-President shall act as President, as in the case of the death or other constitutional disability of the President.—The person having the greatest number of votes as Vice-President, shall be the Vice-President, if such number be a majority of the whole number of Electors appointed, and if no person have a majority, then from the two highest numbers on the list, the Senate shall choose the Vice-President; a quorum for the purpose shall consist of two-thirds of the whole number of Senators, and a majority of the whole number shall be necessary to a choice. But no person constitutionally ineligible to the office of President shall be eligible to that of Vice-President of the United States.

Amendment XIII (Ratified Dec. 6, 1865)

Section 1. Neither slavery nor involuntary servitude, except as a punishment for crime whereof the party shall have been duly convicted, shall exist within the United States, or any place subject to their jurisdiction.

Section 2. Congress shall have power to enforce this article by appropriate legislation.

Amendment XIV (Ratified July 9, 1868)

Section 1. All persons born or naturalized in the United States and subject to the jurisdiction thereof, are citizens of the United States and of the State wherein they reside. No State shall make or enforce any law which shall abridge the privileges or immunities of citizens of the United States; nor shall any State deprive any person of life, liberty, or property, without due process of law; nor deny to any person within its jurisdiction the equal protection of the laws.

Section 2. Representatives shall be apportioned among the several States according to their respective numbers, counting the whole number of persons in each State, excluding Indians not taxed. But when the right to vote at any election for the choice of electors for President and Vice President of the United States, Representatives in Congress, the Executive and Judicial officers of a State, or the members of the Legislature thereof, is denied to any of the male inhabitants of such State, being twenty-one years of age, and citizens of the United States, or in any way abridged, except for participation in rebellion, or other crime, the basis of representation therein shall be reduced in the proportion which the number of such male citizens shall bear to the whole number of male citizens twenty-one years of age in such State.

Section 3. No persons shall be a Senator or Representative in Congress, or elector of President and Vice President, or hold any office, civil or military, under the United States, or under any State, who, having previously taken an oath, as a member of Congress, or as an officer of the United States, or as a member of any State legislature, or as an executive or judicial officer of any State, to support the Constitution of the United States, shall have engaged in insurrection or rebellion against the same, or given aid or comfort to the enemies thereof. But Congress may by a vote of two-thirds of each House, remove such disability.

Section 4. The validity of the public debt of the United States, authorized by law, including debts incurred for payment of pensions and bounties for services in suppressing insurrection or rebellion, shall not be questioned. But neither the United States nor any State shall assume or pay any debt or obligation incurred in aid of insurrection or rebellion against the United States, or any claim for the loss or emancipation of any slave; but all such debts, obligations and claims shall be held illegal and void.

Section 5. The Congress shall have power to enforce, by appropriate legislation, the provisions of this article.

Amendment XV (Ratified Feb. 3, 1870)

Section 1. The right of citizens of the United States to vote shall not be denied or abridged by the United States or by any State on account of race, color, or previous condition of servitude.

Section 2. The Congress shall have power to enforce this article by appropriate legislation.

Amendment XVI (Ratified Feb. 3, 1913)

The Congress shall have power to lay and collect taxes on incomes, from whatever source derived, without apportionment among the several States, and without regard to any census or enumeration.

Amendment XVII (Ratified April 8, 1913)

The Senate of the United States shall be composed of two Senators from each State, elected by the people thereof, for six years; and each Senator shall have one vote. The electors in each State shall have the qualifications requisite for electors of the most numerous branch of the State legislatures.

When vacancies happen in the representation of any State in the Senate, the executive authority of such State shall issue writs of election to fill such vacancies: *Provided,* That the legislature of any State may empower the executive thereof to make temporary appointments until the people fill the vacancies by election as the legislature may direct.

This amendment shall not be so construed as to affect the election or term of any Senator chosen before it becomes valid as part of the Constitution.

Amendment XVIII (Ratified Jan. 16, 1919)

Section 1. After one year from the ratification of this article the manufacture, sale, or transportation of intoxicating liquors within, the importation thereof into, or the exportation thereof from the United States and all territory subject to the jurisdiction thereof for beverage purposes is hereby prohibited.

Section 2. The Congress and the several States shall have concurrent power to enforce this article by appropriate legislation.

Section 3. This article shall be inoperative unless it shall have been ratified as an amendment to the Constitution by the legislatures of the several States, as provided in the Constitution, within seven years from the date of the submission hereof to the States by the Congress.

Amendment XIX (Ratified Aug. 18, 1920)

The right of citizens of the United States to vote shall not be denied or abridged by the United States or by any State on account of sex.

Congress shall have power to enforce this article by appropriate legislation.

Amendment XX (Ratified Jan. 23, 1933)

Section 1. The terms of the President and Vice President shall end at noon on the 20th day of January, and the terms of Senators and Representatives at noon on the 3d day of January, of the years in which such terms would have ended if this article had not been ratified; and the terms of their successors shall then begin.

Section 2. The Congress shall assemble at least once in every year, and such meeting shall begin at noon on the 3d day of January, unless they shall by law appoint a different day.

Section 3. If, at the time fixed for the beginning of the term of the President, the President elect shall have died, the Vice President elect shall become President. If a President shall not have been chosen before the time fixed for the beginning of his term, or if the President elect shall have failed to qualify, then the Vice President elect shall act as President until a President shall have qualified; and the Congress may by law provide for the case wherein neither a President elect nor a Vice President elect shall have qualified, declaring who shall then act as President, or the manner in which one who is to act shall be selected, and such person shall act accordingly until a President or Vice President shall have qualified.

Section 4. The Congress may by law provide for the case of the death of any of the persons from whom the House of Representatives may choose a President whenever the right of choice shall have devolved upon them, and for the case of the death of any of the persons from whom the Senate may choose a Vice President whenever the right of choice shall have devolved upon them.

Section 5. Sections 1 and 2 shall take effect on the 15th day of October following the ratification of this article.

Section 6. This article shall be inoperative unless it shall have been ratified as an amendment to the Constitution by the legislatives of three-fourths of the several States within seven years from the date of its submission.

Amendment XXI (Ratified Dec. 5, 1933)

Section 1. The eighteenth article of amendment to the Constitution of the United States is hereby repealed.

Section 2. The transportation or importation into any State,

Territory or possession of the United States for delivery or use therein of intoxicating liquors, in violation of the laws thereof, is hereby prohibited.

Section 3. This article shall be inoperative unless it shall have been ratified as an amendment to the Constitution by conventions in the several States, as provided in the Constitution, within seven years from the date of the submission hereof to the States by the Congress.

Amendment XXII (Ratified Feb. 27, 1951)

Section 1. No person shall be elected to the office of the President more than twice, and no person who has held the office of President, or acted as President, for more than two years of a term to which some other person was elected President shall be elected to the office of the President more than once. But this Article shall not apply to any person holding the office of President when this Article was proposed by the Congress, and shall not prevent any person who may be holding the office of President, or acting as President, during the term within which this Article become operative from holding the office of President or acting as President during the remainder of such term.

Section 2. This Article shall be inoperative unless it shall have been ratified as an amendment to the Constitution by the legislatures of three-fourths of the several States within seven years from the date of its submission to the States by the Congress.

Amendment XXIII (Ratified March 29, 1961)

Section 1. The District constituting the seat of Government of the United States shall appoint in such manner as the Congress may direct:

A number of electors of President and Vice President equal to the whole number of Senators and Representatives in Congress to which the District would be entitled if it were a State, but in no event more than the least populous State; they shall be in addition to those appointed by the States, but they shall be considered, for the purposes of the election of President and Vice President, to be electors appointed by a State; and they shall meet in the District and perform such duties as provided by the twelfth article of amendment.

Section 2. The Congress shall have power to enforce this article by appropriate legislation.

Amendment XXIV (Ratified Jan. 23, 1964)

Section 1. The right of citizens of the United States to vote in any primary or other election for President or Vice President, for electors for President or Vice President, or for Senator or Representative in Congress, shall not be denied or abridged by the United States or any State by reason of failure to pay any poll tax or other tax.

Section 2. The Congress shall have power to enforce this article by appropriate legislation.

Amendment XXV (Ratified Feb. 10, 1967)

Section 1. In case of the removal of the President from office or of his death or resignation, the Vice President shall become President.

Section 2. Whenever there is a vacancy in the office of the Vice President, the President shall nominate a Vice President who shall take office upon confirmation by a majority vote of both Houses of Congress.

Section 3. Whenever the President transmits to the President pro tempore of the Senate and the Speaker of the House of Representatives his written declaration that he is unable to discharge the powers and duties of his office, and until he transmits to them a written declaration to the contrary, such powers and duties shall be discharged by the Vice President as Acting President.

Section 4. Whenever the Vice President and a majority of either the principal officers of the executive departments or of such other body as Congress may by law provide, transmit to the President pro tempore of the Senate and the Speaker of the House of Representatives their written declaration that the President is unable to discharge the powers and duties of his office, the Vice President shall immediately assume the powers and duties of the office as Acting President.

Thereafter, when the President transmits to the President pro tempore of the Senate and the Speaker of the House of Representatives his written declaration that no inability exists, he shall resume the powers and duties of his office unless the Vice President and a majority of either the principal officers of the executive department or of such other body as Congress may by law provide, transmit within four days to the President pro tempore of the Senate and the Speaker of the House of Representatives their written declaration that the President is unable to discharge the powers and duties of his office. Thereupon Congress shall decide the issue, assembling within forty-eight hours for that purpose if not in session. If the Congress, within twenty-one days after receipt of the latter written declaration, or, if Congress is not in session, within twenty-one days after Congress is required to assemble, determines by two-thirds vote of both houses that the President is unable to discharge the powers and duties of his office, the Vice President shall continue to discharge the same as Acting President; otherwise, the President shall resume the powers and duties of his office.

Amendment XXVI (Ratified July 1, 1971)

Section 1. The right of citizens of the United States, who are eighteen years of age or older, to vote shall not be denied or abridged by the United States or by any State on account of age.

Section 2. The Congress shall have power to enforce this article by appropriate legislation.

APPENDIX B

Justices of the Supreme Court

Justice*	Tenure	Appointed by	Replaced
JOHN JAY	1789–1795	Washington	
John Rutledge	1789–1791	Washington	
William Cushing	1789–1810	Washington	
James Wilson	1789–1798	Washington	
John Blair	1789–1796	Washington	
James Iredell	1790–1799	Washington	
Thomas Johnson	1791–1793	Washington	Rutledge
William Paterson	1793–1806	Washington	Johnson
JOHN RUTLEDGE	1795–1795	Washington	Jay
Samuel Chase	1796–1811	Washington	Blair
OLIVER ELLSWORTH	1796–1800	Washington	Rutledge
Bushrod Washington	1798–1829	John Adams	Wilson
Alfred Moore	1799–1804	John Adams	Iredell
JOHN MARSHALL	1801–1835	John Adams	Ellsworth
William Johnson	1804–1834	Jefferson	Moore
Brockholst Livingston	1806–1823	Jefferson	Paterson
Thomas Todd	1807–1826	Jefferson	(new judgeship)
Gabriel Duval	1811–1835	Madison	Chase
Joseph Story	1811–1845	Madison	Cushing
Smith Thompson	1823–1843	Monroe	Livingston
Robert Trimble	1826–1828	John Q. Adams	Todd
John McLean	1829–1861	Jackson	Trimble
Henry Baldwin	1830–1844	Jackson	Washington
James Wayne	1835–1867	Jackson	Johnson
ROGER B. TANEY	1836–1864	Jackson	Marshall
Phillip P. Barbour	1836–1841	Jackson	Duval
John Catron	1837–1865	Jackson	(new judgeship)
John McKinley	1837–1852	Van Buren	(new judgeship)
Peter V. Daniel	1841–1860	Van Buren	Barbour
Samuel Nelson	1845–1872	Tyler	Thompson
Levi Woodbury	1846–1851	Polk	Story
Robert C. Grier	1846–1870	Polk	Baldwin
Benjamin R. Curtis	1851–1857	Fillmore	Woodbury
John A. Campbell	1853–1861	Pierce	McKinley
Nathan Clifford	1858–1881	Buchanan	Curtis

Justice*	Tenure	Appointed by	Replaced
Noah H. Swayne	1862–1881	Lincoln	McLean
Samuel F. Miller	1862–1890	Lincoln	Daniel
David Davis	1862–1877	Lincoln	Campbell
Stephen J. Field	1863–1897	Lincoln	*(new judgeship)*
SALMON CHASE	1864–1873	Lincoln	Taney
William Strong	1870–1880	Grant	Grier
Joseph P. Bradley	1870–1892	Grant	Wayne
Ward Hunt	1872–1882	Grant	Nelson
MORRISON R. WAITE	1874–1888	Grant	Chase
John Marshall Harlan	1877–1911	Hayes	Davis
William B. Woods	1880–1887	Hayes	Strong
Stanley Matthews	1881–1889	Garfield	Swayne
Horace Gray	1881–1902	Arthur	Clifford
Samuel Blatchford	1882–1893	Arthur	Hunt
Lucius Q. C. Lamar	1888–1893	Cleveland	Woods
MELVILLE W. FULLER	1888–1910	Cleveland	Waite
David J. Brewer	1889–1910	Harrison	Matthews
Henry B. Brown	1890–1906	Harrison	Miller
George Shiras Jr.	1892–1903	Harrison	Bradley
Howell E. Jackson	1893–1895	Harrison	Lamar
Edward D. White	1894–1910	Cleveland	Blatchford
Rufus W. Peckham	1895–1909	Cleveland	Jackson
Joseph McKenna	1898–1925	McKinley	Field
Oliver Wendell Holmes	1902–1932	T. Roosevelt	Gray
William R. Day	1903–1922	T. Roosevelt	Shiras
William H. Moody	1906–1910	T. Roosevelt	Brown
Horace H. Lurton	1909–1914	Taft	Peckham
Charles Evans Hughes	1910–1916	Taft	Brewer
EDWARD D. WHITE	1910–1921	Taft	Fuller
Willis VanDevanter	1910–1937	Taft	White
Joseph R. Lamar	1910–1916	Taft	Moody
Mahlon Pitney	1912–1922	Taft	Harlan
James McReynolds	1914–1941	Wilson	Lurton
Louis D. Brandeis	1916–1939	Wilson	Lamar
John H. Clark	1916–1922	Wilson	Hughes
WILLIAM H. TAFT	1921–1930	Harding	White
George Sutherland	1922–1938	Harding	Clarke
Pierce Butler	1922–1939	Harding	Day
Edward T. Sanford	1923–1930	Harding	Pitney
Harlan F. Stone	1925–1941	Coolidge	McKenna
CHARLES EVANS HUGHES	1930–1941	Hoover	Taft
Owen J. Roberts	1932–1945	Hoover	Sanford
Benjamin N. Cardozo	1932–1938	Hoover	Holmes
Hugo L. Black	1937–1971	F. Roosevelt	VanDevanter
Stanley F. Reed	1938–1957	F. Roosevelt	Sutherland

Justice*	Tenure	Appointed by	Replaced
Felix Frankfurter	1939–1962	F. Roosevelt	Cardozo
William O. Douglas	1939–1975	F. Roosevelt	Brandeis
Frank Murphy	1940–1949	F. Roosevelt	Butler
James F. Byrnes	1941–1942	F. Roosevelt	McReynolds
HARLAN F. STONE	1941–1946	F. Roosevelt	Hughes
Robert H. Jackson	1941–1954	F. Roosevelt	Stone
Wiley B. Rutledge	1943–1949	F. Roosevelt	Byrnes
Harold H. Burton	1945–1958	Truman	Roberts
FRED M. VINSON	1946–1953	Truman	Stone
Tom C. Clark	1949–1967	Truman	Murphy
Sherman Minton	1949–1956	Truman	Rutledge
EARL WARREN	1954–1969	Eisenhower	Vinson
John M. Harlan	1955–1971	Eisenhower	Jackson
William J. Brennan	1957–1990	Eisenhower	Minton
Charles E. Whittaker	1957–1962	Eisenhower	Reed
Potter Stewart	1959–1981	Eisenhower	Burton
Byron R. White	1962–1993	Kennedy	Whittaker
Arthur J. Goldberg	1962–1965	Kennedy	Frankfurter
Abe Fortas	1965–1969	Johnson	Goldberg
Thurgood Marshall	1967–1991	Johnson	Clark
WARREN E. BURGER	1969–1986	Nixon	Warren
Harry A. Blackmun	1970–1994	Nixon	Fortas
Lewis F. Powell	1971–1988	Nixon	Black
William H. Rehnquist	1971–	Nixon	Harlan
John P. Stevens	1975–	Ford	Douglas
Sandra Day O'Connor	1981–	Reagan	Stewart
WILLIAM H. REHNQUIST	1986–	Reagan	Burger
Antonin Scalia	1986–	Reagan	Rehnquist
Anthony M. Kennedy	1988–	Reagan	Powell
David H. Souter	1990–	Bush	Brennan
Clarence Thomas	1991–	Bush	Marshall
Ruth Bader Ginsburg	1993–	Clinton	White
Stephen G. Breyer	1994–	Clinton	Blackmun

*Chief justices are capitalized.

Court Composition since 1900

The table below represents the members of the Supreme Court since 1900. By locating the term in which a particular case was decided, the names of the justices on the Court at the time of the decision may be readily determined.

THE FULLER COURT (1900–1909 Terms)

1900–1901	Fuller	White	Gray	Peckham	Brown	Shiras	Brewer	Harlan	McKenna
1902	Fuller	White	Holmes	Peckham	Brown	Shiras	Brewer	Harlan	McKenna
1903–1905	Fuller	White	Holmes	Peckham	Brown	Day	Brewer	Harlan	McKenna
1906–1908	Fuller	White	Holmes	Peckham	Moody	Day	Brewer	Harlan	McKenna
1909	Fuller	White	Holmes	Lurton	Moody	Day	Brewer	Harlan	McKenna

THE WHITE COURT (1910–1920)

1910–1911	White	VanDevanter	Holmes	Lurton	Lamar	Day	Hughes	Harlan	McKenna
1912–1913	White	VanDevanter	Holmes	Lurton	Lamar	Day	Hughes	Pitney	McKenna
1914–1915	White	VanDevanter	Holmes	McReynolds	Lamar	Day	Hughes	Pitney	McKenna
1916–1920	White	VanDevanter	Holmes	McReynolds	Brandeis	Day	Clarke	Pitney	McKenna

THE TAFT COURT (1921–1929)

1921	Taft	VanDevanter	Holmes	McReynolds	Brandeis	Day	Clarke	Pitney	McKenna
1922	Taft	VanDevanter	Holmes	McReynolds	Brandeis	Butler	Sutherland	Pitney	McKenna
1923–1924	Taft	VanDevanter	Holmes	McReynolds	Brandeis	Butler	Sutherland	Sanford	McKenna
1925–1929	Taft	VanDevanter	Holmes	McReynolds	Brandeis	Butler	Sutherland	Sanford	Stone

THE HUGHES COURT (1930–1940)

1930–1931	Hughes	VanDevanter	Holmes	McReynolds	Brandeis	Butler	Sutherland	Roberts	Stone
1932–1936	Hughes	VanDevanter	Cardozo	McReynolds	Brandeis	Butler	Sutherland	Roberts	Stone
1937	Hughes	Black	Cardozo	McReynolds	Brandeis	Butler	Sutherland	Roberts	Stone
1938	Hughes	Black	Cardozo	McReynolds	Brandeis	Butler	Reed	Roberts	Stone
1939	Hughes	Black	Frankfurter	McReynolds	Douglas	Butler	Reed	Roberts	Stone
1940	Hughes	Black	Frankfurter	McReynolds	Douglas	Murphy	Reed	Roberts	Stone

THE STONE COURT (1941–1945)

1941–1942	Stone	Black	Frankfurter	Byrnes	Douglas	Murphy	Reed	Roberts	Jackson
1943–1944	Stone	Black	Frankfurter	Rutledge	Douglas	Murphy	Reed	Roberts	Jackson
1945	Stone	Black	Frankfurter	Rutledge	Douglas	Murphy	Reed	Burton	Jackson

THE VINSON COURT (1946–1952)

1946–1948	Vinson	Black	Rutledge	Frankfurter	Douglas	Murphy	Reed	Burton	Jackson
1949–1952	Vinson	Black	Minton	Frankfurter	Douglas	Clark	Reed	Burton	Jackson

THE WARREN COURT (1953–1968)

1953–1954	Warren	Black	Minton	Frankfurter	Douglas	Clark	Reed	Burton	Jackson
1955	Warren	Black	Minton	Frankfurter	Douglas	Clark	Reed	Burton	Harlan
1956	Warren	Black	Brennan	Frankfurter	Douglas	Clark	Reed	Burton	Harlan
1957	Warren	Black	Brennan	Frankfurter	Douglas	Clark	Whittaker	Burton	Harlan
1958–1961	Warren	Black	Brennan	Frankfurter	Douglas	Clark	Whittaker	Stewart	Harlan
1962–1965	Warren	Black	Brennan	Goldberg	Douglas	Clark	White	Stewart	Harlan
1965–1967	Warren	Black	Brennan	Fortas	Douglas	Clark	White	Stewart	Harlan
1967–1969	Warren	Black	Brennan	Fortas	Douglas	Marshall	White	Stewart	Harlan

THE BURGER COURT (1969–1985)

1969	Burger	Black	Brennan	Fortas	Douglas	Marshall	White	Stewart	Harlan
1969–1970	Burger	Black	Brennan	Blackmun	Douglas	Marshall	White	Stewart	Harlan
1970	Burger	Black	Brennan	Blackmun	Douglas	Marshall	White	Stewart	Harlan
1971	Burger	Powell	Brennan	Blackmun	Douglas	Marshall	White	Stewart	Rehnquist
1975	Burger	Powell	Brennan	Blackmun	Stevens	Marshall	White	Stewart	Rehnquist
1981	Burger	Powell	Brennan	Blackmun	Stevens	Marshall	White	O'Connor	Rehnquist

THE REHNQUIST COURT (1986–   )

1986	Rehnquist	Powell	Brennan	Blackmun	Stevens	Marshall	White	O'Connor	Scalia
1987	Rehnquist	Kennedy	Brennan	Blackmun	Stevens	Marshall	White	O'Connor	Scalia
1990	Rehnquist	Kennedy	Souter	Blackmun	Stevens	Marshall	White	O'Connor	Scalia
1991	Rehnquist	Kennedy	Souter	Blackmun	Stevens	Thomas	White	O'Connor	Scalia
1993	Rehnquist	Kennedy	Souter	Blackmun	Stevens	Thomas	Ginsburg	O'Connor	Scalia
1994	Rehnquist	Kennedy	Souter	Breyer	Stevens	Thomas	Ginsburg	O'Connor	Scalia

INDEX

741